MOCK TRIAL
CASE FILES AND PROBLEMS

LEXISNEXIS LAW SCHOOL PUBLISHING ADVISORY BOARD

MOCK TRIAL CASE FILES AND PROBLEMS

DAVID A. SCHLUETER
Hardy Professor of Law &
Director of Advocacy Programs
St. Mary's University School of Law
San Antonio, Texas

LexisNexis®

ISBN: 978-0-7698-9196-5 (print)
ISBN: 978-0-7698-9198-9 (ebook)

NOTE TO USERS
To ensure that you are using the latest materials available in this area, please be sure to periodically check the LexisNexis Law School web site for downloadable updates and supplements at www.lexisnexis.com/lawschool.

Editorial Offices
121 Chanlon Rd., New Providence, NJ 07974 (908) 464-6800
201 Mission St., San Francisco, CA 94105-1831 (415) 908-3200
www.lexisnexis.com

MATTHEW BENDER (2014-Pub.3386)

Acknowledgments

The author gratefully acknowledges the invaluable assistance of the following individuals who assisted in preparing the mock trial case files, which were originally prepared for use at the Lone Star Classic®:

Lauren Alberts
Morgan Figueroa
Bianca Frisaura
Celia Garcia
Nicole Hines Glover
Sina Ellis Griffith
Edward Imwinkelried
Christine Ivy
Andrea Koch
Ana Mahrou
Ramona Lampley
Kelsey Leslie
Ana Mahrou
Kelly Pittl
Nathan Roach
Emileigh Stewart
Barbara Schlueter
Jonathan Schlueter
Linda Schlueter
Scott Simpson
Ian Spranger
Kara Spranger
Bill Squires
Morgan Stanley
Marcie Trevino
Shelia Via
Ben Zimmerman

About the Author

David A. Schlueter is the Hardy Professor of Law and Director of Advocacy Programs at St. Mary's University School of Law in San Antonio, Texas. Professor Schlueter teaches evidence, trial advocacy, and constitutional law, and has served as both criminal trial and appellate counsel. He has authored, co-authored, or edited 12 books on procedure and evidence, including the two volume work, FEDERAL EVIDENCE TACTICS (with Imwinkelried). His writings have been cited frequently by state and federal courts, including the Supreme Court of the United States, and legal commentators. Before joining the faculty at St. Mary's in 1983, he served on active duty as an Army JAGC and for two years as legal counsel for the Supreme Court of the United States. He is a fellow in the American Law Institute and a Life Fellow in the American Bar Foundation. From 1988 until 2005, he served as the Reporter for the Federal Rules of Criminal Procedure Advisory Committee.

Table of Contents

Introduction

The mock trial case files and problems in this text are designed to provide opportunities for students to put into practice the theory of courtroom litigation. Each of the first seven chapters presents a series of practical exercises focusing on one of the basic litigation techniques, for example, direct examination of a witness.

The criminal case files were originally prepared for the Lone Star Classic®, a national invitational mock trial competition hosted by St. Mary's University School of Law. The competition is run under the directorship of a full time faculty member, with the able and invaluable assistance of the School's Board of Advocates, who serve as associate and assistant directors. Over the years they have provided invaluable assistance in drafting the mock trial case files that were used each year. Starting in 2007, the case files all involved homicide cases. To expand the case file selections, those homicide cases were developed into wrongful death cases, using essentially the same case file materials, but adding a plaintiff to the case.

The criminal case files require only two witnesses per side. The civil cases involve three witnesses for the plaintiff and two for the defense.

Each case file is designed to be tried in approximately three hours.

Many of the practical exercises are taken from the case files in Chapters 8 through 21. Thus, working on parts of the case files for some of the weekly exercises will expose the students to the information in a way that approximates real trials — understanding that no one piece of evidence or testimony can be taken in isolation. Other problems in this text are "free-standing" to the extent that they do not relate to any particular case or fact pattern in this book.

In order to maintain some realism with the dates of the events, the text uses designated dates that relate to the current year. Thus the date "[YR-0]" means the current year and "[YR-2]' means two years ago. Another example: The date "June 16, [YR-1]" means June 16, one year ago.

Chapter 1
SELECTING A JURY

§ 1-1. Introduction

For the exercises on selecting jurors, use the case file that you are assigned for your mock trial. Using the techniques and examples in your reading assignments, you should be prepared to conduct a short voir dire of prospective jurors for your case.

For this exercise, your instructor may ask students in the section — as prospective jurors — to assume the identity of the persons on the following juror information forms. Or they may simply use the blank juror information forms, which follow, for students to fill in with their own names and information.

§ 1-2. Sample Juror Information Forms

The following juror information forms may filled in and used for the voir dire exercise.

PLEASE TYPE OR PRINT IN INK **JUROR INFORMATION FORM** 6542-98

45356678-99098 **REYES, RACHEL SOPHIE** **2222 WILSON BLVD** **SAN MILANO, TX 55578** PLEASE MAKE CORRECTIONS TO ADDRESS:	**WHEN CALLED FOR JURY SERVICE, BRING THIS FORM WITH YOU. DO NOT MAIL IT.** PHONE # ______________ AGE _____ NO OF CHILDREN ______ GENDER ______ HOW LONG HAVE YOU LIVED IN THIS COUNTY? ________
HAVE YOU EVER SERVED ON A CIVIL JURY? _____YES _____ NO HAVE YOU EVER SERVED ON A CRIMINAL JURY? _____ YES _____ NO HAVE YOU EVER SUSTAINED ACCIDENTAL BODILY INJURY REQUIRING MEDICAL ATTENTION. IF SO, WHAT TYPE? _____ YES _____ NO HAVE YOU BEEN A PARTY TO A LAWSUIT? _____ YES _____ NO	PLACE OF BIRTH: RELIGION: EMPLOYER: OCCUPATION SPOUSE'S NAME: SPOUSE'S EMPLOYER:
HAVE YOU BEEN ACCUSED, COMPLAINANT, OR WITNESS IN CRIMINAL CASE? _____ YES _____ NO	SIGNATURE

PLEASE TYPE OR PRINT IN INK **JUROR INFORMATION FORM** 6542-98

<table>
<tr><td>45356678-99098

SMITH, ROBERT JONES
123 MAIN STREET
SAN MILANO, TX 54678

PLEASE MAKE CORRECTIONS TO ADDRESS:</td><td>WHEN CALLED FOR JURY SERVICE, BRING THIS FORM WITH YOU. DO NOT MAIL IT.
PHONE # ____________________
AGE ______
NO OF CHILDREN ________
GENDER _________
HOW LONG HAVE YOU LIVED IN THIS COUNTY? _____________</td></tr>
<tr><td>HAVE YOU EVER SERVED ON A CIVIL JURY?
_____ YES _____ NO

HAVE YOU EVER SERVED ON A CRIMINAL JURY? _____ YES _____ NO

HAVE YOU EVER SUSTAINED ACCIDENTAL BODILY INJURY REQUIRING MEDICAL ATTENTION. IF SO, WHAT TYPE?
_____ YES _____ NO

HAVE YOU BEEN A PARTY TO A LAWSUIT?
_____ YES _____ NO</td><td>PLACE OF BIRTH:

RELIGION:

EMPLOYER:

OCCUPATION

SPOUSE'S NAME:

SPOUSE'S EMPLOYER:</td></tr>
<tr><td>HAVE YOU BEEN ACCUSED, COMPLAINANT, OR WITNESS IN CRIMINAL CASE?
_____ YES _____ NO</td><td>SIGNATURE</td></tr>
</table>

PLEASE TYPE OR PRINT IN INK **JUROR INFORMATION FORM** 6542-98

<table>
<tr><td>45356678-99098

OLSON, KELLY J.
22123 LAREDO STREET
SAN MILANO, TX 67678

PLEASE MAKE CORRECTIONS TO ADDRESS:</td><td>WHEN CALLED FOR JURY SERVICE, BRING THIS FORM WITH YOU. DO NOT MAIL IT.
PHONE # ____________________
AGE ______
NO OF CHILDREN ________
GENDER _________
HOW LONG HAVE YOU LIVED IN THIS COUNTY? _____________</td></tr>
<tr><td>HAVE YOU EVER SERVED ON A CIVIL JURY?
_____ YES _____ NO

HAVE YOU EVER SERVED ON A CRIMINAL JURY? _____ YES _____ NO

HAVE YOU EVER SUSTAINED ACCIDENTAL BODILY INJURY REQUIRING MEDICAL ATTENTION. IF SO, WHAT TYPE?
_____ YES _____ NO

HAVE YOU BEEN A PARTY TO A LAWSUIT?
_____ YES _____ NO</td><td>PLACE OF BIRTH:

RELIGION:

EMPLOYER:

OCCUPATION

SPOUSE'S NAME:

SPOUSE'S EMPLOYER:</td></tr>
<tr><td>HAVE YOU BEEN ACCUSED, COMPLAINANT, OR WITNESS IN CRIMINAL CASE?
_____ YES _____ NO</td><td>SIGNATURE</td></tr>
</table>

PLEASE TYPE OR PRINT IN INK **JUROR INFORMATION FORM** 6542-98

<table>
<tr><td>45356678-99098

GONZALES, MORGAN WINSLOW
334 MONTENEGRO, APT 321
SAN MILANO, TX 54890

PLEASE MAKE CORRECTIONS TO ADDRESS:</td><td>WHEN CALLED FOR JURY SERVICE, BRING THIS FORM WITH YOU. DO NOT MAIL IT.
PHONE # ________________

AGE _____
NO OF CHILDREN _______
GENDER ________
HOW LONG HAVE YOU LIVED IN THIS COUNTY? ___________</td></tr>
<tr><td>HAVE YOU EVER SERVED ON A CIVIL JURY?
_____ YES _____ NO

HAVE YOU EVER SERVED ON A CRIMINAL JURY? _____ YES _____ NO

HAVE YOU EVER SUSTAINED ACCIDENTAL BODILY INJURY REQUIRING MEDICAL ATTENTION. IF SO, WHAT TYPE?
_____ YES _____ NO

HAVE YOU BEEN A PARTY TO A LAWSUIT?
_____ YES _____ NO</td><td>PLACE OF BIRTH:

RELIGION:

EMPLOYER:

OCCUPATION

SPOUSE'S NAME:

SPOUSE'S EMPLOYER:</td></tr>
<tr><td>HAVE YOU BEEN ACCUSED, COMPLAINANT, OR WITNESS IN CRIMINAL CASE?
_____ YES _____ NO</td><td>SIGNATURE</td></tr>
</table>

PLEASE TYPE OR PRINT IN INK **JUROR INFORMATION FORM** 6542-98

<table>
<tr><td>45356678-99098

DEGATTO, CASS
65454 WOODARD LANE, # 212
SAN MILANO, TX 55468

PLEASE MAKE CORRECTIONS TO ADDRESS:</td><td>WHEN CALLED FOR JURY SERVICE, BRING THIS FORM WITH YOU. DO NOT MAIL IT.
PHONE # ________________

AGE _____
NO OF CHILDREN _______
GENDER ________
HOW LONG HAVE YOU LIVED IN THIS COUNTY? ___________</td></tr>
<tr><td>HAVE YOU EVER SERVED ON A CIVIL JURY?
_____ YES _____ NO

HAVE YOU EVER SERVED ON A CRIMINAL JURY? _____ YES _____ NO

HAVE YOU EVER SUSTAINED ACCIDENTAL BODILY INJURY REQUIRING MEDICAL ATTENTION. IF SO, WHAT TYPE?
_____ YES _____ NO

HAVE YOU BEEN A PARTY TO A LAWSUIT?
_____ YES _____ NO</td><td>PLACE OF BIRTH:

RELIGION:

EMPLOYER:

OCCUPATION

SPOUSE'S NAME:

SPOUSE'S EMPLOYER:</td></tr>
<tr><td>HAVE YOU BEEN ACCUSED, COMPLAINANT, OR WITNESS IN CRIMINAL CASE?
_____ YES _____ NO</td><td>SIGNATURE</td></tr>
</table>

PLEASE TYPE OR PRINT IN INK **JUROR INFORMATION FORM** 6542-98

45356678-99098 **SMITH, KELLY** **456 WHISPER DEW** **SAN MILANO, TX 76678** PLEASE MAKE CORRECTIONS TO ADDRESS:	**WHEN CALLED FOR JURY SERVICE, BRING THIS FORM WITH YOU. DO NOT MAIL IT.** PHONE # ________________ AGE _____ NO OF CHILDREN _______ GENDER ________ HOW LONG HAVE YOU LIVED IN THIS COUNTY? ___________
HAVE YOU EVER SERVED ON A CIVIL JURY? _____ YES _____ NO HAVE YOU EVER SERVED ON A CRIMINAL JURY? _____ YES _____ NO HAVE YOU EVER SUSTAINED ACCIDENTAL BODILY INJURY REQUIRING MEDICAL ATTENTION. IF SO, WHAT TYPE? _____ YES _____ NO HAVE YOU BEEN A PARTY TO A LAWSUIT? _____ YES _____ NO	PLACE OF BIRTH: RELIGION: EMPLOYER: OCCUPATION SPOUSE'S NAME: SPOUSE'S EMPLOYER:
HAVE YOU BEEN ACCUSED, COMPLAINANT, OR WITNESS IN CRIMINAL CASE? _____ YES _____ NO	SIGNATURE

PLEASE TYPE OR PRINT IN INK **JUROR INFORMATION FORM** 6542-98

45356678-99098 **WILSON, SALLY JANE** **8998 CULEBRA STREET** **SAN MILANO, TX 54577** PLEASE MAKE CORRECTIONS TO ADDRESS:	**WHEN CALLED FOR JURY SERVICE, BRING THIS FORM WITH YOU. DO NOT MAIL IT.** PHONE # ________________ AGE _____ NO OF CHILDREN _______ GENDER ________ HOW LONG HAVE YOU LIVED IN THIS COUNTY? ___________
HAVE YOU EVER SERVED ON A CIVIL JURY? _____ YES _____ NO HAVE YOU EVER SERVED ON A CRIMINAL JURY? _____ YES _____ NO HAVE YOU EVER SUSTAINED ACCIDENTAL BODILY INJURY REQUIRING MEDICAL ATTENTION. IF SO, WHAT TYPE? _____ YES _____ NO HAVE YOU BEEN A PARTY TO A LAWSUIT? _____ YES _____ NO	PLACE OF BIRTH: RELIGION: EMPLOYER: OCCUPATION SPOUSE'S NAME: SPOUSE'S EMPLOYER:
HAVE YOU BEEN ACCUSED, COMPLAINANT, OR WITNESS IN CRIMINAL CASE? _____ YES _____ NO	SIGNATURE

PLEASE TYPE OR PRINT IN INK **JUROR INFORMATION FORM** 6542-98

45356678-99098 **SCOTTY, S.C.** **3478 ELM AVENUE** **SAN MILANO, TX 77777** PLEASE MAKE CORRECTIONS TO ADDRESS:	**WHEN CALLED FOR JURY SERVICE, BRING THIS FORM WITH YOU. DO NOT MAIL IT.** PHONE # ________________ AGE _____ NO OF CHILDREN _______ GENDER _______ HOW LONG HAVE YOU LIVED IN THIS COUNTY? ___________
HAVE YOU EVER SERVED ON A CIVIL JURY? _____ YES _____ NO HAVE YOU EVER SERVED ON A CRIMINAL JURY? _____ YES _____ NO HAVE YOU EVER SUSTAINED ACCIDENTAL BODILY INJURY REQUIRING MEDICAL ATTENTION. IF SO, WHAT TYPE? _____ YES _____ NO HAVE YOU BEEN A PARTY TO A LAWSUIT? _____ YES _____ NO	PLACE OF BIRTH: RELIGION: EMPLOYER: OCCUPATION SPOUSE'S NAME: SPOUSE'S EMPLOYER:
HAVE YOU BEEN ACCUSED, COMPLAINANT, OR WITNESS IN CRIMINAL CASE? _____ YES _____ NO	SIGNATURE

PLEASE TYPE OR PRINT IN INK **JUROR INFORMATION FORM** 6542-98

45356678-99098 **NORDSTRUD, JIMMY D.** **56678 STOKES PARKWAY** **# 456** **SAN MILANO, TX 54577** PLEASE MAKE CORRECTIONS TO ADDRESS:	**WHEN CALLED FOR JURY SERVICE, BRING THIS FORM WITH YOU. DO NOT MAIL IT.** PHONE # ________________ AGE _____ NO OF CHILDREN _______ GENDER _______ HOW LONG HAVE YOU LIVED IN THIS COUNTY? ___________
HAVE YOU EVER SERVED ON A CIVIL JURY? _____ YES _____ NO HAVE YOU EVER SERVED ON A CRIMINAL JURY? _____ YES _____ NO HAVE YOU EVER SUSTAINED ACCIDENTAL BODILY INJURY REQUIRING MEDICAL ATTENTION. IF SO, WHAT TYPE? _____ YES _____ NO HAVE YOU BEEN A PARTY TO A LAWSUIT? _____ YES _____ NO	PLACE OF BIRTH: RELIGION: EMPLOYER: OCCUPATION SPOUSE'S NAME: SPOUSE'S EMPLOYER:
HAVE YOU BEEN ACCUSED, COMPLAINANT, OR WITNESS IN CRIMINAL CASE? _____ YES _____ NO	SIGNATURE

PLEASE TYPE OR PRINT IN INK **JUROR INFORMATION FORM** 6542-98

<table>
<tr><td>45356678-99098

Name
Address

PLEASE MAKE CORRECTIONS TO ADDRESS:</td><td>WHEN CALLED FOR JURY SERVICE, BRING THIS FORM WITH YOU. DO NOT MAIL IT.
PHONE # ________________

AGE _____
NO OF CHILDREN _______
GENDER _______
HOW LONG HAVE YOU LIVED IN THIS COUNTY? __________</td></tr>
<tr><td>HAVE YOU EVER SERVED ON A CIVIL JURY?
_____ YES _____ NO

HAVE YOU EVER SERVED ON A CRIMINAL JURY? _____ YES _____ NO

HAVE YOU EVER SUSTAINED ACCIDENTAL BODILY INJURY REQUIRING MEDICAL ATTENTION. IF SO, WHAT TYPE?
_____ YES _____ NO

HAVE YOU BEEN A PARTY TO A LAWSUIT?
_____ YES _____ NO</td><td>PLACE OF BIRTH:

RELIGION:

EMPLOYER:

OCCUPATION

SPOUSE'S NAME:

SPOUSE'S EMPLOYER:</td></tr>
<tr><td>HAVE YOU BEEN ACCUSED, COMPLAINANT, OR WITNESS IN CRIMINAL CASE?
_____ YES _____ NO</td><td>SIGNATURE</td></tr>
</table>

PLEASE TYPE OR PRINT IN INK **JUROR INFORMATION FORM** 6542-98

<table>
<tr><td>45356678-99098

Name
Address

PLEASE MAKE CORRECTIONS TO ADDRESS:</td><td>WHEN CALLED FOR JURY SERVICE, BRING THIS FORM WITH YOU. DO NOT MAIL IT.
PHONE # ________________

AGE _____
NO OF CHILDREN _______
GENDER _______
HOW LONG HAVE YOU LIVED IN THIS COUNTY? __________</td></tr>
<tr><td>HAVE YOU EVER SERVED ON A CIVIL JURY?
_____ YES _____ NO

HAVE YOU EVER SERVED ON A CRIMINAL JURY? _____ YES _____ NO

HAVE YOU EVER SUSTAINED ACCIDENTAL BODILY INJURY REQUIRING MEDICAL ATTENTION. IF SO, WHAT TYPE?
_____ YES _____ NO

HAVE YOU BEEN A PARTY TO A LAWSUIT?
_____ YES _____ NO</td><td>PLACE OF BIRTH:

RELIGION:

EMPLOYER:

OCCUPATION

SPOUSE'S NAME:

SPOUSE'S EMPLOYER:</td></tr>
<tr><td>HAVE YOU BEEN ACCUSED, COMPLAINANT, OR WITNESS IN CRIMINAL CASE?
_____ YES _____ NO</td><td>SIGNATURE</td></tr>
</table>

Chapter 2
Opening Statements

§ 2-1. In General

The case files in Chapters 8 through 11 will provide the basis for the exercises on preparing opening statements. You should be prepared to present an 8 to 10 minute opening statement on one of those cases — to be assigned — using the techniques presented during class and in the reading assignments.

§ 2-2. Opening Statements — A List of Dos and Don'ts

The following chart summarizes some of the basic "dos" and "don'ts" of opening statements.

The "Dos"	The "Don'ts"
Use Themes and Labels; tie rest of opening statement to your theme	Avoid using too much time on preliminary matters
Get to the Point — Explain Theory of Case: Be efficient	Do not argue or state personal opinions
Pay particular attention to opening and closing lines (Start strong and end strong!)	Avoid distracting mannerisms
Consider using exhibits and other visual aids	Do not overstate evidence
Anticipate weaknesses in your case	Do not use the word "I"
Use good techniques of voice inflection and blocking.	In criminal case, avoid referring to defendant's silence — pretrial or trial
Try to speak extemporaneously	Do not read opening statement
Introduce yourself — let them see you	Do not use a lectern.
Personalize individual client	Try to avoid clichés
Get jury's attention and keep it — Grab 'Em	Do not tell jury that what you are saying is not "evidence" i.e. the function of the opening statement.

§ 2-3. Criminal Case — State v. Barkwood

The State of Lone Star has charged Don Barkwood with one count of theft by coercion and one count of manslaughter of his teenage daughter, Tiffany. When Barkwood learned that his daughter was exchanging e-mails with a high school teacher, Johnny Woods, he obtained the court's permission to take a pre-suit deposition of Woods, as provided in the Rules of Civil Procedure, of the Lone Star.

Woods offered to settle the case and paid Barkwood money, which in turn was deposited with a children's cancer foundation. Shortly afterwards, however, Barkwood withdrew the money from the foundation and made a down payment on a new car. When his daughter's pleas to refrain from proceeding against Woods failed, she told Barkwood that she would kill herself. When he ignored her final plea, she committed suicide.

The case file materials for this problem are in Chapter 8. Prepare and give an 8 to 10 minute opening statement:

a. For the prosecution; or

b. For the defense.

For the purposes of this exercise, assume that all of the evidence in the case file is admissible.

§ 2-4. Criminal Case — State v. Lockmore

In Chapter 10, Sissy Lockmore is charged with killing her ex-husband, Bill Lockmore in San Milano, Lone Star. Sissy and Bill were divorced when Bill discovered that Sissy, a financial advisor, was having an affair with a co-worker. The court awarded sole custody of their two children to Bill and ordered Sissy to pay child support. Bill remained in San Milano and Sissy moved to Dallas to be near her family. She failed to make the child support payments and at the time her husband was killed, she owed almost $20,000.

She and Bill were scheduled to appear in a San Milano court to continue their contentious legal battle over custody and child support payments. Bill was killed early in the morning — shot in the back — at his home in San Milano. The police focused their investigation on Sissy and obtained evidence through cell phone records showing that her cell phone was used in San Milano the evening before the killing.

The defendant argues that her business partner provides an alibi at the time of the killing and that the police should have investigated Morgan Walters, a business associate of Bill's. Walters and Bill Lockmore were in the process of dissolving their partnership in a medical practice.

The case file materials for this problem are in Chapter 10. Prepare and present an 8 to 10 minute opening statement:

a. For the prosecution; or

b. For the defense.

For the purposes of this exercise, assume that all of the evidence in the case file is admissible.

§ 2-5. Criminal Case — State v. Moss

In Chapter 14, Sylvia Moss is charged with murder of her husband, Danny Moss. Police responded to Sylvia's 911 call early in the morning and found Danny lying at the bottom of the steps of their home. Sylvia told the police that she had awakened when she heard a loud thump, saw Danny, and dialed 911 without first checking to see if there was anything she could do to help him. The police determined that Danny died as a result of a severe blow to his head, caused when he hit the stair railing. But there was also evidence of a bruise on the back of his neck. Additional evidence showed that Sylvia had reacted with rage whenever Danny ignored her or criticized her cooking.

The State has charged Sylvia with murder, on the theory that she hit him on the neck with a shoe and caused him to fall down the stairs. A prosecution expert has determined that Sylvia suffers from a narcissistic personality disorder, which triggered the attack.

Sylvia's version is that Danny's death was accidental

The case file materials for this problem are in Chapter 14. Prepare and give an 8 to 10 minute opening statement:

a. For the prosecution; or

b. For the defense.

For the purposes of this exercise, assume that all of the evidence in the case file is admissible.

§ 2-6. Civil Case — Barkwood v. Barkwood

Anika Stotward Barkwood has filed a wrongful death lawsuit against her ex-husband, Don Barkwood, for the death of their teenage daughter, Tiffany.

A year earlier Don Barkwood was charged with one count of theft by coercion and one count of manslaughter of their daughter, Tiffany. When Barkwood learned that his daughter was exchanging e-mails with a high school teacher, Johnny Woods, he obtained the court's permission to take a pre-suit deposition of Woods, as provided in the Rules of Civil Procedure, of the Lone Star. Woods offered to settle the case and paid Barkwood money, which in turn was deposited with a children's cancer foundation.

Shortly afterwards, however, Barkwood withdrew the money from the foundation and made a down payment on a new car. When his daughter's pleas to refrain from proceeding against Woods failed, she told Barkwood that she would kill herself. When he ignored her final plea, she committed suicide.

At the time of his criminal trial, Barkwood was separated from the plaintiff. Assume that for reasons unrelated to the merits of the case, the District Attorney later decided to drop the charges against Barkwood. Angered by the DA's action, the plaintiff filed the wrongful death lawsuit against her ex-husband.

Use the case files in Chapter 9 and present an 8 to 10 minute opening statement:

a. For the plaintiff; or

b. For the defense.

For the purposes of this exercise, assume that all of the evidence in the case file is admissible.

§ 2-7. Civil Case — Lockmore v. Lockmore

Sissy and Bill Lockmore were divorced when Bill discovered that Sissy, a financial advisor, was having an affair with a co-worker. The court awarded sole custody of their two children to Bill and ordered Sissy to pay child support. Bill remained in San Milano and Sissy moved to Dallas, State of Lone Star to be near her family.

She failed to make the child support payments and at the time her husband was killed, she owed almost $20,000. She and Bill were scheduled to appear in a San Milano court to continue their contentious legal battle over custody and child support payments. Bill was killed early in the morning — shot in the back — at his home in San Milano. The police focused their investigation on Sissy and obtained evidence through cell phone records showing that her cell phone was used in San Milano the evening before the killing.

At the criminal trial, the defendant argued that her business partner provided an alibi at the time of the killing and that the police should have investigated Morgan Walters, a business associate of Bill's. Walters and Bill Lockmore were in the process of dissolving their partnership in a medical practice.

Sissy Lockmore was tried and acquitted on criminal charges that she killed her ex-husband, Bill Lockmore, in San Milano, Lone Star.

The parents of Bill Lockmore, June and Steve Lockmore, have filed a civil wrongful death suit against Sissy Lockmore, their former daughter-in-law.

Use the case files in Chapter 11 and present an 8 to 10 minute opening statement:

a. For the plaintiff; or

b. For the defense.

For the purposes of this exercise, assume that all of the evidence in the case file is admissible.

§ 2-8. Civil Case — Jones v. Moss

Sylvia Moss was suspected of killing her husband, Danny Moss. Police responded to Sylvia's 911 call early in the morning and found Danny lying at the bottom of the steps of their home. Sylvia told the police that she had awakened when she heard a loud thump, saw Danny, and dialed 911 without first checking to see if there was anything she could do to help him. The police determined that Danny died as a result of a severe blow to his head, caused when he hit the stair railing. But there was also evidence of a bruise on the back of his neck. Additional evidence showed that Sylvia had reacted with rage whenever Danny ignored her or criticized her cooking.

The State's theory was that Sylvia hit him on the neck with a shoe and caused him to fall down the stairs. A prosecution expert determined that Sylvia suffers from a narcissistic personality disorder, which triggered the attack.

Sylvia's version was that Danny's death was accidental. The prosecutor decided not to try her. Shortly thereafter, Danny's step-daughter, Sarah Jones, from a prior marriage filed a wrongful death action against Sylvia.

Use the case files in Chapter 15 and present an 8 to 10 minute opening statement:

a. For the plaintiff, or

b. For the defense.

For the purposes of this exercise, assume that all of the evidence in the case file is admissible.

Chapter 3
DIRECT EXAMINATION

§ 3-1. Introduction

The problems in this chapter are designed to familiarize students with the applicable techniques and rules for conducting direct examination of a witness. For the most part, the problems focus on issues that are likely to recur during a case, and each problem presents the opportunity to develop and hone a particular skill.

Some of the following problems are taken from the case files in Chapters 8 through 15. Others are "free-standing" to the extent that they do not relate to any particular case or fact pattern in this book.

§ 3-2. Direct Examination — A Checklist

In presenting conducting a direct examination, consider the following pointers:

a. Keep it Simple (KISS). This principle applies to not only the form and content of each question (avoid long and confusing questions filled with qualifiers) but also for the scope of the direct examination.

b. Organize Logically: Determine Key Points to be Covered in Examination —
   - Personal Background of Witness
   - Description of Scene
   - Description of the Action (What happened?)
   - Use of Exhibits (for highlighting and repeating)
   - Damages (Civil cases, if applicable)

c. Do not read your questions. (Practice your questions until they sound conversational and natural).

d. Use introductory and transition questions ("Blocking"). (For example, "Now that we have covered your background, I would like to talk about what happened on the day of the accident.").

e. To emphasize key testimony on direct examination, use the techniques of "Parking," "Double Direct," and "Freezing."

f. Be sure to introduce your witness and develop background ("Accredit" your witness).

g. Set the Scene. (Where and when?)

h. Recreate the Action. (What happened?)

i. Use Nonleading Questions. (Use Who?, What?, Where? Why?)

j. Have the witness explain answers, if necessary (do not overdo).

k. Volunteer weaknesses in own case(?)

l. Use exhibits to highlight and summarize the facts.

m. Listen to your witness's answers!

n. Lawyer's position: Where Do I Stand or Sit?

o. Prepare your witness!

§ 3-3. Criminal Case — Prosecution Fact Witness

As counsel for the prosecution, use the case file in Chapter 8, *State v. Barkwood,* and conduct a direct examination of Pat Gonzales, the school counselor, concerning her relationship with Tiffany Barkwood and the fact that she believed that Tiffany had personal problems with her parents. Do not offer her written report or resumé into evidence — those are the subject of other problems.

For this problem, assume that Pat Gonzales is *not* an expert witness.

The direct examination should be about 8 to 10 minutes in length.

As counsel for the defense, be prepared to object to the prosecutor's questions.

§ 3-4. Criminal Case — Defense Fact Witness

As defense counsel, use the case file in Chapter 8, *State v. Barkwood*, and conduct a direct examination of Jordon Thompson. The direct examination should focus on Thompson's relationship with Don Barkwood and Thompson's role in helping Barkwood make a financial contribution to the foundation Thompson worked for.

The direct examination should be about 8 to 10 minutes in length.

As prosecutor, be prepared to object to the defense counsel's questions.

§ 3-5. Criminal Case — Prosecution Fact Witness

As the prosecutor in *State v. Moss*, the case file in Chapter 14, conduct a direct examination of the police detective who investigated the death of Danny Moss. Your direct examination should focus specifically on how the defendant, Sylvia Moss, reacted to her husband's death while the detective was at their house.

Your direct examination should be about 8 to 10 minutes in length.

As the defense counsel, be prepared to object to the prosecutor's questions.

§ 3-6. Criminal Case — Prosecution Fact Witness

As the prosecutor in *State v. Moss*, the case file in Chapter 14, conduct a direct examination of the police detective who investigated the death of Danny Moss. Your direct examination should focus specifically on what the detective observed when he arrived at the Moss residence, e.g., when he arrived, what he observed about the body, the location of the victim's shoe, etc.

Your direct examination should be about 8 to 10 minutes in length.

As defense counsel, be prepared to object to the prosecutor's questions.

§ 3-7. Criminal Case — Defense Fact Witness

As defense counsel, use the case file in Chapter 14, *State v. Moss*, and conduct a direct examination of your client, Sylvia Moss. Your direct examination should focus specifically on her relationship with her husband, the victim, e.g., how long they had been married, her attempt to please him by taking cooking lessons, etc., in an effort to show the jury that she loved him deeply.

Your direct examination should be about 8 to 10 minutes in length.

As prosecutor, be prepared to object to the defense counsel's questions.

§ 3-8. Criminal Case — Defense Fact Witness

As defense counsel, use the case file in Chapter 14, *State v. Moss*, and conduct a direct examination of your client, Sylvia Moss. The case file includes evidence that your client received a written reprimand concerning a confrontation that your client had with a co-worker over comments that the co-worker made about the quality of your client's work. You have decided to take the "sting" out of that evidence and will address that issue during direct examination of your client.

You do not need to introduce the written reprimand she received for the incident.

Your direct examination should be about 8 to 10 minutes in length.

As prosecutor, be prepared to object to the defense counsel's questions.

§ 3-9. Civil Case — Plaintiff Fact Witness

As counsel for the plaintiff, use the case file in Chapter 15, *Jones v. Moss*, and conduct a direct examination of the police detective who investigated the death of Danny Moss. Your direct examination should focus specifically on what the detective observed when he arrived at the Moss residence, e.g., when he arrived, what he observed about the body, the location of the victim's shoe, etc.

Your direct examination should be about 8 to 10 minutes in length.

As defense counsel, be prepared to object to the questions asked by plaintiff's counsel.

§ 3-10. Civil Case — Plaintiff Fact Witness

As plaintiff's counsel, use the case file in Chapter 15, *Jones v. Moss*, and conduct a direct examination of your client, Sarah Jones. Your direct examination should focus specifically on establishing the amount of damages that she has sustained as a result of her step-father's death.

Your direct examination should be about 8 to 10 minutes in length.

As defense counsel, be prepared to object to plaintiff's counsel's questions.

§ 3-11. Civil Case — Defense Fact Witness

As counsel for the defendant in *State v. Moss*, use the case file in Chapter 15, *Jones v. Moss*, and conduct a direct examination of your client, Sylvia Moss. Your direct examination should focus specifically on her relationship with her husband, the victim, e.g., how long they had been married, her attempt to please him by taking cooking lessons, etc., in an effort to show the jury that she loved him deeply.

Your direct examination should be about 8 to 10 minutes in length.

As the prosecutor, be prepared to object to defense counsel's questions.

§ 3-12. Civil Case — Defense Fact Witness

As counsel for Sylvia Moss, the defendant in the Chapter 15 case file, *Jones v Moss*, conduct a direct examination of your client. The case file includes evidence that your client received a written reprimand concerning a confrontation your client had with a co-worker over comments that the co-worker made about the quality of your client's work. You have decided to take the "sting" out of that evidence and will address that issue during direct examination of your client.

You do not need to introduce the written reprimand she received for the incident.

Your direct examination should be about 8 to 10 minutes in length.

As plaintiff's counsel, be prepared to object to the defense counsel's questions.

§ 3-13. Civil Case — Plaintiff Fact Witness

As plaintiff's counsel, use the materials in the case file for *Barkwood v. Barkwood*, in Chapter 9, and conduct a direct examination of Anika Stotward Barkwood. The direct examination should focus on her actions on what she did, or did not do, the day her daughter committed suicide.

Your direct examination should be about 8 to 10 minutes in length.

Acting as defense counsel, be prepared to object to plaintiff's counsel's questions.

§ 3-14. Civil Case — Defense Fact Witness

Acting as counsel for the defendant, use the materials in the case file for *Barkwood v. Barkwood*, in Chapter 9, and conduct a brief direct examination of the defendant, Barkwood. The direct examination should focus on his actions or inactions on the day his daughter committed suicide.

Your direct examination should be about 8 to 10 minutes in length.

As counsel for the plaintiff, be prepared to object to defense counsel's questions.

§ 3-15. Criminal Case — Defense Alibi Witness

Acting as defense counsel, use the case file materials in Chapter 10, *State v. Lockmore*, and conduct a direct examination of Cass Jones, an alibi witness for the defense. The examination should focus on the facts surrounding the witness's interaction with the defendant on the morning of the day her husband was shot, and specifically the time line of that morning.

Your direct examination should be about 8 to 10 minutes in length.

Acting as the prosecutor, be prepared to object to defense counsel's questions.

§ 3-16. Criminal Case — Character Witness

The defendant in *State v. Wilson* is charged with assault on Stan Morts. The defense has decided to present a "good character" defense under Lone Star Rule of Evidence 404(a). The two got into a fight for a parking space at a local bar. The defense theory is that Morts started the fight and that Wilson, who has a peaceful character, acted in self-defense.

One of the defense witnesses is Sammy Stone. Stone has known the defendant for five years. They have worked together at AcmeTech, Inc., a local technology company. They see each other at least two or three times a day. They have visited socially, including their families, at several company events. Stone considers himself a friend of Wilson and is prepared to offer opinion testimony that Wilson is a nonviolent person.

The prosecution has evidence that on April 1, [YR-6], while working for the Zerotech Company, Wilson got into a fight with a co-worker over an office prank where the co-worker added hot sauce to Wilson's sandwich. No charges were ever filed. Wilson was reprimanded in [YR-5] for confronting his boss at Zerotech and was instructed to enroll in an anger management program, offered by the company. Several weeks later, Wilson resigned his position and got the job at Zerotech. The prosecution learned this information while speaking with Wilson's former co-workers. But the prosecution has no documentary evidence to support the information and those co-workers are not willing to testify at the trial.

a. As the defense counsel, conduct the direct examination of Stone and present admissible character evidence about the defendant.

b. As the prosecutor, conduct a cross-examination of Stone.

§ 3-17. Civil Case — Present Memory Refreshed and Past Recollection Recorded

Prisoners at the local county jail filed a civil suit against the County on the grounds that the guards used excessive force. On one particularly hot afternoon, the jail air conditioning unit failed and when the temperatures soared, tempers did as well. Deputies assigned to the jail used force in getting some of the prisoners back into their cells after a morning workout. A question has arisen about the timing of the events on that day, and the names of the deputies and inmates involved.

As counsel for the defendant County, conduct a direct examination of Deputy Mortsworthy to lay the foundation for admitting the following memo as either past recollection recorded or present memory refreshed. For this problem, assume that your witness is not able to remember all of the details about the times and events related in the memo.

a. Establish through direct examination the names of the deputies and inmates involved in the incident on August 3.

b. Establish through direct examination the time that Jones first called Mortsworthy and the content of that conversation, and the time that the DA called Mortsworthy and the content of that conversation.

MEMO FOR RECORD

FROM: **Mortsworthy**
RE: **Problems at Jail**
DATE: **August 3, [YR-1]**
TIME: **1715 hours**

This afternoon we had an incident at the jail. I got a call at 1310 hours from Deputy Jones that the AC had failed in Unit 16-A-10. I asked him to keep me informed.

At 1330 hours, I got another call from Jones. He reported that one of the inmates, Orsen (pending assault charges), was swearing at him in a loud voice and threatening him.

At 1340 hours, I called maintenance to check on status of repairs. No one was there so I left a message saying that we needed the unit fixed as soon as possible.

At 1420 hours, I got a text message from maintenance saying that it was working on problem but that it would be several hours to fix it because a compressor had gone out.

At 1500 hours I went to the jail and personally observed three of our deputies (Jones, Wilson, and Silliman) trying to physically subdue two inmates, Orsen and Juarez. After 5 minutes they were finally able to subdue the inmates.

At 1630 hours, the DA's office called me and recommended that I immediately prepare a memo for record.

Chapter 4
INTRODUCING EXHIBITS

§ 4-1. Introduction

The problems in this chapter focus on the introduction of exhibits. The ability to smoothly and confidently mark, show, and handle exhibits is a skill that can be learned and perfected.

In each of the problems, the student should be prepared to:

1. Mark the exhibit or have it marked by the court reporter, and show it to opposing counsel, and the judge, if necessary;
2. Lay the appropriate foundation;
3. Offer the exhibit into evidence; and
4. Publish the exhibit.

§ 4-2. Criminal Case — E-Mails

As the defense counsel, use the case file in Chapter 8, *State v. Barkwood.* Call the defendant to the stand and introduce into evidence the e-mails sent between Johnny Woods and his student, Tiffany Barkwood.

Use the e-mails to have the defendant explain how he found out about their relationship and his reaction when he read the e-mails.

As the prosecutor, be prepared to object to the defense counsel's questions and the admissibility of the e-mails.

§ 4-3. Criminal Case — School Counselor's Report

As the prosecutor, use the case file materials in Chapter 8, *State v. Barkwood*, and introduce into evidence the written counseling report that Pat Gonzales prepared on Tiffany Barkwood. Your direct examination should explore how Gonzales came to the point of believing that a report was required and its purpose.

As the defense counsel, be prepared to object to the prosecutor's questions and the admissibility of the report.

§ 4-4. Criminal Case — Cancelled Check

For this particular problem, use the case files in Chapter 8, *State v. Barkwood.* Barkwood is charged with theft by coercion of a high school teacher and with manslaughter in the death of his teenage daughter, Tiffany.

Assume that the check was written during the current year of the trial.

a. For the prosecution, using the testimony of Johnny Woods, introduce into evidence the cancelled check from the high school teacher.

b. For the defense, be prepared to object to the introduction of the cancelled check.

§ 4-5. Civil Case — Autopsy Report

As plaintiff's counsel, use the case file materials in Chapter 9, *Barkwood v, Barkwood,* to call Dr. John Rainy, MD, to the stand and introduce into evidence the autopsy report he prepared.

For this problem you need not qualify Dr. Rainy as an expert witness. As part of your direct examination, have him testify as to the time and date of the autopsy, the cause of Tiffany's death, and the fact that the report shows that she was pregnant at the time of death.

As defense counsel, be prepared to object to counsel's questions and the admissibility of the autopsy report.

§ 4-6. Civil Case — Autopsy Report

As plaintiff's counsel, use the case file materials in Chapter 15, *Jones v. Moss*, to call Jasper McCue, M.D., Deputy Medical Examiner, to the stand and introduce into evidence the autopsy report he prepared.

For this problem you need not qualify Dr. McCue as an expert witness. As part of your direct examination, have him testify as to the time and date of the autopsy, the cause of Danny Moss's death, and the fact that the report shows that the level of Prozac in his system did not cause his death.

As defense counsel, be prepared to object to counsel's questions and the admissibility of the autopsy report.

§ 4-7. Criminal Case — Crime Scene Diagram

For this problem, use the criminal case file in Chapter 10, *State v. Lockmore*. The defendant is charged with killing her ex-husband outside his home in San Milano.

a. As the prosecutor, recreate the officer's crime scene diagram, and using the officer's testimony, introduce the diagram (showing the various objects and distances) into evidence as an exhibit.

b. As the defense counsel, be prepared to object to the introduction of the diagram into evidence.

§ 4-8. Criminal Case — Crime Scene Diagram

For this problem, use the criminal case file, *State v. Moss*, at Chapter 14. The defendant is charged with killing her husband at their home in San Milano.

a. As the prosecutor, recreate a larger version the officer's crime scene diagram, and using the officer's testimony introduce the diagram (showing the various objects) into evidence as an exhibit.

b. As the defense counsel, be prepared to object to the introduction of the diagram into evidence.

§ 4-9. Civil Case — Crime Scene Photographs

For this problem, use the case file in Chapter 15, *Jones v. Moss*. The plaintiff has sued the defendant for the wrongful death of the plaintiff's step-father at the Moss residence in San Milano. Police officer Lorson took the crime scene photos.

a. As counsel for the plaintiff, use detective Lorson to introduce the crime scene photograph showing the upstairs hallway and one of the photos showing the victim on the stairway, and have the officer explain what the photographs show.

b. As counsel for the defense, be prepared to object to the introduction of the photographs into evidence.

§ 4-10. Criminal Case — Crime Scene Photographs

For this problem, use the criminal case file in Chapter 10, *State v. Lockmore*. The defendant is charged with killing her ex-husband early one morning, outside his home in San Milano, as he was going outside to pick up his newspaper. Police officer Jamie Gonzales took the crime scene photos.

a. As the prosecutor, use Jamie Gonzales to introduce the crime scene photographs into evidence and have the officer explain what the photographs show.

b. As the defense counsel, be prepared to object to the introduction of the photographs into evidence.

§ 4-11. Criminal Case — Cell Tower Records

As the prosecutor in the Chapter 10 case file, *State v. Lockmore*, call the police detective to the stand and, through the officer's testimony, introduce the cell tower records into evidence.

Assume for this problem that the trial judge has concluded that the cover letter from Sprant is not admissible because it is testimonial hearsay and would violate the Confrontation Clause.

As the defense counsel, be prepared to object to the prosecutor's questions and the admission of the cell tower records.

§ 4-12. Criminal Case — Airline Schedule

As the prosecutor in the Chapter 10 case file, *State v. Lockmore*, call the police detective to the stand and, using his testimony, introduce into evidence the airline schedule for Southeast Airlines, which the detective found on the Internet.

As the defense counsel, be prepared to object to the prosecutor's questions and the admissibility of the schedule.

§ 4-13. Civil Case — Parking Garage Receipt

For this problem, use the case file in Chapter 11, *Lockmore v. Lockmore*. As counsel for the plaintiff, call the police detective to the stand and, using his testimony, introduce into evidence the parking garage receipt that the detective found in Bill Lockmore's backyard.

As defense counsel, be prepared to object to plaintiff's counsel's questions and the admissibility of the receipt.

§ 4-14. Criminal Case — Letter of Reprimand

For this problem, use the case file in Chapter 14, *State v. Moss*. Those materials include a reprimand received by the defendant.

As the defense counsel, you have decided to take the sting out of that issue. Using the defendant's testimony, lay the foundation for the written reprimand to show that she did not assault the co-worker.

As the prosecutor, be prepared to object to defense counsel's questions and the admissibility of the reprimand.

§ 4-15. Civil Case — Newspaper Clipping

For this problem, use the case file in Chapter 15, *Jones v. Moss*. Those materials include a newspaper clipping concerning an incident involving the defendant's younger brother.

As defense counsel, you have decided to take the sting out of that issue. Using the defendant's testimony, lay the foundation for the news clipping to show that her brother's death was an accident.

As the prosecutor, be prepared to object to defense counsel's questions and the admissibility of the clipping.

§ 4-16. Criminal Case — Picture of Shoe

For this problem, use the case file in Chapter 14, *State v. Moss*. Police detective Lorson took a series of pictures at the crime scene.

As the prosecutor, call the police detective to the stand and, using his testimony, introduce into evidence a picture of the victim's shoe, found at the crime scene. In lieu of the photograph, your professor may require you to introduce an actual shoe similar in appearance to the one in the picture.

As defense counsel, be prepared to object to the prosecutor's questions and the admission of the photo.

§ 4-17. Civil Case — Picture of Shoe

For this problem, use the case file in Chapter 15, *Jones v. Moss*. Police detective Lorson took a series of pictures at the crime scene.

As the prosecutor, call the police detective to the stand and, using his testimony, introduce into evidence the picture of the victim's shoe, found at the crime scene. In lieu of the photograph, your professor may require you to introduce an actual shoe similar in appearance to the one in the picture.

As defense counsel, be prepared to object to the prosecutor's questions and the admission of the photo.

Chapter 5

CROSS-EXAMINATION AND IMPEACHMENT

§ 5-1. Introduction

One of the most difficult litigation techniques to master is the art of cross-examination. The exercises in this chapter are designed to assist the student in mastering and honing that skill. In particular, these exercises focus on methods of impeaching a witness. Because the most common form of impeachment is use of a prior inconsistent statement, many of the problems involve that issue.

For each problem, the student should be prepared to impeach or cross-examine the witness by means that effectively inform the jury of the discrediting information, whether it is evidence of bias, prior inconsistent statements, or one of the other recognized forms of impeachment.

Your instructor may ask other students to serve as opponents for your cross-examination

§ 5-2. Cross-Examination Checklist

The following checklist provides a helpful template in preparing for the problems in this chapter:

a. Deciding Whether To Conduct Cross-Examination

1. Has this witness injured my case?
2. Is this witness important?
3. Was the witness's direct testimony credible?
4. Did the witness give less than expected on direct testimony?
5. What are your realistic expectations on your cross-examination?
6. What risks do I need to take?

b. Structure

1. Establish as few points as possible.
2. Make strongest points at beginning and end of examination (primacy and recency).
3. Vary the order of your topics — use "indirection" (be careful lest you confuse the fact finder).
4. Do not simply repeat the direct examination (unless you have a specific goal in mind).

c. Rules for Cross-Examination

1. Start and end "crisply."
2. Know probable answer to your questions (axiom: "Do not ask a question to which you do not know the answer.").
3. Listen carefully to the answers.
4. Do not argue with the witness.

5. Be careful about asking witness to explain answer (unless you know they have a very bad explanation).
6. Avoid the "one question too many" problem.
7. When finished, STOP.

d. Questioning Style

1. Use leading questions.
2. Make statement of fact and have witness agree to it.
3. Use short, clear questions — bit by bit.
4. Keep control over the witness.
5. Project confidence — take charge attitude.
6. Be a good actor.
7. Use a natural style.

d. Traditional Methods of Impeachment

1. Bias, Interest, or Motive (Federal Rule of Evidence 613)
2. Bad Character—Opinion or Reputation Witness (Federal Rule of Evidence 608(a))
3. Prior Convictions (Federal Rule of Evidence 609)
4. Prior Bad Acts (Federal Rule of Evidence 608(b))
5. Contradictory Acts or Facts
6. Prior Inconsistent Statements (Federal Rule of Evidence 613)
7. Common Law Elements of Competency

§ 5-3. Criminal Case — Cross-Examination of Defense Witness

For this problem use the case file in Chapter 8, *State v. Barkwood.* The defendant is charged with theft by coercion of Johnny Woods, his daughter's high school teacher. According to the defendant, Woods paid the defendant a "settlement" of $20,000 which the defendant in turn gave to the Children's Cancer Foundation — with assistance of his friend, Jordan Thompson.

On direct examination, Thompson testified that (1) after the defendant, Don Barkwood, wrote a check for $20,000 to the Children's Cancer Foundation, he deposited $5000.00 in his personal back account; (2) the $5,000 was considered a personal loan from Don Barkwood; and (3) he had repaid the loan several days later when he realized that it would look bad.

a. For the prosecutor, cross-examine Thompson about (1) the "loan," and (2) his relationship with the alleged victim, Johnny Woods.

b. For the defense, be prepared to conduct a redirect examination.

§ 5-4. Criminal Case — Cross-Examination of Prosecution Witness

This problem is taken from Chapter 8, *State v. Barkwood.* Barkwood is charged with theft by coercion from his teenage daughter's teacher, Johnny Woods.

Assume that on direct examination by the prosecutor, Woods testified that the idea of settling the defendant's concerns about his relationship with the defendant's daughter Tiffany, was defendant's idea, and only the defendant's idea.

He also testified that the day before she died, Tiffany told him that she could be pregnant and that she was worried about that fact.

a. As the defense counsel, cross-examine Woods about that testimony.

b. As the prosecutor, be prepared to conduct a redirect examination.

§ 5-5. Criminal Case — Cross-Examination of Prosecution Witness

This problem is taken from Chapter 14, *State v. Moss*. Detective Lorson investigated Mrs. Moss for the murder of her husband, Danny.

Assume that on direct examination by the prosecutor, Lorson testified that he had 10 years of experience as a homicide detective and that he had taken an advanced course in DNA identification, a fact he did not mention in his grand jury testimony.

a. As the defense counsel, cross-examine Lorson about that testimony.

b. As the prosecutor, be prepared to conduct a redirect examination.

§ 5-6. Criminal Case — Cross-Examination of Defendant

In *State v. Barkwood*, Chapter 8, the defendant is charged with theft by coercion of his teenage daughter's high school teacher, Johnny Woods.

On direct examination, the defendant testified that (1) Johnny Woods had never expressed any remorse to him about his (Woods') relationship with Tiffany, and (2) he withdrew his donation to the Children's Cancer Foundation when he heard a news report on a local news station that the Foundation was having some financial difficulties.

a. As the prosecutor, cross-examine the defendant about that testimony.

b. As the defense counsel, be prepared to conduct a redirect examination of the defendant.

§ 5-7. Criminal Case — Cross-Examination of Defendant

For this problem, use the case materials in Chapter 14, *State v. Moss*. The defendant is charged with killing her husband. She has testified on direct examination that she is not an aggressive person and takes criticism very well.

a. As the prosecutor, use the written letter of reprimand that she received at work, and attempt to impeach her with that information.

b. As the defense counsel, be prepared to conduct a redirect examination.

§ 5-8. Criminal Case — Cross-Examination of Prosecution Witness

In Chapter 10, *State v. Lockmore*, the defendant is charged with killing her ex-husband, Bill Lockmore, outside his home in San Milano. At the time of the shooting Lockmore's business partner, Morgan Walters, was inside the house, waiting to go to breakfast with the victim.

Assume that Walters' direct examination testimony was consistent with his grand jury testimony.

a. As the prosecutor, cross-examine Walters' about his actions and inactions when he/she went outside and discovered that Lockmore had been shot in the back.

b. As the defense counsel, be prepared to conduct a redirect examination of the witness.

§ 5-9. Criminal Case — Cross-Examination of Prosecution Witness

This problem is based upon Chapter 10, *State v. Lockmore*. Sissy Lockmore is charged with killing her ex-husband.

On direct examination Detective Gonzales testified about his investigation of the death of Bill Lockmore, and specifically the driving times between the victim's house and the San Milano airport. During the witness' direct testimony, the witness said that he drove the route four times — at approximately the same time of day as the time of the shooting — and that the respective driving times were 30 minutes, 45 minutes, 48 minutes, and 40 minutes.

Further, on direct examination, Gonzales testified that he had carefully reviewed all of the evidence in the case and that after his investigation he believed that Morgan Walters did not have any motive to kill Bill Lockmore, his business partner.

a. As the defense counsel, cross-examine Gonzales about that testimony.

b. As the prosecutor, be prepared to conduct a redirect examination of the witness.

§ 5-10. Criminal Case — Cross-Examination of Defense Alibi Witness

In Chapter 10, *State v. Lockmore*, the defendant is charged with killing her ex-husband in San Milano. Her business partner in Dallas, Cass Jones, was in the office on the morning the victim was killed.

Assume that during Jones' direct examination by the defense counsel, the witness testified that the witness is sure that the defendant came into their office at 10:00 AM on the day that the defendant's husband was killed.

a. As the prosecutor conduct a cross-examination of Jones.

b. As defense counsel, be prepared to conduct a redirect examination of Jones.

§ 5-11. Civil Case — Cross-Examination of Defendant

In Chapter 9, *Barkwood v. Barkwood*, the defendant has been sued for the death of his teenage daughter, Tiffany. The plaintiffs' theory is that Tiffany was despondent over the fact that the defendant was threatening her high-school teacher and that when he refused to back off, she committed suicide by overdosing on drugs.

Assume that on direct examination, the defendant testified that he had taken seriously his daughter's threat to commit suicide and that when he got her last e-mail, he raced home to make sure that she did not harm herself.

a. Acting as plaintiff's counsel, cross-examine the defendant.

b. As defense counsel, be prepared to conduct a redirect examination of the defendant.

§ 5-12. Civil Case — Cross-Examination of Defendant

In Chapter 15, *Jones v. Moss*, the defendant has been sued for the death of her husband. Assume that on direct examination, the defendant testified that taking cooking lessons was a complete waste of $200.00, which she had taken in order to please her husband.

a. Acting as plaintiff's counsel, cross-examine the defendant, using her statement to the police to impeach her.

b. As defense counsel, be prepared to conduct a redirect examination of the defendant.

§ 5-13. Civil Case — Cross-Examination of Plaintiff's Witness

In Chapter 15, *Jones v. Moss*, Dr. Pat Bentley examined the defendant and determined that she had a narcissistic personality disorder, which triggered the attack.

On direct examination Dr. Bentley testified that in evaluating the defendant and in using the Diagnostic and Statistical Manual (DSM), she had not considered any other potential diagnosis for the defendant.

a. Acting as defense counsel, cross-examine the plaintiff's expert witness using the witness's deposition.

b. As plaintiff's counsel, be prepared to conduct a redirect examination of the expert.

For this problem, you do not need to introduce the excerpts from the DSM.

§ 5-14. Civil Case — Cross-Examination of Witness for Plaintiff

For this problem, use the case file in Chapter 9, *Barkwood v. Barkwood*. The defendant's ex-wife has filed a wrongful death suit against the defendant for the death of their teenage daughter, Tiffany.

A witness for the plaintiff, Johnny Woods (Tiffany's teacher) admitted that he and Tiffany had exchanged e-mails concerning "helpers," but denied giving her any Zoloft. His direct testimony is that he only gave Tiffany some Aleve tablets to help with her terrible headaches.

a. As defense counsel, cross-examine Woods about that testimony.

b. As plaintiff's counsel, be prepared to conduct a redirect examination of Woods.

§ 5-15. Civil Case — Cross-Examination of Defendant

In Chapter 11, *Lockmore v. Lockmore*, the plaintiffs have filed a wrongful death suit against their former daughter-in-law, Sissy Lockmore, for killing their son, Bill Lockmore.

The defendant's theory is that she was not even in San Milano on the day her husband was shot and that the real killer is Bill's business partner, Morgan Walters.

On direct examination, the defendant testifies that (1) she used to own a 9 mm Glock but that someone had taken if from a workbench in her garage, when the door was accidentally left open one day; and (2) that she had no motive for killing her ex-husband and that they were working out their problems.

a. As plaintiff's counsel, conduct a cross-examination of the defendant.

b. As defense counsel, be prepared to conduct a redirect examination of the defendant.

§ 5-16. Civil Case — Cross-Examination of Defense Witness

In the case file in Chapter 11, *Lockmore v. Lockmore*, the plaintiffs have filed a wrongful death suit against their former daughter-in-law, for the death of their son, Bill Lockmore.

One of the defense witnesses, the defendant's business partner, Cass Jones, has testified as an alibi witness for the defendant, in an attempt to show that she could not have killed her ex-husband in San Milano. He testifies on direct examination that she was in their office in Dallas on the morning of the shooting.

He also testifies on direct examination that he has no motive or interest to testify in the defendant's behalf.

a. As plaintiff's counsel, cross-examine Jones. Your examination should focus on his testimony that he has no motive or interest to testify on behalf of the defendant.

b. As defense counsel, be prepared to conduct a redirect examination of Jones.

Chapter 6
EXPERT WITNESSES

§ 6-1. Introduction

This chapter focuses on learning the trial techniques relating to expert opinion testimony. Federal Rules of Evidence 702 to 705 address the legal requirements of admitting that type of testimony. The case law, which has interpreted and applied those Rules, generally requires that the proponent of the testimony:

(1) Prove that the witness is qualified to testify as an expert;

(2) Establish that the underlying theories, principles, methodology, techniques, or protocols used by the expert are reliable;

(3) Establish a factual basis for the expert's opinion;

(4) Establish the relationship ("fit") between the underlying principles and facts of the case; and

(5) Offer an opinion, even if it addresses an ultimate issue in the case.

The problems in this chapter present opportunities for the student to put into practice some or all of those 5 steps. As with prior chapters, where possible, the problems draw from the case files in Chapters 8 through 11. In other instances, the problems are free-standing and do not have any relationship to those case files.

§ 6-2. Standards of Admissibility

The following chart provides a summary of the standards of admissibility of expert opinion testimony in federal cases.

	Federal Rules of Evidence
Who Decides?	Judge (Rule 104(a))
Standard for Admissibility	*Daubert*: Validity, i.e. reliability
Burden of Proof	POE
Factors to Be Considered by Judge	(1) Has theory been tested? (2) Peer review? (3) Error rate? (4) Generally accepted?
Applies to What Sort of Evidence? (i.e. "hard" or "soft" science, junk science; or other specialized experience & technical knowledge)?	*Daubert* applies to all forms of expert testimony. *Kumho v. Carmichael*

§ 6-3. Criminal Case — Expert Witness for the Prosecution

In Chapter 8, *State v. Barkwood*, the defendant is charged with causing the suicide of his teenage daughter, Tiffany, who was having an inappropriate relationship with one of her high school teachers. A school counselor, Pat Gonzales, counseled Tiffany and is available as an expert witness on the subject of Tiffany's emotional problems and her relationship with her parents.

Assume that the defense has objected to the testimony of Pat Gonzales and that the judge is holding a pretrial hearing into the admissibility of her testimony:

a. As prosecutor, call Pat Gonzales as one of your witnesses and establish that the witness is qualified to testify as an expert.

b. As defense counsel, be prepared to conduct a voir dire of Pat Gonzales, and object to the witness being qualified to offer expert opinion testimony.

§ 6-4. Criminal Case — Expert Witness for the Prosecution

The case file in Chapter 8 is *State v. Barkwood.* In that case the defendant is charged with manslaughter, i.e., causing the suicide of his teenage daughter, Tiffany, who was having an inappropriate relationship with one of her high school teachers. A school counselor, Pat Gonzales, counseled Tiffany and is available as an expert witness on the subject of Tiffany's emotional problems and her relationship with her parents.

Assume that the trial judge in a pretrial hearing has concluded that Pat Gonzales is qualified as an expert under Rule of Evidence 702:

c. As the prosecutor, conduct a direct examination of Pat Gonzales and present her opinion testimony that Tiffany Barkwood was a very troubled teenager who needed counseling, love, and attention from her parents. You should also establish that Tiffany's parents should have recognized her fragile emotional state.

d. As defense counsel, object to Pat Gonzales' expert testimony and conduct any appropriate cross-examination.

§ 6-5. Criminal Case — Expert Witness for the Prosecution

The case file in Chapter 14 is *State v. Moss*. Sylvia Moss is charged with murdering her husband by pushing him down the stairs of their home after they had a fight about her cooking. An expert witness for the prosecution, Dr. Pat Bentley, has diagnosed Sylvia as having a narcissistic personality disorder.

For the prosecution, conduct a direct examination of Dr. Bentley concerning (1) the Doctor's qualifications to offer opinion testimony on that disorder, and (2) the reliability of the Diagnostic and Statistical Manual (DSM), which the Doctor relied upon. You do not need to establish the details of his diagnosis for opinion.

For this problem, you may need to do some additional research on the DSM — what it is, who authors it, how it is used, etc.

Your examination should run between 8 to 10 minutes in length.

§ 6-6. Criminal Case — Cross-Examination of Prosecution's Expert Witness

The case file in Chapter 14 is *State v. Moss*. Sylvia Moss is charged with murdering her husband by pushing him down the stairs of their home after they had a fight about her cooking. An expert witness for the prosecution, Dr. Pat Bentley, has diagnosed Sylvia as having a narcissistic personality disorder. An expert witness for the defense, Dr. Avery Wilson, has concluded that Mrs. Moss does not suffer from that disorder.

For the defense, conduct a cross-examination of Dr. Bentley. Assume that on direct examination the doctor testified that in the DSM, only four of the diagnostic criteria in 301.81 of the DSM need to be established to reach an opinion that a person has the narcissistic personality disorder. Using the excerpts of the DSM in the case files, cross-examine the doctor about that testimony.

You are to assume that the contents of the DSM are being offered for their truth. Be prepared to address any hearsay objections to your use of the DSM excerpts.

For this problem, you may need to do some additional research on the DSM — what it is, who authors it, how it is used, etc.

Your cross-examination should run not longer than 8 to 10 minutes in length.

§ 6-7. Civil Case — Expert Witness for the Plaintiff

The case file in Chapter 15 is *Jones v. Moss*. Sarah Jones has sued Sylvia Moss for the death of her step-father by pushing him down the stairs of their home after they had a fight about her cooking. An expert witness for the plaintiff, Dr. Pat Bentley, has diagnosed Sylvia as having a narcissistic personality disorder. An expert witness for the defense, Dr. Avery Wilson, has concluded that Mrs. Moss does not suffer from that disorder.

For the plaintiff, conduct a direct examination (8 to 10 minutes) of Dr. Bentley, and establish the prior incidents that he relied upon in forming his opinion: the incident involving a co-worker, and the drowning death of Sylvia's brother.

Be prepared to address the issue of whether the expert may rely on those incidents even if they are not otherwise admissible.

§ 6-8. Civil Case — Expert Witness for the Defense

The case file in Chapter 15 is *Jones v. Moss*. Sarah Jones has sued Sylvia Moss for the death of her step-father by pushing him down the stairs of their home after they had a fight about her cooking. An expert witness for the plaintiff, Dr. Pat Bentley, has diagnosed Sylvia as having a narcissistic personality disorder. An expert witness for the defense, Dr. Avery Wilson, has concluded that Mrs. Moss does not suffer from that disorder.

For the defense, conduct a direct examination of Dr. Wilson (8 to 10 minutes), and establish how the doctor reached the conclusion that Mrs. Moss does not suffer from a narcissistic personality disorder. You should use the relevant portions of the DSM in the case materials to support his testimony.

For the purposes of this problem, you may assume that the DSM is a reliable source for making the sort of diagnosis made by Dr. Wilson.

Chapter 7
CLOSING ARGUMENTS

§ 7-1. Introduction

This chapter focuses on the preparation and execution of closing arguments. The following practical exercises use the case files in Chapters 8 through 15.

§ 7-2. Checklist for Conducting Closing Arguments

In preparing for your closing arguments, review the following checklist as an outline of points and techniques.

a. Use Themes and Labels (Remember Opening Statements)

b. Present Theory of Case

c. Argue Facts, Not *Personal* Opinions

d. Use Exhibits and Other Visual Aids (Grab the Jury with a "Hook").

e. Refer to the Judge's Instructions

f. Use Rhetorical Questions During Argument

g. Use "Stories"

h. Argue Your Case's Strengths

i. Be Candid in Addressing Your Weaknesses

j. Force Opponent to Deal with His/Her Weaknesses.

k. Do Not Read Your Closing Argument — Unless You Are Reading from an Admitted Exhibit

§ 7-3. Criminal Case — *State v. Barkwood*

In the Chapter 8 case file, *State v. Barkwood*, the State has charged Don Barkwood with one count of theft by coercion and one count of manslaughter of his teenage daughter, Tiffany. When Barkwood learned that his daughter was exchanging e-mails with a high school teacher, Johnny Woods, he obtained the court's permission to take a pre-suit deposition of Woods, as provided in the Rules of Civil Procedure of the Lone Star. Woods offered to settle the case and paid Barkwood money, which in turn was deposited with a children's cancer foundation.

Shortly afterwards, however, Barkwood withdrew the money from the foundation and made a down payment on a new car. When his daughter's pleas to refrain from proceeding against Woods failed, she told Barkwood that she would kill herself. When he ignored her final plea, she committed suicide.

Assume that each side was able to present all of its available evidence during the trial. Prepare and give an 8 to 10 minute closing argument:

a. For the prosecution; or

b. For the defense.

§ 7-4. Criminal Case — *State v. Lockmore*

In the Chapter 10 case file, *State v. Lockmore*, the State has charged Sissy Lockmore with killing Bill Lockmore, her ex-husband.

Sissy and Bill were divorced when Bill discovered that Sissy, a financial advisor, was having an affair with a co-worker. The court awarded sole custody of their two children to Bill and ordered Sissy to pay child support. Bill remained in San Milano and Sissy moved to Dallas to be near her family. She failed to make child support payments and at the time her husband was killed, she owed almost $20,000. She and Bill were scheduled to appear in a San Milano court to continue their contentious legal battle over custody and child support payments.

Bill was killed early in the morning — shot in the back — at his home in San Milano. The police focused their investigation on Sissy and obtained evidence through cell phone records showing that her cell phone was used in San Milano the evening before the killing.

The defendant denies killing Bill Lockmore, and her business partner provides an alibi at the time of the killing. She contends that the police should have investigated Morgan Walters, a business associate of Bill's. Walters and Bill Lockmore were in the process of dissolving their partnership in a medical practice.

Assume that each side was able to introduce all of its available evidence. Present an 8 to 10 minute closing argument:

a. For the prosecution, or

b. For the defense.

§ 7-5. Criminal Case — *State v. Moss*

In the Chapter 14 case file, *State v. Moss*, Sylvia Moss is charged with the murder of her husband, Danny Moss. Police responded to Sylvia's 911 call early in the morning, and found Danny lying at the bottom of the steps of their home. Sylvia told the police that she had awakened when she heard a loud thump, saw Danny, and dialed 911 without first checking to see if there was anything she could do to help him. The police determined that Danny died as a result of a severe blow to his head, caused when he hit the stair railing. But there was also evidence of a bruise on the back of his neck. Additional evidence showed that Sylvia had reacted with rage whenever Danny ignored her or criticized her cooking.

The State has charged Sylvia with murder based on the theory that she hit him on the neck with a shoe, which caused him to fall down the stairs. A prosecution expert has determined that Sylvia suffers from a narcissistic personality disorder, which triggered the attack.

Sylvia's version is that Danny's death was accidental.

Prepare and give an 8 to 10 minute closing argument:

a. For the prosecution; or

b. For the defense.

For this problem, assume that all of the evidence in the case file was admitted at trial.

§ 7-6. Civil Case — *Barkwood v. Barkwood*

In the Chapter 9 case file, *Barkwood v. Barkwood*, Anika Stotward Barkwood has filed a wrongful death lawsuit against her ex-husband, Don Barkwood, for the death of their teenage daughter, Tiffany.

A year earlier, Don Barkwood was charged with one count of theft by coercion and one count of manslaughter of their daughter, Tiffany. When Barkwood learned that his daughter was exchanging e-mails with a high school teacher, Johnny Woods, he obtained the court's permission to take a pre-suit deposition of Woods, as provided in the Rules of Civil Procedure of the Lone Star. Woods offered to settle the case and paid Barkwood money, which in turn was deposited with a children's cancer foundation. Shortly afterwards, however, Barkwood withdrew the money from the foundation and made a down payment on a new car.

When his daughter's pleas to refrain from proceeding against Woods failed, she told Barkwood that she would kill herself. When he ignored her final plea, she committed suicide.

At the time of his criminal trial, Barkwood was separated from the plaintiff. Assume that for reasons unrelated to the merits of the case, the District Attorney later decided to drop the charges against Barkwood. Angered by the DA's action, the plaintiff filed the wrongful death lawsuit against her ex-husband.

For this exercise, assume that both the plaintiff and the defense were able to present all of their available evidence. Prepare and present an 8 to 10 minute closing argument:

a. For the plaintiff, or

b. For the defense.

§ 7-7. Civil Case — *Lockmore v. Lockmore*

Refer to the Chapter 11 case file, *Lockmore v. Lockmore*. Sissy and Bill Lockmore were divorced when Bill discovered that Sissy, a financial advisor, was having an affair with a co-worker. The court awarded sole custody of their two children to Bill and ordered Sissy to pay child support. Bill remained in San Milano and Sissy moved to Dallas to be near her family. She failed to make child support payments, and at the time her husband was killed she owed almost $20,000. She and Bill were scheduled to appear in a San Milano court to continue their contentious legal battle over custody and child support payments.

Bill was killed early in the morning — shot in the back—at his home in San Milano. The police focused their investigation on Sissy and obtained evidence through cell phone records showing that her cell phone was used in San Milano the evening before the killing.

At the criminal trial, the defendant argued that her business partner provided an alibi at the time of the killing and that the police should have investigated Morgan Walters, a business associate of Bill's. Walters and Bill Lockmore were in the process of dissolving their partnership in a medical practice.

Sissy Lockmore was tried and acquitted on criminal charges that she killed her ex-husband, Bill Lockmore in San Milano, Lone Star.

The parents of Bill Lockmore, June and Steve Lockmore, have filed a civil wrongful death suit against Sissy Lockmore, their former daughter-in-law.

Assume that both the plaintiffs and the defendant were able to present all of their available evidence. Using the case file, prepare and present an 8 to 10 minute closing argument:

a. For the plaintiff, or

b. For the defense.

§ 7-8. Civil Case — *Jones v. Moss*

In the Chapter 15 case file, *Jones v. Moss*, Sylvia Moss was suspected of killing her husband, Danny Moss. Police responded to Sylvia's 911 call early in the morning, and found Danny lying at the bottom of the steps of their home. Sylvia told the police that she had awakened when she heard a loud thump, saw Danny, and dialed 911 without first checking to see if there was anything she could do to help him. The police determined that Danny died as a result of a severe blow to his head, caused when he hit the stair railing. But there was also evidence of a bruise on the back of his neck. Additional evidence showed that Sylvia had reacted with rage whenever Danny ignored her or criticized her cooking.

The State's theory was that Sylvia hit him on the neck with a shoe and caused him to fall down the stairs. A prosecution expert determined that Sylvia suffers from a narcissistic personality disorder, which triggered the attack.

Sylvia's version was that Danny's death was accidental. The prosecutor decided not to try her. Shortly thereafter, Danny's step-daughter from a prior marriage, Sarah Jones, filed a wrongful death action against Sylvia.

Using the case file, present an 8 to 10 minute closing argument:

a. For the plaintiff, or

b. For the defense.

For this problem, assume that all of the evidence in the case file was admitted at trial.

Chapter 8
State v. Barkwood

§ 8-1. Introduction

The State of Lone Star has charged Don Barkwood with one count of theft by coercion and one count of manslaughter of his daughter, Tiffany. When Barkwood learned that his daughter was exchanging e-mails with a high school teacher, Johnny Woods, he obtained the court's permission to take a pre-suit deposition of Woods, as provided in the Rules of Civil Procedure of the State of Lone Star. Woods offered to settle the case and paid Barkwood money, which in turn was deposited with a children's cancer foundation. Shortly afterwards, however, Barkwood withdrew the money and made a down payment on a new car.

When his daughter's pleas to refrain from proceeding against Woods failed, she told Barkwood that she would kill herself. When he ignored her final plea, she committed suicide.

§ 8-2. Stipulations Regarding Procedural and Evidentiary Matters

1. The case is being tried in a Lone Star state court, but the Federal Rules of Evidence and Criminal Procedure apply.
2. This case will be tried only on the issue of guilt or innocence.
3. All witnesses called to testify, who have in statements or grand jury testimony identified the defendant, other individuals, or tangible evidence, can, if asked, identify the same at trial.
4. The defendant Barkwood signed his statement to the police.
5. Other than what is supplied in the case file, there is nothing exceptional or unusual about the background information of any of the witnesses or the defendant that would bolster or detract from their credibility.
6. This case file does not permit a listed witness or the defendant, while testifying, to "invent" an individual not mentioned in this problem and have testimony or evidence offered to the court or jury from that invented individual.
7. The current year is the year in which this case comes to trial.
8. It is stipulated that the defendant, Don Barkwood, correctly followed the rules of civil procedure concerning pre-suit depositions.
9. For this case, assume that the case law in this State recognizes that a person has an affirmative duty to take reasonable steps to prevent a family member from committing suicide.
10. The e-mails in the problem were all lawfully seized, or obtained, from computers belonging to the defendant, the defendant's family, Pat Gonzales, and Johnny Woods.
11. The autopsy report of Tiffany Barkwood is accurate, authentic, and satisfies the best evidence rule.
12. Although Zoloft tablets were seized from the defendant's house and from Johnny Woods' house, they are not available as evidence.

13. Laboratory tests on the Zoloft tablets revealed that they were indeed Zoloft tablets, containing the drug Atropine.
14. Statements made by Tiffany Barkwood to Pat Gonzales are not privileged. Whatever privilege may have existed was waived by her lawful representative(s).
15. There are no written records of Johnny Woods' legal problems at his prior places of employment.
16. All exhibits in the file are authentic. In addition, each exhibit contained in the file is the original of that document unless otherwise noted on the exhibit or as established by the evidence.
17. The defendant must admit that the check he wrote to Thompson is his personal check and that the signature on the check is his signature.
18. There are no Confrontation Clause problems with any of the hearsay statements in the case file.

§ 8-3. Case File Materials

Students will be expected to use the following case file materials in presenting their cases.

I. Lone Star Penal Code Provisions

§ 79.01. Types of Criminal Homicide

(a) A person commits criminal homicide if he intentionally, knowingly, recklessly, or with criminal negligence causes the death of an individual.

(b) Criminal homicide is murder, capital murder, manslaughter, or criminally negligent homicide.

§ 79.04. Manslaughter

(a) A person commits an offense if he recklessly causes the death of an individual.

(b) An offense under this section is a felony of the second degree.

§ 79.05. Criminally Negligent Homicide

(a) A person commits an offense if he causes the death of an individual by criminal negligence.

(b) An offense under this section is a state jail felony.

* * * * *

§ 131.01. Definitions

In this chapter:

(1) "Deception" means:

(A) creating or confirming by words or conduct a false impression of law or fact that is likely to affect the judgment of another in the transaction, and that the actor does not believe to be true;

(B) failing to correct a false impression of law or fact that is likely to affect the judgment of another in the transaction, that the actor previously created or confirmed by words or conduct, and that the actor does not now believe to be true;

(C) preventing another from acquiring information likely to affect his judgment in the transaction;

(D) selling or otherwise transferring or encumbering property without disclosing a lien, security interest, adverse claim, or other legal impediment to the enjoyment of the property, whether the lien, security interest, claim, or impediment is or is not valid, or is or is not a matter of official record; or

(E) promising performance that is likely to affect the judgment of another in the transaction and that the actor does not intend to perform or knows will not be performed, except that failure to perform the promise in issue without other evidence of intent or knowledge is not sufficient proof that the actor did not intend to perform or knew the promise would not be performed.

(2) "Deprive" means:

(A) to withhold property from the owner permanently or for so extended a period of time that a major portion of the value or enjoyment of the property is lost to the owner;

(B) to restore property only upon payment of reward or other compensation; or

(C) to dispose of property in a manner that makes recovery of the property by the owner unlikely.

(3) "Effective consent" includes consent by a person legally authorized to act for the owner. Consent is not effective if:

(A) induced by deception or coercion;

(B) given by a person the actor knows is not legally authorized to act for the owner;

(C) given by a person who by reason of youth, mental disease or defect, or intoxication is known by the actor to be unable to make reasonable property dispositions;

(D) given solely to detect the commission of an offense; or

(E) given by a person who by reason of advanced age is known by the actor to have a diminished capacity to make informed and rational decisions about the reasonable disposition of property.

(4) "Appropriate" means:

(A) to bring about a transfer or purported transfer of title to or other nonpossessory interest in property, whether to the actor or another; or

(B) to acquire or otherwise exercise control over property other than real property.

(5) "Property" means:

(A) real property;

(B) tangible or intangible personal property including anything severed from land; or

(C) a document, including money, that represents or embodies anything of value.

(6) "Service" includes:

(A) labor and professional service;

(B) telecommunication, public utility, or transportation service;

(C) lodging, restaurant service, and entertainment; and

(D) the supply of a motor vehicle or other property for use.

(7) "Steal" means to acquire property or service by theft.

§ 131.03. Theft

(a) A person commits an offense if he unlawfully appropriates property with intent to deprive the owner of property.

(b) Appropriation of property is unlawful if:

(1) it is without the owner's effective consent;

(2) the property is stolen and the actor appropriates the property knowing it was stolen by another; or

(3) property in the custody of any law enforcement agency was explicitly represented by any law enforcement agent to the actor as being stolen and the actor appropriates the property believing it was stolen by another.

(c) For purposes of Subsection (b):

(1) evidence that the actor has previously participated in recent transactions other than, but similar to, that which the prosecution is based is admissible for the purpose of showing knowledge or intent and the issues of knowledge or intent are raised by the actor's plea of not guilty;

(2) the testimony of an accomplice shall be corroborated by proof that tends to connect the actor to the crime, but the actor's knowledge or intent may be established by the uncorroborated testimony of the accomplice;

(e) An offense under this section is:

* * * * *

(5) a felony of the third degree if the value of the property stolen is $20,000 or more but less than $100,000.

II. Lone Star Rules of Civil Procedure

* * * * * *

Rule 502. Depositions Before Suit or to Investigate Claims

502.a. Generally

A person may petition the court for an order authorizing the taking of a deposition on oral examination or written questions either:

(a) to perpetuate or obtain the person's own testimony or that of any other person for use in an anticipated suit; or

(b) to investigate a potential claim or suit.

502.b. Petition

The petition must:

(a) be verified;

(b) be filed in a proper court of any county:

(1) where venue of the anticipated suit may lie, if suit is anticipated; or

(2) where the witness resides, if no suit is yet anticipated;

(c) be in the name of the petitioner;

(d) state either:

(1) that the petitioner anticipates the institution of a suit in which the petitioner may be a party; or

(2) that the petitioner seeks to investigate a potential claim by or against petitioner;

(e) state the subject matter of the anticipated action, if any, and the petitioner's interest therein;

(f) if suit is anticipated, either:

(1) state the names of the persons petitioner expects to have interests adverse to petitioner's in the anticipated suit, and the addresses and telephone numbers for such persons; or

(2) state that the names, addresses, and telephone numbers of persons petitioner expects to have interests adverse to petitioner's in the anticipated suit cannot be ascertained through diligent inquiry, and describe those persons;

(g) state the names, addresses and telephone numbers of the persons to be deposed, the substance of the testimony that the petitioner expects to elicit from each, and the petitioner's reasons for desiring to obtain the testimony of each; and

(h) request an order authorizing the petitioner to take the depositions of the persons named in the petition.

502.c. Notice and Service

Personal Service on Witnesses and Persons Named. At least 15 days before the date of the hearing on the petition, the petitioner must serve the petition and a notice of the hearing on all persons petitioner seeks to depose and, if suit is anticipated, on all persons petitioner expects to have interests adverse to petitioner's in the anticipated suit.

502.d. Order

(a) *Required Findings.* The court must order a deposition to be taken if, but only if, it finds that:

(1) allowing the petitioner to take the requested deposition may prevent a failure or delay of justice in an anticipated suit, or

(2) the likely benefit of allowing the petitioner to take the requested deposition to investigate a potential claim outweighs the burden or expense of the procedure.

(b) *Contents.* The order must state whether a deposition will be taken on oral examination or written questions. The order may also state the time and place at which a deposition will be taken. If the order does not state the time and place at which a deposition will be taken, the petitioner must notice the deposition as required by these Rules.

502.e. Manner of Taking and Use

Except as otherwise provided in this rule, depositions authorized by this rule are governed by the rules applicable to depositions of nonparties in a pending suit. The scope of discovery in depositions authorized by this rule is the same as if the anticipated suit or potential claim had been filed. A court may restrict or prohibit the use of a deposition taken under this rule in a subsequent suit to protect a person who was not served with notice of the deposition from any unfair prejudice or to prevent abuse of this rule.

* * * * *

INDICTMENT

COURT'S COPY

Name: DON BARKWOOD

Complainants: JOHNNY WOODS and TIFFANY BARKWOOD

Offense Charges: THEFT BY COERCION & MANSLAUGHTER

GJ: 938213 **PH Court:** 290

JN #: 38844-3 **SID #:** 7749332

Witness: State's Attorney

TRUE BILL OF INDICTMENT

IN THE NAME AND BY AUTHORITY OF THE STATE OF LONE STAR, the Grand Jury of Bear County, State of Lone Star, duly organized, empanelled by the Judicial District Court of said County, do present in and to said Court that in the County and State aforesaid, and anterior to the presentment of this indictment, and:

COUNT 1: THEFT BY COERCION

on or about the 25th Day of April, [YR-1], DON BARKWOOD, hereinafter referred to as defendant, then and there unlawfully appropriate, by acquiring or otherwise exercising control over, property, to-wit: cash, of the value of $20,000 or more but less than $100,000, from JOHNNY WOODS, the owner thereof, without the effective consent of the owner, namely, by coercion, and with intent to deprive the owner of the property;

COUNT 2: MANSLAUGHTER

on or about the 7th Day of May, [YR-1], DON BARKWOOD, hereinafter referred to as defendant, did recklessly cause the death of an individual, namely, TIFFANY BARKWOOD, hereinafter referred to as complainant, by recklessly refusing to assist her after she presented a credible threat to committing suicide;

AGAINST THE PEACE AND DIGNITY OF THE STATE.

Johnny Gomez

Johnny Gomez
Grand Jury Foreperson

Defendant's Written Statement to Police

STATE OF LONE STAR
COUNTY OF BEAR

Case Number: 04-9493843

VOLUNTARY STATEMENT OF: DON BARKWOOD

I, Don Barkwood, after first being duly warned by Det. S. Heights #3939 at 0413 hrs, at 214 W. Nueva, on 5-18-[YR-1] that (1) I have the right to remain silent and not make any statement at all, and any statement I do make may be used against me at my trial; (2) Any statement I make may be used as evidence against me in Court; (3) I have the right to have a lawyer present to advise me prior to and during any questioning; (4) If I am unable to employ a lawyer, I have the right to have a lawyer appointed to advise me prior to and during any questioning; (5) I have the right to terminate the interview at any time; and I understand that the above rights are continuing rights and may be urged by me at any stage of the proceedings, and I hereby prior to and during the making of this statement, knowingly, intelligently, and voluntarily waive the above rights and give to the said Det. S. Heights #3939, the person to whom this statement is being given, the following written statement:

My name is Don Barkwood. I live in the State of Lone Star and am licensed to practice law. I am board certified in civil litigation. I am married to Anika Barkwood, but she is in the process of getting a divorce and we are now separated. I had two daughters, Tiffany and Sissy, both teenagers. Tiffany died two weeks ago of a drug overdose. Sissy is now living with her mother and will not talk to me. My wife's name is Anika.

Two months ago, I guess about March 9, I was using the family computer and noticed that my daughter Tiffany was getting e-mails from what appeared to be her high school. At first I thought she was in some sort of trouble at school so I opened one of them and was shocked to see that it was a love note from one of her teachers, Johnny Woods. I had never met him before. In the e-mail he said that he could not wait to see her again and that it was important to keep their friendship private or he could get fired. I was really angry and afraid for my family. I viewed Woods as a predator. My first thought was to confront my daughter but I decided to print out the e-mail and wait a few more days to see if any more came through. The next day I found another e-mail in which he mentioned something about taking pills. I also found several e-mails that she had sent to him. I could tell that she was involved. I printed off his e-mail and her responses and then confronted her. She started crying and said that nothing had happened, that they were just really good friends, and that he understood her. She said that he had gotten some of his wife's anti-depressant pills to help with her depression. Tiffany had had chronic depression problems for several years. She begged me not to say or do anything, that she would take care of it, and that if I did anything that she would not be able to live with herself. I comforted her and said not to worry that I would do the right thing. I did not say anything to my wife or other daughter. I needed to work this out with the least amount of trauma to my family.

After thinking about this problem, on April 14th, I prepared a request or petition with the local district court to take a pre-suit deposition of Woods. This is a little-known tool in the rules of civil procedure. I believe it is Civil Rule 202. It gives a party a chance to see if there is really any need to file a suit and potentially avoid nasty discovery. My thought was to pursue the possibility of filing a civil suit against Woods and to take his statement under oath. I was really embarrassed by this whole thing so I typed up the documents myself, without involving my secretary or staff. I was trying to protect Tiffany. I talked with a law professor at State University School of Law, who specialized in civil procedure, and she said that it sounded like I was doing everything according to the book. Her name was Professor Starnes, I believe. I think I talked to her during the first week in April. I think she is on a sabbatical right now.

I served Woods with notice of the deposition hearing, as required by the rule of procedure, and he immediately called me on the phone on about April 18th and begged me to settle the matter out of court and that he had some money if that is what it took. I don't remember the exact time he called me.

I met him at a local restaurant the next day and told him I was concerned about my daughters and that he could get in a lot of trouble if he did not stop what he was doing and got some professional help. He said he was really sorry and that this was all a big misunderstanding and that he had never done this sort of thing before. I guess at a couple of points I got pretty emotional and started to cry at one point. I just could not stand the thought of my daughter being with this guy. He reminded me of a slick salesman. I do not remember saying anything about going to the police. I suppose in hindsight that would have been okay, too. But I did learn later that Woods had done this sort of thing at least two other times at different schools out of state. But each time the charges were dropped when he agreed to resign and not seek a teaching job in that city.

We agreed on the settlement of $60,000 that he would pay over six months. The first payment would be for $20,000. I told him that a friend of mine, Jordan Thompson was working with a cancer foundation for children and that the money would be deposited there. I did not really need the cash and wanted to do some good with the money from this guy. I figured his actions would someday help a sick kid. He said he would need a week or so to get the money so we set up a meeting in a public place, at his request. I think we met on April 25th at the Lone Tree Hotel, in the lobby. Everything was above board and we shook hands after he gave me the money. It was in cash.

I wrote a $20,000 check to the Children's Cancer Foundation, as recommended by my friend, Thompson. But a week later, I think it was May 2nd or May 3rd, Thompson called and said that the foundation was in real trouble for mismanagement of funds and that I should request the money back fast. So I called the foundation, said that I had changed my mind and wanted my money back. I did not tell them about my conversation with Thompson. They sent it back to me, minus a $5,000 transfer fee or finders' fee, or something like that. They told me to make the check payable to Thompson. I did not really question it because I did not want to make a stink. I just wanted my money back.

I took the $20,000 and deposited it in my personal bank account until I could decide what to do with it. I thought I would look for another foundation. I did buy a new car a few days later but there was absolutely no connection between that money and the money I paid for the car. I paid cash. I think it was for $30,000 or something like that. It was a Nissan.

Several days later, my daughter Tiffany sent me an e-mail on my office e-mail saying that if I did not stop harassing Woods that she would commit suicide. I e-mailed her back and told her that she was exaggerating things and that we would talk when I got home. I found out later that shortly after she got my e-mail that she took the drugs that Woods had given to her. She died a day later. My wife kicked me out of the house.

As far as I know, Tiffany did not have any other steady boyfriends.

I hold Johnny Woods personally responsible for Tiffany's death. Of course I knew that she had problems with depression. We had made arrangements for her to see a school counselor several months ago to talk about her problems with classes and other things. I think the name of the counselor was Gonzales, or something like that. But neither my wife nor I would have ever guessed how bad it was. I feel really sorry about what happened. I had only the best intentions for protecting my family from Woods.

This is the end of my three-page statement. I have read this statement and it is true and correct.

WITNESS: *Wilson Watts*

SIGNATURE: *Don Barkwood*

WITNESS: *Norma Storms*

DATE: 5-18-[YR-1]

Grand Jury Testimony of Johnny Woods

IN RE:	BEFORE THE GRAND JURY
	OF
GRAND JURY INVESTIGATION	BEAR COUNTY, STATE OF LONE STAR

* * * * * *

****

COURT REPORTER'S

Q AND A TRANSCRIPT OF TESTIMONY OF

JOHNNY WOODS

JUNE 9, [YR-1]

****

* * * * *

BE IT REMEMBERED, that heretofore, to-writ on JUNE 9, [YR-1], the above-entitled matter came on for hearing before the Grand Jury of Bear County, sitting in San Milano, State of Lone Star, being presented by ROGER SMITH, Assistant Criminal District Attorney, for consideration by the members thereof.

HEATHER STEVENS was duly sworn as Court Reporter.

WHEREUPON, the following evidence was introduced and proceedings had, to-wit, beginning at 10:42 o'clock a.m. and concluding at 11:08 o'clock a.m.

JOHNNY WOODS, The Witness,

GRAND JURY FOREMAN: Do you solemnly swear that you will not divulge either by words or signs any matter about which you may be interrogated, and that you will keep secret all proceedings of the Grand Jury which may be had in your presence, and that you will true answers make to such questions as may be propounded to you by the Grand Jury or under its direction, so help you God?

THE WITNESS: I do.

EXAMINATION BY ROGER SMITH:

Q: Johnny Woods, as with any witness who comes before the Grand Jury, I need to give you the definitions of perjury and aggravated perjury.

A person commits the offense of perjury if, with intent to deceive and with knowledge of the statement's meaning, that person makes a false statement under oath or swears to the truth of a false statement previously made and the statement is required or authorized by law to be made under oath.

Perjury is a Class A Misdemeanor, which is punishable by anywhere up to one year in the Bear County Jail and/or a fine of up to $4,000.

Perjury becomes aggravated perjury if the person commits perjury, makes that false statement during or in connection with an official proceeding, and Grand Jury proceedings are official proceedings, and the statement is material.

Aggravated perjury is a third-degree felony, which means it's punishable by anywhere from two to ten years in the Lone Star Department of Corrections, and there's a potential fine of up to $10,000. Do you understand this?

A: Yes, sir.

Q: Would you please state your name for the grand jury?

A: Yes, my name is Johnny L. Woods.

Q: Mr. Woods, as we have informed you, you are testifying today under a grant of immunity, which was issued by the court. Do you understand what that means?

A: Yes, my lawyer explained it to me. It means that I have to answer your questions, even if they might incriminate me. The grant of immunity means that my testimony cannot be used against me.

Q: That is correct. And you just swore to tell the truth?

A: Yes.

Q: So, if you do not tell the truth, you can be prosecuted for lying to this grand jury.

A: Yes, I understand that.

Q: Okay. Mr. Woods, I would like you to tell the jurors about your contact with Mr. Don Barkwood in April of this year.

A: I got an official notice in the mail, the second week in April, that Mr. Barkwood wanted to take my deposition and that the court would hold a hearing on whether he could take my deposition. I figured it had to do with his daughter Tiffany, who was in one of my history classes at the time.

Q: What happened?

A: I called him to see what he wanted and he was really, really angry.

Q: What day was that?

A: It was April 18th. He started cursing me and telling me that I was going to have to pay dearly for interfering with his little girl. I also got angry back at him and told him that he had emotionally abused his daughter and that I had simply been there to help her through some really tough emotional times. I told him that nothing had happened.

Q: What happened next?

A: Well, he called me a slimy SOB, or something like that, and hung up. But not more than 30 seconds later the called me and apologized for losing his temper and said he wanted to set up a time to take my deposition.

Q: So what was your relationship with Tiffany?

A: Well, we had talked several times after class, and once in my van. I think I may have given her a small kiss on her cheek to comfort her. She just needed someone to talk to. She kept telling me that her parents were preoccupied with their activities and never listened to her.

Q: So, what happened next in your conversation with Mr. Barkwood?

A: I tried to calm down as well and told him that I hoped we could settle this matter. He wanted to know if I had a lawyer and I said no. He said that was okay because he was a lawyer and could work up any agreement between us to settle the matter out of court.

Q: What happened next?

A: Well we agreed to meet at the Lone Star Grill, which is a few blocks from his law office, the next day.

Q: Did you meet with him?

A: Yes.

Q: What day was that?

A: April 19th, I believe.

Q: Tell us about that meeting.

A: Well, he told me that he intended to take my deposition, under oath, to determine if he had a possible civil suit against me for what I had done to his daughter.

Q: So what were you thinking at this point?

A: I was beginning to think that this might be a shakedown when I asked him if he had talked to the police and he said no, he had not. He said that if I cooperated that we could make the whole thing go away. He said that he did not trust the police to do the right thing and that it was in both of our interests not to involve them, at this point. So I felt like I really did not have a choice.

Q: Did he say what would happen if you did not cooperate?

A: Yes, he said he would make my life hell and see to it that I never taught again and that they would put me under the jail for what I had done. He said that he had friends at the newspaper in the city.

Q: Did you feel threatened by his comments to you?

A: Absolutely. Yes, very much so.

Q: What led you to believe that he would do what he said?

A: Well, first, as I just said, he was really determined. And I guess I can understand why he would feel that way. But he did not appear at first to even want to settle this thing.

Q: So, let's get this straight. Who first raised the issue about settling the matter out of court?

A: I guess I did. I, ah, well [pause] let me put it this way. I figured that he really would cause me major problems and I had heard about settling cases out of court so that you could avoid all of the expense and other problems of going to court. So, I guess . . .

Q: So, you . . .

A: I guess, I . . .

Q: I am sorry to interrupt you, please continue.

A: I guess I hoped that we could work out something.

Q: When you told him that you hoped something could be worked out, what did he say?

A: It was interesting. He did not say anything at first, he got kinda quiet, but then he said something like, "Well I had hoped you would say that." Just like he was setting me up or something.

Q: What do you mean?

A: Well, the tone of his voice changed, pretty quickly, and he said that although he wanted to see me pay, he also wanted to protect his little girl, I think that is what he called her. She hated that when he called her his little girl.

Q: Who hated that?

A: Tiffany.

Q: What happened next, Mr. Woods?

A: He said that he had a dollar amount in mind, which I found also interesting because he did not even hesitate. Nor did he ask me what my proposal was. He sort of gave me his terms as though he had figured it all out.

Q: Go ahead.

A: He told me that a good friend of his, I believe someone named Thompson or Thomasson, something like that, worked for a private foundation for kids with terminal cancer and that he had been thinking about making a donation. He said that the money I gave him would be put to good use, to help someone dying of cancer. In my mind, that seemed like a reasonable proposition. He said that this would be a way to redeem myself. He said that I would give him the money, in cash, and that he would then write a check in that amount to the foundation. He said that it would be better if the foundation did not know about me and start asking questions about why I was so interested in helping them out or asking me for more money.

Q: So what amount did you agree on?

A: I am not sure there was any real agreement. He said the cost to me, and I believe he used those words, would be $60,000.

Q: What did you say?

A: At first I did not say anything. I think I may have said something like, "I need to think about it." And then he said that the offer was going to be good for about 30 seconds or something like that.

Q: So, what happened?

A: I told him okay. By this point in our talk, I had pretty well figured out that there was not going to be any real negotiation. The way I saw it, he was either going to get that money or I was going to lose my job, and maybe my family. So I agreed. But I quickly said that I did not have that kind of money handy and asked if I could pay it out in three equal installments.

Q: Did he agree?

A: Yes, he said that I could do that. But that he wanted the $20,000 as soon as possible so he could give it to the foundation to get Thompson off his back. So we agreed to meet several days later. I explained the situation to my wife who at first told me that I had done nothing wrong and that I should turn Barkwood into the police. But I finally convinced her that he was a real threat, he was a lawyer who seemed to have everything in his favor.

Q: What happened next? Did you pay him the money?

A: Yes, we met at the Lone Tree Hotel here in the city on April 25th. We met in the lobby and I gave him the money in cash — which he demanded — and then he got up and left.

Q: Did you shake hands or anything?

A: No. After I gave him the money, he started to count it. He said that it had been a pleasure doing business with me, that he would contact me in another month or so to get the next installment and then got up quickly and left.

Q: What was his demeanor like during this meeting?

A: Well, he seemed pretty cocky and confident.

Q: Did he say anything else?

A: Oh yes, he said that I should keep the whole thing quiet or that he would have to raise the stakes.

Q: Did you have any more contact with him?

A: No. After he left I went home and told my wife what had happened. I then called our minister and set up a counseling session where I could talk about all of this. But that did not work out and we never talked.

Q: So other than your wife, did you tell anyone else about what Barkwood had done?

A: No.

Q: Now, I draw your attention to several weeks later. When you heard about Tiffany dying. What happened?

A: Well, I was pretty upset. I showed up at the school one morning and girls were crying out in the hallway. I asked them what happened and they said that Tiffany had died during the night of an overdose of drugs. I went to my office and when I turned on my computer I noticed that she had sent me an e-mail.

Q: What did the e-mail say?

A: It said that she was tired of living, that she had a pretty good idea of what her father had done to me and that she had just taken some pills. She said that she had e-mailed her dad but that he had e-mailed her back, calling her a "drama queen," and just like her mother who always wanted attention. She blamed her father for her problems and said that finally, maybe he would pay attention to her.

Q: So, what did you do when you read the e-mail?

A: I immediately called a lawyer who set up a meeting with the police. We met with them and said we would help them get Barkwood for killing his daughter and stealing money from me, if they would grant me some protection against prosecution.

Q: Now, I need to ask you about your relationship with Tiffany. You testified earlier that you were trying to help her work things out with her parents?

A: Yes.

Q: You provided some drugs to her, didn't you? Anti-depressant drugs?

A: Yes.

Q: Were they prescription drugs?

A: Yes.

Q: Where did you get them?

A: I got them from my wife's medicine cabinet when she was not looking.

Q: What drugs were they?

A: Zoloft.

Q: Zoloft?

A: Yes.

Q: Why would you give Tiffany those pills?

A: I was just trying to help her. She told me that she was already taking some anti-depressants but that they did not seem to do the job. So I gave her maybe 10 or 15 pills over the period of about a month.

QUESTION FROM GRAND JUROR

Q: Did you receive any money from Tiffany for those drugs?

A: No.

QUESTION FROM ANOTHER GRAND JUROR

Q: Did you ever have any sexual relations with Tiffany?

A: Absolutely not. I respected her too much to do something like that.

QUESTIONS FROM ANOTHER GRAND JUROR

Q: Did she ever tell you that she had a boyfriend?

A: No.

Q Did she ever tell you that she might be pregnant?

A: No.

QUESTION FROM ANOTHER GRAND JUROR

Q: In your prior jobs, have you ever had similar things like this happen before, I mean, getting really friendly with your students?

A: Yes. Well, maybe not. I am not sure.

QUESTIONING BY ASSISTANT DA ROGER SMITH CONTINUES

Q: Please explain that.

A: Well, several years ago I was teaching at a high school out of state, in Nevada. I had one student who I think had a real crush on me and when it got to the point where it was uncomfortable I told her that I was married and that she had to stop e-mailing me. My wife had found out about it. We went through counseling and when that leaked out the school board gave me an ultimatum. They said either resign and leave the school district or get fired.

Q: So, did you resign?

A: Yes. But I should have stayed and fought it. The girl clearly had mental problems and I am confident that a jury would have sided with me.

QUESTION BY ANOTHER GRAND JUROR

Q: Other than that time did it happen ever again?

A: Yes. At my next job, another student made a pass at me at a football game. I guess I just have lousy luck. I can't believe it.

QUESTION BY ASSISTANT DA ROGER SMITH

Q: A female student?

A: Yes.

Q: One of your students?

A: Yes.

Q: So what happened in that case?

A: Well, this time the girl's mother demanded a payment. I refused. She called my wife and my wife said that for some reason I was a magnet for confused young women and that we needed to leave again. So, I resigned mid-term and moved here. Everything was fine until about six months ago when I met Tiffany. This time, my wife knew that I was meeting Tiffany to counsel her.

A: Did your wife know about the drugs you gave to Tiffany?

Q: No, she did not. And I regret that. She knows now. Thankfully, she has forgiven me for my problems. She knows that I was trying to help this poor girl.

Q: Did you ever give any other money to Mr. Barkwood?

A: No. I only gave him the $20,000.

Q: Do you know what he did with the money you gave him?

Q: No, not really. I assumed he gave the money to his friend's foundation. But it would not surprise me if you told me that he had used the money for himself. That is the sort of guy his daughter said he was. Very manipulative.

ROGER SMITH: Okay. Please step outside for just a few minutes.

THE WITNESS: Okay.

[The Witness leaves the Grand Jury Room at 11:08 a.m., and is subsequently dismissed.]

(END OF TRANSCRIPT)

Grand Jury Testimony of Jordan Thompson

IN RE:	BEFORE THE GRAND JURY
	OF
GRAND JURY INVESTIGATION	BEAR COUNTY, STATE OF LONE STAR

* * * * * *

****

COURT REPORTER'S
Q AND A TRANSCRIPT OF TESTIMONY OF
JORDAN THOMPSON
JUNE 9, [YR-1]

****

* * * * *

BE IT REMEMBERED, that heretofore, to-writ on JUNE 9, [YR-1], the above-entitled matter came on for hearing before the Grand Jury of Bear County, sitting in San Milano, State of Lone Star, being presented by ROGER SMITH, Assistant Criminal District Attorney, for consideration by the members thereof.

HEATHER STEVENS was duly sworn as Court Reporter.

WHEREUPON, the following evidence was introduced and proceedings had, to-wit, beginning at 11:20 o'clock a.m. and concluding at 11:58 o'clock a.m.

JORDAN THOMPSON, The Witness,

GRAND JURY FOREMAN: Do you solemnly swear that you will not divulge either by words or signs any matter about which you may be interrogated, and that you will keep secret all proceedings of the Grand Jury which may be had in your presence, and that you will true answers make to such questions as may be propounded to you by the Grand Jury or under its direction, so help you God?

THE WITNESS: I do.

EXAMINATION BY ROGER SMITH:

Q: Jordan Thompson, as with any witness who comes before the Grand Jury, I need to give you the definitions of perjury and aggravated perjury.

A person commits the offense of perjury if, with intent to deceive and with knowledge of the statement's meaning, that person makes a false statement under oath or swears to the truth of a false statement previously made and the statement is required or authorized by law to be made under oath.

Perjury is a Class A Misdemeanor, which is punishable by anywhere up to one year in the Bear County Jail and/or a fine of up to $4,000.

Perjury becomes aggravated perjury if the person commits perjury, makes that false statement during or in connection with an official proceeding, and Grand Jury proceedings are official proceedings, and the statement is material.

Aggravated perjury is a third-degree felony, which means it's punishable by anywhere from two to ten years in the Lone Star Department of Corrections, and there's a potential fine of up to $10,000. Do you understand this?

A: Yes, sir.

[Jordan Thompson testified as follows before the Grand Jury, after waiving the right to remain silent.]

Q: For the record will you please state your full name?

A: Jordan S. Thompson.

Q: And what is your current employment?

A: I am currently in transition, between jobs.

Q: Are you familiar with the Children's Cancer Foundation?

A: Yes.

Q: How are you familiar with that organization?

A: I used to work there as a fund raiser. Actually, I worked there from about July [YR-4] until just recently, June 12th of this year, to be exact.

Q: Why are you no longer there?

A: They found out that I was connected with Don Barkwood.

Q: So you know Don Barkwood?

A: Sure. Yes, I do.

Q: How do you know him?

A: Well we have known each other for about 10 years.

Q: Are you friends?

A: Some might say that.

Q: Let me repeat the question. Are you friends?

A: Yes.

Q: Did you ever recommend to Mr. Barkwood that he give some money to the foundation that you worked for?

A: I did. Don is a wonderful person, a great husband and loving father, with a big heart. I knew that he had the money and that he would make a difference by giving to the foundation.

Q: Did you ever suggest a particular dollar amount?

A: No.

Q: When did you last talk to him about giving to the foundation?

A: Sometime last year.

Q: I draw your attention to this last spring, in April or May. Did Mr. Barkwood talk to you about making a donation?

A: Yes, he did.

Q: How did that come up?

A: Well, he said that he had found a donor and that he thought he could come up with about 20,000 dollars.

Q: What was your reaction?

A: I was thrilled. Things had been a bit tough on fund raising this last year and I needed to show some donations.

Q: What would have happened if you did not come up with some donors?

A: Well in this business it means you lose your job.

Q: Did he come up with the money?

A: Yes.

Q: Did he tell you the name of his donor?

A: No. And it was not important to me. I trust Don and I believed that everything was on the up and up.

Q: But you did not ask him to give you the name of the donor? That would have been helpful to you, wouldn't it?

A: Not really. I simply listed Don as the donor. Where he got it from was not all that critical to me.

Q: So what happened to his donation?

A: He wrote me a check for $20,000 and I deposited it in our account.

Q: When was that?

A: April 26th.

Q: Did it stay in the account?

A: No. About two weeks later I learned that the foundation was being investigated for fraud and I told Don I felt bad about his donation.

Q: What did he say?

A: He was pretty upset and said he wanted his money back. So I talked to my boss and told him that my donor had had cold feet and wanted his money back. So he said okay.

Q: What happened next?

A: I got a check cut for Don from the foundation.

Q: And when did you do that?

A: Hmmm. May 3rd.

Q: For how much?

A: $20,000.

Q: And did you give it to him?

A: Yes.

Q: We have banking records showing that you deposited $5,000 in your personal account on May 4th and that the check was written by a "D. Barkwood"?

A: Yes.

Q: What was that all about? Could you explain that to the members of the grand jury?

A: Well, Don figured that I was about to lose my job and decided to loan me the $5,000.

Q: Did you ask him for the money?

A: I do not recall whether I asked him or he volunteered it.

Q: Have you paid him back?

A: Not yet.

Q: Have you worked out a repayment plan with Mr. Barkwood?

A: No. He told me that he knew I was good for the money.

Q: You testified earlier that you lost your job with the foundation?

A: Yes, about a month after I helped Don get his money back.

Q: Do you know a Mr. Johnny Woods?

A: Yes.

Q: How do you know him?

A: We shared some of the same friends in college.

Q: Were you friends at the time?

A: Yes.

Q: Are you friends now?

A: Absolutely not.

Q: Why not?

A: Well, during our senior year I found out that he was cheating on his girlfriend, now his wife. I told her about it, she told him, he pushed me down, put a nasty scar on my forehead and said he never wanted to see me again.

Q: How many years ago was that?

A: 5 years ago.

Q: Have you had any contact since then?

A: No.

Q: You sound upset about it.

A: So?

Q: Are you?

A: Yes, I guess so. Johnny Woods is a real loser and both he and his wife can both rot in hell for all I care.

Q: Did you know that he was the donor that Don Barkwood had lined up for you?

A: I believe he told me just recently that that was the connection.

Q: What did he say to you about it?

A: He said that he had found out that Woods was messing with his daughter but that they had reached an amicable financial settlement and that he was ready to put the whole thing behind him. He said that Woods had gotten his due.

Q: How did you feel about that?

A: As I said, I figure that Woods was rotten and that Barkwood did the right thing. And if kids get helped as a result, well then I think that is a good thing. I would believe Barkwood over Woods.

ROGER SMITH: Why don't you go ahead and step outside for just a few minutes.

THE WITNESS: Okay.

[The Witness leaves the Grand Jury Room at 11:58 a.m., and is subsequently dismissed.]

(END OF TRANSCRIPT)

GRAND JURY TESTIMONY OF PAT GONZALES

IN RE:		BEFORE THE GRAND JURY
	}	OF
GRAND JURY INVESTIGATION		BEAR COUNTY, STATE OF LONE STAR

****

COURT REPORTER'S

Q AND A TRANSCRIPT OF TESTIMONY OF

PAT GONZALES

JUNE 10, [YR-1]

****

BE IT REMEMBERED, that heretofore, to-writ on JUNE 10, [YR-1], the above-entitled matter came on for hearing before the Grand Jury of Bear County, sitting in San Milano, State of Lone Star, being presented by ROGER SMITH, Assistant Criminal District Attorney, for consideration by the members thereof.

HEATHER STEVENS was duly sworn as Court Reporter.

WHEREUPON, the following evidence was introduced and proceedings had, to-wit, beginning at 10:05 o'clock a.m. and concluding at 10:50 o'clock a.m.

PAT GONZALES, The Witness,

GRAND JURY FOREMAN: Do you solemnly swear that you will not divulge either by words or signs any matter about which you may be interrogated, and that you will keep secret all proceedings of the Grand Jury which may be had in your presence, and that you will true answers make to such questions as may be propounded to you by the Grand Jury or under its direction, so help you God?

THE WITNESS: I do.

EXAMINATION BY ROGER SMITH:

Q: With any witness who comes before the Grand Jury, I need to give you the definitions of perjury and aggravated perjury.

A person commits the offense of perjury if, with intent to deceive and with knowledge of the statement's meaning, that person makes a false statement under oath or swears to the truth of a false statement previously made and the statement is required or authorized by law to be made under oath.

Perjury is a Class A Misdemeanor, which is punishable by anywhere up to one year in the Bear County Jail and/or a fine of up to $4,000.

Perjury becomes aggravated perjury if the person commits perjury, makes that false statement during or in connection with an official proceeding, and Grand Jury proceedings are official proceedings, and the statement is material.

Aggravated perjury is a third-degree felony, which means it's punishable by anywhere from two to ten years in the Lone Star Department of Corrections, and there's a potential fine of up to $10,000. Do you understand this?

A: Yes, sir.

[Pat Gonzales testified as follows before the Grand Jury, after waiving the right to remain silent.]

Q: Please state your name for the record.

A: Pat Gonzales.

Q: What is your occupation?

A: I am a school counselor at the Wayland Heights High School.

Q: How long have you worked there?

A: About three years.

Q: Are you licensed to perform work as a counselor?

A: Not yet. I am going through that process now.

Q: How is that you were hired by the school without being certified?

A: They needed someone badly and took me on, on a sort of probationary status.

Q: Do you have any experience as a counselor?

A: Oh yes. I have served as a counselor for almost 15 years. For several years in a drug rehab program as a facilitator. And for another several years working in a retirement home as a facilitator in weekly discussion groups.

Q: So what sort of counseling do you perform?

A: It's limited obviously. But I can talk to students, provide a listening ear, and then provide reports to my supervisors who are licensed and certified by the state.

Q: Do you know Tiffany Barkwood?

A: I did know her. She recently committed suicide.

Q: How did she die?

A: She overdosed on anti-depressants.

Q: Had you counseled her?

A: Yes, for almost a year.

Q: Can you tell us what she said?

A: I am not sure I can. I think everything she told me specifically is privileged.

Q: We have spoken to her mother who has filled out a consent form that releases you from the privilege.

A: May I see that?

Q: Certainly. [The Assistant District Attorney shows the properly authorized consent to the witness]

A: All right. Good. [Witness paused] Okay. Okay. I need to tell you what I know.

Q: Go on.

A: Tiffany had a lot of problems. First, she told me that her main problem was getting her folks to listen to her. She was particularly upset by the fact that her father never listened to her and always wrote her off as being, in his words, a drama queen. Second, she had a history of depression and she said that she was, or had been, on a variety of anti-depressants.

Q: Did she say what she was taking?

A: Zoloft, I believe.

Q: Did you give her any prescription drugs?

A: Absolutely not. She showed me the pills she was taking though. As I said, she was using Zoloft, a relatively common anti-depressant.

Q: What other problems did she exhibit?

A: Well, on top of it all, she told me about three months ago that she had found a guy who listened to her and that he was really helping her. She said that he had even given her some Zoloft. I was really shocked by that and told her that she needed to see a physician to have that cleared. That she might take too many at once.

Q: What did she say when you told her that?

A: She laughed nervously and said she knew that. And then she asked me if I had ever thought about committing suicide. I told her I had not and she said she had and that her dad was going to someday push her over the edge. She said that she had told him that several times and each time she did, he told her to go away and quit being, as I said before, a drama queen.

Q: Did she ever identify the guy she said was helping her?

A: No. Not exactly, but I later found out that it was her teacher, Johnny Woods.

Q: Do you know him?

A: Barely.

Q: Did you ever prepare a memo on your conclusions about Tiffany?

A: Yes. I had prepared a memo just a few days before she killed herself.

Q: Is this it? [Assistant DA shows exhibit to witness]

A: Yes, that is the one I prepared in March of this year.

Q: On the memo, there is a handwritten notation that says, "suicide." Is that your handwriting?

A: Yes. I added that to the file when I heard she had died. I knew in my heart before the medical examiner released his report that she had probably committed suicide.

Q: Why do you say that?

A: Just a day before she died, she called me to say that her father had found about her "guy" and that he was going to try and get some money out of him to pay for a new car. I asked her how she knew, and she said that she had overheard her dad talking to a car dealership and said that he expected to come into some money and to hold the car for him.

Q: Did you verify that?

A: No.

Q: What else did she say?

A: She said that she was going to give her dad an ultimatum and that if he did not back off from going after her guy, that she would end it all herself. Then she started sobbing and hung up.

Q: What did you do?

A: I immediately reported this to my supervisor who called and left messages with her parents. I don't think he ever got in touch with them. We learned the next day that she had died. This has really hit the school very hard. I hold her father directly responsible for her death.

Q: Did she say whether she had ever had sexual relations with Mr. Woods?

A: She did not say and I did not ask.

Q: Did she ever tell you that she was pregnant?

A: No. That subject did not come up. And it's not the kind of question I would feel comfortable asking.

ROGER SMITH: Okay. Why don't you go ahead and step outside for just a few minutes.

THE WITNESS: Okay.

[The Witness leaves the Grand Jury Room at 10:50 a.m., and is subsequently dismissed.]

(END OF TRANSCRIPT)

Resume of Pat Gonzales

PAT GONZALES

978 Oak Avenue
San Milano, State of Lone Star 786645

Career Objective

To obtain a challenging position that will allow for growth and a chance to use and contribute my education and job experience.

Summary of Qualifications

Knowledge and ability to work effectively with both Adult and Youth clients; ability to follow instructions both verbally and in writing; ability to maintain confidential case files; PC skills; outstanding organizational and customer service skills.

Work History

[YR-8]-[present] **Wayland Heights High School** – School Counselor.

[YR-13]-[YR-8] **San Milano Area Drug Rehab** – San Milano, Lone Star
Counselor, Adult and Youth Services
Assisting Adult and Youth patients work through their drug problems. Career counseling and planning. Course placement. Degree and occupation exploration. Assist with academic and personal student goal completion. Teacher of student development classes-to include personal and academic success. Time mgt. skills, study skills. Producer of video of occupational and tech. programs to reveal knowledge, skills and abilities for job success. Participated in business and community service to provide information for college enrollment.

[YR-14]-[YR-13] **Wonderful Life Retirement Home** – San Milano, Lone Star
Secretary/Administrative Assistant/Group Discussion Leader
Greeting clients; maintaining and creating all active patient files for Psychology Office; providing administrative support to Counselor; preparing correspondence letters and organizing materials for mailings; light typing, data entry and faxing of documents; basic bookkeeping and medical billing of patients; corresponding with various companies regarding verification of company benefits; scoring tests for counselor and typing exams for students; scheduling meetings, running errands, ordering supplies and inventory; setting up appointments for patients, answering and screening telephone calls; holding weekly group discussions for the patients; performing other duties and special projects as assigned.

Education

[YR-16]-[YR-14]	**The University of San Milano** – San Milano, Lone Star Education Level: Masters Degree Major: Counseling GPA: 3.7 Graduated: Yes
[YR-21]-[YR-16]	**City University** – San Milano, Lone Star Education Level: Bachelors Degree Major: Government Minor: Sociology

Autopsy Report of Tiffany Barkwood

BEAR COUNTY MEDICAL EXAMINER'S OFFICE
1245 MEDICAL BLVD
SAN MILANO. STATE OF LONE STAR 792213

AUTOPSY REPORT

Case No. 1612-0398

Name: Tiffany Barkwood **Age:** 17 **Race:** W **Sex:** F

Date & Time of Autopsy: 8 May [YR-1] @ 08:55 a.m.

GENERAL EXAMINATION

The body is received within a body bag and is that of a normally developed, well nourished, adult Caucasian female, 57 ½ inches tall, weighing 120 lbs and appearing consistent with the listed age of 17 years. Accompanying the body, in a plastic bag, are a pair of cut plaid shorts, white t-shirt, white sneakers, one pair of gold earrings, and undergarments.

Detective Randy Carlisle from the Lone Star Police Department is present for the autopsy.

EXTERNAL EXAMINATION

Rigor mortis is fully developed in all joints. Fixed livor mortis is present posteriorly. The decedent has long, blonde hair averaging 10 inches in length. The eyes are closed; the conjunctivae are pale and without petechiae; the sclerae are white; the corneae are clear; and the irides are brown. The nose, ears, and external auditory canals are unremarkable. The mouth is open revealing natural teeth in good condition.

The neck and chest are symmetrical and atraumatic. The abdomen is soft and flat.

The upper and lower extremities are symmetrical and atraumatic. Multiple small irregular scars involve the anterior knees.

The back is straight and free of trauma.

EVIDENCE OF MEDICAL INTERVENTION

An endotracheal tube protrudes from the mouth and is strapped in place. Multiple cardiac monitor pads are present upon the anterior chest and abdomen. Multiple needle puncture wounds involve the left infraclavicular region and left antecubital fossa. A pulse oximeter monitor is present upon the right index finger.

INTERNAL EXAMINATION

HEAD: An intermastoid incision is made around the cranium and the scalp is retracted. Hemorrhage is present. The brain weighs 1,550 gm. The cerebral and cerebellar hemispheres, midbrain and pons are symmetrical and grossly unremarkable. The cerebral vessels follow the usual distribution and are widely patent.

BODY: The body is opened with the Y-shaped incision. The organs occupy their usual positions and relationships. Inspection of the thoracic and abdominal cavities after evisceration reveals no bony or muscular abnormalities.

NECK: There is no evidence of infection, tumor or trauma.

LUNGS: The right lung weighs 360 gm and the left lung weighs 350 gm. The pleural surfaces are purple, smooth and glistening with a scattered black pigmentation present, consistent with mild anthracotic pigment deposition.

CARDIOVASCULAR SYSTEM: The heart weighs 380 gm. The epicardial surface is smooth and glistening. The coronary arteries follow the usual right dominant distribution and are widely patent. The aorta is open and shows occasional fatty streaks.

GASTROINTESTINAL SYSTEM: The tongue is atraumatic. The esophagus is opened to reveal a gray, wrinkly mucosa. The stomach contains a minimal amount of yellow fluid. The stomach mucosa is erythematous and appropriately folded. The small and large bowels reveal no evidence of natural disease. The appendix is present.

LIVER AND BILIARY TRACT: The liver weighs 990 gm. The capsule is smooth and glistening. On cut sections, the parenchyma is tan-brown and firm.

PANCREAS: Unremarkable.

SPLEEN: The spleen weighs 50 gm. The capsule is purple, smooth and glistening.

GENITOURINARY SYSTEM: The right kidney weighs 70 gm and the left kidney weighs 90 gm. The capsules remove without difficulty revealing smooth and shiny cortical surfaces. The bladder is empty.

FINDINGS

A/N DRUG SCREEN

BLOOD, FEMORAL (GC/MS)

ALCOHOLS

BLOOD, FEMORAL (GC)

NONE DETECTED

VITREOUS (GC)

NONE DETECTED

ALKALINE DRUG SCREEN

BLOOD, FERMORAL (GC, GC/MS)

+ ATROPINE

(+) = PRESENT, NO QUANTITATION

COCAINE AND COCAINE METABOLITES

BLOOD, FERMORAL (ELISA)

NONE DETECTED

NARCOTICS

BLOOD, FERMORAL (ELISA)

NONE DETECTED

PREGNANCY

4 WEEKS

CONCLUSION

It is our opinion that Tiffany Barkwood, a 17 year old Caucasian female, died as a result of an overdose of the antidepressant Zoloft.

MANNER OF DEATH: Overdose.

Lisa D. Bains	JOHN R. RAINY
LISA D. BAINS, M.D.	**JOHN R. RAINY, M.D.**
Chief Medical Examiner	Medical Examiner

Pat Gonzales' Memo

Wayland Heights High School
San Milano, State of Lone Star
Home of the Hornets

MEMO FOR RECORD

FROM: **Pat Gonzales**

RE: **Tiffany Barkwood**

DATE **May 4, [YR-1]**

I have been counseling Ms. Tiffany Barkwood, a junior here at Wayland Heights for the past six months, as instructed by my department head.

I have held approximately 10 sessions with Tiffany, each lasting about 30 minutes. In addition, I have received, but not sent, e-mails from her over the last several weeks.

Her parents initially asked the school for help when they came to the conclusion in December [YR-2], that she was having mild bouts of depression and seemed increasingly moody. At first they thought it was boy problems, but had decided to seek medical help. A doctor (whose name I do not recall) apparently prescribed low doses of an anti-depressant drug in January. They were Zoloft. Tiffany told me that she did not like using drugs and instead of using them had saved them for a "rainy day" in case she got really depressed. I begged her not to do that.

About a month ago, she came to my office. She started sobbing as she related the fact that her father, Don Barkwood, had found out about a "guy" that she was meeting and that he was threatening to sue him and expose him. She did not say who it was but I suspected that it might be an older boy, perhaps an upper classman. It was hard to understand what legal basis her father was supposedly using. She said that she had begged her father to stop but he told her to quit being overly dramatic, and basically ignored her. Tiffany also said that her mother is also distant and of no help to Tiffany and her problems.

In light of these developments I recommend that the school counselor see Tiffany as soon as possible and see if any additional counseling or help is needed.

I am very concerned about the mental health of this young woman!!

Suicide!!

Banking Records for Thompson

1320

Barkwood
1234 Oak Street
San Milano, State of Lone Star 77777

37-65/1119 54

May 4, [YR-1]

Pay to: Jordon Thompson **$ 5000.00**

Five Thousand & 00/100 --------------------------- **Dollars**

For_______________ Don Barkwood

11000111://1 12345634 99882233453

J Thompson

0009 18231
Lone Star Bank
San Milano,
State of Lone Star

Deposited 05/04/[YR-1]

E-Mails from Johnny Woods to Tiffany Barkwood

From: jwoods@waylandhts.edu
Sent: Monday, February 26, [YR-1] 12:10 AM
To: Tiffprincess@bol.com
Subject: Hi

I know you are hurting right now. Please just know that I care about you and do not want to do anything that will hurt you. Believe me. You mean a lot to me. Do you need any more pills?

From: jwoods@waylandhts.edu
Sent: Tuesday, February 27, [YR-1] 11:10 PM
To: Tiffprincess@bol.com
Subject: Hi

I miss you too. I can't get away tonight. We need to talk about the "helpers" I have given to you. My wife said something about missing some from her bottle. I said that I had no idea what she was talking about. ☺

From: jwoods@waylandhts.edu
Sent: Monday, March 12, [YR-1] 11:10 PM
To: Tiffprincess@bol.com
Subject: Oops

Be cool Tiffany. I cannot afford to leave another teaching job. My wife will kill me. I will text message when I figure out where we can meet.

E-Mails from Tiffany Barkwood to Johnny Woods

From: Tiffprincess@bol.com
Sent: Tuesday, February 27, [YR-1] 7:30 AM
To: jwoods@waylandhts.edu
Subject: Hi

I can't live without you. Call me!!!!! My dad and mom may discover us. They don't trust me using the family computer. If they only knew. It serves them right!!!!

From: Tiffprincess@bol.com
Sent: Wednesday, February 28, [YR-1] 7:50 AM
To: jwoods@waylandhts.edu
Subject: Hi

I need to talk to u. Dad is being totally a jerk!! I am really feeling down today. He threatened to stop me from using the family computer. I think he suspects something.

Maybe I will see you after class?

From: Tiffprincess@bol.com
Sent: Monday, March 12, [YR-1] 7:30 AM
To: jwoods@waylandhts.edu
Subject: Oops

I need to see you ASAP. I saw my dad going through my e-mails last night and he started shouting at me. He said that he had been reading my e-mails. I told him that we were just very good friends, right? You are my friend. I miss you. I am going to take a couple of pills before coming to school today.

From: Tiffprincess@bol.com
Sent: Monday, May 7, [YR-1] 4:37 PM
To: jwoods@waylandhts.edu
Subject: Bye

Dad will not stop. He just called me a drama queen. Well I'll give him a little drama. There is no reason to live. I don't think you love me either. I am going to use those pills.

E-Mails from Tiffany Barkwood to the Defendant, Don Barkwood

From: Tiffprincess@bol.com
Sent: Monday, May 7, [YR-1] 4:30 PM
To: DBarkwood@bol.com
Subject: PLEASE

Daddy, please listen to me. PLEASE. PLEASE. PLEASE. I know everything about what you are doing to Mr. Woods. Please stop, Please stop. Please stop. IF YOU DON'T STOP, I WILL KILL MYSELF. I've got the pills to do it. I have them right here. You know the ones I am talking about. If this thing comes out I cannot live anymore. Johnny cares about me and listens to what I need. Please talk to me!!!!!!

From: Tiffprincess@bol.com
Sent: Monday, May 7, [YR-1] 5:25 PM
To: DBarkwood@bol.com
Subject: PLEASE

Daddy. I love U. I did it. No more crap from you or from mommy. I am getting sleeepey. feelsgode. bye;)

E-Mail from the Defendant to Tiffany Barkwood

From: DBarkwood@bol.com
Sent: Monday, May 7, [YR-1] 4:35 PM
To: Tiffprincess@bol.com
Subject: PLEASE

TIFFANY

STOP BEING A DRAMA QUEEN. I AM ONLY DOING THIS FOR YOU AND SISSY. THIS GUY DESERVES TO FRY. AND I AM GOING TO LIGHT THE FIRE. TRUST ME, YOU WILL THANK ME SOMEDAY. I HAVE ONE MORE MEETING HERE AT THE OFFICE AND THEN I AM COMING HOME. DON'T DO ANYTHING STUPID. CALL YOUR MOTHER AND TELL HER I AM RUNNING LATE. WE WILL TALK WHEN I GET HOME.

DAD

E-Mail from Tiffany Barkwood to Pat Gonzales

From: Tiffprincess@bol.com
Sent: Monday, May 7, [YR-1] 4:55 PM
To: Pgonzales@.waylandhts.edu
Subject: Thanks

Thanks for your help. This is not your fault. You tried to help me and I wanted to thank you. It's my dad's fault. But you know that. I just e-mailed him saying that I was going to kill myself. He knows I will do it. I tried it a year ago and they stopped me. Now he does not care. He just called me a drama queen. So its drama he will get. My mom is out shopping with friends, so she is not much help either.

I need to leave for now. Gotta find those pills.

Thanks.

COURT'S COPY

Name: DON BARKWOOD
Complainant: JOHNNY WOODS
Offense Charge: THEFT BY COERCION & MANSLAUGHTER

JURY INSTRUCTIONS

LADIES AND GENTLEMEN OF THE JURY:

The defendant, DON BARKWOOD, stands charged by indictment in COUNT 1 with the offense of theft by coercion, alleged to have been committed on or about the 25th Day of April [YR-1], in BEAR County, State of Lone Star. The defendant has pleaded not guilty.

1.

Our law provides that a person commits the offense of theft if he unlawfully appropriates property with intent to deprive the owner of such property.

Appropriation of property is unlawful if it is without the owner's effective consent; the property is stolen and the person appropriates the property knowing it was stolen by another; property in the custody of any law enforcement agency was explicitly represented by any law enforcement agent to the person as being stolen and the person appropriates the property believing it was stolen by another.

2.

"Appropriate," as used herein, means to acquire or exercise control over personal property. Appropriation of property is unlawful if it is without the owner's effective consent.

"Property" means tangible or intangible personal property, including anything severed from land, or a document, including money, that represents or embodies anything of value.

"Deprive," as used herein, means to withhold property from the owner permanently or to dispose of property in a manner that makes recovery of the property by the owner unlikely or to withhold property from the owner for so extended a period of time that a major portion of the value or enjoyment of the property is lost to the owner.

"Deception," as used herein, means creating or confirming by words or conduct a false impression of law or fact that is likely to affect the judgment of another in the transaction and that the person creating the impression does not believe to be true. It also means failing to correct a false impression of law or fact that is likely to affect the judgment of another in the transaction which impression of fact the person charged previously created or confirmed by words or conduct and which he does not now believe to be true.

"Conduct" means an act or omission and its accompanying mental state.

"Owner" means a person who has title to the property, possession of the property, or a greater right to possession of the property than the person charged.

"Coercion" means a threat, however communicated: to commit an offense; to inflict bodily injury in the future on the person threatened or another; to accuse a person of any offense; to expose a person to hatred, contempt, or ridicule; to harm the credit or business repute of any person; or to take or withhold action as a public servant, or to cause a public servant to take or withhold action.

"Effective consent" includes consent by a person legally authorized to act for the owner. Consent is not effective if: induced by deception or coercion; given by a person the actor knows is not legally authorized to act for the owner; given by a person who by reason of youth, mental disease or defect, or intoxication is known by the actor to be unable to make reasonable property dispositions; given solely to detect the commission of an offense; or given by a person who by reason of advanced age is known by the actor to have a diminished capacity to make informed and rational decisions about the reasonable disposition of property.

"Possession" means actual care, custody, control, or management of the property.

3.

A person acts intentionally, or with intent, with respect to the nature of his conduct, or to a result of his conduct, when it is his conscious objective or desire to engage in the conduct or cause the result.

A person acts knowingly, or with knowledge, with respect to the nature of his conduct or to circumstances surrounding his conduct when he is aware of the nature of his conduct or that the circumstances exist. A person acts knowingly, or with knowledge, with respect to a result of his conduct when he is aware that his conduct is reasonably certain to cause the result.

4.

You are instructed that to constitute theft in this case, it is necessary that the State establish by the evidence beyond a reasonable doubt that the defendant acquired the property in question, that at the time of the acquisition the defendant acquired it by means of coercion, as that term has been defined herein, with the intent at the time of acquisition to deprive the owner of such property and the offense of theft is complete when such property is acquired by the defendant, provided the intent to deprive the owner thereof existed at the very time the property was so acquired by the defendant, and that this is the case notwithstanding that the possession of the property acquired, if it was so acquired, may have been acquired by the defendant by permission of the person from whom it was acquired.

"Proof beyond a reasonable doubt" is proof that leaves you firmly convinced of the defendant's guilt. There are very few things in this world that we know with absolute certainty, and in criminal cases the law does not require proof that overcomes every possible doubt. If, based on your consideration of the evidence, you are firmly convinced that the defendant is guilty of the crime charged, you should find him guilty. If, on the other hand, you think there is a real possibility that he is not guilty, you should give him the benefit of the doubt and find him not guilty.

5.

Now, if you find from the evidence beyond a reasonable doubt that on or about the 25h Day of April [YR-1], in BEAR County, State of Lone Star, the defendant, DON BARKWOOD, then and there unlawfully appropriate, by acquiring or otherwise exercising control over, property, to-wit: cash, of the value of $20,000 or more but less than $100,000, from JOHNNY WOODS, the owner there of, without the effective consent of the owner, namely, by coercion, and with intent to deprive the owner of the property, then you will find the defendant, in COUNT 1, guilty of theft as charged in the indictment.

Unless you so find beyond a reasonable doubt, or if you have a reasonable doubt thereof, you will acquit the defendant and say by your verdict "Not Guilty."

LADIES AND GENTLEMEN OF THE JURY:

The defendant, DON BARKWOOD, stands charged by indictment in COUNT 2 with the offense of manslaughter, alleged to have been committed on or about the 7th Day of May, [YR-1], in BEAR County, State of Lone Star. The defendant has pleaded not guilty.

1.

A person commits the offense of manslaughter if his recklessly causes the death of an individual.

2.

"Individual" means a human being who is alive, including an unborn child at every stage of gestation from fertilization until birth.

A person acts recklessly, or is reckless, with respect to circumstances surrounding his conduct or the result of his conduct when he is aware of but consciously disregards a substantial and unjustifiable risk that the circumstances exist or the result will occur. The risk must be of such a nature and degree that its disregard constitutes a gross deviation from the standard of care that an ordinary person would exercise under all the circumstances, as viewed from the actor's standpoint.

"Proof beyond a reasonable doubt" is proof that leaves you firmly convinced of the defendant's guilt. There are very few things in this world that we know with absolute certainty, and in criminal cases the law does not require proof that overcomes every possible doubt. If, based on your consideration of the evidence, you are firmly convinced that the defendant is guilty of the crime charged, you should find him guilty. If, on the other hand, you think there is a real possibility that he is not guilty, you should give him the benefit of the doubt and find him not guilty.

3.

The law recognizes that a person has an affirmative duty to take reasonable steps to prevent a family member from committing suicide.

4.

Now, if you find from the evidence beyond a reasonable doubt that on or about the 7th Day of May [YR-1], in BEAR County, State of Lone Star, the defendant DON BARKWOOD, did recklessly cause the death of an individual, namely TIFFANY BARKWOOD, by recklessly ignoring her threats to commit suicide, then you will find the defendant guilty of manslaughter as charged in the indictment.

Unless you find that defendant is guilty of manslaughter beyond a reasonable doubt, or if you have a reasonable doubt thereof, you will acquit the defendant and say by your verdict "Not Guilty."

Chapter 9
Barkwood v. Barkwood

§ 9-1. Introduction

Anika Stotward Barkwood has filed a wrongful death lawsuit against her ex-husband, Don Barkwood, for the death of their teenage daughter, Tiffany.

A year earlier Don Barkwood was charged with one count of theft by coercion and one count of manslaughter of his daughter, Tiffany. When Barkwood learned that his daughter was exchanging e-mails with a high school teacher, Johnny Woods, he obtained the court's permission to take a pre-suit deposition of Woods, as provided in the Rules of Civil Procedure of the Lone Star. Woods offered to settle the case and paid Barkwood money, which in turn was deposited with a children's cancer foundation. Shortly afterwards, however, Barkwood withdrew the money and made a down payment on a new car. When his daughter's pleas to refrain from proceeding against Woods failed, she told Barkwood that she would kill herself. When he ignored her final plea, she committed suicide.

At the time of his criminal trial, Barkwood was separated from the plaintiff. For reasons unrelated to the merits of the case, the District Attorney later decided to drop the charges against Barkwood. Angered by the DA's action, the plaintiff filed the lawsuit against her ex-husband.

§ 9-2. Stipulations on Procedural and Evidentiary Matters

The parties have stipulated to the following:

1. The case is being tried in a Lone Star state court. The Federal Rules of Procedure and Evidence apply.
2. This case will be tried on the issues of liability and damages.
3. All witnesses called to testify who, in statements or depositions, have identified the defendant, other individuals, or tangible evidence, can, if asked, identify the same at trial.
4. The defendant Barkwood signed his statement to the police.
5. Other than what is supplied in the case file, there is nothing exceptional or unusual about the background information of any of the witnesses or the defendant that would bolster or detract from their credibility.
6. This case file does not permit a listed witness or the defendant, while testifying, to "invent" an individual not mentioned in this problem and have testimony or evidence offered to the court or jury from that invented individual.
7. The current year is the year in which this case comes to trial.
8. It is stipulated that the defendant, Don Barkwood, correctly followed the rules of civil procedure of the State of Lone Star concerning pre-suit depositions.
9. For this case, assume that the case law in this State recognizes that a person has an affirmative duty to take reasonable steps to prevent a family member from committing suicide.

10. The e-mails in the problem were all lawfully seized, or obtained, from computers belonging to the defendant, the defendant's family, Pat Gonzales, and Johnny Woods.
11. The autopsy report of Tiffany Barkwood is accurate, authentic, and satisfies the best evidence rule.
12. Although Zoloft tablets were seized from the defendant's house and from Johnny Woods' house, they are not available as evidence.
13. Laboratory tests on the Zoloft tablets revealed that they were indeed Zoloft tablets, containing the drug Atropine.
14. Statements made by Tiffany Barkwood to Pat Gonzales are not privileged. Whatever privilege may have existed was waived by her lawful representative(s).
15. There are no written records of Johnny Woods' legal problems at his prior places of employment.
16. All exhibits in the file are authentic. In addition, each exhibit contained in the file is the original of that document unless otherwise noted on the exhibit or as established by the evidence.
17. The defendant must admit that the check he wrote to Thompson is his personal check and that the signature on the check is his signature.
18. At the time of her death, Tiffany Barkwood had an expected life span of another 64 years.

§ 9-3. Case File Materials

The following case file materials should be used for the trial of *Barkwood v. Barkwood.*

Lone Star Wrongful Death Statute

Lone Star Civil Practice & Remedies Code

§ 31.123. Cause of Action

(a) An action for actual damages arising from an injury that causes an individual's death may be brought if liability exists under this section.

(b) A person is liable for damages arising from an injury that causes an individual's death if the injury was caused by the person's or his agent's or servant's wrongful act, neglect, carelessness, unskillfulness, or default.

(c) A person is liable for damages arising from an injury that causes an individual's death if:

(1) the person is a proprietor, owner, charterer, or hirer of an industrial or public utility plant or of a railroad, street railway, steamboat, stagecoach, or other vehicle for the transportation of goods or passengers; and

(2) the injury was caused by the person's or his agent's or servant's wrongful act, neglect, carelessness, unskillfulness, or default.

§ 31.124. Benefitting from Action

(a) An action to recover damages as provided by this subchapter is for the exclusive benefit of the surviving spouse, children, and parents of the deceased.

(b) The surviving spouse, children, and parents of the deceased may bring the action or one or more of those individuals may bring the action for the benefit of all.

§ 31.125. Punitive Damages

When the death is caused by the wilful act or omission or gross negligence of the defendant, punitive as well as actual damages may be recovered.

PLAINTIFF'S PETITION

DISTRICT COURT OF BEAR COUNTY

ANIKA S. BARKWOOD Plaintiff v. DON BACKWOOD Defendant	}	Docket No. 13567-90 COMPLAINT FOR DAMAGES

COMES NOW the above-named Plaintiff and alleges the following:

I. Parties, Jurisdiction, and Venue

A. Plaintiff, Anita Stotward Barkwood, mother to decedent, Tiffany Barkwood, brings this action in her personal capacity.

B. Defendant, Don Barkwood, is a resident of Bear County, State of Lone Star.

C. This Court has jurisdiction over the subject matter of this complaint and over the parties.

D. Venue is proper and appropriate in Bear County because the wrongful death of Tiffany Barkwood, which is the subject matter of this complaint, occurred in Bear County.

II. Factual Basis

A. Plaintiff's and Defendant's daughter was Tiffany Barkwood.

B. Defendant learned that his daughter, Tiffany Barkwood, was exchanging e-mails with a high school teacher, Johnny Woods. Defendant obtained the court's permission to take a pre-suit deposition of him.

C. Woods offered to settle the case and paid Defendant money, which in turn was deposited with a children's cancer foundation. Shortly afterwards, however, Defendant withdrew the money and made a down payment on a new car.

D. Tiffany Barkwood, the decedent, begged her father to refrain from proceeding against Woods. When her pleas failed, she told Barkwood that she would kill herself.

E. Defendant ignored Tiffany Barkwood's pleas, causing her to commit suicide.

F. Defendant's acts or omissions were the sole and proximate cause of Tiffany Barkwood's death.

G. By ignoring his daughter's pleas to refrain from proceeding against Woods and her threats of suicide, Defendant willfully caused the decedent's death, or acted in gross negligence in failing to take steps to prevent her suicide.

III. Causes of Action

A. As a direct and proximate result of the acts of the Defendant, the decedent suffered a wrongful death, entitling Plaintiff to recover actual and punitive damages (including but not limited to medical and hospital expenses, funeral expenses, and all other damages allowable for wrongful death and survival benefits under Lone Star Civil Practice & Remedies Code §§ 31.123-31.125 and any other damages allowable as a result of Defendant's conduct) in amounts not now precisely known, the exact amounts to be proven at or before the time of trial.

B. As a further direct and proximate result of the Defendant's acts and omissions, the Plaintiff of the decedent suffered destruction of the parent-child relationship and loss of parental consortium.

C. As a further direct and proximate result of the negligent acts and omissions of Defendant, Plaintiff is entitled to recover statutory and reasonable attorney's fees and costs in amounts not now precisely known, the court to set such amounts in the future.

IV. Prayer for Relief

WHEREFORE, the plaintiff prays for a judgment of liability against the defendants as follows:

A. For a judgment against Defendant.

B. For an award of actual and punitive damages as set forth in the above complaint herein, including statutory and reasonable fees and costs in such amounts that may be awarded by this Court.

C. For such other and further relief as the Court deems just and appropriate.

DATED this day of April 5, [YR-1].

Chuck W. Rogers

Chuck W. Rogers
The Rogers Law Firm
San Milano, State of Lone Star
Attorney for Plaintiff

Deposition of Anika Stotward Barkwood

ORAL DEPOSITION OF MS. ANIKA STOTWARD BARKWOOD, produced as a witness at the instance of the defendant, DON BARKWOOD, and duly sworn, was taken in the above-styled and numbered cause on October 31, [YR-1] from 2:00 p.m. to 3:10 p.m. before Sally Walker, Certified Shorthand Reporter in and for the State of Lone Star, reported by machine shorthand, at the law offices of Plaintiff, pursuant to the Lone Star Rules of Civil Procedure and the Provisions stated on the record or attached hereto.

This is a deposition of ANIKA STOTWARD BARKWOOD, who having been sworn, testified as follows:

EXAMINATION
QUESTIONS BY DEFENSE COUNSEL:

Q: Good morning, Ms. Barkwood.

A: Hello.

Q: Before we get started I want to make sure that you understand that if you do not understand my questions, please feel free to stop me and ask for a clarification. Okay?

A: Sure.

Q: Okay. First, please state your full name.

A: Anika Stotward Barkwood.

Q: You live here in San Milano?

A: Yes, I do.

Q: You have filed a civil wrongful death lawsuit against Don Barkwood for the death of you minor daughter, Tiffany?

A: Yes.

Q: You are no longer married?

A: No.

Q: But you still use his last name?

A: Yes.

Q: Why?

A: Many of my contacts in the community have known me for years by that last name.

Q: But you hold him responsible?

A: Yes. I hold him responsible for Tiffany's death.

Q: Why?

A: Don was, and probably still is, a workaholic. He would work 24 hours a day if he could.

Q: And that caused the death of your daughter?

A: No, I did not say that.

Q: Well, then please explain.

A: Tiffany was having some severe depression. Don knew about it, but only reluctantly agreed to let her go to counseling. We finally got her linked up with her school counselor, Ms. Garza or something like that.

Q: Do you remember her name?

A: Not really.

Q: Could it have been Pat Gonzales?

A: Yes, that is it.

Q: So how did that lead to Tiffany's death?

A: Well, Don knew about her condition and in spite of that, started causing problems for her by harassing her high school teacher, Johnny Woods.

Q: Did you know about the relationship between Woods and your daughter?

A: Not as such. Tiffany and I would talk often and she mentioned that she had found someone special at school and that he really cared about her and that she felt comfortable and safe talking to him.

Q: So, you are testifying that you did not know it was a teacher?

A: Not at first.

Q: So, at some point you did find out what was happening?

A: Yes. When Don found out about their relationship, he basically overreacted and without talking to me first, he took out after Woods on his own. He basically cut me out. But he did tell me who the special man was.

Q: What was your reaction to getting that information?

A: I had mixed feelings. I knew that what Tiffany was doing was wrong. But on the other hand, she seemed somehow more content and sure about herself. So. . .

Q: So, you approved of the relationship?

A: No, not entirely.

Q: But you objected to Don's attempt to protect his daughter from a predator?

A: Woods was no predator. And even if he was, Don's reaction pushed Tiffany further into her depression.

Q: Did Tiffany come to you to talk about it?

A: Yes. She said that her daddy was being unfair and lacked compassion.

Q: She asked for your help, didn't she?

A: Yes.

Q: And you did not help her, did you?

A: Yes, I did. I helped her. I told her that I would speak to Don, her daddy.

Q: What did you say to Don?

A: I did not get a chance to do so. We were right in the middle of working on a charity ball and I got called away from home on several nights.

Q: I see.

A: No, I don't think you do. Tiffany and I were close and I would have never done anything to hurt her.

Q: Let's move on the amount of money that you are asking for in damages. You are asking for reimbursement for funeral expenses?

A: Yes, 12,370 dollars. That was my share of the expenses.

Q: How is that?

A: Well, Don could not see spending more than 4,000 dollars out of our joint account. So I pitched in the extra money out of my personal and separate bank account — the one I had before we were married.

Q: And you are asking for 30,000 dollars for counseling fees?

A: Yes, I have been in pretty intense weekly therapy for over a year. And that is the actual out-of-pocket expenses. It's actually 30,150 dollars to be exact.

Q: Did you bring the receipts for those expenses with you today?

A: Yes, I did. Here they are.

Q: Okay. Thank you. The total bill for the funeral was 16,370 dollars, right?

A: Yes.

Q: So, your husband and you paid 4,000 out of your joint account. And the remainder, let's see that would be the 12,370 dollars, that you say you paid out of your own separate account? Right?

A: Yes, that is right. I actually paid the whole amount on my account and then Don wrote a check to me on our joint account. [Conferring with counsel] Actually, I should correct that amount. Of the 4,000 he paid out of the joint account, half of that was actually mine. So my total contribution for the funeral expenses was the 12,000 dollars and some cents, plus 2,000.00. The total was 14,370 dollars.

Q: All right. And you are asking for another 50,000 dollars for future therapy expenses?

A: Yes.

Q: That seems a bit high.

A: Well, I am using the best counselors. One of them is Dr. Wellbeshire, who is one of the nation's leading psychiatrists.

Q: You have also claimed 100,000 dollars for pain and suffering?

A: Yes.

Q: Can you please tell me why you are asking for that amount of money.

A: I am taking medications for my depression and the loss of Tiffany has really hit me hard. I don't think I will ever get it over it. I cannot sleep at night without taking sleeping pills. And sometimes, during the middle of the night, I wake up crying.

Q: Is that from feeling guilty about what you did or did not do to save your own daughter?

A: [Confers with counsel] No [pause] not really. I guess we could have all done more to save her. I did what I was capable of doing, under the circumstances.

Q: Okay. One more thing.

A: Okay.

Q: On the day Tiffany died, where were you? What were you doing?

A: As I said, I was working on a major, annual, charity function — a fundraiser dinner for the homeless in our city. Earlier that day, I got a call from one of the people running the fundraiser and they asked me to come to the event center to take care of some problems that had cropped up.

Q: What problems?

A: Apparently several large donors' checks had bounced and we were having an emergency board meeting. And the florist had messed up a 2,000 dollar order for the centerpieces.

Q: So you were working on floral arrangements when your daughter died?

A: No, that is not what I said. No, don't misquote me. We had some major financial issues to work out. Besides, Tiffany knew the kind of work I was involved in and often said [witness starts crying], "Mom, you are doing good in this world." I'm sorry.

Q: Do you want some time?

A: No, let's finish this.

Q: Did you know about Tiffany's e-mail to your ex-husband?

A: No, not at that time.

Q: How did you learn of your daughter's death?

A: I got home about 8:00 p.m. and found that she had overdosed on drugs. I went crazy.

Q: That's all I have. Do you have anything to change or to add to what you have said?

A: No, I don't.

This is to certify that I have read the transcript of my deposition taken on and that the transcript accurately reflects the questions asked and my answers.

SIGNATURE: *Anika S. Barkwood*

Subscribed and sworn to before me on November 15, [YR-1].

Sally Walker

Sally Walker
Certified Shorthand Reporter

Receipt for Funeral Expenses

Wondercare Funeral Services

»«

3456 Silent Acres Blvd

San Milano, State of Lone Star

»«

We Care Because You Care

INVOICE

Casket	$ 5,500.00
Funeral director's basic services fee	$ 2,500.00
Embalming and body preparation	$ 800.00
Funeral ceremony and viewing	$ 2,000.00
Miscellaneous (hearse, death certificates, obituary, etc.)	$ 1,200.00
Rental for Chapel	$ 500.00
Flowers	$ 300.00
Printing Expenses	$ 120.00
Internment Expenses (opening and closing grave)	$ 3000.00
Miscellaneous Expenses	$ 450.00
TOTAL	**$ 16,370.00**

PAID IN FULL (Check # 1890)

Thanks for your prompt payment, Ms.Barkwood. Please let us know if we can serve you in any other way.

Jon Wilson, Funeral Director

Receipt for Counseling Expenses

Office of Dr. Allan D. Wellbeshire
The Wellbeshire Group

54678 Unity Blvd
San Milano, State of Lone Star

Invoice for Professional Counseling Services

Patient: **Anika S. Barkwood**

Service	**Hourly Rate**	**Total Due**
67 hours of counseling	$ 450.00/hr	$ 30,150.00

If you have any questions about this invoice, please call us at 123-555-7890. Thank you.

Paid

DEPOSITION OF DEFENDANT BARKWOOD

ORAL DEPOSITION OF MR. DON BARKWOOD, produced as a witness at the instance of the Plaintiff, ANIKA STOTWARD BARKWOOD, and duly sworn, was taken in the above-styled and numbered cause on November 1, [YR-1], from 10:00 a.m., to 12:10 p.m., before Wanda Wilson, Certified Shorthand, Reporter in and for the State of Lone Star, reported by machine shorthand, at the law offices of Plaintiff, pursuant to the Lone Star Rules of Civil Procedure and the Provisions stated on the record or attached hereto.

This is a deposition of DON BARKWOOD, who having been sworn, testified as follows:

EXAMINATION QUESTIONS BY PLAINTIFF'S COUNSEL:

Q: Good morning, Mr. Barkwood. We are here to take your testimony about the lawsuit that has been filed against you by your ex-wife. Do you understand that?

A: Yes.

Q: And if you have any questions as we go along today, please stop me if you have any concerns about my questions.

A: All right.

Q: For the record, would you please state your full name.

A: Don Barkwood.

Q: Where do you live, Mr. Barkwood?

A: Here in San Milano, Lone Star.

Q: And what is your current occupation?

A: I work in management at a local Walmart Store. I formerly practiced law. I was board certified in civil litigation.

Q: You no longer practice law?

A: No. After my daughter's death I felt really bad and voluntarily ceased practicing law — at least for now. So, technically I am still licensed but my certification in civil litigation has lapsed.

Q: Were you ever disciplined by the State Bar?

A: No.

Q: You were married to Anika Barkwood?

A: Yes.

Q: How many children do you have?

A: We used to have two — Tiffany and Sissy. I had two daughters, Tiffany and Sissy, both teenagers. Tiffany died of a drug overdose. Sissy is now living with her mother and will not talk to me.

Q: I am here to talk to you about how and why your daughter died. First, do you know Johnny Woods?

A: Yes, at the time my daughter died, he was one of her teachers.

Q: And you discovered what you believed was an inappropriate relationship.

A: Yes.

Q: How did you discover that?

A: In March, [YR-2], I was using the family computer and noticed that my daughter Tiffany was getting e-mails from what appeared to be her high school. At first I thought she was in some sort of trouble at school so I opened one of them and was shocked to see that it was a love note from one of her teachers, Johnny Woods. I had never met him before.

Q: Okay.

A: So, in the e-mail he said that he could not wait to see her again and that it was important to keep their friendship private or he could get fired. I was really angry and afraid for my family. I viewed Woods as a predator. My first thought was to confront my daughter but I decided to print out the e-mail and wait a few more days to see if any more came through.

Q: What did you do next?

A: The next day I found another e-mail in which he mentioned something about taking pills. I also found several e-mails that she had sent to him. I could tell that she was involved. I printed off his e-mail and her responses and then confronted her.

Q: What did she say, or do?

A: She started crying and said that nothing had happened, that they were just really good friends, and that he understood her. She said that he had gotten some of his wife's anti-depressant pills to help with her depression. Tiffany had had chronic depression problems for several years. She begged me not to say or do anything, that she would take care of it, and that if I did anything that she would not be able to live with herself. I comforted her and said not to worry that I would do the right thing. I did not say anything to my wife or other daughter. I needed to work this out with the least amount of trauma to my family.

Q: You said that she had problems with depression?

A: Yes.

Q: So, you knew that she was fragile in her emotional life?

A: I did not say that. I said that she had problems with depression. She was a very strong-willed person. Stubborn, if you will.

Q: So what did you do?

A: After thinking about this problem, on April 14th, about a month later, I prepared a request or petition with the local district court to take a pre-suit deposition of Woods. This is a little-known tool in the rules of civil procedure. I believe it is Lone Star Civil Rule 202.

Q: What made you think of using that procedure?

A: Well, I know the rules of procedure very well, or at least I did at the time, and that rule gives a party a chance to see if there is really any need to file a suit and potentially avoid nasty discovery. My thought was to pursue the possibility of filing a civil suit against Woods and to take his statement under oath. I was really embarrassed by this whole thing so I typed up the documents myself, without involving my secretary or staff. I was trying to protect Tiffany.

Q: You have to admit that this whole procedure sounds rather strange to the average attorney.

A: Well, it's not used very often. I talked with a law professor at State University School of Law, who specialized in civil procedure, and she said that it sounded like I was doing everything according to the book. Her name was Professor Starnes, I believe. I think I talked to her during the first week in April.

Q: So, what happened next?

A: I served Woods with notice of the deposition hearing, as required by the rule of procedure, and he immediately called me on the phone on about April 18th and begged me to settle the matter out of court and that he had some money if that is what it took. I don't remember the exact time he called me.

Q: Did you ever meet with him or discuss this issue?

A: Yes, I met him at a local restaurant the next day and told him I was concerned about my daughters and that he could get in a lot of trouble if he did not stop what he was doing and got some professional help. He said he was really sorry and that this was all a big misunderstanding and that he had never done this sort of thing before. I guess at a couple of points I got pretty emotional and started to cry at one point. I just could not stand the thought of my daughter being with this guy. He reminded me of a slick salesman. I do not remember saying anything about going to the police. I suppose in hindsight that would have been okay, too. But I did learn later that Woods had done this sort of thing at least two other times at different schools out of state. But each time the charges were dropped when he agreed to resign and not seek a teaching job in that city.

Q: Did you reach an agreement?

A: Yes. We agreed on the settlement of $60,000 that he would pay over six months. The first payment would be for $20,000. I told him that a friend of mine, Jordan Thompson, was working with a cancer foundation for children and that the money would be deposited there. I did not really need the cash and wanted to do some good with the money from this guy. I figured his actions would someday help a sick kid. He said he would need a week or so to get the money so we set up a meeting in a public place, at his request. I think we met on April 25th at the Lone Tree Hotel, in the lobby. Everything was above board and we shook hands after he gave me the money. It was in cash.

Q: What did you do with the money he gave you?

A: I wrote a $20,000 check to the Children's Cancer Foundation, as recommended by my friend, Thompson.

Q: But the money did not stay with the foundation, did it?

A: No. A week later, I think it was May 2nd or May 3rd, Thompson called and said that the foundation was in real trouble for mismanagement of funds and that I should request the money back fast. So I called the foundation, said that I had changed my mind and wanted my money back. I did not tell them about my conversation with Thompson. They sent it back to me, minus a $5,000 transfer fee or finders' fee, or something like that. They told me to make the check payable to Thompson. I did not really question it because I did not want to make a stink. I just wanted my money back.

Q: What did you do with the money you got back from the foundation?

A: I took the 20,000 dollars and deposited it in my personal bank account until I could decide what to do with it. I thought I would look for another foundation. I did buy a new car a few days later but there was absolutely no connection between that money and the money I paid for the car. I paid cash. I think it was for $30,000 or something like that. It was a Nissan.

Q: I want to ask you some questions about what happened to your daughter after this. What was her reaction to your deal with Woods?

A: Several days later, my daughter, Tiffany, sent me an e-mail on my office e-mail saying that if I did not stop harassing Woods that she would commit suicide. I e-mailed her back and told her that she was exaggerating things and that we would talk when I got home. I found out later that shortly after she got my e-mail she took the drugs that Woods had given to her. She died a day later. My wife kicked me out of the house.

Q: So, after she sent you an e-mail threatening suicide, you did not rush home?

A: No.

Q: How long was it before you went home that day?

A: I cannot remember exactly. Maybe an hour or so.

Q: So, although you knew that Tiffany had problems, you delayed going home that day.

A: Not really. I hold Woods personally responsible for Tiffany's death. Of course I knew that she had problems with depression. We had made arrangements for her to see a school counselor several months ago to talk about her problems with classes and other things. I think the name of the counselor was Gonzales, or something like that. But neither my wife nor I would have ever guessed how bad it was. I feel really sorry about what happened.

I had only the best intentions for protecting my family from Woods. It's not fair that now I get stuck with the responsibility for all of this. You know Tiffany had two parents — my wife is also responsible for what happened.

Q: Why do you say that?

A: Well she was out shopping when Tiffany died. She could have helped her just as easily as I could have.

Q: But your ex-wife did not harass Woods, Tiffany's friend, did she?

A: No. I think she just did not care about that whole thing. She knew what was going on and just blocked it out.

Q: Did you know if Tiffany had any other boyfriends?

A: No, not that I know of.

Q: That is all of the questions I have right now. Do you have anything you would like to correct or add?

A: No.

This is to certify that I have read the transcript of my deposition taken on and that the transcript accurately reflects the questions asked and my answers.

SIGNATURE: Don Barkwood

Subscribed and sworn to before me on November 24 [YR-1].

Wanda Wilson

Wanda Wilson
Certified Shorthand Recorder

DEPOSITION TESTIMONY OF JOHNNY WOODS

ORAL DEPOSITION OF MR. JOHNNY WOODS, produced as a witness at the instance of the Plaintiff, ANIKA STOTWARD BARKWOOD, and duly sworn, was taken in the above-styled and numbered cause on November 5, [YR-1], from 9:00 a.m., to 10:00 am, before Wanda Wilson, Certified Shorthand, Reporter in and for the State of Lone Star, reported by machine shorthand, at the law offices of Plaintiff, pursuant to the Lone Star Rules of Civil Procedure and the Provisions stated on the record or attached hereto.

This is a deposition of JOHNNY WOODS, who having been sworn, testified as follows:

EXAMINATION
QUESTIONS BY PLAINTIFF'S COUNSEL:

Q: Good morning, Mr. Woods.

A: Good morning.

Q: If you have any problems with my questions, please interrupt me. I am sure that you have been told to do so by your attorney, right?

A: Yes, I understand.

Q: Would you please state your name for the record?

A: Yes, my name is Johnny L. Woods.

Q: Okay. Mr. Woods, I would like you to tell us about your contact with Mr. Don Barkwood in April of [YR-2].

A: I got an official notice in the mail, the second week in April, that Mr. Barkwood wanted to take my deposition and that the court would hold a hearing on whether he could take my deposition. I figured it had to do with his daughter Tiffany, who was in one of my history classes at the time.

Q: What happened?

A: I called him to see what he wanted and he was really, really angry.

Q: What day was that?

A: It was April 18th. He started cursing me and telling me that I was going to have to pay dearly for interfering with his little girl. I also got angry back at him and told him that he had emotionally abused his daughter and that I had simply been there to help her through some really tough emotional times. I told him that nothing had happened.

Q: What happened next?

A: Well, he called me a slimy SOB, or something like that, and hung up. But not more than 30 seconds later he called me and apologized for losing his temper and said he wanted to set up a time to take my deposition.

Q: So what was your relationship with Tiffany?

A: Well, we had talked several times after class, and once in my van. I think I may have given her a small kiss on her cheek to comfort her. She just needed someone to talk to. She kept telling me that her parents were preoccupied with their activities and never listened to her.

Q: So, what happened next in your conversation with Mr. Barkwood?

A: I tried to calm down as well and told him that I hoped we could settle this matter. He wanted to know if I had a lawyer and I said no. He said that was okay because he was a lawyer and could work up any agreement between us to settle the matter out of court.

Q: What happened next?

A: Well we agreed to meet at the Lone Star Grill, which is a few blocks from his law office, the next day.

Q: Did you meet with him?

A: Yes.

Q: What day was that?

A: April 19th, I believe.

Q: Tell us about that meeting.

A: Well, he told me that he intended to take my deposition, under oath, to determine if he had a possible civil suit against me for what I had done to his daughter.

Q: So what were you thinking at this point?

A: I was beginning to think that this might be a shakedown when I asked him if he had talked to the police and he said no, he had not. He said that if I cooperated that we could make the whole thing go away. He said that he did not trust the police to do the right thing and that it was in both of our interests not to involve them, at this point. So I felt like I really did not have a choice.

Q: Did he say what would happen if you did not cooperate?

A: Yes, he said he would make my life hell and see to it that I never taught again and that they would put me under the jail for what I had done. He said that he had friends at the newspaper in the city.

Q: Did you feel threatened by his comments to you?

A: Absolutely. Yes, very much so.

Q: What led you to believe that he would do what he said?

A: Well, first, as I just said, he was really determined. And I guess I can understand why he would feel that way. But he did not appear at first to even want to settle this thing.

Q: So, let's get this straight. Who first raised the issue about settling the matter out of court?

A: I guess I did. I, ah. Well. . . . .let me put it this way. I figured that he really would cause me major problems and I had heard about settling cases out of court so that you could avoid all of the expense and other problems of going to court. So, I guess . . .

Q: So, you . . .

A: I guess, I . . .

Q: I am sorry to interrupt you, please continue.

A: I guess I hoped that we could work out something.

Q: When you told him that you hoped something could be worked out, what did he say?

A: It was interesting. He did not say anything at first, he got kinda quiet, but then he said something like, "Well I had hoped you would say that." Just like he was setting me up or something.

Q: What do you mean?

A: Well, the tone of his voice changed, pretty quickly, and he said that although he wanted to see me pay, he also wanted to protect his little girl, I think that is what he called her. She hated that when he called her his little girl.

Q: Who hated that?

A: Tiffany.

Q: What happened next, Mr. Woods?

A: He said that he had a dollar amount in mind, which I found also interesting because he did not even hesitate. Nor did he ask me what my proposal was. He sort of gave me his terms as though he had figured it all out.

Q: Go ahead.

A: He told me that a good friend of his, I believe someone named Thompson or Thomasson, something like that, worked for a private foundation for kids with terminal cancer and that he had been thinking about making a donation. He said that the money I gave him would be put to good use, to help someone dying of cancer. In my mind, that seemed like a reasonable proposition. He said that this would be a way to redeem myself. He said that I would give him the money, in cash, and that he would then write a check in that amount to the foundation. He said that it would be better if the foundation did not know about me and start asking questions about why I was so interested in helping them out or asking me for more money.

Q: So what amount did you agree on?

A: I am not sure there was any real agreement. He said, the cost to me, and I believe he used those words, would be $60,000.

Q: What did you say?

A: At first I did not say anything. I think I may have said something like, "I need to think about it." And then he said that the offer was going to be good for about 30 seconds or something like that.

Q: So, what happened?

A: I told him okay. By this point in our talk, I had pretty well figured out that there was not going to be any real negotiation. The way I saw it, he was either going to get that money or I was going to lose my job, and maybe my family. So I agreed. But I quickly said that I did not have that kind of money handy and asked if I could pay it out in three equal installments.

Q: Did he agree?

A: Yes, he said that I could do that. But that he wanted the $20,000 as soon as possible so he could give it to the foundation to get Thompson off his back. So we agreed to meet several days later. I explained the situation to my wife who at first told me that I had done nothing wrong and that I should turn Barkwood into the police. But I finally convinced her that he was a real threat, he was a lawyer who seemed to have everything in his favor.

Q: What happened next? Did you pay him the money?

A: Yes, we met at the Lone Tree Hotel here in the city on April 25th. We met in the lobby and I gave him the money in cash — which he demanded — and then he got up and left.

Q: Did you shake hands or anything?

A: No. After I gave him the money, he started to count it. He said that it had been a pleasure doing business with me, that he would contact me in another month or so to get the next installment and then got up quickly and left.

Q: What was his demeanor like during this meeting?

A: Well, he seemed pretty cocky and confident.

Q: Did he say anything else?

A: Oh yes, he said that I should keep the whole thing quiet or that he would have to raise the stakes.

Q: Did you have any more contact with him?

A: No. After he left I went home and told my wife what had happened. I then called our minister and set up a counseling session where I could talk about all of this. But that did not work out and we never talked.

Q: So other than your wife, did you tell anyone else about what Barkwood had done?

A: No.

Q: Now, I draw your attention to several weeks later, when you heard about Tiffany dying. What happened?

A: Well, I was pretty upset. I showed up at the school one morning and girls were crying out in the hallway. I asked them what happened and they said that Tiffany had died during the night of an overdose of drugs. I went to my office and when I turned on my computer I noticed that she had sent me an e-mail.

Q: What did the e-mail say?

A: It said that she was tired of living, that she had a pretty good idea of what her father had done to me and that she had just taken some pills. She said that she had e-mailed her dad but that he had e-mailed her back, calling her a "drama queen," and just like her mother who always wanted attention. She blamed her father for her problems and said that finally, maybe he would pay attention to her.

Q: So, what did you do when you read the e-mail?

A: I immediately called a lawyer who set up a meeting with the police. We met with them and said we would help them get Barkwood for killing his daughter and stealing money from me, if they would grant me some protection against prosecution.

Q: Now, I need to ask you about your relationship with Tiffany. You testified earlier that you were trying to help her work things out with her parents?

A: Yes.

Q: You provided some drugs to her, didn't you? Anti-depressant drugs?

A: Yes.

Q: Were they prescription drugs?

A: Yes.

Q: Where did you get them?

A: I got them from my wife's medicine cabinet when she was not looking.

Q: What drugs were they?

A: Zoloft.

Q: Zoloft?

A: Yes.

Q: Why would you give Tiffany those pills?

A: I was just trying to help her. She told me that she was already taking some anti-depressants but that they did not seem to do the job. So I gave her maybe 10 or 15 pills over the period of about a month.

Q: Did you receive any money from Tiffany for those drugs?

A: No.

Q: Did you ever have any sexual relations with Tiffany?

A: Absolutely not. I respected her too much to do something like that.

Q: Did she ever tell you that she had a boyfriend?

A: No.

Q: Did she ever tell you that she might be pregnant?

A: No.

Q: In your prior jobs, have you ever had similar things like this happen before, I mean, getting really friendly with your students?

A: Yes. Well, maybe not. I am not sure.

Q: Please explain that.

A: Well, several years ago I was teaching at a high school out of state, in Nevada. I had one student who I think had a real crush on me and when it got to the point where it was uncomfortable I told her that I was married and that she had to stop e-mailing me. My wife had found out about it. We went through counseling and when that leaked out the school board gave me an ultimatum. They said either resign and leave the school district or get fired.

Q: So, did you resign?

A: Yes. But I should have stayed and fought it. The girl clearly had mental problems and I am confident that a jury would have sided with me.

Q: Other than that time did it happen ever again?

A: Yes. At my next job, another student made a pass at me at a football game. I guess I just have lousy luck. I can't believe it.

Q: A female student?

A: Yes.

Q: One of your students?

A: Yes.

Q: So what happened in that case?

A: Well, this time the girl's mother demanded a payment. I refused. She called my wife and my wife said that for some reason I was a magnet for confused young women and that we needed to leave again. So, I resigned mid-term and moved here. Everything was fine until about six months ago when I met Tiffany. This time, my wife knew that I was meeting Tiffany to counsel her.

A: Did your wife know about the drugs you gave to Tiffany?

Q: No, she did not. And I regret that. She knows now. Thankfully, she has forgiven me for my problems. She knows that I was trying to help this poor girl.

Q: Did you ever give any other money to Mr. Barkwood?

A: No. I only gave him the $20,000.

Q: Do you know what he did with the money you gave him?

A: No, not really. I assumed he gave the money to his friend's foundation. But it would not surprise me if you told me that he had used the money for himself. That is the sort of guy his daughter said he was. He was very manipulative.

Q: Is there anything else you would like to say or correct in your testimony today?

A: Just a minute. [Witness confers with counsel] Yes, I want to make it clear that I was not a predator in this case. I feel terrible about what happened.

(END OF TRANSCRIPT)

This is to certify that I have read the transcript of my deposition taken on and that the transcript accurately reflects the questions asked and my answers.

SIGNATURE: Johnny Woods

Subscribed and sworn to before me on December 12, [YR-1].

Wanda Wilson

Wanda Wilson
Certified Shorthand Reporter

Deposition Testimony of Jordan Thompson

ORAL DEPOSITION OF JORDAN THOMPSON, produced as a witness at the instance of the Plaintiff, ANIKA STOTWARD BARKWOOD, and duly sworn, was taken in the above-styled and numbered cause on November 7, [YR-1], from 11:00 a.m., to 11:46 a.m., before Wanda Wilson, Certified Shorthand Reporter in and for the State of Lone Star, reported by machine shorthand, at the law offices of Plaintiff, pursuant to the Lone Star Rules of Civil Procedure and the Provisions stated on the record or attached hereto.

This is a deposition of JORDAN THOMPSON, who having been sworn, testified as follows:

EXAMINATION
QUESTIONS BY PLAINTIFF'S COUNSEL:

Q: For the record will you please state your full name?

A: Jordan S. Thompson.

Q: I want to be sure that we are clear that if you have any questions about my questions, that you will let me know, so that I can clarify my questions. Okay?

A: Yes.

Q: What is your current employment?

A: I am in transition, between jobs.

Q: Are you familiar with the Children's Cancer Foundation?

A: Yes.

Q: How are you familiar with that organization?

A: I used to work there as a fundraiser. Actually, I worked there from about July [YR-3] until just recently, June 12th of [YR-1], to be exact.

Q: Why are you no longer there?

A: They found out that I was connected with Don Barkwood.

Q: So you know Don Barkwood?

A: Sure. Yes, I do.

Q: How do you know him?

A: Well we have known each other for about 10 years.

Q: Are you friends.

A: Some might say that.

Q: Let me repeat the question. Are you friends?

A: Yes.

Q: Did you ever recommend to Mr. Barkwood that he give some money to the foundation that you worked for?

A: I did. Don is a wonderful person, a great husband and loving father, with a big heart. I knew that he had the money and that he would make a difference by giving to the foundation.

Q: Did you ever suggest a particular dollar amount?

A: No.

Q: When did you last talk to him about giving to the foundation?

A: Sometime last year.

Q: I draw your attention to April or May, [YR-2]. Did Mr. Barkwood talk to you about making a donation?

A: Yes, he did.

Q: How did that come up?

A: Well, he said that he had found a donor and that he thought he could come up with about 20,000 dollars.

Q: What was your reaction?

A: I was thrilled. Things had been a bit tough on fundraising this last year and I needed to show some donations.

Q: What would have happened if you did not come up with some donors?

A: Well in this business it means you lose your job.

Q: Did he come up with the money?

A: Yes.

Q: Did he tell you the name of his donor?

A: No. And it was not important to me. I trust Don and I believed that everything was on the up and up.

Q: But you did not ask him to give you the name of the donor? That would have been helpful to you, wouldn't it?

A: Not really. I simply listed Don as the donor. Where he got it from was not all that critical to me.

Q: So what happened to his donation?

A: He wrote me a check for $20,000 and I deposited it in our account.

Q: When was that?

A: April 26th. [Pause] Yes, April 26th.

Q: Did that money stay in the account?

A: No. About two weeks later I learned that the foundation was being investigated for fraud and I told Don I felt bad about his donation.

Q: What did he say?

A: He was pretty upset and said he wanted his money back. So I talked to my boss and told him that my donor had had cold feet and wanted his money back. So he said okay.

Q: What happened next?

A: I got a check cut for Don from the foundation.

Q: And when did you do that?

A: Hmmm. May 3rd.

Q: For how much?

A: $20,000.

Q: And did you give it to him?

A: Yes.

Q: We have banking records showing that you deposited $5,000 in your personal account on May 4th and that the check was written by a "D. Barkwood"?

A: Yes.

Q: What was that all about? Could you explain that?

A: Well, Don figured that I was about to lose my job and decided to loan me the $5,000.

Q: Did you ask him for the money?

A: I do not recall whether I asked him or he volunteered it.

Q: Have you paid him back?

A: Not yet.

Q: Have you worked out a repayment plan with Mr. Barkwood?

A: No. He told me that he knew I was good for the money.

Q: You testified earlier that you lost your job with the foundation?

A: Yes, about a month after I helped Don get his money back.

Q: Do you know a Mr. Johnny Woods?

A: Yes.

Q: How do you know him?

A: We shared some of the same friends in college.

Q: Were you friends at the time?

A: Yes.

Q: Are you friends now?

A: Absolutely not.

Q: Why not?

A: Well, during our senior year I found out that he was cheating on his girlfriend, now his wife. I told her about it, she told him, he pushed me down, put a nasty scar on my forehead and said he never wanted to see me again.

Q: How many years ago was that?

A: 5 years ago.

Q: Have you had any contact since then?

A: No.

Q: You sound upset about it.

A: So?

Q: Are you?

A: Yes, I guess so. Johnny Woods is a real loser and both he and his wife can both rot in hell for all I care.

Q: Did you know that he was the donor that Don Barkwood had lined up for you?

A: I believe he told me just recently that that was the connection.

Q: What did he say to you about it?

A: He said that he had found out that Woods was messing with his daughter but that they had reached an amicable financial settlement that he was ready to put the whole thing behind him. He said that Woods had gotten his due.

Q: How did you feel about that?

A: As I said, I figure that Woods was rotten and that Barkwood did the right thing. And if kids get helped as a result, well then I think that is a good thing. I would believe Barkwood over Woods.

Q: Is there anything you would like to add to your testimony?

A: [Confers with counsel] No, nothing more to add.

(END OF TRANSCRIPT)

This is to certify that I have read the transcript of my deposition taken on and that the transcript accurately reflects the questions asked and my answers.

SIGNATURE: Jordan S. Thompson

Subscribed and sworn to before me on December 13, [YR-1].

Wanda Wilson

Wanda Wilson
Certified Shorthand Reporter

Deposition Testimony of Pat Gonzales

ORAL DEPOSITION OF PAT GONZALES, produced as a witness at the instance of the Plaintiff, ANIKA STOTWARD BARKWOOD, and duly sworn, was taken in the above-styled and numbered cause on November 6, [YR-1], from 2:00 p.m. to 3:00 p.m., before Wanda Wilson, Certified Shorthand, Reporter in and for the State of Lone Star, reported by machine shorthand, at the law offices of Plaintiff, pursuant to the Lone Star Rules of Civil Procedure and the Provisions stated on the record or attached hereto.

This is a deposition of PAT GONZALES, who having been sworn, testified as follows:

EXAMINATION
QUESTIONS BY PLAINTIFF'S COUNSEL:

Q: Hello.

A: Good afternoon.

Q: Before I ask you any questions, I want to the record to reflect that I informed you that if you have any doubt about my questions or want me to clarify anything, that you stop me so that I can do that. Is that clear?

A: Yes, it's clear.

Q: Good. Please state your name for the record.

A: Pat Gonzales.

Q: What is your occupation?

A: I am a school counselor at the Wayland Heights High School.

Q: How long have you worked there?

A: About eight years.

Q: Are you licensed to perform work as a counselor.

A: Not yet. I am going through that process now.

Q: How is that you were hired by the school without being certified?

A: They needed someone badly and took me on, on a sort of probationary status.

Q: Do you have any experience as a counselor?

A: Oh yes. I have served as a counselor for almost 10 years. For several years in a drug rehab program as a facilitator. And for another several years working in a retirement home as a facilitator in weekly discussion groups.

Q: So what sort of counseling do you perform?

A: It's limited obviously. But I can talk to students, provide a listening ear, and then provide reports to my supervisors who are licensed and certified by the state.

Q: Do you know Tiffany Barkwood?

A: I did know her. She committed suicide.

Q: How did she die?

A: She overdosed on anti-depressants.

Q: Had you counseled her?

A: Yes, for almost a year.

Q: Can you tell us what she said?

A: I am not sure I can. I think everything she told me specifically is privileged.

Q: We have spoken to her mother who has filled out a consent form that releases you from the privilege.

A: May I see that?

Q: Certainly. [Counsel shows the properly authorized consent to the witness]

A: All right. Good. [Witness paused] Okay. Okay. [Witness confers with counsel]

Q: So, please continue.

A: Tiffany had a lot of problems. First, she told me that her main problem was getting her folks to listen to her. She was particularly upset by the fact that her father never listened to her and always wrote her off as being, in his words, a drama queen. Second, she had a history of depression and she said that she was, or had been, on a variety of anti-depressants.

Q: Did she say what she was taking?

A: Zoloft, I believe.

Q: Did you give her any prescription drugs?

A: Absolutely not. She showed me the pills she was taking though. As I said, she was using Zoloft, a relatively common anti-depressant.

Q: What other problems did she exhibit?

A: Well, on top of it all, she told me about three months ago that she had found a guy who listened to her and that he was really helping her. She said that he had even given her some Zoloft. I was really shocked by that and told her that she needed to see a physician to have that cleared. That she might take too many at once.

Q: What did she say when you told her that?

A: She laughed nervously and said she knew that. And then she asked me if I had ever thought about committing suicide. I told her I had not and she said she had and that her dad was going to someday push her over the edge. She said that she had told him that several times and each time she did, he told her to go away and quick being, as I said before, a drama queen.

Q: Did she ever identify the guy she said was helping her?

A: No. Not exactly, but I later found out that it was her teacher, Johnny Woods.

Q: Do you know him?

A: Barely.

Q: Did you ever prepare a memo on your conclusions about Tiffany?

A: Yes. I had prepared a memo just a few days before she killed herself.

Q: Is this it? [Counsel shows exhibit to witness]

A: Yes, that is the one I prepared.

Q: On the memo, there is a handwritten notation that says, "suicide." Is that your handwriting?

A: Yes. I added that to the file when I heard she had died. I knew in my heart before the medical examiner released his report that she had probably committed suicide.

Q: You did not write that word on there until after Tiffany died?

A: No, why would I have written it beforehand?

Q: Well, that is what I am asking.

A: I wrote it after she died. She was depressed but I am not a fortune teller.

Q: But you said that you suspected or believed that she had committed suicide. Why did you just say that?

A: Just a day before she died, she called me to say that her father had found about her "guy" and that he was going to try and get some money out of him to pay for a new car. I asked her how she knew, and she said that she had overheard her dad talking to a car dealership and said that he expected to come into some money and to hold the car for him.

Q: Did you verify that?

A: No.

Q: What else did she say?

A: She said that she was going to give her dad an ultimatum and that if he did not back off from going after her guy, that she would end it all herself. Then she started sobbing and hung up.

Q: What did you do?

A: I immediately reported this to my supervisor who called and left messages with her parents. I don't think he ever got in touch with them. We learned the next day that she had died. This has really hit the school very hard. I hold her father directly responsible for her death.

Q: Did she say whether she had ever had sexual relations with Mr. Woods?

A: She did not say and I did not ask.

Q: Did she ever tell you that she was pregnant?

A: No. That subject did not come up. And it's not the kind of question I would feel comfortable asking.

Q: Is there anything else you would like to add to your testimony today?

A: No, I don't think so.

(END OF TRANSCRIPT)

This is to certify that I have read the transcript of my deposition taken on and that the transcript accurately reflects the questions asked and my answers.

SIGNATURE: Pat Gonzales

Subscribed and sworn to before me on December 16, [YR-1].

Wanda Wilson

Wanda Wilson
Certified Shorthand Reporter

Resume of Pat Gonzales

PAT GONZALES

978 Oak Avenue
San Milano, State of Lone Star 786645

Career Objective

To obtain a challenging position that will allow for growth and a chance to use and contribute my education and job experience.

Summary of Qualifications

Knowledge and ability to work effectively with both Adult and Youth clients; ability to follow instructions both verbally and in writing; ability to maintain confidential case files; PC skills; outstanding organizational and customer service skills.

Work History

[YR-8]-[present]	**Wayland Heights High School** – School Counselor.
[YR-13]-[YR-8]	**San Milano Area Drug Rehab** – San Milano, Lone Star Counselor, Adult and Youth Services Assisting Adult and Youth patients work through their drug problems. Career counseling and planning. Course placement. Degree and occupation exploration. Assist with academic and personal student goal completion. Teacher of student development classes-to include personal and academic success. Time mgt. skills, study skills. Producer of video of occupational and tech. programs to reveal knowledge, skills and abilities for job success. Participated in business and community service to provide information for college enrollment.
[YR-14]-[YR-13]	**Wonderful Life Retirement Home** – San Milano, Lone Star Secretary/Administrative Assistant/Group Discussion Leader Greeting clients; maintaining and creating all active patient files for Psychology Office; providing administrative support to Counselor; preparing correspondence letters and organizing materials for mailings; light typing, data entry and faxing of documents; basic bookkeeping and medical billing of patients; corresponding with various companies regarding verification of company benefits; scoring tests for counselor and typing exams for students; scheduling meetings, running errands, ordering supplies and inventory; setting up appointments for patients, answering and screening telephone calls; holding weekly group discussions for the patients; performing other duties and special projects as assigned.

Education

[YR-16]-[YR-14]	**The University of San Milano** – San Milano, Lone Star Education Level: Masters Degree Major: Counseling GPA: 3.7 Graduated: Yes
[YR-21]-[YR-16]	**City University** – San Milano, Lone Star Education Level: Bachelors Degree Major: Government Minor: Sociology

Autopsy Report of Tiffany Barkwood

Bear County Medical Examiner's Office

1245 MEDICAL BLVD
San Milano. State of Lone Star 792213

AUTOPSY REPORT

Case No. 1612-0398

Name: Tiffany Barkwood **Age:** 17 **Race:** W **Sex:** F

Date & Time of Autopsy: 8 May [YR-2] @ 08:55 a.m.

GENERAL EXAMINATION

The body is received within a body bag and is that of a normally developed, well nourished, adult Caucasian female, 57 ½ inches tall, weighing 120 lbs and appearing consistent with the listed age of 17 years. Accompanying the body, in a plastic bag, are a pair of cut plaid shorts, white t-shirt, white sneakers, one pair of gold earrings, and undergarments.

Detective Randy Carlisle from the Lone Star Police Department is present for the autopsy.

EXTERNAL EXAMINATION

Rigor mortis is fully developed in all joints. Fixed livor mortis is present posteriorly. The decedent has long, blonde hair averaging 10 inches in length. The eyes are closed; the conjunctivae are pale and without petechiae; the sclerae are white; the corneae are clear; and the irides are brown. The nose, ears, and external auditory canals are unremarkable. The mouth is open revealing natural teeth in good condition.

The neck and chest are symmetrical and atraumatic. The abdomen is soft and flat.

The upper and lower extremities are symmetrical and atraumatic. Multiple small irregular scars involve the anterior knees.

The back is straight and free of trauma.

EVIDENCE OF MEDICAL INTERVENTION

An endotracheal tube protrudes from the mouth and is strapped in place. Multiple cardiac monitor pads are present upon the anterior chest and abdomen. Multiple needle puncture wounds involve the left infraclavicular region and left antecubital fossa. A pulse oximeter monitor is present upon the right index finger.

INTERNAL EXAMINATION

HEAD: An intermastoid incision is made around the cranium and the scalp is retracted. Hemorrhage is present. The brain weighs 1,550 gm. The cerebral and cerebellar hemispheres, midbrain and pons are symmetrical and grossly unremarkable. The cerebral vessels follow the usual distribution and are widely patent.

BODY: The body is opened with the Y-shaped incision. The organs occupy their usual positions and relationships. Inspection of the thoracic and abdominal cavities after evisceration reveals no bony or muscular abnormalities.

NECK: There is no evidence of infection, tumor or trauma.

LUNGS: The right lung weighs 360 gm and the left lung weighs 350 gm. The pleural surfaces are purple, smooth and glistening with a scattered black pigmentation present, consistent with mild anthracotic pigment deposition.

CARDIOVASCULAR SYSTEM: The heart weighs 380 gm. The epicardial surface is smooth and glistening. The coronary arteries follow the usual right dominant distribution and are widely patent. The aorta is open and shows occasional fatty streaks.

GASTROINTESTINAL SYSTEM: The tongue is atraumatic. The esophagus is opened to reveal a gray, wrinkly mucosa. The stomach contains a minimal amount of yellow fluid. The stomach mucosa is erythematous and appropriately folded. The small and large bowels reveal no evidence of natural disease. The appendix is present.

LIVER AND BILIARY TRACT: The liver weighs 990 gm. The capsule is smooth and glistening. On cut sections, the parenchyma is tan-brown and firm.

PANCREAS: Unremarkable.

SPLEEN: The spleen weighs 50 gm. The capsule is purple, smooth and glistening.

GENITOURINARY SYSTEM: The right kidney weighs 70 gm and the left kidney weighs 90 gm. The capsules remove without difficulty revealing smooth and shiny cortical surfaces. The bladder is empty.

FINDINGS

A/N DRUG SCREEN
BLOOD, FEMORAL (GC/MS)

ALCOHOLS
BLOOD, FEMORAL (GC)
NONE DETECTED

VITREOUS (GC)
NONE DETECTED

ALKALINE DRUG SCREEN
BLOOD, FERMORAL (GC, GC/MS)
+ ATROPINE
(+) = PRESENT, NO QUANTITATION

COCAINE AND COCAINE METABOLITES
BLOOD, FERMORAL (ELISA)
NONE DETECTED

NARCOTICS
BLOOD, FERMORAL (ELISA)
NONE DETECTED

PREGNANCY
4 WEEKS

CONCLUSION

It is our opinion that Tiffany Barkwood, a 17 year old Caucasian female, died as a result of an overdose of the antidepressant- Zoloft.

MANNER OF DEATH: Overdose.

Lisa D. Bains	JOHN R. RAINY
LISA D. BAINS, M.D. Chief Medical Examiner	**JOHN R. RAINY, M.D.** Medical Examiner

Pat Gonzales' Memo

Wayland Heights High School

San Milano, State of Lone Star
Home of the Hornets

MEMO FOR RECORD

FROM: **Pat Gonzales**
RE: **Tiffany Barkwood**
DATE **May 4, [YR-2]**

I have been counseling Ms. Tiffany Barkwood, a junior here at Wayland Heights for the past six months, as instructed by my department head.

I have held approximately 10 sessions with Tiffany, each lasting about 30 minutes. In addition, I have received, but not sent, e-mails from her over the last several weeks.

Her parents initially asked the school for help when they came to the conclusion in December [YR-3], that she was having mild bouts of depression and seemed increasingly moody. At first they thought it was boy problems, but had decided to seek medical help. A doctor (whose name I do not recall) apparently prescribed low doses of an anti-depressant drug in January. They were Zoloft. Tiffany told me that she did not like using drugs and instead of using them had saved them for a "rainy day" in case she got really depressed. I begged her not to do that.

About a month ago, she came to my office. She started sobbing as she related the fact that her father, Don Barkwood, had found out about a "guy" that she was meeting and that he was threatening to sue him and expose him. She did not say who it was but I suspected that it might be an older boy, perhaps an upper classman. It was hard to understand what legal basis her father was supposedly using. She said that she had begged her father to stop but he told her to quit being overly dramatic, and basically ignored her. Tiffany also said that her mother is also distant and of no help to Tiffany and her problems.

In light of these developments I recommend that the school counselor see Tiffany as soon as possible and see if any additional counseling or help is needed.

I am very concerned about the mental health of this young woman!!

Suicide!!

Banking Records for Thompson

1320

Barkwood
1234 Oak Street
San Milano, State of Lone Star 77777

37-65/1119 54

May 4, [YR-1]

Pay to : Jordon Thompson $ 5000.00

Five Thousand & 00/100 ---------------------------- Dollars

For________________ Don Barkwood

11000111://1 12345634 99882233453

J Thompson

0009 18231
Lone Star Bank
San Milano,
State of Lone Star
Deposited 05/04/[YR-1]

E-mails From Johnny Woods to Tiffany Barkwood

From: jwoods@waylandhts.edu
Sent: Monday, February 26, [YR-2] 12:10 AM
To: Tiffprincess@bol.com
Subject: Hi

I know you are hurting right now. Please just know that I care about you and do not want to do anything that will hurt you. Believe me. You mean a lot to me. Do you need any more pills?

From: jwoods@waylandhts.edu
Sent: Tuesday, February 27, [YR-2] 11:10 PM
To: Tiffprincess@bol.com
Subject: Hi

I miss you too. I can't get away tonight. We need to talk about the "helpers" I have given to you. My wife said something about missing some from her bottle. I said that I had no idea what she was talking about. ☺

From: jwoods@waylandhts.edu
Sent: Monday, March 12, [YR-2] 11:10 PM
To: Tiffprincess@bol.com
Subject: Oops

Be cool Tiffany. I cannot afford to leave another teaching job. My wife will kill me. I will text message when I figure out where we can meet..

E-MAILS FROM TIFFANY BARKWOOD TO JOHNNY WOODS

From: Tiffprincess@bol.com
Sent: Tuesday, February 27, [YR-2] 7:30 AM
To: jwoods@waylandhts.edu
Subject: Hi

I can't live without you. Call me!!!!! My dad and mom may discover us. They don't trust me using the family computer. If they only knew. It serves them right!!!!

From: Tiffprincess@bol.com
Sent: Wednesday, February 28, [YR-2] 7:50 AM
To: jwoods@waylandhts.edu
Subject: Hi

I need to talk to u. Dad is being totally a jerk!! I am really feeling down today. He threatened to stop me from using the family computer. I think he suspects something.

Maybe I will see you after class?

From: Tiffprincess@bol.com
Sent: Monday, March 12, [YR-2] 7:30 AM
To: jwoods@waylandhts.edu
Subject: Oops

I need to see you ASAP. I saw my dad going through my e-mails last night and he started shouting at me. He said that he had been reading my e-mails. I told him that we were just very good friends, right? You are my friend. I miss you. I am going to take a couple of pills before coming to school today.

From: Tiffprincess@bol.com
Sent: Monday, May 7, [YR-2] 4:37 PM
To: jwoods@waylandhts.edu
Subject: Bye

Dad will not stop. He just called me a drama queen. Well I'll give him a little drama. There is no reason to live. I don't think you love me either. I am going to use those pills.

E-MAILS FROM TIFFANY BARKWOOD TO THE DEFENDANT, DON BARKWOOD

From: Tiffprincess@bol.com
Sent: Monday, May 7, [YR-2] 4:30 PM
To: DBarkwood@bol.com
Subject: PLEASE

Daddy, please listen to me. PLEASE. PLEASE. PLEASE. I know everything about what you are doing to Mr. Woods. Please stop, Please stop. Please stop. IF YOU DON'T STOP, I WILL KILL MYSELF. I've got the pills to do it. I have them right here. You know the ones I am talking about. If this thing comes out I cannot live anymore. Johnny cares about me and listens to what I need. Please talk to me!!!!!!

From: Tiffprincess@bol.com
Sent: Monday, May 7, [YR-2] 5:25 PM
To: DBarkwood@bol.com
Subject: PLEASE

Daddy. I love U. I did it. No more crap from you or from mommy. I am getting sleeepey. feelsgode. bye;)

E-mail from the Defendant to Tiffany Barkwood

From: DBarkwood@bol.com
Sent: Monday, May 7, [YR-2] 4:35 PM
To: Tiffprincess@bol.com
Subject: PLEASE

TIFFANY

STOP BEING A DRAMA QUEEN. I AM ONLY DOING THIS FOR YOU AND SISSY. THIS GUY DESERVES TO FRY. AND I AM GOING TO LIGHT THE FIRE. TRUST ME, YOU WILL THANK ME SOME DAY. I HAVE ONE MORE MEETING HERE AT THE OFFICE AND THEN I AM COMING HOME. DON'T DO ANYTHING STUPID. CALL YOUR MOTHER AND TELL HER I AM RUNNING LATE. WE WILL TALK WHEN I GET HOME.

DAD

E-mail from Tiffany Barkwood to Pat Gonzales

From: Tiffprincess@bol.com
Sent: Monday, May 7, [YR-2] 4:55 PM
To: Pgonzales@.waylandhts.edu
Subject: Thanks

Thanks for your help. This is not your fault. You tried to help me and I wanted to thank you. It's my dad's fault. But you know that. I just e-mailed him saying that I was going to kill myself. He knows I will do it. I tried it a year ago and they stopped me. Now he does not care. He just called me a drama queen. So its drama he will get. My mom is out shopping with friends, so she is not much help either.

I need to leave for now. Gotta find those pills.

Thanks.

Jury Instructions

LADIES AND GENTLEMEN OF THE JURY:

I am now going to instruct you about the law governing this case. You are required to accept my instructions as the law. Any ideas you have of what the law is or what the law should be or any statements by the attorneys as to what the law may be must be disregarded by you if they are in conflict with these instructions.

1. Claims of Parties

The plaintiff claims that she sustained damages due to the defendant's negligence in letting their daughter commit suicide. The defendant has denied those claims and also denies that the plaintiff is entitled to recover any damages.

2. Burden of Proof

In this case, the plaintiff has the burden of proving her claims by a preponderance of the evidence. If you find from the evidence, by a preponderance of the evidence, that the defendant acted negligently in regards to responding to his daughter's communications asking for help, and that such negligence was the proximate cause of his daughter's death, then you must find the defendant liable for his negligence.

3. Negligence

When I use the word "negligence" in these instructions, I mean the failure to do something which a reasonably careful person would do, or the doing of something which a reasonably careful person would not do, under circumstances similar to those shown by the evidence. The law does not say how a reasonably careful person would act under those circumstances. It is for you to decide whether the defendant used reasonable care in dealing with his daughter.

4. Reasonable Care & Foreseeability

In determining whether reasonable care has been exercised, you will consider whether the defendant ought to have foreseen, under the attending circumstances, that the natural and probable consequence of his act or omission to act would have been some injury. It is not necessary that the defendant have anticipated the very occurrence which resulted from his wrongdoing but it is sufficient that it was within the realm of foreseeability that some harm might occur thereby. The test is the probable and foreseeable consequences that may reasonably be anticipated from the performance, or the failure to perform, a particular act. If an ordinary person, under similar circumstances and by the use of ordinary care, could have foreseen the result, for example, that some injury or damage would probably result, and either would not have acted or, if he/she did act, would have taken precaution to avoid the result, then the performance of the act or the failure to take such precautions would constitute negligence.

5. Proximate Cause

When I use the expression "proximate cause," I mean a cause that, in the natural or ordinary course of events, produced the plaintiff's injury. It need not be the only cause, nor the last or nearest cause. It is sufficient if it combines with another cause resulting in the injury.

6. Preponderance of the Evidence

The term "preponderance of the evidence" means that amount of evidence that causes you to conclude that the allegation is probably true. To prove an allegation by the preponderance of the evidence, a party must convince you that the allegation is more likely true than not true.

If the evidence on a particular issue is equally balanced, that issue has not been proven by a preponderance of the evidence. Therefore, the party having the burden of proving that issue has failed with respect to that particular issue.

7. Circumstantial Evidence

A fact or a group of facts may, based on logic and common sense, lead you to a conclusion as to other facts. This is known as circumstantial evidence. A fact may be proved by circumstantial evidence. Circumstantial evidence is entitled to the same consideration as any other type of evidence

8. Opinion Testimony

You may have heard a witness give opinions about matters requiring special knowledge or skill. You should judge this testimony in the same way you judge the testimony from any other witness. The fact that such person has given an opinion does not mean that you are required to accept it. Give the testimony whatever weight you think it deserves, considering the reasons given for the opinion, the witness's qualifications, and all of the other evidence in the case.

9. Credibility of Witnesses

It is up to you to decide the credibility of the witnesses. In making the decision you may consider such factors as whether the witness has made a prior inconsistent statement or has been convicted of a crime. Evidence of this kind may be considered by you in connection with all the other facts and circumstances in evidence in deciding the weight to be given to the testimony of that witness.

10. Damages

a. Damages

If you decide the plaintiff is entitled to damages, you shall give such amount as you decide to be fair and just, under all the circumstances, to those persons represented in this case. Such damages may include the following items, to the extent you find they have been proved by the evidence:

- Reasonable medical, hospital, funeral and burial expenses;
- Reasonable compensation for the pain and suffering undergone by the decedent while she was conscious during the time between her injury and her death;

- Loss of financial support;
- Loss of gifts or other valuable gratuities;
- Loss of parental training and guidance;
- Loss of companionship;
- Plaintiff's grief, sorrow, or mental anguish.

Whether the plaintiff has proved these damages is for you to decide, based upon evidence and not upon speculation, guess, or conjecture. The amount of money to be awarded for certain of these elements of damage cannot be proved in a precise dollar amount. The law leaves such amounts to your sound judgment.

b. Punitive Damages

If you find for the plaintiff, you may, but are not required to, award punitive damages. The purposes of punitive damages are to punish a defendant and to deter similar acts in the future. Punitive damages may not be awarded to compensate a plaintiff.

The plaintiff has the burden of proving by a preponderance of the evidence that punitive damages should be awarded, and, if so, the amount of any such damages.

You may award punitive damages only if you find that the defendant's conduct that harmed the plaintiff was a willful act or omission or gross negligence. Gross negligence means conduct or a failure to act that is so reckless that it demonstrates a substantial lack of concern for whether an injury will result.

If you find that punitive damages are appropriate, you must use reason in setting the amount. Punitive damages, if any, should be in an amount sufficient to fulfill their purposes but should not reflect bias, prejudice, or sympathy toward any party. In considering the amount of any punitive damages, consider the degree of reprehensibility of the defendant's conduct.

In addition, you may consider the relationship of any award of punitive damages to any actual harm inflicted on the plaintiff.

11. Insurance

Whether a party is insured or not insured has no bearing on any issue that you must decide. You must refrain from any inference, speculation, or discussion about insurance. If you find for the plaintiff, you shall not speculate about or consider any possible sources of benefits the plaintiff may have received or might receive. After you have returned your verdict, the court will make whatever adjustments are necessary in this regard.

12. Verdict Form

To assist you in deciding these issues, I am giving you a verdict form to use during your deliberations. When you have completed the form, please let the bailiff know that you have completed your deliberations.

VERDICT FORM

1. **Liability**

Do you find by a preponderance of the evidence that the defendant negligently caused the death of his daughter?

______ YES

______ NO

If your answer is "no," then do not answer Question 2. If your answer is "yes," answer Question 2.

2. **Damages**

Do you find by a preponderance of the evidence that the plaintiff suffered damages as a result of the defendant's negligence?

______ YES

______ NO

If you answered "yes," then please enter the amount of damages, in whole dollar amounts, to which the plaintiff is entitled.

$ ______________________

3. **Punitive Damages**

Do you find by a preponderance of the evidence that the plaintiff suffered damages as a result of the defendant's willful act or omission or gross negligence in light of the circumstances?

______ YES

______ NO

If you answered "yes," then please enter the amount of punitive damages, in whole dollar amounts, to which the plaintiff is entitled.

$ ______________________

Chapter 10
State v. Lockmore

§ 10-1. Introduction

Sissy Lockmore is charged with killing her ex-husband, Bill Lockmore in San Milano, Lone Star.

Sissy and Bill were divorced in [YR-5], when Bill discovered that Sissy, a financial advisor, was having an affair with a co-worker. The court awarded sole custody of their two children to Bill and ordered Sissy to pay child support. Bill remained in San Milano and Sissy moved to Dallas to be near her family. She failed to make the child support payments and at the time her husband was killed, she owed almost $20,000. She and Bill were scheduled to appear in a San Milano court to continue their contentious legal battle over custody and child support payments. Bill was killed early in the morning — shot in the back — at his home in San Milano. The police focused their investigation on Sissy and obtained evidence through cell phone records showing that her cell phone was used in San Milano the evening before the killing.

The defendant will argue that her business partner provides an alibi at the time of the killing and that the police should have investigated Morgan Walters, a business associate of Bill's. Walters and Bill Lockmore were in the process of dissolving their partnership in a medical practice.

§ 10-2. Stipulations on Procedural and Evidentiary Matters

1. The case is being tried in a Lone Star court.
2. This case will be tried only on the issue of guilt or innocence.
3. All witnesses called to testify who have in statements or grand jury testimony identified the defendant, other individuals, or tangible evidence, can, if asked, identify the same at trial.
4. The defendant Lockmore and Cass Jones signed their statements to the police.
5. Other than what is supplied in the case file itself, there is nothing exceptional or unusual about the background information of any of the witnesses or the defendant that would bolster or detract from their credibility.
6. This problem does not permit a listed witness or the defendant, while testifying, to "invent" an individual not mentioned in this problem and have testimony or evidence offered to the court or jury from that invented individual.
7. The current year is the year in which this case comes to trial.
8. If any rule of procedure or rule of evidence requires that notice be provided to the court or to the opponent, it will be assumed for the purpose of the problem that the required notice was given.
9. All e-mails were lawfully seized, or obtained, from computers belonging to the defendant, the victim, the defendant's family, Morgan Walters, and/or Cass Jones.
10. The cell tower phone records were obtained pursuant to a valid search warrant.
11. The victim, Bill Lockmore, was killed on April 2, [YR-1], by a single shot in the back, from a 9 mm weapon.

12. The murder weapon was never located.
13. All exhibits in the file are authentic. In addition, each exhibit contained in the file is the original of that document unless otherwise noted on the exhibit or as established by the evidence.

§ 10-3. Case File Materials

Students will be expected to use the following materials for the trial of *State v. Lockmore.*

DEFENDANT'S WRITTEN STATEMENT TO POLICE

LONE STAR **COUNTY OF BEAR**	**Case Number: 04-9493843**

VOLUNTARY STATEMENT OF: SISSY LOCKMORE

I, Sissy Lockmore, after first being duly warned by Det. Jamie Gonzales #3898 at 0925 hrs. at 214 W. Nueva, on 4-4-[YR-1] that (1) I have the right to remain silent and not make any statement at all, and any statement I do make may be used against me at my trial; (2) Any statement I make may be used as evidence against me in Court; (3) I have the right to have a lawyer present to advise me prior to and during any questioning; (4) If I am unable to employ a lawyer, I have the right to have a lawyer appointed to advise me prior to and during any questioning; (5) I have the right to terminate the interview at any time; and I understand that the above rights are continuing rights and may be urged by me at any stage of the proceedings, and I hereby prior to and during the making of this statement, knowingly, intelligently, and voluntarily waive the above rights and give to the said, Det. J. Gonzales #3898, the person to whom this statement is being given, the following written statement:

My name is Sissy Lockmore. I live in Dallas, Lone Star and I am a licensed financial advisor. I am currently single. From 1985 to [YR-5], I was married to Bill Lockmore. I have two children, Zach who is 9 years old, and Andrea, who is 11 years old. In [YR-5], when Bill and I divorced, he got sole custody of the children, at a family court proceeding here in San Milano, Bear County. I was ordered to pay child support payments. I got one visit a month with my kids. I moved back to Dallas to be closer to my family and I moved into a small apartment. I ran into tough financial times and fell behind on my payments. I think I owe about $20,000 in child support. So Bill went to court and got my visitation rights cancelled in February [YR-1], until I could pay the child support payments.

Bill and I continued to talk by phone, but he would always get angry at me and raise the issue about my cheating on him, and that that had broken up our marriage. I would most often talk to the kids either by e-mail or cell phone. From my point of view, his medical practice was the cause of our breakup, and his partnership with Morgan Walters. Morgan was always pressuring him to give up his dream of doing medical research and spend more time with their medical practice, doing general practice. That caused a lot of tension in Bill and he took it out on me. I looked elsewhere for love and affection. He would often scream at me and several times he would get physical with me. He would hit me and push me around. I never reported it to the police because I was afraid it would hurt us professionally.

He refused to be flexible on the timing of my visits with the children so I decided to take him back to court. We were supposed to have a hearing on April 11 to work that out and for me to make arrangements to get paid up on child support payments. He was being really nasty to me and uncooperative.

I went home early on the 1st and in the evening I called my kids to wish them April Fool's Day — it was a part of a running joke in our family. When we were still together we always made it a huge family activity — going out to eat, taking a movie for the kids. I spoke to both kids for a while and told them I loved them. After I talked to them I got so depressed afterwards that I went to several local bars and started drinking. I think one of them was the Chez Monkey, or something like that, and a couple of others. I had an awful lot to drink and I just don't remember all of the details. About midnight I left a message on my business partner's phone — that is Cass Jones — and told him that I was having a few drinks and that I might be in late the next day. I could not find my cell phone so I used the phone at the bar I was in at the time. I don't think anyone would remember me at those bars, because when I went in I would find a quiet corner and keep to myself. I guess it was about 2 AM when I got to my place.

I slept in the next day, April 2nd, until about 9:30 AM. I got up and hurriedly dressed and got to the office about 10:30. I felt terrible. I don't remember the exact time. Cass can probably give you more information. I said hi to him and went into my office to listen to my phone messages. I got a message from you. I did not return your call because I was in a state of shock that something had happened to my kids. I started crying and told Cass that I needed to come to San Milano to check on my kids and to make sure that your call was not a horrible joke. I drove to Love Field in Dallas and caught a Southeast Airways nonstop flight. I got here about 2 PM and rented a car and drove to Bill's house.

I can't believe this has happened. Bill and I had our disagreements but he did not deserve to die. If you think I did it, you are wrong, I did not kill my husband.

I would look into where Morgan Walters was on that day. From what my kids tell me, Bill and Morgan would often shout at each other and fight about their partnership. Morgan had a lot of money riding on that arrangement and if anything happened to it, Morgan stood to lose about $500,000 in business. Bill was bringing in the big bucks for their arrangement. Morgan was a terrible doctor and could not keep patients. I think he was also using drugs which made him a bit crazy.

I cannot explain where my cell phone was on the evening of April 1st. I am sure that I called the kids from my apartment in the early evening. I just don't remember. But I know I called them and they can confirm that. My cell phone number is 555-619-3454. As I said, I was in Dallas the evening of the 1st. I found my cell phone down between my front seats, but that was not until I drove to the airport in Dallas on April 2nd. When and how it got there I can't say. I just don't know.

I do own a gun, a 9 mm Glock, which I purchased for myself several years ago. But someone stole it from me last year when I left my car unlocked. They also took some CDs I had just purchased. I did not report it to the police because it was not worth the effort. I bought it at a gun show in Dallas. I do not have any records on it with a serial number or anything.

This is the end of my statement. I have read this statement and it is true and correct.

WITNESS: *Stephen Morales* SIGNATURE: *Sissy Lockmore*

WITNESS: *Stan Kosinkski*

DATE: **4-4-[YR-1]**

Cass Jones' Written Statement to Police

LONE STAR COUNTY OF BEAR	}	Case Number: 04-9493843

VOLUNTARY STATEMENT OF: CASS JONES

I, Cass Jones, after first being duly warned by Det. Jamie Gonzales #3898 at 1400 hrs. at 513 Soledad Street, Dallas, Lone Star on 4-5-[YR-1] that (1) I have the right to remain silent and not make any statement at all, and nay statement I do make may be used against me at my trial; (2) Any statement I make may be used as evidence against me in Court; (3) I have the right to have a lawyer present to advise me prior to and during any questioning; (4) If I am unable to employ a lawyer, I have the right to have a lawyer appointed to advise me prior to and during any questioning; (5) I have the right to terminate the interview at any time; and I understand that the above rights are continuing rights and may be urged by me at any stage of the proceedings, and I hereby prior to and during the making of this statement, knowingly, intelligently, and voluntarily waive the above rights and give to the said, Det. J. Gonzales #3898, the person to whom this statement is being given, the following written statement:

My name is Cass Jones. I live in Dallas, Lone Star and am a licensed financial advisor at a company called MoneyInc. My office partner is Sissy Lockmore. We have been partners for about five years. She is the senior partner and brings in most of the business, through her contacts.

On April 1, [YR-1], Sissy seemed to be in a real depression. She told me that April 1st was always hard on her because she had a thing about celebrating the day with her kids in San Milano and that because of pending legal problems her husband was not going to let her visit the kids as she always had in the past. She told me that she was going to call them after work.

She left the office about mid-afternoon, complaining of a splitting headache and said she would see me in the morning, the 2nd. I thought nothing of it.

That night she called and left a message on my cell phone saying that she had talked to her kids, was in a major "funk," and that she was having a drink or two. She said that because of that she would probably be in late and not to worry. I think that call came in about 11 PM but I cannot remember and I erased it as I always do with my voice mail.

The next day, April 2nd, she walked into the office about 10:15 or 10:30, something like that, looking really depressed. I am sorry I did not look at the clock at the exact time she came in. She said that she had a hangover and that she was going to get a couple cups of coffee and adjust her attitude. She went into her office and came out a few minutes later telling me that she had just gotten a call from a San Milano detective saying that her ex-husband Bill had just been killed at his home. I comforted her for a while and then she said she had to fly to San Milano to see her kids.

I said that I could drive her to the airport, but she said she would be fine and left the office. She said she would catch a Southeast Airways flight out of Love Field. That airport is about 30 to 40 minutes away from our office. I have made it in less time, but the lights have to be with you and you have to go a bit over the speed limit to do it.

Her demeanor when she told me all of this was somewhat shaken. Given her relationship with her ex-husband, I think she was also more concerned about her children and what would happen to them. She kept me up to date with her legal problems and I was concerned that she might decide to leave the company and move to San Milano. I admit that that really bothered me, because she was the foundation for the company. I am not in the best of health and I really hate to see this happen to Sissy.

We are being questioned or investigated by the Federal Trade Commission. They told us that some of the information that we supplied in one of annual reports last year was wrong and they think we deliberately lied. We have retained counsel and are hopeful that the FTC will see this as an innocent mistake. Sissy is handling most of that problem. If she was not available to help solve that problem, I would be in real trouble.

In my opinion Sissy could not have killed Bill. While she was really angry at him and wanted to see more of her children, she is just not the kind of person who would kill someone.

This is the end of my statement. I have read this statement and it is true and correct.

WITNESS: *Stephen Morales* SIGNATURE: *Cass Jones*

WITNESS: *Stan Kosinkski*

DATE: **4-5-[YR-1]**

Grand Jury Testimony of Jamie Gonzales

IN RE:	BEFORE THE GRAND JURY
	OF
GRAND JURY INVESTIGATION	BEAR COUNTY, STATE OF LONE STAR

* * * * * *

****

COURT REPORTER'S

Q AND A TRANSCRIPT OF TESTIMONY OF

DET. JAMIE GONZALES

JULY 10, [YR-1]

****

* * * * *

BE IT REMEMBERED, that heretofore, to-writ on JULY 10, [YR-1], the above-entitled matter came on for hearing before the Grand Jury of Bear County, sitting in San Milano, Lone Star, being presented by DONALD ROGERS, Assistant Criminal District Attorney, for consideration by the members thereof.

HEATHER STEVENS was duly sworn as Court Reporter.

WHEREUPON, the following evidence was introduced and proceedings had, to-wit, beginning at 10:42 o'clock a.m. and concluding at 11:52 o'clock a.m.

DETECTIVE JAMIE GONZALES, The Witness,

GRAND JURY FOREMAN: Do you solemnly swear that you will not divulge either by words or signs any matter about which you may be interrogated, and that you will keep secret all proceedings of the Grand Jury which may be had in your presence, and that you will true answers make to such questions as may be propounded to you by the Grand Jury or under its direction, so help you God?

THE WITNESS: I do.

EXAMINATION BY DONALD ROGERS:

Q: Detective Gonzales, as with any witness who comes before the Grand Jury, I need to give you the definitions of perjury and aggravated perjury.

A person commits the offense of perjury if, with intent to deceive and with knowledge of the statement's meaning, that person makes a false statement under oath or swears to the truth of a false statement previously made and the statement is required or authorized by law to be made under oath.

Perjury is a Class A Misdemeanor, which is punishable by anywhere up to one year in the Bear County Jail and/or a fine of up to $4,000.

Perjury becomes aggravated perjury if the person commits perjury, makes that false statement during or in connection with an official proceeding, and Grand Jury proceedings are official proceedings, and the statement is material.

Aggravated perjury is a third-degree felony, which means it's punishable by anywhere from two to ten years in the Lone Star Department of Corrections, and there's a potential fine of up to $10,000. Do you understand this?

A: Yes, sir.

Q: Would you please state your name for the grand jury?

A: Yes, my name is Detective Jamie Gonzales.

Q: Could you please tell us your position and duties with the police department?

A: I am a homicide detective, with about 12 years' experience on the force. My duties entail conducting investigations into possible homicides.

Q: Okay. Detective, I would like you to tell the jurors about your investigation into the death of Mr. Bill Lockmore, on April 2nd of this year?

A: I received a call at about 0830 hours of a shooting at 123 Ivy Lane here in the city. It appeared that a male, about 40 years old, had been shot in the back. When I arrived at the scene, I talked with the officers who had been called to the scene at about 0815 hours. The coroner's office was also there. They had secured the scene. CSI was already there taking pictures and gathering whatever forensic evidence they could find. It appeared that the victim had been shot in the back, left side, apparently from someone standing in the garage or close to it. The garage door was open. We found no signs of forced entry at any of the entrances or at the garage door itself. His newspaper was still laying in the driveway so I assume that he was going out to pick it up when he was shot.

Q: Did you interview anyone at the scene?

A: Yes, I spoke to Morgan Walters, who apparently discovered the body at about 0805 hours, I mean 8:05 AM, and placed the 911 call to report the shooting.

Q: Did you obtain a statement from that person?

A: Not a formal statement, no. Walters claimed that the victim and he had gotten together that morning to go to a breakfast meeting to go over their plans for a renewed partnership agreement. Walters had apparently arrived just before the shooting and was in the house at the time. He said that they were on their way out of the house to go and get breakfast when Lockmore said that he needed to get the paper out of the driveway and a short time later he heard what he described as a loud pop. He went outside but did not see anyone leaving the premises. I asked him why the garage door was open and Walters said that the victim was "anal retentive" about his morning paper and had longstanding habit of opening the garage door to go out and get it instead of going out the front door.

Q: What was Walters' demeanor?

A: Walters was badly shaken. Walters said that the victim, Bill Lockmore, had been in a long-standing feud with his ex-wife who was taking him to court to get custody of their two kids. And that he had said that he intended to fight to death to make sure that she did not get any more visitation rights. The victim had told Walters that he figured that she would also fight to the death, given her past history of her nasty tactics during the divorce. He said that in his mind, Sissy Lockmore was responsible.

Q: Did you interview anyone else at the scene?

A: Yes, I spoke briefly to the two children at about 9:00 AM. One of the neighbors had gone to the school to bring them back to the house. They both said that they had left for school at about 7:30 and that their dad was in a bad mood when they saw him, before leaving. He told them that Morgan Walters was coming over to pick him up to take him to breakfast. He also told them that he was going to tell Walters that he was going to finally end their partnership. They also said that their mother, who lived in Dallas, would want to know what happened and said they would call her. I said that I would do that for them. They were grateful — they were pretty shaken up. They gave me her office and cell phone numbers.

Q: Did you call his wife, Sissy Lockmore?

A: Yes, at least I tried to get in touch with her. I left messages on her cell number and office number. She did not return my calls.

Q: What was your message?

A: I said that I needed to talk to her right away and that I had some bad news to give her about her family in San Milano. I do not like giving specifics in a voice mail message.

Q: Did you have an opportunity to speak to Ms. Lockmore personally?

A: Yes, later that day she showed up at the house and one of the neighbors told her what had happened and how to get in touch with me. So she called me at my office and we set up an interview for the next morning, April 3rd.

Q: Did you hold that meeting?

A: Yes.

Q: And what happened?

A: Well she said that she would do anything to help catch the person who had done this terrible thing to her ex-husband.

Q: What was her demeanor?

A: She seemed very confident about herself, calm. She did not cry or show any other emotion. She seemed very focused and determined.

Q: Did she make a written statement?

A: Yes, I asked her questions and typed up her statement, which she then read and signed.

Q: Is this it? [Shows statement to witness]

A: Yes.

Q: Please tell us what other steps you took to investigate the murder.

A: Well, going back to the day of the shooting, the 2nd, while at the scene I made a rough drawing of the crime scene, showing the relative position of the body to the garage and the side of the house.

Q: Is this the drawing? [Shows diagram to witness]

A: Yes, it is.

Q: Is it to scale?

A: No, but I tried to be careful in showing the position and location. You will note that the victim was apparently facing the street, probably going out to pick up his newspaper which was still on the driveway. It appeared that he was shot in the back from someone standing either in the garage or to the side of the house, near the garage door. I walked around the side of the house and it appeared that someone had knocked over a garbage can, perhaps the killer, as he or she ran out through the back yard.

Q: There was a backyard?

A: The house sits on the edge of some sort of greenbelt or park. The backyard adjoins some woods and there is path through there that goes to a small parking lot for hikers about 200 feet from the house.

Q: Did you gather any forensic evidence from the side yard, back yard, or greenbelt.

A: Yes, but not much.

Q: What did you find?

A: As I walked through the back yard, toward the back of the property, I found a parking garage receipt for Love Field, up in Dallas. I picked it up carefully and placed it in a plastic evidence bag. I am sorry, I first initialed it and then placed it in an evidence bag.

Q: Did you investigate this further?

A: Yes, I talked to the owners and managers of this particular parking lot. It's about a block away from the actual terminals, but the property still belongs to the airport. They verified that this ticket was from their machines, but could not give any more information on who had taken it out of the machine on April 1, [YR-1].

Q: Is this it? [Shows exhibit to witness]

A: Yes. Those are my initials, "JG."

Q: Did you ask the parking lot people what someone would do if they lost their ticket?

A: Yes, I did. They explained that if someone loses their ticket they owe the price for full 24 hours of parking. This lot is apparently a short-term, 24-hour lot.

Q: Okay. Ah, did you take any pictures of the crime scene?

A: Yes, I took several.

Q: Are these pictures you took? [Shows photos to witness]

A: Yes. Two views. They show the victim lying in his driveway.

Q: Did you follow up with any forensic testing?

A: Yes, absolutely. I later read the ballistics report and learned that the victim was shot in the back with a 9 mm weapon. The slug recovered from the victim's body was in pretty decent shape but with no gun to match it to that was pretty much all they could say.

Q: Did you execute any search warrants?

A: Yes. We got a warrant to search the victim's computer and with the help of the Dallas police, they got a warrant to search the defendant's office and home computers. They also received consent to search Morgan Walters' computer.

Q: And what were you looking for?

A: E-mails. It appeared that just before the killing, there had been some e-mail traffic between the victim and Ms. Lockmore, and Morgan Walters.

Q: Okay.

A: We also got a warrant to search the records for cell phone towers to see if we could verify whether the defendant had placed her call to her children on April 1st from the Dallas area. The records indicated that she made the call from her cell phone, from a location here in Bear County, certainly not Dallas.

Q: Did you determine what the phone number for her children was?

A: Yes, it was the home phone number for the victim, the house phone, and that was 555-739-5967.

Q: Are these the records? [Shows records to witness]

A: Yes.

Q: Did you check airline schedules and records?

A: Yes, we could find no one with the name Sissy Lockmore who traveled on April 1st to San Milano, or back to Dallas on the 2nd. We did find her travel record for her flight from Dallas to San Milano on the day of the shooting, as she said in her statement to me.

Q: Detective, is this the airline schedule for Southeast Airways? [Shows to witness]

A: Yes, I got this off their official website. You will note that there are regular flights on about an hourly basis from San Milano to Dallas and back.

Q: How did you get this?

A: I went to their official website and printed it off.

Q: Did you check to see if any of the flights listed on the sheet were cancelled or delayed on the 2nd?

A: Yes, three flights were delayed that date. Flights 908 and 123 from Dallas were delayed about 10 minutes. Flights 565, 339, and 222 were delayed going to Dallas. That is the information that Southeast Airways gave me over the phone when I called.

Q: How far is it from the San Milano airport to the victim's house?

A: About 5 miles.

Q: Do you know the driving time?

A: Yes, we drove three different routes and it took us an average of 35 minutes. We tested it at about the same time of day, early to mid-morning. One route took 45 minutes. Shortest was 25 minutes.

Q: So, did you reach any conclusions about whether Sissy Lockmore killed Bill Lockmore?

A: Yes, absolutely. It's clear that she flew to San Milano on the evening of April 1st, placed a call to her kids, pretending to be in Dallas, called her partner to set up an alibi, drove to her husband's house on the morning of the 2nd, waited for him beside the house, shot him in the back, ran through the backyard to her parked rental car, flew back to Dallas and then went into her office. The timeline fits.

Q: Did you look at the possibility that perhaps Morgan Walters had been involved in the killing?

A: Yes, but not really. While there was some evidence that Walters and Bill Lockmore were having some disagreements about their business, it is well known in criminal investigation circles that this type of case is committed almost always by spouses or ex-spouses. All fingers pointed to Sissy Lockmore. Besides, my gut feelings are rarely wrong on this type of case.

Q: Detective, have you ever been wrong about a case?

A: Yes, just once in about 150 cases. But it was a problem with the lab report. Turns out that the DNA did not match.

Q: Did you interview Cass Jones about Sissy's alibi?

A: Yes, well I called him on April 3rd after Sissy made her statement and he said that he was sure that he saw Sissy on the morning of April 2nd at 10:30 AM, when she came into the office.

Q: Did you conduct an interview with him?

A: Yes, I flew to Dallas and interviewed him on April 5th. At that point, it seemed that he was not being entirely truthful and that perhaps he was also involved in the killing. I coordinated all of this with the Dallas Police Department.

Q: Is this his statement? [Shows statement to witness]

A: Yes, that's it.

Q: After interviewing him, did you have any reason to consider him a suspect?

A: No. While his memory was hazy on details, there was not enough there to pursue him as a person of interest. I also had learned beforehand through other sources that the Federal Trade Commission was looking into some irregularities with his and Sissy's company.

Q: What was that about?

A: It appears that in [YR-3], they had filed some misleading information in one of their annual reports and that an investigation is on-going. They are facing some serious jail time from what the FTC told me.

Q: Okay. Please step outside for just a few minutes.

THE WITNESS: Okay.

[The Witness leaves the Grand Jury Room at 11:52 a.m., and is subsequently dismissed.]

(END OF TRANSCRIPT)

Grand Jury Testimony of Morgan Walters

IN RE:		BEFORE THE GRAND JURY
	}	OF
GRAND JURY INVESTIGATION		BEAR COUNTY, Lone Star

* * * * * *

****

COURT REPORTER'S

Q AND A TRANSCRIPT OF TESTIMONY OF

MORGAN WALTERS

JULY 10, [YR-1]

****

* * * * *

BE IT REMEMBERED, that heretofore, to-writ on JULY 10, [YR-1], the above-entitled matter came on for hearing before the Grand Jury of Bear County, sitting in San Milano, Lone Star, being presented by DONALD ROGERS, Assistant Criminal District Attorney, for consideration by the members thereof.

HEATHER STEVENS was duly sworn as Court Reporter.

WHEREUPON, the following evidence was introduced and proceedings had, to-wit, beginning at 1:00 o'clock p.m. and concluding at 2:00 o'clock p.m.

MORGAN WALTERS, The Witness,

GRAND JURY FOREMAN: Do you solemnly swear that you will not divulge either by words or signs any matter about which you may be interrogated, and that you will keep secret all proceedings of the Grand Jury which may be had in your presence, and that you will true answers make to such questions as may be propounded to you by the Grand Jury or under its direction, so help you God?

THE WITNESS: I do.

EXAMINATION BY DONALD ROGERS:

Q: Morgan Walters, as with any witness who comes before the Grand Jury, I need to give you the definitions of perjury and aggravated perjury.

A person commits the offense of perjury if, with intent to deceive and with knowledge of the statement's meaning, that person makes a false statement under oath or swears to the truth of a false statement previously made and the statement is required or authorized by law to be made under oath.

Perjury is a Class A Misdemeanor, which is punishable by anywhere up to one year in the Bear County Jail and/or a fine of up to $4,000.

Perjury becomes aggravated perjury if the person commits perjury, makes that false statement during or in connection with an official proceeding, and Grand Jury proceedings are official proceedings, and the statement is material.

Aggravated perjury is a third-degree felony, which means it's punishable by anywhere from two to ten years in the Lone Star Department of Corrections, and there's a potential fine of up to $10,000. Do you understand this?

A: Yes, sir.

[Morgan Walters testified as follows before the Grand Jury, after waiving the right to remain silent.]

Q: For the record will you please state your full name?

A: Morgan Walters.

Q: And what is your current employment?

A: I am a physician, with the Medical Associates here in the city.

Q: Are you familiar with Bill Lockmore?

A: Yes.

Q: How are you familiar with him?

A: We used to be partners in our medical practice — since 1990. We formed the business together.

Q: Why are you no longer partners?

A: He was killed.

Q: Please tell the Grand Jury what you know about that.

A: Well, I had talked with Bill the day before and he said that we should really try to rethink our business arrangement and plan for an expansion of his medical research part of the practice. I had some concerns about that but agreed that it was probably time to have a heart-to-heart talk.

Q: Okay.

A: Well, he e-mailed me on March 31st and said that he had some open time on the 2nd. He had taken off that whole week, as he said, to think about what he really wanted to do with his life. I guess he also needed some time to sort through the legal issues with his ex-wife, Sissy, who was making his life hell. He said that we could meet for breakfast and take in the large buffet at the Holton Hotel. I agreed. On the morning of the 2nd, I drove to his house at about 7:50 AM and offered to drive us both to breakfast. As he was grabbing his things, he said that he needed to get the paper out of the driveway. So he walked through the kitchen, out the door to the garage, and I could hear the automatic garage door open. Just a few seconds later I heard a large pop.

Q: Gunfire?

A: Not sure. I thought at the time that maybe something in the garage had exploded or broken. I went into the garage and saw Bill lying on the driveway with blood on his back. I quickly went to him, looked around to see if anyone was there, and then called 9 1 1.

Q: So, you did not see anyone else in the area?

A: No. And I guess the gunshot did not cause any alarm in the neighborhood, because for about 5 minutes I was the only one even outside. Finally one of the neighbors came over and started crying. She said she would go to get the kids.

Q: What happened next?

A: I just sat on the grass. I could not believe it. One minute we were going to breakfast and the next he was lying there. A few minutes later a patrol car arrived. They helped me up and moved me to the side and one of them asked me some questions while the other one called for an ambulance, I think.

Q: I want to ask you some questions about your disagreement with Mr. Lockmore about your practice and your future plans. You said that there were problems.

A: I guess. Bill was really into medical research but he was a very gifted physician and the patients loved him. Don't get me wrong. I consider myself to be a very good doctor. But Bill had that little something extra in dealing with his patients. We had a 50-50 split on everything, but Bill was the reason we were so successful. And I really appreciated it. But about a year ago he got a grant to do medical research on cancer and was spending more and more time on that research. He had rented another office in the same building to do that. Consequently, we started to lose patients and their good will. That deeply concerned me and I told Bill that without his attention to our medical practice I was not sure how much longer the practice could continue, with mounting bills and all. At the same time it was all very cordial.

Q: Cordial?

A: Well you know, we never really argued about it. A couple of times it got pretty heated but we always calmed down and took a time out.

Q: Okay. What did you know about Sissy Lockmore?

A: She was a real problem for Bill. He was constantly dealing with some issue with her on a weekly basis. She would call the kids all the time, day and night. She was falling way behind on child support payments, and was going to take him back to court — I think about the time he was killed. He told me several times that he feared that she was crazy enough to hurt him, the kids, and herself. When I asked him to explain, he would say something like: "Don't you watch the evening news with all of the family violence?" I thought he was exaggerating. He said that she would sometimes e-mail him with her threats and then follow it up with an e-mail begging for his forgiveness.

Q: Was Bill dating anyone else at the time of the killing?

A: No. The thing with Sissy pretty well kept that from happening.

DONALD ROGERS: Why don't you go ahead and step outside for just a few minutes.

THE WITNESS: Okay.

[The Witness leaves the Grand Jury Room at 2:00 p.m., and is subsequently dismissed.]

(END OF TRANSCRIPT)

E-MAILS BETWEEN BILL LOCKMORE AND MORGAN WALTERS

From: MBWalters@hmail.com
Sent: Monday, March 31, [YR-1] 4:35 PM
To: bjlockmore@nol.com
Subject: Breakfast?

Sorry Bill. I am having a really bad day. I can see that you have not responded to my tirade from this morning. Sorry.

Yes, lets do breakfast on Wednesday. This is all going to work out. See you at 8 at your house.

My treat. ☺

From: MBWalters@hmail.com
Sent: Monday, March 31, [YR-1] 2:03 PM
To: bjlockmore@nol.com
Subject: Breakfast?

WHAT IN THE HELL ARE YOU TALKING ABOUT? DO YOU WANT TO KILL THE GOOSE THAT IS LAYING OUR COLLECTIVE GOLDEN EGG?

I CAN'T BELIEVE THIS IS WHAT YOU HAVE BEEN ANGLING FOR.

From: bjlockmore@nol.com
Sent: Monday, March 31, [YR-1] 9:15 AM
To: MBWalters@hmail.com
Subject: Breakfast?

Can we have a breakfast meeting on Wednesday? I just checked with our staff and they told me that you don't have a patient until 10 or so.

I really want to finish our discussion about the practice. I pretty well decided over the weekend that the research is for me. We just have to lick this cancer thing.

How about 8:00?

E-mails Between Bill Lockmore and Sissy Lockmore

From: Sissy67@Moneymakers.com
Sent: Monday, March 31, [YR-1] 4:30 PM
To: bjlockmore@nol.com
Subject: Stop It!!

Darling Bill. Stop what? I will see you and your jerk lawyer in court!!!!!!!!

Be careful what you wish for!!!!!

From: bjlockmore@nol.com
Sent: Monday, March 31, [YR-1] 2:30 PM
To: Sissy67@Moneymakers.com
Subject: Stop It!!

My lawyer just called telling me that I need to be in court on the 11th What is up now? Can't we just leave this alone. I told you that as soon as you get some of that child support money to me that I will tell my lawyer to go back to court and get you some more visitation with the kids. I know from my friends in Dallas that you have the money and that you are doing all of this out of spite. Until you pay, it will be over my dead body that you see the kids. Get it? Good.

I am surrounded by jerks. Just leave it alone!!!

Detective Gonzales' Drawing of Crime Scene

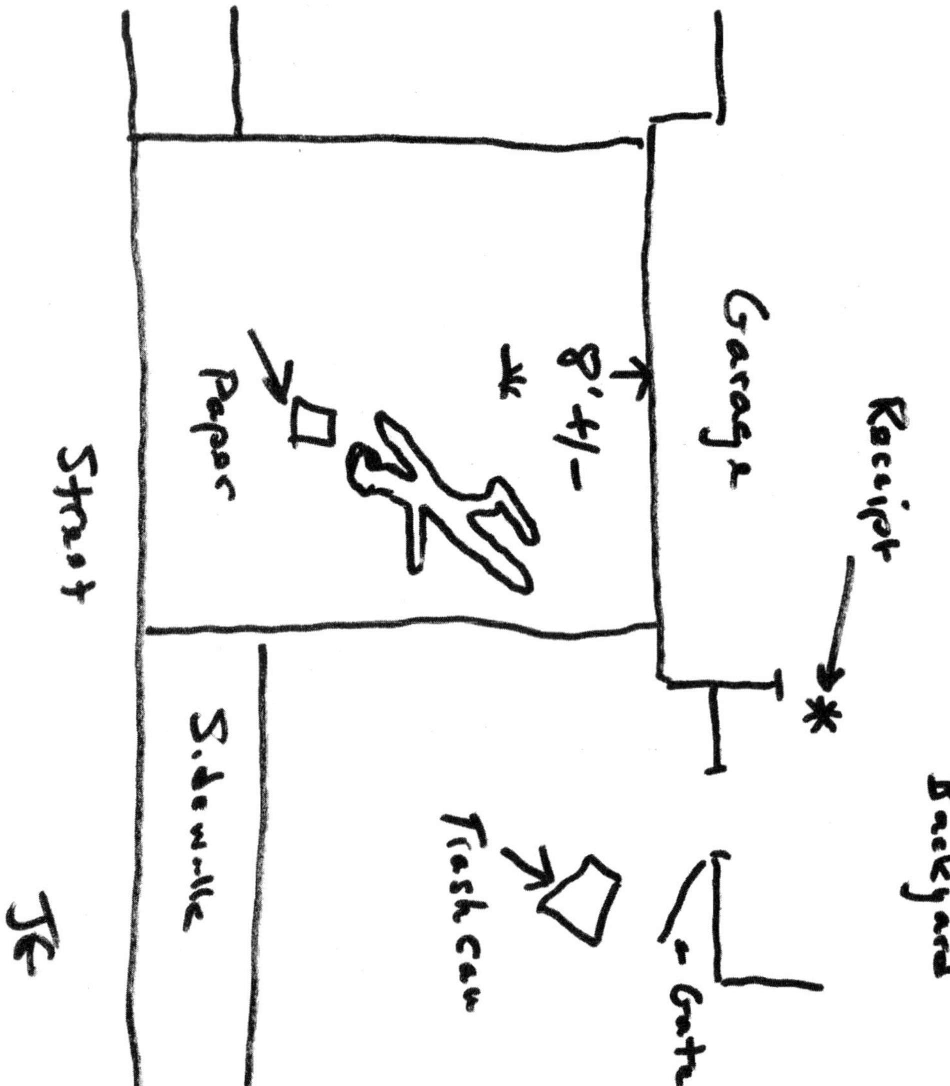

DETECTIVE GONZALES' PHOTOGRAPHS OF CRIME SCENE

Southeast Airways Website — Schedule for April 2

Southeastern Airways	Book Travel	Special Fares!	Rewards	Help!
Plan Trip	Select Flight	Travel Summary	Rental Cars	Hotels

Select Departing Flights
Dallas LS to San Milano LS (Wednesday, April 2, [YR-1])

Flight	*Depart*	*Arrive*	*Stops*	*Travel Time*
012	6:00 am	7:00 am	0	1:00
654	7:00 am	8:00 am	0	1:00
897	8:00 am	9:00 am	0	1:00
908	9:00 am	10:00 am	0	1:00
432	10:00 am	11:00 am	0	1:00
234	12:00 noon	1:00 pm	0	1:00
123	2:00 pm	3:00 pm	0	1:00
789	3:00 pm	4:00 pm	0	1:00
667	5:00 pm	6:00 pm	0	1:00
786	7:00 pm	8:00 pm	0	1:00
211	9:00 pm	10:00 pm	0	1:00

Select Departing Flights
San Milano LS to Dallas LS (Wednesday, April 2, [YR-1]

Flight	*Depart*	*Arrive*	*Stops*	*Travel Time*
565	7:45 am	8:30 am	0	1:00
668	8:00 am	9:00 am	0	1:00
989	9:05 am	10:05 am	0	1:00
888	10:10 am	11:10 am	0	1:00
423	11:15 am	12:15 pm	0	1:00
227	12:00 noon	1:00 pm	0	1:00
321	2:30 pm	3:30 pm	0	1:00
599	3:30 pm	4:30 pm	0	1:00
339	5:30 pm	6:30 pm	0	1:00
677	7:46 pm	8:46 pm	0	1:00
222	9:35 pm	10:35 pm	0	1:00

Go to Next Step	Start Over	Need Help?

CELL TOWER RECORDS FOR APRIL 1

Sprant

Sprant
Corporate Security
3345 Sprant Park Blvd
Medville, N.J. 00233
Office: 555-315-0454 Fax: 555-315-0755

Jamie Warner
Subpoena Specialist

06/25/[YR-1]

Bear County District Attorney
Attention: Donald Rogers
214 West Nueva Street
Bear County, Lone Star 78283

Your Case Name: State v. Lockmore
Sprant Case Number: [YR-1]-010618

Dear Mr. Rogers:

Pursuant to the search warrant in the above-referenced case, please find attached the requested call detail records (CDR) for date 04/01/[YR-1] for subject number 555-619-3454.

These CDRs are computer generated records produced by our wireless server and are created automatically when a call is placed or received using the Sprant wireless network. These CDRs provide Sprant information about recent system usage such as the identities of sources (calling number), the identities of destinations (called numbers), the duration of each call, and repoll numbers (switch and location being used for call). These records are used routinely and on a daily basis for billing and other internal purposes.

The attached printout does not include the phone numbers or other identifiers of any other subscribers, in order to protect their privacy. That information has been deleted manually from this printout. Repoll # 21 is located in San Milano, Bear County, Lone Star. The computer was directed to search for the requested number between the hours of 5:00 pm and 11:50 pm, on April 1. Should you have any questions or further inquiries, please feel free to contact me.

Sincerely,

Jamie Warner
Jamie Warner
Subpoena Compliance

Sprant

Call Detail Record (CDR)

04/01/[YR-1]
17:00:00 to 23:59:00

Record Printed: 06/25/[YR-1]
Requesting Party: Warner

Calling NBR	Called NBR	Dialed Digits	Start Date	End Date	Duration	Repoll	Switch Name
(555) 619-3454	(555) 739-5967	(555) 739-5967	4/1/[YR-1] 19:34:00	4/1/[YR-1] 20:42:03	68:03	21 San Antonio	SA- San Milano-2

Love Field Parking Garage Receipt

Love Field, Dallas, Lone Star
EASY Parking Lot # 32
Short Term (24 Hours)

Time In:	15:34:02
Date	4/1/[YR-1]

___

___

___

___

___

___

___

Please Pay at Kiosk Before Exiting Gates

Not Responsible For Theft of Items from Vehicle

Form23412245

Chapter 11
Lockmore v. Lockmore

§ 11-1. Introduction

Sissy Lockmore was tried and acquitted on charges that she killed her ex-husband, Bill Lockmore, in San Milano, Lone Star.

Sissy and Bill divorced when Bill discovered that Sissy, a financial advisor, was having an affair with a co-worker. The court awarded sole custody of their two children to Bill and ordered Sissy to pay child support. Bill remained in San Milano and Sissy moved to Dallas, Lone Star, to be near her family. She failed to make the child support payments and at the time her husband was killed, she owed almost $20,000. She and Bill were scheduled to appear in a San Milano court to continue their contentious legal battle over custody and child support payments. Bill was killed early in the morning — shot in the back — at his home in San Milano. The police focused their investigation on Sissy and obtained evidence through cell phone records showing that her cell phone was used in San Milano the evening before the killing.

At the criminal trial the defendant argued that her business partner provided an alibi at the time of the killing and that the police should have investigated Morgan Walters, a business associate of Bill's. Walters and Bill Lockmore were in the process of dissolving their partnership in a medical practice.

After her criminal trial, Sissy Lockmore moved back to Bear County, State of Lone Star, to be closer to her children.

The parents of Bill Lockmore, June and Steve Lockmore, have filed a civil wrongful death suit against Sissy Lockmore, their former daughter-in-law, for the death of their son.

§ 11-2. Stipulations Regarding Procedural and Evidentiary Matters

1. The case is being tried in a State court.
2. This case will be tried only on the issues of liability and damages.
3. All witnesses called to testify who have in statements or depositions identified the defendant, other individuals, or tangible evidence can, if asked, identify the same at trial.
4. The parties and witnesses signed their depositions or statements.
5. Other than what is supplied in the problem itself, there is nothing exceptional or unusual about the background information of any of the witnesses or the defendant that would bolster or detract from their credibility.
6. The parties may not "invent" an individual not mentioned in this case file and have testimony or evidence offered to the court or jury from that invented individual.
7. "Beyond the record" must not be entertained as an objection.
8. The current year is the year of the trial.
9. If any rule of procedure or rule of evidence requires that notice be provided to the court or to the opponent, it will be assumed for the purpose of the problem that the required notice was given.

10. All e-mails were lawfully seized, or obtained, from computers belonging to the defendant, the victim, the defendant's family, Morgan Walters, and/or Cass Jones.
11. The cell tower phone records were obtained pursuant to a valid search warrant.
12. The victim, Bill Lockmore, was killed on April 2, [YR-2], by a single shot in the back, from a 9 mm weapon.
13. The murder weapon was never located.
14. All exhibits in the file are authentic. In addition, each exhibit contained in the file is the original of that document unless otherwise noted on the exhibit or as established by the evidence.
15. The case will be tried on the issues of liability and damages.
16. Although Steve Lockmore is considered a plaintiff in this case, he was not available for a deposition and is not available as a witness for the trial.
17. At the time of his death, Bill Lockmore had an expected life span of 48 more years.

§ 11-3. Case File Materials

The following case file materials should be used for the trial of *Lockmore v. Lockmore.*

Lone Star Civil Practice & Remedies Code

§ 31.123. Cause of Action

(a) An action for actual damages arising from an injury that causes an individual's death may be brought if liability exists under this section.

(b) A person is liable for damages arising from an injury that causes an individual's death if the injury was caused by the person's or his agent's or servant's wrongful act, neglect, carelessness, unskillfulness, or default.

(c) A person is liable for damages arising from an injury that causes an individual's death if:

(1) the person is a proprietor, owner, charterer, or hirer of an industrial or public utility plant or of a railroad, street railway, steamboat, stagecoach, or other vehicle for the transportation of goods or passengers; and

(2) the injury was caused by the person's or his agent's or servant's wrongful act, neglect, carelessness, unskillfulness, or default.

§ 31.124. Benefitting From Action

(a) An action to recover damages as provided by this subchapter is for the exclusive benefit of the surviving spouse, children, and parents of the deceased.

(b) The surviving spouse, children, and parents of the deceased may bring the action or one or more of those individuals may bring the action for the benefit of all.

§ 31.125. Exemplary Damages

When the death is caused by the willful act or omission or gross negligence of the defendant, exemplary as well as actual damages may be recovered.

Plaintiff's Petition

DISTRICT COURT OF BEAR COUNTY

JUNE and STEVE LOCKMORE Plaintiffs v. SISSY LOCKMORE Defendant	Docket No. 34678 COMPLAINT FOR DAMAGES

COMES NOW the above-named Plaintiffs and allege the following:

I. Parties, Jurisdiction, and Venue

A. Plaintiffs, June and Steve Lockmore, parents of Bill Lockmore, decedent, bring this action in their personal capacity.

B. Defendant, Sissy Lockmore, is a resident of Bear County, State of Lone Star.

C. This Court has jurisdiction over the subject matter of this complaint and over the parties.

D. Venue is proper and appropriate in Bear County because the death of Bill Lockmore, which is the subject matter of this complaint, occurred in Bear County.

II. Factual Basis

A. Sissy and Bill were divorced when Bill discovered that Sissy was having an affair with a co-worker. The court awarded sole custody of their two children to Bill and ordered Sissy to pay child support.

B. She failed to make the child support payments and at the time she killed her husband, she owed almost $20,000. She and Bill were scheduled to appear in a San Milano court to continue their contentious legal battle over custody and child support payments.

C. Before that hearing, Sissy shot Bill in the back outside his home in San Milano.

D. Defendant's acts were the sole and proximate cause of Sissy Lockmore's death.

III. Causes of Action

A. As a direct and proximate result of the acts of the Defendant, the decedent suffered a wrongful death, entitling Plaintiff to recover actual and exemplary damages (including but not limited to medical and hospital expenses, funeral expenses, and all other damages allowable for wrongful death and survival benefits under Lone Star Civil Practice & Remedies Code §§ 31.123-31.125, and any other damages allowable as a result of Defendant's conduct;) in amounts not now precisely known, the exact amounts to be proven at or before the time of trial.

B. As a further direct and proximate result of the Defendant's acts and omissions, the plaintiffs suffered destruction of the parent-child relationship and loss of parental consortium.

C. As a further direct and proximate result of the intentional acts of Defendant, Plaintiffs are entitled to recover statutory and reasonable attorney's fees and costs in amounts not now precisely known, the court to set such amounts in the future.

IV. Prayer for Relief

WHEREFORE, the plaintiff prays for a judgment of liability against the defendants as follows:

A. For a judgment against defendant.

B. For an award of damages as set forth in the above complaint herein, including statutory and reasonable fees and costs in such amounts that may be awarded by this Court.

C. For such other and further relief as the Court deems just and appropriate.

DATED this day of August 9, [YR-1].

Heather Wetmore

Heather Wetmore
Attorney for Plaintiffs

DEFENDANT'S WRITTEN STATEMENT TO POLICE

LONE STAR **COUNTY OF BEAR**	}	**Case Number: 04-9493843**

VOLUNTARY STATEMENT OF: SISSY LOCKMORE

I, Sissy Lockmore, after first being duly warned by Det. Jamie Gonzales #3898 at 0925 hrs. at 214 W. Nueva, on 4-4-[YR-2] that (1) I have the right to remain silent and not make any statement at all, and any statement I do make may be used against me at my trial; (2) Any statement I make may be used as evidence against me in Court; (3) I have the right to have a lawyer present to advise me prior to and during any questioning; (4) If I am unable to employ a lawyer, I have the right to have a lawyer appointed to advise me prior to and during any questioning; (5) I have the right to terminate the interview at any time; and I understand that the above rights are continuing rights and may be urged by me at any stage of the proceedings, and I hereby prior to and during the making of this statement, knowingly, intelligently, and voluntarily waive the above rights and give to the said, Det. J. Gonzales #3898, the person to whom this statement is being given, the following written statement:

My name is Sissy Lockmore. I live in Dallas, Lone Star, and I am a licensed financial advisor. I am currently single. From 1985 to [YR-6], I was married to Bill Lockmore. I have two children, Zach who is 9 years old, and Andrea, who is 11 years old. In [YR-6], when Bill and I divorced, he got sole custody of the children, at a family court proceeding here in San Milano, Bear County. I was ordered to pay child support payments. I got one visit a month with my kids. I moved back to Dallas to be closer to my family and I moved into a small apartment. I ran into tough financial times and fell behind on my payments. I think I owe about $20,000 in child support. So Bill went to court and got my visitation rights cancelled in February [YR-2], until I could pay the child support payments.

Bill and I continued to talk by phone, but he would always get angry at me and raise the issue about my cheating on him, and that that had broken up our marriage. I would most often talk to the kids, either by e-mail or cell phone. From my point of view, his medical practice was the cause of our breakup, and his partnership with Morgan Walters. Morgan was always pressuring him to give up his dream of doing medical research and spend more time with their medical practice, doing general practice. That caused a lot of tension in Bill and he took it out on me. I looked elsewhere for love and affection. He would often scream at me and several times he would get physical with me. He would hit me and push me around. I never reported it to the police because I was afraid it would hurt us professionally.

He refused to be flexible on the timing of my visits with the children so I decided to take him back to court. We were supposed to have a hearing on April 11 to work that out and for me to make arrangements to get paid up on child support payments. He was being really nasty to me and uncooperative.

I went home early on the 1st and in the evening I called my kids to wish them April Fool's Day — it was a part of a running joke in our family. When we were still together we always made it a huge family activity — going out to eat, taking a movie for the kids. I spoke to both kids for a while and told them I loved them. After I talked to them I got so depressed afterwards that I went to several local bars and started drinking. I think one of them was the Chez Monkey, or something like that, and a couple of others. I had an awful lot to drink and I just don't remember all of the details. About midnight I left a message on my business partner's phone — that is Cass Jones — and told him that I was having a few drinks and that I might be in late the next day. I could not find my cell phone so I used the phone at the bar I was in at the time. I don't think anyone would remember me at those bars, because when I went in I would find a quiet corner and keep to myself. I guess it was about 2 AM when I got to my place.

I slept in the next day, April 2nd, until about 9:30 AM. I got up and hurriedly dressed and got to the office about 10:30. I felt terrible. I don't remember the exact time. Cass can probably give you more information. I said hi to him and went into my office to listen to my phone messages. I got a message from you. I did not return your call because I was in a state of shock that something had happened to my kids. I started crying and told Cass that I needed to come to San Milano to check on my kids and to make sure that your call was not a horrible joke. I drove to Love Field in Dallas and caught a Southeast Airways nonstop flight. I got here about 2 PM and rented a car and drove to Bill's house.

I can't believe this has happened. Bill and I had our disagreements but he did not deserve to die. If you think I did it, you are wrong, I did not kill my husband.

I would look into where Morgan Walters was on that day. From what my kids tell me, Bill and Morgan would often shout at each other and fight about their partnership. Morgan had a lot of money riding on that arrangement and if anything happened to it, Morgan stood to lose about $500,000 in business. Bill was bringing in the big bucks for their arrangement. Morgan was a terrible doctor and could not keep patients. I think he was also using drugs which made him a bit crazy.

I cannot explain where my cell phone was on the evening of April 1st. I am sure that I called the kids from my apartment in the early evening. I just don't remember. But I know I called them and they can confirm that. My cell phone number is 555-619-3454. As I said, I was in Dallas the evening of the 1st. I found my cell phone down between my front seats, but that was not until I drove to the airport in Dallas on April 2nd. When and how it got there I can't say. I just don't know.

I do own a gun, a 9 mm Glock, which I purchased for myself several years ago. But someone stole it from me last year when I left my car unlocked. They also took some CDs I had just purchased. I did not report it to the police because it was not worth the effort. I bought it at a gun show in Dallas. I do not have any records on it with a serial number or anything.

This is the end of my statement. I have read this statement and it is true and correct.

WITNESS: *Stephen Morales* SIGNATURE: *Sissy Lockmore*

WITNESS: *Stan Kosinkski*

DATE: **4-4-[YR-2]**

PLAINTIFF'S DEPOSITION

ORAL DEPOSITION OF JUNE LOCKMORE, produced as a witness at the instance of the Defendant, SISSY LOCKMORE, and duly sworn, was taken in the above-styled and numbered cause on November 4, [YR-1], from 12:00 PM, to 1:00 PM, before Sandy Morales, Certified Shorthand Reporter in and for the State of Lone Star, reported by machine shorthand, at the law offices of Plaintiff, pursuant to the Lone Star Rules of Civil Procedure and the Provisions stated on the record or attached hereto.

This is a deposition of SISSY LOCKMORE, who having been sworn, testified as follows:

EXAMINATION

QUESTIONS BY PLAINTIFF'S COUNSEL:

Q: Would you please state your name for the record?

A: June Lockmore.

Q: And you are one of the plaintiffs in this case, against my client, Sissy Lockmore?

A: Yes.

Q: Okay, before we start going over this, I would like to make sure that you are clear on what we are doing here today. Okay?

A: Yes.

Q: You are under oath, just as if you were testifying in trial. You understand?

A: Yes.

Q: And I want to make it clear that if you do not understand what I am asking about, my questions, please stop me so that we can clear up any confusion. All right?

A: Yes, I understand.

Q: First, your husband Steve is a plaintiff on this case but he is not here?

A: That is correct. This has been so hard on Steve that his doctor has told him not to give his testimony here today. And I expect that he will not be able to testify at trial either. This has been very hard on both of us.

Q: Are you on any medication right now?

A: Yes, I am taking some Valium as a prescription from my doctor. And I sometimes take sleeping pills to go to sleep at night.

Q: How old are you, Mrs. Lockmore?

A: 78 years old.

Q: How old is your husband, Steve?

A: He is 82 years old.

Q: Are you employed?

A: No, I am a retired school teacher. I used to teach elementary school in Idlewood, for 30 years.

Q: Here in the State of Lone Star?

A: Yes.

Q: Okay.

A: Fourth grade, I should add.

Q: And for the record, Bill Lockmore was your son, right?

A: Yes, he was.

Q: But to be perfectly honest, you do not have any personal knowledge about how your son actually died, do you?

A: I know that Sissy killed him — in cold blood.

Q: But you were not there were you?

A: I did not have to be to know what she did to him and to all of us who loved Bill.

Q: So, how did you learn of your son's death?

A: One of our friends lives on the same block with Bill and called us at about 9 o'clock on the morning of his death. We immediately drove to San Milano to be with our grandchildren and help set up the funeral arrangements.

Q: You say in your petition in this lawsuit that you paid for the funeral?

A: Yes, $30,000. Sissy refused to help and Bill's insurance did not cover it. We took it out of our savings, plus a loan. We took $25,000 out of savings and borrowed about $5,000 to make up the difference.

Q: As a retired person, you are certainly drawing a pension, right?

A: Of course.

Q: And your husband?

A: My husband, what?

Q: I'm sorry. Your husband must be drawing some sort of pay right? He is retired military?

A: Yes, we get monthly retirement checks from the military.

Q: So how much to do you get each month in retirement checks and social security combined?

A: About $5,000 a month.

Q: And you own your own house in Idlewood?

A: Yes.

Q: It is paid for?

A: Yes.

Q: And in our request for admissions, you said that you have monthly expenses of only about 2,000 dollars?

A: Right.

Q: You are covered under Medicare and TriCare, right?

A: Yes.

Q: So why are you asking for $500,000 in damages for the death of your son.

A: Like I said, this has been really hard on us. Emotionally. Also, for the last two years of his life, Bill had been sending us a check for 1,000 dollars each month so that we could travel and meet some of our other expenses. He told us that he would do that as long as we lived. He said that his business had been very good to him and that that was not a lot of money for him to send us. He said we were worth it.

Q: You got some of his life insurance money, didn't you?

A: No. It all went to our grandchildren. And they are now living with their mother, Sissy, here in San Milano.

Q: How would you describe your relationship with Sissy?

A: Bad. We never approved of her as a wife for our son. But he was in love and would not listen to us, or the rest of the family for that matter. She was nothing but trouble.

Q: So you approved of their divorce?

A: Absolutely. He found out that she was cheating on him with some guy from her work here in San Milano. She never denied it and seemed proud that she had fooled him.

Q: Do you know Cass Jones?

A: No.

Q: Do you know Morgan Thompson?

A: Yes, of course. Morgan was Bill's partner. Very nice person.

Q: Were you aware that they had been having disagreements over their practice?

A: No.

Q: Is it possible that Morgan was in some way responsible for Bill's death?

A: No. No way.

Q: But you were not there were you?

A: Like I said, I did not have to be to know what happened.

Q: Do you have anything else you want to add?

A: No.

Q: Okay, that is all I have.

(END OF TRANSCRIPT)

This is to certify that I have read the transcript of my deposition taken on and that the transcript accurately reflects the questions asked and my answers.

SIGNATURE: June Lockmore

Subscribed and sworn to before me on January 5, [YR-1].

Sandy Morales

Sandy Morales
Certified Shorthand Reporter

Defendant's Deposition

ORAL DEPOSITION OF SISSY LOCKMORE, produced as a witness at the instance of the Plaintiffs JUNE AND STEVE LOCKMORE, and duly sworn, was taken in the above-styled and numbered cause on November 6, [YR-1], from 2:00 pm., to 3:00 pm, before Charles Wilson, Certified Shorthand Reporter in and for the State of Lone Star, reported by machine shorthand, at the law offices of Plaintiff, pursuant to the Lone Star Rules of Civil Procedure and the Provisions stated on the record or attached hereto.

This is a deposition of SISSY LOCKMORE, who having been sworn, testified as follows:

EXAMINATION

QUESTIONS BY PLAINTIFF'S COUNSEL:

Q: Good morning.

A: Good morning.

Q: Would you please state your name for the record?

A: Sissy Lockmore.

Q: Ms. Lockmore, before we continue I want to be sure that you know that if you have any questions about what I am asking you, that you stop me and ask me to clarify my questions. Do you understand that?

A: Yes, absolutely.

Q: What is your current residence?

A: I live in San Milano, State of Lone Star.

Q: And what is your current employment?

A: I am a licensed financial advisor. I practice alone now.

Q: So you no longer work in Dallas with a partner, Cass Jones?

A: No.

Q: Marital status?

A: I am currently single.

Q: As you may know, your ex-in-laws, June and Steve Lockmore, have filed a wrongful death suit against you for the death of your ex-husband. Bill.

A: Yes, I am aware of that.

Q: What was your relationship with Bill?

A: From [YR-16] to [YR-6], I was married to Bill Lockmore. We have two children, Zach who is 9 years old, and Andrea, who is 11 years old. In [YR-6], when Bill and I divorced, he got sole custody of the children, at a family court proceeding here in San Milano. I was ordered to pay child support payments. I got one visit a month with my kids. I moved back to Dallas to be closer to my family and I moved into a small apartment. I ran into tough financial times and fell behind on my payments. I think I owed about $20,000 in child support. So Bill went to court and got my visitation rights cancelled in February [YR-2], until I could pay the child support payments.

Q: So where are your children living now?

A: They live with me here in San Milano.

Q: So back to your divorce. Your relationship after the divorce was very strained?

A: Yes. Bill and I continued to talk by phone, but he would always get angry at me and raise the issue about my cheating on him, and that that had broken up our marriage. I would most often talk to the kids, either by e-mail or cell phone. From my point of view, his medical practice was the cause of our breakup, and his partnership with Morgan Walters. Morgan was always pressuring him to give up his dream of doing medical research and spend more time with their medical practice, doing general practice. That caused a lot of tension in Bill and he took it out on me.

Q: And you had an affair?

A: Yes, that is one of my failings. I looked elsewhere for love and affection. Bill would often scream at me and several times before we divorced he got physical with me. He would hit me and push me around.

Q: But you did not report it?

A: No. I never reported it to the police because I was afraid it would hurt us professionally.

Q: Tell us about your relationship with the children.

A: Well, they are living with me now.

Q: No, I am sorry. Let's talk about your relationship or contact with them when your husband was still alive.

A: Oh. Well, Bill refused to be flexible on the timing of my visits with the children so I decided to take him back to court. We were supposed to have a hearing on April 11 to work that out and for me to make arrangements to get paid up on child support payments. He was being really nasty to me and uncooperative.

Q: Let's talk about your actions the day before Bill was killed, April 1st. What were you doing?

A: I went home from the office early on the 1st and in the evening I called my kids to wish them April Fool's Day — it was a part of a running joke in our family. When we were still together we always made it a huge family activity — going out to eat, taking a movie for the kids. I spoke to both kids for a while and told them I loved them.

Q: What did you do after you talked to them?

A: After I talked to them I got so depressed afterwards that I went to several local bars and started drinking. I think one of them was the Chez Monkey, or something like that, and a couple of others. I had an awful lot to drink and I just don't remember all of the details. About midnight I left a message on my business partner's phone — that is Cass Jones — and told him that I was having a few drinks and that I might be in late the next day.

Q: And you used your cell phone to make that call.

A: No. I could not find my cell phone so I used the phone at the bar I was in at the time. I don't think anyone would remember me at those bars, because when I went in I would find a quiet corner and keep to myself. I guess it was about 2 AM when I got to my place.

Q: What happened next?

A: I slept in the next day, April 2nd, until about 9:30 AM. I got up and hurriedly dressed and got to the office about 10:30. I felt terrible. I don't remember the exact time. Cass can probably give you more information. I said hi to him and went into my office to listen to my phone messages. I got a message from a police detective in San Milano.

Q: What did he say?

A: Well, I was in shock. He told me that someone had shot Bill in the back and that he was dead.

Q: Did you call back the detective?

A: No. I did not return the call because I was in a state of shock that something had happened to my kids. I started crying and told my business partner Cass that I needed to come to San Milano to check on my kids and to make sure that your call was not a horrible joke. I drove to Love Field in Dallas and caught a Southeast Airways nonstop flight. I got here about 2 PM and rented a car and drove to Bill's house.

Q: Now, you are aware that cell phone records show that you placed a call from your cell phone while in San Milano on April 1st?

A: Yes, but that is physically impossible. I was in Dallas. That is someone's idea of a cruel April Fool's trick. I swear on a stack of Bibles that I did not kill Bill. I did not kill Bill. I can't believe this has happened. Bill and I had our disagreements but he did not deserve to die. If you think I did it, you are wrong, I did not kill my husband.

Q: Well then, [pause] who did?

A: I would check out Bill's business partner, Morgan Walters, and what Morgan was doing that day.

Q: Why?

A: From what my kids tell me, Bill and Morgan would often shout at each other and fight about their partnership. Morgan had a lot of money riding on that arrangement and if anything happened to it, Morgan stood to lose about $500,000 in business. Bill was bringing in the big bucks for their arrangement. Morgan was a terrible doctor and could not keep patients. I think Morgan was also using drugs which made him a bit crazy.

Q: Let me go back to your cell phone. I am confused. So please help me with that.

A: I cannot explain where my cell phone was on the evening of April 1st. I am sure that I called the kids from my apartment in the early evening. I just don't remember. But I know I called them and they can confirm that. My cell phone number is 555-619-3454. As I said, I was in Dallas the evening of the 1st. I found my cell phone down between my front seats, but that was not until I drove to the airport in Dallas on April 2nd. When and how it got there I can't say. I just don't know.

Q: Now, you own a handgun, don't you?

A: No, not currently. I used to own a 9 mm Glock, which I purchased for myself several years ago. But someone stole it from me last year when I left my car unlocked. They also took some CDs I had just purchased. I did not report it to the police because it was not worth the effort. I bought it at a gun show in Dallas. I do not have any records on it with a serial number or anything.

Q: Now, you claim elsewhere that Cass Jones can provide an alibi for you?

A: Yes.

Q: And we have information that your firm was involved in a federal investigation about some reporting problems, or something like that?

A: We worked that out eventually. No charges were filed.

Q: But Cass Jones will say, or has said, that he was counting on you to sort it all out?

A: Yes.

Q: So, if you were in jail for the murder of your husband, he would have had a hard time working out the situation with the federal government. Right?

A: I am sure that Cass could have found a good lawyer to work it out.

Q: But Cass was counting on you. Isn't that correct?

A: Yes, clearly.

Q: Now, you were interviewed by the police as a suspect in this killing, weren't you?

A: Well they did call me a suspect to my face.

Q: Is this the written statement that you made to the police when they interviewed you? [Shows statement]

A: Yes.

Q: Is there anything else that you would like to add to your testimony?

A: No.

Q: Is there anything that you would like to change?

A: [Confers with her counsel] No.

(END OF TRANSCRIPT)

This is to certify that I have read the transcript of my deposition taken on and that the transcript accurately reflects the questions asked and my answers.

SIGNATURE: Sissy Lockmore

Subscribed and sworn to before me on January 16, [YR-1].

Charles Wilson

Charles Wilson
Certified Shorthand Reporter

CASS JONES' DEPOSITION

ORAL DEPOSITION OF CASS JONES, produced as a witness at the instance of the Plaintiffs, JUNE AND STEVE LOCKMORE and duly sworn, was taken in the above-styled and numbered cause on November 7, [YR-1], from 2:30 PM, to 3:30 PM, before Jorge Stency, Certified Shorthand Reporter in and for the State of Lone Star, reported by machine shorthand, at the law offices of Plaintiff, pursuant to the Lone Star Rules of Civil Procedure and the Provisions stated on the record or attached hereto.

EXAMINATION

QUESTIONS BY PLAINTIFF'S COUNSEL:

Q: Hello.

A: Good afternoon.

Q: We are here to take sworn testimony in the case of Lockmore v. Lockmore. You understand that?

A: Yes, I do.

Q: So, before we get started I want you to understand that if you have some problems with my questions that you ask me to clarify my questions. Okay?

A: Sure. I understand.

Q: Please state your name.

A: My name is Cass Jones. I live in Dallas.

Q: And what do you do? What is your current employment?

A: I am a licensed financial advisor at a company called MoneyInc. My office partner used to be Sissy Lockmore. We had been partners for about six years. She is the senior partner and brings in most of the business, through her contacts.

Q: I want to talk to you about your interaction with Sissy on the day of April 1, [YR-2]. What happened that day?

A: Sissy seemed to be in a real depression. She told me that April 1st was always hard on her because she had a thing about celebrating the day with her kids in San Milano and that because of pending legal problems her husband was not going to let her visit the kids as she always had in the past. She told me that she was going to call them after work.

Q: Did she?

A: Well I did not personally hear her make the call. But I assumed that she did.

Q: Did she say anything to you that day about not being able to find her cell phone?

A: No, not that I can recall. But she did have problems with mislaying things, I guess.

Q: When did she leave the office on the 1st?

A: She left the office about mid-afternoon, complaining of a splitting headache and said she would see me in the morning, the 2nd. I thought nothing of it.

Q: Did you have any further contact with her on the 1st?

A: Yes. That night she called and left a message on my cell phone saying that she had talked to her kids, was in a major "funk," and that she was having a drink or two. She said that because of that she would probably be in late and not to worry. I think that call came in about 11 PM but I cannot remember and I erased it as I always do with my voice mail.

Q: When did you next see her?

A: The next day, April 2nd, she walked into the office about 10:15 or 10:30, something like that, looking really depressed. I am sorry I did not look at the clock at the exact time she came in. She said that she had a hangover and that she was going to get a couple cups of coffee and adjust her attitude. She went into her office and came out a few minutes later telling me that she had just gotten a call from a San Milano police detective saying that her ex-husband Bill had just been shot in the back outside his home. I comforted her for a while and then she said she had to fly to San Milano to see her kids.

Q: This is important. What time did she come into the office that day?

A: I know it's important. I have told you what I remember. I am sorry that I cannot be more specific.

Q: So what happened next?

A: I said that I could drive her to the airport, but she said she would be fine and left the office. She said she would catch a Southeast Airways flight out of Love Field. That airport is about 30 to 40 minutes away from our office. I have made it in less time, but the lights have to be with you and you have to go a bit over the speed limit to do it.

Q: How did she appear to you? Was she distraught?

A: Her demeanor when she told me all of this was somewhat shaken. Given her relationship with her ex-husband, I think she was also more concerned about her children and what would happen to them. She kept me up to date with her legal problems and I was concerned that she might decide to leave the company and move to San Milano. I admit that that really bothered me, because she was the foundation for the company. I am not in the best of health and I really hate to see this happen to Sissy.

Q: Tell me about the problems that your company has had with the FTC. Is that still going on?

A: I think it's cleared up. At least I hope so. We were, or are, being questioned or investigated by the Federal Trade Commission. They told us that some of the information that we supplied in one of annual reports last year was wrong and they think we deliberately lied. We have retained counsel and are hopeful that the FTC will see this as an innocent mistake. Sissy was handling most of that problem.

Q: So you are counting on her to get you out of this mess with the FTC.

A: Absolutely.

Q: Do you have anything that you would like to add?

A: Yes. In my opinion Sissy could not have killed Bill. While she was really angry at him and wanted to see more of her children, she is just not the kind of person who would kill someone.

Q: Anything else? Any corrections you want to make?

A: No.

(END OF TRANSCRIPT)

This is to certify that I have read the transcript of my deposition taken on and that the transcript accurately reflects the questions asked and my answers.

SIGNATURE: Cass Jones

Subscribed and sworn to before me on January 16, [YR-1].

Jorge Stency

Jorge Stency
Certified Shorthand Reporter

Deposition Testimony of Jamie Gonzales

ORAL DEPOSITION OF JAMIE GONZALES, produced as a witness at the instance of the PLAINTIFFS, JUNE AND DICK LOCKMORE, and duly sworn, was taken in the above-styled and numbered cause on November 8, [YR-1], from 2:30 PM, to 3:30 PM, before Jorge Stency, Certified Shorthand Reporter in and for the State of Lone Star, reported by machine shorthand, at the law offices of Plaintiff, pursuant to the Lone Star Rules of Civil Procedure and the Provisions stated on the record or attached hereto.

EXAMINATION

QUESTIONS BY PLAINTIFF'S COUNSEL:

Q: Would you please state your name for the record?

A: Yes, my name is Detective Jamie Gonzales.

B Officer, have you given deposition testimony before?

A: Yes.

Q: So you understand that if you do not understand my questions, you can ask me to clarify them, right?

A: Absolutely.

Q: Good. So could you please tell us your position and duties with the police department?

A: I am a homicide detective, with about 12 years' experience on the force. My duties entail conducting investigations into possible homicides.

Q: Okay. Detective, I would like you to tell the jurors about your investigation into the death of Mr. Bill Lockmore, on April 2d of [YR-2].

A: I received a call at about 0830 hours of a shooting at 123 Ivy Lane here in the city. It appeared that a male, about 40 years old, had been shot in the back. When I arrived at the scene, I talked with the officers who had been called to the scene at about 0815 hours. The coroner's office was also there. They had secured the scene. CSI was already there taking pictures and gathering whatever forensic evidence they could find. It appeared that the victim had been shot in the back, left side, apparently from someone standing in the garage or close to it. The garage door was open. We found no signs of forced entry at any of the entrances or at the garage door itself. His newspaper was still laying in the driveway so I assume that he was going out to pick it up when he was shot.

Q: Did you interview anyone at the scene?

A: Yes, I spoke to Morgan Walters, who apparently discovered the body at about 0805 hours, I mean 8:05 AM, and placed the 911 call to report the shooting.

Q: Did you obtain a statement from that person?

A: Not a formal statement, no. Walters claimed that the victim and he had gotten together that morning to go to a breakfast meeting to go over their plans for a renewed partnership agreement. Walters had apparently arrived just before the shooting and was in the house at the time. He said that they were on their way out of the house to go and get breakfast when Lockmore said that he needed to get the paper out of the driveway and a short time later he heard what he described as a loud pop. He went outside but did not see anyone leaving the premises. I asked him why the garage door was open and Walters said that the victim was "anal retentive" about his morning paper and had longstanding habit of opening the garage door to go out and get it instead of going out the front door.

Q: What was Walters' demeanor?

A: Walters was badly shaken. Walters said that the victim, Bill Lockmore, had been in a longstanding feud with his ex-wife who was taking him to court to get custody of their two kids. And that he had said that he intended to fight to death to make sure that she did not get any more visitation rights. The victim had told Walters that he figured that she would also fight to the death, given her past history of her nasty tactics during the divorce. He said that in his mind, Sissy Lockmore was responsible.

Q: Did you interview anyone else at the scene?

A: Yes, I spoke briefly to the two children at about 9:00 AM. One of the neighbors had gone to the school to bring them back to the house. They both said that they had left for school at about 7:30 and that their dad was in a bad mood when they saw him, before leaving. He told them that Morgan Walters was coming over to pick him up to take him to breakfast. He also told them that he was going to tell Walters that he was going to finally end their partnership. They also said that their mother, who lived in Dallas, would want to know what happened and said they would call her. I said that I would do that for them. They were grateful — they were pretty shaken up. They gave me her office and cell phone numbers.

Q: Did you call his wife, Sissy Lockmore?

A: Yes, at least I tried to get in touch with her. I left messages on her cell number and office number. She did not return my calls.

Q: What was your message?

A: I said that I needed to talk to her right away and that I had some bad news to give her about her family in San Milano. I do not like giving specifics in a voice mail message.

Q: Did you have an opportunity to speak to Ms. Lockmore personally?

A: Yes, later that day she showed up at the house and one of the neighbors told her what had happened and how to get in touch with me. So she called me at my office and we set up an interview for the next morning, April 3rd.

Q: Did you hold that meeting?

A: Yes.

Q: And what happened?

A: Well she said that she would do anything to help catch the person who had done this terrible thing to her ex-husband.

Q: What was her demeanor?

A: She seemed very confident about herself, calm. She did not cry or show any other emotion. She seemed very focused and determined.

Q: Did she make a written statement?

A: Yes, I asked her questions and typed up her statement, which she then read and signed.

Q: Is this it? [Shows statement to witness]

A: Yes.

Q: Please tell us what other steps you took to investigate the murder.

A: Well, going back to the day of the shooting, the 2nd, while at the scene I made a rough drawing of the crime scene, showing the relative position of the body to the garage and the side of the house.

Q: Is this the drawing? [Shows diagram to witness]

A: Yes, it is.

Q: Is it to scale?

A: No, but I tried to be careful in showing the position and location. You will note that the victim was apparently facing the street, probably going out to pick up his newspaper which was still on the driveway. It appeared that he was shot in the back from someone standing either in the garage or to the side of the house, near the garage door. I walked around the side of the house and it appeared that someone had knocked over a garbage can, perhaps the killer, as he or she ran out through the back yard.

Q: There was a backyard?

A: The house sits on the edge of some sort of greenbelt or park. The backyard adjoins some woods and there is path through there that goes to a small parking lot for hikers about 200 feet from the house.

Q: Did you gather any forensic evidence from the side yard, back yard, or greenbelt?

A: As I walked through the back yard, toward the back of the property, I found a parking garage receipt for Love Field, up in Dallas. I picked it up carefully and placed it in a plastic evidence bag. I am sorry, I first initialed it and then placed it in an evidence bag.

Q: Did you investigate this further?

A: Yes, I talked to the owners and managers of this particular parking lot. It's about a block away from the actual terminals, but the property still belongs to the airport. They verified that this ticket was from their machines, but could not give any more information on who had taken it out of the machine on April 1, [YR-1].

Q: Is this it? [Shows exhibit to witness]

A: Yes. Those are my initials, "JG."

Q: Did you ask the parking lot people what someone would do if they lost their ticket?

A: Yes, I did. They explained that if someone loses their ticket they owe the price for full 24 hours of parking. This lot is apparently a short-term, 24-hour lot.

Q: In your years of investigating crimes, is that normal procedure if someone loses their ticket?

A: Absolutely. They can get out of the garage — it just costs them a lot of money.

Q: Okay. Ah, did you take any pictures of the crime scene?

A: Yes, I took several.

Q: Are these pictures you took? [Shows photos to witness]

A: Yes. Two views. They show the victim lying in his driveway.

Q: Did you follow up with any forensic testing?

A: Yes, absolutely. I later read the ballistics report and learned that the victim was shot in the back with a 9 mm weapon. The slug recovered from the victim's body was in pretty decent shape but with no gun to match it to that was pretty much all they could say.

Q: Did you execute any search warrants?

A: Yes. We got a warrant to search the victim's computer and with the help of the Dallas police, they got a warrant to search the defendant's office and home computers. They also received consent to search Morgan Walters' computer.

Q: And what were you looking for?

A: E-mails. It appeared that just before the killing, there had been some e-mail traffic between the victim and Ms. Lockmore, and Morgan Walters.

Q: Okay.

A: We also got a warrant to search the records for cell phone towers to see if we could verify whether the defendant had placed her call to her children on April 1st from the Dallas area. The records indicated that she made the call from her cell phone, from a location here in Bear County, certainly not Dallas.

Q: Did you determine what the phone number for her children was?

A: Yes, it was the home phone number for the victim, the house phone, and that was 555-739-5967.

Q: Are these the records? [Shows records to witness]

A: Yes.

Q: Did you check airline schedules and records?

A: Yes, we could find no one with the name Sissy Lockmore who traveled on April 1st to San Milano, or back to Dallas on the 2nd. We did find her travel record for her flight from Dallas to San Milano on the day of the shooting, as she said in her statement to me.

Q: Detective, is this the airline schedule for Southeast Airways? [Shows to witness]

A: Yes, I got this off their official website. You will note that there are regular flights on about an hourly basis from San Milano to Dallas and back.

Q: How did you get this?

A: I went to their official website and printed it off.

Q: Did you check to see if any of the flights listed on the sheet were cancelled or delayed on the 2nd?

A: Yes, three flights were delayed that date. Flights 908 and 123 from Dallas were delayed about 10 minutes. Flights 565, 339, and 222 were delayed going to Dallas. That is the information that Southeast Airways gave me over the phone when I called.

Q: How far is it from the San Milano airport to the victim's house?

A: About 5 miles.

Q: Do you know the driving time?

A: Yes, we drove three different routes and it took us an average of 35 minutes. We tested it at about the same time of day, early to mid-morning. One route took 45 minutes. Shortest was 25 minutes.

Q: So, did you reach any conclusions about whether Sissy Lockmore killed Bill Lockmore?

A: Yes, absolutely. It's clear that she flew to San Milano on the evening of April 1st, placed a call to her kids, pretending to be in Dallas, called her partner to set up an alibi, drove to her husband's house on the morning of the 2nd., waited for him beside the house, shot him in the back, ran through the backyard to her parked rental car, flew back to Dallas and then went into her office. The timeline fits.

Q: Did you look at the possibility that perhaps Morgan Walters had been involved in the killing?

A: Yes, but not really. While there was some evidence that Walters and Bill Lockmore were having some disagreements about their business, it is well known in criminal investigation circles that this type of case is committed almost always by spouses or ex-spouses. All fingers pointed to Sissy Lockmore. Besides, my gut feelings are rarely wrong on this type of case.

Q: Detective, have you ever been wrong about a case?

A: Yes, just once in about 150 cases. But it was a problem with the lab report. Turns out that the DNA did not match.

Q: Did you interview Cass Jones about Sissy's alibi?

A: Yes, well I called him on April 3rd after Sissy made her statement and he said that he was sure that he saw Sissy on the morning of April 2nd at 10:30 AM, when she came into the office.

Q: Did you conduct an interview with him?

A: Yes, I flew to Dallas and interviewed him on April 5th. At that point, it seemed that he was not being entirely truthful and that perhaps he was also involved in the killing. I coordinated all of this with the Dallas Police Department.

Q: Is this his statement? [Shows statement to witness]

A: Yes, that's it.

Q: After interviewing him, did you have any reason to consider him a suspect?

A: No. While his memory was hazy on details, there was not enough there to pursue him as a person of interest. I also had learned beforehand through other sources that the Federal Trade Commission was looking into some irregularities with his and Sissy's company.

Q: What was that about?

A: It appears that in [YR-2], they had filed some misleading information in one of their annual reports and that an investigation is on-going. At least it was when we investigated the murder. They were facing some serious jail time from what the FTC told me.

Q: Do you have anything to add to your testimony today?

A: No.

(END OF TRANSCRIPT)

This is to certify that I have read the transcript of my deposition taken on and that the transcript accurately reflects the questions asked and my answers.

SIGNATURE: *Jamie Gonzales*

Subscribed and sworn to before me on January 18, [YR-1].

Jorge Stency

Jorge Stency
Certified Shorthand Reporter

Deposition of Morgan Walters

ORAL DEPOSITION OF MORGAN WALTERS, produced as a witness at the instance of the DEFENDANT, SISSY LOCKMORE, and duly sworn, was taken in the above-styled and numbered cause on November 9, [YR-1], from 11:30 A.M., to 3:30 P.M., before Sally A. Gallegos, Certified Shorthand Reporter in and for the State of Lone Star, reported by machine shorthand, at the law offices of Defense Counsel, pursuant to the Lone Star Rules of Civil Procedure and the Provisions stated on the record or attached hereto.

EXAMINATION

QUESTIONS BY DEFENDANT'S COUNSEL:

Q: Good morning. Before we get started on your testimony today, I want to make it clear that I want to be as clear as I can in my questions. So if you do not understand what I am asking, please interrupt me. Okay?

A: Sure.

Q: Okay. For the record will you please state your full name?

A: Morgan Walters.

Q: And what is your current employment?

A: I am a physician, with the Medical Associates here in the city.

Q: Are you familiar with Bill Lockmore?

A: Yes.

Q: How are you familiar with him?

A: We used to be partners in our medical practice — since [YR-18]. We formed the business together.

Q: Why are you no longer partners?

A: He was killed in April, [YR-2].

Q: Please tell the Grand Jury what you know about that.

A: Well, I had talked with Bill the day before and he said that we should really try to rethink our business arrangement and plan for an expansion of his medical research part of the practice. I had some concerns about that but agreed that it was probably time to have a heart-to-heart talk.

Q: Okay.

A: Well, he e-mailed me on March 31st and said that he had some open time on the 2nd. He had taken off that whole week, as he said, to think about what he really wanted to do with his life. I guess he also needed some time to sort through the legal issues with his ex-wife, Sissy, who was making his life hell. He said that we could meet for breakfast and take in the large buffet at the Holton Hotel. I agreed. On the morning of the 2nd, I drove to his house at about 7:50 AM and offered to drive us both to breakfast. As he was grabbing his things, he said that he needed to get the paper out of the driveway. So he walked through the kitchen, out the door to the garage, and I could hear the automatic garage door open. Just a few seconds later I heard a large pop.

Q: Gunfire?

A: Not sure. I thought at the time that maybe something in the garage had exploded or broken. I went into the garage and saw Bill lying on the driveway with blood on his back. I quickly went to him, looked around to see if anyone was there, and then called 9 1 1.

Q: So, you did not see anyone else in the area?

A: No. And I guess the gunshot did not cause any alarm in the neighborhood, because for about 5 minutes I was the only one even outside. Finally one of the neighbors came over and started crying. She said she would go to get the kids.

Q: Let me see if I have this right. You are a licensed physician, right?

A: Yes.

Q: But you apparently did not even attempt to apply first aid, right?

A: No, it was clear to me that he was already dead, from the way he looked.

Q: But you did not actually check him out, right?

A: I didn't need to.

Q: Okay. So what happened next?

A: I was in shock. I just sat on the grass. I could not believe it. One minute we were going to breakfast and the next he was lying there. A few minutes later a patrol car arrived. They helped me up and moved me to the side and one of them asked me some questions while the other one called for an ambulance, I think.

Q: I want to ask you some questions about your disagreement with Mr. Lockmore about your practice and your future plans. You said that there were problems. Those ran pretty deep, didn't they?

A: I guess. Bill was really into medical research but he was a very gifted physician and the patients loved him. Don't get me wrong. I consider myself to be a very good doctor. But Bill had that little something extra in dealing with his patients. We had a 50-50 split on everything, but Bill was the reason we were so successful. And I really appreciated it. But about a year ago he got a grant to do medical research on cancer and was spending more and more time on that research. He had rented another office in the same building to do that. Consequently, we started to lose patients and their good will. That deeply concerned me and I told Bill that without his attention to our medical practice I was not sure how much longer the practice could continue, with mounting bills and all. At the same time it was all very cordial.

Q: Cordial?

A: Well you know, we never really argued about it. A couple of times it got pretty heated but we always calmed down and took a time out.

Q: Okay. What did you know about Sissy Lockmore?

A: She was a real problem for Bill. He was constantly dealing with some issue with her on a weekly basis. She would call the kids all the time, day and night. She was falling way behind on child support payments, and was going to take him back to court — I think about the time he was killed. He told me several times that he feared that she was crazy enough to hurt him, the kids, and herself. When I asked him to explain, he would say something like: "Don't you watch the evening news with all of the family violence?" I thought he was exaggerating. He said that she would sometimes e-mail him with her threats and then follow it up with an e-mail begging for his forgiveness.

Q: Was Bill dating anyone else at the time of the killing?

A: No. The thing with Sissy pretty well kept that from happening.

Q: Anything you would like to change or add?

A: No. That's it.

(END OF TRANSCRIPT)

This is to certify that I have read the transcript of my deposition taken on and that the transcript accurately reflects the questions asked and my answers.

SIGNATURE: Morgan Walters

Subscribed and sworn to before me on January 21, [YR-1].

Sally A. Gallegos

Sally A. Gallegos
Certified Shorthand Reporter

E-Mails Between Bill Lockmore and Morgan Walters

From: MBWalters@hmail.com
Sent: Monday, March 31, [YR-2] 4:35 PM
To: bjlockmore@nol.com
Subject: Breakfast?

Sorry Bill. I am having a really bad day. I can see that you have not responded to my tirade from this morning. Sorry.

Yes, lets do breakfast on Wednesday. This is all going to work out. See you at 8 at your house.

My treat. ☺

From: MBWalters@hmail.com
Sent: Monday, March 31, [YR-2] 2:03 PM
To: bjlockmore@nol.com
Subject: Breakfast?

WHAT IN THE HELL ARE YOU TALKING ABOUT? DO YOU WANT TO KILL THE GOOSE THAT IS LAYING OUR COLLECTIVE GOLDEN EGG?

I CAN'T BELIEVE THIS IS WHAT YOU HAVE BEEN ANGLING FOR.

From: bjlockmore@nol.com
Sent: Monday, March 31, [YR-2] 9:15 AM
To: MBWalters@hmail.com
Subject: Breakfast?

Can we have a breakfast meeting on Wednesday? I just checked with our staff and they told me that you don't have a patient until 10 or so.

I really want to finish our discussion about the practice. I pretty well decided over the weekend that the research is for me. We just have to lick this cancer thing.

How about 8:00?

E-Mails Between Bill Lockmore and Sissy Lockmore

From: Sissy67@Moneymakers.com
Sent: Monday, March 31, [YR-2] 4:30 PM
To: bjlockmore@nol.com
Subject: Stop It!!

Darling Bill. Stop what? I will see you and your jerk lawyer in court!!!!!!!!

Be careful what you wish for!!!!!

From: bjlockmore@nol.com
Sent: Monday, March 31, [YR-2] 2:30 PM
To: Sissy67@Moneymakers.com
Subject: Stop It!!

My lawyer just called telling me that I need to be in court on the 11th What is up now? Can't we just leave this alone. I told you that as soon as you get some of that child support money to me that I will tell my lawyer to go back to court and get you some more visitation with the kids. I know from my friends in Dallas that you have the money and that you are doing all of this out of spite. Until you pay, it will be over my dead body that you see the kids. Get it? Good.

I am surrounded by jerks. Just leave it alone!!!

Detective Gonzales' Drawing of Crime Scene

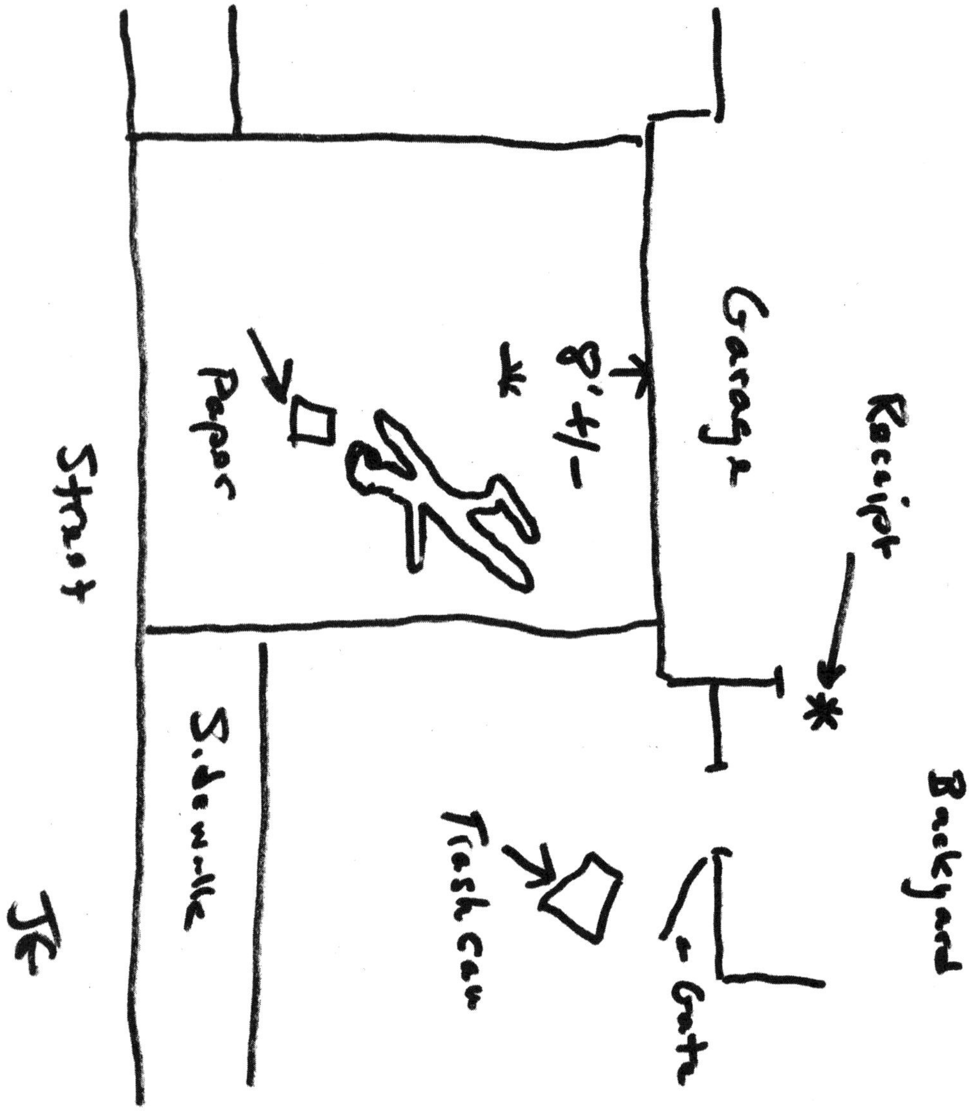

Detective Gonzales' Photographs of Crime Scene

Southeast Airways Website — Schedule for April 2

Southeastern Airways	Book Travel	Special Fares!	Rewards	Help!
Plan Trip	Select Flight	Travel Summary	Rental Cars	Hotels

Select Departing Flights
Dallas LS to San Milano LS (Wednesday, April 2, [YR-2])

Flight	*Depart*	*Arrive*	*Stops*	*Travel Time*
012	6:00 am	7:00 am	0	1:00
654	7:00 am	8:00 am	0	1:00
897	8:00 am	9:00 am	0	1:00
908	9:00 am	10:00 am	0	1:00
432	10:00 am	11:00 am	0	1:00
234	12:00 noon	1:00 pm	0	1:00
123	2:00 pm	3:00 pm	0	1:00
789	3:00 pm	4:00 pm	0	1:00
667	5:00 pm	6:00 pm	0	1:00
786	7:00 pm	8:00 pm	0	1:00
211	9:00 pm	10:00 pm	0	1:00

Select Departing Flights
San Milano LS to Dallas LS (Wednesday, April 2, [YR-2]

Flight	*Depart*	*Arrive*	*Stops*	*Travel Time*
565	7:45 am	8:30 am	0	1:00
668	8:00 am	9:00 am	0	1:00
989	9:05 am	10:05 am	0	1:00
888	10:10 am	11:10 am	0	1:00
423	11:15 am	12:15 pm	0	1:00
227	12:00 noon	1:00 pm	0	1:00
321	2:30 pm	3:30 pm	0	1:00
599	3:30 pm	4:30 pm	0	1:00
339	5:30 pm	6:30 pm	0	1:00
677	7:46 pm	8:46 pm	0	1:00
222	9:35 pm	10:35 pm	0	1:00

Go to Next Step	Start Over	Need Help?

Cell Tower Records for April 1

Sprant

Sprant
Corporate Security
3345 Sprant Park Blvd
Medville, N.J. 00233
Office: 555-315-0454

Jamie Warner
Subpoena Specialist

Fax: 555-315-0755

06/25/[YR-2]

Bear County District Attorney
Attention: Donald Rogers
214 West Nueva Street
Bear County, Lone Star 78283

Your Case Name: State v. Lockmore
Sprant Case Number: [YR-2]-010618

Dear Mr. Rogers:

Pursuant to the search warrant in the above-referenced case, please find attached the requested call detail records (CDR) for date 04/01/[YR-2] for subject number 555-619-3454.

These CDRs are computer generated records produced by our wireless server and are created automatically when a call is placed or received using the Sprant wireless network. These CDRs provide Sprant information about recent system usage such as the identities of sources (calling number), the identities of destinations (called numbers), the duration of each call, and repoll numbers (switch and location being used for call). These records are used routinely and on a daily basis for billing and other internal purposes.

The attached printout does not include the phone numbers or other identifiers of any other subscribers, in order to protect their privacy. That information has been deleted manually from this printout. Repoll # 21 is located in San Milano, Bear County, Lone Star. The computer was directed to search for the requested number between the hours of 5:00 pm and 11:50 pm, on April 1. Should you have any questions or further inquiries, please feel free to contact me.

Sincerely,

Jamie Warner

Jamie Warner
Subpoena Compliance

Sprant

Call Detail Record (CDR)

04/01/[YR-2]
17:00:00 to 23:59:00

Record Printed: 06/25/[YR-2]
Requesting Party: Warner

Calling NBR	Called NBR	Dialed Digits	Start Date	End Date	Duration	Repoll	Switch Name
(555) 619-3454	(555) 739-5967	(555) 739-5967	4/1/[YR-2] 19:34:00	4/1/[YR-2] 20:42:03	68:03	21	SA- San Milano-2

Love Field Parking Garage Receipt

Love Field, Dallas, LS
EASY Parking Lot # 32
Short Term (24 Hours)

Time In: 15:34:02
Date 4/1/[YR-2]

___

___

___

___

___

___

___

Please Pay at Kiosk Before Exiting Gates

Not Responsible For Theft of Items from Vehicle

Form23412245

Jury Instructions

LADIES AND GENTLEMEN OF THE JURY:

I am now going to instruct you about the law governing this case. You are required to accept my instructions as the law. Any ideas you have of what the law is or what the law should be or any statements by the attorneys as to what the law may be, must be disregarded by you, if they are in conflict with these instructions.

1. Claims of Parties

The plaintiffs claim that they sustained damages due to the defendant's wrongful act of shooting their son, Bill Lockmore. The defendant has denied those claims and also denies that the plaintiffs are entitled to recover any damages.

2. Burden of Proof

In this case, the plaintiffs have the burden of proving their claims by a preponderance of the evidence. If you find from the evidence, by a preponderance of the evidence, that the defendant acted intentionally in shooting the plaintiffs's son, and that such actions were the proximate cause of their son's death, then you must find the defendant liable for her actions.

3. Proximate Cause

When I use the expression "proximate cause," I mean a cause that, in the natural or ordinary course of events, produced Bill Lockmore's, the decedent's, death. It need not be the only cause, nor the last or nearest cause. It is sufficient if it combines with another cause resulting in the injury and death.

4. Preponderance of the Evidence

The term "preponderance of the evidence" means that amount of evidence that causes you to conclude that the allegation is probably true. To prove an allegation by the preponderance of the evidence, a party must convince you that the allegation is more likely true than not true.

If the evidence on a particular issue is equally balanced, that issue has not been proven by a preponderance of the evidence. Therefore, the party having the burden of proving that issue has failed with respect to that particular issue.

5. Circumstantial Evidence

A fact or a group of facts may, based on logic and common sense, lead you to a conclusion as to other facts. This is known as circumstantial evidence. A fact may be proved by circumstantial evidence. Circumstantial evidence is entitled to the same consideration as any other type of evidence

6. Opinion Testimony

You may have heard a witness give opinions about matters requiring special knowledge or skill. You should judge this testimony in the same way you judge the testimony from any other witness. The fact that such person has given an opinion does not mean that you are required to accept it. Give the testimony whatever weight you think it deserves, considering the reasons given for the opinion, the witness's qualifications, and all of the other evidence in the case.

7. Credibility of Witnesses

It is up to you to decide the credibility of the witnesses. In making the decision you may consider such factors as whether the witness has made a prior inconsistent statement or has been convicted of a crime. Evidence of this kind may be considered by you in connection with all the other facts and circumstances in evidence in deciding the weight to be given to the testimony of that witness.

8. Damages

a. General

If you decide the plaintiffs are entitled to damages, you shall give such amount as you decide to be fair and just, under all the circumstances. Such damages may include the following items, to the extent you find they have been proved by the evidence:

- Reasonable medical, hospital, funeral and burial expenses;
- Loss of financial support;
- Loss of gifts or other valuable gratuities;
- Loss of parental training and guidance;
- Loss of companionship;
- Plaintiffs's grief, sorrow, or mental anguish.

Whether the plaintiffs have proved these damages is for you to decide, based upon evidence and not upon speculation, guess, or conjecture. The amount of money to be awarded for certain of these elements of damage cannot be proved in a precise dollar amount. The law leaves such amounts to your sound judgment.

b. Punitive Damages

If you find for the plaintiff, you may, but are not required to, award punitive damages. The purposes of punitive damages are to punish a defendant and to deter similar acts in the future. Punitive damages may not be awarded to compensate a plaintiff.

The plaintiff has the burden of proving by a preponderance of the evidence that punitive damages should be awarded, and, if so, the amount of any such damages.

You may award punitive damages only if you find that the defendant's conduct that resulted in the death of Bill Lockmore, the decedent, was a willful act or omission or gross negligence. Gross negligence means conduct or a failure to act that is so reckless that it demonstrates a substantial lack of concern for whether an injury will result.

If you find that punitive damages are appropriate, you must use reason in setting the amount. Punitive damages, if any, should be in an amount sufficient to fulfill their purposes but should not reflect bias, prejudice or sympathy toward any party. In considering the amount of any punitive damages, consider the degree of reprehensibility of the defendant's conduct.

In addition, you may consider the relationship of any award of punitive damages to any actual harm inflicted on the plaintiff.

9. Insurance

Whether a party is insured or not insured has no bearing on any issue that you must decide. You must refrain from any inference, speculation, or discussion about insurance. If you find for the plaintiff, you shall not speculate about or consider any possible sources of benefits the plaintiff may have received or might receive. After you have returned your verdict, the court will make whatever adjustments are necessary in this regard.

10. Verdict Form

To assist you in deciding these issues, I am giving you a verdict form to use during your deliberations. When you have completed the form, please let the bailiff know that you have completed your deliberations.

VERDICT FORM

1. **Liability**

Do you find by a preponderance of the evidence that the defendant caused the death of the plaintiffs's son?

________ YES

________ NO

If your answer is "no," then do not answer Question 2. If your answer is "yes," answer Question 2.

2. **Damages**

Do you find by a preponderance of the evidence that the plaintiffs suffered damages as a result of the defendant's actions?

________ YES

________ NO

If you answered "yes," then please enter the amount of damages, in whole dollar amounts, to which the plaintiffs are entitled.

$ ________________________

3. **Punitive Damages**

Do you find by a preponderance of the evidence that the decedent's death was the result of the defendant's willful act or omission or gross negligence in light of the circumstances?

________ YES

________ NO

If you answered "yes," then please enter the amount of punitive damages, in whole dollar amounts, to which the plaintiffs are entitled.

$ ________________________

Chapter 12
State v. Stonemock

§ 12-1. Introduction

Charlie Stonemock is charged with the murder of his wife, Sally. Responding to a 911 call to their residence, EMT personnel discovered Sally lying on her back on their bed. Charlie told them that he had discovered her submerged in the bathtub when he woke up and realized that she had not come back to bed after getting up earlier in the night. Despite attempts to revive her, Sally was pronounced dead at the scene and an autopsy showed that she had died of drowning.

Although the police initially concluded that Sally's death was an accident, new information was provided a year later by Charlie's second wife, Barbara, and the police reopened the investigation. The State has charged Charlie with Sally's murder, on the theory that he drugged her and then drowned her while she was in the bathtub. Charlie's version is that her drowning was either an accident or a suicide.

§ 12-2. Stipulations Regarding Procedural and Evidentiary Matters.

The following stipulations apply for this case file.

1. The case is being tried in a Lone Star court.
2. This case will be tried only on the issue of guilt or innocence.
3. All witnesses called to testify who have in statements or grand jury testimony identified the defendant, other individuals, or tangible evidence can, if asked, identify the same at trial.
4. The defendant Stonemock signed his statement to the police.
5. Other than what is supplied in the problem itself, there is nothing exceptional or unusual about the background information of any of the witnesses or the defendant that would bolster or detract from their credibility.
6. This case file does not permit a listed witness or the defendant, while testifying, to "invent" an individual not mentioned in this problem and have testimony or evidence offered to the court or jury from that invented individual.
7. "Beyond the record" must not be entertained as an objection.
8. The current year is the year in which this case comes to trial.
9. If any rule of procedure or rule of evidence requires that notice be provided to the court or to the opponent, it will be assumed for the purpose of the problem that the required notice was given.
10. All journal entries and letters by the victim, Sally Stonemock, and the e-mails between Charles and Barbara Stonemock were legally obtained.
11. All entries in Sally Stonemock's journal and her letters were authored by Sally Stonemock.
12. The victim, Sally Stonemock, died on March 30, [YR-2], by drowning, at her home in San Milano, Bear County, State of Lone Star.
13. The autopsy on Sally Stonemock indicated (a) the presence of the drug eszopiclone in her blood but not in a concentration that would have independently caused her death; (b) there were no

visible signs of bruises, contusions, or abrasions on the body; and (c) time of death was between 4:00 and 6:00 A.M.

14. The drug eszopiclone is found in the prescription sleeping pill, Lunesta®.

15. All exhibits in the file are authentic. In addition, each exhibit contained in the file is the original of that document unless otherwise noted on the exhibit or as established by the evidence.

§ 12-3. Case File Materials

Students will be expected to use the following case file materials in presenting their cases.

Statutes — State of Lone Star

I. Lone Star Penal Code Provisions

§ 79.01. Types of Criminal Homicide

(a) A person commits criminal homicide if he intentionally, knowingly, recklessly, or with criminal negligence causes the death of an individual.

(b) Criminal homicide is murder, capital murder, manslaughter, or criminally negligent homicide.

§ 79.02. Murder.

(a) In this Section:

(1) "Adequate cause" means cause that would commonly produce a degree of anger, rage, resentment, or terror in a person of ordinary temper, sufficient to render the mind incapable of cool reflection.

(2) "Sudden passion" means passion directly caused by and arising out of provocation by the individual killed, or another acting with the person killed, which arises at the time of the offense and is not solely the result of former provocation.

(b) A person commits an offense if he:

(1) intentionally or knowingly causes the death of an individual;

(2) intends to cause serious bodily injury and commits an act clearly dangerous to human life that causes the death of an individual; or

(3) commits or attempts to commit a felony, other than manslaughter, and in the course of and in furtherance of the commission or attempt, or in immediate flight from the commission or attempt, he commits or attempts to commit an act clearly dangerous to human life that causes the death of an individual.

(c) Except as provided by Subsection (d), an offense under this section is a felony of the first degree.

(d) At the punishment stage of a trial, the defendant may raise the issue as to whether he caused the death under the immediate influence of sudden passion arising from an adequate cause. If the defendant proves the issue in the affirmative by a preponderance of the evidence, the offense is a felony of the second degree.

* * * * *

§ 79.04. Manslaughter

(a) A person commits an offense if he recklessly causes the death of an individual.

(b) An offense under this section is a felony of the second degree.

§ 79.05. Criminally Negligent Homicide

(a) A person commits an offense if he causes the death of an individual by criminal negligence.

(b) An offense under this section is a state jail felony.

* * * * *

Indictment

COURT'S COPY

Name:	Charles Stonemock
Complainant:	Sally Stonemock
Offense Charge:	Murder
GJ: 1122334	**PH Court: 544**
JN#: 665544	**SID#: 55667788**

Witness: State's Attorney

TRUE BILL OF INDICTMENT

IN THE NAME AND BY AUTHORITY OF THE STATE OF LONE STAR, the Grand Jury of Bear County, State of Lone Star, duly organized, empanelled and sworn as such June term, [YR-1], of the Judicial District Court of said County, at said term, do present in and to said Court that in the County and State aforesaid, and anterior to the presentment of this indictment, and:

COUNT 1: MURDER

on or about March 30, [YR-2], CHARLES STONEMOCK, hereinafter referred to as defendant, then and there intentionally or knowingly, unlawfully, and feloniously kill and murder SALLY STONEMOCK, a human being, hereinafter referred to as complainant, without the authority of law and with deliberate design to effect the death of complainant in violation of Section 79.02, Lone Star Penal Code;

AGAINST THE PEACE AND DIGNITY OF THE STATE.

Frank E. Wilson

Foreperson of the Grand Jury

DEFENDANT'S WRITTEN STATEMENT TO POLICE

STATE OF LONE STAR COUNTY OF BEAR	}	Case Number: 04-9334499

VOLUNTARY STATEMENT OF: CHARLES STONEMOCK

I, Charles Stonemock, after first being duly warned by Det. J. Papparoe #3898 at 0925 hrs, at 214 W. Nueva, on June 16, [YR-1] that (1) I have the right to remain silent and not make any statement at all, and any statement I do make may be used against me at my trial; (2) Any statement I make may be used as evidence against me in Court; (3) I have the right to have a lawyer present to advise me prior to and during any questioning; (4) If I am unable to employ a lawyer, I have the right to have a lawyer appointed to advise me prior to and during any questioning; (5) I have the right to terminate the interview at any time; and I understand that the above rights are continuing rights and may be urged by me at any stage of the proceedings, and I hereby prior to and during the making of this statement, knowingly, intelligently, and voluntarily waive the above rights and give to the said, Det. J. Papparoe #6778, the person to whom this statement is being given, the following written statement:

My name is Charles Stonemock. In [YR-7] I married Sally Worthy, a woman that I had met at work. We also both went to the same church, the Church of the Holy Flame. It's a non-denominational church here in the city. We dated for about a year before getting married. We were very happy together. But in the Spring of [YR-3] I messed up and while we were still married, I had a few dates with a co-worker Barbara Westwood. By dates I mean we had sexual relations.

Sally found out and kicked me out of the house. It was really hard on her and I was a total jerk because she and Barbara had been friends with each other for 10 years. Barbara also went to the same church. We were apart for about six months and then out of the clear blue, in mid-January [YR-2] I think, Sally calls me and says that she has forgiven me and that we should meet and talk about saving our marriage. While Sally and I were apart I did not see Barbara anymore. Barbara felt very guilty about what we had done to Sally and did not want to see me anymore.

When Sally called me she said that she came to the point of understanding that God was telling her that she needed to forgive me and try to reconcile. She said that she had prayed a lot about it and that she had forgiven both Barbara and me for what we had done to her. She said that she was going to talk to Barbara as well. I do not remember the exact date that we had that talk. We finally moved back in together. She insisted that we get more regularly involved in the church and rededicate our lives to each other. I was very happy to be back together with her. I really loved her and wanted to make her happy.

Sally wrote a letter to Barbara, forgiving her, and also met for lunch. Both of them told me that they had worked things out. I do not know what exactly was said, but Sally said that she had forgiven Barbara and Barbara said repeatedly how sorry she was that she had caused Sally so much hurt. I don't think that Barbara ever said anything to either Sally or me about being in love with me.

About that time, I discovered that Sally was journaling, writing out what was on her mind on a fairly regular basis. I saw her writing one day and asked her what she was doing. She told me that during our separation and times of prayer she had seen visions and wanted to record them so she could see if there was a pattern. She told me that she thought that an angel was revealing to her what she needed to do. That was why she decided to get back together with me.

I never really looked at the journal. I may have read one or two entries, but I figured that it was her private property and considering that I needed to walk the narrow line, in light of my unfaithfulness, I did not want to read the whole thing. All I knew was that doing that writing had calmed her and helped her focus on our marriage.

One day in January [YR-2], I believe, she shocked me by saying that she had had a vision the night before in which she had died and that she was going to heaven and that in looking down on earth she had seen Barbara and I together. I told her that was crazy talk and that I did not want to hear about it. I mean, what was she thinking? Here we had just gotten back together and now she is talking about dying. And she told Barbara the same thing.

She started talking more and more about this dying thing and then started complaining about not being able to sleep because of those visions, which became more frequent. After several weeks, I called Barbara and she was very worried about Sally. She said that she had this preoccupation with death and that was not right. Barbara told me that she had fallen in love with me the prior year but had put that behind her when Sally forgave her.

Sally went to a good friend of ours, Pat Campbell, who is an MD. Pat prescribed some powerful sleeping pills, I think Luensta, for Sally but told her to be careful about how many she took. I don't remember what the pills were. I just know that she kept them on the nightstand and would sometimes get up in the middle of the night and take them. She also started taking hot baths at night to help her relax. The next day she would sleep late. So I guess the pills and bath worked.

All this time though, she seemed happy and kept talking about seeing Barbara and me together. It really bothered me. She was restless but happy. She said that I should trust more in God and that I would see that everything was going to work out fine.

In February, I believe, I got a call from Barbara that she needed to see me. We met at a local place and she said that she was really worried about Sally. She said that she had gotten a letter from Sally stating again that if anything happened to her, that she and I were supposed to get back together. She briefly showed me the letter and I said that I was worried about Sally. I read through it quickly.

On March 30, Sally and I went to bed early and about 1:00 AM I was aware that she was getting up. I had my back turned to her. I heard her open her pill bottle and then was aware that water was running into the bathtub. I woke up at 6:30 AM. She was not in the bed. I went into the bathroom and she was in a full tub of water, under the water. I screamed her name and pulled her out. I carried her to the bed and tried to do CPR for a few minutes. I immediately called 911 but did not get any answer. So I called our friend Pat Campbell who came over. When Pat saw what was happening, Pat called 911 and they came over. They said there was nothing they could do. I just slumped into a chair and cried out my eyes. I could not believe it. She was gone.

Pat told the EMT about the sleeping pills and showed them the bottle that was on her nightstand. The police came over and talked to me briefly. They also talked to Pat and afterwards I learned that they had ruled that Sally's death was an accidental overdose.

Several months later Barbara and I got married by the minister of our church, in a small ceremony. We both cried throughout the ceremony, knowing that Sally was looking down and smiling, finally at peace with herself.

I gave Sally's journal to the police when this all happened, if you think that will help you. You can have it. I don't want anything to do with it.

Things got tough between Barbara and me and we are now separated. I guess there was just too much baggage from all of this. Hopefully we can get back together. I think right now she blames me for

Sally's death. I have no idea where she got that idea except that she feels guilty that she and I brought all of this on Sally and drove her crazy.

I did send an e-mail to Barbara several days before Sally died. Based on what Sally had told me I thought that her death was coming quickly. But I had no idea how quickly it would come.

This is the end of my statement. I have read this statement and it is true and correct.

WITNESS: *Danny Mattz* SIGNATURE: *Charles Stonemock*

DATE: **June 16, [YR-1]**

GRAND JURY TESTIMONY OF JESS PAPPAROE

IN RE:	BEFORE THE GRAND JURY
	OF
GRAND JURY INVESTIGATION	BEAR COUNTY, STATE OF LONE STAR

* * * * * *

****

COURT REPORTER'S

Q AND A TRANSCRIPT OF TESTIMONY OF

DET. JESS PAPPAROE

AUGUST 5, [YR-1]

****

* * * * *

BE IT REMEMBERED, that on AUGUST 5, [YR-1], the above-entitled matter came on for hearing before the Grand Jury of Bear County, sitting in San Milano, State of Lone Star, being presented by DALLAS MOSBY, Assistant Criminal District Attorney, for consideration by the members thereof.

HEATHER STEVENS was duly sworn as Court Reporter.

WHEREUPON, the following evidence was introduced and proceedings had, to-wit, beginning at 9:00 o'clock a.m. and concluding at 10:00 o'clock a.m.

DETECTIVE JESS PAPPAROE, The Witness,

GRAND JURY FOREMAN: Do you solemnly swear that you will not divulge either by words or signs any matter about which you may be interrogated, and that you will keep secret all proceedings of the Grand Jury which may be had in your presence, and that you will true answers make to such questions as may be propounded to you by the Grand Jury or under its direction, so help you God?

THE WITNESS: I do.

EXAMINATION BY DALLAS MOSBY:

Q: Detective Papparoe, as with any witness who comes before the Grand Jury, I need to give you the definitions of perjury and aggravated perjury.

A person commits the offense of perjury if, with intent to deceive and with knowledge of the statement's meaning, that person makes a false statement under oath or swears to the truth of a false statement previously made and the statement is required or authorized by law to be made under oath.

Perjury is a Class A Misdemeanor, which is punishable by anywhere up to one year in the Bear County Jail and/or a fine of up to $4,000.

Perjury becomes aggravated perjury if the person commits perjury, makes that false statement during or in connection with an official proceeding, and Grand Jury proceedings are official proceedings, and the statement is material.

Aggravated perjury is a third-degree felony, which means it's punishable by anywhere from two to ten years in the Lone Star Department of Corrections, and there's a potential fine of up to $10,000. Do you understand this?

A: Yes, sir.

Q: Would you please state your name for the grand jury?

A: Yes, my name is Detective Jess Papparoe.

Q: Could you please tell us your position and duties with the police department?

A: I am a homicide detective, with about 9 years experience on the force. My duties entail conducting investigations into possible homicides.

Q: Okay. Detective, I would like you to tell the jurors about your investigation into the death of Mr. Sally Stonemock, on March 30, [YR-1]?

A: Well. I did not work the case in [YR-2]. Another detective, Detective Rod Jones worked it, but he has since moved out of state. The police at that time concluded that her death was accidental. But recently, Barbara Stonemock, she was Barbara Westwood then, called us and said that she had some new information on Sally Stonemock's death.

Q: Okay. First, can you take us back to [YR-2] and briefly tell us what happened, before you get to Ms. Stonemock's information?

A: Right. Our records show that on March 30 at 7:00 AM, EMT was called to the Stonemock residence. The call was placed by a Dr. Campbell. When EMT arrived they found a woman lying on a bed, nude, dry, and covered with a sheet. Her hair was wet. There was no water around the bathtub, which was empty, except for some wet spots. There were several towels on the floor which were wet. A man identified as Charles Stonemock told them that he had found his wife in a full tub of water, under the water. He said that he had tried to call 911 but could not get through and that he had tried CPR, before calling his friend, Dr. Campbell. Efforts to revive the woman, who we now know was Sally Stonemock, failed and she was pronounced dead at the scene by the coroner.

Q: Please continue.

A: Well, in the meantime several police officers arrived and talked with the EMT, Charles Stonemock, and Dr. Campbell. They did not get much information out of Stonemock and Campbell. They interviewed them and reviewed a journal that Sally Stonemock had written shortly before her death and was given to them by Stonemock at the scene. He told them the journal would explain everything. Dr. Campbell said that he had prescribed some sleeping pills for Sally. In his opinion, he believed that she had probably taken a few too many, fell asleep in the tub, and simply slipped under the water and drowned without even waking up. After they reviewed that journal in more detail back at the office, and talked with others who knew Sally, the police officers working the case concluded that the drowning was not a murder. It was either accidental and perhaps even suicide. So after talking to the DA, the case was closed and no charges were brought against anyone.

Q: Thank you. So, now bring us up to date with Barbara Stonemock.

A: As I said, she called us on June 2 [YR-1] and said that she had new information. So I called her in and talked to her. She gave me an e-mail that she said had been sent by Charles Stonemock to her just before Sally died.

Q: Is this it? [Shows to witness]

A: Yes, this is it. You can see that it says that very soon they would be able to be together because he expected Sally's death very shortly.

Q: Did she comment on why that seemed important to the investigation?

A: Yes, I asked her that. She said that she and Charles had earlier had an affair, in [YR-3], and that several weeks before Sally died she and Charlie had started talking regularly again, which led to the e-mail. She responded and asked what that meant, because she was anxious to be together with him, and he said that it was best that she not know the details. She said that she had not shared that with the police in [YR-2] when Sally died, and now regretted it.

Q: Why?

A: Well, they, Charles and Barbara, got married in May [YR-2] but that she had caught him cheating on her a couple of months later, and was concerned that he might try to kill her, the way he killed his first wife. Those were her words. "Kill."

Q: Okay. So what other information do you have that would indicate foul play in this case?

A: I went back through the file and determined that several facts pointed to death as the result of actions, or inactions, by Charles Stonemock. First, there are no records that he ever tried to call 911. Second, her body was dry when the EMT arrived and when he was questioned about that in [YR-2], he said that he guessed that he had dried her off before putting her on the bed, but could not recall. Third, knowing that she was taking pills and getting into the bathtub, he did not try to check on her during the evening. Finally, I have looked at Sally's journal and there are entries that indicate that Charles may have encouraged, or condoned, his wife's belief that she would die and that Charles and Barbara should get together. In short he had the motive and the opportunity to see that Sally died.

Q: Detective, is this Sally's journal? [Shows to witness]

A: Yes, that is it.

Q: Did Barbara Stonemock have anything else to add to the case?

A: She did comment that through the weeks before Sally died, that Charles publicly said that he was concerned about Sally's mental state but that when they talked alone, he admitted that perhaps the best thing was for Sally to die and to be finally at peace.

Q: So what do you think the evidence shows?

A: I think he either gave her the extra pills or let her take the pills. After giving a chance for the pills to take effect, he went into the bathroom and while she was asleep, he pushed her under the water. The estimated time of death was 4 AM to 6 AM. He got back into bed, got up several hours later and put on a charade of being concerned about her death.

Q: Do you recognize these photos? (Shows three photographs to witness)

A: Yes, these are photographs that were taken of the scene by the police photographer and were in the case files. This first one is of the bathroom, this is a picture of the bedroom, and this one is a picture taken in the hallway showing the bathroom on the left and the bedroom on the right.

Q: Okay. Thanks. Now you mentioned that some pills were on the nightstand?

A: Yes, these pictures were taken about an hour after the body was removed from the house. Our records indicate that the officers at the scene picked up the pills for processing and had left the premises before the police photographer was able to take these pictures. He was apparently at another location working another homicide and got delayed. At the time he took the pictures, he had worked for the force for about 8 years. He is very good at what he does.

Q: So, just so we are clear. Mr. Stonemock says that he carried his wife from the bathroom to the bed, right?

A: Yes, through the hallway. There is no door directly connecting the bathroom to the bedroom.

Q: Thank you. Are there any questions from the grand jurors?

QUESTION BY GRAND JUROR

Q: Yes, I have one. Detective, do you have any forensic evidence linking Charles with Sally's death?

A: Well, we don't have fingerprints or other physical evidence, if that is what you mean. But the evidence all points to homicide.

Q: Okay. Please step outside for just a few minutes.

THE WITNESS: Okay.

[The Witness leaves the Grand Jury Room at 10:00 a.m., and is subsequently dismissed.]

(END OF TRANSCRIPT)

GRAND JURY TESTIMONY OF PAT CAMPBELL

IN RE:		BEFORE THE GRAND JURY
	}	OF
GRAND JURY INVESTIGATION		BEAR COUNTY, STATE OF LONE STAR

* * * * * *

****

COURT REPORTER'S

Q AND A TRANSCRIPT OF TESTIMONY OF

PAT CAMPBELL

MAY 5, [YR-1]

****

* * * * *

BE IT REMEMBERED, that heretofore, to-writ on AUGUST 5, [YR-1], the above-entitled matter came on for hearing before the Grand Jury of Bear County, sitting in San Milano, State of Lone Star, being presented by DALLAS MOSBY, Assistant Criminal District Attorney, for consideration by the members thereof.

HEATHER STEVENS was duly sworn as Court Reporter.

WHEREUPON, the following evidence was introduced and proceedings had, to-wit, beginning at 10:15 o'clock a.m. and concluding at 11:10 o'clock a.m.

PAT CAMPBELL, The Witness,

GRAND JURY FOREMAN: Do you solemnly swear that you will not divulge either by words or signs any matter about which you may be interrogated, and that you will keep secret all proceedings of the Grand Jury which may be had in your presence, and that you will true answers make to such questions as may be propounded to you by the Grand Jury or under its direction, so help you God?

THE WITNESS: I do.

EXAMINATION BY DALLAS MOSBY:

Q: Dr. Campbell, as with any witness who comes before the Grand Jury, I need to give you the definitions of perjury and aggravated perjury.

A person commits the offense of perjury if, with intent to deceive and with knowledge of the statement's meaning, that person makes a false statement under oath or swears to the truth of a false statement previously made and the statement is required or authorized by law to be made under oath.

Perjury is a Class A Misdemeanor, which is punishable by anywhere up to one year in the Bear County Jail and/or a fine of up to $4,000.

Perjury becomes aggravated perjury if the person commits perjury, makes that false statement during or in connection with an official proceeding, and Grand Jury proceedings are official proceedings, and the statement is material.

Aggravated perjury is a third-degree felony, which means it's punishable by anywhere from two to ten years in the Lone Star Department of Corrections, and there's a potential fine of up to $10,000. Do you understand this?

A: Yes, sir.

Q: Would you please state your name for the grand jury?

A: My name is Pat Campbell.

Q: Do you know Charles Stonemock?

A: Yes.

Q: Please tell the grand jury about your relationship with Mr. Stonemock.

A: Well, we have been close friends for almost 15 years. I was also good friends with his first wife, Sally. We had all met in high school and stayed friends through college and then when I went to medical school. For the last several years I was their personal physician.

Q: You are a licensed doctor?

A: Yes. I am in general practice. I have been for five years.

Q: So you are authorized to write prescriptions?

A: Yes, of course.

Q: In [YR-2], did you ever write a prescription for sleeping pills for Sally Stonemock?

A: Yes. It was for Lunesta.

Q: Please tell us about that.

A: Sally was going through a difficult time. She and Charles had just gotten back together again after being separated for some months. She said that she was having visions and dreams about dying and about Charles and their friend, Barbara, getting married. She was happy for them and was not afraid of dying. But she was having trouble settling down at night and sleeping. So she asked me for some pills, or something to help her sleep.

Q: Go on.

A: I was concerned about her mental health and recommended that she go through counseling. In my mind, she showed signs of being suicidal. But I wrote her a prescription for a sleeping pill. I told her to be careful not to take too many and again encouraged her to start talking to someone like a counselor or minister. Frankly, I was concerned that she might take too many to fulfill this sort of prophecy about dying. So I talked to Charles as well and told him to make sure that she did not take too many. I was concerned about her.

Q: When she referred to the fact that she thought she was going to die, did she give any specifics?

A: Yes and no. She said that she had a very clear picture that she would die soon. But she never said what she would die from, or of. She, she . . . had a sort of calmness about her when she spoke about it. And she would add that in her visions she saw Barbara and Charles together again, married.

Q: And she was okay with that?

A: Yes. I think so.

Q: What did you think?

A: Frankly, it was too weird for me.

Q: Did you ever talk to Charles about what Sally was saying?

A: Oh yes. I was concerned for both of them. When I mentioned the fact that Sally had told me about Barbara and Charles getting together he simply said that that was crazy. In my mind, well, it crossed my mind that Sally may have had some sort of death wish. When she died, it did not really surprise me.

Q: Okay. Well, did you ever hear Charles say anything about Sally's predictions of dying?

A: He said that she seemed convinced of her vision or premonition, whatever. He also added that what would be would be. Or something like that.

Q: I want to focus on the day that Sally died, March 30, [YR-2]. I understand that you were there?

A: Not when she died, no. But I got a call early in the morning, about 6:45 or so from Charles. He was very excited and said he needed my help immediately. He said something about finding Sally in the bathtub and she was not breathing. I asked him if he had called 911 and he said that he was afraid to do so, but would try. And then he started to cry. So I told him to call 911 and ran over to their house. I got there at about 7 AM. He had placed Sally on their bed with a sheet over her. I checked her pulse and found none. When I asked Charles if he had called 911, he shook his head. So I called them at about 7 AM or so and they arrived at about 7:15. This is hard.

Q: Go ahead.

A: Well, I talked to the EMT and they said that they could not find any signs of life, so they called the coroner and the police showed up shortly thereafter to assist. I told them that I had prescribed sleeping pills for Sally and that I was afraid that she had overdosed or had fallen asleep in the tub and slipped under the water. The bottle of pills was still on her nightstand. She had just refilled the bottle and it looked like four or five were missing — about four days' worth.

Q: Did you hear Charles say anything to the police or EMTs?

A: Yes, he said that he found her in the tub and carried her to the bed and tried to do CPR. He seemed distraught. They took him into the front room to talk with him further and I was not permitted to listen in. Another officer was talking to me.

Q: Did you tell him that you had called 911?

A: Yes.

Q: Did you say anything about whether Mr. Stonemock had called 911?

A: No, at the time I was just concerned that someone had called them.

Q: Okay. Would you please step outside for a few minutes.

A: Yes. [Witness leaves room]

[Witness steps outside at 11:10 a.m. and is subsequently dismissed.]

(END OF TRANSCRIPT)

Grand Jury Testimony of Barbara Stonemock

IN RE:		BEFORE THE GRAND JURY
	}	OF
GRAND JURY INVESTIGATION		BEAR COUNTY, STATE OF LONE STAR

* * * * * *

****

COURT REPORTER'S

Q AND A TRANSCRIPT OF TESTIMONY OF

BARBARA STONEMOCK

AUGUST 5, [YR-1]

****

* * * * *

BE IT REMEMBERED, that heretofore, to-writ on AUGUST 5, [YR-1], the above-entitled matter came on for hearing before the Grand Jury of Bear County, sitting in San Milano, State of Lone Star, being presented by DALLAS MOSBY, Assistant Criminal District Attorney, for consideration by the members thereof.

HEATHER STEVENS was duly sworn as Court Reporter.

WHEREUPON, the following evidence was introduced and proceedings had, to-wit, beginning at 1:30 o'clock P.M. and concluding at 2:20 o'clock p.m.

BARBARA STONEMOCK, The Witness,

GRAND JURY FOREMAN: Do you solemnly swear that you will not divulge either by words or signs any matter about which you may be interrogated, and that you will keep secret all proceedings of the Grand Jury which may be had in your presence, and that you will true answers make to such questions as may be propounded to you by the Grand Jury or under its direction, so help you God?

THE WITNESS: I do.

EXAMINATION BY DALLAS MOSBY:

Q: Please tell us your name.

A: My name is Barbara Stonemock. Before I was married I was Barbara Westwood.

Q: The Grand Jury is looking into the circumstances of the death of Sally Stonemock in March [YR-2].

A: Yes, I know.

Q: And I understand that you may have some information that will assist the Grand Jury?

A: Yes.

Q: First, please tell us about your relationship with Sally Stonemock.

A: Sally and I were friends in high school and college. When Sally met Charlie I thought it was the best thing that could ever happen to her. They seemed really happy. The three of us attended the same church, Church of the Holy Flame. We really loved that environment and Sally seemed to be especially grateful for the spiritual aspects of the church.

Q: At some point you had an affair with Charles Stonemock?

A: Yes, in [YR-3], Charles and I worked in the same office, Willow Office Supply, and fell in love and started seeing each other.

Q: How often would you get together?

A: At least several times a week. For about two months. The chemistry was there. But I realized that eventually, if Sally found out, it would devastate her.

Q: And she did learn of the affair?

A: Yes. In the summer of [YR-3], she learned about what we were doing. I think another mutual friend told her. I guess it does not make any difference now. The damage was done and Sally was crushed. She made Charlie move out but never started divorce proceedings.

Q: Why?

A: I am not sure. At least then I was not sure. About six months later she told Charlie that she had come to the point in her spiritual walk where she could forgive him, and me.

Q: Did you continue your relationship with Charlie?

A: No, when Sally found out, that pretty well killed things for both of us. I quit my job at Willow and Charlie was really torn up. When she called him to make up he jumped at the chance.

Q: What did Sally say to you?

A: Well, she first wrote me a letter in late January [YR-2].

Q: Is this it? [Shows letter to witness]

A: Yes.

Q: Please continue.

A: Well in the letter she said that she forgave me. Then we later met for met lunch a few days later. She told me that she forgave me and wanted to be friends again. Just like that. She was really a special person. I miss her terribly.

Q: At any point did she talk about dying and your eventually getting together with Mr. Stonemock?

A: Yes. After we started talking again she told me that she had been having visions or dreams or something like that. They were very real to her and she believed that God was talking to her. She said that she had written about them in her journal.

Q: Did you ever see the journal?

A: No. I considered that very private.

Q: But she talked about dying?

A: Yes. We talked on the phone several times.

Q: Did she ever say what she expected to be the cause of her death?

A: No. She just said that she did not think she would live to see the new year.

Q: Did you see her again?

A: No. Our lunch in January was the last time we actually saw each other. About two weeks after we met, she wrote me another letter. I read it and immediately called Charlie.

Q: Is this the letter? [Shows letter to witness]

A: Yes. This is it. She says that after she dies she wants Charlie and me to get married. That it's the right thing to do. I called Charlie and he came over. He read it quickly and said that he was really worried about Sally.

Q: Did he seem genuinely worried about Sally?

A: I guess, no, not really. In public he would express deep concern but in private he would say that maybe it would best for Sally if she died.

Q: Go on.

A: Several weeks before Sally died, Charlie started calling me and sending me e-mails saying that he loved me and that it was Sally's wish to get back together. So we did.

Q: At any point in all of this did you have any doubts about whether Sally's death was accidental?

A: Well, I did. But I loved Charlie and I think that I may have wanted it to be accidental.

Q: What do you mean?

A: Well, just a few days before Sally drowned, Charlie sent me an e-mail saying that soon it would all be over and that we would be together, forever.

Q: Did you ever talk to him about that?

A: Yes. I asked him what he meant and he said that he was sure that Sally was right — that she would die shortly and that it would not be good for me to know the details. Then he just kissed me on my cheek and said that he loved me more than ever.

Q: So you got married?

A: Yes. After Sally died. We got married in May [YR-2]. Charlie convinced me that that was what Sally wanted. I was not so sure. But I loved Charlie.

Q: Are you still married to him?

A: We are separated. Shortly after we got married, like months, I found out that Charlie was having an affair with one of his co-workers, again at Willow, where he has worked all this time. I was really angry and kicked him out of the house.

Q: Is that when you called the police?

A: No, I did not. It was months later, in June, [YR-1], and I said that I had some new information about Sally Stonemock's death. They immediately came over and talked to me.

Q: And the new information was?

A: That Charlie told me that he expected Sally to die shortly and that we could be together. I gave them the e-mail. I had not told the police when Sally died and now it all seemed to fit together. Charlie had taken advantage of Sally's state of mind. He was, and is, a real jerk.

Q: Is this the e-mail you are talking about? [Shows exhibit to witness]

A: Yes, that's it.

Q: So do you think that he killed her?

A: Yes. I do. I think he either helped her take too many pills or when she was in the tub, he pushed her underneath the water after she fell asleep in the warm water.

Q: Why did it take you so long to call the police and give them this information?

A: Different reasons. I guess I was a bit scared that he would do the same to me. And a part of me still loved him and I knew that giving the police the e-mail would put him in jail.

Q: I have one more area of inquiry. Our records search showed that you were convicted nine years ago in the State of Oregon for theft of some state government property?

A: Yes.

Q: And the records show that you were charged with a felony count, because of the value of the items you took.

A: Yes.

Q: But you pleaded guilty to one count of felony theft?

A: Yes. My lawyer worked out a deal with the DA. I pled guilty.

Q: And you received a sentence of 5 years, suspended? And a fine of $1,000?

A: Yes, to both of those.

Q: Do you now understand the solemn requirement to tell the truth if you are placed under oath.

A: Absolutely. That was during a very dark period of my life and I know that I did wrong.

Q: So have you told us the truth today?

A: Absolutely.

Q: Okay. Thank you. Would you please step outside for a few minutes? [Witness leaves Grand Jury Room]

A: Witness: Okay.

[Witness leaves the Grand Jury Room at 2:20 p.m., and is subsequently dismissed.]

(END OF TRANSCRIPT)

Sally Stonemock's First Letter to Barbara Stonemock

January 25, [YR-2]

Dearest Barbara,

Please do not tear up this letter, because I know that you probably cannot believe that I would ever want to talk to you again. I do.

I have come to the place in my spiritual life where I can forgive you and Charlie for the hurt that you caused the three of us. I am not sure I will ever understand why it happened but I now believe that God has called me to forgive both of you.

I have talked to Charlie and I have invited him back into my life. It may be difficult at first to trust him completely, but I have never stopped loving him and I pray that this will all work out.

With love and forgiveness,

Sally

Sally Stonemock's Second Letter to Barbara Stonemock

Feb 13, [YR-2]

Barbara,

I just wanted you to know that I have been having visions that you and Charlie will someday be together, with my blessing from heaven. I want you to know that after I am gone, I want you and Charlie to spend the rest of your lives together.

I miss you and look forward to getting together again in the near future.

Love, Sally

Sally Stonemock's Personal Journal

January 1

I have decided to start the new year with a journal. I have been reading some of the books from our church and one of the suggestions for dealing with life's issues is to journal your way to health. Sounds radical. But worth a try. ☺ I pray that it works. Over the last several months there have been days when I thought that it might be best to just lie down and die. I just didn't want to go on. But it's a new day!! And a new year.

Jan 7

Today was an interesting day. First, last night I had the most wonderful vision of heaven. An angel guided me. Not sure what it all means but I am praying that God will open my eyes to whatever message I am supposed to get. Second, I was reading my Bible and focused on the passages dealing with forgiveness. I had the most strange feeling that I had not been as forgiving as I should. Despite my best intentions I don't know that I will journal every day.

January 8

More dreams or visions, or whatever last night. I saw an angel come down out of the bright clouds and say that I was loved and that I should love and forgive in return. I asked the angel what or who I should forgive and the angel said, "you know."

January 10

I missed the journal yesterday. Sorry. I was not feeling well and just could not get out of bed to even eat.

Jan. 11

I am feeling better today. In my dreams last night it was revealed to me that I should forgive Charlie and Barbara for what they did to me. I just don't know, it hurts so bad. I am going to spend the day thinking about this.

Jan 12

I spoke to my pastor today. He said that its not usually unusual that God would use dreams or visions to speak to us but that I should not simply assume that any angel of light is my friend. There are many examples in religious literature.

January 13

Nothing new today. I did not have any dreams last night. Maybe I was just imagining them.

January 14

Nope, they are real. Last night I had the most marvelous and peaceful experience. I dreamed that I had died and was in the heavenly places, with beautiful plants, people, and music. An angel walked with me through a glorious garden and explained that I had one more thing to do on earth before I died, which would be soon. I was supposed to fully forgive Charlie and Barbara.

Jan. 15

I called Charlie today. What a relief. I told him that I forgave him. He started crying and said he was so glad to hear that. He is going to move back into the house. I feel so much better. I feel like I have a new life. Not sure I can forgive Barbara just yet. And not sure I can tell Charlie about my dreams/visions.

January 22

I did it. I had another dream last night that was basically another message that I had to forgive Barbara. I also got the clear message that my time on this earth is coming to a close and that it's important for my own spiritual well-being that I needed to forgive <u>both</u> Charlie and Barbara.

January 24

I finally told Charlie about my dreams and visions. At first he seemed freaked out but then said that if it had meant that we would be together again, that it was fine with him. I told him that I was going to write to Barbara and forgive her as well. He smiled and thanked me for being back in his life.

Jan. 25

Mailed a letter to Barbara today.

January 27

Had lunch with Barbara and told her about what had led me to forgive her. She said that it was pretty "interesting" that I was hearing directly from God in my dreams.

February 3

I have not been good about writing in the journal. So much has happened. Things are good with Charlie. But now I am having dreams that I need to move to the next phase and bless the upcoming union between Charlie and Barbara. It has been revealed to me that I will die soon and that after I am gone, Charlie and Barbara are going to be man and wife. No sign on how I will die.

Feb 11

More dreams last night about my end and Charlie and Barbara. I told Charlie about this at breakfast, along with all of the stuff about my dreams and visions. He was speechless.

February 13

I wrote to Barbara today and told her that I had had a vision about her and Charlie being together and that it was fine with me. I told her that I was going to be going to a better place.

February 20

Charlie told me this morning at breakfast that he had had a dream too. He said that he had seen me in heaven smiling down on him and Barbara. I was so happy!!! I told him that his dream confirmed my visions and dreams. But he looked sad.

March 6

I had another vision. My time is drawing to a close. I have never gotten a clear picture of how I will die. I am simply trusting that God knows best. I am having trouble sleeping, however, and got some sleeping pills. Supposed to be careful with them. Charlie said he would help me remember how many to take. I love him so much!!!! Charlie said that he had had another dream in which he saw me looking down from heaven on him and Barbara. Thank God for the confirmation.

March 12

Still having trouble sleeping without the pills. Have developed a routine. If I cannot sleep, I get up and run a hot bath, take my dosage of pills and relax. It works. Charlie helps me get out of the bath because I am really really relaxed. Ahhhhh. LOL. Sometimes I think it might be best just to slip off to eternity when I fall asleep in the tub. That would be a good way to go.

March 15

Charlie said again that he had had a very vivid dream. He said that he had seen himself and Barbara in a garden with children and I was smiling down on them from heaven. He said that it was so real to him he felt a strange peace come over him. Now I am at peace too.

March 25

Nothing new. Maybe all of this vision stuff is nothing more than hopeful thinking, or deep seated fears of dying. I just don't know. I told Charlie the same thing at breakfast this morning. He took my hand and smiled at me. I love him so much it hurts.

March 28

Another dream last night of my being in heaven. It was so peaceful and the garden was so alive!!! I am not afraid to die.

March 29

Charlie and I had a bad fight today. I am not sure what happened to us. I found out that he had been e-mailing Barbara but felt the need to hide it from me. I felt betrayed. He cried and said that he was sorry that he had done that. He knew that it was wrong. I am really torn. I know that he and Barbara will be together. But I wish that he had told me that he was talking to her again. I told him that his time would come soon enough, that I felt that I was close to my time to go to heaven. Perhaps tonight I will have another vision that will make it all clear for me.

E-MAILS BETWEEN CHARLES AND BARBARA (WESTWOOD) STONEMOCK

From: CStonemock@sssignal.com
Sent: March 27, [YR-2] 8:55 PM
To: BWestwood@.col.com
Subject: Love

Better for you to have plausible deniability.:-)

From: BWestwood@.col.com
Sent: March 27, [YR-2] 8:25 PM
To: CStonemock@sssignal.com
Subject: Love

WHAT?

From: CStonemock@sssignal.com
Sent: March 27, [YR-2] 7:55 PM
To: BWestwood@.col.com
Subject: Love

Things are moving quickly with Sally. You and I will be together very shortly, for a very long time. I love you with all of my heart!

COURT'S COPY

Name: Sally Stonemock
Complainant: Charles Stonemock
Offense Charged: MURDER

JURY INSTRUCTIONS

LADIES AND GENTLEMEN OF THE JURY:

The defendant, CHARLES STONEMOCK, stands charged by indictment COUNT 1 with the offense of murder, alleged to have been committed on or about the March 30, [YR-2], in Bear County, State of Lone Star. The defendant has pleaded not guilty.

1.

Our law provides that a person commits the offense of murder if he or she intentionally or knowingly causes the death of an individual.

2.

A person acts intentionally, or with intent, with respect to a result of his or her conduct when it is his conscious objective or desire to cause the result.

A person acts knowingly, or with knowledge, with respect to a result of his conduct when he is aware that his conduct is reasonably certain to cause the result.

3.

Now, if you find from the evidence beyond a reasonable doubt that on or about March 30, [YR-2], in Bear County, State of Lone Star, that the defendant CHARLES STONEMOCK, did intentionally or knowingly cause the death of an individual, namely SALLY STONEMOCK, by drowning her, then you will find the defendant Charles Stonemock guilty of murder as charged in the indictment.

Unless you so find beyond a reasonable doubt, or if you have a reasonable doubt as to whether the defendant is guilty of murder, then you will find him not guilty.

4.

You are instructed that you may consider all relevant facts and circumstances surrounding the killing, if any, and the previous relationship existing between the accused and the deceased, if any, together with all relevant facts and circumstances going to show the condition of the mind of the defendant at the time of the offense, if any.

The State, however, is not required to prove a motive. If the State has proved the essential elements of the offense beyond a reasonable doubt, the defendant must be found guilty of that offense regardless of the defendant's motive or lack of a motive. If the State, however, has proved a motive, you may consider that insofar as it gives meaning to other circumstances. On the other hand, you may consider the absence of motive in weighing whether or not the defendant is guilty of the crime charged.

5.

"Proof beyond a reasonable doubt" is proof that leaves you firmly convinced of the defendant's guilt. There are very few things in this world that we know with absolute certainty, and in criminal cases the law does not require proof that overcomes every possible doubt. If, based on your consideration of the evidence, you are firmly convinced that the defendant is guilty of the crime charged, you should find him guilty. If, on the other hand, you think there is a real possibility that he is not guilty, you should give him the benefit of the doubt and find him not guilty.

Chapter 13
WORTHY V. STONEMOCK

§ 13-1. Introduction

Charlie Stonemock was tried and acquitted on charges that he killed his first wife, Sally.

Responding to a 911 call to their residence, EMT personnel discovered Sally lying on her back on their bed. Charlie told them he had discovered her submerged in the bathtub when he woke up and realized that she had not come back to bed after getting up earlier in the night. Despite attempts to revive her, Sally was pronounced dead at the scene, and an autopsy showed that she had died of drowning.

Although the police initially concluded that Sally's death was an accident, new information was provided a year later by Charlie's second wife and the police reopened the investigation. The State charged Charlie with Sally's murder, on the theory that he drugged her and then drowned her while she was in the bathtub. Charlie's version at this criminal trial was that her drowning was either an accident or a suicide.

Sally's father, Jim Worthy, has filed a civil wrongful death lawsuit against Charlie Stonemock, for the death of his daughter.

§ 13-2. Stipulations Regarding Procedural and Evidentiary Matters

The following stipulations apply for this case file.

1. The case is being tried in a Lone Star court.
2. This case will be tried only on the issue of liability and damages.
3. All witnesses called to testify who have in statements or depositions identified the defendant, other individuals, or tangible evidence must, if asked, identify the same at trial.
4. The parties and witnesses signed their statements or depositions.
5. Other than what is supplied in the problem itself, there is nothing exceptional or unusual about the background information of any of the witnesses or the defendant that would bolster or detract from their credibility.
6. This case file does not permit a listed witness or the defendant, while testifying, to "invent" an individual not mentioned in this problem and have testimony or evidence offered to the court or jury from that invented individual.
7. "Beyond the record" must not be entertained as an objection.
8. The current year is the year in which this case comes to trial.
9. If any rule of procedure or rule of evidence requires that notice be provided to the court or to the opponent, it will be assumed for the purpose of the problem that the required notice was given.
10. All journal entries and letters by Sally Stonemock, and the e-mails between Charles and Barbara Stonemock were legally obtained.

11. All entries in Sally Stonemock's journal and her letters were authored by Sally Stonemock.
12. The victim, Sally Stonemock, died on March 30, [YR-3], by drowning, at her home in San Milano, Bear County, State of Lone Star.
13. The autopsy on Sally Stonemock indicated (a) the presence of the drug eszopiclone in her blood but not in a concentration that would have independently caused her death; (b) there were no visible signs of bruises, contusions, or abrasions on the body; and (c) time of death was between 4:00 and 6:00 A.M.
14. The drug eszopiclone is found in the prescription sleeping pill, Lunesta®.
15. All exhibits in the file are authentic. In addition, each exhibit contained in the file is the original of that document unless otherwise noted on the exhibit or as established by the evidence.

§ 13-3. Case File Materials

Students will be expected to use the following case file materials in presenting their cases.

Lone Star Wrongful Death Statute

Lone Star Civil Practice & Remedies Code

§ 31.123. Cause of Action

(a) An action for actual damages arising from an injury that causes an individual's death may be brought if liability exists under this section.

(b) A person is liable for damages arising from an injury that causes an individual's death if the injury was caused by the person's or his agent's or servant's wrongful act, neglect, carelessness, unskillfulness, or default.

(c) A person is liable for damages arising from an injury that causes an individual's death if:

(1) the person is a proprietor, owner, charterer, or hirer of an industrial or public utility plant or of a railroad, street railway, steamboat, stagecoach, or other vehicle for the transportation of goods or passengers; and

(2) the injury was caused by the person's or his agent's or servant's wrongful act, neglect, carelessness, unskillfulness, or default.

§ 31.124. Benefitting From Action

(a) An action to recover damages as provided by this subchapter is for the exclusive benefit of the surviving spouse, children, and parents of the deceased.

(b) The surviving spouse, children, and parents of the deceased may bring the action or one or more of those individuals may bring the action for the benefit of all.

§ 31.125. Punitive Damages

When the death is caused by the willful act or omission or gross negligence of the defendant, punitive as well as actual damages may be recovered.

Plaintiff's Petition

DISTRICT COURT OF BEAR COUNTY

JIM WORTHY Plaintiff v. CHARLIE STONEMOCK Defendant	}	Docket No. 1267-45 COMPLAINT FOR DAMAGES

COMES NOW the above-named Plaintiff and alleges the following:

I. Parties, Jurisdiction, and Venue

A. Plaintiff, Jim Worthy, father of Sally Stonemock, brings this action in his personal capacity.

B. Defendant, Charlie Stonemock, is a resident of Bear County, State of Lone Star.

C. This Court has jurisdiction over the subject matter of this complaint and over the parties.

D. Venue is proper and appropriate in Bear County because the death of Sally Stonemock, which is the subject matter of this complaint, occurred in Bear County.

II. Factual Basis

A. Defendant, Charlie Stonemock and Sally Stonemock were husband and wife.

B. Responding to a 911 call to their residence, EMT personnel discovered Sally lying on her back on their bed. Defendant told them that he had discovered her submerged in the bathtub when he woke up and realized that she had not come back to bed after leaving the bed earlier in the night.

C. Despite attempts to revive her, Sally was pronounced dead at the scene and a later autopsy showed that she had died of drowning. The police initially concluded that Sally's death was an accident.

D. A year later, Defendant's second wife, Barbara, provided information that Defendant was responsible for Sally's death.

E. The State charged Defendant with Sally's murder, on the theory that he drugged her and then drowned her while she was in the bathtub. Defendant's version at this criminal trial was that her drowning was either an accident or a suicide. The Defendant was acquitted of the charges.

F. Defendant's acts were the sole and proximate cause of Sally Stonemock's death.

III. Causes of Action

A. As a direct and proximate result of the acts of the Defendant, the decedent suffered a wrongful death, entitling Plaintiff to recover actual and exemplary damages (including but not limited to medical and hospital expenses, funeral expenses, and all other damages allowable for wrongful death and survival benefits under Lone Star Civil Practice & Remedies Code §§ 31.123-31.125 and any other damages allowable as a result of Defendant's conduct) in amounts not now precisely known, the exact amounts to be proven at or before the time of trial.

B. As a further direct and proximate result of the Defendant's acts and omissions, the plaintiff of the decedent suffered destruction of the parent-child relationship and loss of parental consortium.

C. As a further direct and proximate result of the negligent acts and omissions of Defendant, Plaintiff is entitled to recover statutory and reasonable attorney's fees and costs in amounts not now precisely known, the court to set such amounts in the future.

IV. Prayer for Relief

WHEREFORE, the plaintiff prays for a judgment of liability against the defendants as follows:

A. For a judgment against defendant.

B. For an award of damages as set forth in the above complaint herein, including statutory and reasonable fees and costs in such amounts that may be awarded by this Court.

C. For such other and further relief as the Court deems just and appropriate.

DATED this day of October 12, [YR-1].

Doyle F. Younger

Doyle F. Younger
Younger and Associates
Attorney for Plaintiff

Defendant's Written Statement to Police

STATE OF LONE STAR **COUNTY OF BEAR**	}	**Case Number: 04-9334499**

VOLUNTARY STATEMENT OF: CHARLES STONEMOCK

I, Charles Stonemock, after first being duly warned by Det. J. Papparoe #3898 at 0925 hrs. at 214 W. Nueva, on June 16, [YR-2] that (1) I have the right to remain silent and not make any statement at all, and any statement I do make may be used against me at my trial; (2) Any statement I make may be used as evidence against me in Court; (3) I have the right to have a lawyer present to advise me prior to and during any questioning; (4) If I am unable to employ a lawyer, I have the right to have a lawyer appointed to advise me prior to and during any questioning; (5) I have the right to terminate the interview at any time; and I understand that the above rights are continuing rights and may be urged by me at any stage of the proceedings, and I hereby prior to and during the making of this statement, knowingly, intelligently, and voluntarily waive the above rights and give to the said, Det. J. Papparoe #6778, the person to whom this statement is being given, the following written statement:

My name is Charles Stonemock. In [YR-9] I married Sally Worthy, a woman that I had met at work. We also both went to the same church, the Church of the Holy Flame. It's a non-denominational church here in the city. We dated for about a year before getting married. We were very happy together. But in the Spring of [YR-4] I messed up and while we were still married, I had a few dates with a co-worker Barbara Westwood. By dates I mean we had sexual relations.

Sally found out and kicked me out of the house. It was really hard on her and I was a total jerk because she and Barbara had been friends with each other for 10 years. Barbara also went to the same church. We were apart for about six months and then out of the clear blue, in mid-January [YR-3] Ithink, Sally calls me and says that she has forgiven me and that we should meet and talk about saving our marriage. While Sally and I were apart I did not see Barbara anymore. Barbara felt very guilty about what we had done to Sally and did not want to see me anymore.

When Sally called me she said that she come to the point of understanding that God was telling her that she needed to forgive me and try to reconcile. She said that she had prayed a lot about it and that she had forgiven both Barbara and me for what we had done to her. She said that she was going to talk to Barbara as well. I do not remember the exact date that we had that talk. We finally moved back in together. She insisted that we get more regularly involved in the church and rededicate our lives to each other. I was very happy to be back together with her. I really loved her and wanted to make her happy.

Sally wrote a letter to Barbara, forgiving her, and they also met for lunch. Both of them told me that they had worked things out. I do not know what exactly was said, but Sally said that she had forgiven Barbara and Barbara said repeatedly how sorry she was that she had caused Sally so much hurt. I don't think that Barbara ever said anything to either Sally or me about being in love with me.

About that time, I discovered that Sally was journaling, writing out what was on her mind on a fairly regular basis. I saw her writing one day and asked her what she was doing. She told me that during our separation and times of prayer she had seen visions and wanted to record them so she could see if there was a pattern. She told me that she thought that an angel was revealing to her what she needed to do. That was why she decided to get back together with me.

I never really looked at the journal. I may have read one or two entries, but I figured that it was her private property and considering that I needed to walk the narrow line, in light of my unfaithfulness, I did not want to read the whole thing. All I knew was that doing that writing had calmed her and helped her focus on our marriage.

One day in January [YR-3], I believe, she shocked me by saying that she had had a vision the night before in which she had died and that she was going to heaven and that in looking down on earth she had seen Barbara and I together. I told her that was crazy talk and that I did not want to hear about it. I mean, what was she thinking? Here we had just gotten back together and now she is talking about dying. And she told Barbara the same thing.

She started talking more and more about this dying thing and then started complaining about not being able to sleep because of those visions, which became more frequent. After several weeks, I called Barbara and she was very worried about Sally. She said that she had this preoccupation with death and that was not right. Barbara told me that she had fallen in love with me the prior year but had put that behind her when Sally forgave her.

Sally went to a good friend of ours, Pat Campbell, who is an MD. Pat prescribed some powerful sleeping pills, I think Luensta, for Sally but told her to be careful about how many she took. I don't remember what the pills were. I just know that she kept them on the nightstand and would sometimes get up in the middle of the night and take them. She also started taking hot baths at night to help her relax. The next day she would sleep late. So I guess the pills and bath worked.

All this time though, she seemed happy and kept talking about seeing Barbara and me together. It really bothered me. She was restless but happy. She said that I should trust more in God and that I would see that everything was going to work out fine.

In February, I believe, I got a call from Barbara that she needed to see me. We met at a local place and she said that she was really worried about Sally. She said that she had gotten a letter from Sally stating again that if anything happened to her, that she and I were supposed to get back together. She briefly showed me the letter and I said that I was worried about Sally. I read through it quickly.

On March 30, Sally and I went to bed early and about 1:00 AM I was aware that she was getting up. I had my back turned to her. I heard her open her pill bottle and then was aware that water was running into the bathtub. I woke up at 6:30 AM. She was not in the bed. I went into the bathroom and she was in a full tub of water, under the water. I screamed her name and pulled her out. I carried her to the bed and tried to do CPR for a few minutes. I immediately called 911 but did not get any answer. So I called our friend Pat Campbell who came over. When Pat saw what was happening, Pat called 911 and they came over. They said there was nothing they could do. I just slumped into a chair and cried out my eyes. I could not believe it. She was gone.

Pat told the EMT about the sleeping pills and showed them the bottle that was on her nightstand. The police came over and talked to me briefly. They also talked to Pat and afterwards I learned that they had ruled that Sally's death was an accidental overdose.

Several months later Barbara and I got married by the minister of our church, in a small ceremony. We both cried throughout the ceremony, knowing that Sally was looking down and smiling, finally at peace with herself.

I gave Sally's journal to the police last year, if you think that will help you. You can have it. I don't want anything to do with it.

Things got tough between Barbara and me and we are now separated. I guess there was just too much baggage from all of this. Hopefully we can get back together. I think right now she blames me for

Sally's death. I have no idea where she got that idea except that she feels guilty that she and I brought all of this on Sally and drove her crazy.

I did send an e-mail to Barbara several days before Sally died. Based on what Sally had told me I thought that her death was coming quickly. But I had no idea how quickly it would come.

This is the end of my statement. I have read this statement and it is true and correct.

WITNESS: *Danny Mattz* SIGNATURE: *Charles Stonemock*

DATE: **April 16, [YR-2]**

Plaintiff's Deposition

ORAL DEPOSITION OF JIM WORTHY, produced as a witness at the instance of the Defendant, CHARLES STONEMOCK, and duly sworn, was taken in the above-styled and numbered cause on May 4, [YR-1], from 12:00 PM, to 1:00 PM, before Sandy Morales, Certified Shorthand Reporter in and for the State of Lone Star, reported by machine shorthand, at the law offices of Plaintiff, pursuant to the Lone Star Rules of Civil Procedure and the Provisions stated on the record or attached hereto.

This is a deposition of JIM WORTHY, who having been sworn, testified as follows:

EXAMINATION

QUESTIONS BY DEFENSE COUNSEL:

Q: Would you please state your name for the record?

A: Jim Worthy.

Q: And you are the plaintiff in this case, against my client, Charlie Stonemock?

A: Yes.

Q: Okay, before we start going over this, I would like to make sure that you are clear on what we are doing here today. Okay?

A: Yes.

Q: You are under oath, just as if you were testifying in trial. You understand?

A: Yes.

Q: And I want to make it clear that if you do not understand what I am asking about, my questions, please stop me so that we can clear up any confusion. All right?

A: Yes, I understand. This whole thing makes me very nervous. I hope I can make it through this thing.

Q: Are you on any medication right now?

A: Yes, I am taking some Valium as a prescription from my doctor. And I sometimes take sleeping pills to go to sleep at night.

Q: How old are you, Mr. Worthy?

A: 70 years old.

Q: Are you employed?

A: No, not right now. Sally's death affected me deeply. Since she died I have had a hard time getting control of my life and holding a job. My last job was working as a manager at a local dry cleaning establishment.

Q: Okay. What was the name of that business?

A: Spiffy Cleaners, here in San Milano.

Q: When did you last work there?

A: I left there about a month ago.

Q: About the time you filed this lawsuit?

A: Yes.

Q: And for the record, Sally Stonemock was your daughter, right?

A: Yes, she was.

Q: At this point, you do not have any personal knowledge about how your daughter died, do you?

A: I know that Charlie killed her — in cold blood.

Q: You were not there, were you?

A: No. But I did not have to be to know what he did to her and to all of us who loved Sally.

Q: So, how did you learn of her death?

A: One of her friends lives on the same block with Charlie and called me at about 9 o'clock on the morning of Sally's death. I immediately drove to their house. I worked with Charlie to set up the funeral arrangements.

Q: You say in your petition in this lawsuit that you paid for the funeral?

A: Part of it. Yes, $10,000. Charlie wanted to go cheap and he finally agreed to let me pay some of the expenses so we could have a nice service. For some reason the insurance company refused to pay for the funeral. I cashed in a CD to get the money.

Q: Are you drawing any sort of pension or unemployment at this point?

A: Yes, some.

Q: How much?

A: About $800.00 a month, in unemployment checks.

Q: And you own your own house in San Milano?

A: No.

Q: Where do you live?

A: In an apartment.

Q: And in our request for admissions, you said that you have monthly expenses of only about 600.00 dollars?

A: Right.

Q: Do you have any health insurance?

A: No, not now. My church is giving me some assistance until I can find another job.

Q. How much assistance?

A: Well, since I left my last job, they took up an offering and that came to about 200 dollars. They have also given me some food coupons for H.E.B. That was about 100 dollars.

Q: So why are you asking for $500,000 in damages for the death of your daughter?

A: Like I said, this has been really hard on me. Mentally, emotionally. Also, for the last year of her life, Sally had been helping me, financially.

Q: How?

A: Well, she would send me money, like $100 a month out of her personal budget, even when she and Charlie were not together.

Q. Did Charlie know about that?

A: No. She did not want to tell him because Charlie and I do not get along and she was afraid that he would blow up if he knew. She said she would help me as long as it took for me to get back on my feet.

Q: You got some of her life insurance money, didn't you?

A: No. It all went to Charlie. Which he blew on his new wife and new home.

Q: How did you know that?

A: He told me that, several times. He almost sounded like he was rubbing that in my face.

Q: Did you approve of their divorce?

A: No, not at the time. I knew that he had cheated on Sally but I believe that couples should try to work out their troubles. Now I wish that they had never reconciled.

Q: Do you know his second wife, Barbara?

A: Yes. She is a really nice person who got caught up in Charlie's problems.

Q: Do you have anything else you want to add?

A: No.

Q: Okay, that is all I have.

(END OF TRANSCRIPT)

This is to certify that I have read the transcript of my deposition taken on and that the transcript accurately reflects the questions asked and my answers.

SIGNATURE: Jim Worthy

Subscribed and sworn to before me on August 12, [YR-1].

Sandy Morales

Sandy Morales
Certified Shorthand Reporter

Deposition of Jess Papparoe

ORAL DEPOSITION OF JESS PAPPAROE, produced as a witness at the instance of the Defendant, CHARLES STONEMOCK, and duly sworn, was taken in the above-styled and numbered cause on May 4, [YR-1], from 3:00 PM, to 4:00 PM, before Sandy Morales, Certified Shorthand Reporter in and for the State of Lone Star, reported by machine shorthand, at the law offices of Plaintiff, pursuant to the Lone Star Rules of Civil Procedure and the Provisions stated on the record or attached hereto.

This is a deposition of JESS PAPPAROE, who having been sworn, testified as follows:

EXAMINATION

QUESTIONS BY DEFENSE COUNSEL:

Q: Hello, Detective.

A: Hello.

Q: Do you understand that I am representing Charlie Stonemock?

A: Yes, I do.

Q: Would you please state your name for the record?

A: Yes, my name is Detective Jess Papparoe.

Q: Could you please tell us your position and duties with the police department?

A: I am a homicide detective, here in San Milano, with about 10 years experience on the force. My duties entail conducting investigations into possible homicides.

Q: Okay. Detective, please tell me about your investigation into the death of Ms. Sally Stonemock, on March 30, [YR-3]?

A: Well. I did not work the case in [YR-3]. Another detective, Detective Rod Jones worked it, but he has since moved out of state. The police and the DA at the time concluded at that time that her death was accidental. But recently, Barbara Stonemock, she was Barbara Westwood then, called us and said that she had some new information on Sally Stonemock's death.

Q: Okay. First, can you take us back to [YR-3] and briefly tell us what happened, before you get to Ms. Stonemock's information?

A: Right. Our records show that on March 30, [YR-3], at 7:00 AM, EMT was called to the Stonemock residence. The call was placed by a Dr. Campbell. When EMT arrived they found a woman lying on a bed, nude, dry, and covered with a sheet. Her hair was wet. There was no water around the bathtub. The tub did not have any water in it, only some wet spots. And several towels were on the floor, wet. A man identified as Charles Stonemock told them that he had found his wife in a full tub of water, under the water. He said that he had tried to call 911 but could not get through and that he had tried CPR, before calling his friend, Dr. Campbell. Efforts to revive the woman, who we now know was Sally Stonemock, failed, and she was pronounced dead at the scene by the coroner.

Q: Please continue.

A: Well, in the meantime several police officers arrived and talked with the EMT, your client, and Dr. Campbell. They did not get much information out of Stonemock and Campbell. They interviewed them and reviewed a journal that Sally Stonemock had written shortly before her death, which Stonemock gave them. He told them the journal would explain everything. Dr. Campbell said that he had prescribed some sleeping pills for Sally. He told the officers that he believed that she had probably taken a few too many, fell asleep in the tub, and simply slipped under the water and drowned without ever waking up. After the officers working the case reviewed that journal in more detail and talked with others who knew Ms. Stonemock, they concluded that the drowning was not a murder. It was either accidental or perhaps even suicide. So after talking to the DA, the case was closed and no charges were brought against anyone.

Q: So, tell me about Barbara Stonemock.

A: As I said, she called us on June 2, of [YR-2] and said that she had new information. So I called her in and talked to her. She gave me an e-mail that she said had been sent by Charles Stonemock, your client, to her just before Sally died.

Q: Is this it? [Shows exhibit to witness]

A: Yes, this is it. You can see that it says that very soon they would be able to be together because he expected Sally's death very shortly.

Q: Did she comment on why that seemed important to the investigation?

A: Yes, I asked her that. She said that she and Charles had earlier had an affair, in [YR-4], and that several weeks before Sally died she and Charlie had started talking regularly again, which led to the e-mail. She responded and asked what that meant, because she was anxious to be together with him, and he said that it was best that she not know the details. She said that she had not shared that with the police in [YR-3] and now regretted it.

Q: Why?

A: Well, they, Charles and Barbara, got married in May [YR-3], very soon after Sally died, but that she had caught him cheating on her several months later and was concerned that he might try to kill her, the way he killed his first wife. Those were her words. "Kill."

Q: Okay. So what other information do you have that would indicate foul play by my client in this case?

A: I went back through the file and determined that several facts pointed to death as the result of actions, or inactions, by your client. First, there are no records that he ever tried to call 911. Second, her body was dry when the EMT arrived and when he was questioned about that in [YR-3], he said that he guessed that he had dried her off before putting her on the bed, but could not recall. Third, knowing that she was taking pills and getting into the bathtub, he did not try to check on her during the evening. Finally, I have looked at Sally's journal and there are entries that indicate that Charles may have encouraged, or condoned, his wife's belief that she would die, and that Charles and Barbara should get together. In short, he had the motive and the opportunity to see that Sally died.

Q. Detective, is this Sally's journal? [Shows to witness]

A: Yes, that is it.

Q: Let me show you these three exhibits, these photographs. Can you tell me what these are?

A: Sure. This photo is of the bathroom, this is a picture of the bedroom, and this one is a picture taken in the hallway showing the bathroom on the left and the bedroom on the right.

Q: Okay. Thanks. Now you mentioned that some pills were on the nightstand?

A: Yes, these pictures were taken about an hour after the body was removed from the house. Our records indicate that the officers at the scene picked up the pills for processing and had left the premises before the police photographer was able to take these pictures. He was apparently at another location working another homicide and got delayed.

Q: So these pictures are not entirely accurate, are they?

A: They accurately show what the scene of the crime looked like. I would disagree with you.

Q: And you did not take these photos, did you?

A: No, they were taken by a police photographer who has worked for the force for 10 years.

Q: Did Barbara Stonemock have anything else to add to the case?

A: She did comment that through the weeks before Sally died, that Charles publicly said that he was concerned about Sally's mental state but that when they talked alone, he admitted that perhaps the best thing was for Sally to die and to be finally at peace.

Q. So you came to the conclusion, with only this meager evidence, that my client is guilty of murder?

A: I think he either gave her the extra pills or let her take the pills. After giving a chance for the pills to take effect, he went into the bathroom and while she was asleep, he pushed her under the water. The estimated time of death was 4 AM to 6 AM. He got back into bed, got up several hours later and put on a charade of being concerned about her death.

Q: You don't have any forensic evidence linking Charles with Sally's death, do you?

A: Well, we don't have fingerprints or other physical evidence, if that is what you mean.

Q. Okay. That is all I have, Detective.

(END OF TRANSCRIPT)

This is to certify that I have read the transcript of my deposition taken on and that the transcript accurately reflects the questions asked and my answers.

SIGNATURE: *Jess Papparoe*

Subscribed and sworn to before me on June 15, [YR-1].

Sandy Morales

Sandy Morales
Certified Shorthand Reporter

Deposition of Pat Campbell

ORAL DEPOSITION OF PAT CAMPBELL, produced as a witness at the instance of the Defendant, CHARLES STONEMOCK, and duly sworn, was taken in the above-styled and numbered cause on May 5, [YR-1], from 9:00 AM, to 10:00 AM, before Sandy Morales, Certified Shorthand Reporter in and for the State of Lone Star, reported by machine shorthand, at the law offices of Plaintiff, pursuant to the Lone Star Rules of Civil Procedure and the Provisions stated on the record or attached hereto.

This is a deposition of PAT CAMPBELL, who having been sworn, testified as follows:

EXAMINATION

QUESTIONS BY DEFENSE COUNSEL:

Q: Would you please state you name for the court reporter.

A: Yes. I am Pat Campbell.

Q: Do you know Charles Stonemock, my client?

A: Yes.

Q: Please tell me about your relationship with Charles.

A: Well, we have been close friends for almost a number of years. I was also good friends with his first wife, Sally. We had all met in high school and stayed friends through college and then when I went to medical school. For the last several years I was their personal physician.

Q: You are a licensed doctor?

A: Yes. I am in general practice. I have been for five years.

Q: So you are authorized to write prescriptions?

A: Yes, of course.

Q: In [YR-3], did you ever write a prescription for sleeping pills for Sally Stonemock?

A: Yes. It was for Lunesta.

Q: Please tell us about that.

A: Sally was going through a difficult time. She and Charles had just gotten back together again after being separated for some months. She said that she was having visions and dreams about dying and about Charles and their friend, Barbara getting married. She was happy for them and was not afraid of dying. But she was having trouble settling down at night and sleeping. So she asked me for some pills, or something to help her sleep.

Q: Go on.

A: I was concerned about her mental health and recommended that she go through counseling. In my mind, she showed signs of being suicidal. But I wrote her a prescription for a sleeping pill. I told her to be careful not to take too many and again encouraged her to start talking to someone like a counselor or minister. Frankly, I was concerned that she might take too many to fulfill this sort of prophecy about dying. So I talked to Charles as well and told him to make sure that she did not take too many. I was concerned about her.

Q: When she referred to the fact that she thought she was going to die, did she give any specifics?

A: Yes and no. She said that she had a very clear picture that she would die soon. But she never said what she would die from, or of. She, she . . . had a sort of calmness about her when she spoke about it. And she would add that in her visions she saw Barbara and Charles together again, married.

Q: And she was okay with that?

A: Yes. I think so.

Q: What did you think?

A: Frankly, it was too weird for me.

Q: Did you ever talk to Charles about what Sally was saying?

A: Oh, yes. I was concerned for both of them. When I mentioned the fact that Sally had told me about Barbara and Charles getting together he simply said that that was crazy. In my mind, well, it crossed my mind that Sally may have been had some sort of death wish. When she died, it did not really surprise me.

Q: Okay. Well, did you ever hear Charles say anything about Sally's predictions of dying?

A: He said that she seemed convinced of her vision or premonition, whatever. He also added that what would be would be. Or something like that.

Q: I want to focus on the day that Sally died. I understand that you were there?

A: Not when she died, no. But I got a call early in the morning, about 6:45 or so from Charles. He was very excited and said he needed my help immediately. He said something about finding Sally in the bathtub and she was not breathing. I asked him if he had called 911 and he said that he was afraid to do so, but would try. And then he started to cry. So I told him to call 911 and ran over to their house. I got there at about 7 AM. He had placed Sally on their bed with a sheet over her. I checked her pulse and found none. When I asked Charles if he had called 911, he shook his head. So I called them at about 7 AM or so and they arrived at about 7:15. This is hard.

Q: Go ahead.

A: Well, I talked to the EMTs and they said that they could not find any signs of life, so they called the coroner and the police showed up shortly thereafter to assist. I told them that

I had prescribed sleeping pills for Sally and that I was afraid that she had overdosed or had fallen asleep in the tub and slipped under the water. The bottle of pills was still on her nightstand. She had just refilled the bottle and it looked like four or five were missing — about four days' worth.

Q: Did you hear Charles say anything to the police or EMTs?

A: Yes, he said that he found her in the tub and carried her to the bed and tried to do CPR. He seemed distraught. They took him into the front room to talk with him further and I was not permitted to listen in. Another officer was talking to me.

Q: Did you tell him that you had called 911?

A: Yes.

Q: Did you say anything about whether my client had called 911?

A: No, at the time I was just concerned that someone had called them.

Q: Thank you. I don't have any more questions for you.

(END OF TRANSCRIPT)

This is to certify that I have read the transcript of my deposition taken on and that the transcript accurately reflects the questions asked and my answers.

SIGNATURE: Pat Campbell

Subscribed and sworn to before me on July 5, [YR-1].

Sandy Morales

Sandy Morales
Certified Shorthand Reporter

Deposition of Barbara Stonemock

ORAL DEPOSITION OF BARBARA STONEMOCK, produced as a witness at the instance of the Defendant, CHARLES STONEMOCK, and duly sworn, was taken in the above-styled and numbered cause on May 5, [YR-1], from 1:00 PM, to 2:10 PM, before Sandy Morales, Certified Shorthand Reporter in and for the State of Lone Star, reported by machine shorthand, at the law offices of Plaintiff, pursuant to the Lone Star Rules of Civil Procedure and the Provisions stated on the record or attached hereto.

This is a deposition of BARBARA STONEMOCK, who having been sworn, testified as follows:

EXAMINATION

QUESTIONS BY DEFENSE COUNSEL

Q: Good afternoon.

A: Hello.

Q: Could you please state your name?

A: My name is Barbara Stonemock. Before I was married, I was Barbara Westwood.

Q. Okay. And you understand that I am representing your husband, your ex-husband?

A: Yes.

Q: Okay. I want to talk to you about the circumstances of the death of Sally Stonemock.

A: Yes, I know.

Q: And I understand that you may have some information that you provided to the police in the criminal trial against Charles?

A: Yes.

Q: How long have you been divorced?

A: Not quite six months.

Q: Have you remarried?

A: No, I haven't.

Q: First, please tell us about your relationship with Sally Stonemock.

A: Sally and I were friends in high school and college. When Sally met Charlie I thought it was the best thing that could ever happen to her. They seemed really happy. The three of us attended the same church, Church of the Holy Flame. We really loved that environment and Sally seemed to be especially grateful for the spiritual aspects of the church.

Q: At some point you had an affair with Charles Stonemock?

A: Yes, Charles and I worked in the same office, Willow Office Supply, and fell in love and started seeing each other in [YR-4].

Q: How often would you get together?

A: At least several times a week. For about two months. The chemistry was there. But I realized that eventually, if Sally found out, it would devastate her.

Q: And she did learn of the affair?

A: Yes. Early in the summer [YR-4], she learned about what we were doing. I think another mutual friend told her. I guess it does not make any difference now. The damage was done and Sally was crushed. She made Charlie move out but never started divorce proceedings.

Q: Why?

A: I am not sure. At least then I was not sure. About six months later she told Charlie that she had come to the point in her spiritual walk where she could forgive him, and me.

Q: Did you continue your relationship with Charlie?

A: No, when Sally found out, that pretty well killed things for both of us. I quit my job at Willow and Charlie was really torn up. When she called him to make up he jumped at the chance.

Q: What did Sally say to you?

A: Well, she first wrote me a letter in late January [YR-3].

Q: Is this it? [Shows letter to witness]

A: Yes.

Q Please continue.

A: Well in the letter she said that she forgave me. Then we met for lunch a few days later. She told me that she forgave me and wanted to be friends again. Just like that. She was really a special person. I miss her terribly.

Q: At any point did she talk about dying and your eventually getting together with Mr. Stonemock?

A: Yes. After we started talking again she told me that she had been having visions or dreams or something like that. They were very real to her and she believed that God was talking to her. She said that she had written about them in her journal.

Q: Did you ever see the journal?

A: No. I considered that very private.

Q: But she talked about dying?

A: Yes. We talked on the phone several times.

Q: Did she ever say what she expected to be the cause of her death?

A: No. She just said that she did not think she would live to see the new year.

Q: Did you see her again?

A: No. Our lunch in January was the last time we actually saw each other. About two weeks after we met, she wrote me another letter. I read it and immediately called Charlie.

Q: Is this the letter? [Shows letter to witness]

A: Yes. This is it. She says that after she dies she wants Charlie and me to get married. That it's the right thing to do. I called Charlie and he came over. He read it quickly and said that he was really worried about Sally.

Q: Did he seem genuinely worried about Sally?

A: I guess, no, not really. In public he would express deep concern but in private he would say that maybe it would best for Sally if she died.

Q: Go on.

A: Several weeks before Sally died, Charlie started calling me and sending me e-mails saying that he loved me and that it was Sally's wish to get back together. So we did.

Q: At any point in all of this did you have any doubts about whether Sally's death was accidental?

A: Well, I did. But I loved Charlie and I think that I may have wanted it to be accidental.

Q: What do you mean?

A: Well, just a few days before Sally drowned, Charlie sent me an e-mail saying that soon it would all be over and that we would be together, forever.

Q: Did you ever talk to him about that?

A: Yes. I asked him what he meant and he said that he was sure that Sally was right — that she would die shortly and that it would not be good for me to know the details. Then he just kissed me on my cheek and said that he loved me more than ever.

Q: So you got married?

A: Yes. We got married. After Sally died. In May [YR-3]. Charlie convinced me that that was what Sally wanted. I was not so sure. But I loved Charlie.

Q: And you said earlier that you are now divorced?

A: Yes. I found out within months of our getting married that Charlie was having an affair with one of his co-workers, again at Willow, where he has worked all this time. I was really angry and kicked him out of the house.

Q: Is that when you called the police?

A: Not right away. I called them months later in June of [YR-2] and said that I had some new information about Sally Stonemock's death. They immediately came over and talked to me.

Q: And the new information was?

A: That Charlie told me that he expected Sally to die shortly and that we could be together. I gave them the e-mail. I had not told the police that when Sally died and now it all seemed to fit together. Charlie had taken advantage of Sally's state of mind. He was, and is, a real jerk.

Q. Is this the e-mail you are talking about? [Shows exhibit to witness]

A: Yes, that's it.

Q: So do you think that he killed her?

A: Yes. I do. I think he either helped her take too many pills, or when she was in the tub he pushed her underneath the water after she fell asleep in the warm water.

Q: Why did it take you so long to call the police and give them this information?

A: Different reasons. I guess I was a bit scared that he would do the same to me. And a part of me still loved him and I knew that giving the police the email would put him in jail.

Q: I have one more area of inquiry. I understand that you were convicted nine years ago in the State of Oregon for theft of some state government property?

A: Yes.

Q: And the records show that you were charged with a felony count, because of the value of the items you took.

A: Yes.

Q: But you pleaded guilty to one count of felony theft?

A: Yes. My lawyer worked out a deal with the DA. I pled guilty.

Q: And you received a sentence of 5 years, suspended? And a fine of $1,000?

A: Yes, to both of those.

Q: Do you now understand the solemn requirement to tell the truth if you are placed under oath?

A: Absolutely. That was during a very dark period of my life and I know that I did wrong.

Q: Okay. That's all I have.

A: Witness: Okay.

(END OF TRANSCRIPT)

This is to certify that I have read the transcript of my deposition taken on and that the transcript accurately reflects the questions asked and my answers.

SIGNATURE:

Barbara Stonemock

Subscribed and sworn to before me on July 2, [YR-1].

Sandy Morales

Sandy Morales
Certified Shorthand Reporter

Sally Stonemock's First Letter to Barbara Stonemock

January 25, [YR-3]

Dearest Barbara,

Please do not tear up this letter, because I know that you probably cannot believe that I would ever want to talk to you again. I do.

I have come to the place in my spiritual life where I can forgive you and Charlie for the hurt that you caused the three of us. I am not sure I will ever understand why it happened but I now believe that God has called me to forgive both of you.

I have talked to Charlie and I have invited him back into my life. It may be difficult at first to trust him completely, but I have never stopped loving him and I pray that this will all work out.

With love and forgiveness,

Sally

Sally Stonemock's Second Letter to Barbara Stonemock

Feb 13, [YR-3]

Barbara,

I just wanted you to know that I have been having visions that you and Charlie will someday be together, with my blessing from heaven. I want you to know that after I am gone, I want you and Charlie to spend the rest of your lives together.

I miss you and look forward to getting together again in the near future.

Love, Sally

Sally Stonemock's Personal Journal

January 1

I have decided to start the new year with a journal. I have been reading some of the books from our church and one of the suggestions for dealing with life's issues is to journal your way to health. Sounds radical. But worth a try. ☺ I pray that it works. Over the last several months there have been days when I thought that it might be best to just lie down and die. I just didn't want to go on. But it's a new day!! And a new year.

Jan 7

Today was an interesting day. First, last night I had the most wonderful vision of heaven. An angel guided me. Not sure what it all means but I am praying that God will open my eyes to whatever message I am supposed to get. Second, I was reading my Bible and focused on the passages dealing with forgiveness. I had the most strange feeling that I had not been as forgiving as I should. Despite my best intentions I don't know that I will journal every day.

January 8

More dreams or visions, or whatever last night. I saw an angel come down out of the bright clouds and say that I was loved and that I should love and forgive in return. I asked the angel what or who I should forgive and the angel said, "you know."

January 10

I missed the journal yesterday. Sorry. I was not feeling well and just could not get out of bed to even eat.

Jan. 11

I am feeling better today. In my dreams last night it was revealed to me that I should forgive Charlie and Barbara for what they did to me. I just don't know, it hurts so bad. I am going to spend the day thinking about this.

Jan 12

I spoke to my pastor today. He said that its not usually unusual that God would use dreams or visions to speak to us but that I should not simply assume that any angel of light is my friend. There are many examples in religious literature.

January 13

Nothing new today. I did not have any dreams last night. Maybe I was just imagining them.

January 14

Nope, they are real. Last night I had the most marvelous and peaceful experience. I dreamed that I had died and was in the heavenly places, with beautiful plants, people, and music. An angel walked with me through a glorious garden and explained that I had one more thing to do on earth before I died, which would be soon. I was supposed to fully forgive Charlie and Barbara.

Jan. 15

I called Charlie today. What a relief. I told him that I forgave him. He started crying and said he was so glad to hear that. He is going to move back into the house. I feel so much better. I feel like I have a new life. Not sure I can forgive Barbara just yet. And not sure I can tell Charlie about my dreams/visions.

January 22

I did it. I had another dream last night that was basically another message that I had to forgive Barbara. I also got the clear message that my time on this earth is coming to a close and that it's important for my own spiritual well-being that I needed to forgive both Charlie and Barbara.

January 24

I finally told Charlie about my dreams and visions. At first he seemed freaked out but then said that if it had meant that we would be together again, that it was fine with him. I told him that I was going to write to Barbara and forgive her as well. He smiled and thanked me for being back in his life.

Jan. 25

Mailed a letter to Barbara today.

January 27

Had lunch with Barbara and told her about what had led me to forgive her. She said that it was pretty "interesting" that I was hearing directly from God in my dreams.

February 3

I have not been good about writing in the journal. So much has happened. Things are good with Charlie. But now I am having dreams that I need to move to the next phase and bless the upcoming union between Charlie and Barbara. It has been revealed to me that I will die soon and that after I am gone, Charlie and Barbara are going to be man and wife. No sign on how I will die.

Feb 11

More dreams last night about my end and Charlie and Barbara. I told Charlie about this at breakfast, along with all of the stuff about my dreams and visions. He was speechless.

February 13

I wrote to Barbara today and told her that I had had a vision about her and Charlie being together and that it was fine with me. I told her that I was going to be going to a better place.

February 20

Charlie told me this morning at breakfast that he had had a dream too. He said that he had seen me in heaven smiling down on him and Barbara. I was so happy!!! I told him that his dream confirmed my visions and dreams. But he looked sad.

March 6

I had another vision. My time is drawing to a close. I have never gotten a clear picture of how I will die. I am simply trusting that God knows best. I am having trouble sleeping, however, and got some sleeping pills. Supposed to be careful with them. Charlie said he would help me remember how many to take. I love him so much!!!! Charlie said that he had had another dream in which he saw me looking down from heaven on him and Barbara. Thank God for the confirmation.

March 12

Still having trouble sleeping without the pills. Have developed a routine. If I cannot sleep, I get up and run a hot bath, take my dosage of pills and relax. It works. Charlie helps me get out of the bath because I am really really relaxed. Ahhhhh. LOL. Sometimes I think it might be best just to slip off to eternity when I fall asleep in the tub. That would be a good way to go.

March 15

Charlie said again that he had had a very vivid dream. He said that he had seen himself and Barbara in a garden with children and I was smiling down on them from heaven. He said that it was so real to him he felt a strange peace come over him. Now I am at peace too.

March 25

Nothing new. Maybe all of this vision stuff is nothing more than hopeful thinking, or deep seated fears of dying. I just don't know. I told Charlie the same thing at breakfast this morning. He took my hand and smiled at me. I love him so much it hurts.

March 28

Another dream last night of my being in heaven. It was so peaceful and the garden was so alive!!! I am not afraid to die.

March 29

Charlie and I had a bad fight today. I am not sure what happened to us. I found out that he had been e-mailing Barbara but felt the need to hide it from me. I felt betrayed. He cried and said that he was sorry that he had done that. He knew that it was wrong. I am really torn. I know that he and Barbara will be together. But I wish that he had told me that he was talking to her again. I told him that his time would come soon enough, that I felt that I was close to my time to go to heaven. Perhaps tonight I will have another vision that will make it all clear for me.

Crime Scene Photographs

E-MAILS BETWEEN CHARLES AND BARBARA (WESTWOOD) STONEMOCK

From: CStonemock@sssignal.com
Sent: March 27, [YR-3] 8:55 PM
To: BWestwood@.col.com
Subject: Love

Better for you to have plausible deniability.:-)

From: BWestwood@.col.com
Sent: March 27, [YR-3] 8:25 PM
To: CStonemock@sssignal.com
Subject: Love

WHAT?

From: CStonemock@sssignal.com
Sent: March 27, [YR-3] 7:55 PM
To: BWestwood@.col.com
Subject: Love

Things are moving quickly with Sally. You and I will be together very shortly, for a very long time. I love you with all of my heart!

Jury Instructions

LADIES AND GENTLEMEN OF THE JURY:

I am now going to instruct you about the law governing this case. You are required to accept my instructions as the law. Any ideas you have of what the law is or what the law should be or any statements by the attorneys as to what the law may be, must be disregarded by you, if they are in conflict with these instructions.

1. Claims of Parties

The plaintiff claims that he sustained damages due to the defendant's wrongful act of killing his daughter, Sally Stonemock, the decedent. The defendant has denied those claims and also denies that the plaintiff is entitled to recover any damages.

2. Burden of Proof

In this case, the plaintiff has the burden of proving his claims by a preponderance of the evidence. If you find from the evidence, by a preponderance of the evidence, that the defendant acted intentionally in killing the plaintiff's daughter, and that such actions were the proximate cause of his daughter's death, then you must find the defendant liable for her actions.

3. Proximate Cause

When I use the expression "proximate cause," I mean a cause that, in the natural or ordinary course of events, produced Sally Stonemock's, the decedent's, death. It need not be the only cause, nor the last or nearest cause. It is sufficient if it combines with another cause resulting in the injury and death.

4. Preponderance of the Evidence

The term "preponderance of the evidence" means that amount of evidence that causes you to conclude that the allegation is probably true. To prove an allegation by the preponderance of the evidence, a party must convince you that the allegation is more likely true than not true.

If the evidence on a particular issue is equally balanced, that issue has not been proven by a preponderance of the evidence. Therefore, the party having the burden of proving that issue has failed with respect to that particular issue.

5. Circumstantial Evidence

A fact or a group of facts may, based on logic and common sense, lead you to a conclusion as to other facts. This is known as circumstantial evidence. A fact may be proved by circumstantial evidence. Circumstantial evidence is entitled to the same consideration as any other type of evidence

6. Opinion Testimony

You may have heard a witness give opinions about matters requiring special knowledge or skill. You should judge this testimony in the same way you judge the testimony from any other witness. The fact that such person has given an opinion does not mean that you are required to accept it. Give the testimony whatever weight you think it deserves, considering the reasons given for the opinion, the witness's qualifications, and all of the other evidence in the case.

7. Credibility of Witnesses

It is up to you to decide the credibility of the witnesses. In making the decision you may consider such factors as whether the witness has made a prior inconsistent statement or has been convicted of a crime. Evidence of this kind may be considered by you in connection with all the other facts and circumstances in evidence in deciding the weight to be given to the testimony of that witness.

8. Damages

a. General

If you decide the plaintiff is entitled to damages, you shall give such amount as you decide to be fair and just, under all the circumstances. Such damages may include the following items, to the extent you find they have been proved by the evidence:

- Reasonable medical, hospital, funeral and burial expenses;
- Loss of financial support;
- Loss of gifts or other valuable gratuities;
- Loss of parental training and guidance;
- Loss of companionship;
- Plaintiff's grief, sorrow, or mental anguish.

Whether the plaintiff has proved these damages is for you to decide, based upon evidence and not upon speculation, guess, or conjecture. The amount of money to be awarded for certain of these elements of damage cannot be proved in a precise dollar amount. The law leaves such amounts to your sound judgment.

b. Punitive Damages

If you find for the plaintiff, you may, but are not required to, award punitive damages. The purposes of punitive damages are to punish a defendant and to deter similar acts in the future. Punitive damages may not be awarded to compensate a plaintiff.

The plaintiff has the burden of proving by a preponderance of the evidence that punitive damages should be awarded, and, if so, the amount of any such damages.

You may award punitive damages only if you find that the defendant's conduct that resulted in the decedent's death was a willful act or omission or amounted to gross negligence. Gross negligence means conduct or a failure to act that is so reckless that it demonstrates a substantial lack of concern for whether an injury will result.

If you find that punitive damages are appropriate, you must use reason in setting the amount. Punitive damages, if any, should be in an amount sufficient to fulfill their purposes but should not reflect bias, prejudice or sympathy toward any party. In considering the amount of any punitive damages, consider the degree of reprehensibility of the defendant's conduct.

In addition, you may consider the relationship of any award of punitive damages to any actual harm inflicted on the plaintiff.

9. Insurance

Whether a party is insured or not insured has no bearing on any issue that you must decide. You must refrain from any inference, speculation, or discussion about insurance. If you find for the plaintiff, you shall not speculate about or consider any possible sources of benefits the plaintiff may have received or might receive. After you have returned your verdict, the court will make whatever adjustments are necessary in this regard.

10. Verdict Form

To assist you in deciding these issues, I am giving you a verdict form to use during your deliberations. When you have completed the form, please let the bailiff know that you have completed your deliberations.

Verdict Form

1. Liability

Do you find by a preponderance of the evidence that the defendant caused the death of Sally Stonemock, the plaintiff's daughter?

_____ YES

_____ NO

If your answer is "no," then do not answer Question 2. If your answer is "yes," answer Question 2.

2. Damages

Do you find by a preponderance of the evidence that the plaintiff suffered damages as a result of the defendant's actions?

_____ YES

_____ NO

If you answered "yes," then please enter the amount of damages, in whole dollar amounts, to which the plaintiff is entitled.

$ ___________________

3. Punitive Damages

Do you find by a preponderance of the evidence that Sally Stonemock's death resulted from the defendant's willful act or omission or gross negligence in light of the circumstances?

_____ YES

_____ NO

If you answered "yes," then please enter the amount of punitive damages, in whole dollar amounts, to which the plaintiff is entitled.

$ ___________________

Chapter 14
State v. Moss

§ 14-1. Introduction

Sylvia Moss is charged with murder of her husband, Danny Moss. Police responded to Sylvia's 911 call early in the morning, and found Danny lying at the bottom of the steps of their home. Sylvia told the police that she had awakened when she heard a loud thump, saw Danny, and dialed 911 without first checking to see if there was anything she could do to help him. The police determined that Danny died as a result of a severe blow to his head, caused when he hit the stair railing. But there was also evidence of a bruise on the back of his neck. Additional evidence showed that Sylvia had reacted with rage whenever Danny ignored her or criticized her cooking.

The State has charged Sylvia with murder, on the theory that she hit him on the neck with a shoe and caused him to fall down the stairs. A prosecution expert has determined that Sylvia suffers from Narcissistic Personality Disorder, which triggered the attack.

Sylvia's version is that Danny's death was accidental.

§ 14-2. Stipulations Regarding Procedural and Evidentiary Matters

1. The case is being tried in a Lone Star court.
2. This case will be tried only on the issue of guilt or innocence.
3. All witnesses called to testify who have in statements or grand jury testimony identified the defendant, other individuals, or tangible evidence, can, if asked, identify the same at trial.
4. The defendant Moss signed her statement to the police.
5. Any applicable notice and disclosure requirements under the Lone Star Rules of Evidence were met in a timely fashion.
6. Other than what is supplied in the problem itself, there is nothing exceptional or unusual about the background information of any of the witnesses or the defendant that would bolster or detract from their credibility.
7. The parties may not "invent" an individual not mentioned in this problem and have testimony or evidence offered to the court or jury from that invented individual.
8. "Beyond the record" must not be entertained as an objection.
9. There are no Confrontation Clause issues in the problem.
10. The victim, Danny Moss, died on December 5, [YR-1], at his home in San Milano, Bear County, State of Lone Star.
11. All exhibits in the file are authentic. In addition, each exhibit contained in the file is the original of that document unless otherwise noted on the exhibit or as established by the evidence.
12. Only those portions of the DSM-V included in the problem may be introduced, or referred to, by either the prosecution or the defense.

13. The common side effects of Prozac® (fluoxetine) are nausea, insomnia, somnolence, anorexia, anxiety, nervousness, asthenia, and tremor. The most common of these are anxiety, insomnia, and nervousness.

14. A DNA test on the shoe belonging to the victim showed the presence of the victim's DNA and the defendant's DNA on the sides of the shoe.

§ 14-3. Case File Materials

Students will be expected to use the following materials in presenting their cases.

Statutes — State of Lone Star

§ 79.01. Types of Criminal Homicide

(a) A person commits criminal homicide if he intentionally, knowingly, recklessly, or with criminal negligence causes the death of an individual.

(b) Criminal homicide is murder, capital murder, manslaughter, or criminally negligent homicide.

§ 79.02. Murder.

(a) In this Section:

(1) "Adequate cause" means cause that would commonly produce a degree of anger, rage, resentment, or terror in a person of ordinary temper, sufficient to render the mind incapable of cool reflection.

(2) "Sudden passion" means passion directly caused by and arising out of provocation by the individual killed or another acting with the person killed which passion arises at the time of the offense and is not solely the result of former provocation.

(b) A person commits an offense if he:

(1) intentionally or knowingly causes the death of an individual;

(2) intends to cause serious bodily injury and commits an act clearly dangerous to human life that causes the death of an individual; or

(3) commits or attempts to commit a felony, other than manslaughter, and in the course of and in furtherance of the commission or attempt, or in immediate flight from the commission or attempt, he commits or attempts to commit an act clearly dangerous to human life that causes the death of an individual.

(c) Except as provided by Subsection (d), an offense under this section is a felony of the first degree.

(d) At the punishment stage of a trial, the defendant may raise the issue as to whether he caused the death under the immediate influence of sudden passion arising from an adequate cause. If the defendant proves the issue in the affirmative by a preponderance of the evidence, the offense is a felony of the second degree.

* * * * *

§ 79.04. Manslaughter

(a) A person commits an offense if he recklessly causes the death of an individual.

(b) An offense under this section is a felony of the second degree.

§ 79.05. Criminally Negligent Homicide

(a) A person commits an offense if he causes the death of an individual by criminal negligence.

(b) An offense under this section is a Class A misdemeanor.

* * * * *

INDICTMENT

COURT'S COPY
Name: Sylvia Moss
Complainant: Danny Moss
Offense Charge: Murder
GJ: 2212267 **PH Court: 523**
JN#: 556633 **SID#: 2345432**
Witness: State's Attorney

TRUE BILL OF INDICTMENT

IN THE NAME AND BY AUTHORITY OF THE STATE OF LONE STAR, the Grand Jury of Bear County, State of Lone Star, duly organized, empanelled by the Judicial District Court of said County, do present in and to said Court that in the County and State aforesaid, and anterior to the presentment of this indictment, and:

COUNT 1: MURDER

on or about December 5, [YR-1], SYLVIA MOSS, hereinafter referred to as defendant, then and there intentionally or knowingly, unlawfully, and feloniously kill and murder DANNY MOSS, a human being, hereinafter referred to as complainant, without the authority of law and with deliberate design to effect the death of complainant in violation of Section 79.02, Lone Star Penal Code;

AGAINST THE PEACE AND DIGNITY OF THE STATE

Dorothy Flores

Foreperson of the Grand Jury

Defendant's Written Statement to Police

STATE OF LONE STAR
COUNTY OF BEAR } **Case Number: 09-45679**

VOLUNTARY STATEMENT OF: SYLVIA MOSS

I, Sylvia Moss, after first being duly warned by Det. M. Lorson #7779 at 1045 hrs. at 214 W. Nueva, on December 8, [YR-1] that (1) I have the right to remain silent and not make any statement at all, and any statement I do make may be used against me at my trial; (2) Any statement I make may be used as evidence against me in Court; (3) I have the right to have a lawyer present to advise me prior to and during any questioning; (4) If I am unable to employ a lawyer, I have the right to have a lawyer appointed to advise me prior to and during any questioning; (5) I have the right to terminate the interview at any time; and I understand that the above rights are continuing rights and may be urged by me at any stage of the proceedings, and I hereby prior to and during the making of this statement, knowingly, intelligently, and voluntarily waive the above rights and give to the said, Det. Morgan Lorson #7779, the person to whom this statement is being given, the following written statement:

My name is Sylvia Moss. I married my husband, Danny Moss, in [YR-2] here in San Milano. We had dated for about two years before getting married. We met at an office party for Wilson Electronics in July [YR-4] where we had both worked. I started there in [YR-6] and my husband started in [YR-5]. I am still working at Wilson. I like it there and they love me. For the last three years I have received merit pay increases above and beyond what my co-workers receive. I have been told that I have the potential to get promoted to district manager next year. I am not surprised.

I have been told that if I can go back and get a degree that the world is mine for the taking. I started working for Wilson right after high school. I have taken a few evening courses at the Bear County Community College and made high grades in my English and History classes. But I got tired of the poor quality of teaching and decided to wait for the Wilson company to pay for my tuition. They select two people each year for that program and I have been told that I am high on the list.

I loved my husband very much and we had made plans to spend the rest of our lives together. Just like other couples we had our problems. There were times when I did not think that he fully understood my need to be taken care of. And he definitely did not like my cooking. He did not appreciate the fact that I had recently signed up for evening cooking classes at the Southwest School District. It cost me about 50 dollars but I thought it was worth it because I pick up things quickly and assumed that within a couple of weeks I would be able to cook anything that my husband wanted. I have a mind like a steel trap.

I think that what happened is that my husband got up from bed during the night and instead of turning right to go into the bathroom, he took another couple of steps, turned right and fell down the stairs. I guess my cooking lessons went to waste. I woke up when I heard a loud thump and was afraid that someone had broken into the house. When I saw that Danny was not in bed, I called his name, got out of bed, turned on the hall light and saw him at the bottom of the steps. I immediately called 911.

I did not do anything to my husband or try to turn him over. I was afraid of hurting him further. I took a class on first aid several years ago and learned that you can cause more damage sometimes if you try to move someone who has fallen. I know that I called his name and that he did not move or even blink his eyes. That point was on the final exam and I was one of the few in the class to get that question right. Everyone assumes that you should immediately try to move them and make them more comfortable. When the EMT arrived I was clearly in a case of shock and did not fully appreciate my surroundings or the gravity of this horrendous situation. When they told me that my husband was dead, I could not even muster a few tears for him. I was astonished that all of this had happened so quickly. He did not even have a chance to say goodbye to me.

I would never do anything to hurt my husband. I loved him very much. I am not sure what I will do now, but I always land on my feet and am very sure that I will get through this. I have done it before and I will do it again.

By that I mean that when I was a teenager, my brother drowned in a camping accident at the summer camp pool, during the night. He slipped and fell in the deep end of the pool. He could not swim. It really hurt me but I recovered. I jumped in after him but he was already dead.

I have no earthly idea how my husband got the contusion, or whatever, on the back of his neck. I am not an expert but I think he got it when he tripped on one of his shoes, fell and then flipped over before hitting his head on the railing, which clearly killed him.

I am very interested in helping resolve this matter. That is why I waived my lawyer rights and decided to talk to you today.

This is the end of my statement. I have read this statement and it is true and correct.

WITNESS: Johnny Moore SIGNATURE: Sylvia Moss

DATE: Dec. 8, [YR-1]

Grand Jury Testimony of Morgan Lorson

IN RE:	BEFORE THE GRAND JURY
	OF
GRAND JURY INVESTIGATION	BEAR COUNTY, STATE OF LONE STAR

* * * * * *

****

COURT REPORTER'S

Q AND A TRANSCRIPT OF TESTIMONY OF

DET. MORGAN LORSON

MARCH 9, [YR-0]

****

* * * * *

BE IT REMEMBERED, that on MARCH 9, [YR-1], the above-entitled matter came on for hearing before the Grand Jury of BEAR County, sitting in San Milano, State of Lone Star, being presented by DALLAS MOSBY, Assistant Criminal District Attorney, for consideration by the members thereof.

HEATHER STEVENS was duly sworn as Court Reporter.

WHEREUPON, the following evidence was introduced and proceedings had, to-wit, beginning at 9:00 o'clock a.m. and concluding at 10:00 o'clock a.m.

DETECTIVE MORGAN LORSON, the Witness,

GRAND JURY FOREPERSON: Do you solemnly swear that you will not divulge either by words or signs any matter about which you may be interrogated, and that you will keep secret all proceedings of the Grand Jury which may be had in your presence, and that you will true answers make to such questions as may be propounded to you by the Grand Jury or under its direction, so help you God?

THE WITNESS: I do.

EXAMINATION BY DALLAS MOSBY:

Q: Detective Lorson, as with any witness who comes before the Grand Jury, I need to give you the definitions of perjury and aggravated perjury.

A person commits the offense of perjury if, with intent to deceive and with knowledge of the statement's meaning, that person makes a false statement under oath or swears to the truth of a false statement previously made and the statement is required or authorized by law to be made under oath.

Perjury is a Class A Misdemeanor, which is punishable by anywhere up to one year in the Bear County Jail and/or a fine of up to $4,000.

Perjury becomes aggravated perjury if the person commits perjury, makes that false statement during or in connection with an official proceeding, and Grand Jury proceedings are official proceedings, and the statement is material.

Aggravated perjury is a third-degree felony, which means it's punishable by anywhere from two to ten years in the Lone Star Department of Corrections, and there's a potential fine of up to $10,000. Do you understand this?

A: Yes, sir.

Q. Would you please state your name for the grand jury?

A: Yes, my name is Morgan Lorson.

Q: Could you please tell us your position and duties with the police department?

A: I am a homicide detective, with about 7 years' experience on the force. My duties entail conducting investigations into possible homicides.

Q: Could you tell us about your training?

A: Yes, sir. I attended the San Milano Police Academy, graduated in the top 25%. During that course we studied crime reconstruction. I later attended a short course at crime reconstruction at the FBI Academy at Quantico, Virginia. The instructors at that academy, which is nationally recognized, included experienced homicide detectives as well as forensic pathologists. Again, I did well, finished in the top 30%.

Q: Okay. Detective, I would like you to tell the jurors about your investigation into the death of Mr. Danny Moss, on December 5, [YR-1]?

A: Our records show that on December 5, [YR-1], at 2:00 AM, EMT was called to the Moss residence. The call was placed by a Sylvia Moss, Mr. Moss's wife. When EMT arrived they found a man lying at the bottom of the stairs, with no signs of life. They did not try to revive him. I arrived at the scene shortly after they got there. He was pronounced dead at the scene by the coroner. We later identified him as Danny Moss, the husband of Sylvia Moss.

Q: Please go on.

A: Well, things did not seem quite right. Mrs. Moss said that her husband had fallen down the stairs but I noticed a small red spot on the victim's neck and she was acting sort of detached so I decided to take some photos of the scene. I also noticed that a shoe was in the hallway at the top of the stairs. While I was taking the pictures she asked if she could be excused to put on some makeup, so. . .

Q: I am sorry . . .

A: She asked to put on some makeup and I said sure, whatever. She really seemed not to be with it and I thought that she was just in a state of shock.

Q: Did you say anything to her about being in shock and whether she needed any medical attention?

Q: I did. I asked her how she was doing and that is when she said she looked awful and that she wanted to put on her makeup. I think I told her that I was concerned because she seemed to clearly be in a state of shock and she just said "hmmm," or something like that.

Q: Did she say anything else?

A: When I asked her what had happened . . .

Q: Let me interrupt, did you ask her that right away?

A: No, I am sorry I was not clear. When I first got there I asked her if she knew what had happened. That is when she asked if she could put on her makeup first and then she would answer my questions. So, I said yes, she could. That is when I said something about her being in shock. While she was putting on her makeup I took the pictures. About 20 minutes later, after she had put on her makeup she told me that she had awakened when she heard a noise and that is when she saw her husband at the bottom of the stairs.

Q: Okay. Thank you for clarifying that sequence for us. Where did she put on the makeup?

A: She used the upstairs bathroom. Although there was a downstairs bathroom, she went upstairs, which meant she had to step over the victim to get there.

Q: She had to step over his body to get upstairs?

A: Yes, I was stunned when I saw that. I cannot recall ever being at a scene of a crime where a family member did that. She seemed very nonchalant about it.

Q: Can you describe her demeanor during your questioning of her?

A: Yes, I can. She seemed emotionally detached but very interested in my investigation.

Q: How is that?

A: Well she asked me several times if what she had said was helpful. She also asked if I was hungry and whether she could make something for me while we waited for the coroner to arrive.

Q: And?

A: I declined. I said I was fine. But it really seemed odd that she would ask that.

Q: Detective, did she show any concern about her husband?

A: Yes, she said several times that she could not believe that this had happened to him. She said that he was trying so hard to be a good husband and that she was sorry that they had gone to bed angry with one another. She tried to give me the impression that that seemed to bother her.

Q: Did she say what they had fought about?

A: Well she did not use the word fight but when I asked her she said that they had had a disagreement — that was the word she used — about the evening meal. Apparently she burned the vegetables or something. She said that he never really appreciated her efforts to please him and that had led to the quote, disagreement, unquote. I asked her if he had complained about her cooking before, and she said yes, he had, many times. When she was talking about his latest complaint, her face visibly tightened. I could see her clenching her jaw.

Q: Did Mrs. Moss say anything about her husband using any prescription drugs?

A: Yes, she said that he had been taking Prozac, to calm down, and that she was sure that he had taken some earlier in the evening, after dinner. He had a prescription from their family physician.

Q: You mentioned earlier that you saw a shoe at the top of the stairs. Can you tell us more about that?

A: Yes, I asked Mrs. Moss about it and she said that it was her husband's. She said that he must have tripped on it. But the shoe was not on the stairs and was off to one side, which signaled to me that he did not trip on it. It was also odd because the other shoe was in the closet, off the hallway, next to the master bedroom. She could not account for the fact that one of her husband's shoes was in the closet and the other was in the hallway, near the top of the stairs. If there were other shoes or clothes strewn about it would have seemed reasonable to have a shoe in the hallway. But it appeared that everything else was in order. They were neat housekeepers. That is why it caught my eye. The crime lab ran a DNA swipe on the shoe and it showed positive for both the victim's and Mrs. Moss's DNA.

Q: During your contact with Ms. Moss on the evening in question, did she ever show any signs of emotion?

A: Do you mean, did she cry?

Q: Yes.

A: No, she did not cry while I was with her. I didn't see her cry.

Q: Any signs of empathy for her husband?

A: Not really.

Q: Do you recognize these exhibits? [Shows to witness]

A: Yes, I do.

Q: Would you please tell us what they are?

A: These are the pictures I took on December 5th at the Moss residence. These two show Mr. Moss at the bottom of the stairs. I took this one from the top of the stairs and this one from the living room, at the bottom of the stairs. The third photo was taken from the doorway of what I would call the master bedroom looking down the hall, with the closet on the left side. The door on the right is the bathroom door. A few steps beyond that door is the stairway. The victim's shoe is on the floor at the end of the hallway, right outside the other bedroom. And this is a close up picture of the victim's shoe. As I said, the other shoe was in the closet, on the floor, with his other shoes, to the immediate left of the master bedroom door — right across from the bathroom door.

Q: Thank you. Did you have an opportunity to speak to Ms. Moss again?

A: Yes, after thinking about the case I decided I really needed to get a written statement from her and ask her a few more questions. I had a nagging gut feeling that something was not quite right. So I called her a couple of days later and she came in and gave a statement.

Q: Is this her statement? [Shows to witness]

A: Yes. That's it. She was very cooperative and wanted to talk. But at times it was hard to get her to talk about what happened on the night of her husband's death.

Q: After she gave her written statement, did you gather any more information about Ms. Moss?

A: Yes, I did. Very interesting. I learned that when she was a teenager she and her younger brother had attended a youth camp in Missouri for one week. But during that week the brother drowned in the camp swimming pool late one night. He could not swim and although she was with him at the time she did not jump into the water to try and save him. The local police did an investigation and concluded that they did not have enough evidence to take it to trial. I talked to someone in the police department who told me that the police officer who handled the investigation into the drowning had since died, but that they would look for the incident report. They found the report and I believe the DA from Missouri sent a copy to you. I have also reviewed that report as part of this investigation. My sense is that Ms. Moss acted with the same sort of detached interest at the crime scene and that she really never explained why she had not jumped in to save him. The investigator tried to follow up on some of those points, but she lawyered up and he did not get his answers. It appears that the case never went anywhere. Looks like the coroner ruled that it was an accident.

Q: Is this the police report from Missouri that you are referring to? [Shows to witness]

A: Yes, that is it.

Q: Thank you. Anything else?

A: Yes, two years ago there was an incident at Wilson Electronics, where she still works. After I took Ms. Moss's statement, I went over to Wilson and I personally interviewed her co-workers and supervisor. They said that she saw a memo in which one of her co-workers had criticized a report that she had prepared and she, that is Ms. Moss, went, in their words, "ballistic" and screaming at no one in particular. Just an hour later, she confronted the co-worker in the company's cafeteria and started screaming and shouting that the co-worker was quote stupid unquote and did not know a good report from a bad report. She apparently got right into her face, which in turn prompted the co-worker to hit Ms. Moss several times with her fist. That got the co-worker fired for hitting Ms. Moss. Apparently, the company had a zero tolerance policy for physical violence. But Ms. Moss was only reprimanded by the company and was able to keep her job. Her reputation at the company is that she has a very short fuse if anyone questions her. But the management likes her work and keeps her on the payroll. I also got a copy of the company's letter of reprimand that was placed in her file at the time.

Q: Do you recognize this exhibit? [Shows to witness]

A: Yes, this is the letter of reprimand from Wilson Electronics.

Q: And do you recognize this exhibit? [Shows to witness]

A: Yes, I do. This is the official autopsy report on Mr. Moss.

Q: I am sorry, one more. Do you recognize this exhibit? [Shows to witness]

A: Yes, this is a newspaper clipping about her brother's drowning at the camp in Missouri.

Q: Let me go back to the night of December 5th. How long were you at the Moss's residence?

A: I got there at about 2:30 and stayed until about 4:00 a.m. I waited until the coroner had finished and they had removed the body, and then I went to the station.

Q: What happened to Ms. Moss?

A: Before I left, I asked her if she needed to be taken anywhere or needed anything and she said no, that she would be just fine. She said that she was going to make something to eat and then go and stay with friends and make plans for her husband's funeral.

Q: As a result of your investigation have you reached any conclusions about what happened?

A: Yes, in my professional opinion, she hit him on the neck with his shoe, pushed him down the stairs, or did something to make him fall. I think that she is just that kind of person to do that.

Q: What leads you to that conclusion?

A: First, they had had a fight. Second, there is that bruise on his neck that she cannot explain. Third, she showed no emotion during the entire time I was at their home and no emotion during my interview with her when she came to my office. She seemed very cold and detached and more interested in herself and what I thought of her and how she looked.

QUESTION BY GRAND JUROR:

Q: Do you have any forensic evidence that would directly link Ms. Moss with the death of her husband?

A: Well, we don't have any fingerprints. As I said her DNA was on the victim's shoe, if that is what you mean. There was some blood on the carpet from Mr. Moss's head wound, which was fatal. But we did not find any hair fibers or blood on the stair railing. I am trained to examine the scene of the crime, which is part of crime scene reconstruction. As part of that process, I attempt to match up wounds and injuries to possible causes for those injuries, at the scene of the crime. When I examined the bruise, it seemed to match the edge of the shoe and the location and shape of the injury, in my opinion, is more consistent with the hypothesis that he was struck from behind with that shoe before tumbling down the stairs and striking his head on the end of the stair railing.

QUESTION BY ANOTHER GRAND JUROR:

Q: Did you ever ask her flat-out if she had killed her husband?

A: Yes, I did, at the station. She paused, took a deep breath, and then said very slowly that she would never do anything to harm him. It was not a clear "yes" or "no" answer to my question. I got the feeling that she was offended and impatient with me that I even asked the question.

Q: Okay. Thank you, Detective. Would you please step outside for just a few minutes.

THE WITNESS: Okay.

[The Witness leaves the Grand Jury Room at 10:00 a.m., and is subsequently dismissed.]

(END OF TRANSCRIPT)

GRAND JURY TESTIMONY OF DR. PAT BENTLEY

IN RE:	BEFORE THE GRAND JURY
	OF
GRAND JURY INVESTIGATION	BEAR COUNTY, STATE OF LONE STAR

* * * * * *

****

COURT REPORTER'S

Q AND A TRANSCRIPT OF TESTIMONY OF

PAT BENTLEY, M.D.

MARCH 9, [YR-0]

****

* * * * *

BE IT REMEMBERED, that heretofore, to-writ on MARCH 9, [YR-1], the above-entitled matter came on for hearing before the Grand Jury of BEAR County, sitting in San Milano, State of Lone Star, being presented by DALLAS MOSBY, Assistant Criminal District Attorney, for consideration by the members thereof.

HEATHER STEVENS was duly sworn as Court Reporter.

WHEREUPON, the following evidence was introduced and proceedings had, to-wit, beginning at 1:15 o'clock p.m. and concluding at 2:10 o'clock p.m.

PAT BENTLEY, The Witness,

GRAND JURY FOREPERSON: Do you solemnly swear that you will not divulge either by words or signs any matter about which you may be interrogated, and that you will keep secret all proceedings of the Grand Jury which may be had in your presence, and that you will true answers make to such questions as may be propounded to you by the Grand Jury or under its direction, so help you God?

THE WITNESS: I do.

EXAMINATION BY DALLAS MOSBY:

Q: Dr. Bentley, good morning.

A: Good morning.

Q: As with any witness who comes before the Grand Jury, I need to give you the definitions of perjury and aggravated perjury.

A person commits the offense of perjury if, with intent to deceive and with knowledge of the statement's meaning, that person makes a false statement under oath or swears to the truth of a false statement previously made and the statement is required or authorized by law to be made under oath.

Perjury is a Class A Misdemeanor, which is punishable by anywhere up to one year in the Bear County Jail and/or a fine of up to $4,000.

Perjury becomes aggravated perjury if the person commits perjury, makes that false statement during or in connection with an official proceeding, and Grand Jury proceedings are official proceedings, and the statement is material.

Aggravated perjury is a third-degree felony, which means it's punishable by anywhere from two to ten years in the Lone Star Department of Corrections, and there's a potential fine of up to $10,000. Do you understand this?

A: Yes, sir.

Q. Would you please state your name for the grand jury?

A: My name is Pat Bentley.

Q: You are a psychiatrist?

A: Yes, I am.

Q: Could you give the jurors some of your background information and qualifications?

A: Sure. I attended the University of Minnesota and graduated with honors in [YR-23], with a Bachelor of Science. I attended medical school at Johns Hopkins University, specializing in psychiatry. I graduated in [YR-18].

Q: Where did you intern?

A: I interned for about one year at the Central Lone Star Medical Center, in Austin.

Q: Do you have a specialty?

A: Yes, I specialize in psychiatry. I spent three years in residency at the Audy Murphy Veteran's Hospital here in San Milano. I am a diplomate with the American Board of Psychiatry, having passed the written and oral exams. I am now on the faculty of the Baylor University School of Medicine. I continue to practice part-time with three other psychiatrists in our own medical center. I brought a copy of my resume, if that would help. (Witness hands resume to counsel)

Q: Yes, thank you. Have you testified before in a court?

A: Yes, but not often. I have testified in five or six criminal cases, for both prosecution and defense, and in about four civil cases. Mostly in the Dallas area.

Q: Okay. Are you being paid for your help on this case?

A: No, I am not. Well, I should add, that I have been told that I will be reimbursed for my reasonable travel expenses.

Q: Okay. Do you know Sylvia Moss?

A: Yes.

Q: Please tell the grand jury about how you know Ms. Moss.

A: I interviewed her and reviewed her medical history this past month, pursuant to a request from your office.

Q: Can you please tell us what you learned during that examination?

A: I conducted a three-hour interview with Ms. Moss. We talked about her background, her relationships, what, if any, medications she had taken, or was taking, and how she felt about her husband's recent death. I did not have access to any of her past medical records and counted primarily on what she told me.

Q: Did you reach any conclusions about whether Ms. Moss suffers from any mental disease or syndrome?

A: Yes, she is a classic example of what we refer to as Narcissistic Personality Disorder. It is listed in the Diagnostic and Statistical Manual, the most recent edition is number V. We doctors simply refer to it as the "DSM" for short. Every doctor is familiar with that text. The disorder is well-known and in my opinion helps explain her actions and relationships.

Q: In layman terms, what does that mean?

A: Well, in short, she is what I guess you might recognize as being very self-centered and has a strong need to be recognized and valued for what she considers her extraordinary accomplishments. People with this syndrome tend to view others as beneath them. They often show a lack of empathy and if you do not give them adequate attention, it can result in withdrawal or even rage and anger. Frankly, we all have some tendency to focus on ourselves, but that is not what we are talking about in this case. When it goes too far, it falls within the medical disorder described in the Diagnostic and Statistical Manual.

Q: Would you tell us the process of coming to the conclusion that she has the narcissistic personality disorder.

A: Yes. The DSM sets out a list of what we refer to as diagnostic criteria. In this case, the DSM lists nine different criteria. Those have been developed over the years by detailed study and diagnosis. They are not fool-proof but they are very dependable. According to the DSM, permit me to read it: "A pervasive pattern of grandiosity (in fantasy or behavior), need for admiration, and lack of empathy, beginning by early adulthood and present in a variety of contexts, as indicated by five (or more) of the following." And then the DSM lists the nine criteria. I applied that list and found that she satisfied at least five of the criteria — she is often haughty and arrogant, she has what we refer to as a grandiose sense of self-importance, she believes that she is very special and unique and can only be understood by others who have high status, she has a sense of entitlement, she requires excessive admiration, and she lacks empathy.

Q: So, I count six of the criteria.

A: Yes, that is correct.

Q: Were there any others?

A: I could make the case that there were, but the six I listed are very clearly present in Ms. Moss.

Q: What specifically did you consider in applying those criteria?

A: First, I read her statement to the police, I read the incident report from when her younger brother drowned in Missouri, and the discipline report, or reprimand, I guess you call it that, from the company where she works. I took all of those into consideration in making my diagnosis.

Q: Okay. Was that Wilson Electronics where she worked?

A: Yes, I am sorry, that's it.

Q: And you considered your interview with her?

A: Definitely. That carried great weight.

Q: Did she cooperate with you?

A: Yes, absolutely. You see the way the disorder can be manifested is by being arrogant or believing you are better than anyone else. I believe that because I was an MD, she felt that we were equals and that she could impress me with all that she had accomplished. She continued to point out during the interview how she had been so underappreciated for years, by friends, families, and even lovers.

Q: Did you talk at all about her relationship with her husband?

A: Yes, the bottom line was that he did not fully appreciate her and that had led to what she called a number of disagreements. It was clear to me that she has an anger management problem and that it was aggravated by having the syndrome. She described that on the night her husband died, they had had what she called a major disagreement over her cooking. They ended up shouting at each other for over an hour just before they went to bed. She said that to calm down, her husband had taken Prozac before going to sleep, at about 11 p.m.

Q: Would that sort of response, that is, having a major argument or blowup, be consistent with the disorder?

A: Absolutely. The DSM notes that people with this disorder are very sensitive to what the DSM refers to as "injury" from someone's criticism. If you criticize them, they can act with a range of emotions, including anger and rage.

Q: So, if I understand what you are saying, if Mr. Moss criticized her for her cooking, that could account for the anger she felt toward him on the night he died?

A: Yes, but please understand. None of us really likes criticism, whether it's about our cooking, what we are wearing, or about how we do our jobs. People who have this disorder tend to overreact to even the slightest criticism. They need for the camera to be focused on them, all the time, even when the circumstances indicate that the camera should be on someone or something else. I wrote about this in an article in [YR-9].

Q: Did you consider the possibility that there might be any other medical or mental reasons for her actions and attitudes? For example, could her taking drugs explain her behaviors?

A: Yes, I did consider other possible causes. That is what I am required to do as a doctor. First, there was no record that she had ever taken any legal or illegal drugs that would explain her behavior. In fact one of the things she told me in the interview, and she was very proud of this, she said she had never even tried drugs like cocaine, or marijuana. That, she said, was beneath her. I did consider the possibility that she might have what is referred to in the DSM as the Intermittent Explosive Disorder. That is where the patient is unable to control themselves and they act with aggression that results in serious injuries or destruction. Here, even if she has that disorder, the narcissistic personality disorder is more consistent with her words and actions.

Q: Any other possible explanations?

A: I also considered another disorder, or problem. That is what is referred to as the relationship distress with spouse or intimate partner. She clearly had relational problems with her husband. It's also described in the DSM. I felt that, again, even assuming she had a relational problem with her husband, the narcissistic disorder was the key contributing factor. The same would be true for what we often refer to as sibling rivalry problems. In some ways these all tie together in that a person who exhibits severe narcissistic tendencies is bound to have relational problems.

Q: If you learned that right after the EMT and police arrived at the Moss residence, Mrs. Moss wanted to put on her makeup before answering questions about her husband's death, does that fit with this disorder?

A: Yes. Her husband is lying on the steps and instead of showing empathy for his condition, and what happened, she is more concerned about herself.

Q: Okay. If someone had this disorder, could it result in physically attacking the person who was criticizing them?

A: Yes. Clearly.

Q: So, if the evidence showed that Mr. Moss, Sylvia's husband, had a bruise on the back of his neck when he was found dead in his home, is it reasonable to conclude that Sylvia hit him at some point before he died?

A: I would say that that is entirely reasonable. Ms. Moss is a very sick woman, she needs professional medical and mental attention.

Q: Can this disorder be treated?

A: Absolutely. At least we can try to help her.

Q. Okay. Thank you for your testimony, Doctor. Would you please step outside for a few minutes.

A: Yes. [Witness leaves room]

[Witness steps outside at 2:10 PM and is subsequently dismissed.]

(END OF TRANSCIPT)

Curriculum Vitae for Dr. Pat Bentley

Pat Bentley, M.D.
3900 Travis Avenue, Suite 802, Dallas, Sate of Lone Star
214-692-8200—office
headsrus@pmc.com

EDUCATION AND TRAINING

Undergraduate

B.S. [YR-23] University of Minnesota, B.S., Minneapolis, Minnesota
Research fellowship in psychiatry

Medical School

M.D. [YR-18] John Hopkins University School of Medicine, Baltimore, Maryland
National Board of Medical Examiners, honor grade in psychiatry

POSTDOCTORAL

Medical Internship

[YR-18-YR-17] Central Lone Star Medical Center, Austin, State of Lone Star

Residency

[YR-17-YR-14] Resident in Psychiatry, Audy Murphy Veteran's Hospital
San Milano, State of Lone Star

Fellowship

[YR-14-YR-13] Memorial Mental Medical Center
Dallas, State of Lone Star

PROFESSIONAL EXPERIENCE

Private Practice of Psychiatry, Dallas, State of Lone Star

[YR-13] -present (part time since [YR-12])

Academic Appointments

[YR-12-YR-10] Assistant Professor of Psychiatry, Baylor University School of Medicine, Dallas, State of Lone Star

[YR-10] -Present Professor of Psychiatry, Baylor University School of Medicine, Dallas, State of Lone Star

Board Certifications and Memberships

American Board of Psychiatry and Neurology
American Psychiatric Association, Washington, DC
Association for Humanistic Psychology
American Academy of Psychotherapists

State of Lone Star Medical License No. J4356
Maryland State Medical License No. K9032

RESEARCH ACTIVITIES

Peer-reviewed scientific articles

Bentley, P. *Assessing the Narcissistic Personality Disorder.* THE AMERICAN JOURNAL ON PSYCHOLOGY [YR-9]; 73:1006.

Report of Dr. Avery Wilson

Psychiatrics Associates, Inc.
12456 Main Ave.
Dallas, State of Lone Star 86677
(555) 564-9900
(555) 564-9009 (Hotline)

Your Mind is Our Business

REPORT of AVERY WILSON, M.D.
May 27, [YR-1]

I have prepared this report at the request of the defense counsel for Mrs. Sylvia Moss, of San Milano, State of Lone Star.

I am a licensed psychiatrist. My curriculum vitae is attached. I am currently practicing in Dallas, at a clinic with three other doctors specializing in mental disorders and syndromes.

Over the course of two weeks in May, I interviewed Mrs. Sylvia Moss to determine if she has suffered, or is currently suffering from, any significant mental diseases, syndromes, or disorders. During those two weeks I interviewed her three times for a total of 10 hours and 30 minutes. I also read carefully (1) the statement she gave to the police shortly after her husband's death, (2) the police report that was prepared when her younger brother drowned in Missouri some years ago, and (3) the incident report involving a co-worker at Wilson Electronics in San Milano, Lone Star. I also spoke on the phone with the detective who was present at the Moss residence at the time of Mr. Moss's accidental death.

Based on my assessments I did not feel it necessary to have her subjected to a physical examination to determine if any of her problems were caused by an undiagnosed medical condition or the result of any medications that she might have taken, or is currently taking.

Mrs. Moss is a very personable individual who appears to be in very good medical condition. I found no evidence of any drug or alcohol abuse. She is extremely charming and engaging and demonstrates great curiosity about the sciences. She also exhibits a high level of ambition and sees herself as a transformative figure that has great potential. She is very focused and careful about how she presents herself to others.

While she tends to show limited empathy in certain circumstances, she does display emotions at the appropriate time. For example, in discussing the death of her younger brother, she explained that they had been rivals for the attention of their parents, who are both now deceased. She regretted deeply that they had not gotten along and that she missed him terribly. During this conversation, we had to take a break so that she could compose herself. She stated that the great irony was that although the rivalry had existed, the reason for the rivalry, her parents, was no longer present. She no longer remembers the exact details of their argument or what happened. She does recall that it ended up with her chasing him around the pool before he fell into the deep end.

It is clear that she has some relational problems. She said that before she married her husband, she had dated three other men over the course of two years. All of those relationships failed, she said, because they took advantage of her. In one instance, the man used her to get a job with Wilson

Electronics and promptly ended their relationship when he got the job. The second man had a drinking problem, and the third man was still in her words, a "momma's boy" who did not really appreciate or respect her. She reflected some distain for those individuals and expressed empathy for their future partners. Her husband, Danny she said, was the love of her life and they initially were very happy. They were, in her words, soul mates.

The marriage ran into difficulties, however, when he started criticizing her cooking. In response, she took a cooking course and for a while that seemed to appease him. On the night he died, she explained that she probably overreacted to his criticism of how she had fixed his potatoes. That had led to a major argument, she said. Those were the last words that they had shared before he died. She deeply regretted that and still misses him.

Using the criteria listed in the Diagnostic and Statistical Manual V (DSM-V), I have concluded that she does not suffer from a Narcissistic Personality Disorder. Most of the criteria listed for that disorder can be explained through other means. She does tend to believe that she can accomplish much in life but those are not fantasies. She indeed has the means and intelligence to accomplish her goals. I did not find her to be arrogant or haughty. Nor does she view herself as special. She does not display a sense of entitlement. Nor is she "interpersonally exploitive." I found that she displays an appropriate level of empathy. I did not find that she requires excessive attention.

I found that while she has some narcissistic characteristics (e.g., asking to put on makeup while the EMT personnel were attending to her husband), they did not arise to the level of the disorder identified in the DSM. She does exhibit problems with partner-type relationships, i.e., she tends to work better alone. Counseling would be very helpful to help her address those issues.

In my professional opinion, she is not a violent person. While she does have some anger management issues, it's clear from her behavior and past history that she is able to manage her anger for the most part. When rejected or criticized, she tends to use her verbal skills to counterattack the person who has rejected or criticized her.

I recommended to Ms. Moss that she seriously consider seeking professional counseling. She declined, at least for now.

Respectfully submitted,

Avery Wilson,

Avery Wilson, M.D.

Encl.

Curriculum Vitae of Dr. Avery Wilson

Avery Wilson, M.D.

Psychiatrics Associates, Inc.
12456 Main Ave.
Dallas, State of Lone Star 6677
Mobile: (555) 564-9900
Hotline: (555) 564-9009

Objective

- To diagnose and provide expert analysis for all patients suffering from mental diseases, syndromes, and disorders.

Abilities

- I have provided expert psychiatric reports in over 50 criminal trials (primarily for the defense).

Education

- Columbia University, A.B., [YR-20].
- Harvard University Graduate School of Arts and Sciences, A.M. Clinical Psychology, [YR-17].
- Cornell University Medical College, M.D., [YR-13].
- Residency in Psychiatry, Massachusetts Mental Health Center, [YR-13-YR-10].

Professional Experience

- Psychiatrist, Massachusetts Mental Health Center, Boston, MA, [YR-10-YR-8].
- Psychiatrist, University Hospital, San Milano, LS, [YR-8-YR-7].
- Senior Attending Psychiatrist, Shady Acres Mental Health System, Dallas, LS, [YR-7-YR-5].
- Psychiatrist, Psychiatrics Associates, Inc., Dallas, LS, [YR-5-Present].

Board Certification

- American Board of Psychiatry and Neurology, 2000-[YR-0].
- American Psychiatric Association, 2005-[YR-0]
- Massachusetts State Medical License No. L4081
- Lone Star State Medical License No. V8267

Research Activities

Peer-Reviewed Article

- Wilson, A. *Testifying at Trial: Analyzing and Diagnosing Behavioral, Cognitive, and Perceptual Disorders*, THE AMERICAN JOURNAL ON PSYCHOLOGY 44:19-42, [YR-7]

Speech

- Wilson, A. "A Method for Diagnosing Relational and Personality Disorders". State of Lone Star Annual Health Conference, [YR-5].

Excerpts From Diagnostic and Statistical Manual (DSM)*

Intermittent Explosive Disorder

Diagnostic Criteria

312.34 (F63.81)

A. Recurrent behavioral outbursts representing a failure to control aggressive impulses as manifested by either of the following:

   1 Verbal aggression (e.g., temper tantrums, tirades, verbal arguments, or fights) or physical aggression toward property, animals, or other individuals, occurring twice weekly, on average, for a period of 3 months. The physical aggression does not result in damage or destruction of property and does not result in physical injury to animals or other individuals.

   2 Three behavioral outbursts involving damage or destruction of property and/or physical assault involving physical injury against animals or other individuals occurring within a 12-month period.

B. The magnitude of aggressiveness expressed during the recurrent outbursts is grossly out of proportion to the provocation or to any precipitating psychosocial stressors.

C. The recurrent aggressive outbursts are not premeditated (i.e., they are impulsive and/or anger-based) and are not committed to achieve some tangible objective (e.g., money, power, intimidation).

D. The recurrent aggressive outbursts cause either marked distress in the individual or impairment in occupational or interpersonal functioning, or are associated with financial or legal consequences.

E. Chronological age is at least 6 years (or equivalent developmental level).

F. The recurrent aggressive outbursts are not better explained by another mental disorder (e.g., major depressive disorder, bipolar disorder, disruptive mood dysregulation disorder, a psychotic disorder, antisocial personality disorder, borderline personality disorder) and are not attributable to another medical condition (e.g., head trauma, Alzheimer's disease) or to the physiological effects of a substance (e.g., a drug of abuse, a medication). For children ages 6-18 years, aggressive behavior that occurs as part of an adjustment disorder should not be considered for this diagnosis.

Note: This diagnosis can be made in addition to the diagnosis of attention-deficit/hyperactivity disorder, conduct disorder, oppositional defiant disorder, or autism spectrum disorder when recurrent impulsive aggressive outbursts are in excess of those usually seen in these disorders and warrant independent clinical attention.

Diagnostic Features

The impulsive (or anger-based) aggressive outbursts in intermittent explosive disorder have a rapid onset and, typically, little or no prodromal period. Outbursts typically last for less than 30 minutes and commonly occur in response to a minor provocation by a close intimate or associate. Individuals

---

with intermittent explosive disorder often have less severe episodes of verbal and/or nondamaging, nondestructive, or noninjurious physical assault (Criterion A1) in between more severe destructive/assaultive episodes (Criterion A2). Criterion Al defines frequent (i.e., twice weekly, on average, for a period of 3 months) aggressive outbursts characterized by temper tantrums, tirades, verbal arguments or fights, or assault without damage to objects or without injury to animals or other individuals. Criterion A2 defines infrequent (i.e., three in a 1-year period) impulsive aggressive outbursts characterized by damaging or destroying an object, regardless of its tangible value, or by assaulting/striking or otherwise causing physical injury to an animal or to another individual. Regardless of the nature of the impulsive aggressive outburst, the core feature of intermittent explosive disorder is failure to control impulsive aggressive behavior in response to subjectively experienced provocation (i.e., psychosocial stressor) that would not typically result in an aggressive outburst (Criterion B). The aggressive outbursts are generally impulsive and/or anger-based, rather than premeditated or instrumental (Criterion C) and are associated with significant distress or impairment in psychosocial function (Criterion D). A diagnosis of intermittent explosive disorder should not be given to individuals younger than 6 years, or the equivalent developmental level (Criterion E), or to individuals whose aggressive outbursts are better explained by another mental disorder (Criterion F). A diagnosis of intermittent explosive disorder should not be given to individuals with disruptive mood dysregulation disorder or to individuals whose impulsive aggressive outbursts are attributable to another medical condition or to the physiological effects of a substance (Criterion F). In addition, children ages 6-18 years should not receive this diagnosis when impulsive aggressive outbursts occur in the context of an adjustment disorder (Criterion F).

Associated Features Supporting Diagnosis

Mood disorders (unipolar), anxiety disorders, and substance use disorders are associated with intermittent explosive disorder, although onset of these disorders is typically later than that of intermittent explosive disorder.

Prevalence

One-year prevalence data for intermittent explosive disorder in the United States is about 2.7% (narrow definition). Intermittent explosive disorder is more prevalent among younger individuals (e.g., younger than 35-40 years), compared with older individuals (older than 50 years), and in individuals with a high school education or less.

* * * * *

Narcissistic Personality Disorder

Diagnostic Criteria

301.81 (F60.81)

A pervasive pattern of grandiosity (in fantasy or behavior), need for admiration, and lack of empathy, beginning by early adulthood and present in a variety of contexts, as indicated by five (or more) of the following:

1. Has a grandiose sense of self-importance (e.g., exaggerates achievements and talents, expects to be recognized as superior without commensurate achievements).
2. Is preoccupied with fantasies of unlimited success, power, brilliance, beauty, or ideal love.
3. Believes that he or she is "special" and unique and can only be understood by, or should associate with, other special or high-status people (or institutions).
4. Requires excessive admiration.

5. Has a sense of entitlement (i.e., unreasonable expectations of especially favorable treatment of automatic compliance with his or her expectations).

6. Is interpersonally exploitative (i.e., takes advantage of others to achieve his or her own ends).

7. Lacks empathy: is unwilling to recognize or identify with the feelings and needs of others.

8. Is often envious of others or believes that others are envious of him or her.

9. Shows arrogant, haughty behaviors or attitudes.

Diagnostic Features

The essential feature of narcissistic personality disorder is a pervasive pattern of grandiosity, need for admiration, and lack of empathy that begins by early adulthood and is present in a variety of contexts.

Individuals with this disorder have a grandiose sense of self-importance (Criterion 1). They routinely overestimate their abilities and inflate their accomplishments, often appearing boastful and pretentious. They may blithely assume that others attribute the same value to their efforts and may be surprised when the praise they expect and feel they deserve is not forthcoming. Often implicit in the inflated judgments of their own accomplishments is an underestimation (devaluation) of the contributions of others. Individuals with narcissistic personality disorder are often preoccupied with fantasies of unlimited success, power, brilliance, beauty, or ideal love (Criterion 2). They may ruminate about "long overdue" admiration and privilege and compare themselves favorably with famous or privileged people.

Individuals with narcissistic personality disorder believe that they are superior, special, or unique and expect others to recognize them as such (Criterion 3). They may feel that they can only be understood by, and should only associate with, other people who are special or of high status and may attribute "unique," "perfect," or "gifted" qualities to those with whom they associate. Individuals with this disorder believe that their needs are special and beyond the ken of ordinary people. Their own self-esteem is enhanced (i.e., "mirrored") by the idealized value that they assign to those with whom they associate. They are likely to insist on having only the "top" person (doctor, lawyer, hairdresser, instructor) or being affiliated with the "best" institutions but may devalue the credentials of those who disappoint them.

Individuals with this disorder generally require excessive admiration (Criterion4). Their self-esteem is almost invariably very fragile. They may be preoccupied with how well they are doing and how favorably they are regarded by others. This often takes the form of a need for constant attention and admiration. They may expect their arrival to be greeted with great fanfare and are astonished if others do not covet their possessions. They may constantly fish for compliments, often with great charm. A sense of entitlement is evident in these individuals' unreasonable expectation of especially favorable treatment (Criterion 5). They expect to be catered to and are puzzled or furious when this does not happen. For example, they may assume that they do not have to wait in line and that their priorities are so important that others should defer to them, and then get irritated when others fail to assist "in their very important work" This sense of entitlement, combined with a lack of sensitivity to the wants and needs of others, may result in the conscious or unwitting exploitation of others (Criterion 6). They expect to be given whatever they want or feel they need, no matter what it might mean to others. For example, these individuals may expect great dedication from others and may overwork them without regard for the impact on their lives. They tend to form friendships or romantic relationships only if the other person seems likely to advance their purposes or otherwise enhance their self-esteem. They often usurp special privileges and extra resources that they believe they deserve because they are so special.

Individuals with narcissistic personality disorder generally have a lack of empathy and have difficulty recognizing the desires, subjective experiences, and feelings of others (Criterion 7). They may assume that others are totally concerned about their welfare. They tend to discuss their own concerns in inappropriate and lengthy detail, while failing to recognize that others also have feelings and needs. They are often contemptuous and impatient with others who talk about their own problems and concerns. These individuals may be oblivious to the hurt their remarks may inflict (e.g., exuberantly telling a former lover that "I am now in the relationship of a lifetime!" boasting of health in front of someone who is sick). When recognized, the needs, desires, or feelings of others are likely to be viewed disparagingly as signs of weakness or vulnerability. Those who relate to individuals with narcissistic personality disorder typically find an emotional coldness and lack of reciprocal interest.

These individuals are often envious of others or believe that others are envious of them (Criterion 8). They may begrudge others their successes or possessions, feeling that they better deserve those achievements, admiration, or privileges. They may harshly devalue the contributions of others, particularly when those individuals have received acknowledgment or praise for their accomplishments. Arrogant, haughty behaviors characterize these individuals; they often display snobbish, disdainful, or patronizing attitudes (Criterion 9). For example, an individual with this disorder may complain about a clumsy waiter's "rudeness" or "stupidity" or conclude a medical evaluation with a condescending evaluation of the physician.

* * * * *

Other Problems Related to Primary Support Group

V61.10 (Z63.0) Relationship Distress With Spouse or Intimate Partner

This category should be used when the major focus of the clinical contact is to address the quality of the intimate (spouse or partner) relationship or when the quality of that relationship is affecting the course, prognosis, or treatment of a mental or other medical disorder. Partners can be of the same or different genders. Typically, the relationship distress is associated with impaired functioning in behavioral, cognitive, or affective domains. Examples of behavioral problems include conflict resolution difficulty, withdrawal, and overinvolvement. Cognitive problems can manifest as chronic negative attributions of the other's intentions or dismissals of the partner's positive behaviors. Affective problems would include chronic sadness, apathy, and/or anger about the other partner.

OFFICE OF THE DISTRICT ATTORNEY

WALTERS COUNTY, MISSOURI

2445 Mason Lane
Musquire, Missouri 89444

***

--Strength Through Justice--

Mr. Dallas Mosby
Office of the District Attorney
BEAR County
San Milano, State of Lone Star

Re: Sylvia Moss

Mr. Mosby:

Attached is the incident report that was prepared in [YR-11] on the drowning death of Mr. Wilson Moss at a local camp. I am also attaching a copy of a newspaper account that was located in the same file. Unfortunately, the detective who worked the case, Police Detective David Knotts, died of cancer in [YR-3]. The District Attorney at the time is no longer with this office and moved to another state. We have not been successful in contacting him about the file.

Aside from the report and the clipping, there is no other information in the files relating to this case. As noted on the report, no action was taken on the case. And there is no other reference in any of our records relating to Ms. Moss.

This report was prepared and maintained in the regular course of the business of the Musquire Police Department, in accordance with the regulations of that department. The report was found in the incident files for the period, June 1, [YR-11] to September 1, [YR-11]. For what it is worth, Detective Knotts told his other officers that he was sure that Ms. Moss had pushed her brother into the pool.

If I can assist you in any other way, please feel free to contact me.

Sincerely,

Sarah Moores
SARAH T. MOORES
ASSISTANT DISTRICT ATTORNEY
WALTERS COUNTY, MISSOURI

City of Musquire

Police Department
123 Main Ave
Musquire, Missouri 89444
(555) 654-0098

Incident Report

Case Number: *99-34zz5*
Filed Opened: *June 20, [YR-11]*
Time: *1000 hours*
Investigating Officer: *David Knotts, Detective*
Badge Number of Investigating Officer: *456*
Name of Suspect/Person of Interest: *Sylvia Moss*

On June 20, [YR-11], I was called to Camp Munkeewonk at approximately 2:00 a.m. to investigate a drowning of a young man in the camp's swimming pool. The dispatcher related that a 911 call had been placed at 1:52 a.m. from a man identifying himself as the camp manager, Jason Watts.

The young man was identified by camp personnel and by his sister, as Wilson Moss, Jr., a 12-year old male. He had fallen into the deep end of the pool. Suspected cause of death was drowning. I examined his body and did not see any bruises or other unusual marks. Members of the camp staff reported that at about 1:30 a.m. they were awakened by loud screaming and shouting coming from the direction of the pool, followed a few minutes later by complete silence. When they ran toward the pool they were met on the trail by the victim's sister, Sylvia Moss, who was walking toward them and reported that her brother had fallen into the pool and that he could not swim. She told the staff that they had had an argument about their parents and that he had fallen in, when she was chasing him around the pool. The staff did not ask her why she had not jumped in to help him. The staff attempted CPR but could not revive him.

I interviewed Sylvia Moss at the camp for about 15 minutes and she confirmed that she and her brother had been arguing and that when she started to chase him around the pool that he slipped and fell in. She acknowledged that they had been shouting. She said that she knew immediately that he had drowned and ran for help. I asked her how she knew that and she simply said that she was smart and could plainly see that he was dead. She said that they had been arguing about how much time each of them would be spending individually with their parents when they would be visiting the camp the next weekend. I asked her several times why she had not jumped in to save him and she seemed very detached, almost cold, and said that she kept repeating that she did not know why she had not jumped in. She admitted that she knew how to swim.

During the whole time I talked to her, she did not cry or show any other emotion. She seemed concerned about how she would look and what she would say if a newspaper wanted to talk to her. I terminated my questioning at about 3:15 am.

This morning, I was supposed to meet again with Ms Moss to clear up some points. But when she came to the station, she was accompanied by her family lawyer who informed me that she would not be answering any questions about the incident and that she was invoking her right to remain silent.

Recommended Disposition: *No action. Coroner has ruled that death was accidental. J Knotts 6/30/YR-11]*

Signature of Investigating Officer: *Jonathan A Knotts*

Note for File: I know this file is officially closed but there needs to be some follow up on this case. Something tells me that Sylvia Moss has not been entirely truthful about what happened. DA says we don't have enough to convict. But I see real problems in this young woman.
JK, 8-1-[YR-11]

June 21, [YR-11] MUSQUIRE DAILY NEWS 2A

Boy Drowns at Local Camp

Foul Play Suspected

By Justin Knotts

Wilson Moss, a youth from California, attending Camp Munkeewonk, drowned early yesterday morning in the camp's swimming pool. Local police are calling the death a possible homicide.

Moss, and his sister, Sylvia, were arguing by the camp's swimming pool after midnight. Camp staff members heard the fighting and ran toward the pool. They encountered Ms. Moss, who told them that she thought her brother had fallen into the pool as they were chasing each other around the pool decking. The staff found the young Mr. Moss in the deep end of the pool and tried unsuccessfully to revive him. He was later pronounced dead at the scene.

Attempts to contact members of the family were rebuffed by the family's attorney, Sam Nordstop, of Chicago, a member of a criminal defense law firm. A family spokesman simply said that the family needed time to make arrangements for Mr. Moss's funeral. An autopsy is pending.

Mr. Jason Watts, camp director said, "We are all deeply upset about this. In the thirty years that Camp Munkeewonk has been in existence, this is the first tragedy we have experienced." He added that counselors had been brought in to talk to the other campers.

Officer Jonathan Knotts, of the local police department, said that all possible causes of death were under consideration, including a possible homicide. He noted that some things were not adding up about what happened. Other unnamed sources observed that Ms. Moss had given inconsistent accounts of what happened.

Camp Munkeewonk is a privately run camp for children, who have experienced some level of relational problems.

Letter of Reprimand

Wilson Electronics

456 North Main
San Milano, State of Lone Star
210-555-5679
WilsonE.com

June 3, [YR-2]

Ms. Sylvia Moss
Inventory Management Division.
Wilson Electronics

Re: Letter of Reprimand

Ms. Moss:

After investigating the incident last month in which you were involved in an altercation in the company's cafeteria, I have no choice but to issue this formal letter of reprimand.

My investigation indicates that you confronted one of your co-workers, Ms. Nora Gomez, and began shouting at her in a loud voice and in a threatening manner. Your outburst was apparently triggered when you saw a memo prepared by Ms. Gomez, which questioned the quality of your work in the Inventory Management Division of this company. As a result of your actions, Ms. Gomez struck you several times.

As you know, Ms. Gomez has been relieved because of the company's zero tolerance policy on physical violence.

While your work has been above average during your employment here at Wilson, we have received numerous complaints about your inability to accept constructive criticism. This sort of behavior will not be tolerated and if you act in this way again, we may be forced to terminate your employment.

I encourage you to seek professional counseling through our Human Resources Office. A copy of this letter will be placed in your personnel file

Sincerely yours,

Javier Hernandez
Javier Hernandez
CEO, Wilson Electronics

cc Human Resources

Autopsy Report

Office of Chief Medical Examiner
Bear County, State of Lone Star

Autopsy Report

Case No. 0501238

Name: Danny Moss

Approximate Age:	26 years	Sex:	Male
Height:	70 inches (residual)	Weight:	210.5 lbs (residual)

Identified By: Dental Comparison (12-08-[YR-1])

Place of Death: Residence

I hereby certify that I, Jasper McCue, M.D. have performed an autopsy on the body of Danny Moss at the Bear County Medical Examiner's Morgue on the eighth day of December [YR-1], and that the said autopsy revealed:

FINDINGS:

01 Sudden death associated with:

A. Craniocerebral trauma with bibasilar skull fractures due to head trauma

02 Postmortem toxicology studies show an elevated blood concentration of fluoxetine (Prozac®)

03 No evidence of dehydration or electrolyte imbalance:

A. Postmortem vitreous chemistry non-contributory
B. Blood furosemide (Lasix) negative

COMMENT:

Mr. Danny Moss was a 26-year-old White male, who was found dead at his residence at approximately 2:00 a.m. on December 5, [YR-1]. He was discovered by his wife who apparently found him unresponsive at the foot of the stairway in their home. The exact downtime is unknown.

The MedStar ambulance arrived at 2:45 a.m. and Mr. Moss was pronounced dead at 3:27 a.m. Records obtained from Lone Star Medical Facility in Bear County indicate that Mr. Moss had no history of disease. Most significant findings at autopsy included a large contusion on the scalp and massive skull fracture. There was a fresh bruise on the right posterior side of the neck, measuring approximately 6 centimeters, laterally.

Postmortem toxicology was positive for fluoxetine (Prozac®). Fluoxetine is a selective serotonin uptake-inhibitor antidepressant. Because it is highly selective, fluoxetine has fewer side-effects than the older tricyclic antidepressants including dry mouth, blurred vision, memory impairment, constipation, urinary retention, and sinus tachycardia, all which are primarily due to anticholinergic effects. Fluoxetine is well absorbed after oral administration and is not affected by food. The values reflected in Mr. Moss's femoral blood indicate that the amount of fluoxetine was in the toxic range, but was not in lethal range.

In conclusion, Mr. Danny Moss death is attributed to blunt head trauma which resulted in a massive skull fracture. Additionally, even though the amount of fluoxetine was in the toxic range, it did not directly contribute to his death.

CAUSE OF DEATH:

BLUNT HEAD TRAUMA: SKULL FRACTURE.

Jasper McCue

Jasper McCue, M.D.
Deputy Medical Examiner

Drawing of Moss Residence

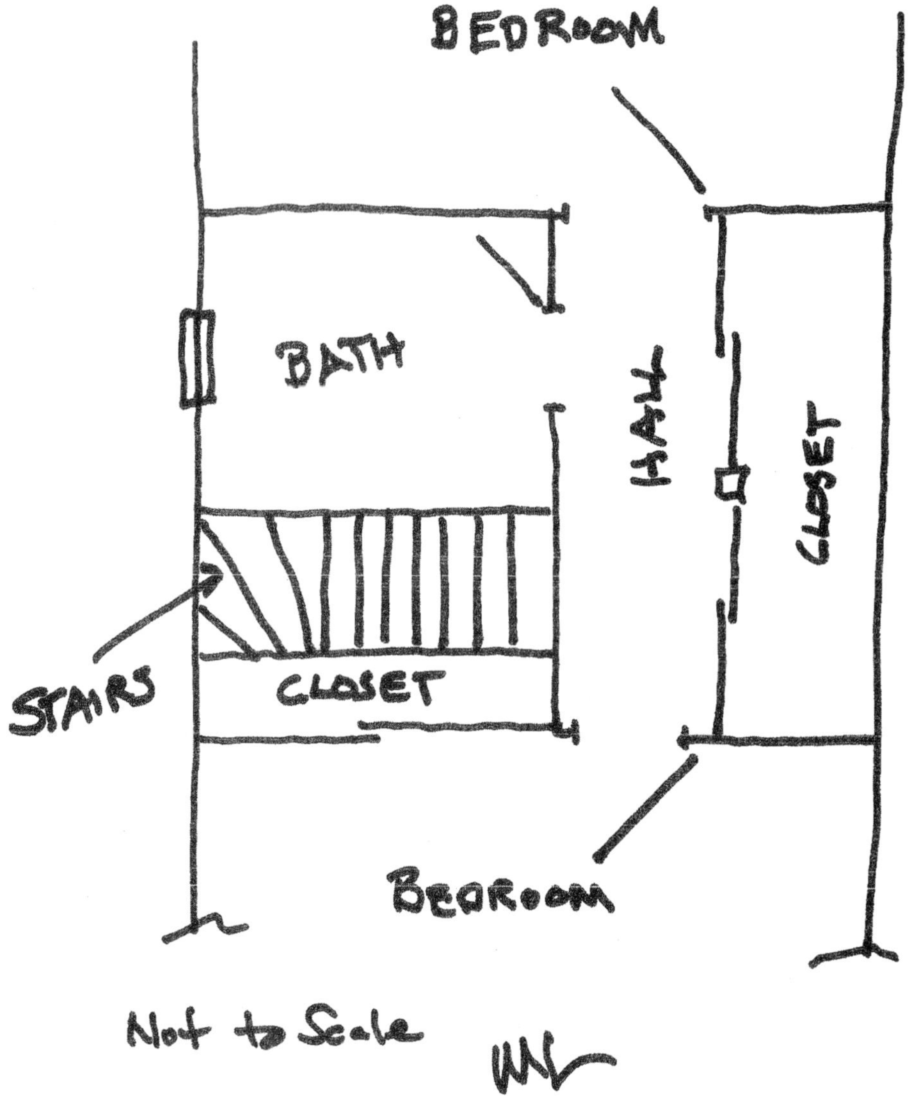

Crime Scene Photographs

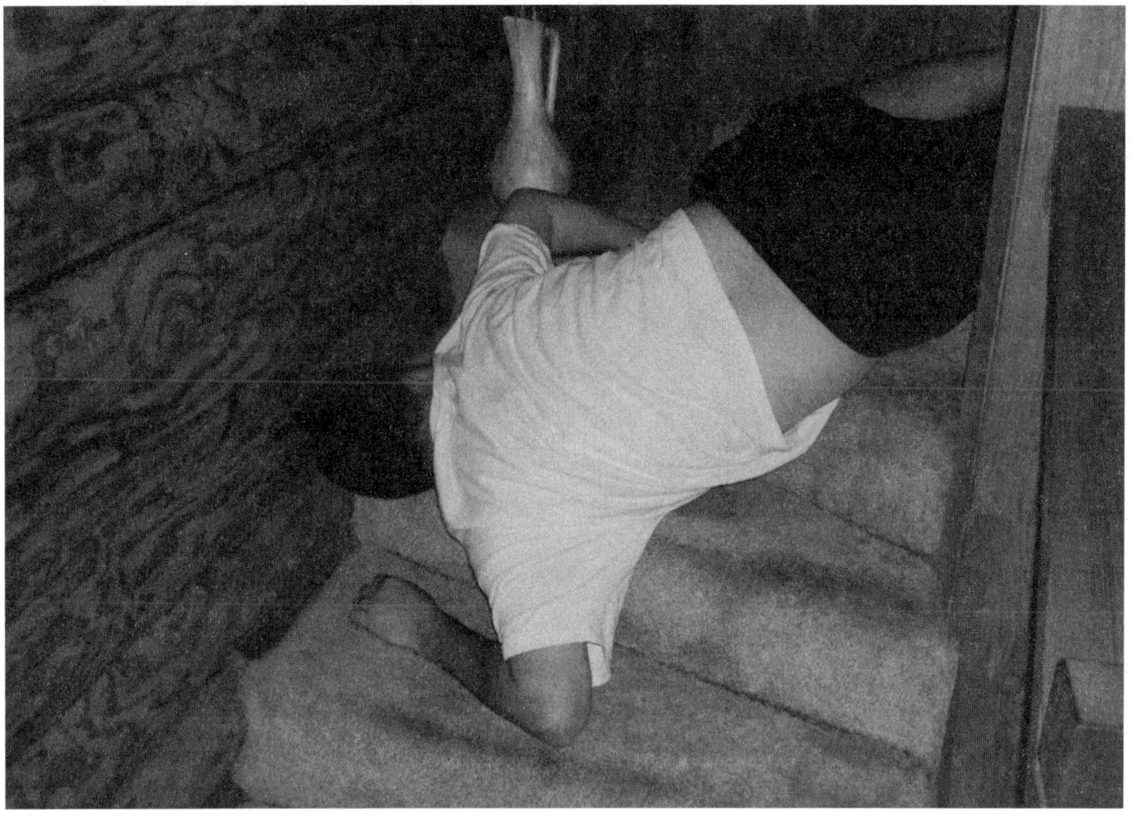

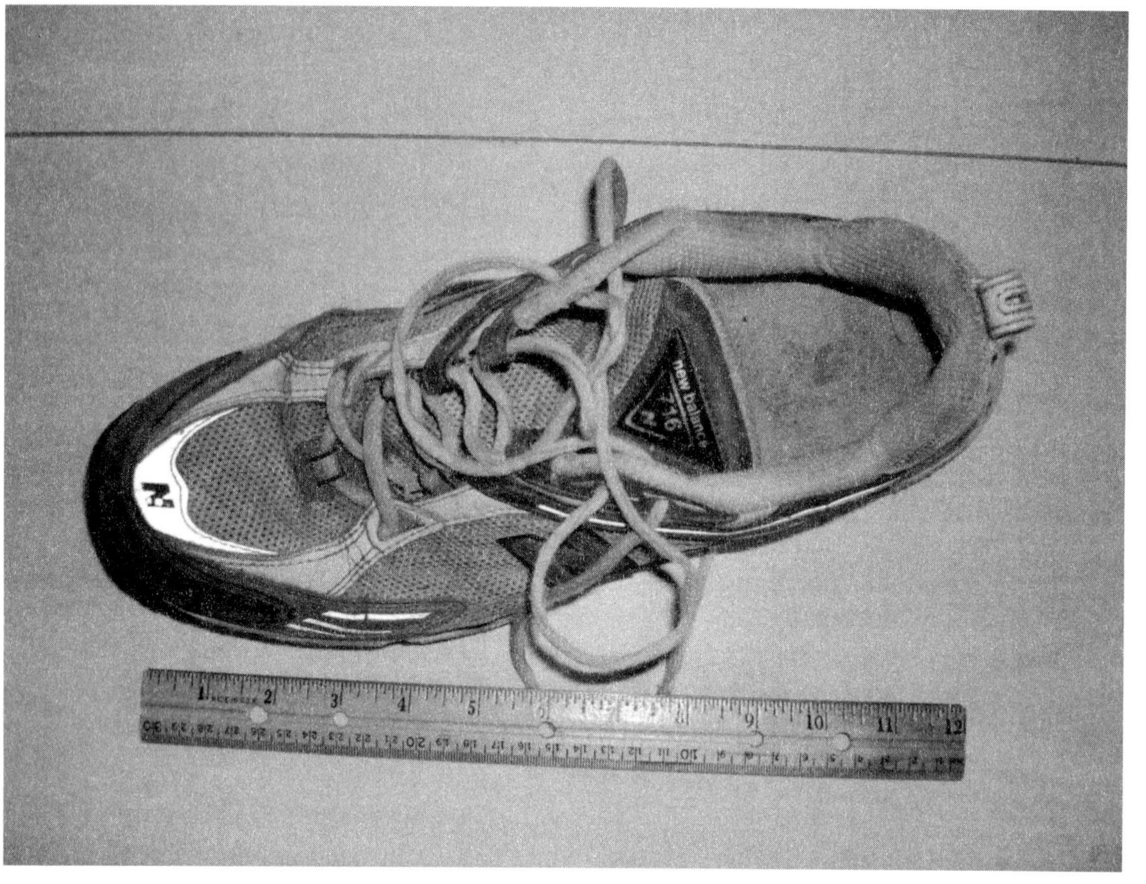
new balance
716

COURT'S COPY

Name: Sylvia Moss
Complainant: Danny Moss
Offense Charged: MURDER

JURY INSTRUCTION

LADIES AND GENTLEMEN OF THE JURY:

The defendant, SYLVIA MOSS, stands charged by indictment COUNT 1 with the offense of murder, alleged to have been committed on or about the December 5, [YR-1], in Bear County, State of Lone Star. The defendant has pleaded not guilty.

1.

Our law provides that a person commits the offense of murder if he or she intentionally or knowingly causes the death of an individual.

2.

A person acts intentionally, or with intent, with respect to a result of his or her conduct when it is his conscious objective or desire to cause the result.

A person acts knowingly, or with knowledge, with respect to a result of his conduct when he or she is aware that his or her conduct is reasonably certain to cause the result.

3.

Now, if you find from the evidence beyond a reasonable doubt that on or about December 5, [YR-1], in Bear County, State of Lone Star, that the defendant SYLVIA MOSS, did intentionally or knowingly cause the death of an individual, namely DANNY MOSS, by applying force to him and causing him to fall down a set of stairs, then you will find the defendant Sylvia Moss guilty of murder as charged in the indictment.

Unless you so find beyond a reasonable doubt, or if you have a reasonable doubt as to whether the defendant is guilty of murder, then you will find her not guilty.

4.

You are instructed that you may consider all relevant facts and circumstances surrounding the killing, if any, and the previous relationship existing between the accused and the deceased, if any, together with all relevant facts and circumstances going to show the condition of the mind of the defendant at the time of the offense, if any.

The State, however, is not required to prove a motive. If the State has proved the essential elements of the offense beyond a reasonable doubt, the defendant must be found guilty of that offense regardless of the defendant's motive or lack of a motive. If the State, however, has proved a motive, you may consider that insofar as it gives meaning to other circumstances. On the other hand, you may consider the absence of motive in weighing whether or not the defendant is guilty of the crime charged.

5.

"Proof beyond a reasonable doubt" is proof that leaves you firmly convinced of the defendant's guilt. There are very few things in this world that we know with absolute certainty, and in criminal cases the law does not require proof that overcomes every possible doubt. If, based on your consideration of the evidence, you are firmly convinced that the defendant is guilty of the crime charged, you should find her guilty. If, on the other hand, you think there is a real possibility that she is not guilty, you should give her the benefit of the doubt and find her not guilty.

Chapter 15
Jones v. Moss

§ 15-1. Introduction

Sylvia Moss was suspected of killing her husband, Danny Moss. Police responded to Sylvia's 911 call early in the morning and found Danny lying at the bottom of the steps of their home. Sylvia told the police that she had awakened when she heard a loud thump, saw Danny, and dialed 911 without first checking to see if there was anything she could do to help him. The police determined that Danny died as a result of a severe blow to his head, caused when he hit the stair railing. But there was also evidence of a bruise on the back of his neck. Additional evidence showed that Sylvia had reacted with rage whenever Danny ignored her or criticized her cooking.

The State's initial theory was that Sylvia hit him on the neck with a shoe and caused him to fall down the stairs. A prosecution expert determined that Sylvia suffers from Narcissistic Personality Disorder, which triggered the attack.

Sylvia's version was that Danny's death was accidental. After further review of the evidence, the prosecutor decided not to try her. Shortly thereafter, Danny's step-daughter from a prior marriage, Sarah Jones, filed a wrongful death action against Sylvia.

§ 15-2. Stipulations Regarding Procedural and Evidentiary Matters

The parties have stipulated to the following:

1. The case is being tried in a Lone Star court.
2. All witnesses called to testify who have in statements or deposition testimony identified the defendant, other individuals, or tangible evidence, can, if asked, identify the same at trial.
3. The defendant Moss signed her statement to the police.
4. Any applicable notice and disclosure requirements under the Federal Rules of Civil Procedure and the Federal Rules of Evidence were met in a timely fashion.
5. Other than what is supplied in the problem itself, there is nothing exceptional or unusual about the background information of any of the witnesses or the defendant that would bolster or detract from their credibility.
6. The parties may not "invent" an individual not mentioned in this problem and have testimony or evidence offered to the court or jury from that invented individual.
7. "Beyond the record" must not be entertained as an objection.
8. Danny Moss died on December 5, [YR-1], at his home in San Milano, Bear County, State of Lone Star.
9. All exhibits in the file are authentic. In addition, each exhibit contained in the file is the original of that document unless otherwise noted on the exhibit or as established by the evidence.
10. Only those portions of the DSM-V included in the problem may be introduced, or referred to, by either the prosecution or the defense.

11. The common side effects of Prozac® (fluoxetine) are nausea, insomnia, somnolence, anorexia, anxiety, nervousness, asthenia, and tremor. The most common of these are anxiety, insomnia, and nervousness.

§ 15-3. Case File Materials

Students will be expected to use the following materials in presenting their cases.

Lone Star Civil Practice & Remedies Code

§ 31.123. Cause of Action

(a) An action for actual damages arising from an injury that causes an individual's death may be brought if liability exists under this section.

(b) A person is liable for damages arising from an injury that causes an individual's death if the injury was caused by the person's or his agent's or servant's wrongful act, neglect, carelessness, unskillfulness, or default.

(c) A person is liable for damages arising from an injury that causes an individual's death if:

(1) the person is a proprietor, owner, charterer, or hirer of an industrial or public utility plant or of a railroad, street railway, steamboat, stagecoach, or other vehicle for the transportation of goods or passengers; and

(2) the injury was caused by the person's or his agent's or servant's wrongful act, neglect, carelessness, unskillfulness, or default.

§ 31.124. Benefitting From Action

(a) An action to recover damages as provided by this subchapter is for the exclusive benefit of the surviving spouse, children, and parents of the deceased.

(b) The surviving spouse, children, and parents of the deceased may bring the action or one or more of those individuals may bring the action for the benefit of all.

§ 31.125. Punitive Damages

When the death is caused by the willful act or omission or gross negligence of the defendant, punitive as well as actual damages may be recovered.

Plaintiff's Petition

District Court of Bear County

SARAH JONES Plaintiff v. SYLVIA MOSS Defendant	}	Docket No. 789-9987 COMPLAINT FOR DAMAGES

COMES NOW the above-named Plaintiff and alleges the following:

I. Parties, Jurisdiction, and Venue

A. Plaintiff, Sarah Jones, the step daughter of Danny Moss, the decedent, brings this action in her personal capacity.

B. Defendant, Sylvia Moss, is a resident of Bear County, State of Lone Star.

C. This Court has jurisdiction over the subject matter of this complaint and over the parties.

D. Venue is proper and appropriate in Bear County because the death of Danny Moss, which is the subject matter of this complaint, occurred in Bear County.

II. Factual Basis

A. Defendant, Sylvia Moss, and Danny Moss were husband and wife.

B. Responding to a 911 call to their residence, EMT personnel discovered Danny Moss lying on the stairwell. Defendant told them that she had discovered her husband after hearing him fall down the stairs.

C. Mr. Moss was pronounced dead at the scene and a later autopsy showed that he had died of injuries including a blow to the back of his neck. The police initially concluded that the death was a homicide.

D. Although a prosecution expert determined that Sylvia suffers from a narcissistic personality disorder, which triggered the attack, the State decided not to prosecute the Defendant for her actions.

E. Defendant's acts were the sole and proximate cause of Danny Moss's death.

III. Causes of Action

A. As a direct and proximate result of the acts of the Defendant, the decedent suffered a wrongful death, entitling Plaintiff to recover actual and exemplary damages (including but not limited to medical and hospital expenses, funeral expenses, and all other damages allowable for wrongful death and survival benefits under Lone Star Civil Practice & Remedies Code §§ 31.123-31.125 and any other damages allowable as a result of Defendant's conduct;) in amounts not now precisely known, the exact amounts to be proven at or before the time of trial.

B. As a further direct and proximate result of the Defendant's acts and omissions, the Plaintiff of the decedent suffered destruction of the parent-child relationship and loss of parental consortium.

C. As a further direct and proximate result of the negligent acts and omissions of Defendant, Plaintiff is entitled to recover statutory and reasonable attorney's fees and costs in amounts not now precisely known, the court to set such amounts in the future.

IV. Prayer for Relief

WHEREFORE, the Plaintiff prays for a judgment of liability against the defendants as follows:

A. For a judgment against Defendant.

B. For an award of damages as set forth in the above complaint herein, including statutory and reasonable fees and costs in such amounts that may be awarded by this Court.

C. For such other and further relief as the Court deems just and appropriate.

DATED this day of October 12, [YR-1].

Jason A. Perez

Jason A. Perez
The Perez Law Firm
Attorney for Plaintiff

DEFENDANT'S WRITTEN STATEMENT TO POLICE

STATE OF LONE STAR COUNTY OF BEAR	}	Case Number: 09-45679

VOLUNTARY STATEMENT OF: SYLVIA MOSS

I, Sylvia Moss, after first being duly warned by Det. M. Lorson #7779 at 1045 hrs, at 214 W. Nueva, on December 8, [YR-1] that (1) I have the right to remain silent and not make any statement at all, and any statement I do make may be used against me at my trial; (2) Any statement I make may be used as evidence against me in Court; (3) I have the right to have a lawyer present to advise me prior to and during any questioning; (4) If I am unable to employ a lawyer, I have the right to have a lawyer appointed to advise me prior to and during any questioning; (5) I have the right to terminate the interview at any time; and I understand that the above rights are continuing rights and may be urged by me at any stage of the proceedings, and I hereby prior to and during the making of this statement, knowingly, intelligently, and voluntarily waive the above rights and give to the said, Det. Morgan Lorson #7779, the person to whom this statement is being given, the following written statement:

My name is Sylvia Moss. I married my husband, Danny Moss, in [YR-2] here in San Milano. We had dated for about two years before getting married. We met at an office party for Wilson Electronics in July [YR-4] where we had both worked. I started there in [YR-6] and my husband started in [YR-5]. I am still working at Wilson. I like it there and they love me. For the last three years I have received merit pay increases above and beyond what my co-workers receive. I have been told that I have the potential to get promoted to district manager next year. I am not surprised.

I have been told that if I can go back and get a degree that the world is mine for the taking. I started working for Wilson right after high school. I have taken a few evening courses at the BEAR County Community College and made high grades in my English and History classes. But I got tired of the poor quality of teaching and decided to wait for the Wilson company to pay for my tuition. They select two people each year for that program and I have been told that I am high on the list.

I loved my husband very much and we had made plans to spend the rest of our lives together. Just like other couples we had our problems. There were times when I did not think that he fully understood my need to be taken care of. And he definitely did not like my cooking. He did not appreciate the fact that I had recently signed up for evening cooking classes at the Southwest School District. It cost me about 50 dollars but I thought it was worth it because I pick up things quickly and assumed that within a couple of weeks I would be able to cook anything that my husband wanted. I have a mind like a steel trap.

I think that what happened is that my husband got up from bed during the night and instead of turning right to go into the bathroom, he took another couple of steps, turned right and fell down the stairs. I guess my cooking lessons went to waste. I woke up when I heard a loud thump and was afraid that someone had broken into the house. When I saw that Danny was not in bed, I called his name, got out of bed, turned on the hall light and saw him at the bottom of the steps. I immediately called 911.

I did not do anything to my husband or try to turn him over. I was afraid of hurting him further. I took a class on first aid several years ago and learned that you can cause more damage sometimes if you try to move someone who has fallen. I know that I called his name and that he did not move or even blink his eyes. That point was on the final exam and I was one of the few in the class to get that question right. Everyone assumes that you should immediately try to move them and make them more comfortable. When the EMT arrived I was clearly in a case of shock and did not fully appreciate my surroundings or the gravity of this horrendous situation. When they told me that my husband was dead, I could not even muster a few tears for him. I was astonished that all of this had happened so quickly. He did not even have a chance to say goodbye to me.

I would never do anything to hurt my husband. I loved him very much. I am not sure what I will do now, but I always land on my feet and am very sure that I will get through this. I have done it before and I will do it again.

By that I mean that when I was a teenager, my brother drowned in a camping accident at the summer camp pool, during the night. He slipped and fell in the deep end of the pool. He could not swim. It really hurt me but I recovered. I jumped in after him but he was already dead.

I have no earthly idea how my husband got the contusion, or whatever, on the back of his neck. I am not an expert but I think he got it when he tripped on one of his shoes, fell and then flipped over before hitting his head on the railing, which clearly killed him.

I am very interested in helping resolve this matter. That is why I waived my lawyer rights and decided to talk to you today.

This is the end of my statement. I have read this statement and it is true and correct.

WITNESS: Johnny Moore SIGNATURE: Sylvia Moss

DATE: Dec. 8, [YR-1]

Deposition of Sarah Jones

ORAL DEPOSITION OF MS. SARAH JONES, produced as a witness at the instance of the defendant, SYLVIA MOSS, and duly sworn, was taken in the above-styled and numbered cause on October 31, [YR-1] from 2:00 PM to 3:10 PM before Sally Walker, Certified Shorthand Reporter in and for the State of Lone Star, reported by machine shorthand, at the law offices of Plaintiff, pursuant to the Lone Star Rules of Civil Procedure and the Provisions stated on the record or attached hereto.

This is a deposition of SARAH JONES, who having been sworn, testified as follows:

EXAMINATION

QUESTIONS BY DEFENSE COUNSEL:

Q: Good morning, Ms. Jones.

A: Good morning.

Q: Before we get started I want to make sure that you understand that if you do not understand my questions, please feel free to stop me and ask for a clarification. Okay?

A: Sure.

Q Okay. First, please state your full name.

A: My name is Sarah Alice Jones.

Q: Okay. How old are you?

A: I am 20 years old.

Q: What was your relationship with Danny Moss?

A: Danny was my stepfather. He and my mother were married some years ago. My birth father was a bit older than Danny was.

Q: How would you describe your relationship with, as you say, Danny.

A: Well we stayed close. I always thought he was more of dad to me than my real father. And I thought it was my mom's fault that they got divorced. He caught her cheating on him.

Q: Now, you are claiming that Danny's death has resulted in damages amounting to three hundred thousand dollars, right?

A: Yes.

Q: That is a lot of money. How do you account for that much?

A: Well, I lost my part-time job about six months before Danny died. And ever since he and my mom split up, Danny gave me $1500 a month to help me get into college and pay for it.

Since he died, I have had to take out more student loans, which now total nearly $75,000. I have been accepted to several law schools and that tuition is going to cost a total of about $100,000. Danny told me that he would pay for all of my education. And the fact that he was paying for my undergraduate costs, shows that.

Q: He paid for everything?

A: About. My part time job flipping burgers covered some costs for books. But Danny really made it possible for me to go to school. I have lost all of that. And I am going through a lot of pain and suffering after his death.

Q: How is that?

A: I am really angry about what happened and have had to see my minister on a very regular basis to deal with all of the anger and grief that I feel. I still cannot bring myself to forgive Sylvia for what she did to Danny, and me.

Q: Are you currently looking for a job?

A: Yes. But so far, nothing has shown up. Plus I expect to start law school in the next year.

Q: Are you receiving any unemployment checks?

A: No, I have not applied for that. I don't like the government paying me.

Q: Food stamps?

A: Nope, have not applied for that either.

Q: So, how are you living right now?

A: I am living with my mom and her new husband. I do odd jobs around the house and they give me a small allowance each month.

Q: How much is that?

A: It varies. About $200 a month.

Q: As I understand it you have no information about the night that your dad died?

A: I was not there, if that's what you mean. But I have no doubt at all that Sylvia killed him. She is crazy and I have never liked her. In her book, I do not even exist. I cannot recall her ever acknowledging me in public as her step-daughter, or anything.

Q: Didn't you get a payment on Danny's life insurance?

A: No, I did not. I am not sure where you got that. As far as I know it all went to Sylvia.

This is to certify that I have read the transcript of my deposition taken on and that the transcript accurately reflects the questions asked and my answers.

SIGNATURE: *Sarah Jones*

Subscribed and sworn to before me on November 15, [YR-1].

Sally Walker

____

Sally Walker
Certified Shorthand Reporter

Deposition of Morgan Lorson

ORAL DEPOSITION OF MORGAN LORSON, produced as a witness at the instance of the Defendant, SYLVIA MOSS, and duly sworn, was taken in the above-styled and numbered cause on November 4, [YR-1], from 9:00 AM, to 11:45 AM, before Sally Walker, Certified Shorthand Reporter in and for the State of Lone Star, reported by machine shorthand, at the law offices of Plaintiff, pursuant to the Lone Star Rules of Civil Procedure and the Provisions stated on the record or attached hereto.

This is a deposition of MORGAN LORSON, who having been sworn, testified as follows:

EXAMINATION

QUESTIONS BY DEFENSE COUNSEL

Q: Good afternoon, Detective. Would you please state your name for the court reporter?

A: Yes, my name is Morgan Lorson.

Q: You are a detective with the San Milano Police Department?

A: Yes. I am a homicide detective, with about 7 years' experience on the force. My duties entail conducting investigations into possible homicides.

Q: What is your training?

A: I attended the San Milano Police Academy, graduated in the top 25%. During that course we studied crime reconstruction. I later attended a short course in crime reconstruction at the FBI Academy at Quantico, Virginia. The instructors at that academy, which is nationally recognized, included experienced homicide detectives as well as forensic pathologists. Again, I did well, finished in the top 30%.

Q: Okay. Detective, I would like you to tell me about your investigation into the death of Mr. Danny Moss, on December 5, [YR-1].

A: On December 5, [YR-1], at 2:00 AM, EMT was called to the Moss residence. The call was placed by a Sylvia Moss, Mr. Moss's wife. When EMT arrived they found a man lying at the bottom of the stairs, with no signs of life. They did not try to revive him. I arrived at the scene shortly after they got there. He was pronounced dead at the scene by the coroner. We later identified him as Danny Moss, the husband of Sylvia Moss.

Q: Please go on.

A: Well, things did not seem quite right. Mrs. Moss said that her husband had fallen down the stairs but I noticed a small red spot on the victim's neck and she was acting sort of detached so I decided to take some photos of the scene. I also noticed that a shoe was in the hallway at the top of the stairs. While I was taking the pictures she asked if she could be excused to put on some makeup, so …

Q: I am sorry …

A: She asked to put on some makeup and I said sure, whatever. She really seemed not to be with it and I thought that she was just in a state of shock.

Q: Did you say anything to her about being in shock and whether she needed any medical attention?

Q: I did. I asked her how she was doing and that is when she said she looked awful and that she wanted to put on her makeup. I think I told her that I was concerned because she seemed to clearly be in a state of shock and she just said "hmmm," or something like that.

Q: Did she say anything else?

A: When I first got there I asked her if she knew what had happened. That is when she asked if she could put on her makeup first and then she would answer my questions. So, I said yes, she could. That is when I said something about her being in shock. While she was putting on her makeup I took the pictures. About 20 minutes later, after she had put on her makeup, she told me that she had awakened when she heard a noise and that is when she saw her husband at the bottom of the stairs.

Q: Okay. Thank you for clarifying that sequence for us. Where did she put on the makeup?

A: She used the upstairs bathroom. Although there was a downstairs bathroom, she went upstairs, which meant she had to step over the victim to get there.

Q: She stepped over his body to get upstairs?

A: Yes, I was stunned when I saw that. I cannot recall ever being at a scene of a crime where a family member did that. She seemed very nonchalant about it.

Q: I assume that you, at some point, stepped over Mr. Moss's body as well?

A: Yes, but in the process of checking the scene, not to use the upstairs bathroom to comb my hair.

Q: Can you describe her demeanor during your questioning of her?

A: Yes, I can. She seemed emotionally detached but very interested in my investigation.

Q: How is that?

A: Well she asked me several times if what she had said was helpful. She also asked if I was hungry and whether she could make something for me while we waited for the coroner to arrive.

Q: And?

A: I declined. I said I was fine. But it really seemed odd that she would ask that.

Q: Detective, she showed concern for her husband, right?

A: No, not in my opinion. Not genuine concern. I got the impression this was all an act to her. Yes, she did say several times that she could not believe that this had happened to him. She said that he was trying so hard to be a good husband and that she was sorry that they had gone to bed angry with one another. She tried to give me the impression that that seemed to bother her.

Q: Did she say what they had fought about?

A: Well she did not use the word fight but when I asked her she said that they had had a disagreement — that was the word she used — about the evening meal. Apparently she burned the vegetables or something. She said that he never really appreciated her efforts to please him and that had led to the quote, disagreement, unquote. I asked her if he had complained about her cooking before, and she said yes, he had, many times. When she was talking about his latest complaint, her face visibly tightened. I could see her clenching her jaw.

Q: Did Mrs. Moss say anything about her husband using any prescription drugs?

A: Yes, she said that he had been taking Prozac, to calm down and that she was sure that he had taken some earlier in the evening, after dinner. He had a prescription from their family physician.

Q: You mentioned earlier that you saw a shoe at the top of the stairs. Can you tell me more about that?

A: Yes, I asked Mrs. Moss about it and she said that it was her husband's. She said that he must have tripped on it. But the shoe was not on the stairs and was off to one side, which signaled to me that he did not trip on it. It was also odd because the other shoe was in the closet, off the hallway, next to the master bedroom. She could not account for the fact that one of her husband's shoes was in the closet and the other was in the hallway, near the top of the stairs. If there were other shoes or clothes strewn about it would have seemed reasonable to have a shoe in the hallway. But it appeared that everything else was in order. They were neat housekeepers. That is why it caught my eye. The crime lab ran a DNA swipe on the shoe and it showed positive for both the victim's and Mrs. Moss's DNA.

Q: During your contact with Ms. Moss on the evening in question, did she ever show any signs of emotion?

A: Do you mean, did she cry?

Q: Yes.

A: No, she did not cry while I was with her. I didn't see her cry.

Q: Any signs of empathy for her husband?

A: Not really.

Q: Do you recognize these exhibits? [Shows to Lorson]

A: Yes, I do.

Q: Would you please tell us what they are?

A: These are the pictures I took on December 5th at the Moss residence. These two show Mr. Moss at the bottom of the stairs. I took this one from the top of the stairs and this one from the living room, at the bottom of the stairs. The third photo was taken from the doorway of what I would call the master bedroom looking down the hall, with the closet on the left side. The door on the right is the bathroom door. A few steps beyond that door is the stairway. The victim's shoe is on the floor at the end of the hallway, right outside the other bedroom. And this is a close up picture of the victim's shoe. As I said, the other shoe was in the closet, on the floor, with his other shoes, to the immediate left of the master bedroom door — right across from the bathroom door.

Q: Thank you. Did you have an opportunity to speak to Ms. Moss again?

A: Yes, after thinking about the case I decided I really needed to get a written statement from her and ask her a few more questions. I had a nagging gut feeling that something was not quite right. So I called her a couple of days later and she came in and gave a statement.

Q: Is this her statement? [Shows to Lorson]

A: Yes. That's it. She was very cooperative and wanted to talk. But at times it was hard to get her to talk about what happened on the night of her husband's death.

Q: After she gave her written statement, did you gather any more information about Ms. Moss?

A: Yes, I did. Very interesting. I learned that when she was a teenager she and her younger brother had attended a youth camp in Missouri for one week. But during that week the brother drowned in the camp swimming pool late one night. He could not swim and although she was with him at the time, she did not jump into the water to try and save him. The local police did an investigation and concluded that they did not have enough evidence to take it to trial. I talked to someone in the police department who told me that the police officer who handled the investigation into the drowning had since died, but that they would look for the incident report. They found the report and I believe the DA from Missouri sent a copy to you. I have also reviewed that report as part of this investigation. My sense is that Ms. Moss acted with the same sort of detached interest at the crime scene and that she really never explained why she had not jumped in to save him. The investigator tried to follow up on some of those points, but she lawyered up and he did not get his answers. It appears that the case never went anywhere. Looks like the coroner ruled that it was an accident.

Q: Is this the police report from Missouri that you are referring to? [Shows to Lorson]

A: Yes, that is it.

Q: Thank you. Anything else?

A: Yes, two years ago there was an incident at Wilson Electronics, where she still works. After I took Ms. Moss's statement, I went over to Wilson and I personally interviewed her co-workers and supervisor. They said that she saw a memo in which one of her co-workers had criticized a report that she had prepared and she, that is Ms. Moss, went, in their words, "ballistic" and screaming at no one in particular. Just an hour later, she confronted the co-worker in the company's cafeteria and started screaming and shouting that the co-worker was quote stupid unquote and did not know a good report from a bad report. She apparently got right into her face, which in turn prompted the co-worker to hit Ms. Moss several times with her fist. That got the co-worker fired for hitting Ms. Moss. Apparently, the company had a zero tolerance policy for physical violence. But Ms. Moss was only reprimanded by the company and was able to keep her job. Her reputation at the company is that she has a very short fuse if anyone questions her. But the management likes her work and keeps her on the payroll. I also got a copy of the company's letter of reprimand that was placed in her file at the time.

Q: Do you recognize this exhibit? [Shows to Lorson]

A: Yes, this is the letter of reprimand from Wilson Electronics.

Q: And do you recognize this exhibit? [Shows to Lorson]

A: Yes I do. This is the official autopsy report on Mr. Moss.

Q: I am sorry, one more. Do you recognize this exhibit? [Shows to Lorson]

A: Yes, this is a newspaper clipping about her brother's drowning at the camp in Missouri.

Q: Let me go back to the night of December 5th. How long were you at the Moss's residence?

A: I got there at about 2:30 and stayed until about 4:00 a.m. I waited until the coroner had finished and they had removed the body, and then I went to the station.

Q: What happened to Ms. Moss?

A: Before I left, I asked her if she needed to be taken anywhere or needed anything and she said no, that she would be just fine. She said that she was going to make something to eat and then go and stay with friends and make plans for her husband's funeral.

Q: As a result of your investigation have you reached any conclusions about what happened?

A: Yes, in my professional opinion, she pushed him down the stairs or did something to make him fall. I think that she is just that kind of person to do that.

Q: What leads you to that conclusion?

A: First, they had had a fight. Second, there is that bruise on his neck that she cannot explain. Third, she showed no emotion during the entire time I was at their home and no emotion during my interview with her when she came to my office. She seemed very cold and detached and more interested in herself and what I thought of her and how she looked.

Q: Do you have any forensic evidence that would directly link Ms. Moss with the death of her husband?

A: Well, we don't have any fingerprints. There was DNA, from Mrs. Moss on her husband's shoe, if that is what you mean. There was some blood on the carpet from Mr. Moss's head wound, which was fatal. But we did not find any hair fibers or blood on the stair railing. I am trained to examine the scene of the crime, which is part of crime scene reconstruction. As part of that process, I attempt to match up wounds and injuries to possible causes for those injuries, at the scene of the crime. When I examined the bruise, it seemed to match the edge of the shoe and the shape of the injury, in my opinion, is more consistent with the hypothesis that he was struck from behind with that shoe before tumbling down the stairs, and striking his head on the end of the stair railing.

Q: You asked her if she had killed her husband?

A: Yes, I did, at the station. She paused, took a deep breath, and then said very slowly that she would never do anything to harm him. It was not a clear "yes" or "no" answer to my question. I got the feeling that she was offended that I even asked the question.

Q: So, after you conducted your investigation, you concluded that my client was responsible for the death of Mr. Moss. Right?

A: Yes, I did. It was very clear to me that she killed him.

Q: But the District Attorney's office did not agree with you?

A: That is also true.

Q: And that was because after they reviewed the file, they did not believe that there was any evidence showing that my client had anything to do with Mr. Moss's death, right?

A: No, I would not say that. They just saw the evidence in a way I did not see. I think they got it wrong.

Q: Okay. Thank you, Detective. That is all I have at this time.

A: Okay.

This is to certify that I have read the transcript of my deposition taken on and that the transcript accurately reflects the questions asked and my answers.

SIGNATURE: *Morgan Lorson*

Subscribed and sworn to before me on December 15, [YR-1].

Sally Walker

Sally Walker
Certified Shorthand Reporter

DEPOSITION OF DR. PAT BENTLEY

ORAL DEPOSITION OF DR. PAT BENTLEY, produced as a witness at the instance of the Defendant, SYLVIA MOSS, and duly sworn, was taken in the above-styled and numbered cause on November 4, [YR-1], from 1:00 PM, to 3:00 PM, before Sally Walker, Certified Shorthand Reporter in and for the State of Lone Star, reported by machine shorthand, at the law offices of Plaintiff, pursuant to the Lone Star Rules of Civil Procedure and the Provisions stated on the record or attached hereto.

This is a deposition of DR. PAT BENTLEY, who having been sworn, testified as follows:

EXAMINATION

QUESTIONS BY DEFENSE COUNSEL:

Q: Dr. Bentley, good afternoon.

A: Hello.

Q: As you know from our phone conversation, I am representing Ms. Sarah Jones, who has sued Mrs. Sylvia Moss, my client, for the wrongful death of her step father.

A: Yes, I understand.

Q: Have you given a deposition before?

A: Yes, I have.

Q: Good, so you know that if you do not understand any of my questions that I want you to stop me so that we can clarify that. Okay?

A: Of course.

Q: Would you please state your name for the court reporter?

A: My name is Pat Bentley.

Q: You are a psychiatrist?

A: Yes, I am.

Q: Could you give me some of your background information and qualifications?

A: Sure. I attended the University of Minnesota and graduated with honors in 1990, with a Bachelor of Science. I attended medical school at Johns Hopkins University, specializing in psychiatry. I graduated in [YR-18], with an MD.

Q: Where did you intern?

A: I interned for about one year at the Central Lone Star Medical Center, in Austin.

Q: Do you have a specialty?

A: Yes, I specialize in psychiatry. I spent three years in residency at the Audy Murphy Veteran's Hospital here in San Milano. I am a diplomate with the American Board of Psychiatry, having passed the written and oral exams. I am now on the faculty of the Baylor University School of Medicine. I continue to practice part-time with three other psychiatrists in our own medical center. I brought a copy of my resume, if that would help. (Witness hands resume to counsel)

Q: Yes, thank you. Have you testified before in a court?

A: Yes, but not often. I have testified in five or six criminal cases, for both prosecution and defense, and in about four civil cases. Mostly in the Dallas area.

Q: Okay. Are you being paid for your help on this case?

A: No, I am not. Well, I should add, that I have been told that I will be reimbursed for my reasonable travel expenses.

Q: Okay. Do you know Sylvia Moss?

A: Yes.

Q: How you know Ms. Moss?

A: I interviewed her and reviewed her medical history this past month, pursuant to a request from your office.

Q: What did you learn during that examination?

A: I conducted a three-hour interview with Ms. Moss. We talked about her background, her relationships, what if any medications she had taken, or was taking, and how she felt about her husband's recent death. I did not have access to any of her past medical records and counted primarily on what she told me.

Q: Did you reach any conclusions about whether Ms. Moss suffers from any mental disease or syndrome?

A: Yes, she is a classic example of what we refer to as Narcissistic Personality Disorder. It is listed in the Diagnostic and Statistical Manual, the most recent edition, DSM-5. We doctors simply refer to it as the "DSM" for short. Every doctor is familiar with that text. The disorder is well-known and in my opinion helps explain her actions and relationships.

Q: In layman terms, what does that mean?

A: Well, in short, she is what I guess you might recognize as being very self-centered and has a strong need to be recognized and valued for what she considers her extraordinary accomplishments. People with this syndrome tend to view others as beneath them. They often show a lack of empathy and if you do not give them adequate attention, it can result in withdrawal or even rage and anger. Frankly, we all have some tendency to focus on ourselves, but that is not what we are talking about in this case. When it goes too far, it falls within the medical disorder described in the Diagnostic and Statistical Manual.

Q: How did you come to the conclusion that she has the narcissistic personality disorder?

A: The DSM sets out a list of what we refer to as diagnostic criteria. In this case, the DSM lists nine different criteria. Those have been developed over the years by detailed study and diagnosis. They are not fool-proof but they are very dependable. According to the DSM, permit me to read it: "A pervasive pattern of grandiosity (in fantasy or behavior), need for admiration, and lack of empathy, beginning by early adulthood and present in a variety of contexts, as indicated by five (or more) of the following." And then the DSM lists the nine criteria. I applied that list and found that she satisfied at least five of the criteria — she is often haughty and arrogant, she has what we refer to as a grandiose sense of self-importance, she believes that she is very special and unique and can only be understood by others who have high status, she has a sense of entitlement, she requires excessive admiration, and she lacks empathy.

Q: So, I count six of the criteria.

A: Yes, that is correct.

Q: Were there any others?

A: I could make the case that there were, but the six I listed are very clearly present in Ms. Moss.

Q: What specifically did you consider in applying those criteria?

A: First, I read her statement to the police, I read the incident report from when her younger brother drowned in Missouri, and the discipline report, or reprimand, I guess you call it that, from the company where she works. I took all of those into consideration in making my diagnosis.

Q: Okay. Was that Wilson Electronics where she worked?

A: Yes, I am sorry, that's it.

Q: And you considered your interview with her?

A: Definitely. That carried great weight.

Q: Did she cooperate with you?

A: Yes, absolutely. You see the way the disorder can be manifested is by being arrogant or believing you are better than anyone else. I believe that because I was an MD, she felt that we were equals and that she could impress me with all that she had accomplished. She continued to point out during the interview how she had been so underappreciated for years, by friends, families, and even lovers.

Q: Did you talk at all about her relationship with her husband?

A: Yes, the bottom line was that he did not fully appreciate her and that had led to what she called a number of disagreements. It was clear to me that she has an anger management problem and that it was aggravated by having the syndrome. She described that on the night her husband died, they had had what she called a major disagreement over her cooking. They ended up shouting at each other for over an hour just before they went to bed. She said that to calm down, her husband had taken Prozac before going to sleep, at about 11 p.m.

Q: Would that sort of response, that is, having a major argument or blowup, be consistent with the disorder?

A: Absolutely. The DSM notes that people with this disorder are very sensitive to what the DSM refers to as "injury" from someone's criticism. If you criticize them, they can act with a range of emotions, including anger and rage.

Q: So, if I understand what you are saying, if Mr. Moss criticized her for her cooking, that could account for the anger she felt toward him on the night he died?

A: Yes, but please understand. None of us really likes criticism, whether it's about our cooking, what we are wearing, or about how we do our jobs. People who have this disorder tend to overreact to even the slightest criticism. They need for the camera to be focused on them, all the time, even when the circumstances indicate that the camera should be on someone or something else. I wrote about this in an article in [YR-9].

Q: Did you consider the possibility that there might be any other medical or mental reasons for her actions and attitudes? For example, could her taking drugs explain her behaviors?

A: Yes, I did consider other possible causes. That is what I am required to do as a doctor. First, there was no record that she had ever taken any legal or illegal drugs that would explain her behavior. In fact one of the things she told me in the interview, and she was very proud of this, she said she had never even tried drugs like cocaine, or marijuana. That, she said, was beneath her. I did consider the possibility that she might have what is referred to in the DSM as the Intermittent Explosive Disorder. That is where the patient is unable to control themselves and they act with aggression that results in serious injuries or destruction. Here, even if she has that disorder, the narcissistic personality disorder is more consistent with her words and actions.

Q: Any other possible explanations?

A: I also considered another disorder, or problem. That is what is referred to as the relationship distress with spouse or intimate partner. She clearly had relational problems with her husband. It's also described in the DSM. I felt that, again, even assuming she had a relational problem with her husband, the narcissistic disorder was the key contributing factor. The same would be true for what we often refer to as sibling rivalry problems. In some ways these all tie together in that a person who exhibits severe narcissistic tendencies is bound to have relational problems.

Q: If you learned that right after the EMT and police arrived at the Moss residence, Mrs. Moss wanted to put on her makeup before answering questions about her husband's death, does that fit with this disorder?

A: Yes. Her husband is lying on the steps and instead of showing empathy for his condition, and what happened, she is more concerned about herself.

Q: Okay. If someone had this disorder, could it result in physically attacking the person who was criticizing them?

A: Yes. Clearly.

Q: So, if the evidence showed that Mr. Moss, Sylvia's husband had a bruise on the back of his neck, when he was found dead in his home, is it reasonable to conclude that Sylvia hit him at some point before he died?

A: I would say that that is entirely reasonable. Ms. Moss is a very sick woman, she needs professional medical and mental attention.

Q: So, in your opinion, can this disorder be treated?

A: Absolutely. At least we can try to help her.

Q: Okay, one last question. She did not ever say to you that she had pushed Danny Moss down the stairs?

A: No. She never said that.

Q: Okay. Thank you, Doctor. That is all of the questions I have for you right now.

This is to certify that I have read the transcript of my deposition taken on and that the transcript accurately reflects the questions asked and my answers.

SIGNATURE: *Pat Bentley*

Subscribed and sworn to before me on December 17, [YR-1].

Sally Walker

Sally Walker
Certified Shorthand Reporter

Curriculum Vitae for Dr. Pat Bentley

Pat Bentley, M.D.

3900 Travis Avenue, Suite 802, Dallas, Sate of Lone Star
214-692-8200—office
headsrus@pmc.com

EDUCATION AND TRAINING

Undergraduate

B.S. [YR-23]	University of Minnesota, B.S., Minneapolis, Minnesota Research fellowship in psychiatry

Medical School

M.D. [YR-18]	John Hopkins University School of Medicine, Baltimore, Maryland National Board of Medical Examiners, honor grade in psychiatry

POSTDOCTORAL

Medical Internship

[YR-18]-[YR-17]	Central Lone Star Medical Center, Austin, State of Lone Star

Residency

[YR-17]-[YR-14]	Resident in Psychiatry, Audy Murphy Veteran's Hospital San Milano, State of Lone Star

Fellowship

[YR-14]-[YR-13]	Memorial Mental Medical Center Dallas, State of Lone Star

PROFESSIONAL EXPERIENCE

Private Practice of Psychiatry, Dallas, State of Lone Star
[YR-13]-present (part time since [YR-12]

Academic Appointments

[YR-12]-[YR-10]	Assistant Professor of Psychiatry, Baylor University School of Medicine, Dallas, State of Lone Star
[YR-10]-Present	Professor of Psychiatry, Baylor University School of Medicine, Dallas, State of Lone Star

Board Certifications and Memberships

American Board of Psychiatry and Neurology
American Psychiatric Association, Washington, DC
Association for Humanistic Psychology

American Academy of Psychotherapists
State of Lone Star Medical License No. J4356
Maryland State Medical License No. K9032

RESEARCH ACTIVITIES

Peer-reviewed scientific articles

Bentley, P. *Assessing the Narcissistic Personality Disorder.* The American Journal on Psychology [YR-7]; 73:1006.

Report of Dr. Avery Wilson

Psychiatrics Associates, Inc.
12456 Main Ave.
Dallas, State of Lone Star 86677
(555) 564-9900
(555) 564-9009 (Hotline)

Your Mind is Our Business

REPORT of AVERY WILSON, M.D.
May 27, [YR-1]

I have prepared this report at the request of the defense counsel for Mrs. Sylvia Moss, of San Milano, State of Lone Star.

I am a licensed psychiatrist. My curriculum vitae is attached. I am currently practicing in Dallas, at a clinic with three other doctors specializing in mental disorders and syndromes.

Over the course of two weeks in May, I interviewed Mrs. Sylvia Moss to determine if she has suffered, or is currently suffering from, any significant mental diseases, syndromes, or disorders. During those two weeks I interviewed her three times for a total of 10 hours and 30 minutes. I also read carefully (1) the statement she gave to the police shortly after her husband's death, (2) the police report that was prepared when her younger brother drowned in Missouri some years ago, and (3) the incident report involving a co-worker at Wilson Electronics in San Milano, Lone Star. I also spoke on the phone with the detective who was present at the Moss residence at the time of Mr. Moss's accidental death.

Based on my assessments I did not feel it necessary to have her subjected to a physical examination to determine if any of her problems were caused by an undiagnosed medical condition or the result of any medications that she might have taken, or is currently taking.

Mrs. Moss is a very personable individual who appears to be in very good medical condition. I found no evidence of any drug or alcohol abuse. She is extremely charming and engaging and demonstrates great curiosity about the sciences. She also exhibits a high level of ambition and sees herself as a transformative figure that has great potential. She is very focused and careful about how she presents herself to others.

While she tends to show limited empathy in certain circumstances, she does display emotions at the appropriate time. For example, in discussing the death of her younger brother, she explained that they had been rivals for the attention of their parents, who are both now deceased. She regretted deeply that they had not gotten along and that she missed him terribly. During this conversation, we had to take a break so that she could compose herself. She stated that the great irony was that although the rivalry had existed, the reason for the rivalry, her parents, was no longer present. She no longer remembers the exact details of their argument or what happened. She does recall that it ended up with her chasing him around the pool before he fell into the deep end.

It is clear that she has some relational problems. She said that before she married her husband, she had dated three other men over the course of two years. All of those relationships failed, she said, because they took advantage of her. In one instance, the man used her to get a job with Wilson Electronics and promptly ended their relationship when he got the job. The second man had a drinking problem, and the third man was still in her words, a "momma's boy" who did not really appreciate or respect her. She reflected some distain for those individuals and expressed empathy for their future partners. Her husband, Danny she said, was the love of her life and they initially were very happy. They were, in her words, soul mates.

The marriage ran into difficulties, however, when he started criticizing her cooking. In response, she took a cooking course and for a while that seemed to appease him. On the night he died, she explained that she probably overreacted to his criticism of how she had fixed his potatoes. That had led to a major argument, she said. Those were the last words that they had shared before he died. She deeply regretted that and still misses him.

Using the criteria listed in the Diagnostic and Statistical Manual V (DSM-V), I have concluded that she does not suffer from a Narcissistic Personality Disorder. Most of the criteria listed for that disorder can be explained through other means. She does tend to believe that she can accomplish much in life but those are not fantasies. She indeed has the means and intelligence to accomplish her goals. I did not find her to be arrogant or haughty. Nor does she view herself as special. She does not display a sense of entitlement. Nor is she "interpersonally exploitive." I found that she displays an appropriate level of empathy. I did not find that she requires excessive attention.

I found that while she has some narcissistic characteristics (e.g., asking to put on makeup while the EMT personnel were attending to her husband), they did not arise to the level of the disorder identified in the DSM. She does exhibit problems with partner-type relationships, i.e., she tends to work better alone. Counseling would be very helpful to help her address those issues.

In my professional opinion, she is not a violent person. While she does have some anger management issues, it's clear from her behavior and past history that she is able to manage her anger for the most part. When rejected or criticized, she tends to use her verbal skills to counterattack the person who has rejected or criticized her.

I recommended to Ms. Moss that she seriously consider seeking professional counseling. She declined, at least for now.

Respectfully submitted,

Avery Wilson,

Avery Wilson, M.D.

Encl.

CURRICULUM VITAE OF DR. AVERY WILSON

AVERY WILSON, M.D.

Psychiatrics Associates, Inc.
12456 Main Ave.
Dallas, State of Lone Star 6677
Mobile: (555) 564-9900
Hotline: (555) 564-9009

Objective

- To diagnose and provide expert analysis for all patients suffering from mental diseases, syndromes and disorders.

Abilities

- I have provided expert psychiatric reports in over 50 criminal trials (primarily for the defense).

Education

- Columbia University, A.B., [YR-20].
- Harvard University Graduate School of Arts and Sciences, A.M. Clinical Psychology, [YR-17].
- Cornell University Medical College, M.D., [YR-13].
- Residency in Psychiatry, Massachusetts Mental Health Center, 2000-2003.

Professional Experience

- Psychiatrist, Massachusetts Mental Health Center, Boston, MA, [YR-10]-[YR-8] Psychiatrist, University Hospital, San Milano, LS, [YR-8]-[YR-7.
- Senior Attending Psychiatrist, Shady Acres Mental Health System, Dallas, LS, [YR-7]-[YR-5].
- Psychiatrist, Psychiatrics Associates, Inc., Dallas, LS, [YR-7]-Present.

Board Certification

- American Board of Psychiatry and Neurology, [YR-13]-Present.
- American Psychiatric Association, [YR-8]-Present
- Massachusetts State Medical License No. L4081
- Lone Star State Medical License No. V8267

Research Activities

Peer-Reviewed Article

- Wilson, A. *Testifying at Trial: Analyzing and Diagnosing Behavioral, Cognitive, and Perceptual Disorders*, THE AMERICAN JOURNAL ON PSYCHOLOGY 44:19-42, [YR-7]

Speech

- Wilson, A. "A Method for Diagnosing Relational and Personality Disorders," State of Lone Star Annual Health Conference, [YR-5]

Intermittent Explosive Disorder

Diagnostic Criteria

312.34 (F63.81)

A. Recurrent behavioral outbursts representing a failure to control aggressive impulses as manifested by either of the following:

   1 Verbal aggression (e.g., temper tantrums, tirades, verbal arguments, or fights) or physical aggression toward property, animals, or other individuals, occurring twice weekly, on average, for a period of 3 months. The physical aggression does not result in damage or destruction of property and does not result in physical injury to animals or other individuals.

   2 Three behavioral outbursts involving damage or destruction of property and/or physical assault involving physical injury against animals or other individuals occurring within a 12-month period.

B. The magnitude of aggressiveness expressed during the recurrent outbursts is grossly out of proportion to the provocation or to any precipitating psychosocial stressors.

C. The recurrent aggressive outbursts are not premeditated (i.e., they are impulsive and/or anger-based) and are not committed to achieve some tangible objective (e.g., money, power, intimidation).

D. The recurrent aggressive outbursts cause either marked distress in the individual or impairment in occupational or interpersonal functioning, or are associated with financial or legal consequences.

E. Chronological age is at least 6 years (or equivalent developmental level).

F. The recurrent aggressive outbursts are not better explained by another mental disorder (e.g., major depressive disorder, bipolar disorder, disruptive mood dysregulation disorder, a psychotic disorder, antisocial personality disorder, borderline personality disorder) and are not attributable to another medical condition (e.g., head trauma, Alzheimer's disease) or to the physiological effects of a substance (e.g., a drug of abuse, a medication). For children ages 6-18 years, aggressive behavior that occurs as part of an adjustment disorder should not be considered for this diagnosis.

Note: This diagnosis can be made in addition to the diagnosis of attention-deficit/hyperactivity disorder, conduct disorder, oppositional defiant disorder, or autism spectrum disorder when recurrent impulsive aggressive outbursts are in excess of those usually seen in these disorders and warrant independent clinical attention.

Diagnostic Features

The impulsive (or anger-based) aggressive outbursts in intermittent explosive disorder have a rapid onset and, typically, little or no prodromal period. Outbursts typically last for less than 30 minutes and commonly occur in response to a minor provocation by a close intimate or associate. Individuals with intermittent explosive disorder often have less severe episodes of verbal and/or nondamaging, nondestructive, or noninjurious physical assault (Criterion A1) in between more severe destructive/assaultive episodes (Criterion A2). Criterion Al defines frequent (i.e., twice weekly, on average, for a period of 3 months) aggressive outbursts characterized by temper tantrums, tirades, verbal arguments or fights, or assault without damage to objects or without injury to animals or other individuals. Criterion A2 defines infrequent (i.e., three in a 1-year period) impulsive aggressive outbursts characterized by damaging or destroying an object, regardless of its tangible value, or by assaulting/striking or otherwise causing physical injury to an animal or to another individual. Regardless of the nature of the impulsive aggressive outburst, the core feature of intermittent explosive disorder is failure to control impulsive aggressive behavior in response to subjectively experienced provocation (i.e., psychosocial stressor) that would not typically result in an aggressive outburst (Criterion B). The aggressive outbursts are generally impulsive and/or anger-based, rather than premeditated or instrumental (Criterion C) and are associated with significant distress or impairment in psychosocial function (Criterion D). A diagnosis of intermittent explosive disorder should not be given to individuals younger than 6 years, or the equivalent developmental level (Criterion E), or to individuals whose aggressive outbursts are better explained by another mental disorder (Criterion F). A diagnosis of intermittent explosive disorder should not be given to individuals with disruptive mood dysregulation disorder or to individuals whose impulsive aggressive outbursts are attributable to another medical condition or to the physiological effects of a substance (Criterion F). In addition, children ages 6-18 years should not receive this diagnosis when impulsive aggressive outbursts occur in the context of an adjustment disorder (Criterion F).

Associated Features Supporting Diagnosis

Mood disorders (unipolar), anxiety disorders, and substance use disorders are associated with intermittent explosive disorder, although onset of these disorders is typically later than that of intermittent explosive disorder.

Prevalence

One-year prevalence data for intermittent explosive disorder in the United States is about 2.7% (narrow definition). Intermittent explosive disorder is more prevalent among younger individuals (e.g., younger than 35-40 years), compared with older individuals (older than 50 years), and in individuals with a high school education or less.

* * * * *

Narcissistic Personality Disorder

Diagnostic Criteria

301.81 (F60.81)

A pervasive pattern of grandiosity (in fantasy or behavior), need for admiration, and lack of empathy, beginning by early adulthood and present in a variety of contexts, as indicated by five (or more) of the following:

1. Has a grandiose sense of self-importance (e.g., exaggerates achievements and talents, expects to be recognized as superior without commensurate achievements).
2. Is preoccupied with fantasies of unlimited success, power, brilliance, beauty, or ideal love.
3. Believes that he or she is "special" and unique and can only be understood by, or should associate with, other special or high-status people (or institutions).
4. Requires excessive admiration.
5. Has a sense of entitlement (i.e., unreasonable expectations of especially favorable treatment of automatic compliance with his or her expectations).
6. Is interpersonally exploitative (i.e., takes advantage of others to achieve his or her own ends).
7. Lacks empathy: is unwilling to recognize or identify with the feelings and needs of others.
8. Is often envious of others or believes that others are envious of him or her.
9. Shows arrogant, haughty behaviors or attitudes.

Diagnostic Features

The essential feature of narcissistic personality disorder is a pervasive pattern of grandiosity, need for admiration, and lack of empathy that begins by early adulthood and is present in a variety of contexts.

Individuals with this disorder have a grandiose sense of self-importance (Criterion 1). They routinely overestimate their abilities and inflate their accomplishments, often appearing boastful and pretentious. They may blithely assume that others attribute the same value to their efforts and may be surprised when the praise they expect and feel they deserve is not forthcoming. Often implicit in the inflated judgments of their own accomplishments is an underestimation (devaluation) of the contributions of others. Individuals with narcissistic personality disorder are often preoccupied with fantasies of unlimited success, power, brilliance, beauty, or ideal love (Criterion 2). They may ruminate about "long overdue" admiration and privilege and compare themselves favorably with famous or privileged people.

Individuals with narcissistic personality disorder believe that they are superior, special, or unique and expect others to recognize them as such (Criterion 3). They may feel that they can only be understood by, and should only associate with, other people who are special or of high status and may attribute "unique," "perfect," or "gifted" qualities to those with whom they associate. Individuals with this disorder believe that their needs are special and beyond the ken of ordinary people. Their own self-esteem is enhanced (i.e., "mirrored") by the idealized value that they assign to those with whom they associate. They are likely to insist on having only the "top" person (doctor, lawyer, hairdresser, instructor) or being affiliated with the "best" institutions but may devalue the credentials of those who disappoint them.

Individuals with this disorder generally require excessive admiration (Criterion4). Their self-esteem is almost invariably very fragile. They may be preoccupied with how well they are doing and how favorably they are regarded by others. This often takes the form of a need for constant attention and admiration. They may expect their arrival to be greeted with great fanfare and are astonished if others do not covet their possessions. They may constantly fish for compliments, often with great charm. A sense of entitlement is evident in these individuals' unreasonable expectation of especially favorable treatment (Criterion 5). They expect to be catered to and are puzzled or furious when this does not happen. For example, they may assume that they do not have to wait in line and that their priorities are so important that others should defer to them, and then get irritated when others fail to assist "in their very important work" This sense of entitlement, combined with a lack of sensitivity to the wants and needs of others, may result in the conscious or unwitting exploitation of others (Criterion 6). They expect to be given whatever they want or feel they need, no matter what it might mean to others. For example, these individuals may expect great dedication from others and may overwork them without regard for the impact on their lives. They tend to form friendships or romantic relationships only if the other person seems likely to advance their purposes or otherwise enhance their self-esteem. They often usurp special privileges and extra resources that they believe they deserve because they are so special.

Individuals with narcissistic personality disorder generally have a lack of empathy and have difficulty recognizing the desires, subjective experiences, and feelings of others (Criterion 7). They may assume that others are totally concerned about their welfare. They tend to discuss their own concerns in inappropriate and lengthy detail, while failing to recognize that others also have feelings and needs. They are often contemptuous and impatient with others who talk about their own problems and concerns. These individuals may be oblivious to the hurt their remarks may inflict (e.g., exuberantly telling a former lover that "I am now in the relationship of a lifetime!" boasting of health in front of someone who is sick). When recognized, the needs, desires, or feelings of others are likely to be viewed disparagingly as signs of weakness or vulnerability. Those who relate to individuals with narcissistic personality disorder typically find an emotional coldness and lack of reciprocal interest.

These individuals are often envious of others or believe that others are envious of them (Criterion 8). They may begrudge others their successes or possessions, feeling that they better deserve those achievements, admiration, or privileges. They may harshly devalue the contributions of others, particularly when those individuals have received acknowledgment or praise for their accomplishments. Arrogant, haughty behaviors characterize these individuals; they often display snobbish, disdainful, or patronizing attitudes (Criterion 9). For example, an individual with this disorder may complain about a clumsy waiter's "rudeness" or "stupidity" or conclude a medical evaluation with a condescending evaluation of the physician.

* * * * *

Other Problems Related to Primary Support Group

V61.10 (Z63.0) Relationship Distress With Spouse or Intimate Partner

This category should be used when the major focus of the clinical contact is to address the quality of the intimate (spouse or partner) relationship or when the quality of that relationship is affecting the course, prognosis, or treatment of a mental or other medical disorder. Partners can be of the same or different genders. Typically, the relationship distress is associated with impaired functioning in behavioral, cognitive, or affective domains. Examples of behavioral problems include conflict resolution difficulty, withdrawal, and overinvolvement. Cognitive problems can manifest as chronic negative attributions of the other's intentions or dismissals of the partner's positive behaviors. Affective problems would include chronic sadness, apathy, and/or anger about the other partner.

OFFICE OF THE DISTRICT ATTORNEY

WALTERS COUNTY, MISSOURI
2445 Mason Lane
Musquire, Missouri 89444

***

–Strength Through Justice–

Mr. Dallas Mosby
Office of the District Attorney
Bear County
San Milano, State of Lone Star

Re: Sylvia Moss

Mr. Mosby:

Attached is the incident report that was prepared in [YR-14] on the drowning death of Mr. Wilson Moss at a local camp. I am also attaching a copy of a newspaper account that was located in the same file. Unfortunately, the detective who worked the case, Police Detective David Knotts, died of cancer in [YR-3]. The District Attorney at the time is no longer with this office and moved to another state. We have not been successful in contacting him about the file.

Aside from the report and the clipping, there is no other information in the files relating to this case. As noted on the report, no action was taken on the case. And there is no other reference in any of our records relating to Ms. Moss.

This report was prepared and maintained in the regular course of the business of the Musquire Police Department, in accordance with the regulations of that department. The report was found in the incident files for the period, June 1, [YR-14] to September 1, [YR-14]. For what it is worth, Detective Knotts told his other officers that he was sure that Ms. Moss had pushed her brother into the pool.

If I can assist you in any other way, please feel free to contact me.

Sincerely,

Sarah Moores

SARAH T. MOORES
ASSISTANT DISTRICT ATTORNEY
WALTERS COUNTY, MISSOURI

City of Musquire
Police Department
123 Main Ave
Musquire, Missouri 89444
(555) 654-0098

Incident Report

Case Number: *99-345*
Filed Opened: *June 20, [YR-14]*
Time: *1000 hours*
Investigating Officer: *David Knotts, Detective*
Badge Number of Investigating Officer: *456*
Name of Suspect/Person of Interest: *Sylvia Moss*

On June 20, [YR-14], I was called to Camp Munkeewonk at approximately 2:00 a.m. to investigate a drowning of a young man in the camp's swimming pool. The dispatcher related that a 911 call had been placed at 1:52 a.m. from a man identifying himself as the camp manager, Jason Watts.

The young man was identified by camp personnel and by his sister, as Wilson Moss, Jr., a 12-year old male. He had fallen into the deep end of the pool. Suspected cause of death was drowning. I examined his body and did not see any bruises or other unusual marks. Members of the camp staff reported that at about 1:30 a.m. they were awakened by loud screaming and shouting coming from the direction of the pool, followed a few minutes later by complete silence. When they ran toward the pool they were met on the trail by the victim's sister, Sylvia Moss, who was walking toward them and reported that her brother had fallen into the pool and that he could not swim. She told the staff that they had had an argument about their parents and that he had fallen in, when she was chasing him around the pool. The staff did not ask her why she had not jumped in to help him. The staff attempted CPR but could not revive him.

I interviewed Sylvia Moss at the camp for about 15 minutes and she confirmed that she and her brother had been arguing and that when she started to chase him around the pool that he slipped and fell in. She acknowledged that they had been shouting. She said that she knew immediately that he had drowned and ran for help. I asked her how she knew that and she simply said that she was smart and could plainly see that he was dead. She said that they had been arguing about how much time each of them would be spending individually with their parents when they would be visiting the camp the next weekend. I asked her several times why she had not jumped in to save him and she seemed very detached, almost cold, and said that she kept repeating that she did not know why she had not jumped in. She admitted that she knew how to swim.

During the whole time I talked to her, she did not cry or show any other emotion. She seemed concerned about how she would look and what she would say if a newspaper wanted to talk to her. I terminated my questioning at about 3:15 am.

This morning, I was supposed to meet again with Ms Moss to clear up some points. But when she came to the station, she was accompanied by her family lawyer who informed me that she would not be answering any questions about the incident and that she was invoking her right to remain silent.

Recommended Disposition: *No action. Coroner has ruled that death was accidental. J Knotts 6/30/99*

Signature of Investigating Officer: *Jonathan A Knotts*

Note for File: I know this file is officially closed but there needs to be some follow up on this case. Something tells me that Sylvia Moss has not been entirely truthful about what happened. DA says we don't have enough to convict. But I see real problems in this young woman. JK, 8-1-[YR-14]

June 21, [YR-14] Musquire Daily News 2A

Boy Drowns at Local Camp

Foul Play Suspected

By Justin Knotts

Wilson Moss, a youth from California, attending Camp Munkeewonk, drowned early yesterday morning in the camp's swimming pool. Local police are calling the death a possible homicide.

Moss, and his sister, Sylvia, were arguing by the camp's swimming pool after midnight. Camp staff members heard the fighting and ran toward the pool. They encountered Ms. Moss, who told them that she thought her brother had fallen into the pool as they were chasing each other around the pool decking. The staff found the young Mr. Moss in the deep end of the pool and tried unsuccessfully to revive him. He was later pronounced dead at the scene.

Attempts to contact members of the family were rebuffed by the family's attorney, Sam Nordstop, of Chicago, a member of a criminal defense law firm. A family spokesman simply said that the family needed time to make arrangements for Mr. Moss's funeral. An autopsy is pending.

Mr. Jason Watts, camp director said, "We are all deeply upset about this. In the thirty years that Camp Munkeewonk has been in existence, this is the first tragedy we have experienced." He added that counselors had been brought in to talk to the other campers.

Officer Jonathan Knotts, of the local police department, said that all possible causes of death were under consideration, including a possible homicide. He noted that some things were not adding up about what happened. Other unnamed sources observed that Ms. Moss had given inconsistent accounts of what happened.

Camp Munkeewonk is a privately run camp for children, who have experienced some level of relational problems.

Letter of Reprimand

Wilson Electronics

456 North Main
San Milano, State of Lone Star
210-555-5679
WilsonE.com

June 3, [YR-2]

Ms. Sylvia Moss
Inventory Management Division.
Wilson Electronics

Re: Letter of Reprimand

Ms. Moss:

After investigating the incident last month in which you were involved in an altercation in the company's cafeteria, I have no choice but to issue this formal letter of reprimand.

My investigation indicates that you confronted one of your co-workers, Ms. Nora Gomez, and began shouting at her in a loud voice and in a threatening manner. Your outburst was apparently triggered when you saw a memo prepared by Ms. Gomez, which questioned the quality of your work in the Inventory Management Division of this company. As a result of your actions, Ms. Gomez struck you several times.

As you know, Ms. Gomez has been relieved because of the company's zero tolerance policy on physical violence.

While your work has been above average during your employment here at Wilson, we have received numerous complaints about your inability to accept constructive criticism. This sort of behavior will not be tolerated and if you act in this way again, we may be forced to terminate your employment.

I encourage you to seek professional counseling through our Human Resources Office. A copy of this letter will be placed in your personnel file

Sincerely yours,

Javier Hernandez
Javier Hernandez
CEO, Wilson Electronics

cc Human Resources

AUTOPSY REPORT

OFFICE OF CHIEF MEDICAL EXAMINER
BEAR COUNTY, STATE OF LONE STAR

AUTOPSY REPORT

Case No. 0501238

Name: Danny Moss

Approximate Age:	26 years	Sex:	Male
Height:	70 inches (residual)	Weight:	210.5 lbs (residual)
Identified By:	Dental Comparison (12-08-[YR-1])		
Place of Death:	Residence		

I hereby certify that I, Jasper McCue, M.D. have performed an autopsy on the body of Danny Moss at the Bear County Medical Examiner's Morgue on the eighth day of December [YR-1], and that the said autopsy revealed:

FINDINGS:

01 Sudden death associated with:
  A. Craniocerebral trauma with bibasilar skull fractures due to head trauma

02 Postmortem toxicology studies show an elevated blood concentration of fluoxetine (Prozac)

03 No evidence of dehydration or electrolyte imbalance:
  A. Postmortem vitreous chemistry non-contributory
  B. Blood furosemide (Lasix) negative

COMMENT:

Mr. Danny Moss was a 26-year-old White male, who was found dead at his residence at approximately 2:00 a.m. on December 5, [YR-1]. He was discovered by his wife who apparently found him unresponsive at the foot of the stairway in their home. The exact downtime is unknown.

The MedStar ambulance arrived at 2:45 a.m. and Mr. Moss was pronounced dead at 3:27 a.m. Records obtained from Lone Star Medical Facility in Bear County indicate that Mr. Moss had no history of disease. Most significant findings at autopsy included a large contusion on the scalp and massive skull fracture. There was a fresh bruise on the right posterior side of the neck, measuring approximately 6 centimeters, laterally.

Postmortem toxicology was positive for fluoxetine (Prozac®). Fluoxetine is a selective serotonin uptake-inhibitor antidepressant. Because it is highly selective, fluoxetine has fewer side-effects than the older tricyclic antidepressants including dry mouth, blurred vision, memory impairment, constipation, urinary retention, and sinus tachycardia, all which are primarily due to anticholinergic effects. Fluoxetine is well absorbed after oral administration and is not affected by food. The values reflected in Mr. Moss's femoral blood indicate that the amount of fluoxetine was in the toxic range, but was not in lethal range.

In conclusion, Mr. Danny Moss death is attributed to blunt head trauma which resulted in a massive skull fracture. Additionally, even though the amount of fluoxetine was in the toxic range, it did not directly contribute to his death.

CAUSE OF DEATH:
BLUNT HEAD TRAUMA: SKULL FRACTURE.

Jasper McCue

Jasper McCue, M.D.
Deputy Medical Examiner

DRAWING OF MOSS RESIDENCE

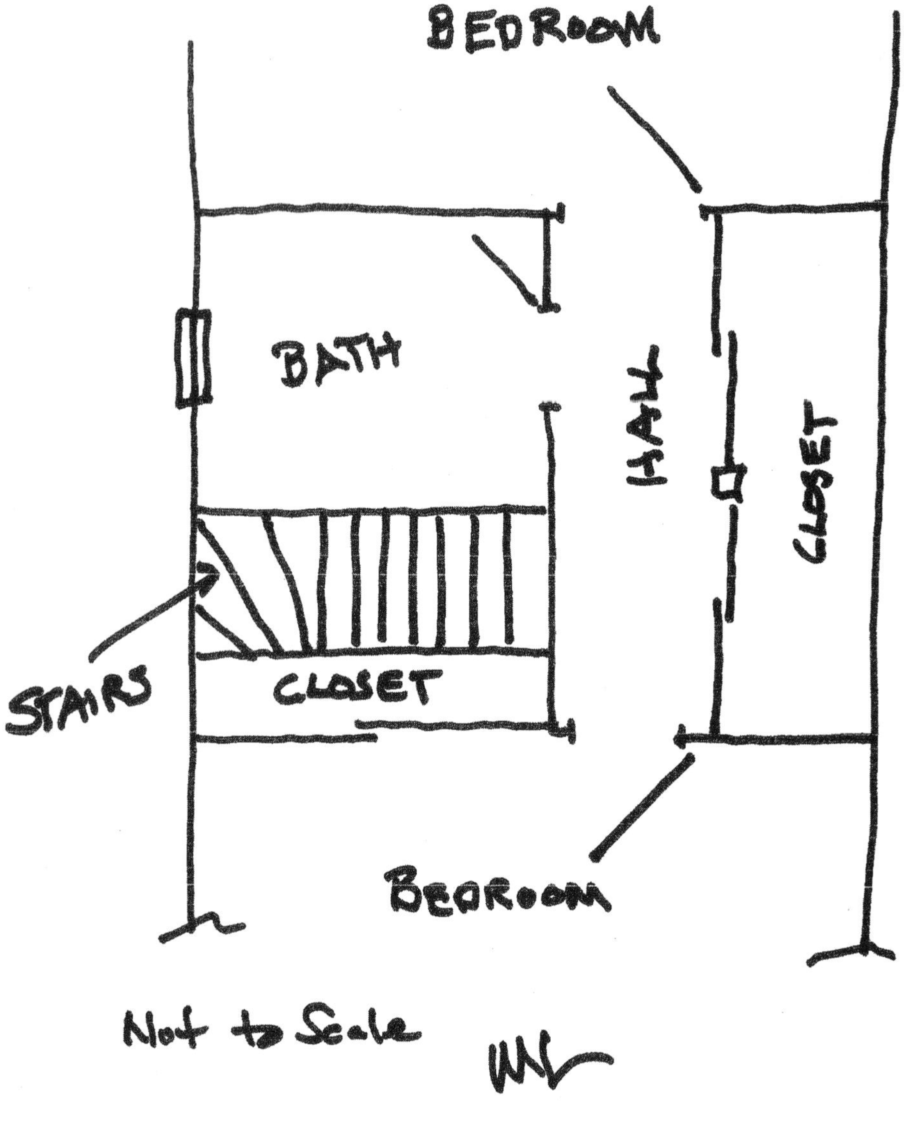

Crime Scene Photographs

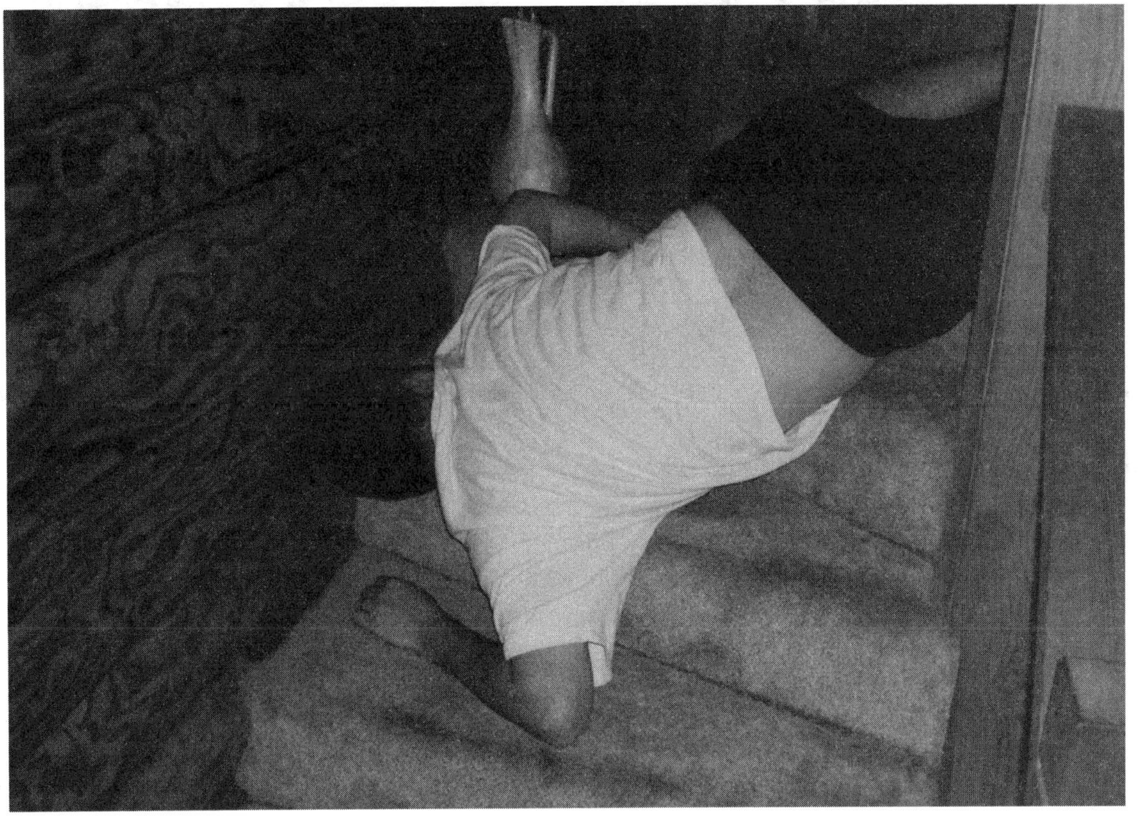

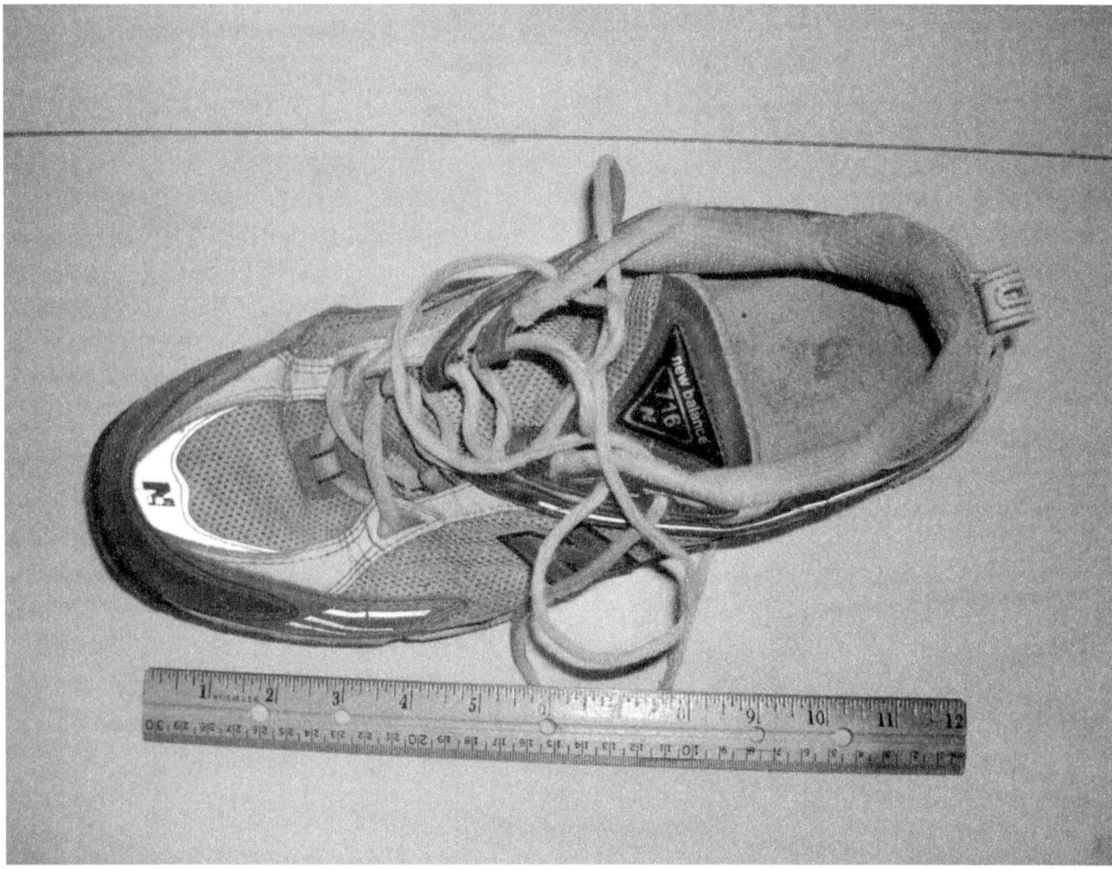
new balance
716

Jury Instructions

LADIES AND GENTLEMEN OF THE JURY:

I am now going to instruct you about the law governing this case. You are required to accept my instructions as the law. Any ideas you have of what the law is or what the law should be or any statements by the attorneys as to what the law may be, must be disregarded by you, if they are in conflict with these instructions.

1. Claims of Parties

The plaintiff claims that she sustained damages due to the defendant's wrongful act of killing her stepfather, Danny Moss. The defendant has denied those claims and also denies that the plaintiff is entitled to recover any damages.

2. Burden of Proof

In this case, the plaintiff has the burden of proving her claims by a preponderance of the evidence. If you find from the evidence, by a preponderance of the evidence, that the defendant acted intentionally in killing her stepfather, and that such actions were the proximate cause of her stepfather's death, then you must find the defendant liable for her actions.

3. Proximate Cause

When I use the expression "proximate cause," I mean a cause that, in the natural or ordinary course of events, produced Danny Moss's, the decedent's, death. It need not be the only cause, nor the last or nearest cause. It is sufficient if it combines with another cause resulting in the injury and death.

4. Preponderance of the Evidence

The term "preponderance of the evidence" means that amount of evidence that causes you to conclude that the allegation is probably true. To prove an allegation by the preponderance of the evidence, a party must convince you that the allegation is more likely true than not true.

If the evidence on a particular issue is equally balanced, that issue has not been proven by a preponderance of the evidence. Therefore, the party having the burden of proving that issue has failed with respect to that particular issue.

5. Circumstantial Evidence

A fact or a group of facts may, based on logic and common sense, lead you to a conclusion as to other facts. This is known as circumstantial evidence. A fact may be proved by circumstantial evidence. Circumstantial evidence is entitled to the same consideration as any other type of evidence

6. Opinion Testimony

You may have heard a witness give opinions about matters requiring special knowledge or skill. You should judge this testimony in the same way you judge the testimony from any other witness. The fact that such person has given an opinion does not mean that you are required to accept it. Give the testimony whatever weight you think it deserves, considering the reasons given for the opinion, the witness's qualifications, and all of the other evidence in the case.

7. Credibility of Witnesses

It is up to you to decide the credibility of the witnesses. In making the decision you may consider such factors as whether the witness has made a prior inconsistent statement or has been convicted of a crime. Evidence of this kind may be considered by you in connection with all the other facts and circumstances in evidence in deciding the weight to be given to the testimony of that witness.

8. Damages

a. General

If you decide the plaintiff is entitled to damages, you should give such amount as you decide to be fair and just, under all the circumstances. Such damages may include the following items, to the extent you find they have been proved by the evidence:

- Reasonable medical, hospital, funeral and burial expenses;
- Loss of financial support;
- Loss of gifts or other valuable gratuities;
- Loss of parental training and guidance;
- Loss of companionship;
- Plaintiff's grief, sorrow, or mental anguish.

Whether the plaintiff has proved these damages is for you to decide, based upon evidence and not upon speculation, guess, or conjecture. The amount of money to be awarded for certain of these elements of damage cannot be proved in a precise dollar amount. The law leaves such amounts to your sound judgment.

b. Punitive Damages

If you find for the plaintiff, you may, but are not required to, award punitive damages. The purposes of punitive damages are to punish a defendant and to deter similar acts in the future. Punitive damages may not be awarded to compensate a plaintiff.

The plaintiff has the burden of proving by a preponderance of the evidence that punitive damages should be awarded, and, if so, the amount of any such damages.

You may award punitive damages only if you find that the defendant's conduct that resulted in the death of Danny Moss, the decedent, was a willful act or omission or gross negligence. Gross negligence means conduct or a failure to act that is so reckless that it demonstrates a substantial lack of concern for whether an injury will result.

If you find that punitive damages are appropriate, you must use reason in setting the amount. Punitive damages, if any, should be in an amount sufficient to fulfill their purposes but should not reflect bias, prejudice or sympathy toward any party. In considering the amount of any punitive damages, consider the degree of reprehensibility of the defendant's conduct.

In addition, you may consider the relationship of any award of punitive damages to any actual harm inflicted on the plaintiff.

9. Insurance

Whether a party is insured or not insured has no bearing on any issue that you must decide. You must refrain from any inference, speculation, or discussion about insurance. If you find for the plaintiff, you shall not speculate about or consider any possible sources of benefits the plaintiff may have received or might receive. After you have returned your verdict, the court will make whatever adjustments are necessary in this regard.

10. Verdict Form

To assist you in deciding these issues, I am giving you a verdict form to use during your deliberations. When you have completed the form, please let the bailiff know that you have completed your deliberations.

Verdict Form

1. **Liability**

Do you find by a preponderance of the evidence that the defendant caused the death of the plaintiff's stepfather?

_________ YES

_________ NO

If your answer is "no," then do not answer Question 2. If your answer is "yes," answer Question 2.

2. **Damages**

Do you find by a preponderance of the evidence that the plaintiff suffered damages as a result of the defendant's actions?

_________ YES

_________ NO

If you answered "yes," then please enter the amount of damages, in whole dollar amounts, to which the plaintiff is entitled.

$ ____________________________

3. **Punitive Damages**

Do you find by a preponderance of the evidence that the decedent's death was the result of the defendant's willful act or omission or gross negligence in light of the circumstances?

_________ YES

_________ NO

If you answered "yes," then please enter the amount of punitive damages, in whole dollar amounts, to which the plaintiff is entitled.

$ ____________________________

Chapter 16
State v. Winston

§ 16-1. Introduction

Don Winston is charged with killing his girlfriend, Nancy Mason. Police received a tip that there was a human hand in the back of Winston's pickup. When they investigated, they found a hand, which was later determined to be that of Mason. Police later learned that Winston had allegedly paid a long-time friend, Frank Norton, to "take care of" Mason, because their relationship had soured after he discovered that Mason was dating someone else. Norton entered into an immunity agreement and a plea agreement for a reduced sentence. He admitted to killing Mason. Mason's body has never been found.

Winston says that he is completely innocent, and that Norton is getting even for a disagreement over a large loan he made to Winston. He also claims that Norton had been dating Mason, had fallen in love with her, and killed her out of jealousy.

§ 16-2. Stipulations Regarding Procedural and Evidentiary Matters

The parties have stipulated to the following:

1. The case is being tried in a State court. But the Federal Rules of Criminal Procedure and Federal Rules of Evidence apply.
2. This case will be tried only on the issue of guilt or innocence.
3. All witnesses called to testify, who have in statements or grand jury testimony identified the defendant, other individuals, or tangible evidence must, if asked, identify the same at trial.
4. Don Winston, Chuck Seeburg, and Morgan Snow signed their statements to the police.
5. All notice and disclosure requirements under the Federal Rules of Criminal Procedure were met in a timely fashion.
6. Other than what is supplied in the problem itself, there is nothing exceptional or unusual about the background information of any of the witnesses or the defendant that would bolster or detract from their credibility.
7. If any rule of procedure or rule of evidence requires that notice be provided to the court or to the opponent, it will be assumed for the purpose of the problem that the required notice was given.
8. All exhibits in the file are authentic. In addition, each exhibit contained in the file is the original of that document unless otherwise noted on the exhibit or as established by the evidence.
9. The lab test confirms that the hand found in the back of the defendant's pickup belongs to Ms. Nancy Mason.
10. There are no Confrontation Clause problems with any hearsay statements made by the witnesses, the defendant, or Chuck Seeburg. Seeburg is unavailable within the meaning of Federal Rule of Evidence 804.
11. Any searches and seizures conducted by the police met the requirements of the Fourth Amendment and the Federal Rules of Criminal Procedure.

12. Chuck Seeburg was convicted in Los Angeles, California, in January [YR-4], for felony possession of cocaine. He was sentenced to two years, but served only one year, having been credited for time served pending trial. He also received a misdemeanor conviction in [YR-6], in Los Angeles, for filing a false official police report, alleging that his friend had stolen his car. He was placed on four months probation after pleading guilty. He successfully completed his probation.
13. Frank Norton received a felony conviction in [YR-8], in Trenton, New Jersey, for assaulting Sally Williams, his girlfriend. As part of plea bargain, he successfully served 6 months probation and also completed an anger-management course.
14. No changes or alterations were made to any of the e-mails.
15. Frank Norton has a plea agreement with the State of Lone Star to testify truthfully against Don Winston and to enter a plea of guilty to the offense of manslaughter in return for a sentence of 5 years. He has not yet entered a plea of guilty.

§ 16-3. Case File Materials

Students will use the following materials in presenting their cases.

Statutes — State of Lone Star

I. Lone Star Penal Code Provisions

§ 79.01. Types of Criminal Homicide

(a) A person commits criminal homicide if he intentionally, knowingly, recklessly, or with criminal negligence causes the death of an individual.

(b) Criminal homicide is murder, capital murder, manslaughter, or criminally negligent homicide.

§ 79.02. Murder.

(a) In this Section:

(1) "Adequate cause" means cause that would commonly produce a degree of anger, rage, resentment, or terror in a person of ordinary temper, sufficient to render the mind incapable of cool reflection.

(2) "Sudden passion" means passion directly caused by and arising out of provocation by the individual killed or another acting with the person killed which passion arises at the time of the offense and is not solely the result of former provocation.

(b) A person commits an offense if he:

(1) intentionally or knowingly causes the death of an individual;

(2) intends to cause serious bodily injury and commits an act clearly dangerous to human life that causes the death of an individual; or

(3) commits or attempts to commit a felony, other than manslaughter, and in the course of and in furtherance of the commission or attempt, or in immediate flight from the commission or attempt, he commits or attempts to commit an act clearly dangerous to human life that causes the death of an individual.

(c) Except as provided by Subsection (d), an offense under this section is a felony of the first degree.

(d) At the punishment stage of a trial, the defendant may raise the issue as to whether he caused the death under the immediate influence of sudden passion arising from an adequate cause. If the defendant proves the issue in the affirmative by a preponderance of the evidence, the offense is a felony of the second degree.

* * * * *

§ 79.04. Manslaughter

(a) A person commits an offense if he recklessly causes the death of an individual.

(b) An offense under this section is a felony of the second degree.

§ 79.05. Criminally Negligent Homicide

(a) A person commits an offense if he causes the death of an individual by criminal negligence.

(b) An offense under this section is a state jail felony.

* * * * *

INDICTMENT

COURT'S COPY

Name:	Don Winston
Complainant:	Nancy Mason
Offense Charge:	Murder
GJ: 223533	**PH Court: 452**
JN#: 783461	**SID#: 4324458**
Witness: State's Attorney	

TRUE BILL OF INDICTMENT

IN THE NAME AND BY AUTHORITY OF THE STATE OF LONE STAR, the Grand Jury of Bear County, State of Lone Star, duly organized, empanelled and sworn as such at the April term, A.D., March 11, [YR-1], of the Judicial District Court of said County, at said term, do present in and to said Court that in the County and State aforesaid, and anterior to the presentment of this indictment, and:

COUNT 1: MURDER

on or about December 30, [YR-2], DON WINSTON, hereinafter referred to as defendant, then and there intentionally or knowingly, unlawfully, and feloniously cause the killing and murder of NANCY MASON, a human being, hereinafter referred to as complainant, without the authority of law and with deliberate design to effect the death of complainant in violation of Section 79.02, Lone Star Penal Code;

AGAINST THE PEACE AND DIGNITY OF THE STATE

Johnny G. Cuellar

Foreman of the Grand Jury

DEFENDANT'S FIRST WRITTEN STATEMENT TO POLICE

STATE OF LONE STAR
COUNTY OF BEAR

Case Number: 11-35672

VOLUNTARY STATEMENT OF: DON WINSTON

I, Don Winston, after first being duly warned by Det. L. Willows #5643 at 0900 hrs. at 214 W. Nueva, on January 4, [YR-1] that (1) I have the right to remain silent and not make any statement at all, and any statement I do make may be used against me at my trial; (2) Any statement I make may be used as evidence against me in Court; (3) I have the right to have a lawyer present to advise me prior to and during any questioning; (4) If I am unable to employ a lawyer, I have the right to have a lawyer appointed to advise me prior to and during any questioning; (5) I have the right to terminate the interview at any time; and I understand that the above rights are continuing rights and may be urged by me at any stage of the proceedings, and I hereby prior to and during the making of this statement, knowingly, intelligently, and voluntarily waive the above rights and give to the said, Det. Leslie Willows #5643, the person to whom this statement is being given, the following written statement:

My name is Don Winston. For about three years I have dated a woman named Nancy Mason. Her nickname is Bunny. For two of those years she lived in my home on Wild Creek Ranch Road and talked about getting married.

In mid-October [YR-2], we had an argument about the fact that I figured out that she was seeing another man on the side. She never denied it but did not tell me who it was. I tried to find out, but could not get the name of the man she was seeing. On November 2, [YR-2], she moved out of my house and moved back in with her parents who lived just outside San Milano.

I tried to call her a number of times to talk to her but she refused to talk to me. Finally, on Christmas day, we got together for dinner that night. She said that she needed some time alone to figure out what to do about us. But we fought again and she left the restaurant. I think she left about 8:30 PM. That was the last time I saw her.

I was away from my home over New Year's Eve and Day. I was visiting family and friends in Dallas, State of Lone Star. I had taxi cabs pick me up and take me to and from the airport. So my truck was at my house during that time.

I have no idea how a hand got into the bed of my pickup. I would not do anything to hurt Nancy. I don't recognize the hand. I love her and hope that she will come back to me. In my opinion she ran off with her new boyfriend.

I do not know who her new boyfriend is.

This is the end of my statement. I have read this statement and it is true and correct.

WITNESS: *Leslie Willows* SIGNATURE: *Don Winston*

DATE: Jan. 4, [YR-1]

Defendant's Second Written Statement to Police

STATE OF LONE STAR **COUNTY OF BEAR**	}	**Case Number: 11-35672**

VOLUNTARY STATEMENT OF: DON WINSTON

I, Don Winston, after first being duly warned by Det. L. Willows #5643 at 1300 hrs, at 214 W. Nueva, on March 6, [YR-1] that (1) I have the right to remain silent and not make any statement at all, and any statement I do make may be used against me at my trial; (2) Any statement I make may be used as evidence against me in Court; (3) I have the right to have a lawyer present to advise me prior to and during any questioning; (4) If I am unable to employ a lawyer, I have the right to have a lawyer appointed to advise me prior to and during any questioning; (5) I have the right to terminate the interview at any time; and I understand that the above rights are continuing rights and may be urged by me at any stage of the proceedings, and I hereby prior to and during the making of this statement, knowingly, intelligently, and voluntarily waive the above rights and give to the said, Det. Leslie Willows #5643, the person to whom this statement is being given, the following written statement:

My name is Don Winston. I work at Simpson Shipping, here in San Milano. I work on the shipping dock. Been there about five years.

I did not kill my girlfriend, Nancy Mason. The last time I saw her was on Christmas Day, in the evening. We had a fight during dinner and she left, saying that she was going to take a few days off to think about things.

You should talk to Frank Norton. I think he killed her out of jealousy. He fell in love with her. Nancy told me during the last meal we had together on December 25 that she and her soul mate were going to take a trip to Austin and spend some time together. She also said that she was going to use the trip to call off their relationship and move back in with me. But she needed time. I did not want to give her that time. I wanted her back immediately. That is when she got mad and walked out of the restaurant. I found out recently from Morgan Snow that Nancy's soul mate was Frank Norton.

I owed Frank some money for a $10,000 loan he gave me over a year ago. I needed the money to buy a new fishing boat. I think I got the money at the end of [YR-3]. I actually bought the boat in January [YR-2]. I finally paid him $5,000.00 cash in November [YR-2] against the loan. All I could afford to pay him back at that time was $5,000.00. He said he wanted the rest soon or I would be sorry. I told him I would have the remaining $5,000.00 by the end of March [YR-1]. He was not happy with that. I thought it was a loan between friends. I had promised to pay him back sooner, but did not expect to have the money to do so until February or March [YR-1], sometime. I don't remember the exact date.

I never paid him any money to kill Nancy. He took care of that himself. I guess he got really mad at her when she told him that it was over between them too. He is obviously out to get me.

I wrote a check for five thousand dollars to Frank for part of the loan at the end of January. He kept bugging me so I scraped up the money and I finally wrote it to him, in partial payment for the loan.

Frank is a born liar. I would not believe anything he told you. I would never trust him with telling the truth. He has a conviction from the state of New Jersey, from before he moved to San Milano. I don't know what it was for, but he seemed proud of the fact that he had gotten off so light. I think he got some sort of probation for only a year or two.

I got to know Frank through some mutual fishing buddies about two years ago. We used to fish on our days off, Thursdays and Fridays, and would often see each other at the boat dock, Adams' Dock, at Canyon Lake, north of San Milano.

When you showed the picture of the hand in our first conversation, in January, I was so shocked that I did not really recognize the ring on the hand in the picture you showed me. Now that I look at it more closely, the ring on the hand looks like the one I gave Nancy last summer.

I have no idea how Nancy's hand ended up in my truck. I did not put it there. I suspect Frank or one of his friends did it to frame me. And it's sickening to think that Frank would have killed her and then left her hand in my truck, where I would get blamed for what happened.

I was gone for about four or five days over New Year's. I went to Dallas, on December 29th, to think things through. I saw a couple of friends but basically hung out in motel room drinking beer and watching TV. I left my truck in my driveway while I was gone. I was having problems with the transmission. I took a cab to the airport and then flew to Dallas.

I do exchange e-mails with Frank. But I never told him to kill Nancy. I am the only one who has access to my computer so I should know if I sent an e-mail telling him to kill her.

You also need to talk to Morgan Snow. Morgan knows Frank well and can give more information about the relationship between Frank and Nancy. Morgan would go fishing with Frank and me sometimes.

WITNESS: Leslie Willows SIGNATURE: Don Winston

DATE: March 6, [YR-1]

MORGAN SNOW'S WRITTEN STATEMENT TO POLICE

STATE OF LONE STAR
COUNTY OF BEAR } **Case Number: 11-35672**

VOLUNTARY STATEMENT OF: MORGAN SNOW

I, Morgan Snow, after first being duly warned by Det. L. Willows #5643 at 1500 hrs. at 214 W. Nueva, on March 7, [YR-1] that (1) I have the right to remain silent and not make any statement at all, and any statement I do make may be used against me at my trial; (2) Any statement I make may be used as evidence against me in Court; (3) I have the right to have a lawyer present to advise me prior to and during any questioning; (4) If I am unable to employ a lawyer, I have the right to have a lawyer appointed to advise me prior to and during any questioning; (5) I have the right to terminate the interview at any time; and I understand that the above rights are continuing rights and may be urged by me at any stage of the proceedings, and I hereby prior to and during the making of this statement, knowingly, intelligently, and voluntarily waive the above rights and give to the said, Det. Leslie Willows #5643, the person to whom this statement is being given, the following written statement:

My name is Morgan Snow. I am a very good friend of Don Winston. I have been told that Don is accused of killing Nancy Mason, another friend of mine. Don could not have killed Nancy. He is too nice a man. He is very peaceful and does not start fights. If someone upsets him, he walks away from them.

I have known Don Winston for about three years. We met each other at Adams' Dock on Canyon Lake. His boat was in pretty bad shape so he would sometimes come onto my boat for a day of fishing. He is an honest and peaceful man. I have never known him to do a violent or aggressive act, or even threaten anyone.

He got a new boat in early [YR-2], after he got a loan from Frank Norton. Sometimes Frank and I would fish together but I never trusted Frank and was never sure where I stood with him. He always had a story to tell about why he was late, or why he could not keep his appointments. I found him to be very undependable. He also hung out with the types of people who always seemed to be in trouble with the law. One of them was Chuck Seeburg. Chuck had problems with the law and I stayed away from him. He told me that there were arrest warrants out for him in Oklahoma for selling drugs. But the three of them would hang out together. Don knows both Frank and Chuck. They fished together.

I also know about Frank and Nancy. One day in September [YR-2], Don brought Nancy to the boat dock and took her out on his boat. But Nancy had eyes for Frank, who was in his own boat. I saw the whole thing.

Nancy later asked me for Frank's phone number and I gave it to her. She told me over Thanksgiving that she had a lot to be thankful for, that she had started seeing Frank and that so far Don did not know about it. She said Don was fine but she was looking for a little excitement in her life. She said that Frank was a "bad boy" and tended to push her around but she liked a strong man who knew what he wanted. She said that Frank told her that he had fallen in madly in love with her and wanted to marry her.

I was sorry to see her move out of Don's home. He was good for her, but I could see that she had a thing for Frank. Don later told me that he had tried everything to keep her and was getting upset that she would not tell him who her new "soul mate" was. After Nancy disappeared I told Don that she had been seeing Frank. And all he said was, "That SOB." I think that was about December 27th. I said to Don that I would not be surprised if Frank had something to do with Nancy's disappearance and he said that could be true.

I was one of those people who got an e-mail from her on Christmas saying that she was taking off for a few days with a "soul mate" to get things sorted out and to let him know that she needed to get back with Don, or something like that. She did not say that she was going to be with Frank, but I figured it out. I still have the e-mail on my computer. You can have it if you want it.

When Nancy went missing, I figured that she had run off with Frank but did not see it as my place to tell Don what I thought had happened. I understand that another friend of ours saw them together in Austin a day or so after Christmas and that they seemed to be having some sort of loud argument. So I guess that is where she went to, Austin.

In early January, I saw Frank at the lake, fishing, and he said that Nancy had been a fine woman and that he had fallen in love with her but that her "time had run out." I am sure about what he said, because I interpreted it to mean that he had killed her. Frank had a bad temper and had a prior conviction from New Jersey for aggravated assault on his girlfriend. He told me that he had a good lawyer who got him off on a guilty plea for assault and one-year's probation. He laughed about it and said that he had really lucked out. I was afraid of what Frank would do to me if I said anything to anyone.

I did not have anything to do with Nancy's death. I am convinced that Frank killed her when he found out that she was going to move back in with Don. I would not believe anything Frank told you. I have caught him in too many lies.

WITNESS: Leslie Willows SIGNATURE: Morgan Snow

DATE: March 7, [YR-1]

Chuck Seeburg's Written Statement to Police

STATE OF LONE STAR **COUNTY OF BEAR**	}	**Case Number: 11-35672**

VOLUNTARY STATEMENT OF: CHUCK SEEBURG

I, Chuck Seeburg, after first being duly warned by Det. L. Willows #5643 at 2000 hrs, at 214 W. Nueva, on March 7, [YR-1] that (1) I have the right to remain silent and not make any statement at all, and any statement I do make may be used against me at my trial; (2) Any statement I make may be used as evidence against me in Court; (3) I have the right to have a lawyer present to advise me prior to and during any questioning; (4) If I am unable to employ a lawyer, I have the right to have a lawyer appointed to advise me prior to and during any questioning; (5) I have the right to terminate the interview at any time; and I understand that the above rights are continuing rights and may be urged by me at any stage of the proceedings, and I hereby prior to and during the making of this statement, knowingly, intelligently, and voluntarily waive the above rights and give to the said, Det. Leslie Willows #5643, the person to whom this statement is being given, the following written statement:

My name is Chuck Seeburg. I am friends with Don Winston and Frank Norton. I do not know anything about what happened to Nancy Mason. I know that she had been dating Don Winston because he always talked about her. I met her just a couple of times. She was a nice lady.

I also know that Frank Norton had dated her for a while but did not know the details. I know that he said once or twice that she was the love of his life.

In September [YR-2], Don talked to me one day while we were fishing in his boat and he said that I could make an easy $3,000 by getting rid of a problem. When I asked him what he meant he said that his girlfriend was cheating on him and that he needed to get rid of her. I told him that he was joking, and he said no, he was for real and that the money was mine if I did it. He said that of course he would need proof. He said that I should make her "disappear." That was his word he used, disappear.

I thought about it for a day or two and finally told him that I was not in the business of killing people. He said, fine, and that he could find someone else willing to make some easy money.

WITNESS: *Leslie Willows*　　　　SIGNATURE: *Chuck Seeburg*

DATE: March 7, [YR-1]

GRAND JURY TESTIMONY OF LESLIE WILLOWS

IN RE:	BEFORE THE GRAND JURY
	OF
GRAND JURY INVESTIGATION	BEAR COUNTY, STATE OF LONE STAR

* * * * * *

****

COURT REPORTER'S

Q AND A TRANSCRIPT OF TESTIMONY OF

DET. LESLIE WILLOWS

MARCH 8, [YR-1]

****

* * * * *

BE IT REMEMBERED, that on MARCH 8, [YR-1], the above-entitled matter came on for hearing before the Grand Jury of Bear County, sitting in San Milano, State of Lone Star, being presented by JOHN GONZALES, Assistant Criminal District Attorney, for consideration by the members thereof.

HEATHER STEVENS was duly sworn as Court Reporter.

WHEREUPON, the following evidence was introduced and proceedings had, to-wit, beginning at 9:00 o'clock a.m. and concluding at 10:00 o'clock a.m.

DETECTIVE LESLIE WILLOWS, The Witness.

GRAND JURY FOREMAN: Do you solemnly swear that you will not divulge either by words or signs any matter about which you may be interrogated, and that you will keep secret all proceedings of the Grand Jury which may be had in your presence, and that you will true answers make to such questions as may be propounded to you by the Grand Jury or under its direction, so help you God?

THE WITNESS: I do.

EXAMINATION BY JOHN GONZALES:

Q: Detective Willows, as with any witness who comes before the Grand Jury, I need to give you the definitions of perjury and aggravated perjury.

A person commits the offense of perjury if, with intent to deceive and with knowledge of the statement's meaning, that person makes a false statement under oath or swears to the truth of a false statement previously made and the statement is required or authorized by law to be made under oath.

Perjury is a Class A Misdemeanor, which is punishable by anywhere up to one year in the Bear County Jail and/or a fine of up to $4,000.

Perjury becomes aggravated perjury if the person commits perjury, makes that false statement during or in connection with an official proceeding, and Grand Jury proceedings are official proceedings, and the statement is material.

Aggravated perjury is a third-degree felony, which means it's punishable by anywhere from two to ten years in the Lone Star Department of Corrections, and there's a potential fine of up to $10,000. Do you understand this?

A: Yes, sir.

Q: Would you please state your name for the grand jury?

A: Yes, my name is Leslie Willows.

Q: Could you please tell us your position and duties with the police department?

A: I am a homicide detective, with about 10 years' experience on the force. My duties entail conducting investigations into possible homicides.

Q: You are a member of the San Milano Police Department?

A: Yes.

Q: Okay. Detective, I would like you to tell the grand jurors about your investigation into the death of Ms. Nancy Mason?

A: Our records show that on December 29, [YR-2], at 4:00 PM, we got a call from Mr. Norris Mason. He said that he was Nancy Mason's father and that he and his wife had been trying to contact her for the last several days. They said that the last time they saw her was on the evening of Christmas when she came back from having dinner with her boyfriend, Don Winston. She told her parents that the two of them had a fight and that she was going to take a few days off with a new friend, who could help her get on with her life. She never told her parents who the new friend was. So we started a missing person's file on her and I told Mr. Mason that we would see what we could do to find her.

Q: What did you do?

A: I tried calling Mr. Winston, and left messages for him to contact me. But I did not hear back from him. I figured he was probably out for the holidays. We also posted her name and information with our department in hopes that someone would run across information about her whereabouts.

Q: Okay. Take us to December 31, [YR-1], New Year's Eve.

A: Yes, our dispatcher got a phone tip at about 3 PM, from an anonymous caller, a man, that there was a hand in the back of the defendant's pickup at his home, which the caller said was parked in front of his garage on Wild Creek Ranch Road. The caller said that it looked like the hand of a female and that it had nice ring on it.

Q: So, did you investigate that?

A: Yes, I immediately drove to the defendant's residence, at 213 Wild Creek Ranch Road, here in Bear County, and saw a Chevrolet Silverado pickup sitting in the driveway. I had figured out early on that Winston was involved in all of this and figured we had caught him. I walked up to the truck and looked into the bed of the pickup. There was a lot of junk in it, but I could clearly see a hand sticking out from the stuff. I knocked on the defendant's door but no one answered. While standing at his door, I called his home number on my cell phone and could hear his phone ringing inside. But no one answered.

Q: Let me go back a bit. So what time was all of this?

A: [Reviewing notes] I got to Winston's house at about 3:30 PM.

Q: What did you do next?

A: I took some pictures of the back of the truck, seized the hand, placed it in an evidence baggie, and took it back to the police station.

Q: Do you recognize these exhibits? [Shows exhibits to witness]

A: Definitely, these are the pictures I took of the hand, the truck, and the scene as I found it at the defendant's residence. I also took pictures of the hand back at the office.

Q: Are these true and accurate photos?

A: Yes, they are. The hand was already in a plastic baggie, so I took this picture of what it looked like when I first seized it. That is not the evidence baggie.

Q: Okay, please continue.

A: When I got back to the police station I processed the hand to send it to the medical examiner's office here in San Milano. Their office was closed so I was not able to deliver it to them until January 3rd. Later that day, the 3rd, I finally heard from Don Winston who said that he had been travelling since December 28th and had just gotten my phone messages. I told him that we had a report that his girlfriend was missing and he acted surprised, saying that as far as he knew, she was with her parents. I asked him to stop by to talk about it and he said that he would do what he could. We decided to meet on January 4th.

Q: Did you question him at that time?

A: Yes, I did. I gave him his rights warnings and he agreed to answer questions. But the interview was very short because he basically said that he had no idea where Ms. Mason was. He admitted that they had a fight and that he figured that she was with her new boyfriend. I showed him pictures of his pickup and he said that he had no idea where the hand came from and who it belonged to. I finally released him and told him that if he thought of anything else to contact me. I also said that I would probably be in touch with him with further questions because we had sent the hand to the lab for analysis.

Q: What was his reaction to that information?

A: He said, "Sure, whatever."

Q: What was your reaction to that statement?

A: My reaction? I knew that he did it. He killed her.

Q: Okay. So what other steps did you take in your investigation?

A: On January 7th, we got a lab report that concluded that the blood on the hand that I found in Don Winston's truck matched Ms. Mason's blood type. So I called her parents and then went over to their house with the pictures I had taken at the crime scene and then at the office. I showed them the pictures and they immediately and positively identified the ring on the hand as belonging to their daughter. They said that it was a ring that the defendant had given to her a couple of months earlier.

Q: So what day did you show them the pictures of the hand?

A: January 7th.

Q: So they identified the hand as belonging to their daughter, Ms. Nancy Mason?

A: Yes, they said it was her hand, same ring, with blue stones.

Q: Did you locate her car?

A: Yes, it had always been at her parents' home. She apparently left it there when she left town. Her parents said that some guy had stopped by to pick her up. Unfortunately, they did not see who picked her up.

Q: Did you search it?

A: Yes, but nothing turned up.

Q: What did you do next in your investigation?

A: We continued to question friends and acquaintances of Ms. Mason to see if anyone had seen her since December 25th. Several friends told us that she had e-mailed them on the evening of December 25th and said that she was going to spend some time with her new "soul mate." We obtained consent from her parents to let us look at her computer and found the e-mail that she had sent.

Q: Do you recognize this exhibit? [Shows to witness]

A: Yes, I do. This is one of the e-mails that we printed off of her computer. We later questioned the people that she had sent it to, to see if they knew anything more. One of them later made a statement, Morgan Snow. She initially told me that all she knew was that Nancy was hanging out with Frank Norton.

Q: Did you attempt to talk again to Mr. Winston?

A: No, not at that time.

Q: Did you subsequently get a good lead on Ms. Mason's whereabouts?

A: Yes, finally, on February 4th we got a lead. One of her friends from work told us that he had seen Ms. Mason and a man named Frank Norton together at a restaurant in Austin, State of Lone Star, on December 27th. They seemed to be having an argument. So we talked to him.

Q: When did you question Mr. Norton?

A: That would have been [pause while consulting notes] on February 7th.

Q: Go ahead.

A: So based on Norton's statements, we obtained a search warrant of his apartment. Later that day we searched his apartment and found blood in the bathtub. We had it tested and it showed that it was a match with Ms. Mason's blood. We arrested him for her murder on February 8th.

Q: Please continue. What did you do next?

A: We brought him in and attempted to question him again. He lawyered up and refused to answer any more questions. He made bail and was released. I believe, on March 5th, his lawyer contacted me and said that his client was ready to talk about Ms. Mason's death. But he wanted immunity. He said that it was a contract killing. He said that Don Winston had paid Frank $5,000 for killing her. So I called the DA and we met up with Norton and his lawyer. Norton got a grant of immunity and agreed to testify against Ms. Mason's boyfriend, Don Winston. He claimed that Winston had paid him to kill Ms. Mason.

Q: Please continue.

A: So I called in Don Winston for a second interview and informed him that he was under arrest for the murder of Nancy Mason. He waived his rights and became very talkative. He finally recognized the hand as belonging to Ms. Mason. He repeatedly continued to deny killing her and said that it was Mr. Norton who had done all this on his own. I later got a search warrant for Mr. Winston's home and was able to retrieve several e-mails that linked him with Mr. Norton.

Q: Do you recognize these exhibits? [Shows to the witness]

A: Yes, definitely. These are the e-mails that I got off of his computer.

Q: Did you interview any other witnesses?

A: Yes, at the suggestion on Mr. Winston, I called Morgan Snow, who readily cooperated and gave me a statement as well.

Q: Is that the same Morgan Snow who got the e-mail from the victim?

A: Yes. Her story was that Mr. Norton must have killed Ms. Mason. I did not tell her that we already had that information and the links between Mr. Winston and Mr. Norton. Did you have any reason to believe that she had any involvement in Ms. Mason's death?

A: No. In my mind she did not have much to offer.

Q: Did you talk to anyone else?

A: Yes, I talked to Chuck Seeburg. His name had come up in my interview with Morgan Snow and with Frank Norton. Chuck told me that Don Winston had talked to him in October [YR-2], and that he needed to get rid of someone. When he asked who, Winston told him his girlfriend because he figured she was cheating on him. Seeburg said that Winston had offered him $3,000 for the job and that he would need proof. Seeburg said the offer was tempting but decided not to. He said he did not trust Winston to keep quiet about it and that he was not in the business of killing people. I did a check on Seeburg and found out that he had a prior felony conviction for drugs out of California, [reviewing notes] in [YR-4]. In [YR-6] he was convicted, following his guilty plea, of filing a false police report. He got four months probation on that one. He apparently filed a false report that his friend had stolen his car.

Q: So, do you have any reason to believe that he was involved in the death of Ms. Mason?

A: No. I had no other information that would have linked him.

Q: Did you take his statement?

A: Yes.

Q: Do you recognize this exhibit?

A: Yes, that is Seeburg's statement.

Q: Did you search the defendant's computer for any e-mails or other information?

A: Yes, as I said, we retrieved the e-mails he had sent to Frank Norton. But we did not find any other information linking him with this crime.

Q: Did you conduct any searches of the defendant's boat?

A: Yes, it was clean. We found nothing.

Q: What about Mr. Norton's boat?

A: Same. It was clean. We did not find any blood or body tissue or any other evidence.

Q: Did you search Morgan Snow's boat and car?

A: No, we did not do a search of her boat or her car. Saw no need to do that.

Q: Okay. Thank you, Detective. Would you please step outside for just a few minutes.

THE WITNESS: Okay.

[The Witness leaves the Grand Jury Room at 10:00 a.m., and is subsequently dismissed.]

(END OF TRANSCRIPT)

GRAND JURY TESTIMONY OF FRANK NORTON

IN RE:	BEFORE THE GRAND JURY
	OF
GRAND JURY INVESTIGATION	BEAR COUNTY, STATE OF LONE STAR

* * * * * *

****

COURT REPORTER'S

Q AND A TRANSCRIPT OF TESTIMONY OF

FRANK NORTON

MARCH 10, [YR-1]

****

* * * * *

BE IT REMEMBERED, that on MARCH 10, [YR-1], the above-entitled matter came on for hearing before the Grand Jury of Bear County, sitting in San Milano, State of Lone Star, being presented by JOHN GONZALES, Assistant Criminal District Attorney, for consideration by the members thereof.

HEATHER STEVENS was duly sworn as Court Reporter.

WHEREUPON, the following evidence was introduced and proceedings had, to-wit, beginning at 1:30 o'clock p.m. and concluding at 2:30 o'clock p.m.

FRANK NORTON, The Witness,

GRAND JURY FOREMAN: Do you solemnly swear that you will not divulge either by words or signs any matter about which you may be interrogated, and that you will keep secret all proceedings of the Grand Jury which may be had in your presence, and that you will true answers make to such questions as may be propounded to you by the Grand Jury or under its direction, so help you God?

THE WITNESS: I do.

EXAMINATION BY JOHN GONZALES:

Q: Mr. Norton, good morning.

A: Good morning.

Q: As with any witness who comes before the Grand Jury, I need to give you the definitions of perjury and aggravated perjury.

A person commits the offense of perjury if, with intent to deceive and with knowledge of the statement's meaning, that person makes a false statement under oath or swears to the truth of a false statement previously made and the statement is required or authorized by law to be made under oath.

Perjury is a Class A Misdemeanor, which is punishable by anywhere up to one year in the Bear County Jail and/or a fine of up to $4,000.

Perjury becomes aggravated perjury if the person commits perjury, makes that false statement during or in connection with an official proceeding, and Grand Jury proceedings are official proceedings, and the statement is material.

Aggravated perjury is a third-degree felony, which means it's punishable by anywhere from two to ten years in the Lone Star Department of Corrections, and there's a potential fine of up to $10,000. Do you understand this?

A: Yes, sir.

Q: Would you please state your name for the grand jury?

A: My name is Frank Norton.

Q: You are testifying today under a grant of immunity concerning the death of Ms. Nancy Mason?

A: Yes.

Q: And that grant of immunity promises you that anything you say to this grand jury and anything you testify to at a trial cannot be used against you. Right?

A: Yes, that is right.

Q: And this grant of immunity does not promise you that you will not be prosecuted for her death, right?

A: That is right. I can still be prosecuted. But I have a deal to plead guilty in return for a lesser offense, I guess they call it.

Q: That deal is contingent on your giving truthful testimony?

A: Of course.

Q: Do you recognize this exhibit? [Shows to witness]

A: Yes, this is my immunity agreement, or whatever you call it.

Q: Okay. Do you, or correction, did you know Ms. Nancy Mason?

A: Yes.

Q: Did you kill her?

A: Yes.

Q: Do you know Mr. Don Winston?

A: Yes, I know him well.

Q: Alright. Please tell us how you got involved in killing Ms. Mason.

A: I first met Ms. Mason last fall when we were at Canyon Lake for the day. She was Don's girlfriend and at the time was living in Don's house. She took a liking to me. She called me later and we had a couple of dates, talking about a lot of things. About a month after we met we had sexual relations. She was a fine woman but not really my type.

Q: What do you mean by that?

A: Well she was clearly a wife type of woman who wanted to settle down, have kids, you know.

Q: And that was not your type?

A: No.

Q: Was she aware of that?

A: I think she finally figured it out.

Q: Were you ever in love with her?

A: No. No way.

Q: So tell us about your contact and agreement with Don Winston.

A: In November, Don called me and said that he was looking for someone to "off" his girlfriend. He had found out that she was seeing someone but could not figure out who it was. Boy was he clueless. It was me.

Q: So what did he say?

A: He said that he had tried to get another mutual friend, Chuck Seeburg, to do it. But Chuck had said he was not going to do it. He offered me the same deal he said that he had offered to Chuck. But I found out later he lied about that. He would pay me $5,000 to do it. I found out later that he only offered Chuck $3000. At least that is what Chuck told me. Don did not want anyone to find the body and said that he would need proof that she was dead. He said that he would leave that to me and said that timing was going to be important and that he would let me know when I should do it. I said that I would think about it and that even if I did it, he still owed me $ 5,000.

Q: How much was the loan for?

A: $ 10,000. But he paid half of it in cash in [YR-2]. So he still owed me $5,000.

Q: What did he say?

A: He said that was fine and that if I did it, he would pay me $5,000 when he got the proof that she was dead. And he said that he would also pay me the other $5,000.

Q: Alright. Please go on.

A: So I thought about it for a day or so and agreed to do it.

Q: So, did he tell you when to do it?

A: As I said, Don told me that he would let me know when to do it and said again that he would need proof that I had done it. So a few days before Christmas I got a call from Nancy and she was ready to spend some time with me to talk about our future. She was really hot for me, she said. So I suggested that she get out of town with me for a few days. I suggested Austin and she said that was fine. She said that she was going to have dinner with Don on Christmas and that we could go afterwards. Well, on Christmas night I got an e-mail from Don saying I should do it.

Q: What did you take that to mean?

A: I took it to mean that the time had arrived. I was supposed to, you know, kill Nancy.

Q: So did you go away with her?

A: Yes. I rented a motel room in south Austin and we hung out there, from the late night of December 25th, for about four or five days. She ended up telling me that she wanted to go back to Don. I acted real disappointed.

Q: Were you really disappointed?

A: Nope, not at all. I think I may have even faked getting angry at her, to throw her off. In fact it made it easier to do it, to kill her, I mean.

Q: Where were you when you had this conversation?

A: We were at an Austin restaurant.

Q: What would you say if someone testified that they saw the two of you having a loud argument?

A: I didn't think it was loud. It was intense, I guess, but not loud. I was trying to act real angry with her. It was all just an act.

Q: So did you kill her in Austin?

A: No, we drove back to my place in San Milano on December 30th. We got there about 11 PM. When she had walked through the door, I strangled her. She died pretty quickly.

Q: Just to be clear, your house is within San Milano city limits?

A: Yes.

Q: And that is within Bear County, State of Lone Star?

A: Of course. Yes.

Q: Okay. What did you do next?

A: Well, I moved her body into the bathtub and cut off one of her hands — the one with a ring on it. I did that for proof for Don. I guess I did not clean up all of the blood because the police found her blood in my tub. Not smart.

Q: What did you use, if anything, to strangle her?

A: My bare hands.

Q: What did you do with Ms. Mason's body?

A: I put it the trunk of my car, drove to Canyon Lake, took out my fishing boat and dumped her body in the deepest part of the lake.

Q: Are you aware that they, the police ... they have never found her body?

A: Yes, that was the idea. I really weighted it down so it would not come to the surface.

Q: Again, when did all of this take place?

A: I killed her on December 30th.

Q: [YR-2]?

A: Yes, December 30, [YR-2]. I drove up to Canyon Lake and dumped her during the middle of the night.

Q: So what did you do with the hand?

A: I put it in a baggie and took it to Don's house the next day, early in the morning of December 31st. I wanted to personally deliver it. But he was not home. He hadn't said he was going to be gone. Someone was driving by the house so I quickly threw the hand into the bed of his truck. I drove home and sent him an e-mail saying that the deed was done.

Q: Did he respond to that e-mail?

A: Yes, he did.

Q: Do you recognize these exhibits? [Shows to witness]

A: Yes, that is the e-mail I sent after I left the hand in his truck. And this is the e-mail back to me. And this one is the one on December 25th where he said I should go ahead and kill her.

Q: Do you recognize this exhibit? [Shows to witness]

A: Yes, that is the check he wrote to me. You can see he wrote on it that it was for the loan. Of course we both knew what it was really for.

Q: Did you see him write this check?

A: Absolutely. Then he handed it to me. He said that the "loan" notation would help if people started nosing around.

Q: Did you deposit this check in your account?

A: Yes.

Q: Have you spent any of the money?

A: Nope. I mean no, sir. Did not get a chance to do so.

Q: Did Don ever ask you what you did with the body?

A: Well, when he gave me the check I asked him if he wanted to know that and he said, "What body?" and then he winked at me.

Q: Do you recognize these exhibits? [Shows to witness]

A: Yes, that is a picture of Nancy's hand in the baggie I used. That is it. And I recognize these other pictures as well. I did not take them but that is her hand.

Q: I want to go back and talk about Don's attempt to get Chuck, I believe his full name is Chuck Seeburg, to kill Nancy Mason. Did I understand you correctly?

A: Yes. Don clearly said that he had talked to Chuck first and offered him the same deal he offered to me. But he said that Chuck thought about it and said it was too risky. So he said no. I should have said no.

Q: Did Don ever say that he had talked to Chuck before you?

A: Yes, he said that Chuck had a chance to make the money but that because he said no, I was going to get the chance to make some money.

Q: Do you regret killing Ms. Mason?

A: I regret getting caught. This makes two for me.

Q: Okay.

QUESTION BY GRAND JUROR

Q: What do you mean by "That makes two?"

A: This is the second time I got caught.

QUESTION BY GRAND JUROR

Q: Please explain what you mean.

A: Before I moved to San Milano four years ago I was charged in New Jersey with beating up my girlfriend who was seeing someone else and got pregnant by him. She had an abortion but I found out about it. I beat her up a little. She was okay but made a big deal about it. The DA charged me with aggravated assault but my lawyer got it reduced to something like regular assault, a misdemeanor. I got it probated for six months and had to complete an anger management course. As soon as I finished my probation, I left Jersey and moved here.

QUESTIONS BY ANOTHER GRAND JUROR

Q: Why did you cut off her hand as proof?

A: No special reason except that I knew that Don had given her that ring on her one hand and that would be proof that I did it. If I just took the ring that would not be proof. I figured that Don might go back on his word so I wanted to make sure he knew that I kept my end of the bargain.

Q: What did you use to cut off her hand?

A: One of my hunting knives. I threw it into the lake.

Q: Thank you, Mr. Norton. Would you please step outside for a few minutes.

A: Yes. [Witness leaves room]

[Witness steps outside at 2:30 p.m. and is subsequently dismissed)

(END OF TRANSCRIPT)

Photographs of Hand

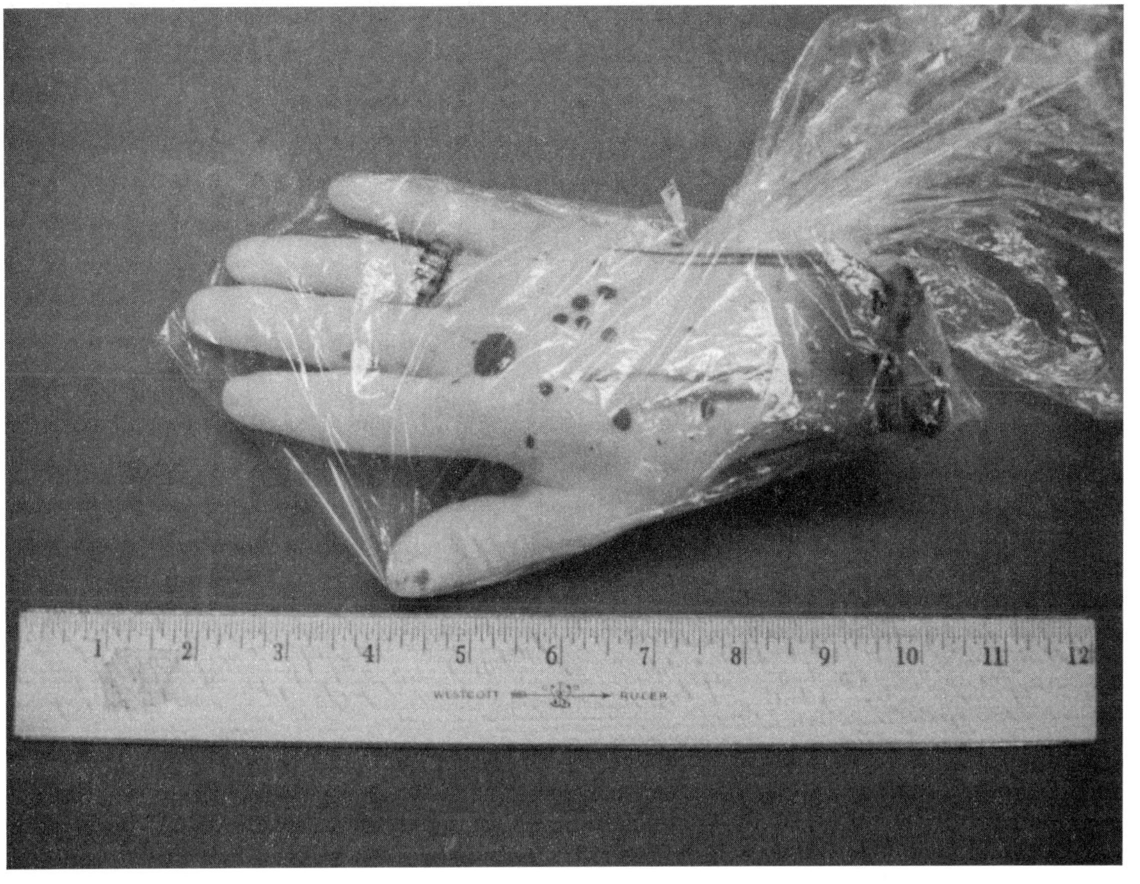

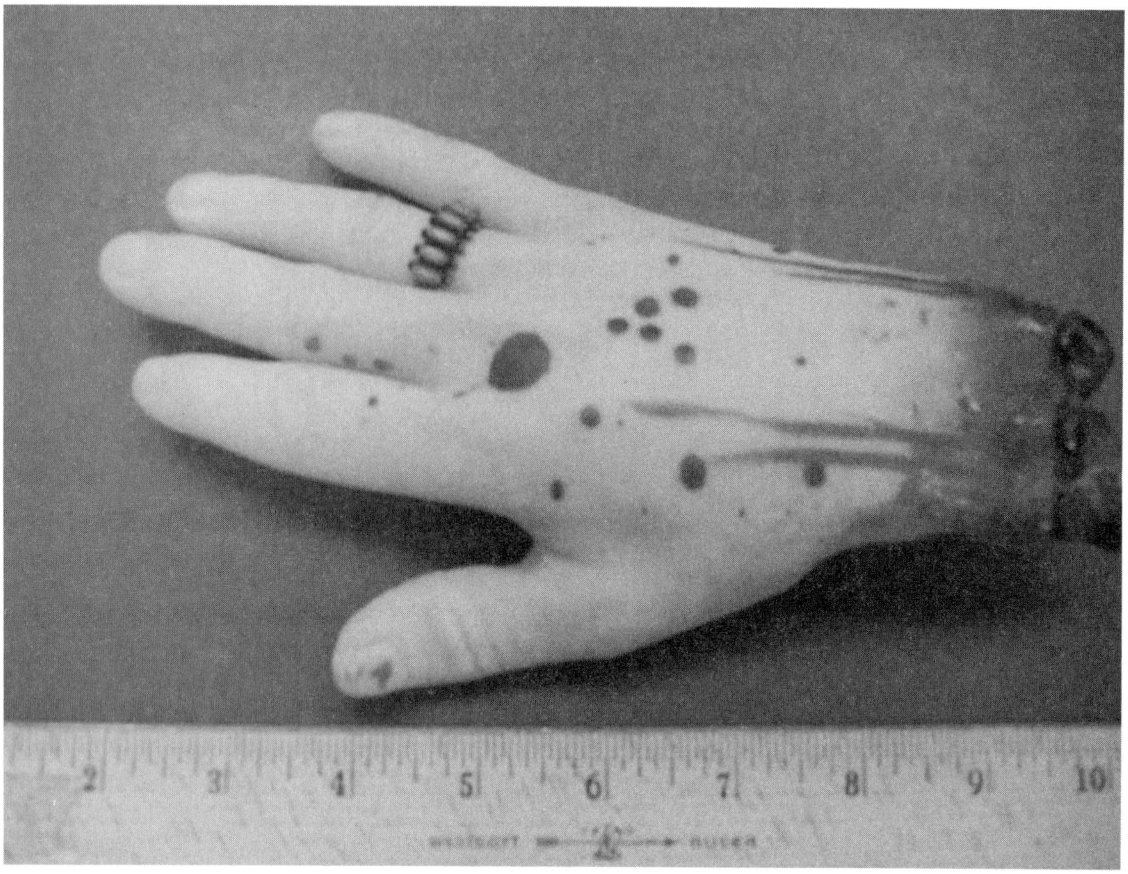
2
3
4
5
6
7
8
9
10

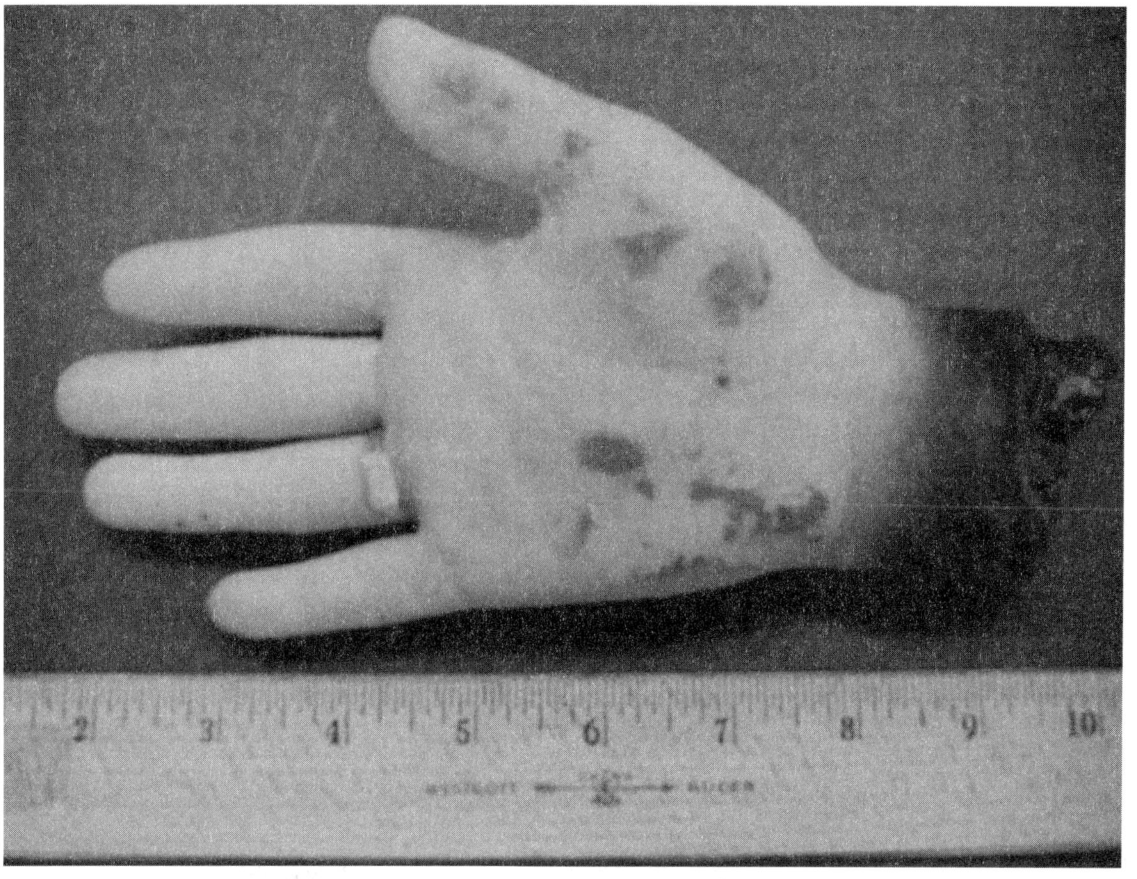
2 3 4 5 6 7 8 9 10

PHOTOGRAPHS OF DEFENDANT'S TRUCK

CHECK WRITTEN BY DON WINSTON TO FRANK NORTON

Don Winston
213 Wild Creek Ranch Rd
San Milano, State of Lone Star

No. 2367

Date *1-31-[YR-2]*

Pay to the Order of *Frank Norton* **$** *5,000.00*

Five Thousand and 00/100 ~~~~~~~~~~~~~~~~~~~ Dollars

First National Bank of Lone Star
1278 Main Street
San Milano, State of Lone Star

For: *Boat Loan*

Don Winston

⑆123⑆ 3432⑈ 4567 ⑈ 7689

E-MAILS BETWEEN DON WINSTON AND FRANK NORTON

From: DWinston@gagacom.net
Sent: January 1, [YR-1] 2:31 PM
To: BNortonTheMan@lol.com
Subject: Done!!!

OK. Thanks man.

From: BNortonTheMan@lol.com
Sent: December 31, [YR-2] 5:00 AM
To: DWinston@gagacom.net
Subject: Done!!!

It's done. Proof is in your truck. Time to show me the money!!!

From: DWinston@gagacom.net
Sent: December 25, [YR-2] 11:40 PM
To: BNortonTheMan@lol.com
Subject: It's that Time

Hey buddy. It's time to do your thing. She is leaving me for some bubba. Remember, I need to know for certain that the deed has been done. Give me a hand on this, OK?

E-Mail Written by Nancy Mason

From: NMason@bol.net
Sent: December 25, [YR-2] 10:30 PM
To: MSnowy@gahoo.com; JulesSnorts@hadmail.com; DoodleDee@bol.com; Jen4Smartsy@gaggle.net
Subject: Leaving Town

Hey y'all

Just had dinner with Don and it's time to leave town for a few days with my BFF ("soul mate" for you Jules) ("lover" for you Morgan). Had big fight with Don tonight so I know I am doing the right thing.

He loves me and says he wants to be with me forever. Going somewhere up north. Should be home in a couple of days. Stay out of trouble. LOL.

Hugs and kisses

Grant of Immunity to Frank Norton

THE STATE OF LONE STAR		IN COURT NO. 999
v.	}	
DON WINSTON		BEAR COUNTY, STATE OF LONE STAR

AGREEMENT FOR IMMUNITY

Whereas, The State of Lone Star is investigating allegations of criminal offenses by Don Winston, the Defendant.

Whereas, The State of Lone Star believes that Frank Norton, hereinafter referred to as "Witness," has material information regarding such criminal offense and that testimony regarding the same is crucial to the prosecution of the case; and whereas, said Witness represented by Jorge Sampson, attorney, is willing to waive his privilege against self-incrimination and to cooperate fully and testify truthfully in return for immunity from his testimony being used against him;

The Undersigned Parties agree to the following:

1. The Witness agrees to make a full and truthful statement to the law enforcement officers investigating the case, and to testify fully and truthfully in any judicial proceeding involving The State of Lone Star v. Don Winston.

2. The State of Lone Star, by and through its District Attorney, agrees to grant said Witness testimonial immunity for this testimony, evidence, or information directly or indirectly derived from such testimony.

3. The Witness agrees and understands that if he perjures himself in the above styled case, the District Attorney can and will prosecute him for aggravated perjury and his involvement, if any, in the criminal conduct of the Defendant.

Agreed as to form and substance on this March 8, A.D., [YR-1].

Sam Ruffinsky

Sam Ruffinsky
Criminal District Attorney
Bear County, State of Lone Star
San Milano, State of Lone Star

Frank Norton

Witness

Jorge Sampson

Jorge Sampson
Attorney for Witness

COURT'S COPY
Name: **Don Winston**
Complainant: **Nancy Mason**
Offense Charged: **MURDER**

JURY INSTRUCTIONS

LADIES AND GENTLEMEN OF THE JURY:

The defendant, DON WINSTON, stands charged by indictment COUNT 1 with the offense of murder, alleged to have been committed on or about the December 30, [YR-2], in Bear County, State of Lone Star. The defendant has pleaded not guilty.

1.

Our law provides that a person commits the offense of murder if he or she intentionally or knowingly causes the death of an individual.

2.

A person acts intentionally, or with intent, with respect to a result of his or her conduct when it is his or her conscious objective or desire to cause the result.

A person acts knowingly, or with knowledge, with respect to a result of his or her conduct when he or she is aware that his or her conduct is reasonably certain to cause the result.

3.

Now, if you find from the evidence beyond a reasonable doubt that on or about December 30th, in Bear County, State of Lone Star, that the defendant DON WINSTON, did intentionally or knowingly cause the death of an individual, namely NANCY MASON, by hiring Frank Norton to kill her then you will find the defendant DON WINSTON guilty of murder as charged in the indictment.

Unless you so find beyond a reasonable doubt, or if you have a reasonable doubt as to whether the defendant is guilty of murder, then you will find him not guilty.

4.

You are instructed that you may consider all relevant facts and circumstances surrounding the killing, if any, and the previous relationship existing between the accused and the deceased, if any, together with all relevant facts and circumstances going to show the condition of the mind of the defendant at the time of the offense, if any.

The State, however, is not required to prove a motive. If the State has proved the essential elements of the offense beyond a reasonable doubt, the defendant must be found guilty of that offense regardless of the defendant's motive or lack of a motive. If the State, however, has proved a motive, you may consider that insofar as it gives meaning to other circumstances. On the other hand, you may consider the absence of motive in weighing whether or not the defendant is guilty of the crime charged.

5.

"Proof beyond a reasonable doubt" is proof that leaves you firmly convinced of the defendant's guilt. There are very few things in this world that we know with absolute certainty, and in criminal cases the law does not require proof that overcomes every possible doubt. If, based on your consideration of the evidence, you are firmly convinced that the defendant is guilty of the crime charged, you should find him guilty. If, on the other hand, you think there is a real possibility that he is not guilty, you should give him the benefit of the doubt and find him not guilty.

Chapter 17
Mason v. Winston

§ 17-1. Introduction

Don Winston was tried for killing his girlfriend, Nancy Mason. Police received a tip that there was a human hand in the back of Winston's pickup. When they investigated, they found a hand, which was later determined to be that of Mason. Police later learned that Winston had allegedly paid a long-time friend, Frank Norton, to "take care of" Mason, because their relationship had soured after he discovered that Mason was dating someone else. Norton entered into an immunity agreement and a plea agreement for a reduced sentence. He admitted to killing Mason. Mason's body has never been found. Winston said that he was completely innocent, and that Norton is getting even for a disagreement over a large loan he made to Winston. He also claimed that Norton had been dating Mason, had fallen in love with her, and killed her out of jealousy.

At Winston's murder trial, Frank Norton testified for the state that he had killed Nancy Mason on orders from Winston. After two days of deliberation, the jury acquitted Winston.

Nancy Mason's father, David Mason, has brought a wrongful death suit against Winston.

§ 17-2. Stipulations Regarding Procedural and Evidentiary Matters

1. The case is being tried in a State court. However, the Federal Rules of Civil Procedure and Federal Rules of Evidence apply.
2. This case will be tried on the issue of liability and damages.
3. All witnesses called to testify who have in depositions, statements, or grand jury testimony identified the defendant, other individuals, or tangible evidence, can, if asked, identify the same at trial.
4. Don Winston, Chuck Seeburg, and Morgan Snow signed their statements to the police.
5. All notice and disclosure requirements under the Federal Rules of Civil Procedure were met in a timely fashion.
6. Other than what is supplied in the problem itself, there is nothing exceptional or unusual about the background information of any of the witnesses or the defendant that would bolster or detract from their credibility.
7. If any rule of procedure or rule of evidence requires that notice be provided to the court or to the opponent, it will be assumed for the purpose of the problem that the required notice was given.
8. All exhibits in the file are authentic. In addition, each exhibit contained in the file is the original of that document unless otherwise noted on the exhibit or as established by the evidence.
9. The lab test confirms that the hand found in the back of the defendant's pickup belongs to Ms. Nancy Mason.
10. Any searches and seizures conducted by the police met the requirements of the Fourth Amendment and the Federal Rules of Criminal Procedure.

11. Chuck Seeburg was convicted in Los Angeles, California, in January [YR-4], for felony possession of cocaine. He was sentenced to two years, but served only one year, having been credited for time served pending trial. He also received a misdemeanor conviction in [YR-6], in Los Angeles, for filing a false official police report, alleging that his friend had stolen his car. He was placed on four months probation after pleading guilty. He successfully completed his probation.
12. Frank Norton received a felony conviction in [YR-8], in Trenton, New Jersey, for assaulting Sally Williams, his girlfriend. As part of the plea bargain, he successfully served 6 months probation and also completed an anger-management course.
13. No changes or alterations were made to any of the e-mails.
14. Frank Norton had a plea agreement with the State of Lone Star to testify truthfully against Don Winston at the criminal trial and to enter a plea of guilty to the offense of manslaughter in return for a sentence of 5 years. He later entered a plea of guilty and was sentenced to 5 years in the state prison. He is available for the trial.

§ 17-3. Case File Materials

Students will be expected to use the following materials in presenting their cases.

Lone Star Civil Practice & Remedies Code

§ 31.123. Cause of Action

(a) An action for actual damages arising from an injury that causes an individual's death may be brought if liability exists under this section.

(b) A person is liable for damages arising from an injury that causes an individual's death if the injury was caused by the person's or his agent's or servant's wrongful act, neglect, carelessness, unskillfulness, or default.

(c) A person is liable for damages arising from an injury that causes an individual's death if:

(1) the person is a proprietor, owner, charterer, or hirer of an industrial or public utility plant or of a railroad, street railway, steamboat, stagecoach, or other vehicle for the transportation of goods or passengers; and

(2) the injury was caused by the person's or his agent's or servant's wrongful act, neglect, carelessness, unskillfulness, or default.

§ 31.124. Benefitting From Action

(a) An action to recover damages as provided by this subchapter is for the exclusive benefit of the surviving spouse, children, and parents of the deceased.

(b) The surviving spouse, children, and parents of the deceased may bring the action or one or more of those individuals may bring the action for the benefit of all.

§ 31.125. Punitive Damages

When the death is caused by the willful act or omission or gross negligence of the defendant, punitive as well as actual damages may be recovered.

Plaintiff's Petition

DISTRICT COURT OF BEAR COUNTY

DAVID MASON Plaintiff v. DON WINSTON Defendant	Docket No. 9876 COMPLAINT FOR DAMAGES

COMES NOW the above-named Plaintiff and alleges the following:

I. Parties, Jurisdiction, and Venue

A. Plaintiff, David Mason, father of Nancy Mason, brings this action in his personal capacity.

B. Defendant, Don Winston, is a resident of Bear County, State of Lone Star.

C. This Court has jurisdiction over the subject matter of this complaint and over the parties.

D. Venue is proper and appropriate in Bear County because the death of Nancy Mason, which is the subject matter of this complaint, occurred in Bear County.

II. Factual Basis

A. Defendant, Don Winston, was in a relationship with Nancy Mason.

B. Police received a tip that there was a human hand in the back of Don Winston's pickup. When they investigated, they found a hand, which was later determined to be that of Mason.

C. Police later learned that Winston had allegedly paid a long-time friend, Frank Norton, to "take care of" Mason, because their relationship had soured after he discovered that Mason was dating someone else.

D. Norton entered into an immunity agreement and a plea agreement for a reduced sentence. He admitted to killing Mason.

E. Mason's body has never been found.

F. Defendant was tried, and acquitted, of charges that he killed Nancy Mason.

G. Defendant's acts were the sole and proximate cause of Nancy Mason.

III. Causes of Action

A. As a direct and proximate result of the acts of the Defendant, the decedent suffered a wrongful death, entitling Plaintiff to recover actual and exemplary damages (including but not limited to medical and hospital expenses, funeral expenses, and all other damages allowable for wrongful death and survival benefits under Lone Star Civil Practice & Remedies Code §§ 31.123-31.125 and any other damages allowable as a result of Defendant's conduct;) in amounts not now precisely known, the exact amounts to be proven at or before the time of trial.

B. As a further direct and proximate result of the Defendant's acts and omissions, the plaintiff of the decedent suffered destruction of the parent-child relationship and loss of parental consortium.

C. As a further direct and proximate result of the negligent acts and omissions of Defendant, Plaintiff is entitled to recover statutory and reasonable attorney's fees and costs in amounts not now precisely known, the court to set such amounts in the future.

IV. Prayer for Relief

WHEREFORE, the plaintiff prays for a judgment of liability against the defendants as follows:

A. For a judgment against defendant.

B. For an award of damages as set forth in the above complaint herein, including statutory and reasonable fees and costs in such amounts that may be awarded by this Court.

C. For such other and further relief as the Court deems just and appropriate.

DATED this day of December 2, [YR-1].

Johnson H. Watters, Jr

Johnson H. Watters, Jr.

Attorney for Plaintiff

Defendant's Written Statement to Police

STATE OF LONE STAR
COUNTY OF BEAR

Case Number: 11-35672

VOLUNTARY STATEMENT OF: DON WINSTON

I, Don Winston, after first being duly warned by Det. L. Willows #5643 at 0900 hrs, at 214 W. Nueva, on January 4, [YR-2] that (1) I have the right to remain silent and not make any statement at all, and any statement I do make may be used against me at my trial; (2) Any statement I make may be used as evidence against me in Court; (3) I have the right to have a lawyer present to advise me prior to and during any questioning; (4) If I am unable to employ a lawyer, I have the right to have a lawyer appointed to advise me prior to and during any questioning; (5) I have the right to terminate the interview at any time; and I understand that the above rights are continuing rights and may be urged by me at any stage of the proceedings, and I hereby prior to and during the making of this statement, knowingly, intelligently, and voluntarily waive the above rights and give to the said, Det. Leslie Willows #5643, the person to whom this statement is being given, the following written statement:

My name is Don Winston. For about three years I have dated a woman named Nancy Mason. Her nickname is Bunny. For two of those years she lived in my home on Wild Creek Ranch Road and talked about getting married.

In mid-October [YR-3], we had an argument about the fact that I figured out that she was seeing another man on the side. She never denied it but did not tell me who it was. I tried to find out, but could not get the name of the man she was seeing. On November 2, [YR-3], she moved out of my house and moved back in with her parents who lived just outside San Milano.

I tried to call her a number of times to talk to her but she refused to talk to me. Finally, on Christmas day, we got together for dinner that night. She said that she needed some time alone to figure out what to do about us. But we fought again and she left the restaurant. I think she left about 8:30 PM. That was the last time I saw her.

I was away from my home over New Year's Eve and Day. I was visiting family and friends in Dallas, State of Lone Star. I had taxi cabs pick me up and take me to and from the airport. So my truck was at my house during that time.

I have no idea how a hand got into the bed of my pickup. I would not do anything to hurt Nancy. I don't recognize the hand. I love her and hope that she will come back to me. In my opinion she ran off with her new boyfriend.

I do not know who her new boyfriend is.

This is the end of my statement. I have read this statement and it is true and correct.

WITNESS: *Leslie Willows* SIGNATURE: *Don Winston*

DATE: Jan. 4, [YR-2]

Chuck Seeburg's Written Statement to Police

STATE OF LONE STAR
COUNTY OF BEAR

Case Number: 11-35672

VOLUNTARY STATEMENT OF: CHUCK SEEBURG

I, Chuck Seeburg, after first being duly warned by Det. L. Willows #5643 at 2000 hrs, at 214 W. Nueva, on March 7, [YR-2] that (1) I have the right to remain silent and not make any statement at all, and any statement I do make may be used against me at my trial; (2) Any statement I make may be used as evidence against me in Court; (3) I have the right to have a lawyer present to advise me prior to and during any questioning; (4) If I am unable to employ a lawyer, I have the right to have a lawyer appointed to advise me prior to and during any questioning; (5) I have the right to terminate the interview at any time; and I understand that the above rights are continuing rights and may be urged by me at any stage of the proceedings, and I hereby prior to and during the making of this statement, knowingly, intelligently, and voluntarily waive the above rights and give to the said, Det. Leslie Willows #5643, the person to whom this statement is being given, the following written statement:

My name is Chuck Seeburg. I am friends with Don Winston and Frank Norton. I do not know anything about what happened to Nancy Mason. I know that she had been dating Don Winston because he always talked about her. I met her just a couple of times. She was a nice lady.

I also know that Frank Norton had dated her for a while but did not know the details. I know that he said once or twice that she was the love of his life.

In September [YR-3] Don talked to me one day while we were fishing in his boat and he said that I could make an easy $3,000 by getting rid of a problem. When I asked him what he meant he said that his girlfriend was cheating on him and that he needed to get rid of her. I told him that he was joking, and he said no, he was for real and that the money was mine if I did it. He said that of course he would need proof. He said that I should make her "disappear." That was his word he used, disappear.

I thought about it for a day or two and finally told him that I was not in the business of killing people. He said, fine and that he could find someone else willing to make some easy money.

WITNESS: *Leslie Willows* SIGNATURE: *Chuck Seeburg*

DATE: March 7, [YR-2]

Deposition of Don Winston

ORAL DEPOSITION OF DON WINSTON, produced as a witness at the instance of the plaintiff, DAVID MASON, and duly sworn, was taken in the above-styled and numbered cause on October 30, [YR-1] from 8:00 AM to 10:00 AM before Sydney Jones, Certified Shorthand Reporter in and for the State of Lone Star, reported by machine shorthand, at the law offices of Defendant, pursuant to the Lone Star Rules of Civil Procedure and the Provisions stated on the record or attached hereto.

This is a deposition of DON WINSTON, who having been sworn, testified as follows:

EXAMINATION

QUESTIONS BY PLAINTIFF'S COUNSEL:

Q: Good morning Mr. Winston.

A: Good morning.

Q: Would you please state your name for the record.

A: Sure, my name is Don Winston.

Q: Do you live and work here, in San Milano?

A: Yes, live here and I work at Simpson Shipping, here in San Milano. I work in on the shipping dock. Been there about five years.

Q: Do you understand why we are taking your deposition this morning?

A: Nancy's father has sued me. He says I killed his daughter? I did not kill my girlfriend, Nancy. Never. I did not have anything to do with her death.

Q: When was the last time you saw her?

A: The last time I saw her was on Christmas Day, in the evening. We had a fight during dinner and she left, saying that she was going to take a few days off to think about things.

Q: And you blamed Frank Norton for her death, right?

A: Yes, and he admitted it. He pleaded guilty to killing her and because he got a deal, he only got a few years. He lied about me at my murder trial.

Q: Let's talk about Frank's involvement in this.

A: Absolutely, he killed her out of jealousy. He fell in love with her. Nancy told me during the last meal we had together on December 25th that she and her soul mate were going to take a trip to Austin and spend some time together. She also said that she was going to use the trip to call off their relationship and move back in with me. But she needed time. I did not want to give her that time. I wanted her back immediately. That is when she got mad and walked out of the restaurant. I later found out from Morgan Snow that Nancy's soul mate was Frank Norton.

Q: Now, you owed Frank Norton a lot of money, right?

A: Well, I did.

Q: It was $ 10,000, right?

A: Yes, I owed Frank some money for a $10,000 loan he gave me over a year ago. I needed the money to buy a new fishing boat. I think I got the money at the end of [YR-4]. I actually bought the boat in January [YR-3]. I finally paid him $5,000 cash in November [YR-3] against the loan. All I could afford to pay him back at that time was $5,000. He said he wanted the rest soon or I would be sorry. I told him I would have the remaining $5,000 by the end of March [YR-2]. He was not happy with that. I thought it was a loan between friends. I had promised to pay him back sooner, but did expect to have the money to do so until February or March [YR-2], sometime. I don't remember the exact date.

Q: So, you want us to believe that the money was for the boat and not for killing Nancy?

A: I never paid him any money to kill Nancy. He took care of that himself. I guess he got really mad at her when she told him that it was over between them two. He was obviously out to get me. I wrote a check for five thousand dollars to Frank for part of the loan at the end of January. He kept bugging me so I scraped up the money and I finally wrote it to him, in partial payment for the loan.

Q: Tell me how you became acquainted with Frank Norton.

A: I got to know Frank through some mutual fishing buddies about two years ago. We used to fish on our days off, Thursdays and Fridays, and would often see each other at the boat dock, Adams' Dock, at Canyon Lake, north of San Milano.

Q: Now Frank testified under oath at your criminal trial that this whole scheme to kill Nancy was your idea.

A: Frank is a born liar. I would not believe anything he told you. I would never trust him with telling the truth. He has a conviction from the state of New Jersey, from before he moved to San Milano. I don't know what it was for, but he seemed proud of the fact that he had gotten off so light. I think he got some sort of probation for only a year or two.

Q: The police investigation revealed that when you were shown a picture of Nancy's hand that you were not able to identify it. But you did recognize it as Nancy's, didn't you?

A: When the police officer showed me the picture of the hand in our first conversation, in January, I was so shocked that I did not really recognize the ring on the hand in the picture he showed me. After I looked at it again, the ring on the hand looks like the one I gave Nancy.

Q: Her hand was found in your truck.

A: Yes, Frank testified at my trial that he put it there. I have no doubt that he did it to frame me for Nancy's death. It's sickening to think that Frank would have killed her and then left her hand in my truck, where I would get blamed for what happened.

Q: Apparently, you had an unexplained absence from your house about the time Nancy disappeared.

A: I was gone for about four or five days over New Year's. I went to Dallas, on December 29th to think things through. I saw a couple of friends but basically hung out in my motel room drinking beer and watching TV. I left my truck in my driveway while I was gone. I was having problems with the transmission. I took a cab to the airport and then flew to Dallas.

Q: You exchanged some e-mails with Frank Norton, right?

A: Yes.

Q: These are the e-mails, right? [Counsel shows exhibits to witness]

A: Yes. But I never told him to kill Nancy. I am the only one who has access to my computer so I should know if I sent an e-mail telling him to kill her.

Q: That is all I have for today.

A: Okay

(END OF TRANSCRIPT)

This is to certify that I have read the transcript of my deposition taken on and that the transcript accurately reflects the questions asked and my answers.

SIGNATURE: *Don Winston*

Subscribed and sworn to before me on November 15, [YR-1].

Syndey W. Jones

Sydney W. Jones
Certified Shorthand

Deposition of Morgan Snow

ORAL DEPOSITION OF MORGAN SNOW, produced as a witness at the instance of the defendant, DON WINSTON, and duly sworn, was taken in the above-styled and numbered cause on October 31, [YR-1] from 1:00 PM to 3:10 PM, before Sydney Jones, Certified Shorthand Reporter in and for the State of Lone Star, reported by machine shorthand, at the law offices of Defendant, pursuant to the Lone Star Rules of Civil Procedure and the Provisions stated on the record or attached hereto.

This is a deposition of MORGAN SNOW, who having been sworn, testified as follows:

EXAMINATION

QUESTIONS BY DEFENSE COUNSEL:

Q: Good afternoon.

A: Hello.

Q: Before we get started, please let me know if you do not understand my questions. So, please feel free to stop me and ask for a clarification.

A: Sure. I understand.

Q: First, please state your full name.

A: My name is Morgan Snow.

Q: Okay. How old are you?

A: I am 23 years old.

Q: Do you understand that we are taking this deposition in conjunction with a law suit filed by Mr. David Mason?

A: Yes.

Q: And that he is alleging that Mr. Winston killed his daughter?

A: Yes.

Q: And you know Mr. Winston?

A: Yes, I am a very good friend of Don Winston.

Q: And how long have you known him?

A: Probably 3 years or more. I am not exactly sure.

Q: How do you know him?

A: We met each other at Adams' Dock on Canyon Lake. His fishing boat was in pretty bad shape so he would sometimes come onto my boat for a day of fishing. He is an honest and peaceful man. I have never known him to do a violent or aggressive act, or even threaten anyone.

Q: Okay. Well we can get into that.

A: Well, I just want to go on the record to say that. Don could not have killed Nancy. He is too nice a man. He is very peaceful and does not start fights. If someone upsets him, he walks away from them.

Q: Alright. Please tell me what you know about his financial relations with Mr. Frank Norton. I guess I should ask, do you know Frank Norton?

A: Yes, I know him, too.

Q: Okay. So now tell us about their arrangements.

A: Well, Don got a new boat in early [YR-3], after he got a loan from Frank Norton.

Q: And did you ever socialize with Frank Norton?

A: Yes, of course. Sometimes Frank and I would fish together but I never trusted Frank and was never sure where I stood with him. He always had a story to tell about why he was late, or why he could not keep his appointments. I found him to be very undependable. He also hung out with the types of people who always seemed to be in trouble with the law. One of them was Chuck Seeburg. Chuck had problems with the law and I stayed away from him. He told me that there were arrest warrants out for him in Oklahoma for selling drugs. But the three of them would hang out together. Don knows both Frank and Chuck. They fished together.

Q: Did you know Nancy Mason?

A: Yes, and I also know about Frank and Nancy. One day in September [YR-3], Don brought Nancy to the boat dock and took her out on his boat. But Nancy had eyes for Frank, who was in his own boat. I saw the whole thing.

Q: What else to you know about the relationship between Frank and Nancy?

A: Well, Nancy later asked me for Frank's phone number and I gave it to her. She told me over Thanksgiving that she had a lot to be thankful for, that she had started seeing Frank and that so far Don did not know about it. She said Don was fine but she was looking for a little excitement in her life. She said that Frank was a "bad boy" and tended to push her around but she liked a strong man who knew what he wanted. She said that Frank told her that he had fallen madly in love with her and wanted to marry her.

Q: Did you learn at some point that she had moved out of Don Winston's home?

A: Yes, and I was sorry to see her move out of Don's home. He was good for her, but I could see that she had a thing for Frank. Don later told me that he had tried everything to keep her and was getting upset that she would not tell him who her new "soul mate" was.

Q: Did you have an opportunity to tell Mr. Winston about what you knew about the relationship between Frank and Nancy?

A: Yes, after Nancy disappeared I told Don that she had been seeing Frank. And all he said was, "That SOB." I think that was about December 27th. I said to Don that I would not be surprised if Frank had something to do with Nancy's disappearance and he said that could be true.

Q: Did you ever hear from Nancy on her travel plans before she disappeared?

A: Yes, I did. I was one of those people who got an e-mail from her on Christmas saying that she was taking off for a few days with a "soul mate" to get things sorted out and to let him know that she needed to get back with Don, or something like that. She did not say that she was going to be with Frank, but I figured it out. I still have the e-mail on my computer. You can have it if you want it.

Q: What did you think happened to Nancy?

A: When Nancy went missing, I figured that she had run off with Frank but did not see it as my place to tell Don what I thought had happened. I understand that another friend of ours saw them together in Austin a day or so after Christmas and that they seemed to be having some sort of loud argument. So I guess that is where she went to, Austin.

Q: Tell us about your subsequent conversation with Mr. Winston.

A: Well, in early January, I saw Frank at the lake, fishing, and he said that Nancy had been a fine woman and that he had fallen in love with her but that her "time had run out." I am sure about what he said, because I interpreted it to mean that he had killed her. Frank had a bad temper and had a prior conviction from New Jersey for aggravated assault on his girlfriend. He told me that he had a good lawyer who got him off on a guilty plea for assault and one-year's probation. He laughed about it and said that he had really lucked out. I was afraid of what Frank would do to me if I said anything to anyone.

Q: What else do you know about Nancy's death?

A: That is all. I sure did not have anything to do with Nancy's death. I am convinced that Frank killed her when he found out that she was going to move back in with Don. I would not believe anything Frank told you. I have caught him in too many lies.

This is to certify that I have read the transcript of my deposition taken on and that the transcript accurately reflects the questions asked and my answers.

SIGNATURE: Morgan Snow
Subscribed and sworn to before me on November 15, [YR-1].

Sydney W. Jones

Sydney W. Jones
Certified Shorthand Reporter

Deposition of David Mason

ORAL DEPOSITION OF DAVID MASON, produced as a witness at the instance of the defendant, DAVID MASON, and duly sworn, was taken in the above-styled and numbered cause on November 6, [YR-1] from 9:15 AM, to 10:30 AM, before Sydney Jones, Certified Shorthand Reporter in and for the State of Lone Star, reported by machine shorthand, at the law offices of Plaintiff, pursuant to the Lone Star Rules of Civil Procedure and the Provisions stated on the record or attached hereto.

This is a deposition of DAVID MASON, who having been sworn, testified as follows:

EXAMINATION

QUESTIONS BY DEFENSE COUNSEL:

Q: Good morning Mr. Mason.

A: Good morning.

Q: Just let me say that we are all saddened by the loss of your daughter, Nancy.

A: Thank you.

Q: As you know I represent Mr. Donald Winston in the law suit that you have brought against him.

A: Yes, I know that.

Q: Alright. Well the purpose of this deposition is to determine what, if anything, you know about Nancy's death.

A: Yes.

Q: And to determine other facts that may be relevant to the case.

A: Okay.

Q: First, let me say that if you, if I am not clear in my questions, please stop me and ask me to restate the question. Okay?

A: Sure.

Q: Well, let me start by asking you to state your name for the reporter.

A: My name is David Mason.

Q: And where to you currently live?

A: I live at Scenic Acres retirement home, here in San Milano.

Q: Are you retired?

A: I retired several years ago.

Q: Mr. Mason, how old are you?

A: I am 70 years old.

Q: Okay. Now let's talk about the day that you heard about Nancy's death. Can you tell me about that?

A: My wife and I were shocked. All we knew was that Nancy had gone on a trip with someone and the next thing we know, a detective was calling to ask us to come to the station.

Q: And did you go to the station?

A: Yes, we did.

Q: And what happened.

A: We talked with a Detective Willows who took us into a room and closed the door. She told us that they had reason to believe that Nancy was dead and that they wanted us to look at a picture of a person's hand to see if we could identify it. The detective said that we should brace ourselves.

Q: Did you look at the picture?

A: Yes, actually several pictures. The hand clearly belonged to Nancy. We both recognized her hand, in particular the distinctive ring that she always wore. A sort of blue stone, turquoise, I believe.

Q: That must have been hard.

A: Absolutely.

Q: You were in a state of shock?

A: Yes.

Q: Is it possible that the hand actually belonged to someone else who had a similar ring on?

A: I don't think so.

Q: You would agree though, that that is a possibility?

A: I suppose. But that was clearly her hand in the picture. It was so clear to us that it was Nancy's hand, that my wife fainted and hit her head on the edge of the table in the detective's office.

Q: Was she injured?

A: Yes, it knocked her out and they needed to call EMT to take her to the hospital where she stayed for a week.

Q: I notice that you are asking for damages incurred because of your wife's hospital stay?

A: Yes. My lawyer should have given you the receipts for the expenses. It came to about $ 10,000 for the stay, and then for several weeks of rehabilitation.

Q: Okay. Now, you are also claiming $ 240,000 in damages for lost income and another $200,000 for pain and suffering, right?

A: Yes.

Q: Can you please tell me how you arrived at those figures?

A: Yes, Nancy was giving my wife and I, sorry, my wife and me, some money each month to supplement our social security payments. She was sending us about $ 500.00 a month to help us pay the rent, and for other things. We calculated her potential life span and how much she would send to us each month and we figured she would send us money until she retired, in about 30 years.

Q: I see. But you are currently 70 years old. Right?

A: Yes.

Q: And the actuarial tables indicate that you are likely to pass away long before your daughter Nancy would have retired, right?

A: Not necessarily.

Q: But given the difference in your ages, if she was in her 20's when she died, and she lived long enough to retire, say at 65, you would be about 110 years old at that point, right?

A: Absolutely. I expect to live that long.

Q: All right. But the actuarial tables would indicate that you could reasonably expect to live to the age 82.

A: I don't agree with those tables.

Q: You have other income, right?

A: No, I do not. Just social security, which is about $2,000.00 per month. I never had a high paying job.

Q: But you are living in a fairly nice retirement community?

A: We were able to do that because we had to sell our home last year and used that money to buy a very small apartment in the community. I do not owe any money on that. It's paid for. But I am on the meal plan and that runs several hundred dollars a month. Plus, I have some travel expenses, when the community organizes tours. Trust me, the money I get from Social Security does not go very far each month.

Q: All right. What about the pain and suffering? Can you explain to me how you arrived at that figure?

A: Sure.

Q: My wife and I both loved Nancy dearly. She was our only daughter. I have never recovered from her death, especially the way it happened. And my wife's death several months ago is, in my mind, directly the result of Nancy's death. After she got home from rehab, she was never the same. She couldn't eat or sleep. She died of a broken heart.

A: And you?

Q: I am devastated by my wife's death. I grieve for both of them. I visit my wife's grave every week. You will never know how much this has hurt. I just want what is due to me for Nancy's death.

Q: Now, I have received information that before Nancy's death, that you and your wife were no longer talking to Nancy. Because you disagreed with her decision to move in with Mr. Winston.

A: Well, I don't know where you got that so-called information but we were like every other family. We had our ups and downs. And yes, for several months before she died, we were having one of the down times. But, I need to say, we never stopped loving her. The fact that we were upset with her life decisions did not stop us from loving her.

Q: Okay. But it's true, isn't it, that during that time, over three months, she had stopped giving you and your wife the money that she had been giving to you to supplement your income?

A: That is true. But as I said, the fact that were in experiencing some difficulties does not mean that we would have not made up and she would have started paying again.

A: Okay, Mr. Mason, that is all I have today.

(END OF TRANSCRIPT)

This is to certify that I have read the transcript of my deposition taken on and that the transcript accurately reflects the questions asked and my answers.

SIGNATURE: *David Mason*

Subscribed and sworn to before me on November 24, [YR-1].

Sydney W. Jones

Sydney W. Jones
Certified Shorthand Reporter

Deposition of Detective Leslie Willows

ORAL DEPOSITION OF DETECTIVE LESLIE WILLOWS, produced as a witness at the instance of the plaintiff, DAVID MASON, and duly sworn, was taken in the above-styled and numbered cause on November 4, [YR-1] from 12:10 PM to 2:45 PM before Sydney Jones, Certified Shorthand Reporter in and for the State of Lone Star, reported by machine shorthand, at the law offices of Plaintiff, pursuant to the Lone Star Rules of Civil Procedure and the Provisions stated on the record or attached hereto.

This is a deposition of LESLIE WILLOWS, who having been sworn, testified as follows:

EXAMINATION

QUESTIONS BY DEFENSE COUNSEL:

Q: Good afternoon, Detective.

A: Good afternoon.

Q: Before we get started, please let me know if you do not understand my questions, and if you want any clarification.

A: I will.

Q: And you understand that this deposition is being taken at the request of Mr. David Mason, who has filed a wrongful death suit against Mr. Donald Winston?

A: Yes, I understand that.

Q: Okay, First, please state your full name.

A: My name is Detective Leslie Willows.

Q: Could you please tell me your position and duties with the police department?

A: I am a homicide detective, with about 12 years' experience on the force. My duties entail conducting investigations into possible homicides.

Q: You are a member of the San Milano Police Department?

A: Yes.

Q: Okay. Detective, I would like you to tell me about your investigation into the death of Ms. Nancy Mason?

A: Our records show that on December 29, [YR-3], at 4:00 PM, we got a call from Mr. David Mason. He said that he was Nancy Mason's father and that he and his wife had been trying to contact her for the last several days. They said that the last time they saw her was on the evening of Christmas when she came back from having dinner with her boyfriend, Don Winston. She told her parents that the two of them had a fight and that she was going to take a few days off with a new friend, who could help her get on with her life. She never told her parents who the new friend was. So we started a missing person's file on her and I told Mr. Mason that we would see what we could do to find her.

Q: What did you do?

A: I tried calling Mr. Winston, and left messages for him to contact me. But I did not hear back from him. I figured he was probably out for the holidays. We also posted her name and information with our department in hopes that someone would run across information about her whereabouts.

Q: Okay. Let's talk about December 31, [YR-3], New Year's Eve.

A: Yes, our dispatcher got a phone tip at about 3 PM, from an anonymous caller, a man, that there was a hand in the back of the defendant's pickup at his home, which the caller said was parked in front of his garage on Wild Creek Ranch Road. The caller said that it looked like the hand of a female and that it had nice ring on it.

Q: So, did you investigate that?

A: Yes, I immediately drove to the defendant's residence, at 213 Wild Creek Ranch Road, here in Bear County, and saw a 2003 Chevrolet Silverado pickup sitting in the driveway. I had figured out early on that Winston was involved in all of this and figured we had caught him. I walked up to the truck and looked into the bed of the pickup. There was a lot of junk in it, but I could clearly see a hand sticking out from the stuff. I knocked on the defendant's door but no one answered. While standing at his door, I called his home number on my cell phone and could hear his phone ringing inside. But no one answered.

Q: Let me go back a bit. So what time was all of this?

A: [Reviewing notes] I got to Winston's house at about 3:30 PM.

Q: What did you do next?

A: I took some pictures of the back of the truck, seized the hand, placed it in an evidence baggie, and took it back to the police station.

Q: Do you recognize these exhibits? [Shows exhibits to witness]

A: Definitely, these are the pictures I took of the hand, the truck, and the scene as I found it at the defendant's residence. I also took pictures of the hand back at the office.

Q: Are these true and accurate photos?

A: Yes, they are. The hand was already in a plastic baggie, so I took this picture of what it looked like when I first seized it. That is not the evidence baggie.

Q: Okay, please continue.

A: When I got back to the police station I processed the hand to send it to the medical examiner's office here in San Milano. Their office was closed so I was not able to deliver it to them until January 3rd. Later that day, the 3rd, I finally heard from Don Winston who said that he had been travelling since December 28th and had just gotten my phone messages. I told him that we had a report that his girlfriend was missing and he acted surprised, saying that as far as he knew, she was with her parents. I asked him to stop by to talk about it and he said that he would do what he could. We decided to meet on January 4th.

Q: Did you question him at that time?

A: Yes, I did. I gave him his rights warnings and he agreed to answer questions. But the interview was very short because he basically said that he had no idea where Ms. Mason was. He admitted that they had a fight and that he figured that she was with her new boyfriend. I showed him pictures of his pickup and he said that he had no idea where the hand came from and who it belonged to. I finally released him and told him that if he thought of anything else to contact me. I also said that I would probably be in touch with him with further questions because we had sent the hand to the lab for analysis.

Q: What was his reaction to that information?

A: He said, "Sure, whatever."

Q: What was your reaction to that statement?

A: My reaction? I knew that he did it. He killed her.

Q: Okay. So what other steps did you take in your investigation?

A: On January 7th, [YR-2], we got a lab report that concluded that the blood on the hand that I found in Don Winston's truck matched Ms. Mason's blood type. So I called her parents and then went over to their house with the pictures I had taken at the crime scene and then at the office. I showed them the pictures and they immediately and positively identified the ring on the hand as belonging to their daughter. They said that it was a ring that the defendant had given to her a couple of months earlier.

Q: So what day did you show them the pictures of the hand?

A: January 7th.

Q: So they identified the hand as belonging to their daughter, Ms. Nancy Mason?

A: Yes, they said it was her hand, same ring, with blue stones.

Q: Could you please tell me how they reacted?

A: They were completely devastated. As I recall, Mrs. Mason collapsed and had to be taken to the hospital. I really hated having to give them the news. It was clear to me that they dearly loved their daughter.

Q: Yes, they did. Did you locate her car?

A: Yes, it had always been at her parents' home. She apparently left it there when she left town. Her parents said that some guy had stopped by to pick her up. Unfortunately, they did not see who picked her up.

Q: Did you search it?

A: Yes, but nothing turned up.

Q: What did you do next in your investigation?

A: We continued to question friends and acquaintances of Ms. Mason to see if anyone had seen her since December 25th. Several friends told us that she had e-mailed them on the evening of December 25th and said that she was going to spend some time with her new "soul mate." We obtained consent from her parents to let us look at her computer and found the e-mail that she had sent.

Q: Do you recognize this exhibit? [Shows to witness]

A: Yes, I do. This is one of the e-mails that we printed off of her computer. We later questioned the people that she had sent it to, to see if they knew anything more. One of them later made a statement, Morgan Snow. She initially told me that all she knew was that Nancy was hanging out with Frank Norton.

Q: Did you attempt to talk again to Mr. Winston?

A: No, not at that time.

Q: Did you subsequently get a good lead on Ms. Mason's whereabouts?

A: Yes, finally, on February 4th we got a lead. One of her friends from work told us that he had seen Ms. Mason and a man named Frank Norton together at a restaurant in Austin, State of Lone Star, on December 27th. They seemed to be having an argument. So we talked to him.

Q: When did you question Mr. Norton?

A: That would have been [pause while consulting notes] on February 7th.

Q: Go ahead.

A: So based on Norton's statements, we obtained a search warrant of his apartment. Later that day we searched his apartment and found blood in the bathtub. We had it tested and it showed that it was a match with Ms. Mason's blood. We arrested him for her murder on February 8th.

Q: Please continue. What did you do next?

A: We brought him in and attempted to question him again. He lawyered up and refused to answer any more questions. He made bail and was released. I believe, on March 5th, his lawyer contacted me and said that his client was ready to talk about Ms. Mason's death. But he wanted immunity. He said that it was a contract killing. He said that Don Winston had paid Frank $5,000 for killing her. So I called the DA and we met up with Norton and his lawyer. Norton got a grant of immunity and agreed to testify against Ms. Mason's boyfriend, Don Winston. He claimed that Winston had paid him to kill Ms. Mason.

Q: Please continue.

A: So I called in Don Winston for a second interview and informed him that he was under arrest for the murder of Nancy Mason. He also invoked his rights and refused to answer any questions. I later got a search warrant for Mr. Winston's home and was able to retrieve several e-mails that linked him with Mr. Norton.

Q: Do you recognize these exhibits? [Shows to the witness]

A: Yes, definitely. These are the e-mails that I got off of his computer.

Q: Did you interview any other witnesses?

A: Yes, I called Morgan Snow, who readily cooperated and gave me a statement as well.

Q: Is that the same Morgan Snow who got the e-mail from the victim?

A: Yes. Her story was that Mr. Norton must have killed Ms. Mason. I did not tell her that we already had that information and the links between Mr. Winston and Mr. Norton.

Q: Did you have any reason to believe that she had any involvement in Ms. Mason's death?

A: No. In my mind she did not have much to offer.

Q: Did you talk to anyone else?

A: Yes, I talked to Chuck Seeburg. His name had come up in my interview with Morgan Snow and with Frank Norton. Chuck told me that Don Winston had talked to him in October [YR-3], and that he needed to get rid of someone. When he asked who, Winston told him his girlfriend because he figured she was cheating on him. Seeburg said that Winston had offered him $3,000 for the job and that he would need proof. Seeburg said the offer was tempting but decided not to. He said he did not trust Winston to keep quiet about it and that he was not in the business of killing people. I did a check on Seeburg and found out that he had a prior felony conviction for drugs out of California, in [reviewing notes] [YR-4]. In [YR-6] he was convicted, following his guilty plea, of filing a false police report. He got four months' probation on that one. He apparently filed a false report that his friend had stolen his car.

Q: So, do you have any reason to believe that he was involved in the death of Ms. Mason?

A: No. I had no other information that would have linked him.

Q: Did you take his statement?

A: Yes.

Q: Do you recognize this exhibit?

A: Yes, that is Seeburg's statement.

Q: Did you search the defendant's computer for any e-mails or other information?

A: Yes, as I said, we retrieved the e-mails he had sent to Frank Norton. But we did not find any other information linking him with this crime.

Q: Did you conduct any searches of the defendant's boat?

A: Yes, it was clean. We found nothing.

Q: What about Mr. Norton's boat?

A: Same. It was clean. We did not find any blood or body tissue or any other evidence?

Q: Did you search Morgan Snow's boat and car?

A: No, we did not do a search of her boat or her car. Saw no need to do that.

Q: Okay. Thank you, Detective. That is all the questions I have for you.

(END OF TRANSCRIPT)

This is to certify that I have read the transcript of my deposition taken on and that the transcript accurately reflects the questions asked and my answers.

SIGNATURE: *Leslie Willows*

Subscribed and sworn to before me on November 20, [YR-1].

Sydney W. Jones

Sydney W. Jones
Certified Shorthand Reporter

GRAND JURY TESTIMONY OF FRANK NORTON

IN RE:		BEFORE THE GRAND JURY
	}	OF
GRAND JURY INVESTIGATION		BEAR COUNTY, STATE OF LONE STAR

* * * * * *

****

COURT REPORTER'S

Q AND A TRANSCRIPT OF TESTIMONY OF

FRANK NORTON

MARCH 10, [YR-2]

****

* * * * *

BE IT REMEMBERED, that heretofore, to-writ on MARCH 10, [YR-2], the above-entitled matter came on for hearing before the Grand Jury of Bear County, sitting in San Milano, State of Lone Star, being presented by JOHN GONZALES, Assistant Criminal District Attorney, for consideration by the members thereof.

HEATHER STEVENS was duly sworn as Court Reporter.

WHEREUPON, the following evidence was introduced and proceedings had, to-wit, beginning at 1:30 o'clock p.m. and concluding at 2:30 o'clock p.m.

FRANK NORTON, The Witness,

GRAND JURY FOREMAN: Do you solemnly swear that you will not divulge either by words or signs any matter about which you may be interrogated, and that you will keep secret all proceedings of the Grand Jury which may be had in your presence, and that you will true answers make to such questions as may be propounded to you by the Grand Jury or under its direction, so help you God?

THE WITNESS: I do.

EXAMINATION BY JOHN GONZALES:

Q: Mr. Norton, good morning.

A: Good morning.

Q: As with any witness who comes before the Grand Jury, I need to give you the definitions of perjury and aggravated perjury.

A person commits the offense of perjury if, with intent to deceive and with knowledge of the statement's meaning, that person makes a false statement under oath or swears to the truth of a false statement previously made and the statement is required or authorized by law to be made under oath.

Perjury is a Class A Misdemeanor, which is punishable by anywhere up to one year in the Bear County Jail and/or a fine of up to $4,000.

Perjury becomes aggravated perjury if the person commits perjury, makes that false statement during or in connection with an official proceeding, and Grand Jury proceedings are official proceedings, and the statement is material.

Aggravated perjury is a third-degree felony, which means it's punishable by anywhere from two to ten years in the Lone Star Department of Corrections, and there's a potential fine of up to $10,000. Do you understand this?

A: Yes, sir.

Q: Would you please state your name for the grand jury?

A: My name is Frank Norton.

Q: You are testifying today under a grant of immunity concerning the death of Ms. Nancy Mason?

A: Yes.

Q: And that grant of immunity promises you that anything you say to this grand jury and anything you testify to at a trial cannot be used against you. Right?

A: Yes, that is right.

Q: And this grant of immunity does not promise you that you will not be prosecuted for her death, right?

A: That is right. I can still be prosecuted. But I have a deal to plead guilty in return for a lesser offense, I guess they call it.

Q: That deal is contingent on your giving truthful testimony?

A: Of course.

Q: Do you recognize this exhibit? [Shows to witness]

A: Yes, this is my immunity paper.

Q: Okay. Do you, or correction, did you know Ms. Nancy Mason?

A: Yes.

Q: Did you kill her?

A: Yes.

Q: Do you know Mr. Don Winston?

A: Yes, I know him well.

Q: Alright. Please tell us how you got involved in killing Ms. Mason.

A: I first met Ms. Mason last fall when we were at Canyon Lake for the day. She was Don's girlfriend and at the time was living in Don's house. She took a liking to me. She called me later and we had a couple of dates, talking about a lot of things. About a month after we met we had sexual relations. She was a fine woman but not really my type.

Q: What do you mean by that?

A: Well she was clearly a wife type of woman who wanted to settle down, have kids, you know.

Q: And that was not your type?

A: No.

Q: Was she aware of that?

A: I think she finally figured it out.

Q: Were you ever in love with her?

A: No. No way.

Q: So tell us about your contact and agreement with Don Winston.

A: In November, Don called me and said that he was looking for someone to "off" his girlfriend. He had found out that she was seeing someone but could not figure out who it was. Boy was he clueless. It was me.

Q: So what did he say?

A: He said that he had tried to get another mutual friend, Chuck Seeburg, to do it. But Chuck had said he was not going to do it. He offered me the same deal he said that he had offered to Chuck. But I found out later he lied about that. He would pay me $5,000 to do it. I found out later that he only offered Chuck $3000. At least that is what Chuck told me. Don did not want anyone to find the body and said that he would need proof that she was dead. He said that he would leave that to me and said that timing was going to be important and that he would let me know when I should do it. I said that I would think about it and that even if I did it, he still owed me $ 5,000.

Q: How much was the loan for?

A: $ 10,000. But he paid half of it in cash in [YR-3]. So he still owed me $ 5,000.

Q: What did he say?

A: He said that was fine and that if I did it, he would pay me $5,000 when he got the proof that she was dead. And he said that he would also pay me the other $5,000.

Q: Alright. Please go on.

A: So I thought about it for a day or so and agreed to do it.

Q: So, did he tell you when to do it?

A: As I said, Don told me that he would let me know when to do it and said again that he would need proof that I had done it. So a few days before Christmas I got a call from Nancy and she was ready to spend some time with me to talk about our future. She was really hot for me, she said. So I suggested that she get out of town with me for a few days. I suggested Austin and she said that was fine. She said that she was going to have dinner with Don on Christmas and that we could go afterwards. Well, on Christmas night I got an e-mail from Don saying I should do it.

Q: What did you take that to mean?

A: I took it to mean that the time had arrived. I was supposed to, you know, kill Nancy.

Q: So did you go away with her?

A: Yes. I rented a motel room in south Austin and we hung out there, from the late night of December 25th, for about four or five days. She ended up telling me that she wanted to go back to Don. I acted real disappointed.

Q: Were you really disappointed?

A: Nope, not at all. I think I may have even faked getting angry at her, to throw her off. In fact it made it easier to do it, to kill her, I mean.

Q: Where were you when you had this conversation?

A: We were at an Austin restaurant.

Q: What would you say if someone testified that they saw the two of you having a loud argument?

A: I didn't think it was loud. It was intense, I guess, but not loud. I was trying to act real angry with her. It was all just an act.

Q: So did you kill her in Austin?

A: No, we drove back to my place in San Milano on December 30th. We got there about 11 PM. When she had walked through the door, I strangled her. She died pretty quickly.

Q: Just to be clear, your house is within San Milano city limits?

A: Yes.

Q: And that is within Bear County, State of Lone Star?

A: Of course. Yes.

Q: Okay. What did you do next?

A: Well, I moved her body into the bathtub and cut off one of her hands — the one with a ring on it. I did that for proof for Don. I guess I did not clean up all of the blood because the police found her blood in my tub. Not smart.

Q: What did you use, if anything, to strangle her?

A: My bare hands.

Q: What did you do with Ms. Mason's body?

A: I put it the trunk of my car, drove to Canyon Lake, took out my fishing boat and dumped her body in the deepest part of the lake.

Q: Are you aware that they, the police ... they have never found her body?

A: Yes, that was the idea. I really weighted it down so it would not come to the surface.

Q: Again, when did all of this take place?

A: I killed her on December 30th.

Q: [YR-3]?

A: Yes, December 30, [YR-3]. I drove up to Canyon Lake and dumped her during the middle of the night.

Q: So what did you do with the hand?

A: I put it in a baggie and took it to Don's house the next day, early in the morning of December 31st. I wanted to personally deliver it. But he was not home. He hadn't said he was going to be gone. Someone was driving by the house so I quickly threw the hand into the bed of his truck. I drove home and sent him an e-mail saying that the deed was done.

Q: Did he respond to that e-mail?

A: Yes, he did.

Q: Do you recognize these exhibits? [Shows to witness]

A: Yes, that is the e-mail I sent after I left the hand in his truck. And this is e-mail back to me. And this one is the one on December 25th where he said I should go ahead and kill her.

Q: Do you recognize this exhibit? [Shows to witness]

A: Yes, that is the check he wrote to me. You can see he wrote on it that it was for the loan. Of course we both knew what it was really for.

Q: Did you see him write this check?

A: Absolutely. Then he handed it to me. He said that the "loan" notation would help if people started nosing around.

Q: Did you deposit this check in your account?

A: Yes.

Q: Have you spent any of the money?

A: Nope. I mean no, sir. Did not get a chance to do so.

Q: Did Don ever ask you what you did with the body?

A: Well, when he gave me the check I asked him if he wanted to know that and he said, "What body?" and then he winked at me.

Q: Do you recognize these exhibits? [Shows to witness]

A: Yes, that is a picture of Nancy's hand in the baggie I used. That is it. And I recognize these other pictures as well. I did not take them but that is her hand.

Q: I want to go back and talk about Don's attempt to get Chuck, I believe his full name is Chuck Seeburg, to kill Nancy Mason. Did I understand you correctly?

A: Yes. Don clearly said that he had talked to Chuck first and offered him the same deal he offered to me. But he said that Chuck thought about it and said it was too risky. So he said no. I should have said no.

Q: Did Don ever say that he had talked to Chuck before you?

A: Yes, he said that Chuck had a chance to make the money but that because he said no, I was going to get the chance to make some money.

Q: Do you regret killing Ms. Mason?

A: I regret getting caught. This makes two for me.

Q: Okay.

QUESTION BY GRAND JUROR

Q: What do you mean by "That makes two?"

A: This is the second time I got caught.

QUESTION BY GRAND JUROR

Q: Please explain what you mean.

A: Before I moved to San Milano four years ago I was charged in New Jersey with beating up my girlfriend who was seeing someone else and got pregnant by him. She had an abortion but I found out about it. I beat her up a little. She was okay but made a big deal about it. The DA charged me with aggravated assault but my lawyer got it reduced to something like regular assault, a misdemeanor. I got it probated for six months and had to complete an anger management course. As soon as I finished my probation, I left Jersey and moved here.

QUESTIONS BY ANOTHER GRAND JUROR

Q: Why did you cut off her hand as proof?

A: No special reason except that I knew that Don had given her that ring on her one hand and that would be proof that I did it. If I just took the ring that would not be proof. I figured that Don might go back on his word so I wanted to make sure he knew that I kept my end of the bargain.

Q: What did you use to cut off her hand?

A: One of my hunting knives. I threw it into the lake.

Q: Thank you, Mr. Norton. Would you please step outside for a few minutes.

A: Yes. [Witness leaves room]

[Witness steps outside at 2:30 p.m. and is subsequently dismissed.]

(END OF TRANSCRIPT)

PHOTOGRAPHS OF HAND

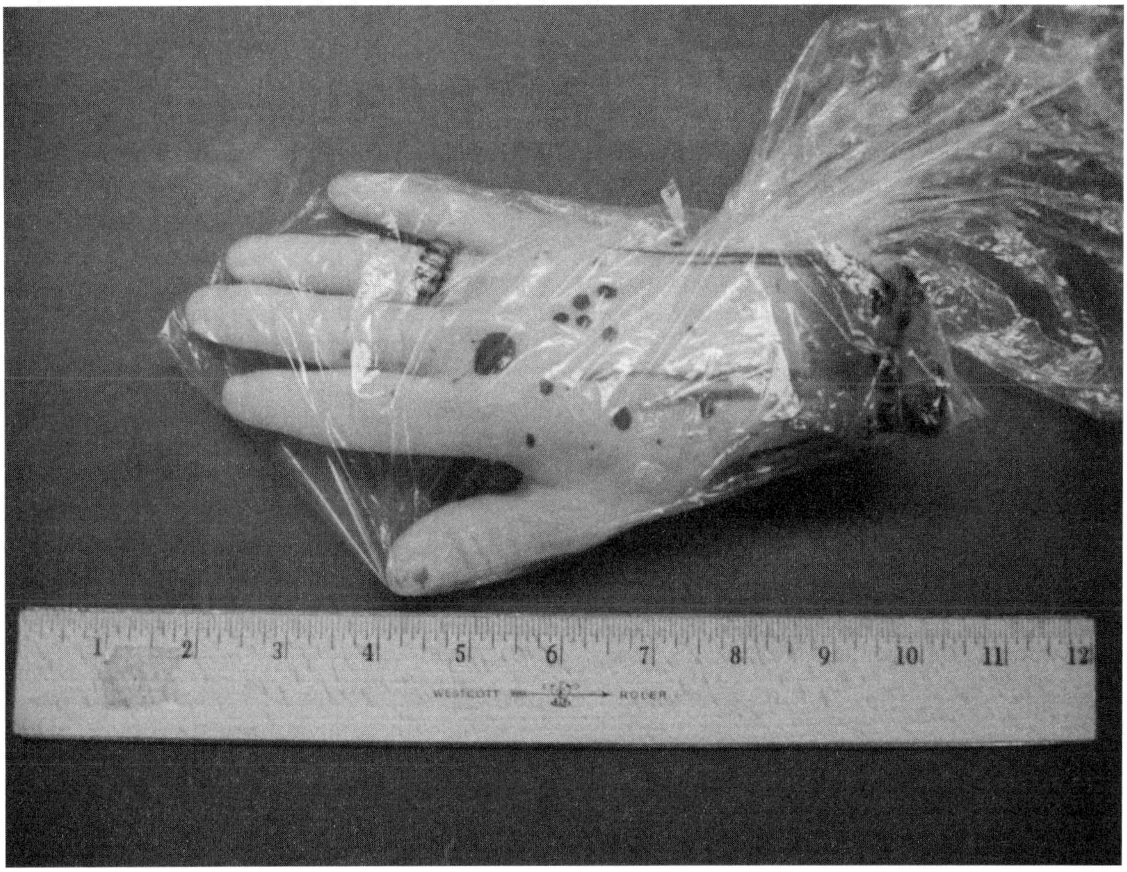

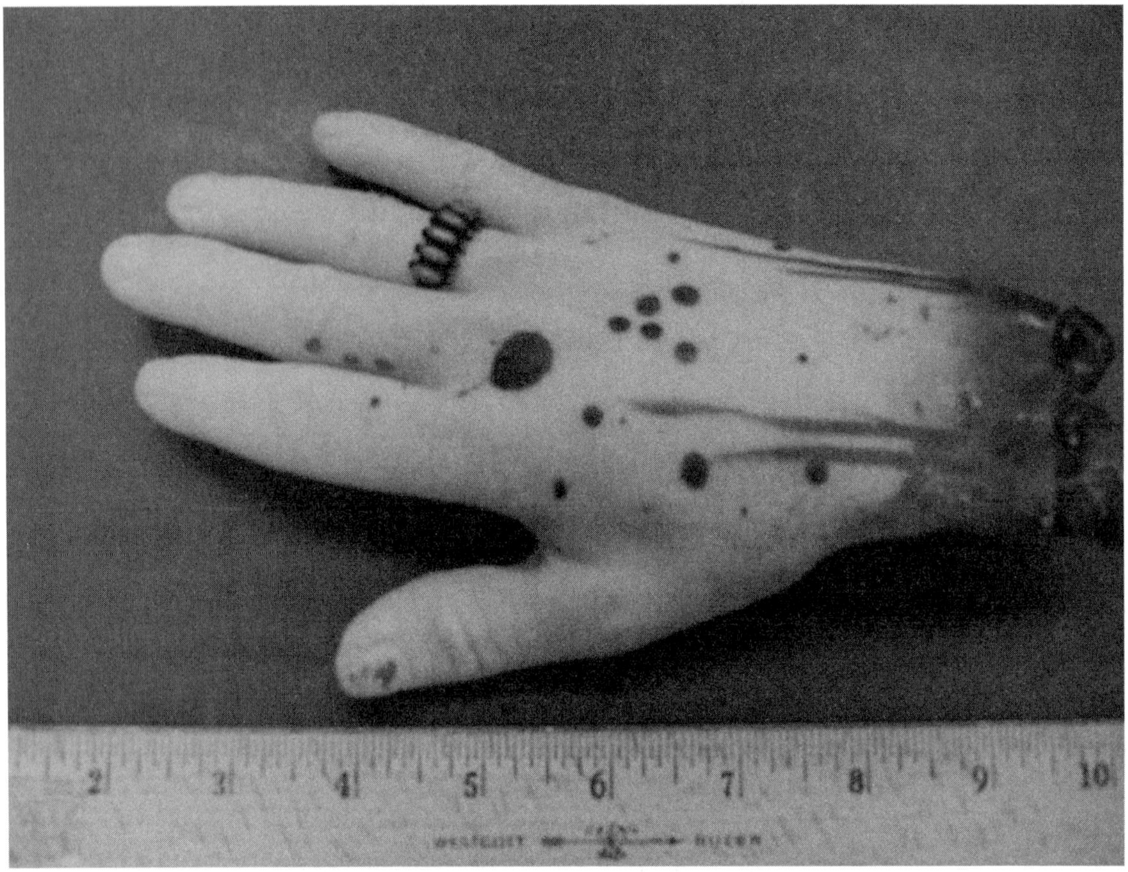
2 3 4 5 6 7 8 9 10

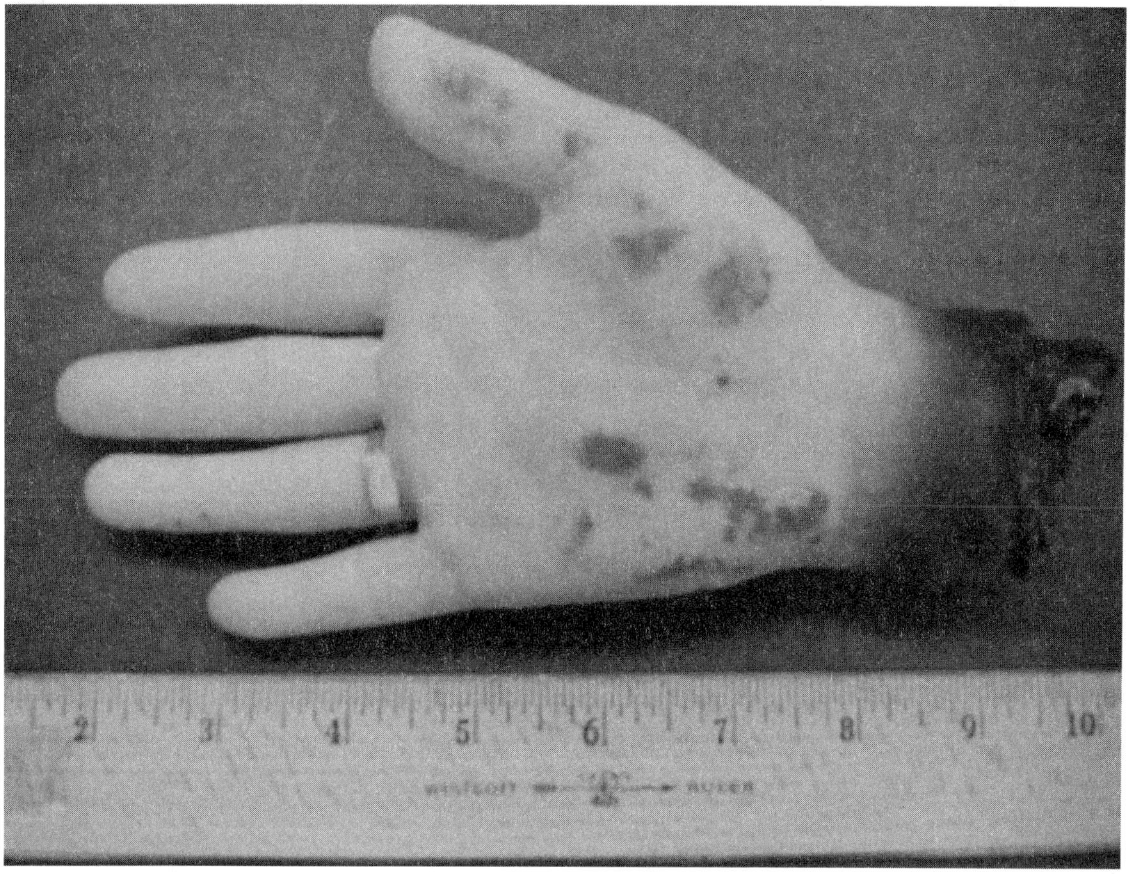

Photographs of Defendant's Truck

Check Written by Don Winston to Frank Norton

Don Winston
213 Wild Creek Ranch Rd
San Milano, State of Lone Star

No. 2367

Date *1-31-[YR-2]*

Pay to the Order of *Frank Norton* **$** *5,000.00*

Five Thousand and 00/100 ~~~~~~~~~~~~~~~~~~ ~~ **Dollars**

First National Bank of Lone Star
1278 Main Street
San Milano, State of Lone Star

For: *Boat Loan*

Don Winston

∞123⁝ 3432⁝ □4567 □ 7689

E-Mails Between Don Winston and Frank Norton

From: DWinston@gagacom.net
Sent: January 1, [YR-2] 2:31 PM
To: BNortonTheMan@lol.com
Subject: Done!!!

OK. Thanks man.

From: BNortonTheMan@lol.com
Sent: December 31, [YR-3] 5:00 AM
To: DWinston@gagacom.net
Subject: Done!!!

It's done. Proof is in your truck. Time to show me the money!!!

From: DWinston@gagacom.net
Sent: December 25, [YR-3] 11:40 PM
To: BNortonTheMan@lol.com
Subject: It's that Time

Hey buddy. It's time to do your thing. She is leaving me for some bubba. Remember, I need to know for certain that the deed has been done. Give me a hand on this, OK?

E-Mail Written by Nancy Mason

From: NMason@bol.net
Sent: December 25, [YR-3] 10:30 PM
To: MSnowy@gahoo.com; JulesSnorts@hadmail.com; DoodleDee@bol.com; Jen4Smartsy@gaggle.net
Subject: Leaving Town

Hey y'all

Just had dinner with Don and it's time to leave town for a few days with my BFF ("soul mate" for you Jules)("lover" for you Morgan). Had big fight with Don tonight so I know I am doing the right thing.

He loves me and says he wants to be with me forever. Going somewhere up north. Should be home in a couple of days. Stay out of trouble. LOL.

Hugs and kisses

GRANT OF IMMUNITY TO FRANK NORTON

THE STATE OF LONE STAR		IN COURT NO. 999
v.	}	
DON WINSTON		BEAR COUNTY, STATE OF LONE STAR

AGREEMENT FOR IMMUNITY

Whereas, The State of Lone Star is investigating allegations of criminal offenses by Don Winston, the Defendant.

Whereas, The State of Lone Star believes that Frank Norton, hereinafter referred to as "Witness," has material information regarding such criminal offense and that testimony regarding the same is crucial to the prosecution of the case; and whereas, said Witness represented by Jorge Sampson, attorney, is willing to waive his privilege against self-incrimination and to cooperate fully and testify truthfully in return for immunity from his testimony being used against him;

The Undersigned Parties agree to the following:

1. The Witness agrees to make a full and truthful statement to the law enforcement officers investigating the case, and to testify fully and truthfully in any judicial proceeding involving The State of Lone Star v. Don Winston.

2. The State of Lone Star, by and through its District Attorney, agree to grant said Witness testimonial immunity for this testimony, evidence, or information directly or indirectly derived from such testimony.

3. The Witness agrees and understands that if he perjures himself in the above styled case, the District Attorney can and will prosecute him for aggravated perjury and his involvement, if any, in the criminal conduct of the Defendant.

Agreed as to form and substance on this March 8, A.D., [YR-2].

Sam Ruffinsky

Sam Ruffinsky
Criminal District Attorney
Bear County, State of Lone Star
San Milano, State of Lone Star

Frank Norton
Witness

Jorge Sampson

Jorge Sampson
Attorney for Witness

Jury Instructions

LADIES AND GENTLEMEN OF THE JURY:

I am now going to instruct you about the law governing this case. You are required to accept my instructions as the law. Any ideas you have of what the law is or what the law should be or any statements by the attorneys as to what the law may be, must be disregarded by you, if they are in conflict with these instructions.

1. Claims of Parties

The plaintiff claims that he sustained damages due to the defendant's wrongful act of killing his daughter, Nancy Mason, the decedent. The defendant has denied those claims and also denies that the plaintiff is entitled to recover any damages.

2. Burden of Proof

In this case, the plaintiff has the burden of proving his claims by a preponderance of the evidence. If you find from the evidence, by a preponderance of the evidence, that the defendant acted intentionally in killing plaintiff's daughter, and that such actions were the proximate cause of his daughter's death, then you must find the defendant liable for his actions.

3. Proximate Cause

When I use the expression "proximate cause," I mean a cause that, in the natural or ordinary course of events, produced Nancy Mason's, the decedent's, death. It need not be the only cause, nor the last or nearest cause. It is sufficient if it combines with another cause resulting in the injury and death.

4. Preponderance of the Evidence

The term "preponderance of the evidence" means that amount of evidence that causes you to conclude that the allegation is probably true. To prove an allegation by the preponderance of the evidence, a party must convince you that the allegation is more likely true than not true.

If the evidence on a particular issue is equally balanced, that issue has not been proven by a preponderance of the evidence. Therefore, the party having the burden of proving that issue has failed with respect to that particular issue.

5. Circumstantial Evidence

A fact or a group of facts may, based on logic and common sense, lead you to a conclusion as to other facts. This is known as circumstantial evidence. A fact may be proved by circumstantial evidence. Circumstantial evidence is entitled to the same consideration as any other type of evidence

6. Opinion Testimony

You may have heard a witness give opinions about matters requiring special knowledge or skill. You should judge this testimony in the same way you judge the testimony from any other witness. The fact that such person has given an opinion does not mean that you are required to accept it. Give the testimony whatever weight you think it deserves, considering the reasons given for the opinion, the witness's qualifications, and all of the other evidence in the case.

7. Credibility of Witnesses

It is up to you to decide the credibility of the witnesses. In making the decision you may consider such factors as whether the witness has made a prior inconsistent statement or has been convicted of a crime. Evidence of this kind may be considered by you in connection with all the other facts and circumstances in evidence in deciding the weight to be given to the testimony of that witness.

8. Damages

a. General

If you decide the plaintiff is entitled to damages, you should give such amount as you decide to be fair and just, under all the circumstances. Such damages may include the following items, to the extent you find they have been proved by the evidence:

- Reasonable medical, hospital, funeral and burial expenses;
- Loss of financial support;
- Loss of gifts or other valuable gratuities;
- Loss of parental training and guidance;
- Loss of companionship;
- Plaintiff's grief, sorrow, or mental anguish.

Whether the plaintiff has proved these damages is for you to decide, based upon evidence and not upon speculation, guess, or conjecture. The amount of money to be awarded for certain of these elements of damage cannot be proved in a precise dollar amount. The law leaves such amounts to your sound judgment.

b. Punitive Damages

If you find for the plaintiff, you may, but are not required to, award punitive damages. The purposes of punitive damages are to punish a defendant and to deter similar acts in the future. Punitive damages may not be awarded to compensate a plaintiff.

The plaintiff has the burden of proving by a preponderance of the evidence that punitive damages should be awarded, and, if so, the amount of any such damages.

You may award punitive damages only if you find that the defendant's conduct that resulted in the death of Nancy Mason, the decedent, was a willful act or omission or gross negligence. Gross negligence means conduct or a failure to act that is so reckless that it demonstrates a substantial lack of concern for whether an injury will result.

If you find that punitive damages are appropriate, you must use reason in setting the amount. Punitive damages, if any, should be in an amount sufficient to fulfill their purposes but should not reflect bias, prejudice, or sympathy toward any party. In considering the amount of any punitive damages, consider the degree of reprehensibility of the defendant's conduct.

In addition, you may consider the relationship of any award of punitive damages to any actual harm inflicted on the plaintiff.

9. Insurance

Whether a party is insured or not insured has no bearing on any issue that you must decide. You must refrain from any inference, speculation, or discussion about insurance. If you find for the plaintiff, you shall not speculate about or consider any possible sources of benefits the plaintiff may have received or might receive. After you have returned your verdict, the court will make whatever adjustments are necessary in this regard.

10. Verdict Form

To assist you in deciding these issues, I am giving you a verdict form to use during your deliberations. When you have completed the form, please let the bailiff know that you have completed your deliberations.

VERDICT FORM

1. Liability

Do you find by a preponderance of the evidence that the defendant caused the death of the plaintiff's daughter?

_____ YES

_____ NO

If your answer is "no," then do not answer Question 2. If your answer is "yes," answer Question 2.

2. Damages

Do you find by a preponderance of the evidence that the plaintiff suffered damages as a result of the defendant's actions?

_____ YES

_____ NO

If you answered "yes," then please enter the amount of damages, in whole dollar amounts, to which the plaintiff is entitled.

$ ____________________

3. Punitive Damages

Do you find by a preponderance of the evidence that the decedent's death was the result of the defendant's willful act or omission or gross negligence in light of the circumstances?

_____ YES

_____ NO

If you answered "yes," then please enter the amount of punitive damages, in whole dollar amounts, to which the plaintiff is entitled.

$ ____________________

Chapter 18
State v. Moore

§ 18-1. Introduction

Alex Moore is charged with killing his sister, Robin Warren. On the night she was killed, the defendant, the victim, and the victim's husband Bradley Warren, had been drinking and arguing about a range of subjects including the victim's marriage and money that the victim owed the defendant. The defendant told the police that Bradley was the one who killed Robin and that the police had the wrong man.

§ 18-2. Stipulations Regarding Procedural and Evidentiary Matters

1. The case is being tried in a Lone Star court.
2. This case will be tried only on the issue of guilt or innocence.
3. All witnesses called to testify who made statements or grand jury testimony identifying the defendant, other individuals, or tangible evidence must, if asked, identify the same at trial.
4. Alex Moore, Jaime Hill and Bradley Warren signed their statements to the police.
5. Other than what is supplied in the problem itself, there is nothing exceptional or unusual about the background information of any of the witnesses or the defendant that would bolster or detract from their credibility.
6. The parties may not "invent" an individual not mentioned in this problem or to have testimony or evidence offered to the court or jury from that invented individual.
7. "Beyond the record" must not be made or entertained as an objection.
8. The current year is the year in which this case comes to trial.
9. If any rule of procedure or rule of evidence requires that notice be provided to the court or to the opponent, it will be assumed for the purpose of the problem that the required notice was given.
10. All exhibits in the file are authentic. In addition, each exhibit contained in the file is the original of that document unless otherwise noted on the exhibit or as established by the evidence.
11. Any searches and seizures conducted by the police met the requirements of the Fourth Amendment and the State's Rules of Criminal Procedure.
12. No changes or alterations were made to any of the exhibits.
13. There are no Confrontation Clause issues with regard to any written or oral hearsay statements.
14. The victim's lake house is located within Bear County, Lone Star.

15. At the time of trial, Jamie Hill is a clergy member.
16. The defendant's DNA was found under the victim's fingernails.

§ 18-3. Case File Materials

Students will be expected to use the following materials in presenting their cases.

I. Lone Star Penal Code Provisions

§ 79.01. Types of Criminal Homicide

(a) A person commits criminal homicide if he intentionally, knowingly, recklessly, or with criminal negligence causes the death of an individual.

(b) Criminal homicide is murder, capital murder, manslaughter, or criminally negligent homicide.

§ 79.02. Murder

(a) In this Section:

(1) "Adequate cause" means cause that would commonly produce a degree of anger, rage, resentment, or terror in a person of ordinary temper, sufficient to render the mind incapable of cool reflection.

(2) "Sudden passion" means passion directly caused by and arising out of provocation by the individual killed or another acting with the person killed which passion arises at the time of the offense and is not solely the result of former provocation.

(b) A person commits an offense if he:

(1) intentionally or knowingly causes the death of an individual;

(2) intends to cause serious bodily injury and commits an act clearly dangerous to human life that causes the death of an individual; or

(3) commits or attempts to commit a felony, other than manslaughter, and in the course of and in furtherance of the commission or attempt, or in immediate flight from the commission or attempt, he commits or attempts to commit an act clearly dangerous to human life that causes the death of an individual.

(c) Except as provided by Subsection (d), an offense under this section is a felony of the first degree.

(d) At the punishment stage of a trial, the defendant may raise the issue as to whether he caused the death under the immediate influence of sudden passion arising from an adequate cause. If the defendant proves the issue in the affirmative by a preponderance of the evidence, the offense is a felony of the second degree.

* * * * *

§ 79.04. Manslaughter

(a) A person commits an offense if he recklessly causes the death of an individual.

(b) An offense under this section is a felony of the second degree.

§ 79.05. Criminally Negligent Homicide

(a) A person commits an offense if he causes the death of an individual by criminal negligence.

(b) An offense under this section is a state jail felony.

Privilege for Clergy-Penitent Confidential Communications

Lone Star Statutory Clergy Privilege

§ 12-505. Communications to Members of the Clergy

(a) Definitions. As used in this rule:

(1) A "member of the clergy" is a minister, priest, rabbi, accredited Christian Science Practitioner, or other similar functionary of a religious organization or an individual reasonably believed so to be by the person consulting with such individual.

(2) A communication is "confidential" if made privately and not intended for further disclosure except to other persons present in furtherance of the purpose of the communication.

(b) General Rule of Privilege. A person has a privilege to refuse to disclose and to prevent another from disclosing a confidential communication by the person to a member of the clergy in the member's professional character as spiritual adviser.

(c) Who May Claim the Privilege. The privilege may be claimed by the person, by the person's guardian or conservator, or by the personal representative of the person if the person is deceased. The member of the clergy to whom the communication was made is presumed to have authority to claim or waive the privilege, but only on behalf of the communicant.

INDICTMENT

COURT'S COPY

Name:	Alex Moore
Complainant:	Robin Warren
Offense Charge:	Murder
GJ: 643421	**PH Court: 681**
JN#: 119352	**SID#: 1863184**

Witness: State's Attorney

TRUE BILL OF INDICTMENT

IN THE NAME AND BY AUTHORITY OF THE STATE OF LONE STAR, the Grand Jury of Bear County, State of Lone Star, duly organized, empanelled by the Judicial District Court of said County, at said term, do present in and to said Court that in the County and State aforesaid, and anterior to the presentment of this indictment, and:

COUNT 1: MURDER

on or about August 6, [YR-1], ALEX MOORE, hereinafter referred to as defendant, then and there intentionally or knowingly, unlawfully, and feloniously cause the killing and murder of ROBIN WARREN, a human being, hereinafter referred to as complainant, without the authority of law and with deliberate design to effect the death of complainant in violation of Section 79.02, Lone Star Penal Code;

AGAINST THE PEACE AND DIGNITY OF THE STATE

Charles A. Tripp
Foreperson of the Grand Jury

DEFENDANT'S FIRST WRITTEN STATEMENT TO POLICE

STATE OF LONE STAR } **Case Number: 12-81377**
COUNTY OF BEAR }

VOLUNTARY STATEMENT OF: ALEX MOORE

I, Alex Moore, after first being duly warned by Det. B. Rodriguez #6387 at 0730 hrs, at 214 W. Nueva, on August 6, [YR-1] that (1) I have the right to remain silent and not make any statement at all, and any statement I do make may be used against me at my trial; (2) Any statement I make may be used as evidence against me in Court; (3) I have the right to have a lawyer present to advise me prior to and during any questioning; (4) If I am unable to employ a lawyer, I have the right to have a lawyer appointed to advise me prior to and during any questioning; (5) I have the right to terminate the interview at any time; and I understand that the above rights are continuing rights and may be urged by me at any stage of the proceedings, and I hereby prior to and during the making of this statement, knowingly, intelligently, and voluntarily waive the above rights and give to the said, Det. Blair Rodriguez #6387, the person to whom this statement is being given, the following written statement:

My name is Alex Moore. Robin Warren was my sister.

Like I told you earlier at the house, I was in bed sleeping until about 1 a.m. We had stayed up late together and crashed about 11 p.m. I fell asleep, clothes and all. When I woke up about 4 a.m., I had to use the bathroom. So I got up and walked out of my room.

When I was coming back from the bathroom, I heard Bradley yelling to call 911 as he came in from the dock, and yelling that something had happened to Robin. I was shocked and disoriented. I remember fumbling for my cell phone from the nightstand, and running out to the dock while on the phone with 911.

When I got to the dock I saw Robin laying face down on the boat, toward the front of the boat. I tried to check her to see if she had a pulse and held her in my arms and screamed her name.

I came back up to the house to wait for you guys to show up after I realized there was nothing I could do. Robin was dead.

The scratches on my arms are from an argument I had with my sister earlier this evening. She was going to leave Bradley, but became angry when I told her that she needed to do it the next day. She told me she wanted to do it on her own terms, yelling at me and scratching me.

Bradley overheard us arguing about her leaving him. He became very angry and we argued as well. He yelled at me, "Our relationship is none of your business." Then he leaned in and said, "Keep your nose out of it or I'll make sure you never see her again."

I honestly think you guys should be looking at him for murdering my sister. He started abusing her about a year after they were married, and she's called 911 several times. He's an abusive, mean guy.

I also do not remember if he had blood on him when he came in yelling for me to call 911.

This is the end of my statement. I have read this statement and it is true and correct.

WITNESS: *Blair Rodriguez* SIGNATURE: *Alex Moore*

DATE: Aug. 6, [-1]

DEFENDANT'S SECOND WRITTEN STATEMENT TO POLICE

STATE OF LONE STAR COUNTY OF BEAR	}	Case Number: 12-81377

VOLUNTARY STATEMENT OF: ALEX MOORE

I, Alex Moore, after first being duly warned by Det. B. Rodriguez #6387 at 0730 hrs, at 214 W. Nueva, on August 8, [YR-1] that (1) I have the right to remain silent and not make any statement at all, and any statement I do make may be used against me at my trial; (2) Any statement I make may be used as evidence against me in Court; (3) I have the right to have a lawyer present to advise me prior to and during any questioning; (4) If I am unable to employ a lawyer, I have the right to have a lawyer appointed to advise me prior to and during any questioning; (5) I have the right to terminate the interview at any time; and I understand that the above rights are continuing rights and may be urged by me at any stage of the proceedings, and I hereby prior to and during the making of this statement, knowingly, intelligently, and voluntarily waive the above rights and give to the said, Det. Blair Rodriguez #6387, the person to whom this statement is being given, the following written statement:

I did not kill my sister, Robin Warren. I am certain that her husband, Bradley Warren, killed her in a violent fit of rage.

It is my understanding that Bradley has attempted to blame me for Robin's death. I would NEVER kill my sister over money.

Robin started college in [YR-8] and graduated in [YR-4]. She went to Altross State University here in the State of Lone Star. She got a bachelor's degree in business, as I recall. During the time she was in school, I paid for her tuition and living expenses so that she could focus on school. Our dad had died in [YR-12], when she was just 14, so I had become the man of the house. I wanted to make sure Robin got a good education. Although I insisted it be a gift, she insisted on paying me back. Ultimately, we agreed it would be a loan, but with no interest.

All total, I loaned her about $100,000.00 for her education.

In February of [YR-4], our mom was killed in a horrific car accident. I didn't handle it well. Although I had been undercover a couple years, and was making good progress on the case I was working, I blew it. Losing our mom killed me. I started drinking heavily and doing drugs. Sometime in April of [YR-4] I disappeared for a few months. I am not even sure what I was doing during that time. I wasn't around when Robin met Bradley. I wish every day I had been so that I could have kept her from marrying him. Maybe I could have pointed out the warning signs I saw. Maybe I could have showed her what he was really like.

I guess it was sometime in June that I was arrested and charged with my first crime, drug possession. After a couple more charges, I was discharged from the police department in October of [YR-4].

The first charge was that drug possession in June of [YR-4]. In connection with that I had an aggravated assault charge. While undercover I stabbed a female drug trafficker. She had come at me with a knife during an argument, and I wrestled with her to get it away from her. Somewhere in the scuffle I stabbed her once, but I was still charged with the crime. I also had a small baggie of crack cocaine on me, so that's where the drug possession came from.

My other charge before I was discharged from the force in October of '09 was another aggravated assault. I got into a heated argument with a superior officer. She refused to let me handle some information I had received from an informant the way I wanted to, and I guess I pulled a knife. I know I would never have hurt her, but I was so into the drugs and alcohol at that point I wasn't thinking clearly.

Within a couple weeks of my discharge from the police department, I checked myself into rehab. I knew I needed help.

When I got out in May of [YR-3], I got my own place and started working. I wanted to make something of myself again before I went back around Robin. She deserved the brother she used to have, not what I was then. But I relapsed again in July of [YR-3]. I spent another six months in rehab, and then started again. By June of [YR-2], a good five months after I got out of rehab, I looked Robin up. I hoped our relationship would be like it was before I disappeared.

Unfortunately, it wasn't. Robin's husband Bradley didn't want me around. At first, I couldn't blame him. I figured Robin had told him about my past. That I had just up and disappeared on her when she must have been grieving, too. But then I realized it was more sinister than that. Robin and I had talked about her paying me back to help get me back on my feet. I guess Bradley felt that Robin didn't owe me a thing. He did not have a clue as to how much I had sacrificed to get Robin through school.

Robin and I had a friend we grew up with, Jaime Hill, who became a minister about the time Robin graduated from college. When I came back around in June of [YR-2], I also started talking to Jaime again. Jaime told me that Robin had come to talk about her marriage to Bradley because he had become abusive and Robin didn't know what to do. Jaime tried to give Robin some spiritual advice, referred Robin to various agencies when she still wasn't sure what to do, and even had started arrangements for Robin to leave Bradley at one point. Jaime told me that there were times that Robin may have called 911.

I started poking around and found out that Robin had called 911 about Bradley's violence before. You guys should really be looking at him. I would never, NEVER hurt Robin for money. I knew she would pay me back eventually.

Like I said before, our fight the night of the 5th was because Robin and I were arguing about when she was going to leave Bradley. We had been drinking that day and probably weren't thinking as clear as we would have been if we had been sober. But it wasn't a question of "if" Robin was leaving him. It was a question of "when." I wanted Robin to leave him the next day, and it was just that Robin wanted more time to plan her escape from him.

It was my job to protect her. I feel like I failed by not talking to her in a place where Bradley couldn't hear us, and that I should have insisted she leave with me that night instead of staying one more night with him. I'm sure if I had, Robin would still be alive.

WITNESS: *Jane Hernandez* SIGNATURE: Alex Moore

DATE: Aug. 8, [YR-1]

Jamie Hill's Letter to The Police

To Whom It May Concern: Aug. 8, [YR-1]

My name is Jaime Hill. I am a family friend of Alex Moore, and was a long-time friend of Robin Warren before her death. I am writing this letter because I have learned of Robin's death and have information to assist you in your investigation of her death.

I spoke with Robin numerous times before her death about leaving Bradley. She had confided in me that Bradley had become very abusive after their marriage. She told me on several occasions, "I'm scared for my life. I believe Bradley may kill me one of these days." Robin also told me she believed Bradley had taken out a life insurance policy on her for that very reason.

Although Alex has made mistakes in his past, that in no way affects his love for his sister. I've known Alex and Robin since the three of us were children. He would never, ever, have hurt Robin.

Robin told me several times that if anything happened to her that I should contact the police and tell them everything she told me about her husband.

Please let me know if I can be of further assistance,

Respectfully yours,

Jaime Hill

JAIME HILL'S WRITTEN STATEMENT TO POLICE

STATE OF LONE STAR **COUNTY OF BEAR**	}	**Case Number: 12-81377**

VOLUNTARY STATEMENT OF: JAIME HILL

I, Jaime Hill, after first being duly warned by Det. B. Rodriguez #6387 at 0700 hrs, at 214 W. Nueva, on August 14, [YR-1] that (1) I have the right to remain silent and not make any statement at all, and any statement I do make may be used against me at my trial; (2) Any statement I make may be used as evidence against me in Court; (3) I have the right to have a lawyer present to advise me prior to and during any questioning; (4) If I am unable to employ a lawyer, I have the right to have a lawyer appointed to advise me prior to and during any questioning; (5) I have the right to terminate the interview at any time; and I understand that the above rights are continuing rights and may be urged by me at any stage of the proceedings, and I hereby prior to and during the making of this statement, knowingly, intelligently, and voluntarily waive the above rights and give to the said, Det. Blair Rodriguez #6387, the person to whom this statement is being given, the following written statement:

My name is Jaime Hill. I am a very good friend to Alex Moore, and was a very good friend of Robin Warren when she was alive.

I grew up with Alex and Robin, and had known Alex and Robin since long before their father died in [YR-12]. They were very close growing up, but when their father died, Alex stepped in and became more of a father to Robin. He's always tried to be there for her and do everything he can to help her, no matter what the cost to himself.

When Alex disappeared, Robin was very vulnerable. I believe she fell into the relationship with Bradley Warren because he provided what appeared to be a steady rock for her. They met the same month that Alex disappeared, and were married just three months later. However, I realized quickly that Bradley's apparent steadiness was a façade for his abusive nature.

Robin came to me several times after she married Bradley in August of [YR-4] and told me that he had become abusive. I was working as a minister at that point, and Robin would come to the church to speak with me, or would call me at home if I weren't at the church. Several times she showed me the bruises that she got when Bradley hit her.

I attempted to provide spiritual guidance for Robin, but when that didn't seem to help, I also provided a shoulder to cry on and personal advice. Many times it seemed like Robin wanted to leave Bradley, and I even helped her begin preparing an escape plan shortly before her death in August. I think it was about July 5th or 6th.

In the days leading up to the 4th of July they had been in their honeymoon phase. Everything was wonderful and Bradley had been surprising Robin with all sorts of surprises like flowers and chocolates. I knew that it was only a matter of time before he snapped again. Sure enough, on the 4th of July Bradley viciously attacked Robin again. She came to me while I was at the church the next day, very distraught, and told me vehemently, "I am leaving him, no matter what it takes."

Robin had also discovered Bradley had taken out a very high dollar amount life insurance policy on her and the idea terrified her. I do not know the amount of the policy. But she was very worried he might try to make her death look like an accident, or that someone else had murdered her, just to get away with killing her, then take the money to start over and find another woman to abuse and control.

Robin was convinced she needed to plan when she left perfectly. Robin wouldn't leave Bradley without planning every last detail. When I talked to Alex the day after Robin's death, and he told me about their fight, I realized that Robin probably panicked when Bradley overheard her saying she was leaving him. Robin told me once, "He will never let me leave him. It'll be over his dead body."

I am 100% sure that Bradley murdered Robin because he would never have let her leave him. Alex would never have hurt Robin. Never. He is not that kind of man. The Alex I know is a changed man and has turned his life around and is non-aggressive.

WITNESS: Blair Rodriguez SIGNATURE: Jaime Hill

DATE: Aug. 14, [YR-1]

BRADLEY WARREN'S WRITTEN STATEMENT TO POLICE

STATE OF LONE STAR **COUNTY OF BEAR**	}	**Case Number: 12-81377**

VOLUNTARY STATEMENT OF: BRADLEY WARREN

I, Bradley Warren, after first being duly warned by Det. B. Rodriguez #6387 at 0800 hrs, at 214 W. Nueva, on August 7, [YR-1] that (1) I have the right to remain silent and not make any statement at all, and any statement I do make may be used against me at my trial; (2) Any statement I make may be used as evidence against me in Court; (3) I have the right to have a lawyer present to advise me prior to and during any questioning; (4) If I am unable to employ a lawyer, I have the right to have a lawyer appointed to advise me prior to and during any questioning; (5) I have the right to terminate the interview at any time; and I understand that the above rights are continuing rights and may be urged by me at any stage of the proceedings, and I hereby prior to and during the making of this statement, knowingly, intelligently, and voluntarily waive the above rights and give to the said, Det. Blair Rodriguez #6387, the person to whom this statement is being given, the following written statement:

My name is Bradley Warren. I am giving this statement because my wife, Robin Warren, was murdered two days ago. By her brother, Alex Moore. I know it had something to do with the money he loaned her.

We all went to bed about 11 p.m. While I was lying in bed, Robin told me she thought the boat wasn't secured to the dock. I was very tired, so she offered to check it. She left to go check it and I must have fallen asleep.

The next thing I remember was waking up and Robin wasn't in bed. I think it was about 4 a.m. I went to find her. When I passed by the guest room I noticed the door was standing open about a foot and a half. Robin's brother Alex was staying in that room. I looked in and he wasn't there.

I looked into the living room and the dining room, but neither of them was there.

I ran out to the dock because I saw a light on it. It was not moving. I was afraid something had happened to my wife. When I got there, I saw it was our flashlight. We keep the flashlight, an industrial one, in the kitchen. I picked it up and found Robin on the boat. I tried to help her, but there was nothing I could do. One of our knives that we keep on the boat was next to her. I picked it up and ran back to the house.

I ran back to the house and screamed for Alex to call 911. The next thing I remember was trying to get Robin's blood off of me, and then the police showing up.

I think I must have put the knife on the sink. It's a hunting type knife that we have had for years and use it on the boat for general stuff like cutting bait. I am not sure whether I cleaned it or not. I was in such as state of shock I guess I just don't know.

WITNESS: *Blair Rodriguez* SIGNATURE: *Bradley Warren*

DATE: Aug. 7, [YR-1]

Grand Jury Testimony of Bradley Warren

IN RE:		BEFORE THE GRAND JURY
	}	OF
GRAND JURY INVESTIGATION		BEAR COUNTY, STATE OF LONE STAR

* * * * * *

****

COURT REPORTER'S

Q AND A TRANSCRIPT OF TESTIMONY OF

BRADLEY WARREN

AUGUST 9, [YR-1]

****

* * * * *

BE IT REMEMBERED, that on AUGUST 9, [YR-1], the above-entitled matter came on for hearing before the Grand Jury of Bear County, sitting in San Milano, State of Lone Star, being presented by DAVID ANDERSON, Assistant Criminal District Attorney, for consideration by the members thereof.

VERONICA GARCIA was duly sworn as Court Reporter.

WHEREUPON, the following evidence was introduced and proceedings had, to-wit, beginning at 12:30 o'clock p.m. and concluding at 1:30 o'clock p.m.

BRADLEY WARREN, The Witness.

GRAND JURY FOREMAN: Do you solemnly swear that you will not divulge either by words or signs any matter about which you may be interrogated, and that you will keep secret all proceedings of the Grand Jury which may be had in your presence, and that you will true answers make to such questions as may be propounded to you by the Grand Jury or under its direction, so help you God?

THE WITNESS: I do.

EXAMINATION BY DAVID ANDERSON:

Q: Good morning Mr. Warren.

A: Good morning, sir.

Q: Before we get started, as with any witness who comes before the Grand Jury, I need to give you the definitions of perjury and aggravated perjury.

A: Of course.

Q: A person commits the offense of perjury if, with intent to deceive and with knowledge of the statement's meaning, that person makes a false statement under oath or swears to the truth of a false statement previously made and the statement is required or authorized by law to be made under oath.

Perjury is a Class A Misdemeanor, which is punishable by anywhere up to one year in the Bear County Jail and/or a fine of up to $4,000.

Perjury becomes aggravated perjury if the person commits perjury, makes that false statement during or in connection with an official proceeding, and Grand Jury proceedings are official proceedings, and the statement is material.

Aggravated perjury is a third-degree felony, which means it's punishable by anywhere from two to ten years in the Lone Star Department of Corrections, and there's a potential fine of up to $10,000. Do you understand this?

A: Yes, sir.

Q: Would you please state your name for the grand jury?

A: Yes, my name is Bradley Warren.

Q: Could you please tell us your relationship to Mrs. Warren?

A: Yes, she was my wife. She was murdered the night of August 5th.

Q: Do you mean the early morning of August 6th?

A: Yes, that is what I meant.

Q: Can you tell us about that night?

A: We were at our vacation home, just outside of San Milano on Town Lake.

Q: Here in Bear County?

A: Yes.

Q: Okay. Go ahead.

A: We, that is my wife — Robin — and her brother — Alex. [Clears throat and pauses.] The three of us had been drinking a good bit and spending some time visiting before we all headed home the next morning. It got pretty loud at some points. Alex and Robin started arguing about the money that Alex claimed Robin owed him and she said that he was a loser and that she did not intend to pay him back. She accused him of having gotten the money by selling drugs and that he had no right to ask her to repay him. At one point they shoved each other around a bit. I stayed out of it until Alex started to tell Robin that she needed to leave me and that the only reason that she was saying those things was because she was afraid of me. That is when I got into it with Alex and told him to shut up and go to bed. I had heard the two of them talking earlier in the day about her leaving me. Well, we all headed to bed around 11 p.m. I was exhausted and crashed almost as soon as I hit the bed. I vaguely remember Robin telling me she thought the boat wasn't secure. Then I heard her say she was going down to check it. I glanced at the clock as she walked out and saw it was about 11:15.

Q: What happened next?

A: I woke up about 4 a.m. and I realized Robin was not in the bed. I was really worried. I got out of bed to go find her. I walked out of our bedroom still sleepy. I noticed the guest door was standing partially open as I passed by it and glanced in. I saw the blanket had been laid on, and the pillow was . . . what's the word I'm looking for. . . scrunched? But the blankets hadn't been pulled back and slept under. Anyway, I figured that Alex and Robin might be talking in the living area, or outside.

Q: Is that where you headed?

A: Yes. I walked to the front rooms of the house, but didn't see them. It was eerily quiet. I walked over to the kitchen sink and looked down the path toward the dock. I noticed that there was a light coming from the end of the dock. By this point I had woken up enough to realize that wasn't right. As I walked down to the dock, it hit me that the light was coming from a flashlight on the path. I later recognized it as the industrial one we keep in our kitchen.

Q: What happened next?

A: Once I reached the flashlight, I picked it up and started looking for Robin. I saw her lying on the deck of the boat as I shined the flashlight in that direction. I jumped on the boat and dropped the flashlight to check her and see if she was okay.

Q: Did you say anything?

A: I don't remember . . . I just remember dropping to my knees. She was lying face down. I tried to pull her into my lap and feel for a pulse on her throat, but there wasn't one and she was cold. I panicked. There was blood all over her blouse, on the front.

Q: What happened then?

A: I don't remember everything in detail. I just gently put her back down. I remember yelling out for Alex. But he did not come out. So I ran up the path toward the house yelling for him to call the police and yelling Robin's name. I was so out of it. I know I cleaned up in the kitchen sink before the police arrived. I couldn't stand having Robin's blood on me.

Q: What happened once the police arrived?

A: I spoke with Detective Rodriguez and then Detective Rodriguez spoke with Alex. After that, Detective Rodriguez went out back to look around and shortly after took Alex down to the police station.

Q: Did you wonder why Detective Rodriguez was taking Alex into custody?

A: No. I remember telling Detective Rodriguez that I thought Alex was responsible for Robin's death. I know he murdered Robin. Rodriguez asked me if I thought that anyone else might have done it and I said that we had seen a strange man walking around the lake at night, but that based on what I saw, I was convinced that Alex killed her.

Q: How do you know that?

A: Alex isn't a good person. Alex has been in trouble since Robin was a teenager. From what Robin told me, Alex was a police officer, but ended up a dirty cop. He went undercover a couple years before their mother passed away and disappeared entirely after she died. Alex dabbled in drugs, alcohol, and even got kicked off the force for some violent incidents. There was even talk that he had stolen drugs from the evidence room and sold them to get some extra money. Robin wouldn't tell me exactly what that was all about, but when he came looking for her a couple of years ago. I can tell you I wasn't pleased. I didn't want him back in her life. All he would talk about was getting his money.

Q: Did anything else make you think Alex was responsible for her death?

A: Well, I didn't see him in bed when I passed by looking for Robin. And like I said, the sheets didn't look slept in, just laid on. He probably would have gotten away with it if I wouldn't have passed by his room and noticed that.

Q: Mr. Warren, could you tell us some more about the money that Alex said Robin owed to him?

A: Well, Robin had borrowed money from Alex. I didn't know about it until well after Robin and I had been involved for some time. Honestly, it was more a gift than a loan. He had offered to pay for her education and her expenses while she was in college. . . . But she insisted that he let her pay him back once she graduated. For the four years she was in college, he paid everything.

Q: Please continue.

A: Well, when Alex came back into Robin's life, I knew he was just after his money. She was so happy to have him back in her life, but then that all changed when he asked about the money. Robin wasn't sure if she still wanted a relationship with him, or if she was going to just pay him some money to go away, or what to do.

Q: Did you know anything else about the money?

A: Yeah, the weekend he was visiting us she was still deciding what she wanted to do about Alex. She told me that she had found out the money was dirty money from his days undercover and she told me she wouldn't be a part of that by paying it back. I know that Alex just wanted the money, one way or another.

Q: Do you know how much Alex was alleging Robin owed him?

A: Yes, about $100,000 in total.

Q: Do you have anything else to tell the Grand Jury?

A: No.

QUESTION FROM GRAND JUROR

Q: You told Detective Rodriguez that there was a stranger in the area?

A: Yes. I didn't think it was of much importance, so I didn't mention it until later. It was just some strange guy I noticed off and on, standing on the shoreline.

QUESTION FROM ANOTHER GRAND JUROR

Q: But you said that that person would be the only other suspect?

A: I did not murder my wife. Nor would anyone I know who lives up by our lake house. So yes that would be the only other suspect.

QUESTION FROM THIRD GRAND JUROR

Q: Did you have a life insurance policy out on your wife?

A: Yes, I did. My work offers life insurance for both employees and their spouses. I took one out simply because it seemed like the responsible thing to do.

Q: Did you file a claim?

A: Yes.

Q: When?

A: Shortly after she died. I needed the money to help pay bills that I had incurred. Funeral expenses. Lawyer costs for doing her estate, you know.

Q: Have you been paid?

A: No, not yet.

QUESTION FROM SECOND GRAND JUROR

Q: Did you ever harm your wife?

A: We had our fights. But they weren't as bad as they may sound.

DAVID ANDERSON

Q: Thank you Mr. Warren. Would you please step outside for a few minutes?

A: Yes.

[Witness steps outside at 1:30 p.m. and is subsequently dismissed.]

(END OF TRANSCRIPT)

Resume of Blair Rodriguez

Blair Rodriguez

Homicide Detective
San Milano, State of Lone Star

Experience

Homicide Detective, City of San Milano, State of Lone Star — July [YR-1] – Present

- Responsible for approximately 50 homicide investigations to date, with 20 convictions resulting from those investigations. Only two homicide investigations currently open. Currently certified in Forensics Collection.

Police Officer, City of San Milano, State of Lone Star — August [YR-5] – July [YR-0]

Education

- Forensics Collection — May [YR-5] – August [YR-5]

  Training in proper collection of evidence, including DNA, fingerprints, and weapons. Training on what evidence to collect as well; although the evidence may not appear out of the ordinary, it could be critical to an investigation.

- Police Academy — May [YR-6] – May [YR-5]

  Top 5% of the City of San Milano Police Training Academy.

- Brackettville High School — Graduated May [YR-5]

Additional

Have testified regarding investigations in 48 cases.

Currently researching to write an article entitled "Proper Homicide Investigation: A Fail-Proof Checklist for Correct Identification of the Culprit."

Grand Jury Testimony of Blair Rodriguez

IN RE:		BEFORE THE GRAND JURY
	}	OF
GRAND JURY INVESTIGATION		BEAR COUNTY, STATE OF LONE STAR

****

COURT REPORTER'S

Q AND A TRANSCRIPT OF TESTIMONY OF

DET. BLAIR RODRIGUEZ

AUGUST 9, [YR-1]

****

* * * * *

BE IT REMEMBERED, that on AUGUST 9, [YR-1], the above-entitled matter came on for hearing before the Grand Jury of Bear County, sitting in San Milano, State of Lone Star, being presented by DAVID ANDERSON, Assistant Criminal District Attorney, for consideration by the members thereof.

VERONICA GARCIA was duly sworn as Court Reporter.

WHEREUPON, the following evidence was introduced and proceedings had, to-wit, beginning at 10:00 o'clock a.m. and concluding at 11:00 o'clock a.m.

DETECTIVE BLAIR RODRIGUEZ, The Witness.

GRAND JURY FOREMAN: Do you solemnly swear that you will not divulge either by words or signs any matter about which you may be interrogated, and that you will keep secret all proceedings of the Grand Jury which may be had in your presence, and that you will true answers make to such questions as may be propounded to you by the Grand Jury or under its direction, so help you God?

THE WITNESS: I do.

EXAMINATION BY DAVID ANDERSON:

Q: Detective Rodriguez, as with any witness who comes before the Grand Jury, I need to give you the definitions of perjury and aggravated perjury.

A person commits the offense of perjury if, with intent to deceive and with knowledge of the statement's meaning, that person makes a false statement under oath or swears to the truth of a false statement previously made and the statement is required or authorized by law to be made under oath.

Perjury is a Class A Misdemeanor, which is punishable by anywhere up to one year in the Bear County Jail and/or a fine of up to $4,000.

Perjury becomes aggravated perjury if the person commits perjury, makes that false statement during or in connection with an official proceeding, and Grand Jury proceedings are official proceedings, and the statement is material.

Aggravated perjury is a third-degree felony, which means it's punishable by anywhere from two to ten years in the Lone Star Department of Corrections, and there's a potential fine of up to $10,000. Do you understand this?

A: Yes, sir.

Q: Would you please state your name for the grand jury?

A: Yes, my name is Blair Rodriguez.

Q: Could you please tell us your position and duties with the police department?

A: I am a homicide detective, with about 5 years' experience on the force. My duties entail conducting investigations into possible homicides.

Q: You are a member of the San Milano Police Department?

A: Yes.

Q: Okay. Detective, I would like you to tell the grand jurors about your investigation into the death of Mrs. Robin Warren.

A: Our records show that on August 6, [YR-1], at 4:06 a.m. we received a 911 call requesting emergency medical services and police, to 143 Cottonwood Lane, here in Bear County. I was dispatched to that location and arrived on scene at about 4:15 a.m.

Q: What happened once you arrived?

A: Once I arrived on scene, I proceeded to the front door of the residence and was met by a man identified to me as Bradley Warren, the decedent's husband. He was clearly distraught; his eyes were red and it looked as though he had been rubbing at his face and pulling on his hair.

Q: Did you notice anything else?

A: Yes. He was wearing a bloody t-shirt and bloody pajama pants. However his arms had no blood on them. He also had no shoes on.

Q: What happened after he met you at the door?

A: First I spoke with Mr. Warren regarding what had occurred that evening. EMS had informed me that Robin Warren had been deceased for some length of time, enough that they could not resuscitate her.

Q: And what did you learn from that conversation with Mr. Warren?

A: I learned that Mrs. Warren's brother, Alex Moore, had been visiting at their lake house, the residence I was called to, for the weekend. The three of them had been visiting until about 11 p.m. at which point they went to their respective rooms of the home to go to bed.

Q: What else did you learn?

A: Not much. Mr. Warren was only able to tell me bits and pieces of what had occurred that night, as he was very emotionally distraught. He was unable to give me a complete, comprehensive version of what had occurred that evening.

Q: Please tell us what you were able to gather from the bits and pieces.

A: I gathered that Mr. Warren had been sleeping until about 4:00 a.m., or so, at which point he realized his wife had never come to bed. At that point he went to go find her.

Q: And he found her?

A: Yes, he told me he had seen a light on the path down to the dock. I understood from the bits and pieces he was able to say that once he got out to the dock he recognized the light as the industrial strength flashlight from their kitchen. He said he picked it up to look for her and found her on the deck of the boat. At this point he became so unintelligible that I told him I would go speak to Mr. Moore.

Q: Did he say anything else of importance?

A: Not at that point. Before I left, he did manage to convey that he believed Mr. Moore was responsible for her death.

Q: At any point did you think that Mr. Warren was a suspect?

A: No. His visible reaction was consistent with that I've seen in the spouses of homicide victims.

Q: Did Mr. Warren explain the lack of blood on his hands or arms?

A: I later asked him about it and he informed me that he had checked Mrs. Warren when he found her on the boat. After checking his wife he couldn't stand having her blood on him. He told me he had washed off in the kitchen sink while Mr. Moore called 911.

Q: What did you do after speaking with Mr. Warren, Detective?

A: Again, at this point, I told Mr. Warren I would be speaking to Mr. Moore. He pointed me to the bedrooms, where I found Mr. Moore.

Q: What can you tell us about Mr. Moore?

A: Mr. Moore was sitting in his bedroom. He seemed to be very calm for the circumstances, but it was a strange kind of calm. Something was off. I also noticed he had bloodshot eyes, blood on his shirt and arms, as well as fresh scratches on his arms.

Q: Did you speak with Mr. Moore?

A: Yes, I did. I asked him what he could tell me about the evening before and what had happened up until we arrived on scene.

Q: What did he tell you?

A: Mr. Moore told me that the three of them had gone to bed around 11:00 or 11:30 p.m. after arguing about what he described as "meaningless stuff." He said that he would always regret that his last words to his sister were words of anger. He told me he had awakened around 4:00 a.m. needing to use the bathroom. He had just returned to his bed when Mr. Warren came in screaming to call 911.

Q: Did he tell you anything else of importance?

A: Yes. Mr. Moore told me that he grabbed his cell phone and called 911 as he ran out to the dock. He told me that he thought maybe he could help his sister and attempted to check her, getting blood on himself in the process.

Q: Did Mr. Moore explain how he had gotten the scratches on his arms?

A: No, he did not.

Q: Did you ask him?

A: I did. And he just looked at the scratches and mumbled that he did not know. And he added that he did not care.

Q: What did you do next, Detective?

A: I proceeded outside to investigate the scene.

Q: And what can you tell us about that?

A: Well, the deputies that had arrived on scene with me had already gone out back to preserve the scene. By the time I got out there, it was around 5:00 a.m. I did not have my camera at the time. We had to wait for the medical examiner to arrive, so we did not take the picture of the victim until later in the morning. I took the knife that we found on the kitchen sink and processed it. I also looked for other relevant evidence.

Q: Such as?

A: Anything else that could have been relevant. In other cases there have been footprints in the blood of the victim, or something the attacker dropped.

Q: Did you find any of that here?

A: No, I did not. However, there was something that stood out to me. We were unable to find the industrial flashlight that Mr. Warren alleged he had seen on the dock and used in finding Mrs. Warren.

Q: Did you ask Mr. Warren about the flashlight?

A: I did at a later point in time, I don't remember if it was that evening, and he told me that in his panic to seek help he didn't remember what had happened to it.

Q: Please proceed with what happened during your investigation that night.

A: Well, while I was waiting for the coroner and someone with the camera to take a picture of the scene, I took Mr. Moore to the station.

Q: And why did you take him into the station?

A: The fact that he had fresh scratches on his arms, his strange demeanor, and the fact I didn't consider Mr. Warren a suspect.

Q: Do you recognize these exhibits? [Shows the exhibits to witness]

A: Absolutely. Those are the photographs of the victim and the knife. This is a drawing I made of the scene. And this is a floor plan of the lake house. I did an original sketch and turned it over to our computer folks who made this more detailed image.

Q: Are these true and accurate representations of what they show?

A: Yes, they are.

Q: Can you tell us what kind of boat this is and where the victim was located?

A: Yes, I think they call this a bay boat and it has a very shallow draft for being used in shallow water. It's used for fishing. The victim was lying on the front of the boat, a sort of platform where someone can stand while fishing. That is a small electric motor there that can be used for trolling.

Q: Okay. Is your drawing to scale?

A: No. I wanted to show the general layout of things outside the house.

Q: What about the house? Is it to scale?

A: Yes, pretty close. I took some rough measurements, but did not include them on my drawing. So what you see is very accurate in terms of the layout and where the doors and windows are.

Q: Did you take the pictures?

A: Like I said, I did not have a camera with me. Detective Jones took the picture of the victim later in the morning. I took the picture of the knife at the station. But those pictures are definitely accurate.

Q: Where is Detective Jones now?

A: He moved back to Wisconsin to be closer to his family.

Q: Okay. Just one more question before we discuss your interrogation of Mr. Moore, was there any other evidence collected from the scene?

A: Yes, there was. A thorough search by the officers remaining at the scene led to the discovery of forensic evidence within the home.

Q: And what did that evidence consist of?

A: They found blood belonging to the victim in the kitchen sink, as well as fingerprints belonging to all three individuals on that sink. There was also blood belonging to the victim in the guest bathroom and only Mr. Moore's prints were present on that sink.

Q: Did you check the knife for fingerprints?

A: Yes, we did. The results were inconclusive.

Q: Did you check it for blood?

A: Yes, there was no blood on it to test. And after the autopsy of the victim, I learned that the defendant's DNA was found under several of the victim's fingernails.

Q: Okay. Now, once you arrived at the police station that night, what happened?

A: I arrived back at the police station and proceeded to interview Mr. Moore at roughly 6:30 a.m.

Q: What did this interview reveal?

A: Mr. Moore told the same story he gave me at the lake residence. I asked him about the scratches on his arms, at which point he told me that he had now remembered that they were from a fight earlier that evening with his sister. He told me that she had become angry and upset with him, becoming physically violent with him.

Q: Did you ask him what made her so angry and upset?

A: I did. He informed me that she was angry with him for trying to get her to leave her husband that weekend. Mr. Moore told me that Mrs. Warren had been planning on leaving Mr. Warren, but wanted to do it on her own terms.

Q: Did he tell you anything else of importance?

A: Yes, Mr. Moore also told me that Mr. Warren overheard the argument between his sister and himself. He said Mr. Warren became angry and that they — Mr. Moore and Mr. Warren — got into an argument as well.

Q: Was there anything else?

A: Yes, at this point in the interview Mr. Moore paused and asked me if Mr. Warren was also being questioned at the police station. He asked if what Mr. Warren was saying added up.

Q: What else can you tell us about this?

A: Mr. Moore came across like he honestly believed Mr. Warren was responsible for his sister's death. When I informed him that Mr. Warren was not currently being questioned, he became irritated. He asked me something to the effect of "Why the hell not? She's only called 911 about him beating her five or six times!"

Q: Did you look into that claim?

A: I did. After I finished my questioning of Mr. Moore about 8:00 a.m., I continued investigating what we had so far. This included finding several domestic disturbance calls from a woman who identified herself as Robin Warren.

Q: Did Mr. Moore say anything else before you finished questioning him?

A: The only other thing he told me was that he couldn't remember if there was blood on Mr. Warren when he came in screaming to call 911. I didn't give this much weight. It was dark in the house when Mr. Warren came in and Mr. Moore was clearly running past him to get out the front door, looking at his phone to call 911.

Q: What else can you tell us about your investigation?

A: I met with Mr. Warren the next day to follow up. He told me essentially the same story he had the night before, but in a much more collected manner. I asked him to come in and give a statement, which he did the next day.

Q: Did he tell you anything else of importance to your investigation during your follow up?

A: Yes, he told me he remembered a stranger watching them over the weekend on the lakeshore. He told me if Mr. Moore didn't murder Mrs. Warren, that stranger would be the only other suspect.

Q: Did Mr. Moore remember this same strange person?

A: Yes, he later informed me there was a male stranger watching them from a neighbor's lot on the lakefront. He said that when the so-called stranger saw them looking right at him, he ran back into the bushes and disappeared.

Q: Did you follow up on that lead?

A: [Reviews notes] No, I did not consider that a credible lead. But [reviewing notes] I need to correct that, I did follow up and we found a 911 call. But it was anonymous and after a patrol office went to the area and found nothing, we considered it to be a false alarm. There had been no other reports of so-called strangers in the area so I did not consider it credible.

Q: Did you interview any other witnesses?

A: No, I did not.

Q: Okay. Thank you, Detective. Would you please step outside for just a few minutes?

A: Of course.

[The Witness leaves the Grand Jury Room at 11:00 a.m. and is subsequently dismissed.]

(END OF TRANSCRIPT)

911 TRANSCRIPTS

911 TRANSCRIPT
August 28, [YR-2]
2:00 A.M.

Dispatch: 911, what is your emergency?

Caller: My husband just attacked me!

Dispatch: Is he with you?

Caller: I ran to the neighbors, and I'm using their phone. Please, send the police!

Dispatch: Ma'am, I'm sending someone out there now. Do you need medical attention?

Caller: I don't know. . . (unintelligible). . . I don't know. . .

Dispatch: What is your name honey?

Caller: It's Robin Warren. Please hurry. Please.

Dispatch: Robin, the police are on their way. I'll send medical as well. What happened?

Caller: He attacked me! He came at me, hitting me, hit me several times. . . He was so angry. . . I didn't do anything. . . Then he hit me in the face. . . I ran when I saw him grab a knife. . .

Dispatch: Did he stab you?

Caller: No. . . I ran. . . I ran here.

Dispatch: I'll stay on the phone with you until the police arrive, alright?

Caller: (Unintelligible. . . talking to neighbors)

Dispatch: Robin? I'll stay here on the phone with you until the police and medical arrive.

Caller: Okay. (Unintelligible. . . talking to neighbors)

Dispatch: I see the police and medical say they've arrived

Caller: They're next door now. I can see them. . . Thank you.

(END OF TRANSCRIPT)

911 TRANSCRIPT
November 2, [YR-2]
4:11 P.M.

Dispatch: 911, what is your emergency?

Caller: Please send the police! Please! Help!

Dispatch: Ma'am, what is happening?

Caller: Oh please! He's so angry. I'm hiding. He's looking for me and I'm hiding in my own damn house. Please send the police.

Dispatch: What is your address?

Caller: 6789 Whispering Way, here in San Milano.

Dispatch: Okay. Ma'am, the police are on their way. Who is he?

Caller: My husband, Brad. Bradley Warren. He hit me. My face is swollen, I can feel it.

Dispatch: Ma'am, the police are on their way. I'll send medical as well. Do you have any other injuries?

Caller: He hit me in the face, the arms, the chest, my stomach, all over. Where are the police?

Dispatch: Ma'am, the police are almost there. Are you still hiding?

Caller: Yes, I'm hiding in the guest room. He's looking for me. He's almost to this room.

Dispatch: Ma'am, they say they are outside. If you can get out of the house while he's at the front door, or if you can yell when he opens the door to the police.

Caller: They're at the door now. . . HELP! I'M IN HERE!

(END OF TRANSCRIPT)

911 TRANSCRIPT
February 6, [YR-1]
3:09 AM

Dispatch: 911, what is your emergency?

Caller: I think my neighbor is hitting his wife. Please send the police.

Dispatch: What is the address?

Caller: They live at 6788, I mean 6789 Whispering Way.

Dispatch: Sir, I'm sending the police. Can you tell me more?

Caller: I heard them arguing earlier, outside. Then I heard her yell out, like she was in pain, and by the time I got to the window I saw what looked like him dragging her into the house.

Dispatch: Sir, is there anything else you can tell me?

Caller: She came over here and called the police late last year about him abusing her. I am really scared for her. For her safety. Please, get someone here quickly.

Dispatch: Sir, the police are on their way. I'll send medical too.

Caller: Thank you.

(END OF TRANSCRIPT)

911 TRANSCRIPT
August 5, [YR-1]
11:48 P.M.

Dispatch: 911, what is your emergency?

Caller: I think someone is looking into my window.

Dispatch: What is the address?

Caller: I would rather not give it.

Dispatch: Sir, I cannot help you if do not give me your address.

Caller: I live on Town Lake.

Dispatch: Sir, is there anything else you can tell me?

Caller: I have seen him several other times walking slowly on the path around the lake. Whenever I glance his way he turns and walks quickly the other way. Some of my neighbors have also noticed him. No one knows who he is.

Dispatch: Sir, I will send the police to drive through the area.

Caller: Thank you.

(END OF TRANSCRIPT)

MEDICAL EXAMINER'S AUTOPSY REPORT

Date: August 6, [YR-1]

Time: 3:00 p.m.

Examiner: Henry Martin, M.D.

Witness: Detective Blair Rodriguez

Deceased: Robin Warren

Date of Birth: May 18, [YR-26]

Height: 5' 5"

Weight: 128 pounds

Observations: The deceased has one stab wound to the chest. The stab wound is directly through the heart. It is roughly 1" wide and 6" deep. The wound is consistent with a knife blade ranging from 7" to 8".

Based on the location of the wound and the minimal blood flow from it, it is clear the victim died very quickly.

Upon further examination it was also determined the deceased suffered blunt force trauma to the back of the head prior to death.

Cause/Manner of Death: Stab wound to chest, homicide

Submitted August 6, [YR-1]

Henry Martin

Henry Martin, M.D.
Medical Examiner

Medical Examiner's Death Certificate

Name of Deceased: Robin Warren

Date and Time of Death: August 6th, [YR-1] at approximately 3:00 a.m.

Primary Cause of Death: Stab wound to chest

Survivors: Husband, Bradley Warren
Brother, Alex Moore

Submitted August 7, [YR-1]

Henry Martin

Henry Martin, M.D.
Medical Examiner

Forensics Report

Bear County Crime Laboratory
Bear County
State of Lone Star

WEAPONS:

The weapon gathered was a 7.5-inch knife. Bradley and Robin Warren owned the weapon.

FINGERPRINTS:

Fingerprints were taken from the knife. The prints on the knife belong to Robin Warren, Bradley Warren, and Alex Moore.

Fingerprints were not taken from the kitchen sink.

Fingerprints were not taken from the master bathroom.

Fingerprints taken from the guest bathroom sink were only those of Alex Moore.

DNA:

DNA was collected from the knife. However, it was unidentified.

DNA was also collected from the kitchen sink. The DNA proved to be Robin Warren's blood.

Additional DNA was collected from the guest bathroom sink and was proven to be Robin Warren's blood.

No DNA testing was performed in the master bathroom.

DNA belonging to Alex More was found under victim's fingernails.

Submitted: September 5, [YR-1]

Jane Gilbert

Jane Gilbert
Lab Technician

Life Insurance Policy on Robin Warren

Warm Heart Life Insurance
Providing for your loved ones as if they were our own since 1971

LIFE INSURANCE POLICY
Summary

Policy Number: 338285764-3

Type of Policy: Term Life
Policy Holder: Bradley Warren
The Insured: Warren, Robin
Gender: Female
Date of Birth: May 18, [YR-26]
Age: 26 years of age
Occupation: Office Manager

Beginning Date of Coverage: August 10, [YR-4]
Expiration Date of Coverage: August 10, [YR-1]
Amount of Coverage: $100,000
Premium Due: Paid In Full

This life insurance policy for $100,000 is payable in full upon the death of the insured, Robin Warren, to the policyholder, Bradley Warren.

Limitations:

> This policy will be null and void should the insured become deceased due to any act by the policyholder.

Floor Plan of Lake House

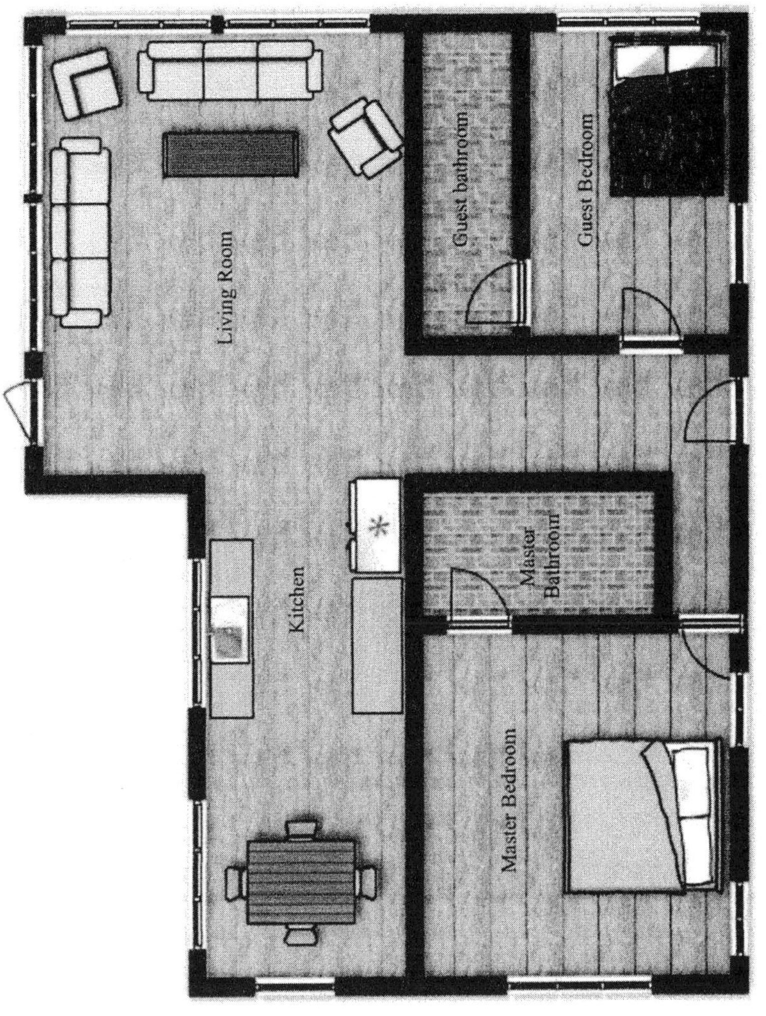

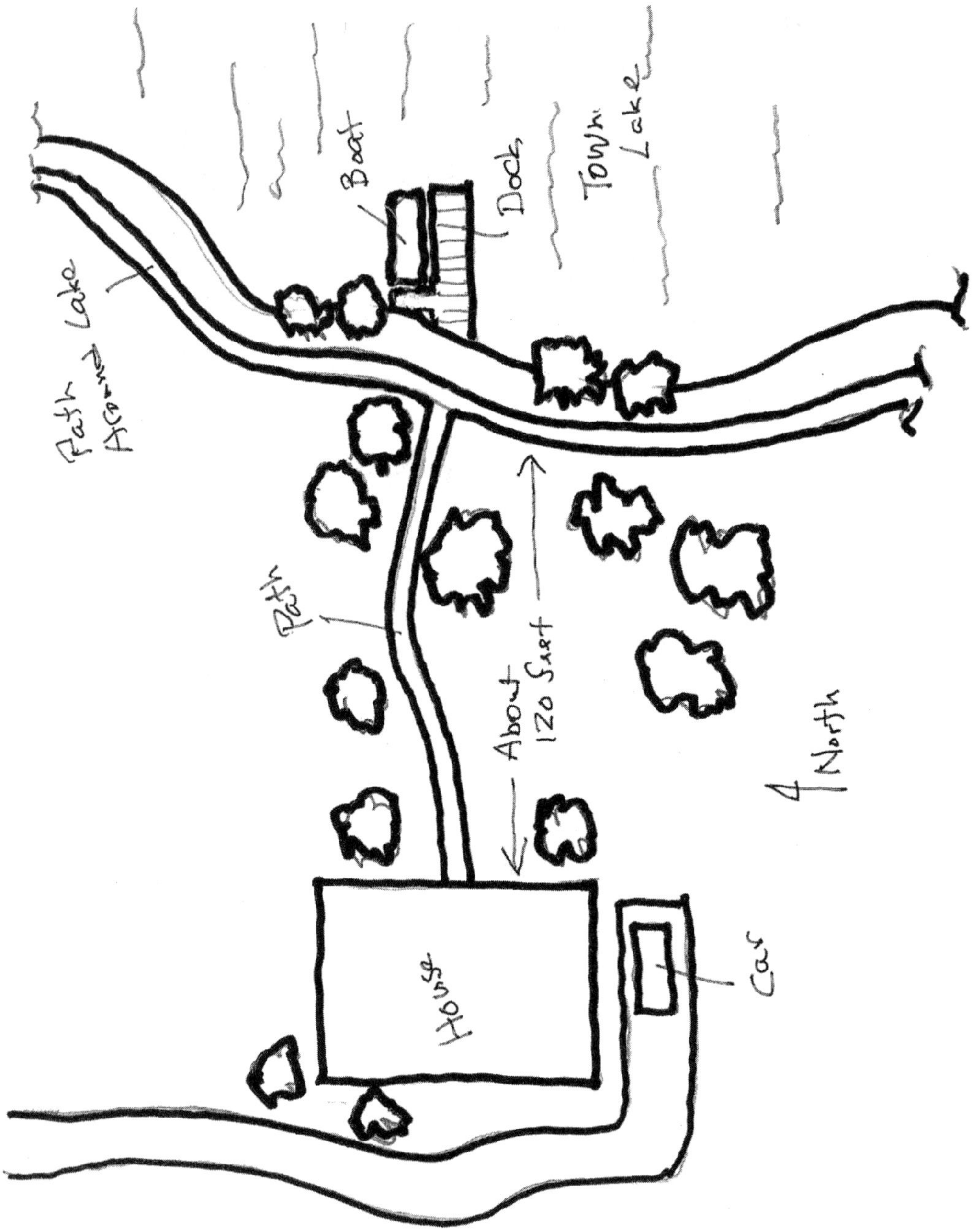
Boat
Dock
Town Lake
Path Around Lake
Path
About 120 feet
North
House
Car

PHOTOGRAPH OF VICTIM

Photograph of Knife

August 7, [-1] **The San Milano Times** **2B**

Local Woman Murdered at Lake

Reported by: Trisha Green
August 7, [-1]

Police responded early yesterday morning to a homicide here in San Milano, Lone Star. The deceased victim was Mrs. Robin Warren. Her husband, Bradley Warren, told investigators that he found her just after four in the morning, outside their lake house on Town Lake. Although it is reported that both her husband and her brother attempted to resuscitate her, Mrs. Warren was pronounced dead at the scene by paramedics who arrived some time later.

A phone call to the medical examiner's office indicates that she died from a single knife wound to the chest.

Her husband talked to police at the scene but was not taken in for questioning.

According to an inside source, the police have cleared Mr. Warren as a suspect based on evidence collected at the scene.

Police have taken her brother, Alex Moore, into custody for her murder. Alex Moore is not new to law enforcement. A former police officer, he was discharged from the San Milano Police Department in late 2009. Since then, he has been in and out of rehabilitation facilities. Our inside source is confident he is responsible for the murder of Mrs. Robin Warren.

Detective Rodriguez, who is working the case, states that he is confident that they have their man.

Interviews with some neighbors, however, seem to point to an unknown man who has been seen in the area after dark for the last several nights.

The investigation continues.

Jury Instructions

LADIES AND GENTLEMEN OF THE JURY:

The defendant, ALEX MOORE, stands charged by indictment COUNT 1 with the offense of murder, alleged to have been committed on or about the August 6, [YR-1] in Bear County, State of Lone Star. The defendant has pleaded not guilty.

1.

Our law provides that a person commits the offense of murder if he or she intentionally or knowingly causes the death of an individual.

2.

A person acts intentionally, or with intent, with respect to a result of his or her conduct when it is his or her conscious objective or desire to cause the result.

A person acts knowingly, or with knowledge, with respect to a result of his conduct when he or she is aware that his or her conduct is reasonably certain to cause the result.

3.

Now, if you find from the evidence beyond a reasonable doubt that on or about August 6, [YR-1], in Bear County, State of Lone Star, that the defendant ALEX MOORE, did intentionally or knowingly cause the death of an individual, namely ROBIN WARREN then you will find the defendant ALEX MOORE guilty of murder as charged in the indictment.

Unless you so find beyond a reasonable doubt, or if you have a reasonable doubt as to whether the defendant is guilty of murder, then you will find him not guilty.

4.

You are instructed that you may consider all relevant facts and circumstances surrounding the killing, if any, and the previous relationship existing between the accused and the deceased, if any, together with all relevant facts and circumstances going to show the condition of the mind of the defendant at the time of the offense, if any.

The State, however, is not required to prove a motive. If the State has proved the essential elements of the offense beyond a reasonable doubt, the defendant must be found guilty of that offense regardless of the defendant's motive or lack of a motive. If the State, however, has proved a motive, you may consider that insofar as it gives meaning to other circumstances. On the other hand, you may consider the absence of motive in weighing whether or not the defendant is guilty of the crime charged.

5.

"Proof beyond a reasonable doubt" is proof that leaves you firmly convinced of the defendant's guilt. There are very few things in this world that we know with absolute certainty, and in criminal cases the law does not require proof that overcomes every possible doubt. If, based on your consideration of the evidence, you are firmly convinced that the defendant is guilty of the crime charged, you should find him guilty. If, on the other hand, you think there is a real possibility that he is not guilty, you should give him the benefit of the doubt and find him not guilty.

Chapter 19
Warren v. Moore

§ 19-1. Introduction

Alex Moore is charged with killing his sister, Robin Warren. On the night she was killed, the defendant, the victim, and the victim's husband Bradley Warren, had been drinking and arguing about a range of subjects including the victim's marriage and money that the victim owed the defendant. The defendant told the police that Bradley was the one who killed Robin and that the police had the wrong man.

The defendant was acquitted at his criminal trial. The victim's husband, Bradley Warren, filed a wrongful death suit against Moore.

§ 19-2. Stipulations Regarding Procedural and Evidentiary Matters

1. The case is being tried in a Lone Star court. The Federal Rules of Civil Procedure and Evidence apply.
2. All witnesses called to testify who made statements or deposition testimony identifying the defendant, other individuals, or tangible evidence must, if asked, identify the same at trial.
3. Alex Moore, Jaime Hill, and Bradley Warren signed their statements to the police.
4. Other than what is supplied in the problem itself, there is nothing exceptional or unusual about the background information of any of the witnesses or the defendant that would bolster or detract from their credibility.
5. The parties may not "invent" an individual not mentioned in this problem or to have testimony or evidence offered to the court or jury from that invented individual.
6. "Beyond the record" must not be made or entertained as an objection.
7. If any rule of procedure or rule of evidence requires that notice be provided to the court or to the opponent, it will be assumed for the purpose of the problem that the required notice was given.
8. All exhibits in the file are authentic. In addition, each exhibit contained in the file is the original of that document unless otherwise noted on the exhibit or as established by the evidence.
9. Any searches and seizures conducted by the police met the requirements of the Fourth Amendment and the State's Rules of Criminal Procedure.
10. No changes or alterations were made to any of the exhibits.
11. The victim's lake house is located within Bear County, Lone Star.
12. At the time of trial, Jamie Hill is a clergy member.
13. The defendant's DNA was found under the victim's fingernails.

§ 19-3. Case File Materials

Students will use the following materials for the mock trial.

Lone Star Wrongful Death Statute

Lone Star Civil Practice & Remedies Code

§ 31.123. Cause of Action

(a) An action for actual damages arising from an injury that causes an individual's death may be brought if liability exists under this section.

(b) A person is liable for damages arising from an injury that causes an individual's death if the injury was caused by the person's or his agent's or servant's wrongful act, neglect, carelessness, unskillfulness, or default.

(c) A person is liable for damages arising from an injury that causes an individual's death if:

(1) the person is a proprietor, owner, charterer, or hirer of an industrial or public utility plant or of a railroad, street railway, steamboat, stagecoach, or other vehicle for the transportation of goods or passengers; and

(2) the injury was caused by the person's or his agent's or servant's wrongful act, neglect, carelessness, unskillfulness, or default.

§ 31.124. Benefitting From Action

(a) An action to recover damages as provided by this subchapter is for the exclusive benefit of the surviving spouse, children, and parents of the deceased.

(b) The surviving spouse, children, and parents of the deceased may bring the action or one or more of those individuals may bring the action for the benefit of all.

§ 31.125. Exemplary Damages

When the death is caused by the wilful act or omission or gross negligence of the defendant, exemplary as well as actual damages may be recovered.

PLAINTIFF'S PETITION

DISTRICT COURT OF BEAR COUNTY

BRADLEY WARREN Plaintiff v. ALEX MOORE Defendant	}	Docket No. 13567-90 COMPLAINT FOR DAMAGES

COMES NOW the above-named Plaintiff and alleges the following:

I. Parties, Jurisdiction, and Venue

A. Plaintiff, Bradley Warren, husband to decedent, Robin Warren, brings this action in his personal capacity.

B. Defendant, Alex Moore, is a resident of Bear County, State of Lone Star.

C. This Court has jurisdiction over the subject matter of this complaint and over the parties.

D. Venue is proper and appropriate in Bear County because the wrongful death of Robin Warren, which is the subject matter of this complaint, occurred in Bear County.

II. Factual Basis

A. Plaintiff's wife was Robin Warren.

B. On the night she was killed, the plaintiff, the defendant, and the decedent were staying the plaintiff's home.

C. During the evening an argument broke out between the defendant and the decedent over a range of subjects including the large amount of money that the decedent owed the defendant.

D. Later that evening, the defendant confronted the decedent and stabbed her in the heart, causing her death.

E. Defendant's acts or omissions were the sole and proximate cause of Robin Warren's death.

III. Causes of Action

A. As a direct and proximate result of the acts of the Defendant, the decedent suffered a wrongful death, entitling Plaintiff to recover actual and exemplary damages (including but not limited to medical and hospital expenses, funeral expenses, and all other damages allowable for wrongful death and survival benefits under Lone Star Civil Practice & Remedies Code §§ 31.123-31.125 and any other damages allowable as a result of Defendant's conduct;) in amounts not now precisely known, the exact amounts to be proven at or before the time of trial.

B. As a further direct and proximate result of the Defendant's acts and omissions, the Plaintiff of the decedent suffered destruction of the parent-child relationship and loss of parental consortium.

C. As a further direct and proximate result of the intentional acts of Defendant, Plaintiff is entitled to recover statutory and reasonable attorney's fees and costs in amounts not now precisely known, the court to set such amounts in the future.

IV. Prayer for Relief

WHEREFORE, the plaintiff prays for a judgment of liability against the defendants as follows:

A. For a judgment against defendant.

B. For an award of damages as set forth in the above complaint herein, including statutory and reasonable fees and costs in such amounts that may be awarded by this Court.

C. For such other and further relief as the Court deems just and appropriate.

DATED this day of June 20, [YR-1].

Yvette Gonzales

Yvette Gonzales
Attorney for Plaintiff

Defendant's First Written Statement to Police

STATE OF LONE STAR
COUNTY OF BEAR

Case Number: 12-81377

VOLUNTARY STATEMENT OF: ALEX MOORE

I, Alex Moore, after first being duly warned by Det. B. Rodriguez #6387 at 0730 hrs. at 214 W. Nueva, on August 6, [YR-2] that (1) I have the right to remain silent and not make any statement at all, and any statement I do make may be used against me at my trial; (2) Any statement I make may be used as evidence against me in Court; (3) I have the right to have a lawyer present to advise me prior to and during any questioning; (4) If I am unable to employ a lawyer, I have the right to have a lawyer appointed to advise me prior to and during any questioning; (5) I have the right to terminate the interview at any time; and I understand that the above rights are continuing rights and may be urged by me at any stage of the proceedings, and I hereby prior to and during the making of this statement, knowingly, intelligently, and voluntarily waive the above rights and give to the said, Det. Blair Rodriguez #6387, the person to whom this statement is being given, the following written statement:

My name is Alex Moore. Robin Warren was my sister.

Like I told you earlier at the house, I was in bed sleeping until about 1 a.m. We had stayed up late together and crashed about 11 p.m. I fell asleep, clothes and all. When I woke up about 4 a.m., I had to use the bathroom. So I got up and walked out of my room.

When I was coming back from the bathroom, I heard Bradley yelling to call 911 as he came in from the dock, and yelling that something had happened to Robin. I was shocked and disoriented. I remember fumbling for my cell phone from the nightstand, and running out to the dock while on the phone with 911.

When I got to the dock I saw Robin laying face down on the boat, toward the front of the boat. I tried to check her to see if she had a pulse and held her in my arms and screamed her name.

I came back up to the house to wait for you guys to show up after I realized there was nothing I could do. Robin was dead.

The scratches on my arms are from an argument I had with my sister earlier this evening. She was going to leave Bradley, but became angry when I told her that she needed to do it the next day. She told me she wanted to do it on her own terms, yelling at me and scratching me.

Bradley overheard us arguing about her leaving him. He became very angry and we argued as well. He yelled at me, "Our relationship is none of your business." Then he leaned in and said, "Keep your nose out of it or I'll make sure you never see her again."

I honestly think you guys should be looking at him for murdering my sister. He started abusing her about a year after they were married, and she's called 911 several times. He's an abusive, mean guy.

I also do not remember if he had blood on him when he came in yelling for me to call 911.

This is the end of my statement. I have read this statement and it is true and correct.

WITNESS: *Blair Rodriguez*

SIGNATURE: *Alex Moore*

DATE: Aug. 6, [YR-2]

DEFENDANT'S SECOND WRITTEN STATEMENT TO POLICE

STATE OF LONE STAR } **Case Number: 12-81377**
COUNTY OF BEAR }

VOLUNTARY STATEMENT OF: ALEX MOORE

I, Alex Moore, after first being duly warned by Det. B. Rodriguez #6387 at 0730 hrs, at 214 W. Nueva, on August 8, [YR-2] that (1) I have the right to remain silent and not make any statement at all, and any statement I do make may be used against me at my trial; (2) Any statement I make may be used as evidence against me in Court; (3) I have the right to have a lawyer present to advise me prior to and during any questioning; (4) If I am unable to employ a lawyer, I have the right to have a lawyer appointed to advise me prior to and during any questioning; (5) I have the right to terminate the interview at any time; and I understand that the above rights are continuing rights and may be urged by me at any stage of the proceedings, and I hereby prior to and during the making of this statement, knowingly, intelligently, and voluntarily waive the above rights and give to the said, Det. Blair Rodriguez #6387, the person to whom this statement is being given, the following written statement:

I did not kill my sister, Robin Warren. I am certain that her husband, Bradley Warren, killed her in a violent fit of rage.

It is my understanding that Bradley has attempted to blame me for Robin's death. I would NEVER kill my sister over money.

Robin started college in [YR-8] and graduated in [YR-4]. She went to Altross State University here in the State of Lone Star. She got a bachelor's degree in business, as I recall. During the time she was in school, I paid for her tuition and living expenses so that she could focus on school. Our dad had died in [YR-12], when she was just 14, so I had become the man of the house. I wanted to make sure Robin got a good education. Although I insisted it be a gift, she insisted on paying me back. Ultimately, we agreed it would be a loan, but with no interest.

All total, I loaned her about $100,000.00 for her education.

In February of [YR-4], our mom was killed in a horrific car accident. I didn't handle it well. Although I had been undercover a couple years, and was making good progress on the case I was working, I blew it. Losing our mom killed me. I started drinking heavily and doing drugs. Sometime in April of [YR-4] I disappeared for a few months. I am not even sure what I was doing during that time. I wasn't around when Robin met Bradley. I wish every day I had been so that I could have kept her from marrying him. Maybe I could have pointed out the warning signs I saw. Maybe I could have showed her what he was really like.

I guess it was sometime in June that I was arrested and charged with my first crime, drug possession. After a couple more charges, I was discharged from the police department in October of [YR-3].

The first charge was that drug possession in June of [YR-4]. In connection with that I had an aggravated assault charge. While undercover I stabbed a female drug trafficker. She had come at me with a knife during an argument, and I wrestled with her to get it away from her. Somewhere in the scuffle I stabbed her once, but I was still charged with the crime. I also had a small baggie of crack cocaine on me, so that's where the drug possession came from.

My other charge before I was discharged from the force in October of [YR-3] was another aggravated assault. I got into a heated argument with a superior officer. She refused to let me handle some information I had received from an informant the way I wanted to, and I guess I pulled a knife.

I know I would never have hurt her, but I was so into the drugs and alcohol at that point I wasn't thinking clearly.

Within a couple weeks of my discharge from the police department, I checked myself into rehab. I knew I needed help.

When I got out in May of [YR-3], I got my own place and started working. I wanted to make something of myself again before I went back around Robin. She deserved the brother she used to have, not what I was then. But I relapsed again in July of [YR-3]. I spent another six months in rehab, and then started again. By June of [YR-2], a good five months after I got out of rehab, I looked Robin up. I hoped our relationship would be like it was before I disappeared.

Unfortunately, it wasn't. Robin's husband Bradley didn't want me around. At first, I couldn't blame him. I figured Robin had told him about my past. That I had just up and disappeared on her when she must have been grieving, too. But then I realized it was more sinister than that. Robin and I had talked about her paying me back to help get me back on my feet. I guess Bradley felt that Robin didn't owe me a thing. He did not have a clue as to how much I had sacrificed to get Robin through school.

Robin and I had a friend we grew up with, Jaime Hill, who became a minister about the time Robin graduated from college. When I came back around in June of [YR-2], I also started talking to Jaime again. Jaime told me that Robin had come to talk about her marriage to Bradley because he had become abusive and Robin didn't know what to do. Jaime tried to give Robin some spiritual advice, referred Robin to various agencies when she still wasn't sure what to do, and even had started arrangements for Robin to leave Bradley at one point. Jaime told me that there were times that Robin may have called 911.

I started poking around and found out that Robin had called 911 about Bradley's violence before. You guys should really be looking at him. I would never, NEVER hurt Robin for money. I knew she would pay me back eventually.

Like I said before, our fight the night of the 5th was because Robin and I were arguing about when she was going to leave Bradley. We had been drinking that day and probably weren't thinking as clear as we would have been if we had been sober. But it wasn't a question of "if" Robin was leaving him. It was a question of "when." I wanted Robin to leave him the next day, and it was just that Robin wanted more time to plan her escape from him.

It was my job to protect her. I feel like I failed by not talking to her in a place where Bradley couldn't hear us, and that I should have insisted she leave with me that night instead of staying one more night with him. I'm sure if I had, Robin would still be alive.

WITNESS: *Jane Hernandez* SIGNATURE: Alex Moore

DATE: Aug. 8, [YR-2]

Jamie Hill's Letter to the Police

To Whom It May Concern:

Aug. 8, [-2]

My name is Jaime Hill. I am a family friend of Alex Moore, and was a long-time friend of Robin Warren before her death. I am writing this letter because I have learned of Robin's death and have information to assist you in your investigation of her death.

I spoke with Robin numerous times before her death about leaving Bradley. She had confided in me that Bradley had become very abusive after their marriage. She told me on several occasions, "I'm scared for my life. I believe Bradley may kill me one of these days." Robin also told me she believed Bradley had taken out a life insurance policy on her for that very reason.

Although Alex has made mistakes in his past, that in no way affects his love for his sister. I've known Alex and Robin since the three of us were children. He would never, ever, have hurt Robin.

Robin told me several times that if anything happened to her that I should contact the police and tell them everything she told me about her husband.

Please let me know if I can be of further assistance,

Respectfully yours,

Jaime Hill

Jaime Hill's Written Statement to Police

STATE OF LONE STAR
COUNTY OF BEAR } **Case Number: 12-81377**

VOLUNTARY STATEMENT OF: JAIME HILL

I, Jaime Hill, after first being duly warned by Det. B. Rodriguez #6387 at 0700 hrs, at 214 W. Nueva, on August 14, [YR-2] that (1) I have the right to remain silent and not make any statement at all, and any statement I do make may be used against me at my trial; (2) Any statement I make may be used as evidence against me in Court; (3) I have the right to have a lawyer present to advise me prior to and during any questioning; (4) If I am unable to employ a lawyer, I have the right to have a lawyer appointed to advise me prior to and during any questioning; (5) I have the right to terminate the interview at any time; and I understand that the above rights are continuing rights and may be urged by me at any stage of the proceedings, and I hereby prior to and during the making of this statement, knowingly, intelligently, and voluntarily waive the above rights and give to the said, Det. Blair Rodriguez #6387, the person to whom this statement is being given, the following written statement:

My name is Jaime Hill. I am a very good friend to Alex Moore, and was a very good friend of Robin Warren when she was alive.

I grew up with Alex and Robin, and had known Alex and Robin since long before their father died in [YR-12]. They were very close growing up, but when their father died, Alex stepped in and became more of a father to Robin. He's always tried to be there for her and do everything he can to help her, no matter what the cost to himself.

When Alex disappeared, Robin was very vulnerable. I believe she fell into the relationship with Bradley Warren because he provided what appeared to be a steady rock for her. They met the same month that Alex disappeared, and were married just three months later. However, I realized quickly that Bradley's apparent steadiness was a façade for his abusive nature.

Robin came to me several times after she married Bradley in August of [YR-4] and told me that he had become abusive. I was working as a minister at that point, and Robin would come to the church to speak with me, or would call me at home if I weren't at the church. Several times she showed me the bruises that she got when Bradley hit her.

I attempted to provide spiritual guidance for Robin, but when that didn't seem to help, I also provided a shoulder to cry on and personal advice. Many times it seemed like Robin wanted to leave Bradley, and I even helped her begin preparing an escape plan shortly before her death in August. I think it was about July 5th or 6th.

In the days leading up to the 4th of July they had been in their honeymoon phase. Everything was wonderful and Bradley had been surprising Robin with all sorts of surprises like flowers and chocolates. I knew that it was only a matter of time before he snapped again. Sure enough, the 4th of July Bradley viciously attacked Robin again. She came to me while I was at the church the next day, very distraught, and told me vehemently, "I am leaving him, no matter what it takes."

Robin had also discovered Bradley had taken out a very high dollar amount life insurance policy on her and the idea terrified her. I do not know the amount of the policy. But she was very worried he might try to make her death look like an accident, or that someone else had murdered her, just to get away with killing her, then take the money to start over and find another woman to abuse and control.

Robin was convinced she needed to plan when she left perfectly. Robin wouldn't leave Bradley without planning every last detail. When I talked to Alex the day after Robin's death, and he told me about their fight, I realized that Robin probably panicked when Bradley overheard her saying she was leaving him. Robin told me once, "He will never let me leave him. It'll be over his dead body."

I am 100% sure that Bradley murdered Robin because he would never have let her leave him. Alex would never have hurt Robin. Never. He is not that kind of man. The Alex I know is a changed man and has turned his life around and is non-aggressive.

WITNESS: *Blair Rodriguez* SIGNATURE: *Jaime Hill*

DATE: Aug. 14, [YR-2]

Bradley Warren's Written Statement to Police

STATE OF LONE STAR
COUNTY OF BEAR }

Case Number: 12-81377

VOLUNTARY STATEMENT OF: BRADLEY WARREN

I, Bradley Warren, after first being duly warned by Det. B. Rodriguez #6387 at 0800 hrs. at 214 W. Nueva, on August 7, [YR-2] that (1) I have the right to remain silent and not make any statement at all, and any statement I do make may be used against me at my trial; (2) Any statement I make may be used as evidence against me in Court; (3) I have the right to have a lawyer present to advise me prior to and during any questioning; (4) If I am unable to employ a lawyer, I have the right to have a lawyer appointed to advise me prior to and during any questioning; (5) I have the right to terminate the interview at any time; and I understand that the above rights are continuing rights and may be urged by me at any stage of the proceedings, and I hereby prior to and during the making of this statement, knowingly, intelligently, and voluntarily waive the above rights and give to the said, Det. Blair Rodriguez #6387, the person to whom this statement is being given, the following written statement:

My name is Bradley Warren. I am giving this statement because my wife, Robin Warren, was murdered two days ago. By her brother, Alex Moore. I know it had something to do with the money he loaned her.

We all went to bed about 11 p.m. While I was lying in bed, Robin told me she thought the boat wasn't secured to the dock. I was very tired, so she offered to check it. She left to go check it and I must have fallen asleep.

The next thing I remember was waking up and Robin wasn't in bed. I think it was about 4 a.m. I went to find her. When I passed by the guest room I noticed the door was standing open about a foot and a half. Robin's brother Alex was staying in that room. I looked in and he wasn't there.

I looked into the living room and the dining room, but neither of them was there.

I ran out to the dock because I saw a light on it. It was not moving. I was afraid something had happened to my wife. When I got there, I saw it was our flashlight. We keep the flashlight, an industrial one, in the kitchen. I picked it up and found Robin on the boat. I tried to help her, but there was nothing I could do. One of our knives that we keep on the boat was next to her. I picked it up and ran back to the house.

I ran back to the house and screamed for Alex to call 911. The next thing I remember was trying to get Robin's blood off of me, and then the police showing up.

I think I must have put the knife on the sink. It's a hunting type knife that we have had for years and use it on the boat for general stuff like cutting bait. I am not sure whether I cleaned it or not. I was in such as state of shock I guess I just don't know.

WITNESS: *Blair Rodriguez* SIGNATURE: Bradley Warren

DATE: Aug. 7, [YR-2]

DEPOSITION OF BRADLEY WARREN

ORAL DEPOSITION OF BRADLEY WARREN, produced as a witness at the instance of the Defendant, ALEX MOORE, and duly sworn, was taken in the above-styled and numbered cause on October 30, [YR-1] from 8:00 p.m. to 10:00 a.m. before Sydney Jones, Certified Shorthand Reporter in and for the State of Lone Star, reported by machine shorthand, at the law offices of Defendant, pursuant to the Federal Rules of Civil Procedure and the Provisions stated on the record or attached hereto.

This is a deposition of BRADLEY WARREN, who having been sworn, testified as follows:

EXAMINATION

QUESTIONS BY DEFENDANT'S COUNSEL:

Q: Good morning Mr. Warren.

A: Good morning, sir.

Q: First, I would like the record to reflect that you are here this morning with your counsel, who will be given the opportunity ask you questions as well. Also present is our reporter, Sydney Jones. Also, if I am unclear on any of my questions, please let me know so that we can clarify the question. Okay?

A: Sure.

Q: Would you please state your name for the reporter.

A: Yes, my name is Bradley Warren.

Q: Could you please tell us your relationship to Mrs. Warren?

A: Yes, she was my wife. She was murdered the night of August 5th.

Q: Do you mean the early morning of August 6th?

A: Yes, that is what I meant.

Q: Can you tell us about that night?

A: We were at our vacation home, just outside of San Milano on Town Lake.

Q: Here in Bear County?

A: Yes.

Q: Okay. Go ahead.

A: We, that is my wife, Robin, and her brother, Alex. [Clears throat and pauses] Alex Moore, your client. The three of us had been drinking a good bit and spending some time visiting before we all headed home the next morning. It got pretty loud at some points. Alex and Robin started arguing about the money that Alex claimed Robin owed him and she said that he was a loser and that she did not intend to pay him back. She accused him of having gotten the money by selling drugs and that he had no right to ask her to repay him. At one point they shoved each other around a bit. I stayed out of it until Alex started to tell Robin that she needed to leave me and that the only reason that she was saying those things was because she was afraid of me. That is when I got into it with Alex and told him to shut up and go to bed. I had heard the two of them talking earlier in the day about her leaving me. Well, we all headed to bed around 11 p.m. I was exhausted and crashed almost as soon as I hit the bed. I vaguely remember Robin telling me she thought the boat wasn't secure. Then I heard her say she was going down to check it. I glanced at the clock as she walked out and saw it was about 11:15.

Q: What happened next?

A: I woke up about 4 a.m. and I realized Robin was not in the bed. I was really worried. I got out of bed to go find her. I walked out of our bedroom still sleepy. I noticed the guest door was standing partially open as I passed by it and glanced in. I saw the blanket had been laid on, and the pillow was . . . what's the word I'm looking for . . . scrunched? But the blankets hadn't been pulled back and slept under. Anyway, I figured that Alex and Robin might be talking in the living area, or outside.

Q: Is that where you headed?

A: Yes. I walked to the front rooms of the house, but didn't see them. It was eerily quiet. I walked over to the kitchen sink and looked down the path toward the dock. I noticed that there was a light coming from the end of the dock. By this point I had woken up enough to realize that wasn't right. As I walked down to the dock, it hit me that the light was coming from a flashlight on the path. I later recognized it as the industrial one we keep in our kitchen.

Q: What happened next?

A: Once I reached the flashlight, I picked it up and started looking for Robin. I saw her lying on the deck of the boat as I shined the flashlight in that direction. I jumped on the boat and dropped the flashlight to check her and see if she was okay.

Q: Did you say anything?

A: I don't remember . . . I just remember dropping to my knees. She was lying face down. I tried to pull her into my lap and feel for a pulse on her throat, but there wasn't one and she was cold. I panicked. There was blood all over her blouse, on the front.

Q: What happened then?

A: I don't remember everything in detail. I just gently put her back down. I remember yelling out for Alex. But he did not come out. So I ran up the path toward the house yelling for him to call the police and yelling Robin's name. I was so out of it. I know I cleaned up in the kitchen sink before the police arrived. I couldn't stand having Robin's blood on me.

Q: What happened once the police arrived?

A: I spoke with Detective Rodriguez and then Detective Rodriguez spoke with Alex. After that, Detective Rodriguez went out back to look around and shortly after took Alex down to the police station.

Q: Did you wonder why Detective Rodriguez was taking Alex into custody?

A: No. I remember telling Detective Rodriguez that I thought Alex was responsible for Robin's death. I know he murdered Robin. Rodriguez asked me if I thought that anyone else might have done it and I said that we had seen a strange man walking around the lake at night, but that based on what I saw, I was convinced that Alex killed her.

Q: How do you know that?

A: Alex isn't a good person. Alex has been in trouble since Robin was a teenager. From what Robin told me, Alex was a police officer, but ended up a dirty cop. He went undercover a couple years before their mother passed away and disappeared entirely after she died. Alex dabbled in drugs, alcohol, and even got kicked off the force for some violent incidents. There was even talk that he had stolen drugs from the evidence room and sold them to get some extra money. Robin wouldn't tell me exactly what that was all about, but when he came looking for her a couple of years ago. I can tell you I wasn't pleased. I didn't want him back in her life. All he would talk about was getting his money.

Q: Did anything else make you think Alex was responsible for her death?

A: Well, I didn't see him in bed when I passed by looking for Robin. And like I said, the sheets didn't look slept in, just laid on. He probably would have gotten away with it if I wouldn't have passed by his room and noticed that.

Q: Mr. Warren, could you tell us some more about the money that Alex said Robin owed to him?

A: Well, Robin had borrowed money from Alex. I didn't know about it until well after Robin and I had been involved for some time. Honestly, it was more a gift than a loan. He had offered to pay for her education and her expenses while she was in college. . . . But she insisted that he let her pay him back once she graduated. For the four years she was in college, he paid everything.

Q: Please continue.

A: Well, when Alex came back into Robin's life, I knew he was just after his money. She was so happy to have him back in her life, but then that all changed when he asked about the money. Robin wasn't sure if she still wanted a relationship with him, or if she was going to just pay him some money to go away, or what to do.

Q: Did you know anything else about the money?

A: Yeah, the weekend he was visiting us she was still deciding what she wanted to do about Alex. She told me that she had found out the money was dirty money from his days undercover and she told me she wouldn't be a part of that by paying it back. I know that Alex just wanted the money, one way or another.

Q: Do you know how much Alex was alleging Robin owed him?

A: Yes, about $100,000 in total.

Q: Do you have anything else to tell the Grand Jury?

A: No.

Q: You told Detective Rodriguez that there was a stranger in the area?

A: Yes. I didn't think it was of much importance, so I didn't mention it until later. It was just some strange guy I noticed off and on, standing on the shoreline.

Q: But you said that that person would be the only other suspect?

A: I did not murder my wife. Nor would anyone I know who lives up by our lake house. So yes that would be the only other suspect.

Q: Now, you had a life insurance policy on your wife, right?

A: Yes, I did. My work offers life insurance for both employees and their spouses. I took one out simply because it seemed like the responsible thing to do.

Q: Did you file a claim?

A: Yes.

Q: When?

A: Shortly after she died. I needed the money to help pay bills that I had incurred. Funeral expenses. Lawyer costs for doing her estate, you know.

Q: Have you been paid?

A: Yes, I got the money about six months ago.

Q: Now, you have harmed your wife in the past, isn't that correct?

A: We had our fights. But they weren't as bad as they may sound.

Q: Thank you, Mr. Warren. That is all I have.

A: Okay.

(END OF TRANSCRIPT)

This is to certify that I have read the transcript of my deposition taken on and that the transcript accurately reflects the questions asked and my answers.

SIGNATURE: Bradley Warren

Subscribed and sworn to before me on December 4, [YR-1].

Syndey W. Jones

Sydney W. Jones
Certified Shorthand

RESUME OF BLAIR RODRIGUEZ

BLAIR RODRIGUEZ

Homicide Detective
San Milano, State of Lone Star

Experience —

Homicide Detective, City of San Milano, State of Lone Star — July [YR-2] – Present

- Responsible for approximately 50 homicide investigations to date, with 40 convictions resulting from those investigations. Only two homicide investigations currently open. Currently certified in Forensics Collection.

Police Officer, City of San Milano, State of Lone Star — August [YR-5] – July [YR-0]

Education —

- Forensics Collection — May [YR-5] – August [YR-5]

Training in proper collection of evidence, including DNA, fingerprints, and weapons. Training on what evidence to collect as well; although the evidence may not appear out of the ordinary, it could be critical to an investigation.

- Police Academy — May [YR-6] – May [YR-5]

Top 5% of the City of San Milano Police Training Academy.

- Brackettville High School Graduated — May [YR-5]

Additional —

Have testified regarding investigations in 48 cases.

Currently researching to write an article entitled "Proper Homicide Investigation: A Fail-Proof Checklist for Correct Identification of the Culprit."

DEPOSTION OF BLAIR RODRIGUEZ

ORAL DEPOSITION OF BLAIR RODRIGUEZ, produced as a witness at the instance of the Defendant, ALEX MOORE, and duly sworn, was taken in the above-styled and numbered cause on November 5, [YR-1] from 9:10 AM to 11:00 AM before Sydney Jones, Certified Shorthand Reporter in and for the State of Lone Star, reported by machine shorthand, at the law offices of Defendant, pursuant to the Federal Rules of Civil Procedure and the Provisions stated on the record or attached hereto.

This is a deposition of BLAIR RODRIGUEZ, who having been sworn, testified as follows:

EXAMINATION

QUESTIONS BY DEFENDANT'S COUNSEL:

Q: Good morning, Detective Rodriguez.

A: Good morning.

Q: I am representing Mr. Alex Moore, who is the defendant in a civil lawsuit brought by Mr. Bradley Warren. Do you remember them?

A: Yes, of course.

Q: Good. Before we get started, I would like to note for the record that plaintiff's counsel is present and has an opportunity to ask you questions as well. Do you understand?

A: Yes, I do.

Q: Also present today is a certified reporter, Sydney Jones, who will be recording all of this.

A: I understand.

Q: And I would also like to state at the outset of this deposition that I want you to know that if for any reason you do not understand my questions, please let me know so that we can clear that up.

A: I will.

Q: Okay, good. To start, would you please state your name for the reporter?

A: Yes, my name is Blair Rodriguez.

Q: Could you please tell us your position and duties with the police department?

A: I am a homicide detective, with about 7 years' experience on the force. My duties entail conducting investigations into possible homicides.

Q: You are a member of the San Milano Police Department?

A: Yes.

Q: Okay. Detective, I would like you to tell me about your investigation into the death of Mrs. Robin Warren.

A: Our records show that on August 6, [YR-2], at 4:06 a.m., we received a 911 call requesting emergency medical services and police, to 143 Cottonwood Lane, here in Bear County. I was dispatched to that location and arrived on scene at about 4:15 a.m.

Q: What happened once you arrived?

A: Once I arrived on scene, I proceeded to the front door of the residence and was met by a man identified to me as Bradley Warren, the decedent's husband. He was clearly distraught; his eyes were red, and it looked as though he had been rubbing at his face and pulling on his hair.

Q: Did you notice anything else?

A: Yes. He was wearing a bloody t-shirt and bloody pajama pants. However his arms had no blood on them. He also had no shoes on.

Q: What happened after he met you at the door?

A: First I spoke with Mr. Warren regarding what had occurred that evening. EMS had informed me that Robin Warren had been deceased for some length of time, enough that they could not resuscitate her.

Q: And what did you learn from that conversation with Mr. Warren?

A: I learned that Mrs. Warren's brother, Alex Moore, had been visiting at their lake house, the residence I was called to, for the weekend. The three of them had been visiting until about 11 p.m. at which point they went to their respective rooms of the home to go to bed.

Q: What else did you learn?

A: Not much. Mr. Warren was only able to tell me bits and pieces of what had occurred that night, as he was very emotionally distraught. He was unable to give me a complete, comprehensive version of what had occurred that evening.

Q: Please tell us what you were able to gather from the bits and pieces.

A: I gathered that Mr. Warren had been sleeping until about 4:00 a.m., or so, at which point he realized his wife had never come to bed. At that point he went to go find her.

Q: And he found her?

A: Yes, he told me he had seen a light on the path down to the dock. I understood from the bits and pieces he was able to say that once he got out to the dock he recognized the light as the industrial strength flashlight from their kitchen. He said he picked it up to look for her and found her on the deck of the boat. At this point he became so unintelligible that I told him I would go speak to Mr. Moore.

Q: Did he say anything else of importance?

A: Not at that point. Before I left, he did manage to convey that he believed Mr. Moore was responsible for her death.

Q: At any point did you think that Mr. Warren was a suspect?

A: No. His visible reaction was consistent with that I've seen in the spouses of homicide victims.

Q: Did Mr. Warren explain the lack of blood on his hands or arms?

A: I later asked him about it and he informed me that he had checked Mrs. Warren when he found her on the boat. After checking his wife he couldn't stand having her blood on him. He told me he had washed off in the kitchen sink while Mr. Moore called 911.

Q: What did you do after speaking with Mr. Warren, Detective?

A: Again, at this point, I told Mr. Warren I would be speaking to Mr. Moore. He pointed me to the bedrooms, where I found Mr. Moore.

Q: What can you tell us about Mr. Moore?

A: Mr. Moore was sitting in his bedroom. He seemed to be very calm for the circumstances, but it was a strange kind of calm. Something was off. I also noticed he had bloodshot eyes, blood on his shirt and arms, as well as fresh scratches on his arms.

Q: Did you speak with Mr. Moore?

A: Yes, I did. I asked him what he could tell me about the evening before and what had happened up until we arrived on scene.

Q: What did he tell you?

A: Mr. Moore told me that the three of them had gone to bed around 11:00 or 11:30 p.m. after arguing about what he described as "meaningless stuff". He said that he would always regret that his last words to his sister were words of anger. He told me he had awakened around 4:00 a.m. needing to use the bathroom. He had just returned to his bed when Mr. Warren came in screaming to call 911.

Q: Did he tell you anything else of importance?

A: Yes. Mr. Moore told me that he grabbed his cell phone and called 911 as he ran out to the dock. He told me that he thought maybe he could help his sister and attempted to check her, getting blood on himself in the process.

Q: Did Mr. Moore explain how he had gotten the scratches on his arms?

A: No, he did not.

Q: Did you ask him?

A: I did. And he just looked at the scratches and mumbled that he did not know. And he added that he did not care.

Q: What did you do next, Detective?

A: I proceeded outside to investigate the scene.

Q: And what can you tell us about that?

A: Well, the deputies that had arrived on scene with me had already gone out back to preserve the scene. By the time I got out there, it was around 5:00 a.m. I did not have my camera at the time. We had to wait for the medical examiner to arrive, so we did not take the picture of the victim until later in the morning. I took the knife that we found on the kitchen sink and processed it. I also looked for other relevant evidence.

Q: Such as?

A: Anything else that could have been relevant. In other cases there have been footprints in the blood of the victim, or something the attacker dropped.

Q: Did you find any of that here?

A: No, I did not. However, there was something that stood out to me. We were unable to find the industrial flashlight that Mr. Warren alleged he had seen on the dock and used in finding Mrs. Warren.

Q: Did you ask Mr. Warren about the flashlight?

A: I did at a later point in time, I don't remember if it was that evening, and he told me that in his panic to seek help he didn't remember what had happened to it.

Q: Please proceed with what happened during your investigation that night.

A: Well, while I was waiting for the coroner and someone with the camera to take a picture of the scene, I took Mr. Moore to the station.

Q: And why did you take him into the station?

A: The fact that he had fresh scratches on his arms, his strange demeanor, and the fact I didn't consider Mr. Warren a suspect.

Q: Do you recognize these exhibits? [Shows the exhibits to witness]

A: Absolutely. Those are the photographs of the victim and the knife. This is a drawing I made of the scene. And this is a floor plan of the lake house. I did an original sketch and turned it over to our computer folks who made this more detailed image.

Q: Are these true and accurate representations of what they show?

A: Yes, they are.

Q: Can you tell us what kind of boat this is and where the victim was located?

A: Yes, I think they call this a bay boat and it has a very shallow draft for being used in shallow water. It's used for fishing. The victim was lying on the front of the boat, a sort of platform where someone can stand while fishing. That is a small electric motor there that can be used for trolling.

Q: Okay. Is your drawing to scale?

A: No. I wanted to show the general layout of things outside the house.

Q: What about the house? Is it to scale?

A: Yes, pretty close. I took some rough measurements, but did not include them on my drawing. So what you see is very accurate in terms of the layout and where the doors and windows are.

Q: Did you take the pictures?

A: Like I said, I did not have a camera with me. Detective Jones took the picture of the victim later in the morning. I took the picture of the knife at the station. But those pictures are definitely accurate.

Q: Where is Detective Jones now?

A: He moved back to Wisconsin to be closer to his family.

Q: Okay. Just one more question before we discuss your interrogation of Mr. Moore, was there any other evidence collected from the scene?

A: Yes, there was. A thorough search by the officers remaining at the scene led to the discovery of forensic evidence within the home.

Q: And what did that evidence consist of?

A: They found blood belonging to the victim in the kitchen sink, as well as fingerprints belonging to all three individuals on that sink. There was also blood belonging to the victim in the guest bathroom and only Mr. Moore's prints were present on that sink.

Q: Did you check the knife for fingerprints?

A: Yes, we did. The results were inconclusive.

Q: Did you check it for blood?

A: Yes, there was no blood on it to test. And after the autopsy of the victim, I learned that the defendant's DNA was found under several of the victim's fingernails.

Q: Okay. Now, once you arrived at the police station that night, what happened?

A: I arrived back at the police station and proceeded to interview Mr. Moore at roughly 6:30 a.m.

Q: What did this interview reveal?

A: Mr. Moore told the same story he gave me at the lake residence. I asked him about the scratches on his arms, at which point he told me that he had now remembered that they were from a fight earlier that evening with his sister. He told me that she had become angry and upset with him, becoming physically violent with him.

Q: Did you ask him what made her so angry and upset?

A: I did. He informed me that she was angry with him for trying to get her to leave her husband that weekend. Mr. Moore told me that Mrs. Warren had been planning on leaving Mr. Warren, but wanted to do it on her own terms.

Q: Did he tell you anything else of importance?

A: Yes, Mr. Moore also told me that Mr. Warren overheard the argument between his sister and himself. He said Mr. Warren became angry and that they — Mr. Moore and Mr. Warren — got into an argument as well.

Q: Was there anything else?

A: Yes, at this point in the interview Mr. Moore paused and asked me if Mr. Warren was also being questioned at the police station. He asked if what Mr. Warren was saying added up.

Q: What else can you tell us about this?

A: Mr. Moore came across like he honestly believed Mr. Warren was responsible for his sister's death. When I informed him that Mr. Warren was not currently being questioned, he became irritated. He asked me something to the effect of "Why the hell not? She's only called 911 about him beating her five or six times!"

Q: Did you look into that claim?

A: I did. After I finished my questioning of Mr. Moore about 8:00 a.m., I continued investigating what we had so far. This included finding several domestic disturbance calls from a woman who identified herself as Robin Warren.

Q: Did Mr. Moore say anything else before you finished questioning him?

A: The only other thing he told me was that he couldn't remember if there was blood on Mr. Warren when he came in screaming to call 911. I didn't give this much weight. It was dark in the house when Mr. Warren came in and Mr. Moore was clearly running past him to get out the front door, looking at his phone to call 911.

Q: What else can you tell us about your investigation?

A: I met with Mr. Warren the next day to follow up. He told me essentially the same story he had the night before, but in a much more collected manner. I asked him to come in and give a statement, which he did the next day.

Q: Did he tell you anything else of importance to your investigation during your follow up?

A: Yes, he told me he remembered a stranger watching them over the weekend on the lakeshore. He told me if Mr. Moore didn't murder Mrs. Warren, that stranger would be the only other suspect.

Q: Did Mr. Moore remember this same strange person?

A: Yes, he later informed me there was a male stranger watching them from a neighbor's lot on the lakefront. He said that when the so-called stranger saw them looking right at him, he ran back into the bushes and disappeared.

Q: Did you follow up on that lead?

A: [Reviews notes] No, I did not consider that a credible lead. But [reviewing notes] I need to correct that, I did follow up and we found a 911 call. But it was anonymous and after a patrol office went to the area and found nothing, we considered it to be a false alarm. There had been no other reports of so-called strangers in the area so I did not consider it credible.

Q: Did you interview any other witnesses?

A: No, I did not.

Q: Okay. Thank you, Detective. I think that covers all I need for now.

(END OF TRANSCRIPT)

This is to certify that I have read the transcript of my deposition taken on and that the transcript accurately reflects the questions asked and my answers.

SIGNATURE: Blair Rodriguez

Subscribed and sworn to before me on December 20, [YR-1].

Syndey W. Jones

Sydney W. Jones
Certified Shorthand

911 TRANSCRIPTS

911 TRANSCRIPT
August 28, [-2]
2:00 A.M.

Dispatch: 911, what is your emergency?

Caller: My husband just attacked me!

Dispatch: Is here with you?

Caller: I ran to the neighbors, and I'm using their phone. Please, send the police!

Dispatch: Ma'am, I'm sending someone out there now. Do you need medical attention?

Caller: I don't know . . . (unintelligible) . . . I don't know . . .

Dispatch: What is your name, honey?

Caller: It's Robin Warren. Please hurry. Please.

Dispatch: Robin, the police are on their way. I'll send medical as well. What happened?

Caller: He attacked me! He came at me, hitting me, hit me several times . . . He was so angry . . . I didn't do anything . . . Then he hit me in the face . . . I ran when I saw him grab a knife . . .

Dispatch: Did he stab you?

Caller: No . . . I ran . . . I ran here.

Dispatch: I'll stay on the phone with you until the police arrive, alright?

Caller: (Unintelligible . . . talking to neighbors)

Dispatch: Robin? I'll stay here on the phone with you until the police and medical arrive.

Caller: Okay. (Unintelligible . . . talking to neighbors)

Dispatch: I see the police and medical say they've arrived

Caller: They're next door now. I can see them. . . . Thank you.

(END OF TRANSCRIPT)

911 TRANSCRIPT
November 2, [-2]
4:11 P.M.

Dispatch: 911, what is your emergency?

Caller: Please send the police! Please! Help!

Dispatch: Ma'am, what is happening?

Caller: Oh please! He's so angry. I'm hiding. He's looking for me and I'm hiding in my own damn house. Please send the police.

Dispatch: What is your address?

Caller: 6789 Whispering Way, here in San Milano.

Dispatch: Okay. Ma'am, the police are on their way. Who is he?

Caller: My husband, Brad. Bradley Warren. He hit me. My face is swollen, I can feel it.

Dispatch: Ma'am, the police are on their way. I'll send medical as well. Do you have any other injuries?

Caller: He hit me in the face, the arms, the chest, my stomach, all over. Where are the police?

Dispatch: Ma'am, the police are almost there. Are you still hiding?

Caller: Yes, I'm hiding in the guest room. He's looking for me. He's almost to this room.

Dispatch: Ma'am, they say they are outside. If you can get out of the house while he's at the front door, or if you can yell when he opens the door to the police.

Caller: They're at the door now. . . HELP! I'M IN HERE!

(END OF TRANSCRIPT)

911 TRANSCRIPT
February 6, [YR-2]
3:09 AM

Dispatch: 911, what is your emergency?

Caller: I think my neighbor is hitting his wife. Please send the police.

Dispatch: What is the address?

Caller: They live at 6788, I mean 6789 Whispering Way.

Dispatch: Sir, I'm sending the police. Can you tell me more?

Caller: I heard them arguing earlier, outside. Then I heard her yell out, like she was in pain, and by the time I got to the window I saw what looked like him dragging her into the house.

Dispatch: Sir, is there anything else you can tell me?

Caller: She came over here and called the police late last year about him abusing her. I am really scared for her. For her safety. Please, get someone here quickly.

Dispatch: Sir, the police are on their way. I'll send medical, too.

Caller: Thank you.

(END OF TRANSCRIPT)

911 TRANSCRIPT
August 5, [YR-2]
11:48 P.M.

Dispatch: 911, what is your emergency?

Caller: I think someone is looking into my window.

Dispatch: What is the address?

Caller: I would rather not give it.

Dispatch: Sir, I cannot help you if do not give me your address.

Caller: I live on Town Lake.

Dispatch: Sir, is there anything else you can tell me?

Caller: I have seen him several other times walking slowly on the path around the lake. Whenever I glance his way he turns and walks quickly the other way. Some of my neighbors have also noticed him. No one knows who he is.

Dispatch: Sir, I will send the police to drive through the area.

Caller: Thank you.

(END OF TRANSCRIPT)

Medical Examiner's Autopsy Report

Date:	August 6, [YR-2]
Time:	3:00 p.m.
Examiner:	Henry Martin, M.D.
Witness:	Detective Blair Rodriguez
Deceased:	Robin Warren
Date of Birth:	May 18, [-26]
Height:	5' 5"
Weight:	128 pounds

Observations: The deceased has one stab wound to the chest. The stab wound is directly through the heart. It is roughly 1" wide and 6" deep. The wound is consistent with a knife blade ranging from 7" to 8".

Based on the location of the wound and the minimal blood flow from it, it is clear the victim died very quickly.

Upon further examination it was also determined the deceased suffered blunt force trauma to the back of the head prior to death.

Cause/Manner of Death: Stab wound to chest, homicide

Submitted August 6, [YR-2]

Henry Martin

Henry Martin, M.D.

Medical Examiner

MEDICAL EXAMINER'S DEATH CERTIFICATE

Name of Deceased: Robin Warren

Date and Time of Death: August 6th, [YR-2] at approximately 3:00 a.m.

Primary Cause of Death: Stab wound to chest

Survivors: Husband, Bradley Warren
Brother, Alex Moore

Submitted August 7, [YR-2]

HENRY MARTIN

Henry Martin, M.D.
Medical Examiner

Forensics Report

Bear County Crime Laboratory
Bear County
State of Lone Star

WEAPONS:

The weapon gathered was a 7.5-inch knife. Bradley and Robin Warren owned the weapon.

FINGERPRINTS:

Fingerprints were taken from the knife. The prints on the knife belong to Robin Warren, Bradley Warren, and Alex Moore.

Fingerprints were not taken from the kitchen sink.

Fingerprints were not taken from the master bathroom.

Fingerprints taken from the guest bathroom sink were only those of Alex Moore.

DNA:

DNA was collected from the knife. However, it was unidentified.

DNA was also collected from the kitchen sink. The DNA proved to be Robin Warren's blood.

Additional DNA was collected from the guest bathroom sink and was proven to be Robin Warren's blood.

No DNA testing was performed in the master bathroom.

DNA belonging to Alex More was found under victim's fingernails.

Jane Gilbert

Jane Gilbert
Lab Technician
Submitted: September 5, [YR-1]

Life Insurance Policy on Robin Warren

Warm Heart Life Insurance
Providing for your loved ones as if they were our own since 1971

LIFE INSURANCE POLICY
Summary

Policy Number: 338285764-3

Type of Policy: Term Life
Policy Holder: Bradley Warren
The Insured: Warren, Robin
Gender: Female
Date of Birth: May 18, [-26]
Age: 26 years of age
Occupation: Office Manager

Beginning Date of Coverage: August 10, [-4]
Expiration Date of Coverage: August 10, [YR-2]
Amount of Coverage: $100,000
Premium Due: Paid In Full

This life insurance policy for $100,000 is payable in full upon the death of the insured, Robin Warren, to the policyholder, Bradley Warren.

Limitations:

This policy will be null and void should the insured become deceased due to any act by the policyholder.

This policy will only be paid to the amount of the premiums paid should the policyholder commit suicide.

Floor Plan of Lake House

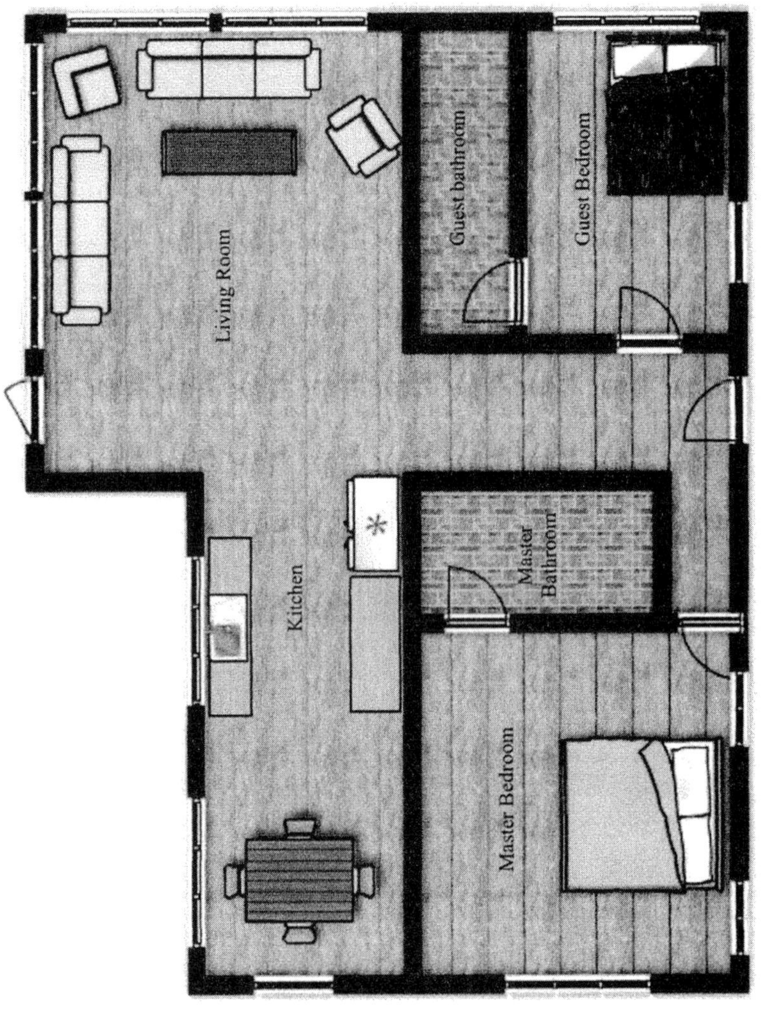

Drawing of Scene

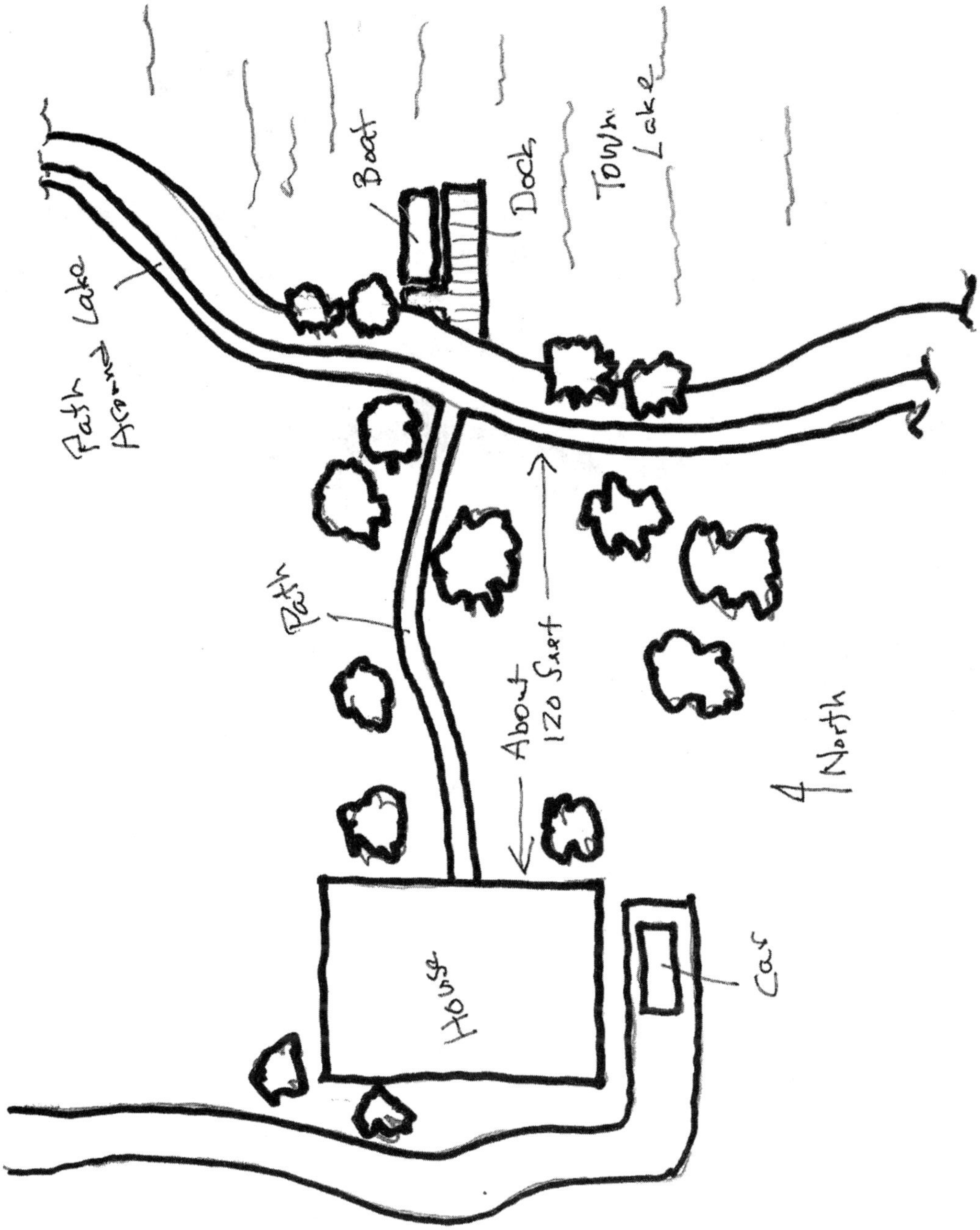

PHOTOGRAPH OF VICTIM

Photograph of Knife

Newspaper Article

Local Woman Murdered at Lake

Reported by: Trisha Green
August 7, [YR-2]

Police responded early yesterday morning to a homicide here in San Milano, Lone Star. The deceased victim was Mrs. Robin Warren. Her husband, Bradley Warren, told investigators that he found her just after four in the morning, outside their lake house on Town Lake. Although it is reported that both her husband and her brother attempted to resuscitate her, Mrs. Warren was pronounced dead at the scene by paramedics who arrived some time later.

A phone call to the medical examiner's office indicates that she died from a single knife wound to the chest.

Her husband talked to police at the scene but was not taken in for questioning.

According to an inside source, the police have cleared Mr. Warren as a suspect based on evidence collected at the scene.

Police have taken her brother, Alex Moore, into custody for her murder. Alex Moore is not new to law enforcement. A former police officer, he was discharged from the San Milano Police Department in late 2009. Since then, he has been in and out of rehabilitation facilities. Our inside source is confident he is responsible for the murder of Mrs. Robin Warren.

Detective Rodriguez, who is working the case, states that he is confident that they have their man.

Interviews with some neighbors, however, seem to point to an unknown man who has been seen in the area after dark for the last several nights.

The investigation continues.

Jury Instructions

LADIES AND GENTLEMEN OF THE JURY:

I am now going to instruct you about the law governing this case. You are required to accept my instructions as the law. Any ideas you have of what the law is or what the law should be or any statements by the attorneys as to what the law may be, must be disregarded by you, if they are in conflict with these instructions.

1. Claims of Parties

The plaintiff claims that he sustained damages due to the defendant's wrongful act of killing his wife, Robin Warren. The defendant has denied those claims and also denies that the plaintiff is entitled to recover any damages.

2. Burden of Proof

In this case, the plaintiff has the burden of proving his claims by a preponderance of the evidence. If you find from the evidence, by a preponderance of the evidence, that the defendant acted intentionally in killing plaintiff's wife, and that such actions were the proximate cause of his wife's death, then you must find the defendant liable for his actions.

3. Proximate Cause

When I use the expression "proximate cause," I mean a cause that, in the natural or ordinary course of events, produced Robin Warren's, the decedent's, death. It need not be the only cause, nor the last or nearest cause. It is sufficient if it combines with another cause resulting in the injury and death.

4. Preponderance of the Evidence

The term "preponderance of the evidence" means that amount of evidence that causes you to conclude that the allegation is probably true. To prove an allegation by the preponderance of the evidence, a party must convince you that the allegation is more likely true than not true.

If the evidence on a particular issue is equally balanced, that issue has not been proven by a preponderance of the evidence. Therefore, the party having the burden of proving that issue has failed with respect to that particular issue.

5. Circumstantial Evidence

A fact or a group of facts may, based on logic and common sense, lead you to a conclusion as to other facts. This is known as circumstantial evidence. A fact may be proved by circumstantial evidence. Circumstantial evidence is entitled to the same consideration as any other type of evidence

6. Opinion Testimony

You may have heard a witness give opinions about matters requiring special knowledge or skill. You should judge this testimony in the same way you judge the testimony from any other witness. The fact that such person has given an opinion does not mean that you are required to accept it. Give the testimony whatever weight you think it deserves, considering the reasons given for the opinion, the witness's qualifications, and all of the other evidence in the case.

7. Credibility of Witnesses

It is up to you to decide the credibility of the witnesses. In making the decision you may consider such factors as whether the witness has made a prior inconsistent statement or has been convicted of a crime. Evidence of this kind may be considered by you in connection with all the other facts and circumstances in evidence in deciding the weight to be given to the testimony of that witness.

8. Damages

a. General

If you decide the plaintiff is entitled to damages, you should give such amount as you decide to be fair and just, under all the circumstances. Such damages may include the following items, to the extent you find they have been proved by the evidence:

- Reasonable medical, hospital, funeral and burial expenses;
- Loss of financial support;
- Loss of gifts or other valuable gratuities;
- Loss of parental training and guidance;
- Loss of companionship;
- Plaintiff's grief, sorrow, or mental anguish.

Whether the plaintiff has proved these damages is for you to decide, based upon evidence and not upon speculation, guess, or conjecture. The amount of money to be awarded for certain of these elements of damage cannot be proved in a precise dollar amount. The law leaves such amounts to your sound judgment.

b. Punitive Damages

If you find for the plaintiff, you may, but are not required to, award punitive damages. The purposes of punitive damages are to punish a defendant and to deter similar acts in the future. Punitive damages may not be awarded to compensate a plaintiff.

The plaintiff has the burden of proving by a preponderance of the evidence that punitive damages should be awarded, and, if so, the amount of any such damages.

You may award punitive damages only if you find that the defendant's conduct that resulted in the death of Robin Warren, the decedent, was a willful act or omission or gross negligence. Gross negligence means conduct or a failure to act that is so reckless that it demonstrates a substantial lack of concern for whether an injury will result.

If you find that punitive damages are appropriate, you must use reason in setting the amount. Punitive damages, if any, should be in an amount sufficient to fulfill their purposes but should not reflect bias, prejudice, or sympathy toward any party. In considering the amount of any punitive damages, consider the degree of reprehensibility of the defendant's conduct.

In addition, you may consider the relationship of any award of punitive damages to any actual harm inflicted on the plaintiff.

9. Insurance

Whether a party is insured or not insured has no bearing on any issue that you must decide. You must refrain from any inference, speculation, or discussion about insurance. If you find for the plaintiff, you shall not speculate about or consider any possible sources of benefits the plaintiff may have received or might receive. After you have returned your verdict, the court will make whatever adjustments are necessary in this regard.

10. Verdict Form

To assist you in deciding these issues, I am giving you a verdict form to use during your deliberations. When you have completed the form, please let the bailiff know that you have completed your deliberations.

VERDICT FORM

1. **Liability**

Do you find by a preponderance of the evidence that the defendant caused the death of the plaintiff's wife?

_________ YES

_________ NO

If your answer is "no," then do not answer Question 2. If your answer is "yes," answer Question 2.

2. **Damages**

Do you find by a preponderance of the evidence that the plaintiff suffered damages as a result of the defendant's actions?

_________ YES

_________ NO

If you answered "yes," then please enter the amount of damages, in whole dollar amounts, to which the plaintiff is entitled.

$ ______________________

3. **Punitive Damages**

Do you find by a preponderance of the evidence that the decedent's death was the result of the defendant's willful act or omission or gross negligence in light of the circumstances?

_________YES

_________ NO

If you answered "yes," then please enter the amount of punitive damages, in whole dollar amounts, to which the plaintiff is entitled.

$ ______________________

Chapter 20
State v. Winslet

§ 20-1. Introduction

Charles Winslet has been charged with murdering his girlfriend, Sadie Norris. Her skeletal remains were found by hunters on Winslet's ranch, which he had shared with Ms. Norris for two years before he reported her missing in [YR-2]. Evidence indicates that she died from being shot in the back with a crossbow bolt.

Winslet claims that he knows nothing of her death and urged the police to investigate Johnny Bleu, someone he thinks was having an affair with Ms. Norris at the time of her disappearance.

§ 20-2. Stipulations Regarding Procedural and Evidentiary Matters

1. Although the case is being tried in a State court, the Federal Rules of Criminal Procedure and Federal Rules of Evidence apply.
2. This case will be tried only on the issue of guilt or innocence.
3. All witnesses called to testify who made statements or grand jury testimony identifying the defendant, other individuals, or tangible evidence must, if asked, identify the same at trial.
4. Charles Winslet and Taylor Dodds signed their statements to the police.
5. All notice and disclosure requirements under the Federal Rules of Criminal Procedure and the Federal Rules of Evidence were met in a timely fashion.
6. Other than what is supplied in the problem itself, there is nothing exceptional or unusual about the background information of any of the witnesses or the defendant that would bolster or detract from their credibility.
7. This competition does not permit a listed witness or the defendant, while testifying, to "invent" an individual not mentioned in this problem, or to have testimony or evidence offered to the court or jury from that invented individual.
8. "Beyond the record" must not be entertained as an objection.
9. Contact with the competition officials concerning this problem must be pursuant to the rules of the competition.
10. The year [YR-0] is the current year in which this case comes to trial.
11. All exhibits in the file are authentic. In addition, each exhibit contained in the file is the original of that document unless otherwise noted on the exhibit or as established by the evidence.
12. Any searches and seizures conducted by the police met the requirements of the Fourth Amendment and the Federal Rules of Criminal Procedure.
13. No changes or alterations were made to any of the exhibits.
14. There are no Confrontation Clause issues with regard to any written or oral hearsay statements.

15. The victim's body was located in Bear County, State of Lone Star.
16. The e-mails in the packet may be presented at trial as a string of e-mails or individually.
17. Sadie Norris' remains were identified by DNA testing on May 14 [YR-1] by the Bear County Crime Laboratory.

I. Lone Star Penal Code Provisions

§ 81.01. Types of Criminal Homicide

(a) A person commits criminal homicide if he intentionally, knowingly, recklessly, or with criminal negligence causes the death of an individual.

(b) Criminal homicide is murder, capital murder, manslaughter, or criminally negligent homicide.

§ 81.02. Murder.

(a) In this Section:

(1) "Adequate cause" means cause that would commonly produce a degree of anger, rage, resentment, or terror in a person of ordinary temper, sufficient to render the mind incapable of cool reflection.

(2) "Sudden passion" means passion directly caused by and arising out of provocation by the individual killed or another acting with the person killed which passion arises at the time of the offense and is not solely the result of former provocation.

(b) A person commits an offense if he:

(1) intentionally or knowingly causes the death of an individual;

(2) intends to cause serious bodily injury and commits an act clearly dangerous to human life that causes the death of an individual; or

(3) commits or attempts to commit a felony, other than manslaughter, and in the course of and in furtherance of the commission or attempt, or in immediate flight from the commission or attempt, he commits or attempts to commit an act clearly dangerous to human life that causes the death of an individual.

(c) Except as provided by Subsection (d), an offense under this section is a felony of the first degree.

(d) At the punishment stage of a trial, the defendant may raise the issue as to whether he caused the death under the immediate influence of sudden passion arising from an adequate cause. If the defendant proves the issue in the affirmative by a preponderance of the evidence, the offense is a felony of the second degree.

* * * * *

§ 81.04. Manslaughter

(a) A person commits an offense if he recklessly causes the death of an individual.

(b) An offense under this section is a felony of the second degree.

§ 81.05. Criminally Negligent Homicide

(a) A person commits an offense if he causes the death of an individual by criminal negligence.

(b) An offense under this section is a state jail felony.

INDICTMENT

COURT'S COPY
Name: Charles Winslet
Complainant: Sadie Norris
Offense Charge: Murder
GJ: 3456721 **PH Court: 546**
JN#: 143245 **SID#: 14563**
Witness: State's Attorney

TRUE BILL OF INDICTMENT

IN THE NAME AND BY AUTHORITY OF THE STATE OF LONE STAR, the Grand Jury of Bear County, State of Lone Star, duly organized, empanelled and sworn as such at the April term, A.D., July 12, [YR-1], of the Judicial District Court of said County, at said term, do present in and to said Court that in the County and State aforesaid, and anterior to the presentment of this indictment, and:

COUNT 1: MURDER

on or about June 8, [YR-2], CHARLES WINSLET, hereinafter referred to as defendant, then and there intentionally or knowingly, unlawfully, and feloniously cause the killing and murder of SADIE NORRIS, a human being, hereinafter referred to as complainant, without the authority of law and with deliberate design to effect the death of complainant in violation of Section 81.02, Lone Star Penal Code;

AGAINST THE PEACE AND DIGNITY OF THE STATE

David S. Warren

Foreperson of the Grand Jury

Defendant's First Written Statement to Police

STATE OF LONE STAR }
COUNTY OF BEAR }

Case Number: 13-3214

VOLUNTARY STATEMENT OF: CHARLES WINSLET

I, Charles Winslet, after first being duly warned by Det. Roger Stone #3489 at 0930 hrs, at 214 W. Nueva, on June 13, [YR-2], that (1) I have the right to remain silent and not make any statement at all, and any statement I do make may be used against me at my trial; (2) Any statement I make may be used as evidence against me in Court; (3) I have the right to have a lawyer present to advise me prior to and during any questioning; (4) If I am unable to employ a lawyer, I have the right to have a lawyer appointed to advise me prior to and during any questioning; (5) I have the right to terminate the interview at any time; and I understand that the above rights are continuing rights and may be urged by me at any stage of the proceedings, and I hereby prior to and during the making of this statement, knowingly, intelligently, and voluntarily waive the above rights and give to the said, Det. Roger Stone #3489, the person to whom this statement is being given, the following written statement:

My name is Charles Winslet. Several days ago, my girlfriend and I had a big argument over an affair she was having with someone on the Internet. I want to make a statement now in case something happens to me and to investigate someone named Johnny Bleu.

At about 11 PM on June 8th, Sadie said that she was tired of arguing and that she was leaving for a drive and that she needed to cool off. She walked out the door. I did not follow her. I heard her get in her car and drive off. We live in the country without many lights so it was hard to see in which direction she was headed.

I stayed in the house. I was pretty angry as well. When she did not show up the next day, I called 911 and reported her missing. She has never done anything like that. I think she is with this Bleu guy. I saw some of the e-mails that they were sharing and it's clear that he was trying to break us up. She denied it and I guess that is why she got so angry when I accused her of cheating on me.

A couple of weeks ago, I woke up at about 3 AM and I thought that I heard someone driving off from our house. I got up and could not see anything.

She has no family in the area. I am not really sure what I should do next or who to contact and that is why I am here making a statement. She is my life and I cannot go on without her. We were supposed to get married later this year.

I really think this guy Bleu knows what happened. I tried to find a person by that name but have not had any luck. She must be with him somewhere.

I have not heard anything from her. I can't find her car.

She did not take any clothes or other stuff with her. Just her purse and car keys, is all that she took to the best of my memory.

WITNESS: *Bill Blair* SIGNATURE: *Charles Winslet*

DATE: June 13, [YR-2]

Defendant's Second Written Statement to Police

STATE OF LONE STAR **COUNTY OF BEAR**	}	**Case Number: 12-81377**

VOLUNTARY STATEMENT OF: CHARLES WINSLET

I, Charles Winslet, after first being duly warned by Det. Lanny Davidson #4587 at 0930 hrs, at 214 W. Nueva, on May 21, [YR-1] that (1) I have the right to remain silent and not make any statement at all, and any statement I do make may be used against me at my trial; (2) Any statement I make may be used as evidence against me in Court; (3) I have the right to have a lawyer present to advise me prior to and during any questioning; (4) If I am unable to employ a lawyer, I have the right to have a lawyer appointed to advise me prior to and during any questioning; (5) I have the right to terminate the interview at any time; and I understand that the above rights are continuing rights and may be urged by me at any stage of the proceedings, and I hereby prior to and during the making of this statement, knowingly, intelligently, and voluntarily waive the above rights and give to the said, Det. Lanny Davidson #4587, the person to whom this statement is being given, the following written statement:

I did not kill my girlfriend. I know who did. I said that two years ago that Johnny Bleu did something to her. And the police did nothing to find her. I kept looking for her and found nothing. I could not even find her car. No one found her car.

Like I said, when I talked to police detective in [YR-2], Sadie had walked out and said she needed time to think. She packed a bag with some of her personal stuff and then walked out of the house and drove off. I have not seen her since.

I loved her and we planned to get married.

I tried finding Johnny Bleu and sent out some e-mails to my friends, after I talked to the police to see if anyone knew where she was. I begged them to help me. One of my friends is Taylor Dodds.

I know that you will probably search my computer. I have nothing to hide.

I do own a crossbow but have not used it in a couple of years. I bought it at Sports Paradise where I work in the camping section. I used it once during the fall hunting season in 2010. I got a deer with it but do not have the patience to sit quietly waiting for the deer to come in close enough to use it. My weapon of choice now for hunting deer is a 30-06 Remington. I am not even sure where I put the crossbow.

Since 2009, I have leased out the back part of my property to deer hunters. I go back there only once or twice a year to make sure the deer stand is okay.

The ranch is in my name, not Sadie's. I bought it about 5 years ago, about 2 years before Sadie moved in with me.

Sadie worked at a local Walmart, here in San Milano. She worked in several different sections of the store, I believe. Our ranch is in Bear County, about 6 miles outside San Milano.

I have had deer hunting leases on my ranch for the last five years. Some of them use archery equipment, like crossbows, which are legal in this state.

When I saw the remains on my ranch the other day, my first thought was that I was in real trouble because one of my hunters must have accidently killed someone. The place where the remains were found is between the deer blind and an active trail that deer use to get to the other side of my property.

I do not know anyone named Johnny Bleu or whatever he or she called themselves.

WITNESS: *Sally E. Hernandez*   SIGNATURE: Charles Winslet

DATE: May 21, [YR-1]

Taylor Dodds's Statement to Police

STATE OF LONE STAR
COUNTY OF BEAR

Case Number: 12-81377

VOLUNTARY STATEMENT OF: Taylor Dodds

I, Taylor Dodds, after first being duly warned by Det. Lanny Davidson #4587 at 0700 hrs, at 214 W. Nueva, on June 5, [YR-1], that (1) I have the right to remain silent and not make any statement at all, and any statement I do make may be used against me at my trial; (2) Any statement I make may be used as evidence against me in Court; (3) I have the right to have a lawyer present to advise me prior to and during any questioning; (4) If I am unable to employ a lawyer, I have the right to have a lawyer appointed to advise me prior to and during any questioning; (5) I have the right to terminate the interview at any time; and I understand that the above rights are continuing rights and may be urged by me at any stage of the proceedings, and I hereby prior to and during the making of this statement, knowingly, intelligently, and voluntarily waive the above rights and give to the said, Det. Lanny Davidson #3489, the person to whom this statement is being given, the following written statement:

I am making this statement because I am afraid that the police are going to convict an innocent man, Charles Winslet. He did not kill his girlfriend, Sadie. Ken Lott did.

I have worked with both men for the last three years at the local Sports Paradise. Ken works in archery and Charles in camping, where I also work. Ken has a terrible temper and is always getting in trouble with management. He has been threatened with being fired on at least two occasions. But he is such a charmer that he talks his way out of trouble. You cannot believe him.

He also sees himself as a real ladies' man. Everyone at the store knows that he goes on the Internet and has so-called Internet affairs with different women. When things get really serious and they want to meet him, he calls it off. He talks about doing that all the time. He kept telling me that he was doing it for the fun of it.

When it came to connecting with Sadie, things changed. He met her when she came to see Charles in the store and she and Ken hit it off real quick. I watched them flirting with each other. I mean serious flirting. I heard him tell her one day that he would see her on the "net." That was the word he used. Ken told me that Sadie was way too good for Charles and that he and Sadie planned to run off. He said that he was finally in love and was going to stop having, what he called, "Internet sex." He also said something about making it look like she had left Charles. He said that he would even things up with Charles. Ken was jealous of Charles because Charles kept getting pay raises when he did not. I know because I saw their pay stubs a couple of times.

Ken told me that he had gone out to see Sadie at the ranch at least twice where she lived with Winslet. But later he denied that he had ever been to the ranch. I know that is a lie because Charles and Sadie hosted a BBQ out there before Sadie disappeared and we were all invited and got a tour of the house and the grounds. So Ken knows where things are out there. I think the BBQ was in April before Sadie disappeared. By then, Ken and Sadie could not hide their feelings for each other. Whenever she came in the store, supposedly to see Charles, Ken would get all fluttery. Sickening.

I am not sure what finally happened but it sounded like Sadie finally told both of them that she was finished playing games and was leaving town. Ken was checking his e-mails at work about the time Sadie disappeared and said something that I overheard about Sadie was making a really big mistake and she would regret it big time. He muttered that she had broken his heart, or something like that.

The next thing I knew, Charles came into the store one day, and said that Sadie had left him the night before for some guy named Johnny Bleu who she met on the Internet. I looked at Ken who did not say anything. But he was nervous all day and kept asking if Charles had found Sadie. Eventually, they both quit talking about her. But I am convinced that Ken, the one with the bad temper, killed her. He had access to crossbows and I just don't think that Charles could have done it. Charles is a very calm, even-tempered man, who has never shown signs of anger when things do not go his way.

I never told Charles who Johnny Bleu really was. I figured I did not want to get between them.

Charles loved Sadie and after she left he used Facebook to try and find her. I will give you a printout of his posting.

You need to follow up on Ken Lott.

WITNESS: Susan Blair SIGNATURE: Taylor Dodds

DATE: June 5, [YR-1]

Grand Jury Testimony of Lanny Davidson

IN RE:	BEFORE THE GRAND JURY
	OF
GRAND JURY INVESTIGATION	BEAR COUNTY, STATE OF LONE STAR

* * * * * *

****

COURT REPORTER'S

Q AND A TRANSCRIPT OF TESTIMONY OF

LANNY DAVIDSON

JUNE 24, [YR-1]

****

* * * * *

BE IT REMEMBERED, that on JUNE 24, [YR-1], the above-entitled matter came on for hearing before the Grand Jury of Bear County, sitting in San Milano, State of Lone Star, being presented by JAMES HERNANDEZ, Assistant Criminal District Attorney, for consideration by the members thereof.

VERONICA GARCIA was duly sworn as Court Reporter.

WHEREUPON, the following evidence was introduced and proceedings had, to-wit, beginning at 9:30 o'clock a.m. and concluding at 11:03 o'clock a.m.

DETECTIVE LANNY DAVIDSON, The Witness.

GRAND JURY FOREMAN: Do you solemnly swear that you will not divulge either by words or signs any matter about which you may be interrogated, and that you will keep secret all proceedings of the Grand Jury which may be had in your presence, and that you will true answers make to such questions as may be propounded to you by the Grand Jury or under its direction, so help you God?

THE WITNESS: I do.

EXAMINATION BY JAMES HERNANDEZ:

Q: Good morning, Detective Davidson.

A: Hello.

Q: Before we get started, as with any witness who comes before the Grand Jury, I need to give you the definitions of perjury and aggravated perjury.

A: Of course.

Q: A person commits the offense of perjury if, with intent to deceive and with knowledge of the statement's meaning, that person makes a false statement under oath or swears to the truth of a false statement previously made and the statement is required or authorized by law to be made under oath.

Perjury is a Class A Misdemeanor, which is punishable by anywhere up to one year in the Bear County Jail and/or a fine of up to $4,000.

Perjury becomes aggravated perjury if the person commits perjury, makes that false statement during or in connection with an official proceeding, and Grand Jury proceedings are official proceedings, and the statement is material.

Aggravated perjury is a third-degree felony, which means it's punishable by anywhere from two to ten years in the Lone Star Department of Corrections, and there's a potential fine of up to $10,000. Do you understand this?

A: Yes, sir.

Q: Would you please state your name for the grand jury?

A: Yes, my name is Lanny Davidson.

Q: You are a detective with the San Milano Police Department?

A: Yes.

Q: Tell us about your work experience.

A: I joined the force about 10 years ago. I have been a homicide detective for about five years and have worked on about 75 cases, homicide. I have taken several forensic courses in the last two years, which were offered by the FBI at Quantico Virginia. I scored very high on the end of the course tests and received an award of merit.

Q: Do you have any college education?

A: Yes, from Texas Tech. I got a BA in sociology with a minor in criminal justice studies. I brought a copy of my resume, like you asked.

Q: Okay. Good. Can I see it? [Witness hands exhibit to prosecutor.] Thank you. Now, let's turn to this case. Do you know Charles Winslet?

A: Yes, I do. I met him for the first time in April of this year when I questioned him about the death of his girlfriend, Sadie Norris.

Q: That was the first time?

A: Yes. We, actually someone else in our office, actually had talked to him in [YR-2], when he said he wanted to make a statement about his girlfriend's running off, as he said it, with someone she had met on the Internet.

Q: Who did he give his statement to?

A: Detective Roger Stone. He has since left the force to take a job with the Dallas police force.

Q: Okay. Let's go back a bit. Why did you interview Mr. Winslet?

A: Earlier in April, on April 22, we got a report from two deer hunters that they had found skeletal remains on Winslet's property. They were there apparently scouting the area to see if they wanted to lease the property for the fall [YR-1] hunting season. They told us that it looked like there was an arrow sticking out of the remains and immediately called 911.

Q: Did you investigate it?

A: Yes, I immediately drove to the ranch and talked to Mr. Winslet. He said that two men had just been at the back of his property and said that they had found a body. He said that he did not call us because he had not yet checked it out for himself. He said that he was getting ready to do so when I drove up.

Q: So what happened next?

A: The hunters had already left the property, after telling him generally where the remains were located. I asked him to take me to the back of his property.

Q: Did he?

A: Yes, it took us about 30 minutes to locate the remains. As we drove to the location, he seemed to be wandering around the property rather than driving directly to the location stated by the two men who found the remains.

Q: Do you recognize this exhibit? [Prosecutor shows photo to witness]

A: Yes, definitely, that is the photo I took of the remains. As you can see it's basically what appears to be skeletal remains, with an arrow, or more technically a crossbow bolt, coming out of the rib cage. And it looks like someone had tried to cover it up at some point. It looked like they had tried to cover the remains with branches.

Q: Did you take this picture?

A: Yes.

Q: And do you recognize these exhibits? [Shows to witness]

A: Yes, I took these as well. From different angles and distances.

Q: Now, it looks like there are clothing fragments on the remains, right?

A: That is also correct.

Q: It appears to be a t-shirt so something like that. Did you find any other remnants of clothing such as pants, or even undergarments?

A: No, we did not.

Q: What did you do next?

A: I called the medical examiner's office and they got there about 30 minutes later to gather the remains and other evidence and take it to their office for processing.

Q: Can you tell us what Mr. Winslet's reaction was at this time?

A: He just stared at the remains. He did not say anything, which I found very strange. In my experience there are appropriate responses to seeing a dead body. And he just stared, sort of zombie like. He did not say anything, like oh crap, or any other signs of shock that we had found a dead body on his property. I asked him to not disturb anything. I asked him to sit down about 30 feet away from the remains while I quickly took the pictures and called for backup and the medical examiner.

Q: So, did it seem to you that he was not surprised by the whole scene?

A: No, he did not seem shocked, surprised, sorry, or anything.

Q: Was he in a state of medical shock?

A: No, he was very coherent and did not complain of dizziness. It was clear to me that he was very much aware of what was going on.

Q: Did you ask him any other questions at that point?

A: I did. I asked him if he recognized what appeared to an arrow and he said no, he did not. I also asked him if he knew who the remains belonged to and he said no. His eyes looked cold and distant.

Q: After the medical examiner arrived, what did you do?

A: I waited for a few minutes, took Mr. Winslet back to his house, and told him we would probably need to talk to him further. He finally said something about the body maybe belonging to his fiancée, Sadie Norris, who had disappeared in [YR-2]. I asked him about that and he said that it was my fault that the police had not found her. He said that he had made 911 calls and talked to a detective in our office, asking for his help. I told him I would look into that and then I drove back to my office. I looked through our files and reviewed Mr. Winslet's statement to Detective Stone in [YR-2] and also the 911 call that he had made. He had told me that he made several calls, but I could only find one. I also found a transcript of a 911 call that his girlfriend, Sadie Norris, had made in May [YR-2]. The transcript indicates that police officers showed up at their ranch. But there is no report from the police on what happened when they got there and talked to the parties involved. Apparently, that matter was resolved and they saw no need to file a report, or charges.

Q: Did you have another opportunity to interview Mr. Winslet?

A: Yes, I did. After we got a positive ID on the remains, I called him in and talked with him. He made a statement. I told him that we had information that the remains belonged to his girlfriend, Sadie. He did not cry or show any signs of grief. During the questioning he maintained his innocence and said that he had urged the police to look for Johnny Bleu, and said that although he owned a crossbow, he could not even say where it was. I got his consent to search his ranch.

Q: Did you conduct the search?

A: When the reports and evidence started pointing at Winslet, we got a warrant to search. We conducted the search on [reviewing notes] May 23rd and found incriminating evidence. A crossbow and two bolts in the machine shed. They were in a case back in a corner and had stuff stacked around it.

Q: Anything else?

A: Yes, in searching his computer in his house we found some e-mails between Winslet and someone named Johnny Bleu, which were shortly before Sadie Norris disappeared in [YR-2]. The e-mails give some indication that Winslet told Bleu to leave Norris alone or that there would be consequences. Computer forensics showed that one e-mail between Winslet's computer and Bleu had been deleted. We, actually our computer experts in the police department, were able to recover the actual text of that missing e-mail. We also found Facebook entries linked to Winslet.

Q: Is this that e-mail? [Shows exhibit to witness]

A: Yes, this is the one that someone deleted but we recovered. In it Winslet threatened both Sadie Norris and the person named Johnny Bleu and said something about piercing her heart if she left him. It was actually sent to Bleu.

Q: Were there any e-mails between the victim and either Winslet or Johnny Bleu?

A: As I said, there were several other e-mails that were still on the computer from Winslet to Bleu. But none from Bleu back to Winslet.

Q: Are these the e-mails? [Shows exhibits to witness]

A: Yes, the ones from April [YR-2], where Winslet suspects something and is trying to figure out who Bleu is.

Q: Okay, thanks. And what are these exhibits? [Shows exhibits to witness].

A: These are the e-mail exchanges between Sadie Norris and Johnny Bleu. It looked like Bleu was trying hard to get the victim to leave Winslet and run away with him. And it appears that there was some sort of physical relationship between Bleu and the victim.

Q: Do you recognize these exhibits? [Prosecutor shows several exhibits to the witness]

A: Yes, these are pictures of the crossbow and the case, and where it was found in the machine shed. Right in front of a John Deere tractor, with a front loader on it. It was pretty easy to spot when we walked into the building, the machine shed. This is a picture of the crossbow and arrows, or bolts, as they are sometimes called, we found in the case.

Q: And what are these?

A These are Winslet's Facebook entries that we found on his computer. The one is from just after Sadie Norris disappeared, and the other was posted after he found out that she was dead.

Q: Okay. Thanks. And what about this picture?

A: This is a picture of the bolt that was found in the victim's remains.

Q: Where were these pictures taken?

A: At our police station.

Q: There does not appear to be much blood on the head of the bolt.

A: It's hard to see in the picture but there was what appeared to be blood residue on the head, when I examined it.

Q: Now, did you have a chance to compare the bolt that was found in the victim and the two bolts found in the quiver attached to the crossbow?

A: They all matched. Same make, length, and type of point on the bolt. The points were three-sided. The type used for hunting.

Q: Okay. Were you able to identify the victim?

A: Yes, the remains were positively identified as those of Sadie Norris.

Q: How was the identification made?

A: DNA results. It took a couple of weeks to get the results.

Q: Was there any forensic evidence linking the crossbow found in the defendant's machine shed with the bolt found in the victim?

A: Our lab looked for some sort of residue, paint, anything, and they came up empty. I should add that unlike firearm ballistic testing, linking an arrow, or a bolt, to a particular crossbow is very difficult, if not impossible.

Q: Do you recognize this exhibit?

A: Yes, these are the defendant's statements. One to Detective Stone and the other one he gave to me.

Q: And what about these exhibits?

A: These are [pausing to review exhibits]. This is the transcript of the 911 call that Mr. Winslet made in June [YR-2].

Q: Detective, based on your experience, could you tell us whether you think that the victim was killed at another location and then her body moved to where it was found?

A: I believe she died where she was standing, or walking. She was shot in the back and fell forward. Based on the penetration of the bolt, I would say that she was shot from a distance of, say, at least 40 or 50 yards.

Q: Isn't that awfully far away for a crossbow?

A: No, not really. Most crossbows these days have a scope on them. So a kill shot from as far as 60 yards is not impossible. At that distance the penetration of the bolt is not as significant, but it's still fatal.

Q: Let me ask the question this way. Is it possible that the victim was on the ground and then shot through the back?

A: No, if she had been shot at close range, while on the ground, the bolt would have gone at a lot further into the soil. As it was, I think the tip of the bolt was only in the ground an inch or two. It was pretty rocky and hard soil there.

Q: Could she have been running when she was shot?

A: Of course.

Q: Now, I notice that the remains seem to be located amongst some brush, or trees. . . .

A: Yes, I examined the vegetation and it appeared that there was one bush that had seemed to have actually grown up and over the remains. The others had been pulled from the ground and it appeared to be an attempt to cover up the remains, and hide them.

Q: So, the bushes or whatever in the picture are consistent with your opinion that she was shot from behind, and not somewhere else and dragged to this position, under the vegetation?

A: Yes, that is correct. She was shot in the back while either walking or standing, or even running, I guess.

Q: Do you have any experience with crossbows?

A: Absolutely. A lot. I have hunted with crossbows for at least 10 years. And when I am not hunting I am working on mine and practicing with it. I also know how to repair them and occasionally give classes on crossbow usage and safety.

Q: Now, in looking at these pictures of the skeletal remains, there seems to be little or no signs of blood at the point of entry in the back.

A: Yes, that is sometimes the case with an arrow. If the arrow remains in the body, it can act like a plug, sorry for being so graphic, and very little blood comes out at that point. On the exit wound, however, which does not show on this picture, there was more blood, or actually some residue of what appeared to be blood. After two years, there was not much to see or test.

Q: Okay. Were any forensic tests done on the crossbow and the bolts?

A: Yes, Mr. Winslet's fingerprints were found on the crossbow. Mr. Winslet's fingerprints were found on the bolt that was found in the remains of the victim. There was also another set of what appeared to be partial fingerprints, but could not be identified. His fingerprints were also found on the crossbow arrows that were found in the case containing the crossbow.

Q: Early in the investigation, I believe you testified earlier, that Mr. Winslet said that his girlfriend was having an affair with someone?

A: Yes, he said that she was e-mailing Johnny Bleu. We had a computer expert check the computer that Winslet and the victim had used and we determined that Johnny Bleu was actually Ken Lott, who worked at Sports Paradise, here in San Milano. He worked in the archery department. Mr. Winslet also worked at Sports Paradise.

Q: What else did you learn about Mr. Lott?

A: I interviewed him as well and learned that he apparently created several online personas, with women, and sweet-talked them into communicating with them. He said that he never really had an actual affair with the women. He said that in his mind he had no doubt that Winslet had killed Sadie.

Q: And why is that?

A: He said that Sadie had e-mailed him and told him that she was afraid of Winslet and that he had threatened to kill her if she ever left him.

Q: Do you have any record of that?

A: Yes, on Winslet's computer we found an e-mail that suggested that. But Lott also showed us an e-mail message that he had received from Ms. Norris the same day she disappeared.

Q: Is this the e-mail? [Shows exhibit to witness]

A: Yes, that is a printout that he gave me.

QUESTION FROM GRAND JUROR

Q: When you and Mr. Winslet saw the remains, you said that you thought it odd that he had not said anything. But it's hard to see from the photos that the body is even that of a woman, right?

A: Yes.

Q: So, there might have been some other reason for his actions?

A: No. [Pausing] I didn't think so.

QUESTION FROM ANOTHER GRAND JUROR

Q: Did you run a check for fingerprints on the case for the crossbow?

A: Yes, we did. We found two sets of prints on the case, one for Winslet and the other set for Ken Lott. But that seemed normal because Lott worked in the archery department and his prints would have been all over the case when he sold it to Winslet. We ran the tests on the crossbow itself and the bolts in the quiver, which was attached to the crossbow, in the case. I forgot to mention the tests on the bolts in the case. The only fingerprints on those bolts belonged to Mr. Winslet.

QUESTION FROM ANOTHER GRAND JUROR

Q: Did you ever consider that there might be other suspects, for example, Johnny Bleu, or I guess Ken Lott?

A: No, I did not. I considered the statement of Taylor Dodds who said that Ken Lott killed Sadie. But I found that statement to be incredible because Dodds and Winslet are friends. I am convinced that the evidence all pointed to Winslet and no one else in this case.

Q: One more question, Detective. Did you ever try to contact the two deer hunters who had originally discovered the victim's remains?

A: I tried to talk to them. They never returned my calls. And, besides, from what I had seen, I did not think that they would have anything else to add to the case.

JAMES HERNANDEZ

Q: Thank you, Detective Davidson. Would you please step outside for a few minutes?

A: Yes.

[Witness steps outside at 11:03 a.m. and is subsequently dismissed.]

(END OF TRANSCRIPT)

RESUME OF LANNY DAVIDSON

Lanny Davidson

Homicide Detective
San Antonio, State of Lone Star

Experience

Police Officer, City of San Antonio, State of Lone Star — Oct [YR-10] – July [YR-4]

Homicide Detective, City of San Antonio, State of Lone Star — July [YR-4] – Present

Responsible for approximately 75 homicide investigations to date, with 20 convictions resulting from those investigations. Only two homicide investigations currently open. Currently certified in Forensics Collection.

Education

- Texas Tech University (BA, Sociology) — January [YR-10]
- Police Academy — May [YR-10] – Oct [YR-10]
- Top 5% of the City of San Antonio Police Training Academy.
- Forensics Collection — Oct. 2009 & Nov. [YR-1]

  Forensic Courses at FBA Academy, Quantico, VA. Training in proper collection of evidence including DNA, fingerprints, and weapons. Training on what evidence to collect as well; although the evidence may not appear out of the ordinary, it could be critical to an investigation. Award of Merit in both courses.

Additional

- Have testified regarding investigations in 48 cases.
- Currently researching to write an article entitled "Proper Homicide Investigation: A Fail-Proof Checklist for Correct Identification of the Culprit".
- Married, two young children. Hobbies include hunting with crossbows, aquatic sports.

GRAND JURY TESTIMONY OF KEN LOTT

IN RE:	BEFORE THE GRAND JURY
	OF
GRAND JURY INVESTIGATION	BEAR COUNTY, STATE OF LONE STAR

* * * * * *

****

COURT REPORTER'S

Q AND A TRANSCRIPT OF TESTIMONY OF

KEN LOTT

JUNE 24, [YR-1]

****

* * * * *

BE IT REMEMBERED, that ON JUNE 24, [YR-1], the above-entitled matter came on for hearing before the Grand Jury of Bear County, sitting in San Milano, State of Lone Star, being presented by JAMES HERNANDEZ, Assistant Criminal District Attorney, for consideration by the members thereof.

VERONICA GARCIA was duly sworn as Court Reporter.

WHEREUPON, the following evidence was introduced and proceedings had, to-wit, beginning at 2:00 o'clock p.m and concluding at 3:05 o'clock p.m.

KEN LOTT, The Witness.

GRAND JURY FOREMAN: Do you solemnly swear that you will not divulge either by words or signs any matter about which you may be interrogated, and that you will keep secret all proceedings of the Grand Jury which may be had in your presence, and that you will true answers make to such questions as may be propounded to you by the Grand Jury or under its direction, so help you God?

THE WITNESS: I do.

EXAMINATION BY JAMES HERNANDEZ:

Q: As with any witness who comes before the Grand Jury, I need to give you the definitions of perjury and aggravated perjury.

A person commits the offense of perjury if, with intent to deceive and with knowledge of the statement's meaning, that person makes a false statement under oath or swears to the truth of a false statement previously made and the statement is required or authorized by law to be made under oath.

Perjury is a Class A Misdemeanor, which is punishable by anywhere up to one year in the Bear County Jail and/or a fine of up to $4,000.

Perjury becomes aggravated perjury if the person commits perjury, makes that false statement during or in connection with an official proceeding, and Grand Jury proceedings are official proceedings, and the statement is material.

Aggravated perjury is a third-degree felony, which means it's punishable by anywhere from two to ten years in the Lone Star Department of Corrections, and there's a potential fine of up to $10,000. Do you understand this?

A. Yes, sir.

Q: Would you please state your name for the grand jury?

A: Yes, my name is Ken Lott.

Q: Thank you. Where do you live?

A: Here in San Milano.

Q: And where do you work?

A: I work at Sports Paradise, here in San Milano. I have worked there for about six years.

Q: And where do you work in that store?

A: I have always worked in the archery section. The whole time I have been there.

Q: Do you know Charles Winslet?

A: Yes.

Q: How do you know him?

A: Well, he also works at Sports Paradise — in the camping section, which is just around the corner from where I work. I don't socialize with him but I did sell him a crossbow — a Parker Crossbow—several years ago.

Q: So, you know him from work?

A: Yes, that is pretty much it.

Q: Do you recognize these exhibits? [Shows witness pictures of crossbow and bolt]

A: Yes, that is a Parker crossbow and a Parker arrow, or bolt, that you are supposed to use with that particular crossbow.

Q: Have you had a chance to observe Mr. Winslet at work?

A: Yes, I have. A lot.

Q: How would you describe his behavior?

A: Erratic and prone to fits of temper. Once he was visiting with me in the archery section and got upset with the way a female customer was acting. When she walked away from the counter, he picked up the crossbow that she had been looking at buying, raised it to his shoulder, pointed it at her back and said something like, "zing, thwap," and then laughed.

Q: Zing, thwap?

A: Yes, I guess he was trying to imitate the sounds of firing the crossbow and the sound the arrow or bolt makes when it hits something.

Q: What did you do?

A: I grabbed it from him and told him that it was not funny. He then got made at me and said that I did not enjoy good humor, or something like that.

Q: Did you ever observe any other behavior?

A: No, but I heard that a couple of years ago, he got a written reprimand for anger management problems at work.

Q: Did you ever know Sadie Norris?

A: Yes, I did. Very nice girl.

Q: Tell us about her.

A: She was dating Winslet and I met her a couple of times when she would come to visit Winslet at the store. She was always smiling and sort of shy. Why she stayed with him I will never know.

Q: Tell us about Johnny Bleu.

A: [Pause] I guess that was not one of the smartest things I have ever done.

Q: Go ahead.

A: I got lonely a couple of years ago. I had broken up with another girl and I went online and created a fake person, Johnny Bleu, to meet women.

Q: Did you ever actually meet women?

A: No, I came close a couple of times. But, no, I never actually met anyone.

Q: Is it true that you carried on long-term Internet relationships with several women?

A: Yes, I did.

Q: How many?

A: [Pause] Four or five.

Q: Was Sadie Norris one of them?

A: Yes.

Q: How did you happen to link up with her?

A: I had seen her in the store and liked her. I never worked up the nerve to talk to her in person other than when she showed up at the store.

Q: How did you link up with her?

A: About two years ago, about 3 months before she disappeared, she logged on to a dating site and used her real name. I logged on as Johnny Bleu and started connecting with her. We had a great relationship. She told me a lot of things. She told me that her boyfriend, Winslet, was mean to her and although she was living with him, she was afraid of him and his temper. She mentioned several times that she was thinking of leaving him and I encouraged her to do so. I think in some ways, that I contributed to her death.

Q: Why do you say that?

A: The day she disappeared I got an e-mail from Winslet to my account for Johnny Bleu. I don't think he knew who I really was. He told me to back away from his fiancée, or he would come looking for me and kill me. He said something like, if she broke his heart, he would pierce hers. That really freaked me out. He didn't say he would break hers. He said he would pierce her heart. I remember those words.

Q: Did you respond to that e-mail?

A: No. I did not. I had e-mailed her earlier and told her it was time to leave. She said she was going to leave and that she was packed and ready to go. So I breathed easier when I read that.

Q: When did this take place?

A: I think that it was a day or so before she disappeared. Because Winslet came into the store one day, right after that, and said that his girlfriend had left him. That is when I thought that she had finally left him and was hiding somewhere. He said that he would find her and that she would regret the day she left him. He said that he was convinced that she had run off with some guy named Bleu. I kept my mouth shut and played dumb, like I had no idea what he was talking about. Shortly after that, I quit using that name on the Internet, hoping that no one would find out what I had done.

Q: Had you developed feelings for Sadie?

A: She was an angel. I think she fell in love with me, or maybe Johnny Bleu.

Q: Did you ever reveal to Sadie who you really were?

A: I don' think it happened quite that way. We saw each other, if that is what you mean.

Q: Well, I am not sure. Can you explain?

A: On the Internet I was Johnny and in real life, as Ken, we connected at some level. We played along on the Internet as though we had never actually met in person. But actually we had, in person, when she came to visit Charles, for example, at the store. So, I am not positive if she knew that Johnny and I were the same person. I am not sure. It was our way of hiding our relationship from Charles.

Q: Did Winslet ever figure out who you were?

A: I don't think so. At least I never told him. All I know is that after Sadie left, I have not been the same. It's been a very hard two years. I am glad we finally know what happened to Sadie.

Q: I understand that you had some run-ins with your boss?

A: Yes, after Sadie disappeared, I was not myself and said and did some things I am not proud of. I think I am better now.

Q: Do you recognize this photo? [Shows picture to witness]

A: Yes, absolutely. That is Sadie. I took this picture during a lunch break when she came out to Sports Paradise before she disappeared. It was taken at the mall, where Sports Paradise is located.

Q: Okay. Thank you. That is all I have for now.

QUESTION BY GRAND JUROR

Q: Did you love Sadie?

A: Yes, I did. I really fell in love with her and cared about her deeply.

Q Do you own a crossbow?

A: Yes, I do.

Q: What kind?

A: Like the one I sold to Charles, a Buck Buster. It's made by Parker. It's at my home. I think.

Q: Did you ever visit Sadie at Winslet's ranch?

A: No.

Q: Were you ever at his ranch?

A: Not that I can recall, no.

JAMES HERNANDEZ

Q: Okay. Thank you. Would you please step outside for just a few minutes?

A: Of course.

[The Witness leaves the Grand Jury Room at 3:05 p.m. and is subsequently dismissed.]

(END OF TRANSCRIPT)

911 TRANSCRIPTS

911 TRANSCRIPT
May 2, [YR-2]
6:13 PM

Dispatch: 911, what is your emergency?

Caller: My boyfriend, Charles, just threatened me

Dispatch: Is he there with you?

Caller: No, he is outside. Please, send the police!

Dispatch: Ma'am, do you need help? Do you need medical attention?

Caller: I don't know . . . (unintelligible) . . . I don't know. . .

Dispatch: What is your name, honey?

Caller: It's Sadie Norris.

Dispatch: Sadie, I am sending help, the police are on their way. What happened?

Caller: He threatened to cut me with a hunting knife. He has been drinking and he is scaring me. I don't think he would actually do it, but I am really scared.

Dispatch: Did he threaten you?

Caller: Yes, briefly. He is waving it around.

Dispatch: I will stay on the phone with you until the police arrive, alright?

Caller: (Unintelligible . . . talking to a man)

Dispatch: Sadie? I'll stay here on the phone with you until the police and medical arrive.

Caller: Okay. (Unintelligible. . . talking to man). Okay, he hears the police and he is putting the knife back in his hunting bag.

Dispatch: I see the police say they've arrived

Caller: They're here. Thank you.

(END OF TRANSCRIPT)

911 TRANSCRIPT
June 11, [YR-2]
9:09 AM

Dispatch: 911, what is your emergency?

Caller: My girlfriend is missing and I can't find her.

Dispatch: When did you last see her?

Caller: Hmmm, several nights ago, I guess.

Dispatch: What is your name?

Caller: Winslet, Charlie Winslet.

Dispatch: Do you have reason to believe that she is hurt?

Caller: Oh God, I hope not. We had a fight about another man and she just walked out the door, saying that she would be back when she had cooled down. But that was almost two days ago.

Dispatch: Have you tried contacting her family and friends?

Caller: Yes. I have. I have asked them for help on Facebook. You are recording this right?

Dispatch: Yes. Why are you asking?

Caller: Sorry, I have another call coming in. I'll stop by the police station and get them to help.

Dispatch: Okay.

(END OF TRANSCRIPT)

Medical Examiner's Autopsy Report

Office of Medical Examiner
Bear County
State of Lone Star

Date: April 23, [YR-1]
Time: 9:00 a.m.
Examiner: Brandon Lane, M.D.
Witness: Detective Lanny Davidson
Deceased: Unknown
Date of Birth: Unknown
Height: 4'11"- 5'2"
Weight: Unknown
Race: Unknown
Gender: Female

Observations: The remains consisted of a skull, a mostly intact rib cage and assorted arm and leg bones, and pelvic bones, which were collected personally by the undersigned on April 22, [YR-1]. A crossbow bolt, 20 inches long penetrated the rib cage, from the posterior side, left lateral, approximately 1 inch from the spine, between the fifth and sixth ribs, and extending approximately 2 inches from the anterior rib cage. Small blood residue around entry point of bolt.

Size and structure of pelvic bones indicates that victim was likely female.

Based on the location of the bolt, it appears that the bolt penetrated the heart.

Penetration of bolt into the ground was minimal, suggesting that bolt entered the body before the body fell to the ground.

Cause/Manner of Death: Bolt wound in back, through the heart, homicide

Submitted April 24, [YR-1]

Brandon D. Lane
Brandon D. Lane, M.D.
Medical Examiner
Bear County

Medical Examiner's Death Certificate

Office of Medical Examiner
Bear County
State of Lone Star

Death Certificate

Name of Deceased:	Sadie Norris
Date and Time of Death:	June [YR-2]
Primary Cause of Death:	Bolt wound in back
Survivors:	Mother, Janey Norris

Submitted May 15, [YR-1]

Brandon D. Lane
Brandon D. Lane, M.D.
Medical Examiner
Bear County

Forensics Report

STATE OF LONE STAR		
v.		DOCKET NO.13456
CHARLES WINSLET Defendant		

Before me, the undersigned authority, personally appeared Sandra Borland, who, being by me duly sworn, deposed as follows:

My name is Sandra Borland, I am of sound mind, capable of making this affidavit, and personally acquainted with the facts herein stated:

> I am the custodian of the records of Bear County Crime Laboratory. Attached hereto is one (1) page of the records of the forensic reports from the Bear County Crime Laboratory. This page is from those records kept by the Bear County Crime Laboratory in the regular course of business, and it was the regular course of business of Bear County Crime Laboratory for an employee or representative of that office, with knowledge of the act, event, condition, opinion, or diagnosis, recorded to make the record or to transmit information thereof to be included in such record; and the record was made at or near the time or reasonably soon thereafter. The record attached hereto is the original.

Sandra Borland
Affiant

SWORN TO AND SUBSCRIBED before me on the 20 day of June, [YR-1].

Danny Muniz
Notary Public, State of Lone Start

Notary's printed name:
Danny Muniz

My commission expires: January 1, [YR+1]

BEAR COUNTY CRIME LABORATORY
BEAR COUNTY
STATE OF LONE STAR

WEAPONS:

The weapon gathered was a crossbow bolt, 20 inches in length, and a crossbow manufactured by Parker Company.

FINGERPRINTS:

Fingerprints were taken from the crossbow. The prints on the crossbow belong to Charles Winslet.

Fingerprints were taken of the crossbow case. They belonged to Charles Winslet and Ken Lott.

Two sets of fingerprints were taken from the bolt found in the victim's remains. One set belongs to Charles Winslet. The other set of fingerprints could not be identified.

One set of fingerprints was found on the two bolts found in crossbow case. Those prints belong to Charles Winslet.

DNA:

DNA was collected from the victim's remains. That DNA indicates that the victim is Sadie Norris (Test results — May 14).

Jane Gilbert

Jane Gilbert
Lab Technician
June 13, [YR-1]

Photograph of Victim

Photograph of Crossbow Case in Machine Shed

Photograph of Machine Shed

PHOTOGRAPHS OF CROSSBOW AND BOLT

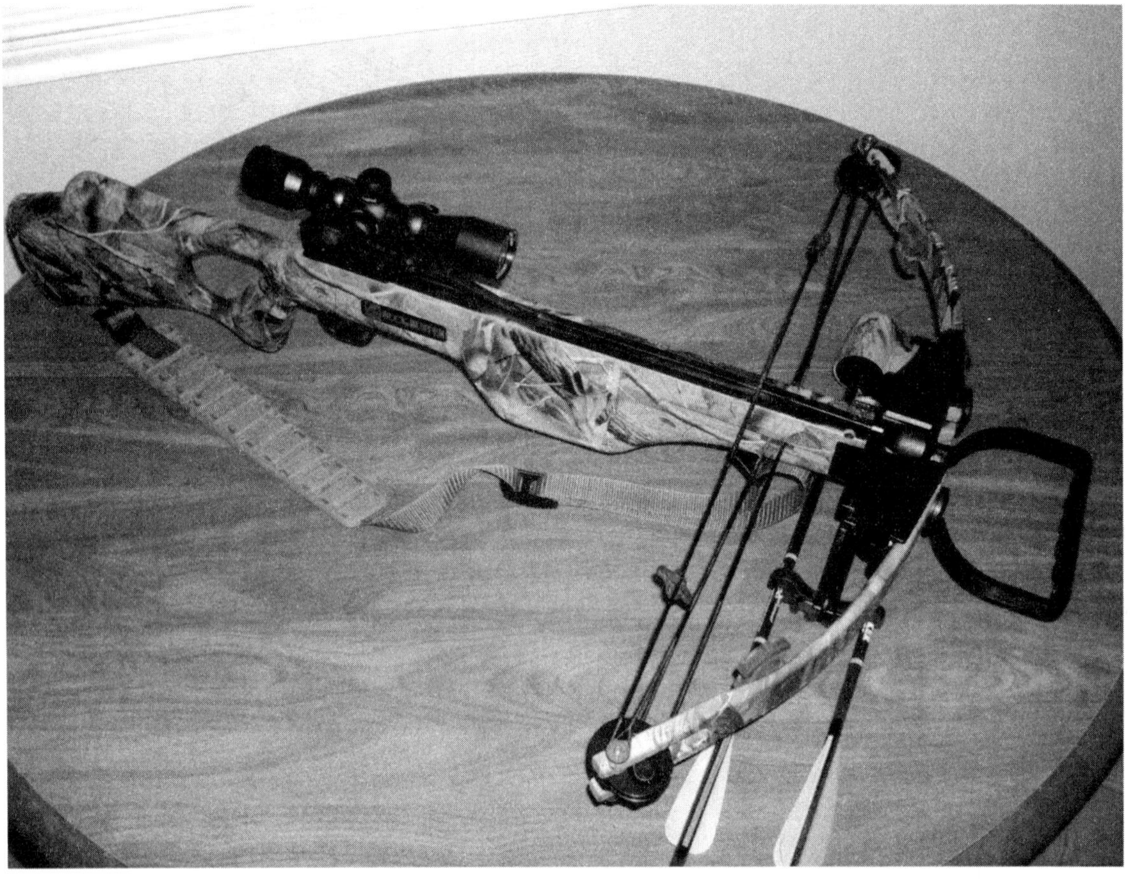

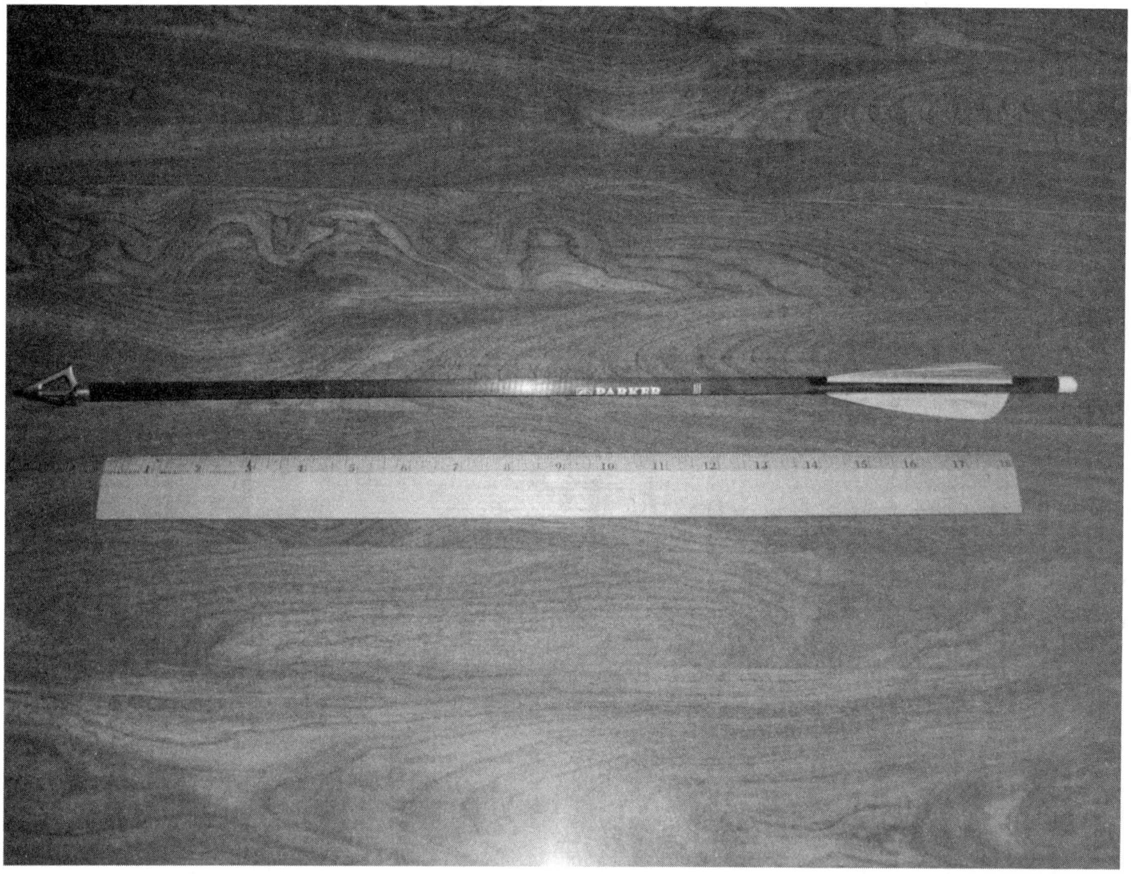

Photographs of Remains

April 23, [YR-1] THE LONE STAR TIMES **4B**

Remains Located on Ranch

Reported by: Trisha Green
April 23, [YR-1]

Two area deer hunters got the surprise of their lives yesterday when they discovered human remains on a local ranch, while scouting out locations for the fall deer season.

According to a source close to the investigation, the remains had an arrow in them, indicating that the victim was killed intentionally.

One of the men, who asked to remain unnamed, said that he and his friend had spent several hours hiking the ranch to look for deer signs and locate a place for their deer blind. When they noticed the remains, they took a closer look but did not touch anything. They immediately returned to the owner's ranch house, told him what they had found, and then called the police. He said that the owner appeared very nervous when he heard that there was a dead body on his ranch. He said that he and his friend were no longer interested in leasing the land for hunting.

The ranch's owner, Charles Winslet, said that he had no idea about who the remains might belong to. Neighbors say that Winslet's girlfriend, Sadie Norris, went missing a couple of years ago and they think that mystery will now be solved.

The police have declined to comment on the case, stating simply that their investigation continues.

Written Reprimand to Taylor Dodds

SPORTS PARADISE
124 Lakeview Drive
555-342-9765
San Milano, State of Lone Star

Where Great Things Happen Outdoors

Memo to: **Taylor Dodds**
Camping Department

From: **John "Bear" Schwartz**
President and CEO

Date: **December 4, [YR-3]**

Re: **Written Reprimand**

As you know, it has come to my attention that several weeks ago that in filling out your monthly sales report for the second quarter of this past fiscal year, you falsified that report. You inflated your sales by more than 5 percent, which then qualified you for our company's annual "Trophy" bonus.

Your correct sales figures were discovered during a random audit by an independent CPA firm.

We gave you ample opportunity to explain your actions and your answer was that it was simple mistake.

Thus, the bonus that was paid to you, in the amount of $1,000.00, will be deducted from your next three paychecks. In addition you will be placed on probationary status for 90 days, beginning today. If for any reason your conduct again falls below that expected of our employees, you will be terminated.

As you know, Taylor, we take pride in being a family here at Sports Paradise. We are giving you another chance.

If you have any questions, please feel free to contact me.

WRITTEN REPRIMAND TO KEN LOTT

SPORTS PARADISE
124 Lakeview Drive
555-342-9765
San Milano, State of Lone Star

Where Great Things Happen Outdoors

Memo to: **Ken Lott**
Archery Department

From: **John "Bear" Schwartz**
President and CEO

Date: **December 4, [YR-2]**

Re: **Written Reprimand**

I learned last week that you had threatened one of your co-workers in the camping department of our store, on November 20th. This is the second incident involving aggressive behavior on your part. The first, as you well know, involved one of our patrons, in July [YR-2].

You are now on a 120-day probation. If we receive any further complaints about your behavior, you will be terminated.

Until these incidents arose you had been a model employee. That is why I am giving you another chance.

You told me in our conversation last week that the last year has been very hard on you because you lost a good friend. I recommend that you get professional counseling to deal with that issue and avoid any further problems in our store.

If you have any questions, please feel free to contact me.

E-Mails Between Sadie Norris and Johnny Bleu

From: SadieNorris@nol.com
To: johnnybleu@BOl.com
Sent: April 1, [YR-2], 3:00 AM
Subject: Help

Johnny, I am scared. Charles has become very threatening lately. He says that he is getting tired of me running around behind his back and that if I ever betray him, he will make sure I don't forget it.

What should I do?

Please hclp.

From: SadieNorris@nol.com
To: johnnybleu@BOl.com
Sent: April 3, [YR-2], 2:00 AM
Subject: Help

Johnny, why aren't you responding? I am scared and need someone to tell me what to do.

I want to leave Charles but am afraid that he will follow me and kill me.

From: SadieNorris@nol.com
To: johnnybleu@BOI.com
Sent: May 3, [YR-2], 3:30 PM
Subject: I'm in Trouble

I think I am pregnant. What have I done? I HATE YOU. I HATE YOU. I HATE YOU.

Where are you?

From: johnnybleu@BOI.com
To: SadieNorris@nol.com
Sent: May 3, [YR-2], 4:30 PM
Subject: I'm in Trouble

A baby? I love you. Is it mine?

Let's get outta here and start somewhere else. You are too good for Charles!!!

From: SadieNorris@nol.com
To: johnnybleu@BOl.com
Sent: May 3, [YR-2], 8:30 PM
Subject: I'm in Trouble

No. I am leaving both of you. Just as soon as I can find a time to do it.

Don't email me, tweet me, call me or try to see me. We are done!

From: johnnybleu@BOl.com
To: SadieNorris@nol.com
Sent: May 4, [YR-2], 9:30 PM
Subject: I'm in Trouble

No. No.

Don't do that. I love you and cannot live without you. I am giving up my internet affairs. You are the only one. Don't leave me. If you do, you will regret it.

I will find you. I love you.

From: SadieNorris@nol.com
To: johnnybleu@BOl.com
Sent: June 8, [YR-2], 9:21 PM
Subject: Leaving

I am out of here. Car is gassed. Bags are packed and Charles is outside in machine shed messing around. Good riddance to both of you. . . . . Ken!!

GO TO HELL.

I was wrong. I am not pregnant. But if I was, I would never admit that it was your's.

PS. You had better hope and pray that I don't turn you in to "Bear", Mr. Internet Lover!!!! You are already in trouble with him

---

E-MAILS FROM CHARLES WINSLET TO JOHNNY BLEU

From: CWinslet34@nol.com
To: johnnybleu@BOl.com
Sent: April 4, [YR-2], 2:23 AM
Subject: Who Are You?

HEY JOHNNY, OR WHOEVER YOU ARE. WHO ARE YOU REALLY?

I DON'T APPRECIATE YOU MESSING WITH MY FUTURE WIFE!

From: CWinslet34@nol.com
To: johnnybleu@BOl.com
Sent: April 9, [YR-2], 1:56 AM
To: Subject: Who are You!!!!

You had better stop contacting my girlfriend. She and I are getting married and messing with her (and me) will not go well for you.

IF YOU ARE A REAL MAN YOU WILL STEP UP AND TELL ME WHO YOU ARE.

From: CWinslet34@nol.com
To: johnnybleu@BOl.com
Sent: May 15, [YR-2], 4:15 PM
To: Subject: Breaking My Heart

Hey Johnny Blue, whoever you are.

I know that you and my girlfriend have a thing going on the internet and that she is thinking of leaving me.

You had better not be involved in that plan or I will kill you with my bare hands.

If she leaves me it will break my heart and I will pierce her's. And she will leave with only the shirt on her back.

Got it? I hope so.

Winslet's Facebook Postings

Charles Winslet
June 9, [YR-2] at 8:34 am

Hey everyone. If anyone sees Sadie, please let me know. She left me last night and I have not heard from her. Be sure to save this message for future reference. I really miss her. Please please please help me.

2 likes **0 comment**

Like **Comment** **Share**

Charles Winslet
May 21 [YR-1] at 12:14 pm

Looks like the police finally found Sadie.

Libre al fin! Libre al fin!

3 likes **0 comment**

Like **Comment** **Share**

JURY INSTRUCTIONS

COURT'S COPY

Name:	**Charles Winslet**
Complainant:	**Sadie Norris**
Offense Charged:	**MURDER**

JURY INSTRUCTION

LADIES AND GENTLEMEN OF THE JURY:

The defendant, CHARLES WINSLET, stands charged by indictment COUNT 1 with the offense of murder, alleged to have been committed on or about the June 8, [YR-2] in Bear County, State of Lone Star. The defendant has pleaded not guilty.

1.

Our law provides that a person commits the offense of murder if he or she intentionally or knowingly causes the death of an individual.

2.

A person acts intentionally, or with intent, with respect to a result of his or her conduct when it is his or her conscious objective or desire to cause the result.

A person acts knowingly, or with knowledge, with respect to a result of his or her conduct when he or she is aware that his or her conduct is reasonably certain to cause the result.

3.

Now, if you find from the evidence beyond a reasonable doubt that on or about June 8, [YR-2], in Bear County, State of Lone Star, that the defendant CHARLES WINSLET, did intentionally or knowingly cause the death of an individual, namely SADIE NORRIS then you will find the defendant CHARLES WINSLET guilty of murder as charged in the indictment.

Unless you so find beyond a reasonable doubt, or if you have a reasonable doubt as to whether the defendant is guilty of murder, then you will find him not guilty.

4.

You are instructed that you may consider all relevant facts and circumstances surrounding the killing, if any, and the previous relationship existing between the accused and the deceased, if any, together with all relevant facts and circumstances going to show the condition of the mind of the defendant at the time of the offense, if any.

The State, however, is not required to prove a motive. If the State has proved the essential elements of the offense beyond a reasonable doubt, the defendant must be found guilty of that offense regardless of the defendant's motive or lack of a motive. If the State, however, has proved a motive, you may consider that insofar as it gives meaning to other circumstances. On the other hand, you may consider the absence of motive in weighing whether or not the defendant is guilty of the crime charged.

5.

"Proof beyond a reasonable doubt" is proof that leaves you firmly convinced of the defendant's guilt. There are very few things in this world that we know with absolute certainty, and in criminal cases the law does not require proof that overcomes every possible doubt. If, based on your consideration of the evidence, you are firmly convinced that the defendant is guilty of the crime charged, you should find him guilty. If, on the other hand, you think there is a real possibility that he is not guilty, you should give him the benefit of the doubt and find him not guilty.

Chapter 21

NORRIS V. WINSLET

§ 21-1. Introduction

Charles Winslet was tried for murdering his girlfriend, Sadie Norris. Her skeletal remains were found by hunters on Winslet's ranch, which he had shared with Ms. Norris before he reported her missing in [YR-3]. Evidence indicates that she died from being shot in the back with a crossbow bolt.

Winslet claimed that he knew nothing of her death and urged the police to investigate Johnny Bleu, someone he thought was having an affair with Ms. Norris at the time of her disappearance.

At his trial for murder, Winslet was acquitted. Sadie Norris's mother, Janey Norris, has filed a wrongful death suit against Winslet.

§ 21-2. Stipulations Regarding Procedural and Evidentiary Matters

1. Although the case is being tried in a State court, the Federal Rules of Civil Procedure and Federal Rules of Evidence apply.
2. All witnesses called to testify who made statements or grand jury or deposition testimony identifying the defendant, other individuals, or tangible evidence must, if asked, identify the same at trial.
3. Charles Winslet and Taylor Dodds signed their statements to the police.
4. All notice and disclosure requirements under the Federal Rules of Civil Procedure and the Federal Rules of Evidence were met in a timely fashion.
5. Other than what is supplied in the problem itself, there is nothing exceptional or unusual about the background information of any of the witnesses or the defendant that would bolster or detract from their credibility.
6. This competition does not permit a listed witness or the defendant, while testifying, to "invent" an individual not mentioned in this problem or to have testimony or evidence offered to the court or jury from that invented individual.
7. "Beyond the record" must not be entertained as an objection.
8. Contact with the competition officials concerning this problem must be pursuant to the rules of the competition.
9. The year [YR-0] is the current year in which this case comes to trial.
10. All exhibits in the file are authentic. In addition, each exhibit contained in the file is the original of that document unless otherwise noted on the exhibit or as established by the evidence.
11. Any searches and seizures conducted by the police met the requirements of the Fourth Amendment and the Federal Rules of Criminal Procedure.
12. No changes or alterations were made to any of the exhibits.
13. The victim's body was located in Bear County, State of Lone Star.

14. The e-mails in the packet may be presented at trial as a string of e-mails or individually.
15. Sadie Norris' remains were identified by DNA testing on May 14, [YR-2], by the Bear County Crime Laboratory.

§ 21-3. Case File Materials

Students will be expected to use the following materials in presenting their cases.

Lone Star Wrongful Death Statute

Lone Star Civil Practice & Remedies Code

§ 31.123. Cause of Action

(a) An action for actual damages arising from an injury that causes an individual's death may be brought if liability exists under this section.

(b) A person is liable for damages arising from an injury that causes an individual's death if the injury was caused by the person's or his agent's or servant's wrongful act, neglect, carelessness, unskillfulness, or default.

(c) A person is liable for damages arising from an injury that causes an individual's death if:

(1) the person is a proprietor, owner, charterer, or hirer of an industrial or public utility plant or of a railroad, street railway, steamboat, stagecoach, or other vehicle for the transportation of goods or passengers; and

(2) the injury was caused by the person's or his agent's or servant's wrongful act, neglect, carelessness, unskillfulness, or default.

§ 31.124. Benefitting From Action

(a) An action to recover damages as provided by this subchapter is for the exclusive benefit of the surviving spouse, children, and parents of the deceased.

(b) The surviving spouse, children, and parents of the deceased may bring the action or one or more of those individuals may bring the action for the benefit of all.

§ 31.125. Exemplary Damages

When the death is caused by the willful act or omission or gross negligence of the defendant, exemplary as well as actual damages may be recovered.

Plaintiff's Petition

District Court of Bear County

JANEY NORRIS Plaintiff v. CHARLES WINSLET Defendant	}	Docket No. 789-9987 COMPLAINT FOR DAMAGES

COMES NOW the above-named Plaintiff and alleges the following:

I. Parties, Jurisdiction, and Venue

A. Plaintiff, Janey Norris, the mother of Sadie Norris the decedent, brings this action in his personal capacity.

B. Defendant, Charles Winslet, is a resident of Bear County, State of Lone Star.

C. This Court has jurisdiction over the subject matter of this complaint and over the parties.

D. Venue is proper and appropriate in Bear County because the death of Sadie Norris, which is the subject matter of this complaint, occurred in Bear County.

II. Factual Basis

A. Defendant, Charles Winslet, and Sadie Norris lived at Winslet's ranch.

B. Following an argument in June [YR-3], Sadie Norris left the ranch. When she failed to return to the ranch, Defendant made some attempts to locate her and denied that he had anything to do with her disappearance.

C. In [YR-2] deer hunters located skeletal remains on the Defendant's ranch. Forensic tests showed that the remains were those of Sadie Norris. The police concluded that Ms. Norris had died as a result of a crossbow bolt shot into her back.

D. Evidence seized from the Defendant's ranch and computer indicated that the Defendant killed Ms. Norris, using his crossbow.

E. Defendant's acts were the sole and proximate cause of Sadie Norris's death.

III. Causes of Action

A. As a direct and proximate result of the acts of the Defendant, the decedent suffered a wrongful death, entitling Plaintiff to recover actual and exemplary damages (including but not limited to medical and hospital expenses, funeral expenses, and all other damages allowable for wrongful death and survival benefits under Lone Star Civil Practice & Remedies Code §§ 31.123-31.125 and any other damages allowable as a result of Defendant's conduct;) in amounts not now precisely known, the exact amounts to be proven at or before the time of trial.

B. As a further direct and proximate result of the Defendant's acts and omissions, the Plaintiff of the decedent suffered destruction of the parent-child relationship and loss of parental consortium.

C. As a further direct and proximate result of the negligent acts and omissions of Defendant, Plaintiff is entitled to recover statutory and reasonable attorney's fees and costs in amounts not now precisely known, the court to set such amounts in the future.

IV. Prayer for Relief

WHEREFORE, the Plaintiff prays for a judgment of liability against the defendants as follows:

A. For a judgment against Defendant.

B. For an award of damages in the amount of $ 100,000.00 as set forth in the above complaint herein, including statutory and reasonable fees and costs in such amounts that may be awarded by this Court.

C. For such other and further relief as the Court deems just and appropriate.

DATED this day of October 12, [YR-1].

Nancy Dettmann

Nancy Dettmann
The Jones Firm
Attorney for Plaintiff

Defendant's First Written Statement to Police

STATE OF LONE STAR
COUNTY OF BEAR

Case Number: 13-3214

VOLUNTARY STATEMENT OF: CHARLES WINSLET

I, Charles Winslet, after first being duly warned by Det. Roger Stone #3489 at 0930 hrs, at 214 W. Nueva, on June 13, [YR-2], that (1) I have the right to remain silent and not make any statement at all, and any statement I do make may be used against me at my trial; (2) Any statement I make may be used as evidence against me in Court; (3) I have the right to have a lawyer present to advise me prior to and during any questioning; (4) If I am unable to employ a lawyer, I have the right to have a lawyer appointed to advise me prior to and during any questioning; (5) I have the right to terminate the interview at any time; and I understand that the above rights are continuing rights and may be urged by me at any stage of the proceedings, and I hereby prior to and during the making of this statement, knowingly, intelligently, and voluntarily waive the above rights and give to the said, Det. Roger Stone #3489, the person to whom this statement is being given, the following written statement:

My name is Charles Winslet. Several days ago, my girlfriend and I had a big argument over an affair she was having with someone on the Internet. I want to make a statement now in case something happens to me and to investigate someone named Johnny Bleu.

At about 11 PM on June 8th, Sadie said that she was tired of arguing and that she was leaving for a drive and that she needed to cool off. She walked out the door. I did not follow her. I heard her get in her car and drive off. We live in the country without many lights so it was hard to see in which direction she was headed.

I stayed in the house. I was pretty angry as well. When she did not show up the next day, I called 911 and reported her missing. She has never done anything like that. I think she is with this Bleu guy. I saw some of the e-mails that they were sharing and it's clear that he was trying to break us up. She denied it and I guess that is why she got so angry when I accused her of cheating on me.

A couple of weeks ago, I woke up at about 3 AM and I thought that I heard someone driving off from our house. I got up and could not see anything.

She has no family in the area. I am not really sure what I should do next or who to contact and that is why I am here making a statement. She is my life and I cannot go on without her. We were supposed to get married later this year.

I really think this guy Bleu knows what happened. I tried to find a person by that name but have not had any luck. She must be with him somewhere.

I have not heard anything from her. I can't find her car.

She did not take any clothes or other stuff with her. Just her purse and car keys, is all that she took to the best of my memory.

WITNESS: *Bill Blair* SIGNATURE: *Charles Winslet*

DATE: June 13, [YR-3]

DEFENDANT'S SECOND WRITTEN STATEMENT TO POLICE

STATE OF LONE STAR COUNTY OF BEAR	}	Case Number: 12-81377

VOLUNTARY STATEMENT OF: CHARLES WINSLET

I, Charles Winslet, after first being duly warned by Det. Lanny Davidson #4587 at 0930 hrs, at 214 W. Nueva, on May 21, [YR-2] that (1) I have the right to remain silent and not make any statement at all, and any statement I do make may be used against me at my trial; (2) Any statement I make may be used as evidence against me in Court; (3) I have the right to have a lawyer present to advise me prior to and during any questioning; (4) If I am unable to employ a lawyer, I have the right to have a lawyer appointed to advise me prior to and during any questioning; (5) I have the right to terminate the interview at any time; and I understand that the above rights are continuing rights and may be urged by me at any stage of the proceedings, and I hereby prior to and during the making of this statement, knowingly, intelligently, and voluntarily waive the above rights and give to the said, Det. Lanny Davidson #4587, the person to whom this statement is being given, the following written statement:

I did not kill my girlfriend. I know who did. I said that two years ago that Johnny Bleu did something to her. And the police did nothing to find her. I kept looking for her and found nothing. I could not even find her car. No one found her car.

Like I said, when I talked to police detective in [YR-3], Sadie had walked out and said she needed time to think. She packed a bag with some of her personal stuff and then walked out of the house and drove off. I have not seen her since.

I loved her and we planned to get married.

I tried finding Johnny Bleu and sent out some e-mails to my friends, after I talked to the police to see if anyone knew where she was. I begged them to help me. One of my friends is Taylor Dodds.

I know that you will probably search my computer. I have nothing to hide.

I do own a crossbow but have not used it in a couple of years. I bought at Sports Paradise where I work in the camping section. I used it once during the fall hunting season in [YR-4]. I got a deer with it but do not have the patience to sit quietly waiting for the deer to come in close enough to use it. My weapon of choice now for hunting deer is a 30-06 Remington. I am not even sure where I put the crossbow.

Since [YR-4], I have leased out the back part of my property to deer hunters. I go back there only once or twice a year to make sure the deer stand is okay.

The ranch is in my name, not Sadie's. I bought it about 5 years ago, about 2 years before Sadie moved in with me.

Sadie worked at a local Walmart, here in San Milano. She worked in several different sections of the store, I believe. Our ranch is in Bear County, about 6 miles outside San Milano.

I have had deer hunting leases on my ranch for the last five years. Some of them use archery equipment, like crossbows, which are legal in this state.

When I saw the remains on my ranch the other day, my first thought was that I was in real trouble because one of my hunters must have accidently killed someone. The place where the remains were found is between the deer blind and an active trail that deer use to get to the other side of my property.

I do not know anyone named Johnny Bleu or whatever he or she called themselves.

WITNESS: *Sally E. Hernandez* SIGNATURE: Charles Winslet

DATE: May 21, [YR-2]

Taylor Dodds's Statement to Police

STATE OF LONE STAR COUNTY OF BEAR	}	**Case Number: 12-81377**

VOLUNTARY STATEMENT OF: Taylor Dodds

I, Taylor Dodds, after first being duly warned by Det. Lanny Davidson #4587 at 0700 hrs, at 214 W. Nueva, on June 5, [YR-2] that (1) I have the right to remain silent and not make any statement at all, and any statement I do make may be used against me at my trial; (2) Any statement I make may be used as evidence against me in Court; (3) I have the right to have a lawyer present to advise me prior to and during any questioning; (4) If I am unable to employ a lawyer, I have the right to have a lawyer appointed to advise me prior to and during any questioning; (5) I have the right to terminate the interview at any time; and I understand that the above rights are continuing rights and may be urged by me at any stage of the proceedings, and I hereby prior to and during the making of this statement, knowingly, intelligently, and voluntarily waive the above rights and give to the said, Det. Lanny Davidson #3489, the person to whom this statement is being given, the following written statement:

I am making this statement because I am afraid that the police are going to convict an innocent man, Charles Winslet. He did not kill his girlfriend, Sadie. Ken Lott did.

I have worked with both men for the last three years at the local Sports Paradise. Ken works in archery and Charles in camping, where I also work. Ken has a terrible temper and is always getting in trouble with management. He has been threatened with being fired on at least two occasions. But he is such a charmer that he talks his way out of trouble. You cannot believe him.

He also sees himself as a real ladies' man. Everyone at the store knows that he goes on the Internet and has so-called Internet affairs with different women. When things get really serious and they want to meet him, he calls it off. He talks about doing that all the time. He kept telling me that he was doing it for the fun of it.

When it came to connecting with Sadie, things changed. He met her when she came to see Charles in the store and she and Ken hit it off real quick. I watched them flirting with each other. I mean serious flirting. I heard him tell her one day that he would see her on the "net." That was the word he used. Ken told me that Sadie was way too good for Charles and that he and Sadie planned to run off. He said that he was finally in love and was going to stop having, what he called, "Internet sex." He also said something about making it look like she had left Charles. He said that he would even things up with Charles. Ken was jealous of Charles because Charles kept getting pay raises when he did not. I know because I saw their pay stubs a couple of times.

Ken told me that he had gone out to see Sadie at the ranch at least twice where she lived with Winslet. But later he denied that he had ever been to the ranch. I know that is a lie because Charles and Sadie hosted a BBQ out there before Sadie disappeared and we were all invited and got a tour of the house and the grounds. So Ken knows where things are out there. I think the BBQ was in April before Sadie disappeared. By then, Ken and Sadie could not hide their feelings for each other. Whenever she came in the store, supposedly to see Charles, Ken would get all fluttery. Sickening.

I am not sure what finally happened but it sounded like Sadie finally told both of them that she was finished playing games and was leaving town. Ken was checking his e-mails at work about the time Sadie disappeared and said something that I overheard about Sadie was making a really big mistake and she would regret it big time. He muttered that she had broken his heart, or something like that.

The next thing I knew, Charles came into the store one day, and said that Sadie had left him the night before for some guy named Johnny Bleu who she met on the Internet. I looked at Ken who did not say anything. But he was nervous all day and kept asking if Charles had found Sadie. Eventually, they both quit talking about her. But I am convinced that Ken, the one with the bad temper, killed her. He had access to crossbows and I just don't think that Charles could have done it. Charles is a very calm, even-tempered man, who has never shown signs of anger when things do not go his way.

I never told Charles who Johnny Bleu really was. I figured I did not want to get between them.

Charles loved Sadie and after she left he used Facebook to try and find her. I will give you a print-out of his posting.

You need to follow up on Ken Lott.

WITNESS: Susan Blair SIGNATURE: Taylor Dodds

DATE: June 5, [YR-2]

DEPOSITION OF JANEY NORRIS

DEPOSITION OF JANEY NORRIS, produced as a witness at the instance of the Defendant, CHARLES WINSLET, and duly sworn, was taken in the above-styled and numbered cause on October 1, [YR-1] from 8:00 AM to 10:00 AM before Sydney Jones, Certified Shorthand Reporter in and for the State of Lone Star, reported by machine shorthand, at the law offices of Defendant, pursuant to the Federal Rules of Civil Procedure and the Provisions stated on the record or attached hereto.

This is a deposition of JANEY NORRIS, who having been sworn, testified as follows:

EXAMINATION

QUESTIONS BY DEFENDANT'S COUNSEL:

Q: Good morning. Ms. Norris.

A: Hello.

Q: First, I would like the record to reflect that you are here this morning with your counsel, who will be given the opportunity ask you questions as well. Also present is our reporter, Sydney Jones. Also, if I am unclear on any of my questions, please let me know so that we can clarify the question. Okay?

A: That is fine, sure.

Q: Would you please state your name for the reporter.

A: Yes, my name is Janey Norris.

Q: Could you spell that please for the court reporter?

A: Yes, it is spelled J A N E Y N O R R I S.

Q: Thank you. Could you please tell us your relationship to Sadie Norris?

A: Yes, she was my daughter. Your client killed her.

Q: Well, you understand that we do not believe that is the case.

A: We will see about that.

Q: Yes, that is true. In your petition you are asking for a lot of money.

A: And Charles will pay it all up.

Q: If you will give me a chance Ms. Norris, our purpose today is to ask some questions about what justifications or reasons you have for asking the court to give you that much money. I am not here today to argue with you. Okay?

A: [Confers with counsel] Yes, I understand.

Q: I understand you are asking my client to pay for the funeral expenses that you incurred for your daughter?

A: Yes.

Q: And how much was that?

A: It was 20,345 dollars.

Q: Okay. And how did you arrive at that amount?

A: That was the bill I got from the Jackson Funeral Home and Crematory, here in San Marino.

Q: Do you have a copy of the bill?

A: Yes, here it is. [Hands to counsel who reviews it]

Q: Thank you. When you arranged the funeral did you do any comparison shopping to see if you could save some money on these expenses?

A: I did not. I loved Sadie with my whole heart and I wanted the best for her. The funeral director said she deserved the best and I agreed with him.

Q: All right. Now, what other expenses did you incur as a result of your daughter's death?

A: The rest of it is pain and suffering, or whatever you call it.

Q: And how did you arrive at the figure of one hundred thousand dollars?

A: You must understand. Sadie was my only child. I loved her very much. It has really been hard on me. I cannot sleep. I go to the doctor's office to get sleeping pills but those make me sick, so it's either sleep or be sick during the day. Some days I don't know which end is up.

Q: Now you say that you loved her. But it's true, isn't it, that you two had a major fight several years ago when she moved in with my client and that you did not even talk to each other?

A: We had a disagreement, that is true.

Q: And it's a fact that after she moved into my client's home you never talked again, right?

A: We never could find a time to talk.

Q: In fact, when the police finally turned over your daughter's things to you, you discovered that she did not even have your phone number in her list of contacts on her cell phone, or on her computer. Isn't that right?

A: She didn't need to have it in there. She knew it by heart. I never changed my number.

Q: So, you would agree that you were not on speaking terms with her?

A: It is not like you put it. The fact that we did not get a chance to make up makes it even harder to think about living without her.

Q: You do not live here in San Marino, do you?

A: No. I live in New Orleans.

Q: And what do you do for a living?

A: I am in sort of transition right now. I used to waitress in the French Quarter.

Q: And what happened with that job?

A: I had a disagreement with the owner. So I left.

Q: You got fired.

A: That is not how I view it.

Q: So when did you get fired?

A: I said that is one way to describe it, and that was last year.

Q: So, you are not currently employed?

A: No, I am still looking.

Q: I understand that you got some insurance money from Sadie's death? Fifty thousand dollars, I believe?

A: Yes, that was not nearly enough.

Q: Are you currently married?

A: No, Sadie's father left us when she was only five years old. So it was just me and Sadie, trying to make it on our own.

Q: You mentioned that you see doctors about not being able to sleep. Do you have any receipts for those visits?

A: No, I don't think so.

Q: That is all I have.

(END OF TRANSCRIPT)

This is to certify that I have read the transcript of my deposition taken on and that the transcript accurately reflects the questions asked and my answers.

SIGNATURE: *Janey Norris*

Subscribed and sworn to before me on December 12 [YR-1].

Syndey W. Jones

Sydney W. Jones
Certified Shorthand

Deposition of Lanny Davidson

ORAL DEPOSITION OF DETECTIVE LANNY DAVIDSON, produced as a witness at the instance of the defendant, CHARLES WINSLET, and duly sworn, was taken in the above-styled and numbered cause on September 13, [YR-1] from 1:00 PM to 2:10 PM, before Norma Rogers, Certified Shorthand Reporter in and for the State of Lone Star, reported by machine shorthand, at the law offices of Plaintiff, pursuant to the Federal Rules of Civil Procedure.

This is a deposition of LANNY DAVIDSON, who having been sworn, testified as follows:

EXAMINATION
QUESTIONS BY DEFENSE COUNSEL:

Q: Good afternoon, Detective.

A: Good afternoon.

Q: Before we get started, do you understand that I represent Mr. Charles Winslet?

A: Yes.

Q: He is being sued for the death of Ms. Sadie Norris. You know that?

A: Yes.

Q: Before we get started I want to make sure that you understand that if you do not understand my questions, please feel free to stop me and ask for a clarification. Okay?

A: Sure.

Q: Would you please state your name for the court reporter, and also spell it.

A: Yes, my name is Lanny Davidson. It's spelled L A N N Y D A V I D S O N.

Q: Thank you. You are a detective with the San Milano police department?

A: Yes.

Q: Tell me about your work experience.

A: I joined the force about 10 years ago. I have been a homicide detective for about five years and have worked on about 75 cases, homicide. I have taken several forensic courses in the last two years, which were offered by the FBI at Quantico Virginia. I scored very high on the end of the course tests and received an award of merit.

Q: Do you have any college education?

A: Yes, from Texas Tech. I got a BA in sociology with a minor in criminal justice studies. I brought a copy of my resume, like you asked.

Q: Okay. Good. Can I see it? [Witness hands exhibit to counsel] Thank you. Now, let's turn to this case. Do you know Charles Winslet?

A: Yes, I do. I met him for the first time in April of two years ago when I questioned him about the death of his girlfriend, Sadie Norris.

Q: That was the first time?

A: Yes. We, actually someone else in our office, actually had talked to him in [YR-3], when he said he wanted to make a statement about his girlfriend's running off, as he said it, with someone she had met on the Internet.

Q: Who did he give his statement to?

A: Detective Roger Stone. He has since left the force to take a job with the Dallas police force.

Q: Okay. Let's go back a bit. Why did you interview Mr. Winslet?

A: Earlier in April, on April 22, [YR-2] we got a report from two deer hunters that they had found skeletal remains on Winslet's property. They were there apparently scouting the area to see if they wanted to lease the property for the fall [YR-2] hunting season. They told us that it looked like there was an arrow sticking out of the remains and immediately called 911.

Q: Did you investigate it?

A: Yes, I immediately drove to the ranch and talked to Mr. Winslet. He said that two men had just been at the back of his property and said that they had found a body. He said that he did not call us because he had not yet checked it out for himself. He said that he was getting ready to do so when I drove up.

Q: So what happened next?

A: The hunters had already left the property, after telling him generally where the remains were located. I asked him to take me to the back of his property.

Q: Did he?

A: Yes, it took us about 30 minutes to locate the remains. As we drove to the location, he seemed to be wandering around the property rather than driving directly to the location stated by the two men who found the remains.

Q: Do you recognize this exhibit? [Counsel shows photo to witness]

A: Yes, definitely, that is the photo I took of the remains. As you can see it's basically what appears to be skeletal remains, with an arrow, or more technically a crossbow bolt, coming out of the rib cage. And it looks like someone had tried to cover it up at some point. It looked like they had tried to cover the remains with branches.

Q: Did you take this picture?

A: Yes.

Q: And do you recognize these exhibits? [Shows to witness]

A: Yes, I took these as well. From different angles and distances.

Q: Now, it looks like there are clothing fragments on the remains, right?

A: That is also correct.

Q: It appears to be a t-shirt so something like that. Did you find any other remnants of clothing such as pants, or even undergarments?

A: No, we did not.

Q: What did you do next?

A: I called the medical examiner's office and they got there about 30 minutes later to gather the remains and other evidence and take it to their office for processing.

Q: Can you tell us what Mr. Winslet's reaction was at this time?

A: He just stared at the remains. He did not say anything, which I found very strange. In my experience there are appropriate responses to seeing a dead body. And he just stared, sort of zombie like. He did not say anything, like oh crap, or any other signs of shock that we had found a dead body on his property. I asked him to not disturb anything. I asked him to sit down about 30 feet away from the remains while I quickly took the pictures and called for backup and the medical examiner.

Q: So, did it seem to you that he was not surprised by the whole scene?

A: No, he did not seem shocked, surprised, sorry, or anything.

Q: Was he in a state of medical shock?

A: No, he was very coherent and did not complain of dizziness. It was clear to me that he was very much aware of what was going on.

Q: Did you ask him any other questions at that point?

A: I did. I asked him if he recognized what appeared to be an arrow and he said no, he did not. I also asked him if he knew who the remains belonged to and he said no. His eyes looked cold and distant.

Q: After the medical examiner arrived, what did you do?

A: I waited for a few minutes, took Mr. Winslet back to his house, and told him we would probably need to talk to him further. He finally said something about the body maybe belonging to his fiancée, Sadie Norris, who had disappeared in [YR-2]. I asked him about that and he said that it was my fault that the police had not found her. He said that he had made 911 calls and talked to a detective in our office, asking for his help. I told him I would look into that and then I drove back to my office. I looked through our files and reviewed Mr. Winslet's statement to Detective Stone in [YR-3] and also the 911 call that he had made. He had told me that he made several calls, but I could only find one. I also found a transcript of a 911 call that his girlfriend, Sadie Norris, had made in May [YR-3]. The transcript indicates that police officers showed up at their ranch. But there is no report from the police on what happened when they got there and talked to the parties involved. Apparently, that matter was resolved and they saw no need to file a report, or charges.

Q: Did you have another opportunity to interview Mr. Winslet?

A: Yes, I did. After we got a positive ID on the remains, I called him in and talked with him. He made a statement. I told him that we had information that the remains belonged to his girlfriend, Sadie. He did not cry or show any signs of grief. During the questioning he maintained his innocence and said that he had urged the police to look for Johnny Bleu, and said that although he owned a crossbow, he could not even say where it was. I got his consent to search his ranch.

Q: Did you conduct the search?

A: When the reports and evidence started pointing at Winslet, we got a warrant to search. We conducted the search on (reviewing notes) May 23rd and found incriminating evidence. A crossbow and two bolts in the machine shed. They were in a case back in a corner and had stuff stacked around it.

Q: Anything else?

A: Yes, in searching his computer in his house we found some e-mails between Winslet and someone named Johnny Bleu, which were shortly before Sadie Norris disappeared in [YR-3]. The e-mails give some indication that Winslet told Bleu to leave Norris alone or that there would be consequences. Computer forensics showed that one e-mail between Winslet's computer and Bleu had been deleted. We, actually our computer experts in the police department, were able to recover the actual text of that missing e-mail. We also found Facebook entries linked to Winslet.

Q: Is this that e-mail? [Shows exhibit to witness]

A: Yes, this is the one that someone deleted but we recovered. In it Winslet threatened both Sadie Norris and the person named Johnny Bleu and said something about piercing her heart if she left him. It was actually sent to Bleu.

Q: Were there any e-mails between the victim and either Winslet or Johnny Bleu?

A: As I said, there were several other e-mails that were still on the computer from Winslet to Bleu. But none from Bleu back to Winslet.

Q: Are these the e-mails? [Shows exhibits to witness]

A: Yes, the ones from April [YR-3], where Winslet suspects something and is trying to figure out who Bleu is.

Q: Okay, thanks. And what are these exhibits? [Shows exhibits to witness].

A: These are the e-mail exchanges between Sadie Norris and Johnny Bleu. It looked like Bleu was trying hard to get the victim to leave Winslet and run away with him. And it appears that there was some sort of physical relationship between Bleu and the victim.

Q: Do you recognize these exhibits? [Prosecutor shows several exhibits to the witness]

A: Yes, these are pictures of the crossbow and the case, and where it was found in the machine shed. Right in front of a John Deere tractor, with a front loader on it. It was pretty easy to spot when we walked into the building, the machine shed. This is a picture of the crossbow and arrows, or bolts, as they are sometimes called, we found in the case.

Q: And what are these?

A: These are Winslet's Facebook entries that we found on his computer. The one is from just after Sadie Norris disappeared, and the other was posted after he found out that she was dead.

Q: Okay. Thanks. And what about this picture?

A: This is a picture of the bolt that was found in the victim's remains.

Q: Where were these pictures taken?

A: At our police station.

Q: There does not appear to be much blood on the head of the bolt.

A: It's hard to see in the picture but there was what appeared to be blood residue on the head, when I examined it.

Q: Now, did you have a chance to compare the bolt that was found in the victim and the two bolts found in the quiver attached to the crossbow?

A: They all matched. Same make, length, and type of point on the bolt. The points were three-sided. The type used for hunting.

Q: Okay. Were you able to identify the victim?

A: Yes, the remains were positively identified as those of Sadie Norris.

Q: How was the identification made?

A: DNA results. It took a couple of weeks to get the results.

Q: Was there any forensic evidence linking the crossbow found in the defendant's machine shed with the bolt found in the victim?

A: Our lab looked for some sort of residue, paint, anything and they came up empty. I should add that unlike firearm ballistic testing, linking an arrow, or a bolt, to a particular crossbow is very difficult, if not impossible.

Q: Do you recognize this exhibit?

A: Yes, these are the defendant's statements. One to Detective Stone and the other one he gave to me.

Q: And what about these exhibits?

A: These are. [Pausing to review exhibits] This is the transcript of the 911 call that Mr. Winslet made in June [YR-3].

Q: Detective, based on your experience, could you tell us whether you think that the victim was killed at another location and then her body moved to where it was found?

A: I believe she died where she was standing, or walking. She was shot in the back and fell forward. Based on the penetration of the bolt, I would say that she was shot from a distance of say, at least 40 or 50 yards.

Q: Isn't that awfully far away for a crossbow?

A: No, not really. Most crossbows these days have a scope on them. So a kill shot from as far as 60 yards is not impossible. At that distance the penetration of the bolt is not as significant, but it's still fatal.

Q: Let me ask the question this way. Is it possible that the victim was on the ground and then shot through the back?

A: No, if she had been shot at close range, while on the ground, the bolt would have gone at a lot further into the soil. As it was, I think the tip of the bolt was only in the ground an inch or two. It was pretty rocky and hard soil there.

Q: Could she have been running when she was shot?

A: Of course.

Q: Now, I notice that the remains seem to be located amongst some brush, or trees . . .

A: Yes, I examined the vegetation and it appeared that there was one bush that had seemed to have actually grown up and over the remains. The others had been pulled from the ground and it appeared to be an attempt to cover up the remains, and hide them.

Q: So, the bushes or whatever in the picture are consistent with your opinion that she was shot from behind, and not somewhere else and dragged to this position, under the vegetation?

A: Yes, that is correct. She was shot in the back while either walking or standing, or even running, I guess.

Q: Do you have any experience with crossbows?

A: Absolutely. A lot. I have hunted with crossbows for at least 10 years. And when I am not hunting I am working on mine and practicing with it. I also know how to repair them and occasionally give classes on crossbow usage and safety.

Q: Now, in looking at these pictures of the skeletal remains, there seems to be little or no signs of blood at the point of entry in the back.

A: Yes, that is sometimes the case with an arrow. If the arrow remains in the body, it can act like a plug, sorry for being so graphic, and very little blood comes out at that point. On the exit wound, however, which does not show on this picture, there was more blood, or actually some residue of what appeared to be blood. After two years, there was not much to see or test.

Q: Okay. Were any forensic tests done on the crossbow and the bolts?

A: Yes, Mr. Winslet's fingerprints were found on the crossbow. Mr. Winslet's fingerprints were found on the bolt that was found in the remains of the victim. There was also another set of what appeared to be partial fingerprints, but could not be identified. His fingerprints were also found on the crossbow arrows that were found in the case containing the crossbow.

Q: Early in the investigation, I believe you testified earlier, that Mr. Winslet said that his girlfriend was having an affair with someone?

A: Yes, he said that she was e-mailing Johnny Bleu. We had a computer expert check the computer that Winslet and the victim had used and we determined that Johnny Bleu was actually Ken Lott, who worked at Sports Paradise, here in San Milano. He worked in the archery department. Mr. Winslet also worked at Sports Paradise.

Q: What else did you learn about Mr. Lott?

A: I interviewed him as well and learned that he apparently created several online personas, with women, and sweet-talked them into communicating with them. He said that he never really had an actual affair with the women. He said that in his mind he had no doubt that Winslet had killed Sadie.

Q: And why is that?

A: He said that Sadie had e-mailed him and told him that she was afraid of Winslet and that he had threatened to kill her if she ever left him.

Q: Do you have any record of that?

A: Yes, on Winslet's computer we found an e-mail that suggested that. But Lott also showed us an e-mail message that he had received from Ms. Norris the same day she disappeared.

Q: Is this the e-mail? [Shows exhibit to witness]

A: Yes, that is a printout that he gave me.

Q: Let me go back a second. When you and Mr. Winslet saw the remains, you said that you thought it odd that he had not said anything. But it's hard to see from the photos that the body is even that of a woman, right?

A: Yes.

Q: So, there might have been some other reason for his actions?

A: No, I didn't think so.

Q: Did you run a check for fingerprints on the case for the crossbow?

A: Yes, we did. We found two sets of prints on the case, one for Winslet and the other set for Ken Lott. But that seemed normal because Lott worked in the archery department and his prints would have been all over the case when he sold it to Winslet. We ran the tests on the crossbow itself and the bolts in the quiver, which was attached to the crossbow, in the case. I forgot to mention the tests on the bolts in the case. The only fingerprints on those bolts belonged to Mr. Winslet.

Q: Did you ever consider that there might be other suspects, for example, Johnny Bleu, or I guess Ken Lott?

A: No, I did not. I considered the statement of Taylor Dodds who said that Ken Lott killed Sadie. But I found that statement to be incredible because Dodds and Winslet are friends. I am convinced that the evidence all pointed to Winslet and no one else in this case.

Q: One more question, detective. Did you ever try to contact the two deer hunters who had originally discovered the victim's remains?

A: I tried to talk to them. They never returned my calls. And, besides, from what I had seen, I did not think that they would have anything else to add to the case.

Q: Thank you, Detective Davidson. That is all I have for now.

(END OF TRANSCRIPT)

This is to certify that I have read the transcript of my deposition taken on and that the transcript accurately reflects the questions asked and my answers.

SIGNATURE: *Lanny Davidson*

Subscribed and sworn to before me on November 15, [YR-1].

Norma Rogers

Norma Rogers
Certified Shorthand Reporter

Resume of Lanny Davidson

Lanny Davidson

Homicide Detective
San Antonio, State of Lone Star

Experience

Police Officer, City of San Antonio, State of Lone Star — Oct [YR-10] – July [YR-4]

Homicide Detective, City of San Antonio, State of Lone Star — July [YR-4] – Present

Responsible for approximately 75 homicide investigations to date, with 20 convictions resulting from those investigations. Only two homicide investigations currently open. Currently certified in Forensics Collection.

Education

- Texas Tech University (BA, Sociology) — January [YR-10]
- Police Academy — May [YR-10] – Oct [YR-10]

  Top 5% of the City of San Antonio Police Training Academy.
- Forensics Collection — Oct. 2009 & Nov. [YR-1]

  Forensic Courses at FBA Academy, Quantico, VA. Training in proper collection of evidence including DNA, fingerprints, and weapons. Training on what evidence to collect as well; although the evidence may not appear out of the ordinary, it could be critical to an investigation. Award of Merit in both courses.

Additional

- Have testified regarding investigations in 48 cases.
- Currently researching to write an article entitled "Proper Homicide Investigation: A Fail-Proof Checklist for Correct Identification of the Culprit".
- Married, two young children. Hobbies include hunting with crossbows, aquatic sports.

Grand Jury Testimony of Ken Lott

IN RE:	BEFORE THE GRAND JURY
	OF
GRAND JURY INVESTIGATION	BEAR COUNTY, STATE OF LONE STAR

* * * * * *

****

COURT REPORTER'S

Q AND A TRANSCRIPT OF TESTIMONY OF

KEN LOTT

JUNE 24, [YR-2]

****

* * * * *

BE IT REMEMBERED, that ON JUNE 24, [YR-2], the above-entitled matter came on for hearing before the Grand Jury of Bear County, sitting in San Milano, State of Lone Star, being presented by JAMES HERNANDEZ, Assistant Criminal District Attorney, for consideration by the members thereof.

VERONICA GARCIA was duly sworn as Court Reporter.

WHEREUPON, the following evidence was introduced and proceedings had, to-wit, beginning at 2:00 o'clock p.m and concluding at 3:05 o'clock p.m.

KEN LOTT, The Witness.

GRAND JURY FOREMAN: Do you solemnly swear that you will not divulge either by words or signs any matter about which you may be interrogated, and that you will keep secret all proceedings of the Grand Jury which may be had in your presence, and that you will true answers make to such questions as may be propounded to you by the Grand Jury or under its direction, so help you God?

THE WITNESS: I do.

EXAMINATION BY JAMES HERNANDEZ:

Q: As with any witness who comes before the Grand Jury, I need to give you the definitions of perjury and aggravated perjury.

A person commits the offense of perjury if, with intent to deceive and with knowledge of the statement's meaning, that person makes a false statement under oath or swears to the truth of a false statement previously made and the statement is required or authorized by law to be made under oath.

Perjury is a Class A Misdemeanor, which is punishable by anywhere up to one year in the Bear County Jail and/or a fine of up to $4,000.

Perjury becomes aggravated perjury if the person commits perjury, makes that false statement during or in connection with an official proceeding, and Grand Jury proceedings are official proceedings, and the statement is material.

Aggravated perjury is a third-degree felony, which means it's punishable by anywhere from two to ten years in the Lone Star Department of Corrections, and there's a potential fine of up to $10,000. Do you understand this?

A: Yes, sir.

Q: Would you please state your name for the grand jury?

A: Yes, my name is Ken Lott.

Q: Thank you. Where do you live?

A: Here in San Milano.

Q: And where do you work?

A: I work at Sports Paradise, here in San Milano. I have worked there for about six years.

Q: And where do you work in that store?

A: I have always worked in the archery section. The whole time I have been there.

Q: Do you know Charles Winslet?

A: Yes.

Q: How do you know him?

A: Well, he also works at Sports Paradise — in the camping section, which is just around the corner from where I work. I don't socialize with him but I did sell him a crossbow — a Parker Crossbow—several years ago.

Q: So, you know him from work?

A: Yes, that is pretty much it.

Q: Do you recognize these exhibits? [Shows witness pictures of crossbow and bolt]

A: Yes, that is a Parker crossbow and a Parker arrow, or bolt, that you are supposed to use with that particular crossbow.

Q: Have you had a chance to observe Mr. Winslet at work?

A: Yes, I have. A lot.

Q: How would you describe his behavior?

A: Erratic and prone to fits of temper. Once he was visiting with me in the archery section and got upset with the way a female customer was acting. When she walked away from the counter, he picked up the crossbow that she had been looking at buying, raised it to his shoulder, pointed it at her back and said something like, "zing, thwap," and then laughed.

Q: Zing, thwap?

A: Yes, I guess he was trying to imitate the sounds of firing the crossbow and the sound the arrow or bolt makes when it hits something.

Q: What did you do?

A: I grabbed it from him and told him that it was not funny. He then got made at me and said that I did not enjoy good humor, or something like that.

Q: Did you ever observe any other behavior?

A: No, but I heard that a couple of years ago, he got a written reprimand for anger management problems at work.

Q: Did you ever know Sadie Norris?

A: Yes, I did. Very nice girl.

Q: Tell us about her.

A: She was dating Winslet and I met her a couple of times when she would come to visit Winslet at the store. She was always smiling and sort of shy. Why she stayed with him I will never know.

Q: Tell us about Johnny Bleu.

A: [Pause] I guess that was not one of the smartest things I have ever done.

Q: Go ahead.

A: I got lonely a couple of years ago. I had broken up with another girl and I went online and created a fake person, Johnny Bleu, to meet women.

Q: Did you ever actually meet women?

A: No, I came close a couple of times. But, no I never actually met anyone.

Q: Is it true that you carried on long-term Internet relationships with several women?

A: Yes, I did.

Q: How many?

A: [Pause] Four or five.

Q: Was Sadie Norris one of them?

A: Yes.

Q: How did you happen to link up with her?

A: I had seen her in the store and liked her. I never worked up the nerve to talk to her in person other than when she showed up at the store.

Q: How did you link up with her?

A: About two years ago, about 3 months before she disappeared, she logged on to a dating site and used her real name. I logged on as Johnny Bleu and started connecting with her. We had a great relationship. She told me a lot of things. She told me that her boyfriend, Winslet, was mean to her and although she was living with him, she was afraid of him and his temper. She mentioned several times that she was thinking of leaving him and I encouraged her to do so. I think in some ways, that I contributed to her death.

Q: Why do you say that?

A: The day she disappeared I got an e-mail from Winslet to my account for Johnny Bleu. I don't think he knew who I really was. He told me to back away from his fiancée, or he would come looking for me and kill me. He said something like, if she broke his heart, he would pierce hers. That really freaked me out. He didn't say he would break hers. He said he would pierce her heart. I remember those words.

Q: Did you respond to that e-mail?

A: No. I did not. I had e-mailed her earlier and told her it was time to leave. She said she was going to leave and that she was packed and ready to go. So I breathed easier when I read that.

Q: When did this take place?

A: I think that it was a day or so before she disappeared. Because Winslet came into the store one day, right after that, and said that his girlfriend had left him. That is when I thought that she had finally left him and was hiding somewhere. He said that he would find her and that she would regret the day she left him. He said that he was convinced that she had run off with some guy named Bleu. I kept my mouth shut and played dumb, like I had no idea what he was talking about. Shortly after that, I quit using that name on the Internet, hoping that no one would find out what I had done.

Q: Had you developed feelings for Sadie?

A: She was an angel. I think she fell in love with me, or maybe Johnny Bleu.

Q: Did you ever reveal to Sadie who you really were?

A: I don' think it happened quite that way. We saw each other, if that is what you mean.

Q: Well, I am not sure. Can you explain?

A: On the Internet I was Johnny and in real life, as Ken, we connected at some level. We played along on the Internet as though we had never actually met in person. But actually we had, in person, when she came to visit Charles, for example, at the store. So, I am not positive if she knew that Johnny and I were the same person. I am not sure. It was our way of hiding our relationship from Charles.

Q: Did Winslet ever figure out who you were?

A: I don't think so. At least I never told him. All I know is that after Sadie left, I have not been the same. It's been a very hard two years. I am glad we finally know what happened to Sadie.

Q: I understand that you had some run-ins with your boss?

A: Yes, after Sadie disappeared, I was not myself and said and did some things I am not proud of. I think I am better now.

Q: Do you recognize this photo? [Shows picture to witness]

A: Yes, absolutely. That is Sadie. I took this picture during a lunch break when she came out to Sports Paradise before she disappeared. It was taken at the mall, where Sports Paradise is located.

Q: Okay. Thank you. That is all I have for now.

QUESTION BY GRAND JUROR

Q: Did you love Sadie?

A: Yes, I did. I really fell in love with her and cared about her deeply.

Q: Do you own a crossbow?

A: Yes, I do.

Q: What kind?

A: Like the one I sold to Charles, a Buck Buster. It's made by Parker. It's at my home. I think.

Q: Did you ever visit Sadie at Winslet's ranch?

A: No.

Q: Were you ever at his ranch?

A: Not that I can recall, no.

JAMES HERNANDEZ

Q: Okay. Thank you. Would you please step outside for just a few minutes?

A: Of course.

(The Witness leaves the Grand Jury Room at 3:05 p.m. and is subsequently dismissed.)

(END OF TRANSCRIPT)

911 Transcripts

911 TRANSCRIPT
May 2, [YR-3]
6:13 PM

Dispatch: 911, what is your emergency?

Caller: My boyfriend, Charles, just threatened me.

Dispatch: Is he there with you?

Caller: No, he is outside. Please, send the police!

Dispatch: Ma'am, do you need help? Do you need medical attention?

Caller: I don't know . . . (unintelligible) . . . I don't know. . .

Dispatch: What is your name, honey?

Caller: It's Sadie Norris.

Dispatch: Sadie, I am sending help, the police are on their way. What happened?

Caller: He threatened to cut me with a hunting knife. He has been drinking and he is scaring me. I don't think he would actually do it, but I am really scared.

Dispatch: Did he threaten you?

Caller: Yes, briefly. He is waving it around.

Dispatch: I will stay on the phone with you until the police arrive, alright?

Caller: (Unintelligible . . . talking to a man)

Dispatch: Sadie? I'll stay here on the phone with you until the police and medical arrive.

Caller: Okay. (Unintelligible . . . talking to man). Okay, he hears the police and he is putting the knife back in his hunting bag.

Dispatch: I see the police say they've arrived

Caller: They're here. Thank you.

(END OF TRANSCRIPT)

911 TRANSCRIPT
June 11, [YR-3]
9:09 AM

Dispatch: 911, what is your emergency?

Caller: My girlfriend is missing and I can't find her.

Dispatch: When did you last see her?

Caller: Hmmm, several nights ago, I guess.

Dispatch: What is your name?

Caller: Winslet, Charlie Winslet.

Dispatch: Do you have reason to believe that she is hurt?

Caller: Oh God, I hope not. We had a fight about another man and she just walked out the door, saying that she would be back when she had cooled down. But that was almost two days ago.

Dispatch: Have you tried contacting her family and friends?

Caller: Yes. I have. I have asked them for help on Facebook. You are recording this right?

Dispatch: Yes. Why are you asking?

Caller: Sorry, I have another call coming in. I'll stop by the police station and get them to help.

Dispatch: Okay.

(END OF TRANSCRIPT)

MEDICAL EXAMINER'S AUTOPSY REPORT

Office of Medical Examiner
Bear County
State of Lone Star

Date:	April 23, [YR-2]
Time:	9:00 a.m.
Examiner:	Brandon Lane, M.D.
Witness:	Detective Lanny Davidson
Deceased:	Unknown
Date of Birth:	Unknown
Height:	4'11"– 5'2"
Weight:	Unknown
Race:	Unknown
Gender:	Female

Observations: The remains consisted of a skull, a mostly intact rib cage and assorted arm and leg bones, and pelvic bones, which were collected personally by the undersigned on April 22, [YR-2]. A crossbow bolt, 20 inches long penetrated the rib cage, from the posterior side, left lateral, approximately 1 inch from the spine, between the fifth and sixth ribs, and extending approximately 2 inches from the anterior rib cage. Small blood residue around entry point of bolt.

Size and structure of pelvic bones indicates that victim was likely female.

Based on the location of the bolt, it appears that the bolt penetrated the heart.

Penetration of bolt into the ground was minimal, suggesting that bolt entered the body before the body fell to the ground.

Cause/Manner of Death: Bolt wound in back, through the heart, homicide

Submitted April 24, [YR-2]

Brandon D. Lane
Brandon D. Lane, M.D.
Medical Examiner
Bear County

Medical Examiner's Death Certificate

Office of Medical Examiner
Bear County
State of Lone Star

Death Certificate

Name of Deceased:	Sadie Norris
Date and Time of Death:	June [YR-3]
Primary Cause of Death:	Bolt wound in back
Survivors:	Mother, Janey Norris
Submitted May 15, [YR-2]	

Brandon D. Lane
Brandon D. Lane, M.D.
Medical Examiner
Bear County

Forensics Report

JANEY NORRIS Plaintiff v. CHARLES WINSLET Defendant	}	CIVIL DOCKET NO. 5674678

Before me, the undersigned authority, personally appeared Sandra Borland, who, being by me duly sworn, deposed as follows:

My name is Sandra Borland, I am of sound mind, capable of making this affidavit, and personally acquainted with the facts herein stated:

> I am the custodian of the records of Bear County Crime Laboratory. Attached hereto is one (1) page of the forensic report records from the Bear County Crime Laboratory. This page is from the records kept by the Bear County Crime Laboratory in the regular course of business, and it was the regular course of business of Bear County Crime Laboratory for an employee or representative of that office, with knowledge of the act, event, condition, opinion, or diagnosis, recorded to make the record or to transmit information thereof to be included in such record; and the record was made at or near the time or reasonably soon thereafter. The record attached hereto is the original.

Sandra Borland
Affiant

SWORN TO AND SUBSCRIBED before me on the 15th day of August, [YR-1].

Linda Castel
Notary Public, State of Lone Start

Notary's printed name:
Linda Castel

My commission expires: January 1, [YR+1]

Bear County Crime Laboratory

Bear County

State of Lone Star

WEAPONS:

The weapon gathered was a crossbow bolt, 20 inches in length, and a crossbow manufactured by Parker Company.

FINGERPRINTS:

Fingerprints were taken from the crossbow. The prints on the crossbow belong to Charles Winslet.

Fingerprints were taken of the crossbow case. They belonged to Charles Winslet and Ken Lott.

Two sets of fingerprints were taken from the bolt found in the victim's remains. One set belongs to Charles Winslet. The other set of fingerprints could not be identified.

One set of fingerprints was found on the two bolts found in crossbow case. Those prints belong to Charles Winslet.

DNA:

DNA was collected from the victim's remains. That DNA indicates that the victim is Sadie Norris (Test Results — May 14).

Jane Gilbert

Jane Gilbert
Lab Technician
June 13, [YR-2]

Receipt for Funeral Expenses

Evermore Funeral Home and Crematory

456 Center Street

San Milano, State of Lone Star

INVOICE

Casket	$ 8,500.00
Funeral director's basic services fee	$ 2,500.00
Embalming and body preparation	$ 900.00
Funeral ceremony and viewing	$ 3,100.00
Miscellaneous (hearse, death certificates, obituary, etc.)	$ 2,000.00
Flowers	$ 300.00
Internment Expenses (opening and closing grave)	$ 3,800.00
Rental for Chapel	$ 500.00
TOTAL	**$ 21,600.00**

PAID IN FULL
(Check # 2345)

Photograph of Victim

Photograph of Crossbow Case in Machine Shed

Photograph of Machine Shed

PHOTOGRAPHS OF CROSSBOW AND BOLT

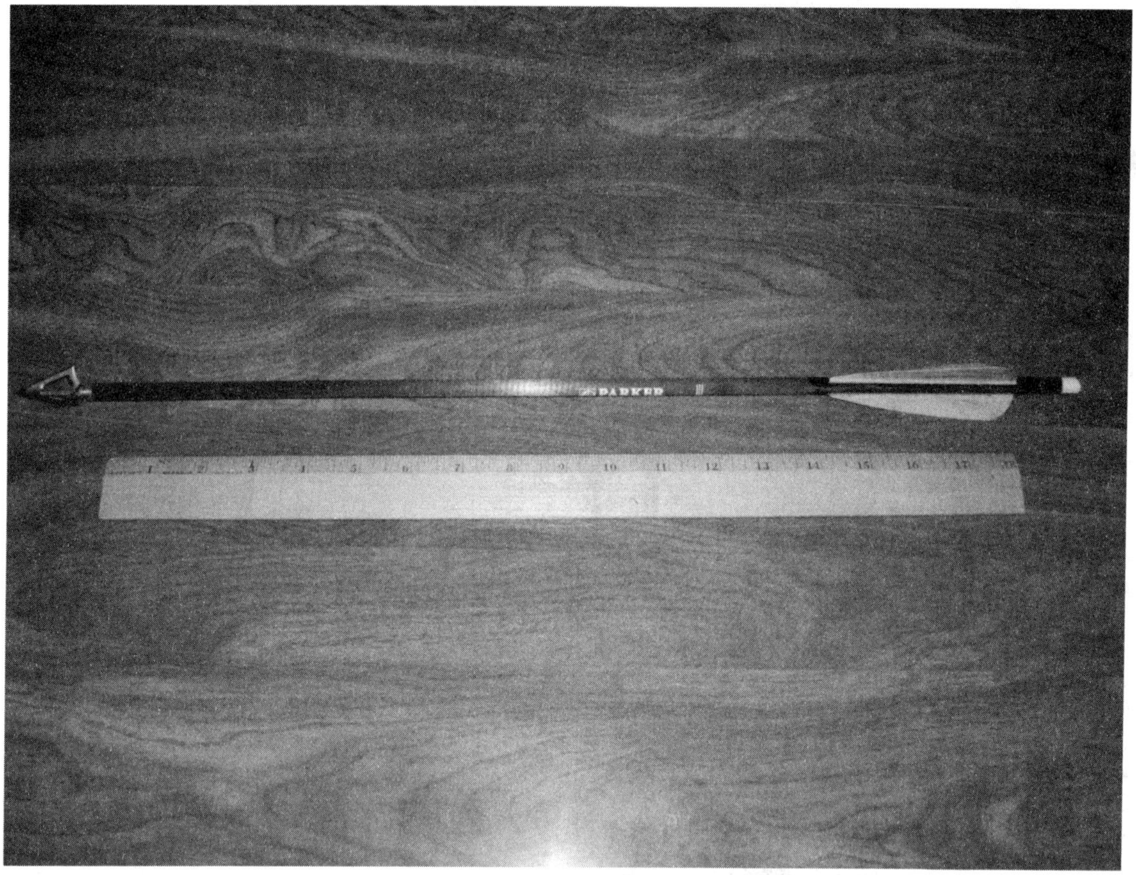

Photographs of Remains

April 23, [YR-1] | The Lone Star Times | 4B

Remains Located on Ranch

Reported by: Trisha Green
April 23, [YR-2]

Two area deer hunters got the surprise of their lives yesterday when they discovered human remains on a local ranch, while scouting out locations for the fall deer season.

According to a source close to the investigation, the remains had an arrow in them, indicating that the victim was killed intentionally.

One of the men, who asked to remain unnamed, said that he and his friend had spent several hours hiking the ranch to look for deer signs and locate a place for their deer blind. When they noticed the remains, they took a closer look but did not touch anything. They immediately returned to the owner's ranch house, told him what they had found, and then called the police. He said that the owner appeared very nervous when he heard that there was a dead body on his ranch. He said that he and his friend were no longer interested in leasing the land for hunting.

The ranch's owner, Charles Winslet, said that he had no idea about who the remains might belong to. Neighbors say that Winslet's girlfriend, Sadie Norris, went missing a couple of years ago and they think that mystery will now be solved.

The police have declined to comment on the case, stating simply that their investigation continues.

Written Reprimand to Taylor Dodds

SPORTS PARADISE
124 Lakeview Drive
555-342-9765
San Milano, State of Lone Star

Where Great Things Happen Outdoors

Memo to: **Taylor Dodds**
Camping Department

From: **John "Bear" Schwartz**
President and CEO

Date: **December 4, [YR-4]**

Re: **Written Reprimand**

As you know, it has come to my attention that several weeks ago that in filling out your monthly sales report for the second quarter of this past fiscal year, you falsified that report. You inflated your sales by more than 5 percent, which then qualified you for our company's annual "Trophy" bonus.

Your correct sales figures were discovered during a random audit by an independent CPA firm.

We gave you ample opportunity to explain your actions and your answer was that it was simple mistake.

Thus, the bonus that was paid to you, in the amount of $1,000.00, will be deducted from your next three paychecks. In addition you will be placed on probationary status for 90 days, beginning today. If for any reason your conduct again falls below that expected of our employees, you will be terminated.

As you know, Taylor, we take pride in being a family here at Sports Paradise. We are giving you another chance.

If you have any questions, please feel free to contact me.

WRITTEN REPRIMAND TO KEN LOTT

SPORTS PARADISE
124 Lakeview Drive
555-342-9765
San Milano, State of Lone Star

Where Great Things Happen Outdoors

Memo to: **Ken Lott**
Archery Department

From: **John "Bear" Schwartz**
President and CEO

Date: **December 4, [YR-3]**

Re: **Written Reprimand**

I learned last week that you had threatened one of your co-workers in the camping department of our store, on November 20th. This is the second incident involving aggressive behavior on your part. The first, as you well know, involved one of our patrons, in July [YR-3].

You are now on a 120-day probation. If we receive any further complaints about your behavior, you will be terminated.

Until these incidents arose you had been a model employee. That is why I am giving you another chance.

You told me in our conversation last week that the last year has been very hard on you because you lost a good friend. I recommend that you get professional counseling to deal with that issue and avoid any further problems in our store.

If you have any questions, please feel free to contact me.

From: SadieNorris@nol.com
To: johnnybleu@BOl.com
Sent: April 1, [YR-3], 3:00 AM
Subject: Help

Johnny, I am scared. Charles has become very threatening lately. He says that he is getting tired of me running around behind his back and that if I ever betray him, he will make sure I don't forget it.

What should I do?

Please help.

From: SadieNorris@nol.com
To: johnnybleu@BOl.com
Sent: April 3, [YR-3], 2:00 AM
Subject: Help

Johnny, why aren't you responding? I am scared and need someone to tell me what to do.

I want to leave Charles but am afraid that he will follow me and kill me.

From: SadieNorris@nol.com
To: johnnybleu@BOl.com
Sent: May 3, [YR-3], 3:30 PM
Subject: I'm in Trouble

I think I am pregnant. What have I done? I HATE YOU. I HATE YOU. I HATE YOU.

Where are you?

From: johnnybleu@BOl.com
To: SadieNorris@nol.com
Sent: May 3, [YR-3], 4:30 PM
Subject: I'm in Trouble

A baby? I love you. Is it mine?

Let's get outta here and start somewhere else. You are too good for Charles!!!

From: SadieNorris@nol.com
To: johnnybleu@BOl.com
Sent: May 3, [YR-3], 8:30 PM
Subject: I'm in Trouble

No. I am leaving both of you. Just as soon as I can find a time to do it.

Don't email me, tweet me, call me or try to see me. We are done!

From: johnnybleu@BOl.com
To: SadieNorris@nol.com
Sent: May 4, [YR-3], 9:30 PM
Subject: I'm in Trouble

No. No.

Don't do that. I love you and cannot live without you. I am giving up my internet affairs. You are the only one. Don't leave me. If you do, you will regret it.

I will find you. I love you.

From: SadieNorris@nol.com
To: johnnybleu@BOI.com
Sent: June 8, [YR-3], 9:21 PM
Subject: Leaving

I am out of here. Car is gassed. Bags are packed and Charles is outside in machine shed messing around. Good riddance to both of you. . . . . Ken!!

GO TO HELL.

I was wrong. I am not pregnant. But if I was, I would never admit that it was your's.

PS. You had better hope and pray that I don't turn you in to "Bear", Mr. Internet Lover!!!! You are already in trouble with him

---

E-Mails From Charles Winslet to Johnny Bleu

From: CWinslet34@nol.com
To: johnnybleu@BOI.com
Sent: April 4, [YR-3], 2:23 AM
Subject: Who Are You?

HEY JOHNNY, OR WHOEVER YOU ARE. WHO ARE YOU REALLY?

I DON'T APPRECIATE YOU MESSING WITH MY FUTURE WIFE!

From: CWinslet34@nol.com
To: johnnybleu@BOI.com
Sent: April 9, [YR-3], 1:56 AM
To: Subject: Who are You!!!!

You had better stop contacting my girlfriend. She and I are getting married and messing with her (and me) will not go well for you.

IF YOU ARE A REAL MAN YOU WILL STEP UP AND TELL ME WHO YOU ARE.

From: CWinslet34@nol.com
To: johnnybleu@BOI.com
Sent: May 15, [YR-3], 4:15 PM
To: Subject: Breaking My Heart

Hey Johnny Blue, whoever you are.

I know that you and my girlfriend have a thing going on the internet and that she is thinking of leaving me.

You had better not be involved in that plan or I will kill you with my bare hands.

If she leaves me it will break my heart and I will pierce her's. And she will leave with only the shirt on her back.

Got it? I hope so.

Charles Winslet
June 9, [YR-3] at 8:34 am

Hey everyone. If anyone sees Sadie, please let me know. She left me last night and I have not heard from her. Be sure to save this message for future reference. I really miss her. Please please please help me.

2 likes **0 comment**

Like **Comment** **Share**

Charles Winslet

May 21 [YR-2] at 12:14 pm

Looks like the police finally found Sadie.

Libre al fin! Libre al fin!

3 likes **0 comment**

Like **Comment** **Share**

Jury Instructions

LADIES AND GENTLEMEN OF THE JURY:

I am now going to instruct you about the law governing this case. You are required to accept my instructions as the law. Any ideas you have of what the law is or what the law should be or any statements by the attorneys as to what the law may be, must be disregarded by you, if they are in conflict with these instructions.

1. Claims of Parties

The plaintiff claims that she sustained damages due to the defendant's wrongful act of killing her daughter, Sadie Norris. The defendant has denied those claims and also denies that the plaintiff is entitled to recover any damages.

2. Burden of Proof

In this case, the plaintiff has the burden of proving her claims by a preponderance of the evidence. If you find from the evidence, by a preponderance of the evidence, that the defendant killed the plaintiff's daughter by wrongful act, neglect, or carelessness, and that such actions were the proximate cause of her daughter's death, then you must find the defendant liable for his actions.

3. Proximate Cause

When I use the expression "proximate cause," I mean a cause that, in the natural or ordinary course of events, produced Sadie Norris's, the decedent's, death. It need not be the only cause, nor the last or nearest cause. It is sufficient if it combines with another cause resulting in the injury and death.

4. Preponderance of the Evidence

The term "preponderance of the evidence" means that amount of evidence that causes you to conclude that the allegation is probably true. To prove an allegation by the preponderance of the evidence, a party must convince you that the allegation is more likely true than not true.

If the evidence on a particular issue is equally balanced, that issue has not been proven by a preponderance of the evidence. Therefore, the party having the burden of proving that issue has failed with respect to that particular issue.

5. Circumstantial Evidence

A fact or a group of facts may, based on logic and common sense, lead you to a conclusion as to other facts. This is known as circumstantial evidence. A fact may be proved by circumstantial evidence. Circumstantial evidence is entitled to the same consideration as any other type of evidence

6. Opinion Testimony

You may have heard a witness give opinions about matters requiring special knowledge or skill. You should judge this testimony in the same way you judge the testimony from any other witness. The fact that such person has given an opinion does not mean that you are required to accept it. Give the testimony whatever weight you think it deserves, considering the reasons given for the opinion, the witness's qualifications, and all of the other evidence in the case.

7. Credibility of Witnesses

It is up to you to decide the credibility of the witnesses. In making the decision you may consider such factors as whether the witness has made a prior inconsistent statement or has been convicted of a crime. Evidence of this kind may be considered by you in connection with all the other facts and circumstances in evidence in deciding the weight to be given to the testimony of that witness.

8. Damages

a. General

If you decide the plaintiff is entitled to damages, you shall give such amount as you decide to be fair and just, under all the circumstances. Such damages may include the following items, to the extent you find they have been proved by the evidence:

- Reasonable medical, hospital, funeral and burial expenses;
- Loss of financial support;
- Loss of gifts or other valuable gratuities;
- Loss of parental training and guidance;
- Loss of companionship;
- Plaintiff's grief, sorrow, or mental anguish.

Whether the plaintiff has proved these damages is for you to decide, based upon evidence and not upon speculation, guess, or conjecture. The amount of money to be awarded for certain of these elements of damage cannot be proved in a precise dollar amount. The law leaves such amounts to your sound judgment.

b. Punitive Damages

If you find for the plaintiff, you may, but are not required to, award punitive damages. The purposes of punitive damages are to punish a defendant and to deter similar acts in the future. Punitive damages may not be awarded to compensate a plaintiff.

The plaintiff has the burden of proving by a preponderance of the evidence that punitive damages should be awarded, and, if so, the amount of any such damages.

You may award punitive damages only if you find that the defendant's conduct that resulted in the death of Sadie Norris, the decedent, was a willful act or omission or gross negligence. Gross negligence means conduct or a failure to act that is so reckless that it demonstrates a substantial lack of concern for whether an injury will result.

If you find that punitive damages are appropriate, you must use reason in setting the amount. Punitive damages, if any, should be in an amount sufficient to fulfill their purposes but should not reflect bias, prejudice, or sympathy toward any party. In considering the amount of any punitive damages, consider the degree of reprehensibility of the defendant's conduct.

In addition, you may consider the relationship of any award of punitive damages to any actual harm inflicted on the plaintiff.

9. Insurance

Whether a party is insured or not insured has no bearing on any issue that you must decide. You must refrain from any inference, speculation, or discussion about insurance. If you find for the plaintiff, you shall not speculate about or consider any possible sources of benefits the plaintiff may have received or might receive. After you have returned your verdict, the court will make whatever adjustments are necessary in this regard.

10. Verdict Form

To assist you in deciding these issues, I am giving you a verdict form to use during your deliberations. When you have completed the form, please let the bailiff know that you have completed your deliberations.

VERDICT FORM

1. **Liability**

Do you find by a preponderance of the evidence that the defendant caused the death of the plaintiff's daughter?

________ YES

________ NO

If your answer is "no," then do not answer Question 2. If your answer is "yes," answer Question 2.

2. **Damages**

Do you find by a preponderance of the evidence that the plaintiff suffered damages as a result of the defendant's actions?

________ YES

________ NO

If you answered "yes," then please enter the amount of damages, in whole dollar amounts, to which the plaintiffs are entitled.

$ ______________________________

3. **Punitive Damages**

Do you find by a preponderance of the evidence that the decedent's death was the result of the defendant's willful act or omission or gross negligence in light of the circumstances?

________ YES

________ NO

If you answered "yes," then please enter the amount of punitive damages, in whole dollar amounts, to which the plaintiff is entitled.

$ ______________________________